AMERICAN INDIAN POLICY
AND AMERICAN REFORM

AMERICAN INDIAN POLICY AND AMERICAN REFORM

Case Studies of the Campaign to Assimilate the American Indians

CHRISTINE BOLT

Professor of American History
University of Kent at Canterbury

London
ALLEN & UNWIN
Boston Sydney Wellington

Allen & Unwin, the academic imprint of
Unwin Hyman Ltd
PO Box 18, Park Lane, Hemel Hempstead, Herts HP2 4TE, UK
40 Museum Street, London WC1A 1LU, UK
37/39 Queen Elizabeth Street, London SE1 2QB

Allen & Unwin Inc.,
8 Winchester Place, Winchester, Mass. 01890, USA

Allen & Unwin (Australia) Ltd,
8 Napier Street, North Sydney, NSW 2060, Australia

Allen & Unwin (New Zealand) Ltd in association with the
Port Nicholson Press Ltd,
60 Cambridge Terrace, Wellington, New Zealand

First published in 1987

British Library Cataloguing in Publication Data

Bolt, Christine
    American Indian policy and American reform: case studies of the
campaign to assimilate the American Indians.
1. Indians of North America – Government relations – History
I. Title
323.1'197'073   E93
ISBN 0–04–00037–3
ISBN 0–04–900039–X Pbk

Library of Congress Cataloging-in-Publication Data

Bolt, Christine.
    American Indian policy and American reform.
Bibliography: p.
Includes index.
1. Indians of North America – Cultural assimilation. 2. Indians of North
America – Cultural assimilation – Case studies. 3. Indians of North
America – Government relations. 4. Indians of North America –
Government relations – Case studies. 5. United States – Social policy –
Case studies. I. Title.
E98.C89B65 1986   973'.0497   86–22240
ISBN 0–04–900037–3 (alk. paper)
ISBN 0–04–900039–X (pbk.: alk. paper)

Typeset in 10 on 12 point Palatino by Computape (Pickering) Limited
and printed in Great Britain by Mackays of Chatham.

For IAN, again

Contents

Foreword   *Page* ix

PART ONE: The Context

Introduction   3
1   The Colonial Legacy   13
2   White Power Grows, Reformer Hopes Fluc-
    tuate: the 1770s to the 1850s   36
3   Assimilationist Pressures Mount: the 1860s
    to 1920   71
4   The Uncertain Road to Self-Determination:
    the 1920s to the 1960s   103

PART TWO: The Case Studies

5   Slavery, Red and Black   149
6   Red, Black and White: Reconstruction and
    Beyond   166
7   American Indians and American
    Anthropologists   189
8   Indian Education: Goals and Illusions   209
9   Indian Education in the Twentieth Century   231
10 Indian Women in Fancy and Fact   252
11 Urban Indians since the Second World War   270
12 Indian Political Protest Groups   287

Notes and References   307

Index   426

Maps

1 American Indian peoples c.1600   16
2 Indian Country after the Removal Act of 1830   63
3 Indian Country after the Mexican War of 1846–8   66
4 Indian reservations today, showing the impact of allotment   98
5 Chief locations of 173 Indian peoples in the USA in 1970   142
6 The Indian Territory in 1888   168

Note

Throughout this book the word Indian has generally been used. The term Native American is now, of course, often more acceptable. But commentators from colonial times onwards have usually employed the misnomer 'Indian', and given the historical scope and focus of the present study it has therefore seemed sensible to utilize the most common description of America's original peoples.

Foreword

The debts accumulated in the course of a long study are numerous and pleasant to acknowledge. I should like to express warm thanks to the Wolfson Foundation and the Leverhulme Trust for generous grants which funded research in various American libraries and visits to American Indian communities in the Southwest. My sincere appreciation goes also to the staff of the institutions from which materials used in this book were collected. I am extremely grateful for information received over the years from the National Congress of American Indians, the National Indian Youth Council and the National Tribal Chairmen's Association and I would like to acknowledge the advice received at the National Archives in Washington from Mr Richard Crawford and at the Bureau of Indian Affairs in Washington, where I worked on post-1945 BIA records, from the head of the Mails and Files section, Mr Robinson. My thanks go to Professor Norman Crockett of the University of Oklahoma, to Professor John Ezell and the inestimable Mr Jack Haley of the University of Oklahoma's Western History Collections and to Mrs Martha Blaine of the Indian Archives Division of the Oklahoma Historical Society. At the Special Collections Department of the University of New Mexico Library in Albuquerque, I received valued guidance about the Doris Duke Indian Oral History Collection (the Doris Duke collections in Oklahoma and Arizona were consulted, too, and are of great interest to scholars). I benefited from the advice of Ms Jan Bell at the Arizona State Museum and from staff aid at the Special Collections Division of the University of Arizona Library, the Arizona Historical Society and the Newberry Library, Chicago.

Professor Alice Schlegel of the University of Arizona offered some excellent leads about anthropological work on Native American women and I am grateful to Professor Roger Nichols and Professor Karen Anderson of the University of Arizona for a number of helpful suggestions. Colleagues in Britain have commented usefully on papers which summarized some of the themes pursued in the book and Professor Michael L. Tate of the University of Nebraska, who read the manuscript for Allen & Unwin, provided invaluable criticisms of its content and organization, as well as making some much appreciated bibliographical points and saving me from a number of errors. Ms Enid Dixon of the Inter-Library Loan service of the University of Kent's library has coped with a long stream of requests for books with her customary promptness, while the British Library has been a rich resource. And, finally, my thanks go to the charming, efficient and unflappable secretarial staff of Eliot College: to two galvanizing secretarial supervisors, Mrs Jan Galbraith and Mrs Ros Webb, and to those who uncomplainingly typed, and retyped, the manuscript, Mrs Linda Williams, Ms Joanna Snow, Mrs Val Oswald and Mrs Viv Howard.

For all assistance, I am most grateful; for all errors of fact or interpretation which may remain, I am, of course, responsible.

Christine Bolt,
Eliot College,
University of Kent at Canterbury,
April 1986.

PART ONE

The Context

Introduction

In writing this book, it has been my purpose, through a series of case studies preceded by a broad chronological introduction, to examine some key aspects of American Indian policy and reform in the context of ethnic problems generally and the American reform tradition as a whole. To further point up the distinctiveness or otherwise of American Indian policy, it is compared, when appropriate, with the administration of Indian affairs in Canada.

The next four chapters in Part One seek to develop a number of themes within the history of Indian policy from colonial times to the 1960s. First, I have attempted to establish how far racial prejudice was a factor in determining policy, and what the consequences were if the Native Americans were admired or condemned by whites on cultural rather than racial grounds. I have given prominence to economic issues in order to show why it proved so difficult to give an economic dimension to Indian policy and philanthropy that would actually benefit the Indians. Since early white reformers in the United States have been condemned for their inability to channel individual and group enthusiasms into institutions which would ensure the continuation of reform once enthusiasm had faded, considerable time is spent on gauging the advantages and disadvantages to the Indians of the Bureau of Indian Affairs (BIA), founded in 1824. For the same reason, I have dealt with the extraordinary involvement in their affairs of missionary societies working in co-operation with the government. And because whites on the whole did not grasp or applaud the political complexity of the Indian groups they encountered, I examine here their consequent attempts to elevate native leaders they found useful and impose on native communities political institutions that resembled their own.

The aim is to show that Indian reform both proceeded in parallel with other liberal reform movements in America, and in certain respects followed an organization and momentum of its own. At once a basic paradox emerges. Indian policy-makers and reformers, like those concerned with other minorities, hoped to assimilate their constituents into white society. Only in the 1930s and the period from

3

the 1960s has this not been their objective. Yet their endeavours served to delay or prevent assimilation.* It is therefore tempting to judge them solely by results, not rhetoric; to write off both elements as hypocritical and to search simply for their ulterior motives. But to genuinely understand their history one needs to know what sustained their confidence and how far their policies failed because they were misconceived, supported by the self-interested, misapplied, or opposed. When this has been done, however, there is still no altering the basic fact that reformers and policy-makers, until well on into the twentieth century and unlike their Canadian counterparts, made extravagant promises that they could not keep, and failed to secure the Indians in even the reduced territories of the reservation era. Why the promises were made relates to concern with realizing the nation's founding commitment to create a moral and egalitarian society. Why they were broken relates to the larger numbers of whites and Indians at odds in the United States and the whites' primary interest, from the seventeenth century onwards, in settling and exploiting the land.[1]

Though detailing the struggles of philanthropists and administrators with Indians they had to some extent invented and thus essentially writing a 'white' history, in Part One and Part Two alike I have also tried to remind the reader of the Indian actors who, while their powers of resistance to white assimilationist efforts may have differed according to the strength of their political institutions, the nature of their terrain, their numbers and their distance from the main white settlements, none the less critically affected the outcome of those struggles. In so doing, I have attempted to point up the variety of Indian peoples and the contrasts in outlook between Indians and whites. And without belittling humanitarian efforts, I have aimed to indicate the damaging impact of underfunded, coercive reform, which took little account of Indian wishes and diversity.

In Part Two, the obstacles in the way of harmonious race relations are first examined in a survey of two particular areas: the South and Indian Territory. They are then considered in chapters on assimilationist campaigns which often receive skimpy treatment in surveys of Indian policy: education, the transformation of Indian women and the urbanization of Native Americans. Additional case studies look at the relationship of anthropology to the assimilationist crusade and at

---

* The term assimilation, though it can have various meanings, is used here to encompass the desire of whites to see 'greater homogeneity in society', with Indian individuals, indeed Indians as a whole, being persuaded to merge into the 'dominant Anglo-Saxon Protestant ethnicity' (see discussion in S. Thernstrom (ed.), *Harvard Encyclopedia of American Ethnic Groups* (Cambridge, Mass., Harvard University Press, 1981 edn), pp. 31–58, 150–60). Acculturation is taken to be the process whereby Indian and white cultures met and altered, without one absorbing the other.

the efforts of Indians to shape their own affairs through new forms of political organization.

The opening case study, contained in Chapters 5 and 6, is concerned with the interaction of Indians, blacks and, to a lesser extent, whites, initially in the southern states and subsequently in Indian Territory, following the removal there between the 1820s and 1840s of the southern Indians: the Cherokees, Choctaws, Chickasaws, Creeks and Seminoles, eventually known as the Five Civilized Tribes. These are the two areas where such interaction is most important before large numbers of blacks and Indians joined whites in the cities during the twentieth century.

By the late colonial period, it was only in the Carolinas and Georgia that all three races were numerically strong. It was only in this region that they had many opportunities for intermarriage and trade with each other and took advantage of their opportunities. And although the white and Indian settlements did not merge, while the blacks were deliberately segregated in slavery or freedom, southern whites worried that Indians and blacks might combine against them. They had some cause for concern. Blacks were given refuge among the Indians, despite whites' efforts to exact the return of runaways and their employment of blacks in the colonial militia to fight against the tribes. Yet whites were able to contain the fraternization they feared. If the treatment of blacks and Indians alike cast doubts on the sincerity of Revolutionary idealism, the different cultures and economic circumstances of Native and Afro-Americans caused them to be regarded and presented rather differently by the colonists. It is my contention that whites in time passed on to the southern Indians some of their more derogatory perceptions of the blacks and that instead of real solidarity developing between the similarly exploited and initially amicable Indians and blacks, the Five Civilized Tribes followed whites in enslaving, disliking and pulling apart from blacks.

In showing how and why this happened, I have ranged from colonial times to the twentieth century, and have briefly looked at significant instances of Indian–black contacts outside my two chosen regions. I have placed a heavy emphasis upon the social context of the Indians' antipathy. Far more than was the case with whites, their responses to blacks were shaped by economic and political considerations rather than theoretical speculations or emotional reactions. Indeed, I have generally tried to bring out the distinctive aspects of race relations among the Five Tribes and to demonstrate that, all difficulties notwithstanding, instances of amity between Indians and blacks can be found up to and beyond the end of Indian Territory in 1907. Through studying the three races in the South and Indian

Territory, it has been possible to confirm the general belief that, as late as the end of the nineteenth century, America remained a nation of distinct ethnic communities, with race being the most fundamental division.[2]

The Five Tribes are also the ideal group to study if one wants to test the sincerity of white claims to be interested in civilizing the Native Americans and willing to respect the rights of those tribes who accepted the white way. We do not really know why some native peoples adapted more readily than others to white civilization. The usual argument is that groups most culturally 'advanced', from the white point of view, came out best.[3] Whatever the reason, in terms of adaptability to white culture, the powerful, horticulturalist southern tribes occupied a position analogous to that of the Bantu people who were brought to North America and enslaved there.[4] But as we shall see, their 'progressive' strain did not save the protesting Five Tribes from removal west of the Mississippi, not least because, with the aid of black slaves, they had revealed the rich potential of their lands to acquisitive white neighbours. However, the Indian Territory to which the southern Indians were despatched was supposedly their inviolable home and their progress in the Territory, where they ostensibly enjoyed domestic autonomy, earned them their collective title. Even after their support for black slavery and a number of other factors had drawn sections of the Five Tribes into the Civil War on the side of the South, resulting in punitive renegotiation of their treaties by the federal government, they continued to enjoy self-government within a reduced territory, were initially exempt from the 1887 allotment legislation and seemed to be holding out, with real prospects of success, for separate statehood from Oklahoma Territory (created out of their 'surplus' lands in 1890).

Just before the battle was lost, the mixed-blood Creek chief, Pleasant Porter, testified to a senatorial committee visiting Indian Territory that[5]

> We have striven in our own way for our elevation and uplifting, and for a time it seemed that we were actually going to evolve a sort of civilization that would suit our temperament; and we probably would if it had not been for this white and black invasion.

Chief Porter was referring to the inrush of black and white immigrants in the last quarter of the nineteenth century which, added to the ex-slaves and whites already there, had by 1890 reduced the Indians to about 28 per cent of the population of Indian Territory. At that date blacks constituted some 10 per cent of the Territory's total population of over 178,000 and formed a larger fraction of the individual Five Tribes than they had in 1860.

6

In Chapters 5 and 6, I try to establish that the southern Indians reached this low point because, instead of being allowed to experience what the anthropologists Edward Spicer, Ralph Linton and Evon Vogt have called 'non-directed' or voluntary 'incorporative' change,[6] that is, a process of slow adaptation to alien cultures in which their own core culture was retained, they were forced along the unwanted path towards assimilation by white pressures and evasions. It has been suggested by Joan Chandler that since whites have intervened in all Indian societies and that some forms of intervention have been welcomed, then the distinction between directed and non-directed change is of limited value.[7] But I think it is important to see why whites would not accept a type of change which a particularly accommodating group of Indians was willing to embark upon and which, if allowed, might have made for a much more harmonious relationship between native societies and the Bureau of Indian Affairs.

Black slaves were agents of acculturation that the Five Tribes were ready to accept; they had enhanced the power and wealth of the warrior class and the mixed bloods, changed the character of Indian agriculture and increased Indian involvement with white traders and politics. Unfortunately, native society did not alter fast enough for whites and they therefore followed up removal of the Five Tribes from the South by manipulation of 'the Negro problem' in Indian Territory in order to destroy Indian nationality. Earlier in the book (Chapters 2 and 3), attention is given to additional devices employed by whites to produce directed change among the southern Indians, notably the use of government agents to limit tribal authority, and the modernization of tribal economies via the railroad, town and corporation.

Following on from this treatment of race relations, Chapter 7 is concerned with American Indians and American anthropologists. While the role of other 'friends of the Indian' is usually outlined in broad surveys of Indian–white relations, the contribution of anthropologists to the making of Indian policy is less often considered. One reason for the initially poor showing of administrators of native affairs in many parts of the world may be that they had no 'scientific' basis upon which to build:[8] in other words, they either could not or would not utilize the work of those whose primary interest was the scholarly study of native societies. In the early years of the United States, politicians like Thomas Jefferson and Albert Gallatin were also amateur anthropologists, but for the most part anthropologists and their findings were not determinedly consulted by policy-makers until the twentieth century. When they were, those who had hoped for a major improvement in Indian policy were often disappointed, while the relations between anthropologists and the peoples they studied sometimes deteriorated. An effort is therefore made here to assess the difficulties involved in the emergence of the discipline and its practical application, as well as the long-term contribution of anthropology to a better understanding between Indians and whites.

Chapters 8 and 9 move on to the subject of American Indian education. Here was something which whites had no hesitation in making an integral part of their Indian policy, not least because the missionaries who first worked among the tribes believed that the advance of religion and civility were intimately connected. Up to the 1920s, certain assumptions and objectives in the campaign for Indian education remained constant. It was acknowledged that Indians were teachable and could benefit from both academic and practical training. It was assumed that the federal government had a duty to find the means and establish the framework for education, even if this meant its subcontracting work to missionaries or helping itself out by adding some of the Indians' own funds to general appropriations. This commitment, albeit imperfectly honoured, underlined the government's special relationship with Indian peoples; federal aid to education for the American population as a whole was delayed until the mid 1960s, for fear of stirring up racial and religious antagonisms.[9] Education, it was further held, could be used to alter the sexual division of labour in Indian communities, thus emancipating Indian women. And it was believed that education would civilize the Indians and assimilate them as individuals into white society.

We may now endorse with equanimity Carl Degler's view that the principal conflicts in American history have been related to racial and ethnic consciousness and that the writing of American history is therefore more difficult than it was when confident, WASP-centred accounts of the national experience predominated.[10] It is scarcely surprising, however, that policy-makers in a country divided along ethnic lines, racked by racial tensions and beset by growing economic cleavages, should regard diversity with alarm and seek ways of securing national unity and strengthening the entrenched, but numerically threatened, social groups from which they themselves generally came. Education was one of those ways. The account of the instruction of the American Indians in Chapters 8 and 9 is accordingly set in the context of a wider debate about the ability of schools to 'uplift' and integrate ethnics, and since uplift was intended to proceed just so far, an effort is made to determine whether the Native Americans were as rigorously educated for 'place' as American blacks.

The desire to educate the Indians was not, of course, equally strong at all times, nor was the progress of instruction evenly achieved over time. Consequently, Chapter 8 looks at the causes of the failure of colonial efforts at Indian schooling and at the reasons for renewing efforts in the second and sixth decades of the nineteenth century. Consideration is also given to the disruption and dismay caused by Indian removal west of the Mississippi, the pacification of the warlike tribes and land allotment. Account is taken of the government failure to fulfil treaty promises and reformers' inability to decide on the best means to achieve their end of an Indian education system run according to white precepts. And there is an assessment of the impact of the First World War and the ensuing period of political reaction. In explaining the Indian opposition to white schools (albeit this was not uniform among the tribes), attention is paid to the Indians' own educational institutions and endeavours, as well as to the deficiencies of the white institutions and their operators, missionary and lay, and the reactions of whites to Indian attendance at the public schools. Given the generally gloomy tenor of the story, it is worth noting at the outset that whites frequently offered to Native Americans the best that contemporary pedagogy had to give, and that the gap between theory and practice in Indian schools was often no greater than that prevailing in other rural schools, or in the big city educational systems of the era.

Taking the account of education from the 1920s to the 1970s, Chapter 9 records the continuing struggles of Indian parents to control the instruction of their children against the background of a slow, erratic shift in white thinking away from assimilation as the main goal of schooling and towards the more modest objective of improving and extending educational facilities. Again, developments in Indian schooling are related to trends in American education as a whole and to changes in the overall direction of Indian policy. Hence a period of reappraisal in the late 1920s was followed by a 'new day' for the Indians, in which community schools under community control gained more official backing than they had previously experienced. The reforming 1930s were in turn succeeded by years of retrenchment and conservatism, beginning with the cutbacks necessitated during the Second World War, a disastrous time generally for education in the United States. Caution continued through the 1950s, being challenged in the liberal 1960s and reaffirmed by the mid 1970s.

Yet some of the progress made during the 1930s and 1960s was retained, despite the subsequent reactions and remaining difficulties. These difficulties were daunting. It was not easy for parents who had traditionally been powerless in this area to get used to exerting influence on school matters, and it was not clear how bicultural education could be achieved, or even whether it improved the academic performance as opposed to the morale of minority children.

9

When Indians moved to cities they might enhance their economic prospects, but (as I also suggest in Chapter 11) their children encountered the kinds of problems in large and run-down city schools that had long faced the offspring of other minorities enrolled there. And it was uncertain where the agents or money for bicultural instruction were to be found, or whether disillusionment with education could be prevented if all the reforms failed to bring the sort of returns to Indian (and other minority) children that schooling brought to fortunate whites.

The situation of Indian women, touched on in the education section and in the discussion of economics and politics in twentieth-century Indian societies in Chapter 4, and of urban Indians and pan-Indian political groups in Chapters 11 and 12, is examined further in Chapter 10. It is argued that whereas whites appreciated the appearance of Indian women and did not rule out miscegenation as a means of assimilating Native Americans, they initially married and cohabited with them only to a limited degree, due to lack of opportunity, the greater suitability of European women for white farm life, the Indians' preference for partners of their own race, and white prejudice. In particular, whites deplored the Indians' sexual division of labour (though it was not that different from their own) and denounced the natives for their promiscuity, polygamy, child-rearing methods and lack of sentimentality about marriage and divorce. The general aim of reformers was to impose upon the Indians the conjugal family of the white middle class, and so to increase the responsibilities of allegedly idle Indian men and the dignity of allegedly servile Indian women. Such attempts to alter Indian family life were singularly unfortunate, partly because they stemmed from a distorted appraisal of the lot of Indian women and partly because their customary effect, wherever they have been made by colonizers, has been to decrease the economic independence of native women, upon which such power as they had depended, and to bring upon them the complaints of their undermined and disgruntled menfolk.

A feminist critique of the second-class status of Indian women is, like the observations of nineteenth-century reformers, open to the charge of arrogantly ignoring the apparent acceptance of their circumstances by Indian women themselves. On the other hand, the feminist approach also seeks to value women's experiences, domestic or otherwise. Accordingly, using the findings of feminist-inspired modern scholarship on women, I have attempted to establish the consequences for Indian women of matriliny and matrilocality and, in broad terms, to depict their roles in the family, work, religion and politics. What emerges clearly is that, while Indian women were best placed in horticulturalist tribes where they could combine their responsibilities for children with crop production, they were generally better off in some respects than white women. They were not, for example, as liable to be driven into organized prostitution; witches were not exclusively female; and Indian communities, with a few exceptions, were not autocratic societies supporting similarly autocratic family structures.

Just as white hopes of transforming Indian women were defeated by Indian conservatism and resentment, so the campaigns to 'modernize' Native Americans in an urban environment, outlined in Chapter 11, were embarrassed by the problems awaiting latecomers to the cities and the unwillingness of Indian migrants to sever their reservation roots. Indians have not been deliberately recruited by city employers, as native peasants have been wooed in other parts of the world, because American immigrants, blacks and other ethnics were closer to hand and responded sooner and more readily to employer needs; these groups also aroused fewer white qualms about their long-term reliability as workers. But a considerable degree of Indian urbanization was probably inevitable, in view of the limited economic openings on many Indian reservations, the expansion of the Indian population in the twentieth century, and such periods of obvious urban opportunity as the Second World War. It is likely to continue on a voluntary basis, as Native Americans seek in the cities material opportunities, a change from traditional community ways and contact with Indians from other backgrounds. In this chapter, however, the main focus is upon the BIA's relocation programme. Consideration is given to Indian and white criticism of the programme. Indian gains from relocation are assessed and their experiences with regard to urban housing, health, education, welfare, family relations and institution-making are outlined.

In conclusion, Chapter 12 looks at the emergence of pan-Indian political protest groups. Their advent was welcomed by white reformers as a sign of the Indians' political maturity, as an indication of their willingness to set their own priorities and interest themselves in the political world beyond the reservation or native enclave. Although the first leaders of these groups shared many of the assimilationist goals of their white counterparts, and limited Indian numbers will always make them dependent on white allies, I have argued here that co-operation between the two was uneasy. The Indian organizations undoubtedly encountered many of the same problems and employed some of the same tactics as the other American pressure groups alluded to in Chapter 12. They likewise benefited or suffered from changing political circumstances. Yet in the existence of a territorial

base and treaty heritage, the divided political loyalties of their reservation constituents, the differences between urban and reservation
Indians, the lack of a congressional caucus and the special relationship
with the BIA, they faced distinctive challenges which they have
struggled to resolve on their own terms. The diversity of Indians
precludes unanimity among their protest groups, but they have, by
avoiding dangerous reliance on a handful of artificially chosen leaders,
by never losing sight of local issues and by linking up with Indian
campaigners outside the United States, evolved an obviously Indian
stance in American pressure politics.

1

The Colonial Legacy

I

RACE, CULTURE AND THE INDIAN

For a number of years there has been disagreement about the importance of white racism to the institutionalization of black slavery in the
North American colonies, although there is no doubt that allegations
about black inferiority were invaluable in the defence of slavery, once
it came under attack.[1] Similar differences of opinion exist regarding
early white responses to Indian groups in North America.

There are those who contend that, from the first, English settlers
considered the Native Americans to be an alien race and treated them
accordingly.[2] Others maintain that the Indians' tawny hue, unlike the
blackness of the African, was often attributed to paint and accorded no
special significance. Indians were not referred to as red men before the
end of the seventeenth century and the term was not in common
usage until the late colonial period. In other words, Indians, unlike
blacks, were either included in the white race or not viewed as a
separate, 'lower' race, set apart by their physical characteristics.[3] Some
writers suggest that ethnocentrism* gradually gave way to racism, so
far as Indians were concerned, but they debate whether this had
happened by the close of the eighteenth century, or by the 1850s.[4] No
agreement has been reached about claims that, among all the English
settlers, the Puritans were particularly contemptuous of Indian cul-

* *Ethocentrism* is usually taken to be a conviction of the invariable cultural superiority
of one's own ethnic group; whereas *racism* is a supposedly scientific theory that men and
women can be divided into higher and lower biological stocks, possessing specific
cultural attributes, a theory which leads those who subscribe to it to practise discrimination against, to conflict with and to coerce the allegedly inferior races. A distinction has
been made between racialism – the theory, and racism – the practice, but the
terminological distinction will not be drawn in this book. Clearly many who expounded
racist theories did not have the opportunity to practise discrimination; some may not
have had the inclination. Yet their ideas gave respectability to those who did discriminate and it seems fair that the two groups should be linked together even while
their different roles are duly noted.

13

tures because they saw themselves as a totally distinctive, chosen people.[5] Finally, even if one accepts that colonial whites condemned Indian cultures rather than the Indian race, controversy arises as to whether cultural arrogance may be as harmful as racial prejudice. And if so, then did Indian peoples gain nothing from initially being seen as very different from imported Africans? Did they, like blacks, suffer because the English came to the New World from an extremely parochial country, whose inhabitants were obsessed with the need to impose order on themselves and others in an age of change and entertained a broad set of hostile assumptions about dark-skinned peoples?[6]

There is no easy way out of this thicket. My own view, already expressed elsewhere,[7] is that white prejudices led to the lumping together of non-whites in times of crisis and that the distinction between ethnocentrism and racism has always been clearer to scholars than to the victims of either. None the less, I believe that Indian peoples were at times helped by the fact that they were regarded by many as culturally, rather than racially, distinct from whites. But the long-term benefits they gained were not large, while the reformers who became involved in their affairs in the nineteenth century were very similar in outlook and background to those who campaigned on behalf of American blacks, whose status as a separate race was never in question.

It is important to establish not only what Englishmen believed about Indian societies, but also when they believed it, and the nature of the commentators. On the whole, the most outlandish judgements were made by writers with little first-hand experience of the natives and the most hostile were pronounced during times of conflict, which varied from colony to colony. Some give us a better idea of what Englishmen feared or wished to reaffirm in their own society than they do of the realities of Indian society. The majority of English observers were drawn from what contemporaries called the 'better sort' and Karen Kupperman maintains that they judged the Indians they met, who usually were not, as they would have judged poor Englishmen at home. Thus even if we accept Kupperman's point that 'status, not race, was the category which counted for English people of the early years of colonization', we cannot expect the bulk of the natives to be very favourably presented.[8]

The Indian peoples encountered by the European colonists have been divided into eight basic culture areas: (1) the northeastern woodlands, the region above the South and east of the Mississippi; (2) the Southeast, which comprised all the southern territory east of the Mississippi; (3) the Great Plains, stretching between the Rocky Mountains and the Mississippi; (4) the Southwest, encompassing Arizona, the western two-thirds of New Mexico and parts of Utah, Colorado and Texas; (5) California; (6) the Great Basin, ranging across Nevada and Utah from the Rockies to the Sierra Nevada and including sections of Idaho, Oregon, California, Arizona and Wyoming; (7) the Plateau country between the Rocky Mountains and the Cascade Mountains; and (8) the northwestern Pacific Coast, taking in western Oregon and Washington. Settlers in what became the thirteen American colonies came into contact with Indians of the first two regions. In the Southeast, there were mainly sedentary, game-hunting and farming tribes, who lived in towns. They included the Cherokees in the Carolinas, Tennessee, Alabama and Georgia; the Choctaws in south-eastern Mississippi and southwestern Alabama; the Chickasaws in northern Mississippi; and the Creeks in Alabama and Georgia. In the northeastern woodlands, between the Mississippi and the Atlantic, and reaching north from the Carolinas and the Ohio River, most of the tribes farmed and hunted. They also lived in settled communities. Exceptions were the largely nomadic northern Ojibwas (Chippewas) and the buffalo hunters of Illinois. Among the New England peoples were the Penobscots, Pennacooks, Massachusets, Wampanoags, Niantics, Narragansets, Pequots and Mohegans. The Hudson River valley was the home of the Iroquois confederacy, which comprised the Mohawks, Oneidas, Onondagas, Cayugas, Senecas and, after 1722, the Tuscaroras. The region from the Great Lakes to the Ohio River contained the Menominees, Ottawas, Potawatomis, Sauk and Fox, Winnebagos, Kickapoos, the Illinois confederacy, Miamis, Shawnees, Conestogas (Susquehannocks) and Eries. And in the east, south of the Iroquois and into the Carolinas, were the Delawares, Nanticokes and Powhatans, the Pamunkeys, Chickahominys, Mattaponis, Notta-ways, Pamlicos, Tuscaroras and Catawbas (see Map 1).

In commenting on some of these diverse groups, Europeans, despite the prejudices just noted, were generally complimentary about their appearance, and the Indians' clothes, though frequently scanty, were thought to suit their environment and to take proper account of divisions of rank and sex.[9] Whatever the peculiarities of Indian sexual mores, from the white point of view, it was recognized that relations between the sexes were carefully regulated.[10] There was some acknowledgement that civil government existed among the Indians and that they revered their leaders.[11] The early seventeenth-century confederacy of Virginian Algonquian tribes, numbering some '12,000 Indians in thirty different tribal groupings' and headed by Powhatan, commanded grudging white respect as well as exciting suspicion.[12] Colonists, in order to survive, were obliged to learn from

15

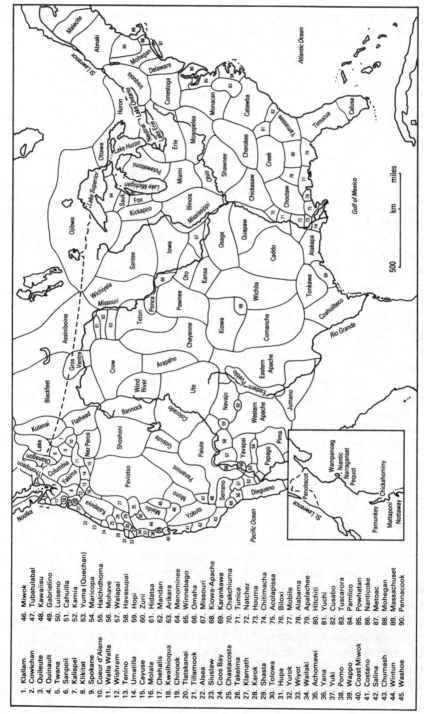

Map 1 American Indian peoples c.1600.

Source: S. Thernstrom (ed.), *Harvard Encyclopedia of Ethnic Groups* (Cambridge, Mass. and London: Belknap Press of Harvard University Press, 1980; 1981 edn); adapted from George Peter Murdock, *Ethnographic Bibliography of North America* (New Haven, Ct., Human Relations Area Files Press, 1960, 3rd edn).

1. Klallam
2. Cowichan
3. Quileute
4. Quinault
5. Twana
6. Sanpoil
7. Kalispel
8. Ktikitat
9. Spokane
10. Coeur d'Alene
11. Walla Walla
12. Wishram
13. Tenino
14. Umatilla
15. Cayuse
16. Molala
17. Chehalis
18. Kwalhioqua
19. Chinook
20. Tlatskanai
21. Tillamook
22. Alsea
23. Siuslaw
24. Coos Bay
25. Chastacosta
26. Takelma
27. Klamath
28. Karok
29. Shasta
30. Tolowa
31. Hupa
32. Yurok
33. Wiyot
34. Wailaki
35. Achomawi
36. Yana
37. Yuki
38. Pomo
39. Wappo
40. Coast Miwok
41. Costano
42. Salina
43. Chumash
44. Wintun
45. Washoe
46. Miwok
47. Tubatulabal
48. Kawaiisu
49. Gabrielino
50. Luiseno
51. Cahuilla
52. Kamia
53. Yuma (Quechan)
54. Maricopa
55. Halchidhoma
56. Mohave
57. Walapai
58. Havasupai
59. Hopi
60. Zuni
61. Hidatsa
62. Mandan
63. Arikara
64. Menominee
65. Winnebago
66. Omaha
67. Missouri
68. Kiowa-Apache
69. Karankawa
70. Chakchiuma
71. Tunica
72. Natchez
73. Houma
74. Chitimacha
75. Acolapissa
76. Biloxi
77. Mobile
78. Alabama
79. Apalachee
80. Hitchiti
81. Yuchi
82. Cusabo
83. Tuscarora
84. Pamlico
85. Powhatan
86. Nanticoke
87. Metoac
88. Mohegan
89. Massachuset
90. Pennacook

the natives how to obtain food and other resources, how to apply herb medicines and how to travel and fight effectively in wilderness conditions. They admitted that the native population engaged in 'hunting, farming, and trade' and that some groups were 'more competent than others'. Indian corn was highly valued, Indian towns, houses and products remarked, and in these matters, too, the fact that the Indians were ingeniously at one with their surroundings was appreciated.[13]

The importance of religion to native peoples was generally accepted; and to Puritans, at least, the Indians were initially less offensive than such 'unregenerate' Christians as Catholics and Quakers.[14] Certain aspects of the Indian character evoked considerable admiration: courage, dignity, good humour, generosity, hospitality and strong family feeling.[15] And the ultimate proof that Indian cultures were not regarded as unapproachably alien by whites were the runaways from the various colonies who went to live as Indians, or chose to remain with them when captured. In New England before 1782, for example, approximately 15 per cent of captives elected to become 'full-fledged Indians'.[16] Yet the point is, what, if any, advantage did these acknowledgements of the Indians' 'civility' bring to them?

In English areas of settlement, recognition that the Indians were not culturelesss only rarely led to consistent respect for their rights. Pennsylvania was one of the regions where it did. Very often kindly comment about the natives was made for promotional purposes by interested individuals and William Penn, the founder of Pennsylvania, when he described in glowing terms the 'Persons, Language, Manners, Religion and Government' of the Delaware Indians with whom he had to deal, intended thereby to recommend his colony to prospective settlers. He also believed in the superiority of white civilization. None the less, he was convinced that the Indians could adapt to that civilization. He was determined to convert them 'by gentle and just manners to the love of civil society and Christian Religion' and, in the process of enlarging the English empire and trade, to deal 'justly and lovingly towards' the natives, whether in the matter of land negotiations, refraining from liquor sales, the conduct of trade, or providing for the settlement of differences between the two races.

This determination bore fruit. Although Shawnees, Miamis and Tuscaroras joined the Delawares in Pennsylvania, the Quaker settlers avoided involvement in Indian wars from the last quarter of the seventeenth century to the 1750s, when they relinquished political dominance of the colony and their control over Indian affairs had ceased. In New England and the South the Quaker record, if less impressive, was still good, and granting that Indian slaves were at first bought and sold by Quakers, the sect moved against this traffic in the early eighteenth century. But their stance seems to have owed as much to the Quakers' pacifism, aloofness and aversion to practising against others the persecution that they had experienced, as it did to advanced opinions about the Indians' 'Lofty' language, liberality, sagacity, and possible link with 'the Jewish Race'. Moreover, comparative tolerance of Indian ways does not appear to have made Quakers willing to contemplate miscegenation with the natives, while the dealings with the Indians of John and Thomas Penn and the merchant and proprietary agent, James Logan, were distinctly grasping.[17]

Elsewhere in North America, Alden T. Vaughan suggests that such colonial leaders as 'George Thorpe in early Virginia, the second Lord Baltimore in Maryland . . . and Edward Winslow and the elder Jonathan Mayhew in New England' were genuinely 'solicitous of Indian welfare' and the legal rights of Indians were at least sporadically defended by colonial authorities in the seventeenth century, before Indians came to be regarded as an alien race.[18] Indians were not enslaved on the same scale or with the same confidence as blacks. Yet, as we argue in Chapter 5, this advantage cannot be explained simply with reference to the Indians' cultural claims, and it should not, in any event, be exaggerated. Indian enslavement remained important in the Carolinas and in Canada until the eighteenth century, while the association of slavery with race and colour was damaging to Indians as well as to blacks. Nevertheless, as late as the eighteenth century there were public officials, traders and pioneer ethnologists who, though they did not restrain a public disenchanted by encounters with desperate or demoralized natives, kept alive a degree of interest in Indian cultures which greatly surpassed the curiosity displayed in African societies.[19] They did so despite the growth of ominous intellectual challenges to the Christian view of man's origins. This interest in turn helped to make federal Indian policy in the Revolutionary and early republican years less cynically dedicated to white expansion at any cost than it might otherwise have been.[20]

On the other hand, whites' moderate respect for Indian attributes tended to vanish during conflicts with the tribes, notably the 1622 uprising of Virginia natives and the 1637 white attack on Pequots in Connecticut. At such times especially, Indians were described as savages, a designation which expressed settler insecurity, 'justified' whites' efforts at aggrandizement and partly restored their badly threatened sense of solidarity.[21] Furthermore, appreciation of Indian civility did not prevent ethnocentric English efforts to deliberately destroy aspects of native culture. Missionary endeavour is a good case in point.

Since it was recognized that Indian religion intermeshed vitally with other elements of Indian society, it was logical that Christian missionaries should argue that conversion and the adoption of white civilization had to proceed together. Their labours are detailed in later chapters. It is enough here to note that they failed, and Sheehan maintains that the failure strengthened English convictions about Indian savagery.[22] But the missionaries themselves, though they may have had some doubts about the Indian ability to adapt to civility,[23] did not generally surrender to racism, not least because they remained convinced of the possibility of training native preachers to sustain the converts.

It could be contended that a greater effort, achieving more recruits, might have produced a much greater compliance among the Indians, some of whom were inclined to attribute the growth of English power on the continent to the strength of the whites' god, and to accommodate themselves to Christianity as a means of cultural survival.[24] Alternatively, we have suggested that the Quakers' slowness to proselytize may have been the key to their successes with the Indians, and as Jacobs has noted, a similar restraint on the part of the religious liberal and Rhode Island statesman, Roger Williams (1603–82/3), initially helped to secure peace between Rhode Island whites and the local Narraganset Indians.[25] Yet English aloofness is frequently cited as evidence of English race prejudice and is certainly demonstrated in the low level of Indian–white miscegenation in the colonial period, the reluctance of whites as a whole to live in scattered settlements among the Indians and their failure to find any role for 'civilized' Indians or 'Indianized' whites in their own communities.[26]

We should not suppose that because native spokesmen occasionally complained about this English reluctance to fraternize and intermarry with their people, the Indians were, by contrast, free of ethnocentrism.[27] They found a niche for the newcomers in their societies essentially because they needed them. Those adopted replaced kinsmen lost in wars and epidemics and were especially valuable as white immigrants poured into the New World and the white population came to exceed the native population in coastal regions. Whites may have been co-opted as Indians with a wholeheartedness that whites did not extend to Indians who moved into their society; yet in each case the admitting society set the terms of entry, as one would expect. The crucial difference between them was that, when the whites arrived to settle rather than to trade, and their beachheads survived, the Indians' land became more useful than the friendly contacts with native peoples which had ensured that survival. It may be that whereas whites were inclined to destroy what was strange to them, Indians were prepared to add aspects of white culture to their own: European trade goods, technology, religious practices and even education might be accepted.[28] But white destructiveness, as Salisbury argues, seems to have been more the result of white numbers, diseases and firearms than of an inevitably fatal culture conflict.[29]

No one can deny, however, that a culture conflict damaging to the Indians did exist, and that although the natives did not entertain the concept of race, Indian pride in their own ways was a formidable challenge to English cultural imperialism. Thus, while whites congratulated themselves on the superiority of their religion, technology and social organization, Indian commentators derided the sexual division of labour among whites, mocked the assertiveness of English women and deplored the wasteful destructiveness of English methods of warfare.[30] Indian individuals were taken into colonial settlements and homes and back to England, with a view to showing them the glories of European civilization and making them into its agents. Even when impressed by what they saw, the Indians usually declined to act as intended, or did not live long to tell their tales. Amerindian views of French culture in the seventeenth century seem to have been similarly critical and the Indians had good reason to dislike the cruelty of the Spanish colonists, whose lust for precious metals they also despised. The resulting resistance to white culture might provoke tensions as fatal to the integrity of Indian societies as too much compliance with white ways turned out to be.[31]

II

Economics and Demography

At the heart of the cultural conflict between whites and Indians was a series of economic activities and exchanges which were not fatal in themselves to native societies. Since both groups traded, hunted and farmed, there was scope for coexistence while their numbers remained roughly comparable. Some of the eastern tribes and bands who came into contact with whites were both accustomed to trade with neighbours and to seeking a bargain. As an aid to commerce, and a valued item in it, the Indians had devised a shell currency usually known as wampum, which became more widespread after white settlement but was already in use in pre-contact days in New England and elsewhere in the eastern parts of North America.[32] The short-term benefits of trade with the settlers seemed obvious and its long-term consequences were difficult to predict, because the native peoples initially had no means of gauging white intentions and advantages. It is therefore not surprising that Indians were willing to deal with the newcomers and to exploit the contest for tribal custom that evolved among English, French and Dutch traders.[33] The Iroquois, in particular, were sufficiently well-organized and ruthless to benefit from European rivalries until as late as the 1750s, playing an uneasy balancing role between the French and the English, first as actors and then as middlemen in the fur trade.[34]

Competition for Indian trade also grew up between the different English colonies, from which the tribesmen were happy to profit.[35] And when, by the middle of the eighteenth century, these colonies were able to manufacture cheaply some of the goods required for the traffic, rather than having to rely on European imports, a development that made their products more desirable than those of the French, the tribesmen did not hesitate to switch allegiances in search of commercial gain. Thus as R. David Edmunds has demonstrated, in the 1740s the Miami chief 'Old Briton' emerged as the most vocal critic of France's trading system among its Indian allies, albeit his attempt to transfer his support to the British, with their encouragement, failed and resulted in his own death in 1752.[36]

As this example makes plain, for all their ability to get their trading preferences across and to seek the best terms available to them, Indians might find that the price they had to pay took the form of destructive military alliances from which it was difficult or impossible to escape. Hence the Iroquois, with the aid of European firearms, not only maintained a dominant position in the fur trade but assisted in the devastation of the Illinois and Hurons (who were not effectively armed) and the displacement further west of the Ohio and Great Lakes tribes. Moreover, their constant warfare, prompted by the ramifications of the fur trade and considerations of prestige or revenge, reduced their numbers and necessitated a policy of wholesale adoptions, while the Iroquois' partial support of the English proved disastrous to their fortunes during the American Revolution. Among the southern Indians, European trade goods were exchanged for deerskins and war captives destined for slavery. The new traffic subjected the tribes to pressures for their support from the English, French and Spanish and brought them into extra conflicts with one another.[37]

There were further dangers involved in white–Indian trade. Early contacts produced a mutual benefit but whites disliked and feared their reliance on the natives, and colonial authorities moved to end it as soon as they could.[38] The Indians could not feed themselves and a

21

steady stream of newcomers indefinitely and disputes over food quickly produced dangerous friction between the two races.[39] Many items of trade received from Europeans simply replaced similar artefacts produced in native societies, without destroying the traditional function of those artefacts. Needles, kettles, traps and fish-hooks came into this category. White firearms and fermented liquor, however, had a more dramatic impact. Although European weapons may have given the receiving Indians a better chance of resisting white encroachments, the tribes also used them against each other to deadly effect. With the aid of liquor the colonists cheated Indians out of their land. Under its influence Indian lawlessless grew, and tribesmen lost that dignity which whites regarded as one of their most attractive qualities. In addition, the recipients of liquor and arms became dangerously dependent on whites for replacement stocks.[40]

Commerce with Europeans came in time to replace the old intertribal and localized Indian trade networks. Indian reliance on whites was consequently increased, with most of the coastal tribes drawing heavily on imported goods by the time of the Revolution.[41] It was therefore particularly unfortunate that the new traffic did not materially benefit the natives to the same degree as it benefited the colonists. White traders made a personal profit and their explorations revealed the rich agricultural and settlement possibilities of much eastern Indian land.[42] Europeans could quickly see the individual and collective advantages to be reaped from the commerce. There were only two drawbacks to the traders' activities from the white point of view, though they could at times seem considerable ones. The first was that they provoked Indian hostilities which the newcomers dreaded and could not afford. And, secondly, the traders themselves opposed and hampered the settlement that they ultimately made possible. Things were different for the Indians. Strong groupings like the Iroquois or dominant individuals like Powhatan might use trade wealth to enhance their power and advance their political ambitions in a manner that whites could understand. But for many more Indians, the new acquisitions were used to sustain traditional hospitality and ceremony, to avert group censure and to establish purely personal, perhaps fleeting, prestige. When Indian individuals did see the usefulness of accumulating and retaining wealth, and this was feasible in tribes like the Cherokees, which distinguished between property belonging to the tribe, the lineage and the individual, their subsequent elevation through an involvement in a market economy stretching beyond their boundaries could seriously aggravate the factionalism that was 'a common form of Indian politics'.[43]

Of all the new types of interracial trade, the fur trade presented at once the most opportunities and the most dangers for the Indians. As Jennings has argued, European demand for pelts generated a shift from subsistence hunting, broke down the Indians' respect for the well-recognized territorial boundaries between tribes and for the balance of natural forces in their environment and eventually led them to assist in the exhaustion of the commodity which rendered them important to the white traders.[44] Of course, self-interest made these traders show some concern about not overhunting the fur-bearing animals or destroying the native societies that depended on them. But their concern was more pronounced in Canada than further south.[45] Even in Canada it was not successful in the long run among the hunter-gatherer tribes.[46] The fact that the fur traders were rather more prepared than most whites to acknowledge the great variety of the Indians they met with did not, in any event, make them into humanitarians, or positive friends of the Indian. Traders were inclined to think best of the tribes who fitted most easily into their commerce. They projected the Indians as incorrigibly self-interested, were uneasy over miscegenation and mixed-blood offspring and expressed pessimism about Indian prospects of adjusting to 'civilized' life.[47]

The hardships endured by the Indian fur traders and the variety of tasks they performed in an enterprise which has been likened by Jennings to a European cottage industry, did not, until modern times, essentially change the European view of Indians as primitive hunters. Still more importantly, the dislocations caused by linking Indian trade to a very different, highly commercialized, market, could not be undone. In colonial New England, as Salisbury has shown, the result was a rupturing of the reciprocal, functional and sacred relationship between man and nature. Once the commerce in skins declined, Indians sought the European goods they then needed by offering their labour and land for sale.[48] Some of that land was already carefully cultivated.

It is now argued that while the Indians' practice of burning their fields and the woodland undergrowth may have destroyed flora and fauna, it increased nutrients in the ground, facilitated hunting and improved the availability of pasture and wild foods for man and animal alike. In addition, the native habit of planting beans and corn together helped productivity because the legumes fixed nitrogen in the soil. If Indian fields were not cleared as thoroughly as those of whites before cultivation, they were scrupulously tended, the surpluses were stored and out of native stocks, as we have seen, the colonists were fed. In overall terms, food production in the western hemisphere was efficient enough, combined with other factors, to sustain between 90 and 112 million people, in Dobyns's estimate, at

23

the time of European contact, of whom some 10 to 12 million lived in North America. Yet the advantages to the Indians from contacts with whites were even less in agriculture than they were in trade.

White animals strayed into Indian fields and the Indians were held responsible, whereas the English continued to intrude on Indian lands without compunction. Tribal orchards, garden plots and food stores were also deliberately destroyed by whites when they were at war with the Indians, albeit they in their turn, in such circumstances, slaughtered the settlers' cattle. The stable village life which had been supported through agriculture was disrupted, and in terms of crops and techniques of cultivation, the tribes gained nothing from the English. During the colonial period, whites had little to offer the Indians apart from stronger, metal implements. Content with their own way of life, the natives were reluctant to adopt the newcomers' domesticated animals and forage grasses. Coming into a continent where soil yields were initially rich and land was more plentiful than in Europe, however problematic its acquisition, the colonists often underused or misused the terrain and then moved on. Although intensive methods of agriculture may have been less necessary in the New World than in the Old, the newcomers were certainly not the bringers of an agricultural revolution, except to the extent that their incursions led to the abandonment of Indian fields and firing, so that the forest encroached again in the east before it was finally pushed back by large-scale white settlement.

Subsistence agriculture was 'pervasive throughout the colonies', among whites, just as it was among the sedentary Indians. And since agriculture remained the chief economic activity in the colonies, the economic gulf between the two races was not as great as it would become in the nineteenth century. None the less, by the time of the break with Britain, as Walton and Shepherd point out, the whites' initial collective methods of agricultural production had been abandoned as unpopular and discredited as inefficient. Overseas markets had developed for colonial tobacco, rice, flour, fish and indigo, and shipping and trade were flourishing. The distribution of wealth and income had become more unequal and urbanization and industrialization had given rise to a free labour class which owned no property.[49] In this increasingly unequal and diverse society, juxtaposed against the Indians' reciprocal communities, the prospects for future co-operation between natives and settlers looked poor.

Moreover, by the middle of the eighteenth century, the Indians were no longer able to block white settlement. Before the coming of the whites, not least because of their geographical isolation, they appear to have been comparatively healthy and long-lived peoples.

But traders, missionaries and settlers brought with them diseases to which the natives had no immunity. These included smallpox and tuberculosis, which of course could be very serious for whites, and ailments such as measles and mumps, which were childhood problems in Europe. Syphilis, though native to the western hemisphere, was brought into North America by Europeans and the various new infections were carried there by white fishermen and explorers even before settlement began. In Virginia, the Indians were ravaged by smallpox epidemics in the 1660s, 1679–80 and 1696. Other southern tribes, both close to and distant from the main areas of white colonization, also felt the impact of European diseases.[50] Assorted epidemics similarly devastated the tribes of New England in 1616–18, 1622 and 1633. Precise figures are lacking, but the Massachusets, for example, may have been reduced by smallpox from 3,000 to 1,000.[51]

Within a generation or so, the impact of such epidemics on particular Indian groups tailed off dramatically.[52] However, by that time the damage was done. Whites were quick to draw conclusions from Indian losses and, given the state of medical knowledge in the colonial period, these were self-interested rather than scientific. The settlers were disposed to see disease in their own communities as a sign of divine displeasure. Fortunately for them, the Indians suffered more severely and this appeared to indicate that God was on the side of the English. In the demoralization produced when native cures and medicine men proved ineffective, some Indians inclined to the same opinion. After all, the ghastly plagues that took life also broke down the kinship networks, skills, customs and leadership of the afflicted societies.[53]

The high level of Indian mortality did not prevent Europeans from enslaving the natives, but it did have the grim side-effect of stimulating the demand for black slaves. As Kiple and King remark, whereas whites were discouraged from settling in Africa because they were fatally susceptible to its diseases, they were encouraged to settle in the New World, where both they and imported Africans could survive, the latter being resistant to European and tropical diseases alike. The African slave traffic then introduced American Indians to ulriparium malaria and yellow fever, by which their numbers were further reduced, while the African ability to withstand these two diseases was used by whites as 'proof' that blacks were intended to labour in hot regions and that they were not. In short, the colonists were conveniently able to conclude that the Indians would vanish before civilization, while the Africans were ordained to be its servants.[54]

As far as the economy was concerned, those Indians who survived might possibly have hoped to benefit from this situation. Jennings has suggested that in their relations with the white colonists, who drew them into a wider market, polity and world, the native peoples constituted peasant rather than 'primitive' communities.[55] With the labour shortage substantially met by blacks in the late colonial era, whites did not need to deprive these peasant societies of their land in order to force their members to work for wages, as settlers disposssessed the black peasantry in South Africa more than a century later.[56] But no benefit materialized. Indian vulnerability was too tempting to be ignored by a white population convinced of its cultural superiority and growing rapidly, due to a high rate of immigration and of natural increase in a relatively salubrious, largely rural, environment. Between 1620 and 1770, as disease, a declining birthrate, war and enslavement reduced the Indians, white numbers grew from 2,000 to 2,205,000.

III

POLITICS

If Indians and Europeans conflicted with each other over cultural and economic matters, it was in the realm of politics that the settlers tried to bring about the most obviously 'directed' change, though the direction was not necessarily intended to be disastrous to the Indians. Indeed, local leaders were sometimes able to advance their own concerns as a result of white patronage or intervention, and whites had to take note of the factionalism among Indian societies that pre-dated their arrival.[57] Thus Richard Metcalf has demonstrated that in eastern Connecticut during the first half of the seventeenth century, the ambitious renegade sachem from the Pequot grouping, the Mohegan Uncas, who aspired to supremacy over the New England Indians, used his friendship with the English to overthrow the established Pequot sachem, Sassacus, and subsequently to destroy the Narraganset sachem, Miantonomo, and the power of his supporters. From 1645 to the 1670s, Uncas then enjoyed the pre-eminence he had sought, still with English support.[58] On the other hand, Miantonomo in New England, the lesser chiefs under Powhatan's rule in Virginia, and Powhatan himself, saw no prospect of resolving inter- or intra-tribal difficulties by means of an English alliance.[59] Their caution was wise.

Whenever possible, English politicians tried to turn the power of Indian spokesmen to their own, non-traditional uses. Hence local sachems in New England were given the unenviable task of enforcing against Indians punishments which had been decreed by white courts in cases involving both races.[60] In the same way, when the English entered into a tribute relationship with an Indian people it was not the same as that imposed by Indian leaders upon their subordinate allies. Accordingly, after peace was agreed in 1646 between the English and the Virginia Indians, the latter were obliged not only to pay an annual tribute of bearskins and to aid the English against their native enemies, but also to accept constraints upon their freedom of movement.[61] The extension of European protection over a native group was, in addition, likely to involve it in more damaging military commitments than an Indian suzerain could exact, European warfare and ambitions being what they were.

The English were glad to find distinctions of rank in Indian societies and to single out prominent individuals with whom they could deal. However, the contacts between the two races were not sufficiently intimate to provide either with genuine insights into the workings of the other's political systems. In fact, detailed information about and interest in the workings of native politics have only recently emerged. In these circumstances, the English – like colonizers in many parts of the world – decided that they were dealing with tribes or nations and, in Fried's words, provided 'vaguely defined and grossly overlapping populations ... with the minimal organisation required for their manipulation, even though they had little or no internal organisation of their own other than that based on conceptions of kinship'. Modern research may indicate that a tribe is frequently difficult to define in terms of common cultural traits, ideologies, political or economic systems, the power to make war and peace, language or breeding populations. It may show that, before contact with whites, none of the so-called tribes in the United States were sovereign states in the European sense and that the Iroquois, Powhatan and Illinois confederacies lacked strong central authority by white standards.[62] But the colonists did not appreciate the role of kinship within Indian societies, albeit they might have to deal with the resulting political factions, as Anderson's study of early white–Dakota contacts in the upper Mississippi valley has established.[63] What was important to whites was to locate a body, appropriate or otherwise, that could negotiate the sale of land.

Determination to do business with a tribe led, in turn, to a search for its head chief. Historians disagree about whether efforts to achieve tribal-wide government resulted from native values and concerns as well as from white manipulation. Whatever the case, the office of head chief does not appear to have existed among the Cherokees, Choctaws, Chickasaws and Creeks, for example, until the English and French came on the scene. Even then, Cotterill suggests, the 'head chief's authority was legally little and actually only what his influence and ability could make it'.[64] This state of affairs could be as irritating to the settlers as the whites' elaborate penal codes, delays between the arrest and punishment of offenders and fondness for imprisoning wrongdoers were alarming to the Indians. The ultimate irony came when whites held Indians as a group responsible for decisions made on their behalf by unrepresentative leaders, while the Indians held whites as a group answerable for offences committed against them by individuals acting on their own initiative.

Had better information been available to the English colonists, it is likely that they would merely have used it to exploit Indian political divisions more effectively, although it might thereafter have saved the early anthropologists and historians from some of their sweeping comments on Indian government and made administrators less optimistic about the acceptability of the governments modelled on white practices that they imposed on re-formed tribal units in the twentieth century (see below, Chapter 4). As it was, the settlers were content to benefit from what they rather despised, namely the failure of Indian communities to differentiate sharply, as they themselves did, between different kinds of power.[65] It followed that just as the inability of a holy man to resist white missionaries could undermine faith in Indian medicine, for which he was responsible,[66] so the demise of the military leader of a tribe or band might mean the simultaneous loss of its wisest, or most ambitious, politician. Such was the case when the Ottawa chief, Pontiac, died in 1769, depriving his people and his northwestern allies of unusual military, diplomatic and political skills in their struggle against the British.[67]

Opinions will always vary about how far, amid all these complexities, colonial governments strove for justice to the Indians, settler aggrandizement or their own advantage. It has to be acknowledged that, though they were largely untroubled by the home government until the late colonial period, the colonial authorities attempted to secure Indian support, invalidated land sales by Indians which lacked their approval, tried to prevent the sale of firearms and liquor to the tribes and struggled to license Indian traders in order that ruffians might be excluded. Their record was so undistinguished, and the complaints of the Indians were so strong, that in 1755–6 the British government established northern and southern departments of Indian affairs, whose superintendents were to carry out these duties and prevent the tribes from supporting the French. But trade and settlers proved impossible to control and the Indians became more resentful, not least about the colonies' own purchases of land. And while no rigid segregation of the two races developed, Indians were already

28

being confined to reservations in Massachusetts, Connecticut, Pennsylvania, Maryland, Virginia and the Carolinas. As A. Grenfell Price observes, since the English and Scots had employed this institution 'in the Scottish and Irish borderlands' before 1607, the development of reservations in colonial America was a predictable one.[68] It was further encouraged by bitterness born of military confrontations, growing white numbers and an awareness that the natives were unwilling to give up their way of life.

The right of the Indians to the soil was recognized by the colonies and purchase was the approved way of transferring that right.[69] Unfortunately, Europeans spent much ingenuity in defending their rights to New World territory, based upon discovery, royal grant, occupancy and cultural superiority. On these occasions, Wilcomb Washburn reminds us, whites chose to ignore what they knew about Indian horticulture and settled habitations, and to create the myth of nomadic savages that they wished to use. As a result, Indian lands continued to change hands through wars between the European powers in America and between Indians and whites. Consequently, the separation of Indian territory west of the Appalachian Mountains from that of the settlers, ordained by the British Proclamation of 1763, seemed both a sensible security measure and a way of ensuring a consolidation of the white population in the east. Westward expansion was temporarily curbed, governors were to punish intruders on Indian lands, and those lands were only to be sold with royal permission. Neither the boundary line nor ensuing imperial attempts to regulate Indian commerce proved effective. The colonies and their inhabitants remained intractably expansionist and Indian trade a generally dishonest business. It was left to the Continental Congress in the 1770s to see whether a just Indian policy could be devised.

Even if the Indians had thought better of the newcomers than they did and raised no objection to land losses, the tasks facing the colonial and imperial governments would have been herculean. None the less, it cannot be denied that the colonial authorities normally yielded to the claims of advantage, while the British government yielded to those of expediency, security and frugality. New York and Pennsylvania in the North and Georgia and North Carolina in the South were particularly determined to defend their interest in Indian lands from outside interference.[70] And the concept of a separate Indian country, though it might be said to take account of the very real independence still possessed by the western Indians at least, could only encourage the damaging view catching hold of the Revolutionary generation: that the Indians were a separate and alien race.

IV

ENGLAND, SPAIN AND FRANCE ABROAD

By way of concluding this opening survey, it may be useful to consider the frequently advanced judgement that the English can be distinguished as colonists from the Spanish and French by their distance from the native peoples: by their inability to find a place for non-whites in the imperial regime they were trying to erect. The differences between these three powers would seem to have been exaggerated, however, never more neatly than in Parkman's contention that 'Spanish civilization crushed the Indian; English civilization scorned and neglected him; French civilization embraced and cherished him'.[71]

The fifteenth- and sixteenth-century Spanish explorers set out from a country which had absorbed dark-skinned peoples and was fairly tolerant of racial diversity and mixing.[72] This tolerance was not immediately evident in the New World, where the early settlers were primarily interested in obtaining fame and wealth. In the Caribbean, and then in Mexico and South America, the native inhabitants were ruthlessly exploited or killed by the invaders, both directly and through the introduction of disease. Walton and Shepherd note that whereas the population of Spanish America in 1500 was close to that of Europe, it was only one-tenth the size by 1600. Survivors were obliged to work for the Spanish, producing the raw materials they craved and the goods they needed for survival.[73]

If Spanish and Indian craftsmanship combined to produce an impressive architecture throughout Mexico and Peru, in a fashion that was impossible in the more austere French and English settlements,[74] the physical and economic contacts of the two peoples were less admirable. The early Spanish colonists, like other Europeans, came to the Americas expecting to encounter wild men and savages.[75] They had acted accordingly before the Spanish Crown, influenced by the conquistador-turned-priest, Bartolomé de Las Casas, exhorted them to acknowledge the Indians' basic human rights. The Spanish, like the English and the French, enslaved the Indians when they could (see Chapter 5) and edicts against the institution issued in metropolitan Spain proved extremely difficult to enforce.[76] Although, under the *encomienda* system, through which grantees were entitled to Indian land and labour in a particular region, Indian ownership of the land was retained and Indian leaders acted as intermediaries, the Indians were reduced to virtual slavery. The eventual supplanting of this system by more direct means of exploiting local labour merely replaced semi-slavery by peonage. As was the case in the English colonies, native agriculture was disrupted and declined in efficiency, though there were eventual dietary gains to be derived from the introduction of European crops and livestock.

The Spanish, in common with the French and the English, argued that colonization and Christianization were partners. But their missionaries ultimately won more converts than the English, primarily because they were more adventurous and readier to overlook what they could not immediately alter. They were also more willing to learn native languages and less deferential to settler, soldier and metropolitan pressures. In the North American settlements of Florida (from the 1560s), the Pueblo regions of the Southwest (from the 1590s) and California (from the 1790s), where missionary objectives dominated, Spain's record was better than elsewhere in the Americas. Yet the missionaries were intolerant of many Indian customs, demanding that the natives accept Spanish law, marriage practices, dress and lifestyle, as well as Catholicism. They inadvertently introduced the Indians to European diseases and regulated neophytes at their missions with great severity. As a result, the native population dwindled and converts were ill equipped to cope once the mission system crumbled. Spanish hostilities with the English and their Creek allies had, by the middle of the eighteenth century, resulted in the destruction of the Florida missions and in 1763 the province was temporarily lost to Britain. Conflict between civilian and religious personnel became a serious problem in the American Southwest. And the fact that Indians often simply combined Catholic practices with traditional beliefs and ways can scarcely be seen as a triumph for Catholic tolerance, since such syncretism was not the basic intention.

In many of the areas they invaded, the Spanish were lucky in facing peaceful tribes or groups, accustomed to strong government, who were more suitable subjects for exploitation and conversion than the scattered peoples of tropical America.[77] By the 1790s the Spanish in West Florida (recovered from Britain in 1783, along with East Florida) and Louisiana (acquired from France in 1763) were willing to treat the local Indians well. They employed competent officials who learned their various languages, distributed goods generously and helped the natives to resist American encroachment on their lands.[78] But this policy reflects not so much pure humanitarianism as a need for alliances with the Indians against Spain's American enemies. The Indians did indeed have a clear place in the Spanish imperial order, in a way that the tribes in English areas of colonization did not. Yet it is hard to see that they gained any advantage from being accorded a place that meant they were 'conquered, converted, and used'.[79]

The French showed interest in colonization later than the Spanish and the northern regions with which their explorers, fishermen and traders became most involved contained no easy riches. They were therefore unable to emulate the merely exploitative role of the Spanish, and neither the French nor the English wished to repeat the well-published atrocities against the natives attendant on Spain's search for gold in the New World.[80] The Indians encountered were largely hunters and what they chiefly had to offer the newcomers were furs. In order to obtain these and keep out European competitors, it was necessary to enter into military alliances with the tribes and to preserve their basic way of life. Moreover, it was advantageous to cohabit with them and since the way of life of the two peoples was not greatly different, and white women were scarce, cohabitation was common.[81] Having no need to 'maintain a large standing army to defend its frontiers', England, as Eccles observes, had manpower that 'could be exported overseas', whereas the French only slowly found either the men or the money to further their colonial ambitions.[82] The small number of French colonists in Canada and Louisiana, and their primary interest in trade, in turn meant that they avoided struggles for land to exploit or settle on the scale of those which soured relations between the Spanish and English colonists and the Indians.[83] They had the additional advantage that the native population, perhaps 300,000, including Alaska and the Arctic region, was smaller at the time of discovery than that faced in the United States (*c.* 1,000,000), Mexico (*c.* 4,000,000), or Central and South America and the West Indies (*c.* 8,000,000). (The figures used here are conservative and should be compared with those of Dobyns.)[84]

None the less, it would be a mistake to romanticize the French–Indian connection, just because both peoples had an important place in the French empire and their relationship was one of mutual dependence. Favourable demographic and economic factors did not prevent the destruction of the natives by white diseases, firearms and alcohol, or the undermining of their social order by political intervention and unduly exploitative trade. The dealings of the French with the Indians could be ruthless, as when they abandoned their Chippewa trading partners in the Great Lakes region in pursuit of trade relations with more westerly tribes, such as the Santee Sioux. The French hold over the Indian peoples of both the upper and lower Mississippi was fragile by the 1740s because of the competition afforded by American traders. France's early superiority over England in the fur trade was the result of getting in first and showing greater flexibility, and the natives' support for Europeans, the French included, seems to have been based on realism, not sentiment.[85] It was an integral part of

European colonial rivalries that the different powers criticized their opponents' handling of native affairs, reminded their Indian allies of indignities meted out by rival whites and congratulated themselves on their superiority in this area.[86] But Lewis Saum has shown convincingly that there was neither general acknowledgement nor evidence that the French were particularly successful with the Indians while the English were peculiarly aloof and inept.[87]

There *is* some evidence to show that the French habit of 'going native' strengthened the Indians' belief in their own cultural superiority and reduced their incentive to learn French.[88] For their part the French came to regard their vital Indian allies as conquered peoples, who had to be granted titles to the lands they cultivated. This situation left little room for illusions and the French were said to view the Louisiana Choctaws as the greatest cheats, liars, drunkards and beggars among the southern tribes.[89] The 'noble savage' theories which fortified French anti-colonialism may have found stronger expression in French than in English culture.[90] Yet they flourished in Spain and England as well as France, usually among those who had little contact with native peoples, or at times of amity between natives and colonists. The French often merely used the word 'savage', which could mean 'noble savage' or not, depending on who was writing. Like all forms of sympathetic comment upon the Indians, the 'noble savage' concept tells us more about contemporary Europeans' anxieties concerning their own corrupt and restless societies than anything else.[91]

It is, however, pre-eminently the French missionaries who are said to have 'embraced and cherished' the Indians. We do not have to accept Parkman's judgement that Catholicism was 'the only form of Christianity likely to take root in . . . [the Indian's] crude and barbarous nature'[92] to acknowledge that the Catholic evangelists undoubtedly had some advantages over their English, Protestant counterparts. Their ceremony and display appealed to the natives.[93] Free from parish duties and direction, the Jesuits took their message to the Indian villages. They learned the Indian languages, tolerated native rites that they could not displace, avoided 'a dictatorial or overbearing tone' and adapted themselves to Indian life.[94] Catholic missionaries generally did not require Indians to go through such a rigorous conversion process as the Protestant sects, with their 'emphasis on individual piety external to the rituals of the church, on the directness of the individual's relationship with God, and on the importance of scripture'.[95]

On the other hand, the French found their Indian converts hard to keep and the French government looked upon them with scepticism.[96]

Notwithstanding their powers of accommodation to native culture, French missionaries, like those of their rivals for empire, required neophytes to give up much that was dear to them and were engaged in an uphill struggle against native holy men.[97] Greater contact between cultures does not necessarily lead to greater understanding and this was certainly the case with Anglo-French contacts. Thus, while Indians might be attracted by the French missionaries' physical courage, they disliked their schools and found their attitude to human sexuality bewildering. Priestly celibacy also meant that the missionaries could not strengthen their intimacy with the natives, whose illicit liaisons with whites they strove to prevent.[98] Native realism was involved here too: Indian converts sometimes hoped, as Christians, to preserve their property from traditional gift-giving or to obtain preferential treatment from French traders and officials.[99] By the end of the colonial period, neither the English nor the French missions had converted more than a fraction of the natives within their sphere of influence.[100]

The charter of the Company of New France offered full French citizenship, including the right to settle in France, to Indians who became practising Roman Catholics, an offer nor formally paralleled by any other European colonizer in the Americas. But Récollets and Jesuits alike substantially failed to interest the natives in this offer. The success enjoyed among the Hurons availed the missionaries little, since that nation was destroyed by the Iroquois.[101] In Louisiana, unlike Canada, there was not even a grand missionary campaign among the Indians; missionaries and religious enthusiasm were scarce and there was no more desire to assimilate the native population than there was to integrate the imported blacks. Indeed, white intermarriage with either was forbidden, although the church was unable to persuade settlers to give up their Indian or black concubines.[102]

Yet while the Spanish and French colonists shared many characteristics with their English contemporaries, Parkman's indictment of 'English civilization' remains telling. There were, of course, some variations in relations between Indians and whites in the thirteen colonies. By comparison with the Quakers, the Puritans may have been especially intolerant of native peoples on religious grounds, while the southern settlers were peculiarly grasping after Indian land because it would yield valuable export crops, and displayed a callousness on race matters that went hand in hand with the enslavement of both Indians and blacks. But in North and South alike, the Indians were 'scorned and neglected' and the impact on their fortunes was invariably damaging.

Accordingly, in New England, the tribes had substantially lost their land base by the end of the seventeenth century and their numbers may have plummeted by as much as 80 per cent by the middle of the eighteenth. In the middle states, such once powerful groups as the Delawares and Nanticokes were pushed westwards, while by the 1760s even the proud Iroquois were a reduced force. The Virginia tribes felt the brunt of early white expansion in the South and Nash estimates that between 1607 and the first decade of the eighteenth century the Indian population of the colony declined from perhaps 18,000 to 2,000. By the 1770s, the Cherokees, Creeks and Choctaws had also been obliged to cede ominous amounts of land to the colonists. And though a few small native enclaves survived in New England and Virginia, they had a hard struggle to retain their identity, as did the larger Indian groupings remaining in the East. The eastern Indians did not vanish. As Alfred Tamarin has established, the Native Americans of the Atlantic coastal regions have reversed their population decline in the twentieth century, living on reservations and communities outside them, earning a living in city and country alike, some still retaining their own languages, and joined by Indians from other parts of America. They have, just the same, been reduced from more than a hundred peoples at the time of European colonization to about thirty recognized tribes.[103]

When the colonial era closed, all the major ideas, policies and paradoxes that would dominate Indian policy and reform until the 1930s had emerged. Treaty-making was firmly established and would leave an enduring legacy after the system was abolished in 1871. Reservations and the allotting of land to tribesmen on an individual basis had both been tried. Wishing to disarm the Indians and impress the world, American leaders had looked for legal ways of obtaining Indian land and urged the civilization of the tribes on white terms. But they had bowed to the circumstances, including Indian and white preoccupation with their own affairs, which encouraged separation of the races and neglect of cultural crusades. For security reasons, Indian policy was unusually important during these years. Yet many other issues were more pressing and it was never accorded the attention and resources necessary to achieve racial justice. National policy guidelines had been devised, but they had proved ineffective when local governments and people were unwilling to honour them. As we shall now see, after the break with Britain, American citizens were increasingly indifferent about extending justice to Indians, provided that justice was done to whites; and even philanthropists regarded tribal claims with ambivalence.

2

White Power Grows, Reformer Hopes Fluctuate: the 1770s to the 1850s

I

THE AMERICAN REVOLUTION AND AFTER

During the War of Independence, the English hoped to use their Indian allies but to restrain them until they could be militarily supervised. The Americans established southern, middle and northern Indian departments, whose commissioners were to try to keep the tribes out of the conflict. As in earlier and later white quarrels, prudence should have told the Indians to remain neutral. However, a number of Indian leaders recognized the threat that American acquisitiveness posed to their lands and white pressures combined with native loyalties, resentments and opportunism to make neutrality impossible. Although the resulting hostilities were unsatisfactory to all the participants, the British and the Indians were the losers in the long run, a fact that was obscured by the unsettled situation immediately at the end of the war.[1]

While the new republic was being consolidated, whites needed peace with the native population. Yet they proposed to treat the Indians as conquered nations, having a misguided estimate of what the tribes would accept. Northwestern Indians had not been resoundingly beaten and the Iroquois led by the Mohawk warrior, Joseph Brant, were not reconciled to defeat. Other Iroquois, Delawares, Chippewas, Ottawas, Shawnees and Wyandots resented the dictated treaties of 1784–6, which asserted United States claims to much of their land without compensation. The British were happy to assure the Indians that they had not intended to deliver to their conquerors the right to Indian lands as far as the Mississippi. And the jurisdiction of the American government was not sufficiently clear for it to implement a forceful Indian policy.

Under the Articles of Confederation, the first national constitution which was in effect from 1781, there were some continuities with the past. The national government, like the British government before it, was authorized to supervise relations with the Indians and recognized that its mandate ran in an Indian country beyond existing state boundary lines, from which settlers and unlicensed traders were to be excluded. This authorization was strongly opposed by South Carolina, which did not feel so vulnerable on its frontiers as neighbouring Georgia and North Carolina, and benefited from the prevailing, ill-regulated state of Indian trade. As a result of South Carolina's stance, a clause was inserted in the Articles which specified that Congress, when acting in Indian affairs, was not to infringe or violate 'the legislative right of any State within its own interest'. The government therefore found it impossible to prevent North Carolina and Georgia in the South, and New York and Pennsylvania in the North, from dealing independently with the tribes inside their borders. The result, not surprisingly, was to incline the southern Indians towards the Spanish, who remained in Florida, and to stir up the tribes of the Northwest, where the British retained a foothold until 1794.

Allan Nevins has suggested that by 1788, the year of the ratification of the Constitution, which replaced the Articles, the conflict between Indians and whites was such that it gave an impulse to solidarity among the states. They knew, he argues, that 'it would be easier to bring the struggle to a quick and successful conclusion if they submitted to Federal direction'. They were forcibly reminded of their transgressions under the Articles during the Constitutional Convention and in the *Federalist Papers*, which were designed to secure the ratification of the Constitution. As the *Papers'* authors, James Madison, John Jay and Alexander Hamilton complained, the states had made war and peace with the Indians, proved 'unable or unwilling to restrain or punish offenses' and were incapable of resolving their jurisdiction over the Indians. The day of submission was nevertheless put off for as long as possible. It was, after all, unreasonable to expect speedy unity between states which, in the words of the contemporary Congress, differed 'in habits, produce, commerce, and internal police', and whose inhabitants knew and cared for each other but little.[2]

It is unlikely that the United States could quickly have found an effective policy which would have satisfied all those involved. American citizens, remembering wartime losses, and with Congress engaged in protracted negotiations for the release of white prisoners held by the Indians, tended to think of their adversaries as savages, as they had done during colonial wars. This tendency was strengthened by the temporary association of blacks and Indians in the public mind. The colonial authorities had always employed divide-and-rule tactics to prevent an alliance developing between non-whites. Despite their efforts, blacks and Indians made considerable contacts with each other (see Chapter 5) and had even collaborated in actual or threatened slave revolts, as in New England between 1657 and 1775 and New York city in 1712. The Revolution seemed to offer another opportunity for co-operation and revenge, by courtesy of the Loyalists and the British. Recruitment of blacks and Indians to help suppress the Revolution created more bitterness than simply the numbers raised would have warranted. The bitterness was at the prospect of 'savage' enemies within America being pitted against the forces of freedom and civilization and the Declaration of Independence sternly accused George III of exciting 'domestic Insurrections amongst us' and endeavouring 'to bring on the Inhabitants of our Frontiers, the merciless Indian Savages, whose known Rule of Warfare, is an undistinguished Distinction of all Ages, Sexes and Conditions'.[3]

The popular prejudice against non-whites, which Revolutionary tensions compounded, had a number of sources. In the case of blacks, there was their association with poverty and enslavement; and emancipation was feared as an assault on property rights, an offence against the South and a step which would increase the power of the unruly mob. As far as the Indians were concerned, frontier whites hated their attacks and regarded their demoralization through dispossession, disease and alcohol, as a sign of inferiority. Both Indians and blacks suffered from the odium attached to inequality before the law, as well as from the confidence induced in the colonists by their economic progress and triumph over the British. And although the need for national unity made white Americans willing to ignore the profound cultural and ethnic differences which existed among themselves,[4] this was the extent of their toleration. By the late eighteenth century, vigorous defenders of Americans' Anglo-Saxon greatness had appeared, among them the Virginia statesman and future president, Thomas Jefferson, while naturalists like Charles Linnaeus, the Comte de Buffon, John Mitchell and Bernard Romans had produced treatises which emphasized the distinctions between the races of the world.[5] Yet it must also be admitted that the views of the racial theorizers were not dominant in official or philanthropic circles and that the Revolutionary debate about whether slavery could be condoned in a free nation, which ironically intensified existing prejudices and the search for racial 'justifications' of black bondage,[6] was not paralleled by an equally damaging discussion about the place of Indian peoples in American society.

In the early years of the republic, the objectives of Indian policy attracted a degree of attention from prominent statesmen that they would not receive once the Indian 'menace' was overcome. The funding and implementation of policy were a sorry contrast. Although social and political reforms were achieved during these years, money for everything was short under a system which depended on the willingness of states to respond to congressional requisitions. At the end of the Revolutionary War the Continental Army was rapidly disbanded, dwindling to a mere eighty or so men by 1784. The superintendents of Indian affairs for the northern and southern Indian departments established in 1786 had too much to do and so did the commanders of frontier posts who were meant to assist them. Hence the Secretary of War, Henry Knox, was reduced to futile affirmations of federal authority and censure of white acquisitiveness.[7]

None the less, the Confederation government spent $580,103.4 between 1776 and 1789 on conducting relations with the tribes, which, though utterly inadequate, was more than it could afford. If both Canada and the United States felt the need to give presents to their calculating Indian allies, the American government consistently spent more on Indian policy than did Canadian administrators.[8] It had more Indians to consider and more pangs of conscience to appease and Americans fell early into the habit of applying pecuniary remedies to complicated social problems. But most of the money went on land bargains with the Indians; a sizeable 'Indian office' bureaucracy or expenditure on native welfare were not yet the cause of large outlays.

Whatever its deficiencies, the government was anxious to avoid damaging the honour of the young country. It could scarcely eliminate ethical considerations in its dealings with the Indians so long as Americans hoped to show Europeans that 'nations as well as individuals could live by moral standards'. One might suppose, of course, that the imposed treaties of 1784–6 revealed few moral scruples, but the notion of confiscation of enemy property after a 'just' war could be conveniently used then, as it would be again, all wars seeming just to the victors.[9] Moreover, there were strict limits to white respect for Indian rights.

In their impressive plea for greater tribal autonomy, Barsh and Henderson maintain that European states recognized the sovereignty of the American Indian nations and that 'British law was explicit in its regard for tribal sovereignty'. During the Revolutionary War, they argue, the Indian tribes were free to choose sides as commitment and inclination dictated and their power was shown by the Cherokee refusal to agree to peace with the United States until the Treaty of Hopewell in 1785 and by the American treaty with the Delawares in

1778, which invited them 'with other tribes, "to join the present confederation, and to form a state, whereby the Delaware nation shall be the head, and have a representation in Congress" '. The main problem after the Revolution, they further suggest, was not whether Indian affairs should be 'conducted by treaty in accordance with the law of nations, as they had been conducted before the war', but how the power to treat with the tribes was to be divided between the national government and the states.[10]

This division certainly did present problems, as we have seen. Yet we have also tried to show that, in colonial times, tribal sovereignty as acknowledged through treaty-making was mainly a device to legitimize white land purchases and was negated both by the frequently superior power of whites and by the frequent failure of Indian tribes to act as cohesive entities. Similarly, in the Revolutionary era, some Senecas, Mohawks and Oneidas opposed Six Nation support for the British, despite the efforts of Joseph Brant; the majority of Creeks remained at peace, despite the efforts of the disenchanted chief Dragging Canoe; while the Creeks divided into pro-British and pro-American factions, despite the efforts of their mixed-blood leader, Alexander McGillivray, to rally them behind Britain. And small factions continued to alienate tribal land, regardless of their authority to do so, as when two Creek chiefs in 1783 ceded to Georgia the area between the Tugalo and Apalachee rivers. Cotterill says of the transaction that it was unclear 'whether the right to alienate land lay in the tribe as a whole or in that portion which had occupied it'.[11] Such uncertainty was exploited with great cynicism by whites before and after the Revolution, as was the willingness of Indian leaders to ignore the sovereignty of other tribes and sell land which was not theirs to dispose of, a case in point being the Iroquois cession of Cherokee territory north of the Tennessee in 1768.[12]

It would seem that whites, from the colonial period onwards, were less inclined to explicitly acknowledge tribal sovereignty than to take it for granted when it suited them and to disavow it when it did not – as in the peace of 1783, which omitted to involve the Indians as though they were on equal terms with the other combatants. We may further note that the British, after the peace, were no more disposed than the Americans to rigour on this point, denying that the proclamation of 1763 had recognized anything other than Indian rights of 'prior occupancy' and rejecting Joseph Brant's contention that they had acknowledged the sovereignty of their Iroquois allies when resettling them in Ontario.[13]

The final obstacle to the evolution of a just Indian policy under the Confederation was the general economic situation. In the course of the

Revolutionary War, American exports had plummeted and the price level had soared; when the conflict ended, shipping and its supporting industries were in the doldrums before trade links were built up outside the British Empire and there was a large national debt to fund.[14] Small wonder that hard-pressed officials looked forward to the revenues to be obtained from the sale of land in the western regions ceded by the states to the Confederation government. These territories were obtained with difficulty (North Carolina holding out until 1789, Georgia until 1802), and the subsequent organization for potential statehood of the area between the Mississippi, Ohio and Appalachians, by the Northwest Ordinance of 1787, was one of the government's few achievements. The reversal of Britain's previously generous land policy by the proclamation of 1763 may have 'reduced colonial incomes somewhat', but it probably helped eastern farmers and was not generally too onerous.[15] None the less, the postwar relaxation of restraints on expansion was welcomed and too much concern for the rights of Indians – of whom there were some 45,000 in the Northwest alone in 1787 – might have jeopardized policy, revenue and prestige altogether.

By the end of the eighteenth century, American economic trends as a whole held out little encouragement to the Indian population. That small element of native people who lived in American towns and cities shared the insecurity and opprobrium attached to the poor of all races by the better-off members of society. The emphasis of the artisan class upon self-discipline, thrift and self-improvement, and its determination not to be associated with the dependent poor, contained nothing that could direct its interest either to Indians who had cut loose from their tribes or to those who remained within traditional groupings. The labour movement did develop an interest in anti-slavery in the nineteenth century, but by then most slaves were black and in any case labour leaders objected to concern for black slavery if it distracted attention from the plight of workers enduring wage slavery, or from the fact that capitalists and slave-owners alike were 'non-producers who fattened on the fruits of the labor of others'.[16]

When contemporary radicalism took on an agrarian dimension, associating republicanism with an agrarianism which argued for a rough equality of property, there should perhaps have been more hope for a check on popular antipathy towards the Indians. The surviving Indian groups in the East were, after all, engaged in agriculture, derived much of their independence from it and, partly through holding land in common, had avoided the institutionalized poverty tolerated by 'civilization'. Yet while Thomas Paine and other

41

radicals might urge the compensation of citizens for 'the loss of the national right to land which private property in land caused', most Americans did not favour the abolition of private property. Nor did they favour the confiscation and redistribution of existing property belonging to fortunate whites.[17] The answer to the land hunger which, when satisfied, would produce the class necessary to a virtuous republic, lay in confiscating Indian land. And to make this respectable, Indian societies were projected as warrior-hunter communities, lacking effective government and so unable to suppress the ignorance and vice that the American republican government was expected to curb. Many frontiersmen, of course, did not care much about respectable justifications for expropriating the Indians. By 1800, as Henry Adams put it,

> pioneers were at work, cutting into the forests with the energy of so many beavers, and with no more express moral purpose than the beavers they drove away. The civilisation that they carried with them was rarely illumined by an idea; they sought room for a new truth, and aimed neither at creating, like the Puritans, a government of saints, nor, like the Quakers, one of love and peace.[18]

Since Indians were commonly regarded as incorrigible individualists who nevertheless entertained a sense of nationality,[19] they should have won more respect than they did from white Americans, whose society was committed to protecting individual liberties in a new nation. Unfortunately, Indian individualism was seen to threaten America's security, as well as the opportunity of its citizens to add actual property in land to that form of property which was individual freedom.[20] Just as the property interests and ambitions of slaveholders undermined the effort to rethink the American involvement in slavery during the Revolutionary era, so the aspirations of white land speculators, frontiersmen and farmers undermined the attempts of a concerned few to force their countrymen to reshape American Indian policy and the assumptions on which it rested.

The nostalgia of white agrarians for a golden age, untainted by the growth of commerce and urbanization, should also have led them to sympathize with the Indians' widely remarked respect for tradition and the past. But again, the breach with England had symbolized a break with traditional society, to which there was no going back, while the vastness of the western lands held out hope that the golden age could be extended into the future in the United States.[21] Moreover Jefferson, agrarianism's most illustrious spokesman, was a practical politician who eventually resigned himself to economic change and meanwhile could take comfort in his optimism about the malleability of human nature, which led him to argue that the Indians could be brought to share in the economic and moral advantages he associated with farming in the white manner.

II

FROM ASSIMILATION TO REMOVAL

By the end of the Confederation period, American Indian policy had been set on a track from which it would subsequently be hard to deviate. The economic interests of whites were given absolute priority, despite efforts by the federal government to restrain their worst excesses and curb the independence of state authorities. Money spent on Indian policy was generally sufficient to satisfy men of conscience, yet inadequate to ensure a just or efficient administration of Indian affairs. Prejudice against Indians, most marked at the popular level, was growing in elite circles. The fledgeling secular reformers, to the limited extent that they tried to close the gap between Revolutionary ideals and republican practice in matters of race, directed their energies to containing slavery: terminating the African slave trade, prohibiting slavery in the Northwest Territory and ending it in the northern states. And though politically vulnerable, native peoples were not reconciled to white pretensions.

From the 1790s to the 1820s, while reformer and missionary interest in assimilating the Indians increased, most of these problems and deficiencies were again apparent. The constitution gave Congress the power to regulate commerce with the Indians 'within the limits of any State, not subject to the laws thereof', thus ending the weakness endured under the Articles. A series of acts 'to regulate trade and intercourse with the Indian tribes', passed between 1790 and 1802, involved the licensing of Indian traders and the promotion of civilization through the release of funds to teach the Indians 'agriculture and domestic manufacture'. The invalidation of private land deals with the Indians was provided for, together with the protection of Indian boundaries, the removal of intruders on Indian lands and the regulation of the liquor traffic. In addition, provision was made for the punishment of crimes committed by whites against Indians in the Indian country. This legislation was supplemented by a system of government trading houses, which operated from 1795 to 1822 and were to make Indian trade goods available at cost, and by treaty appropriations for civilization, as envisaged by the acts. With the setting up in 1819 of a Civilization Fund, in response to the entreaties of humanitarians, $10,000 was provided annually for the purpose.

If the Indian Department was established in 1787 under the jurisdiction of the Secretary of War, presidents from George Washington onwards were concerned to convert and civilize, as well as to control, the Indians. The British and colonial policy of purchasing Indian land title was reverted to, several land grabs were paid for or revoked and the government, from the 1790s, began to pay annuities, or annual payments under treaty obligations. Acknowledging the destructive thrust of white settlement, it felt honour bound to offer Indians the options of either retreating westwards or accommodating themselves to white ways, in close contact with white society and through the acquisition of land in fee simple.[22]

These policies foundered not only because of the greed and opposition of their enemies, but also because of the weaknesses of their architects and agents. It would be foolish to expect whites not to put the interests of their people first; the Indians did the same. It would be equally unreasonable to claim that because reformers and their opponents alike were convinced of white superiority and conditioned by the cultural and economic priorities of white society, then there is nothing to choose between them. Yet the prejudices and delusions of those ostensibly pledged to seeking justice and progress for the Indians must be noted, if only so that we can understand their failures.

Although both George Washington and his successor, John Adams, were interested in the Indians, Washington's anxiety about the nation's security led him to describe the native peoples as savages and his anxiety about the nation's honour led him to exaggerate the promise of the civilization programme launched in 1793. Even the limited funds allocated for this purpose were drained off for other purposes. Adams, for his part, tempered respect for the Indians' basic human rights with a conviction that whites had behaved fairly towards them and with resignation about their declining numbers. When white intrusions on Cherokee lands provoked a crisis between 1796 and 1798, Adams took the part of the white settlers and the Cherokees were pressured into ceding more territory to accommodate them.[23] But Jefferson was the president whose ideas and actions had the most fateful impact upon the Indians before 1830.

As Winthrop Jordan has shown, while Jefferson opposed slavery he used financial excuses for not freeing his own slaves, believed that blacks belonged to an inferior race and argued that they were incapable of being 'incorporated into white society on equal terms'. Indians, by contrast, were 'in body and mind equal to the white man'. By means of 'agriculture and the domestic arts', and perhaps intermarriage, they were therefore to be given the opportunity of assimilating with whites. However, other scholars have gone on to demonstrate that Jefferson, though backed up by a sympathetic Secretary of

44

War, Henry Dearborn, was no more interested in giving force to his views on Indians, when they clashed with the political and economic realities of the white world, than he was in finding practical application for his anti-slavery sentiment.[24] Moreover, even before they met any practical test, Jefferson's assumptions about the native population were at odds with other, more strongly held convictions.

As president, Jefferson began by addressing Indian delegations and leaders as 'brothers', but soon hailed them as his 'children'.[25] Such paternalism came naturally to a man of Jefferson's affluence, rank and accomplishments, but it suggests a form of race prejudice all too prevalent in the nineteenth and twentieth centuries. It is clear that the President regarded blacks, Indians and women alike as prisoners of their instincts and incapable of the self-government which republicanism demanded. He ranked them with a number of elements – including assorted urban interests and cliques of allegedly monarchist leanings – which might threaten the security, purity and progress of the new country.[26] Given that the Indians' right to collective self-government and stubborn affection for old ways threatened Jefferson's sanguine hope of creating an agrarian republic sustained by the open frontier, it is easy to see how his intellectual concern for them unravelled. Jefferson did not have the sort of overpowering personal interest in land speculation that he had in plantation slavery, but he did inherit his surveyor and speculator father's share in the claims of the Loyal Company, and one of his guardians was a prominent land speculator. While in no sense the direct mouthpiece for frontiersmen, Jefferson was certainly associated with those of his class who, like him, favoured expansionism.[27] Paternalists also expect their charges to show respect and gratitude. And so although Jefferson, jealous of his own and the nation's reputation for virtue, was anxious to reject British suggestions that Americans intended to take Indian lands and exterminate their owners, he could not forgive the tribes' ungrateful willingness to respond to British overtures when they had been offered civilization by the Americans.[28]

On some issues – notably the need for state-supported education and for religious toleration – Jefferson was prepared to stand out against popular prejudices. But no politician can afford to do this too often and, in view of his reserve, sensitivity to criticism and only moderate flair as a political manipulator, Jefferson was unlikely to do so. At the end of his term as governor of Virginia, and equally at the end of his two terms as president, he left office surrounded by controversy and criticism. It would have required an individual of exceptional courage and intellectual detachment to compound his problems by advancing the right of the Indian minority at the expense of the white majority, particularly when his party had achieved success, once in office, by its pragmatism and respect for the people. Jefferson was not that individual, though he was fully alive to the necessity of safeguarding minority rights in a democracy.

The President's invitation to native peoples to intermingle with whites was made in the knowledge that they were declining in numbers and in the belief that they were no sexual threat to whites. He did nothing to highlight or discredit the discriminatory treatment of Indians before the law in white society, discrimination which ironically included state laws against the intermarriage of Indians and whites. Nor did he press for the extension of citizenship to Indians within the states, or in Louisiana Territory after it was bought from France in 1803.[29] The negative view of government entertained by the Jeffersonian Republicans, in particular the commitment to frugal government, might indeed have exempted the President from even the inadequate level of expenditure he was willing to commit to the programme for civilizing and assimilating the Indians. From 1802, Congress authorized $15,000 annually for Indian affairs, but as in the Confederation period, much of the money went on gifts and negotiations. Little was directed into the civilization campaign.

Jefferson and his supporters are more culpable for the combination of naivety and cynicism which marked their Indian policy. As Bernard Sheehan has shown, many Jeffersonians saw the Indians as an admirable part of the American environment. They tried to offer the tribes the best of white civilization and expected them to embrace it rapidly. Such an assumption ignored the known white and Indian opposition to the civilization programme, and the slowness and uncertainty of actual culture change. It also disregarded the dismay produced among the Indians by accompanying efforts to manoeuvre them into indebtedness to government traders and thus into parting with their lands and possibly moving west. Some 853,760 acres were obtained from the Choctaws by this means. The coercive tactics employed by humanitarians did not transform native society as they hoped, while making it difficult for the Indians to distinguish their friends from their enemies. When every acknowledgement of honourable intentions has been made, it is undeniable that the main consequence of philanthropy, during Jefferson's time in office and beyond, was to increase the dependence on white society of disrupted Indian groups, rather than to produce the confident independence believed to be central to civilization.[30] The linking together of white expansion and reform, by humanitarians as well as their opponents, was understandable, but it was fatal to reform.

As far as Jefferson was concerned, the most promising way out of his difficulties presented itself with the Louisiana Purchase. Through the purchase, the United States fortuitously doubled its size, obtaining an ill-defined region which included the Isle of Orleans on the east bank of the Mississippi and the area westward from that river to the Rockies and Spain's southwestern territories. The legality of the acquisition being doubtful, Jefferson proposed a constitutional amendment to validate it and authorize the removal of eastern tribes to the upper part of the newly acquired territory. The proceeds from the sale of their land were to be used to clear off the National Debt. Since the proposed amendment was deemed an unwise delay by the President's advisers, it was abandoned and the Indian project lapsed with it. But Jefferson did not abandon the idea of removal, which he had cherished before 1803, believing that 'our Indians could constitute a Maréchaussée to prevent emigrants crossing the river, until we have filled up all the vacant country on this side'. The Chickasaws were invited to go west in 1805, the Choctaws and Cherokees in 1808, notwithstanding the fact that Indians generally were averse to removal, while the Cherokees had for years been adapting themselves to white civilization.[31]

It is not quite clear what would have happened to plans for civilizing such tribes, if they had complied *en masse* instead of in small parties. Jefferson, Gibson reminds us, seems to have envisaged a western colonization zone where Indians could live in isolation until they were ready for assimilation. The Lewis and Clark expedition to the far West in 1804 gathered information on which the government could base its plans. But since plentiful game was held up to the Indians as one of the attractions of the trans-Mississippi west and since civilization in the form of white settlers was supposedly to be kept at bay, we may assume that changes in the lifestyles of the removing tribes would have been made with difficulty. As it was, the intention of holding back white settlement was swiftly abandoned and trade contacts between the two peoples ultimately brought the same mixed results in the West as they had in the East. This is not to say, however, that the President expected Indian hunting grounds beyond the Mississippi to be quickly destroyed, Zebulon M. Pike's exploring expeditions of 1805–7 having suggested that much of the Louisiana territory was too arid for agriculture, a judgement confirmed by Stephen H. Long's expedition of 1820.[32]

By 1808, Jefferson would appear to have retreated from his position in the 1776 Declaration of Independence 'that all Men are created equal' and to have reached what would be Abraham Lincoln's view in the 1850s and 1860s: namely, that the Revolution involved the *proposition* that men were equal. Jefferson, the philosopher statesman, was satisfied to claim for the civilization programme a success that it never enjoyed and to make his most eloquent commitments to Indian equality in the safe confines of his *Notes on the State of Virginia*, private correspondence and discussions within the meetings of the American Philosophical Society. Principles had to some extent to substitute for policy[33] and along the way Jefferson's attitudes to blacks and Indians converged. Indeed, he hoped that free blacks would be colonized in Louisiana together with the tribes. This resolution, and evasion, of the race issue by removing the victims of prejudice to more suitable environments would be advocated by a growing number of ostensibly well-meaning whites in the next few decades.[34] They included James Monroe, the fifth President of the United States; the administrator of Indian affairs, Thomas L. McKenney, and his collaborator on *History of the Indian Tribes of North America*, James Hall; and the Whig statesman, Henry Clay, who deplored forced removal but hoped that the Indians would emigrate of their own accord.[35]

The proposals to colonize both races were extremely dangerous because they could bring their friends and enemies into an uneasy but influential alliance. Whereas black emancipation and Indian independence would mean whites exchanging economic advantages for security worries, colonization projects preserved the whites' self-esteem and advanced their interests. The American Colonization Society, established in 1816, was supported by southern slaveholders who regarded free or emancipated blacks as a menace and by northerners who felt that blacks would have a better chance of developing outside the hostile atmosphere of the United States. Similarly, the campaign for the removal of the Indians, though pressed most strongly by the southern states, also attracted backing from northern humanitarians who were convinced that the Indians were being destroyed rather than civilized by the press of white settlers into their territory. With respect to blacks and Indians alike, whites were consulting their own wishes. The majority of the intended beneficiaries were uncooperative, while those who did choose to remove often desired, for self-protection, to do so under their own steam. Colonization efforts in fact aggravated existing political differences within the two minority communities. In each instance, the federal government was willing to finance the movement (though only marginally in the case of the Colonization Society). In each instance, support was forthcoming from religious groups, while unsympathetic whites were willing to make life as unpleasant as they could for the uncooperative, in the hope of driving them out.[36]

Although Americans before and after Jefferson claimed that they would never seek to buy the Indians' land against their wishes, the results of the civilization and 'voluntary' sale policy between the late 1780s and the 1820s were huge land losses and ill feeling between the two races. The federal government abandoned its early opposition to rapid expansion when the economic and political strains it had expected to follow did not materialize. And westward migrations were further fed and facilitated by a growing white population, improved transport, enhanced awareness of the desirability of Indian lands, and Indian military and treaty defeats.

Through the Treaty of Greenville in 1795, the United States acquired two-thirds of Ohio and parts of Michigan and Indiana. Between 1800 and 1812, a series of treaties consolidated or established the American hold on New York, Ohio, Indiana, Illinois, Michigan, Wisconsin, Arkansas and Missouri. With the cessation of English aid after the War of 1819 and of Spanish support following the American acquisition of the whole of Florida in 1821, both the northern and southern tribes were on their own against the westward movement of whites. Self-interested and unreliable allies as the Spanish and English had been, the Indians were subsequently more vulnerable. Accordingly, from 1814 to 1823 they were pressured into giving up large tracts of land in Illinois, Wisconsin, Michigan, Indiana, Missouri, Kansas, Oklahoma, Tennessee, Kentucky, Alabama and Florida, while treaties even before the policy was officially adopted and enforced after 1830 provided for immediate or eventual removal. If, later in the century, it would appear that the warlike tribes won the best treatment from whites,[37] this was not necessarily the case in the years leading up to removal. As their own strength grew, white Americans could afford to treat the peaceable and belligerent alike, though it certainly seemed that the meek did not inherit the earth.

The affairs of the Indian peoples during these difficult times continued for the most part to reflect Indian social organization, factionalism, traditional alliances and enmities, upon which white directives acted variously as irritant, opportunity and disaster. In the North, the best hope of staying the white advance was destroyed with the defeat and death of the Shawnee war chief, Tecumseh, in 1813. Tecumseh and his brother, Tenskwatawa, the Prophet, had urged the concerted resistance of Great Lakes, Ohio Valley and southern Indians to further land cessions. Yet despite winning support from the Potawatomis, Winnebagos, Ojibwas and others, the brothers did not inspire the Indian unity they needed. Fear of the war that would be necessary for Tecumseh's success, jealousy of his prominence, ancient differences between the tribes and factionalism within them may explain why. Among the Sauk, for example, the Shawnees' appeals had to be weighed in the context of customary hostility towards the Sioux,

Omahas and Menominees, concern about the aftermath of a controversial cession of Illinois lands in 1804, and the struggle of Black Hawk and Keokuk for supremacy in the Sauks' loosely organized, clan-based polity. Black Hawk declined to follow Tecumseh and tried to stay out of the War of 1812, but his caution did not pay off. Because his opponents were pro-American, he eventually ended up backing Tecumseh's allies, the British. Black Hawk's stance, culminating in his refusal to leave Illinois and in the brief Black Hawk War of 1832, gave victory to his rival, although it was only one factor in that rivalry. Keokuk's reward was that he, and later his son, were recognized as leaders of the Sauks, but they exercised power over a defeated people.[38]

The experience of other Indian groups confirms that there was no obvious path towards autonomy and peace. In the South, Creek particularism, reflected in autonomous towns, the sharing of government between warriors and civil councils, and a divided National Council, hampered McGillivray's attempts to secure Creek sovereignty by playing off the Americans against the Spanish. Conservative resentment of his diplomacy and political innovation, aggravated by subsequent white encroachments on Creek territory and by Jefferson's civilization programme, led to sympathy for Tecumseh and ultimately to the Creek civil war of 1813–14. The war in turn brought conflict with the United States, followed by additional land losses. During the early nineteenth century, the pre-eminent head chief of the Choctaws, Pushmataha, was engaged, like McGillivray, in a struggle for both personal and group advantage. His rejection of Tecumseh, support for America in the Creek civil war and conciliatory land cessions to whites did not, however, preserve his people from demands for their removal westwards. In Wisconsin, violent resistance to white demands by the Winnebagos proved just as frustrating as the Creek stand; the outcome was simply territorial losses for the tribe in 1828 and the death of one of their leaders, Red Bird. A rather different approach was made possible in the course of the decade when the Cherokees adopted a centralized government on the white pattern, encompassing a written constitution, chief, vice chief, bicameral legislature and supreme court. Although the erosion of native practices involved caused enduring controversy, the sense of nationality which this kind of government helped to foster made the Cherokees more determined to resist white coercion, and by means of 'civilized' tactics that the whites would find embarrassing.[39]

These sour and complex interactions between Indians and whites might have improved had the civilization programme proved more welcome and effective. Its difficulties cannot be attributed to the lack of a religious component. In the first two decades of the nineteenth century, a 'resurgent evangelical Protestantism' aimed at making America 'a Christian nation'[40] and this involved whites in operations among both blacks and Indians. But whereas missionaries to the blacks were hampered by the hostility of slaveowners and their own anxiety not to provoke class or racial conflict,[41] missionaries to the Indians were buoyed up by the encouragement of successive presidents and money from the Civilization Fund. It has been estimated that between 1818 and 1845 the federal government provided over half the funds needed by Indian missions, despite the official American commitment to the non-establishment of religion. The American Board of Commissioners for Foreign Missions (a Presbyterian and Congregational organization, founded in 1810), the Baptist General Missionary Convention for Foreign Missions (established in 1814) and the United Foreign Mission Society (formed in 1817) were the principal beneficiaries of the Fund. A consequently revitalized missionary campaign drew upon Catholics as well as Protestants and the latter now included the Quakers, who had shaken off the quietism of their early years in America.[42]

As had been the case in the eighteenth century, and for many of the same reasons, the business of conversion proceeded slowly. According to the Baptist evangelist, Isaac McCoy, missionaries[43]

> should be men of good sense, ardent piety, persevering disposition, conciliating manners, ... industrious, frugal, and economical, ready to enlist for life, and willing to labor through life without laying up a dollar for those of their family who may outlive them.

They might, in addition, have to face danger and discomfort in remote regions devoid of 'civilized' amenities. Such individuals are always hard to find, even allowing for the importance of self-sacrifice in the reformer's make-up. It was also an extraordinary missionary family, generally overworked and with the first misplaced optimism seeping away, that could endure the illnesses, deaths and neglect that were the lot of Mrs McCoy and her circle.[44] Problems arose from the high turnover of missionaries and from their disputes with those who paid their salaries and were usually themselves short of money. Under the circumstances, it is not surprising that suitable evangelists were hard to find, that some sects still had no Indian missions and that a number of oddities and scoundrels found their way into the field. Recruitment difficulties were compounded because the various denominations were distracted by the need to establish themselves in the white communities of frontier areas. And then there were other good causes to consider, including overseas missions, temperance and anti-slavery. Indian missions were never popular. McCoy complained that foreign missions were not short of volunteers; perhaps they had greater glamour. More probably, potential evangelists discounted the public confidence of established missionaries and shared the contemporary belief that the Indians were doomed to extinction, making Christian efforts among them futile.

Missionary methods and Indian opposition aggravated the disappointments involved in the organization of the work. Protestant missionaries especially demanded a total change in lifestyle from their neophytes, the point of which frequently eluded Indians in wild regions where they were more at home than the evangelists and where many of the whites they encountered scarcely measured up to the Christian code. This extremism affected even Quaker missionaries, who tended to concentrate on imparting practical skills and improving the material lot of their converts. Being associated with a government which had extracted a whole series of unwanted treaties from the tribesmen, the evangelists were often regarded with hostility by the Indians before they began their operations. When the demoralization of some northwestern tribes resulting from defeat, migrations, liquor and dependence on annuities led certain missionaries to advocate Indian removal to a permanent home west of the Mississippi, tribal suspicions were confirmed, while the disagreements of evangelists over removal proposals could only disillusion their supporters and the Indians alike. Equally dispiriting were the antagonisms which emerged between Christian and unconverted Indians, and the damaging effects on tribes when they were proselytized by several different and competing missionary groups.[45]

Although the evangelists offered some of their converts an advanced education in the East that their white counterparts might have been pleased to obtain, the fact that most missionaries worked with the Indians inside native territory increased their problems. Few evangelists were linguists and while we can defend their belief that a knowledge of English would help the Indians in an increasingly white world, the missionaries were unable to penetrate far into the native world because of their reluctance or inability to learn Indian languages. Evangelists customarily had no training in how to teach practical skills, and where these were imparted, they seemed simply to be directed at keeping the mission station going. The fact that tribal funds were sometimes given to the missionaries for their educational work further alienated Indians who were unconvinced of the usefulness of Christian instruction or deterred by the treatment of converts by fellow tribesmen. One of the 'revitalization' or 'amalgamation' movements in native religion which developed despite and in reaction to the white onslaught might subsequently enlist the alienated.[46]

From the Delaware prophet, Neolin, in the 1760s, and Handsome Lake of the Iroquois at the end of the eighteenth century, to the Shawnee Tenskwatawa and Hillis Hadjo among the Creeks and Seminoles in the early nineteenth century, native holy men had emerged who urged moral reformation and a return to the old ways.[47] And other Indian peoples, for instance the Indiana followers of the 'Potawatomi Preacher', Menominee, merely added Christian beliefs to native practices, as they had done from colonial times. Of course black Americans did the same,[48] and such syncretism was achieved in each case because the non-whites' original intimate relationship with their natural environment had been disrupted. But the degree of disruption was crucial in determining the outcome. For Indian groups like those of the South, with a powerful mixed-blood element, or for tribes whose defeats were so severe as to shake their faith in the old order, white religion might have some attraction. It did not, however, have the sort of appeal that evangelical Christianity in particular held for blacks who were permanently cut off from their African roots or had been born in the United States. During the 1770s and 1780s they were finding hope in a religion which initially 'knew no class, caste, race or sex', and 'invited them to participate in worship through the evocative similarity of the conversion experience to religious rituals and expression bequeathed them by Mother Africa'.[49] By the 1850s, they had adjusted the institutions and emphases of that religion to their own needs and heritage on a scale not paralleled in the Indian community.

It would be unfair, none the less, to imply that the pioneer American missionaries were uniquely inept or unfortunate. In Canada, the Society for the Propagation of the Gospel in Foreign Parts struggled to sustain Christianity among the Iroquois Six Nations, not least in the face of the Handsome Lake movement. Although the first church in Upper Canada was established at the Mohawk village of Brantford in 1785, attempts to use Mohawk texts as a medium of instruction ran into difficulties and educational endeavours fared poorly. A little more progress was made by the New England Company, which moved to Canada at the outbreak of the Revolutionary War, and the Methodist and Baptist missionaries who next entered the field issued optimistic reports, especially about the mission schools. But they were hard pressed to minister both to the Indians and the frontier whites, and to counteract the bad example of white Christians. A report in 1844 estimated that 'a large Majority of the Upper and lower Cayugas, Onondagas, Senecas, and some of the [neighbouring] Delawares are still Heathens'.[50] In the territory of the Hudson's Bay Company, where missionaries were cautiously tolerated, there was tension between the Protestants and the traders and between the Protestants and the Catholics, and if the Protestants were more congenial to the company, the Catholics were more at ease with the Indians and mixed bloods.[51]

Missionaries, in common with other reformers, generally had to be content with counting small gains. Hence they took pleasure in new ventures begun, more Indians speaking English, abandoning native dress, living in better houses, showing an interest in farming and professing Christianity. There was no point in advertising that their successes were very variable and the new Christians frequently very nominal. The evangelists persisted in their labours despite an awareness that they had not made America 'a Christian nation' and that the missions had not compensated Indian peoples for the unfair deal whereby they exchanged their lands for white vices.[52] They could seek comfort in the knowledge that, all other considerations aside, the institutional resources of philanthropy were inadequate to cope with such an enormous undertaking. So, too, were those of the federal government.

While the Civilization Fund endured under the supervision of the War Department, the government's factory trading operation, headed by Thomas L. McKenney, was abolished in 1822 because it had proved unpopular with the Indians and private traders, as well as disillusioning to reformers.[53] Thereafter, the work of co-ordinating the Indian superintendents, agents, sub-agents and lesser personnel rested entirely on the Secretary of War and a few clerks. The men in the field had to rely on local marshals, district attorneys, territorial courts and the commanders of military posts for help in implementing the Trade and Intercourse Acts, and relations between them were not always harmonious. Army personnel were hampered by their limited numbers and arresting powers over civilians, while the territorial governors who were *ex-officio* Indian superintendents were torn between the conflicting interests of whites and Indians within their jurisdiction, besides facing the inconvenience of having to report to the Secretary of State in their first capacity and to the Secretary of War in their second. Since an Indian superintendent had charge of negotiating treaties, making any resulting payments to the tribes and overseeing a range of administrative duties, his was obviously a full-time job in itself. To make things worse, Indian matters were governed by a confused mass of laws and treaties, and loosely directed field officials were allowed to deflect funds voted by Congress for one purpose to another (a practice known as counter-warranting).[54]

Hoping to improve this whole system, Secretary of War John C.

Calhoun created a Bureau of Indian Affairs within his department in 1824. (It was quickly known by contemporaries as the Office of Indian Affairs; the name Bureau of Indian Affairs was not formally adopted until 1947. In 1849, the bureau was transferred to the newly established Department of the Interior and has remained there.) The first man to take charge of the Indian Bureau was Thomas McKenney, who pressed strongly for the regularization of its work, eventually achieved in 1834, and the appointment of a Commissioner of Indian Afairs. By the time Congress created the post of commissioner in 1832, at an annual salary of $3,000, the ill-paid and luckless McKenney had been two years out of office, having made an enemy of Andrew Jackson by supporting Calhoun, his rival for the presidency in 1824, and John Quincy Adams, his opponent in 1828.

On first reflection, leaving aside its obvious practical usefulness, the creation of the bureau seems an odd political development in the Jacksonian era. The Democratic administration installed in 1829 had promised retrenchment and it initially procured some.[55] Jackson, it has been argued, saw administration 'in terms of individual office-holders rather than as a process of government' and had little in the way of a 'philosophy of party or of government'.[56] His followers have been presented as advocates of limited government, in contrast to the Whigs, and Jackson's most famous fight as president was against that mighty institution, the second Bank of the United States. As Lynn L. Marshall sees it, however, the Jacksonians acted on the advice of the president's adviser, Amos Kendall, to 'Organize, organize'; they put together an efficient national party machine, and tried to reorder the executive department so as to give greater weight to efficient rules and regulations than to the special claims of individual character. The Jacksonians' negativism, professed egalitarianism and agrarianism did, of course, often seem in conflict with the expanding and exploitative economic order developing from the 1820s. But as Marshall maintains, 'Jacksonian party development and administrative reform' were very much in tune with other experiments in social organization in the economy, religious and secular reform, though the Democrats certainly appear to have attached more importance to a flexible and pragmatic approach than did the moral reformers.[57]

The involvement of the Indian Bureau in the politics of patronage is, by contrast with its creation, anything but odd. It is entirely fitting that the Jacksonian era, which witnessed the elevation in national politics of the partisan allocation of government offices, should have seen personal and political considerations result in the dismissal of

McKenney and the preferment of Elbert Herring, Carey Allen Harris, T. Hartley Crawford and William Medill for the top job in the Indian Bureau, regardless of their inexperience in Indian affairs. Indeed, the position of Commissioner of Indian Affairs had come to be seen 'as an important patronage office' by the 1840s. And while there was some continuity in the expanded personnel of the Indian Bureau, its members were likewise affected by changes due to the patronage system.[58] It is equally fitting that the Indian Service Reorganization Act of 1834 was pushed as an economy measure. Twelve agencies were provided for but it was assumed that their numbers would be reduced once Indian removal was over. Savings were meanwhile made by obliging agents to serve as acting superintendents, by increasing the burdens of frontier military commanders and, contrary to the intention of the Act, by continuing the practice of using territorial governors as *ex-officio* Indian superintendents. Furthermore, since the duties of the two were not distinguished, sub-agents were often expected to do the same work as agents, for half the pay.

Even after the shake-up of 1834, the Indian service had many flaws. Agents went into the field without proper briefing until the production of a rule book for bureau employees in 1850. They continued to find communication with Washington difficult, to indulge in counter-warranting and to escape on-the-spot inspection. The provision of Indian supplies, together with the negotiation and ratification of Indian treaties, still gave rise to much corruption. Agents and sub-agents remained overburdened by a work-load that could involve issuing and revoking traders' licences, overseeing the civilization and education programmes, resolving Indian–white disputes, paying annuities and settling intertribal conflicts. There were too many patronage appointments and too few Indians on the bureau's payroll. Satz has shown that in the context of the federal government's weakness and incompetence when directing the territories and public land policy, matters might have been worse. Some attempts were made to get rid of corrupt or inefficient officials, for example, while the exaggeration of agents' misdemeanours for political reasons obscured the achievements of individuals like Henry R. Schoolcraft among the Lake Superior tribes and Lawrence Taliaferro among the Sioux. Nevertheless, public apathy, political partisanship, a seven-year economic depression from 1837 and the Indians' political powerlessness all made substantial improvements hard to achieve. Thus was the huge upheaval in Indian affairs necessitated by removal rendered more painful.[59]

III

INDIAN REMOVAL

Following the example of Thomas Jefferson, but with an ever growing degree of urgency, presidents James Monroe and John Quincy Adams urged the voluntary removal of eastern Indians to a permanent location west of the Mississippi. The southern states stood to gain most from the removal of over 50,000 Cherokees, Choctaws, Chickasaws, Creeks and Seminoles, living on 33 million acres of land. And the southerners' mouthpiece was Georgia, whose western land claims had been relinquished in 1802 in return for a promise from the federal government to extinguish the Indian land title within the state. After 1815, the total value of cotton exports mounted steadily and cotton constituted an increasingly large share of the total value of exports. Its share of the total, together with receipts from public land sales in the South, rose particularly markedly during the removal years of the 1830s, and as Takaki and others have shown, the emergence of the cotton kingdom plainly depended on Indian dispossession, the accompanying expansion of white settlement, and black slavery. Repeated cessions of territory by the southern Indians between 1814 and 1824 had whetted rather than dulled the whites' appetite for land which was not only suitable for cotton growing but also contained valuable mineral resources. Southerners asserted that they would use this territory better than the Indians and the acquisition of rich new land was especially welcome at a time when town life and work were exerting a growing attraction for country dwellers in unrewarding regions.

The point that tribes like the Cherokees were becoming civilized could be met by a variety of arguments. Only the mixed bloods, it was suggested, had made any progress and they were selfishly exploiting the rest of their people. Alternatively, if the tribes really were civilized, contended Georgia, Tennessee, Alabama and Mississippi, then it would do no harm to extend state jurisdiction over the tribal enclaves and treat their inhabitants like other Americans. Georgia was the first state to adopt this course, in 1828, and its three neighbours followed suit. It was pointed out that the Indian domain attracted runaway slaves, and was therefore a threat to white property rights and security (see Chapter 5). In addition, the 1823 *Johnson and Graham's Lessee v. William McIntosh* ruling of the Supreme Court had, when upholding the sovereignty of the United States in matters pertaining to Indian land sales, referred to the tribes as merely *occupying* territory owned by the United States, thereby encouraging southerners anxious to characterize the Indians as 'dependent tenants' in their midst.[60]

Running beneath these arguments was a strong vein of race prejudice. It seems clear that the whites of the South did not want Indians among them, civilized or otherwise. Northerners who protested against removal were dismissed as hypocrites who themselves believed in Anglo-Saxon superiority and conveniently forgot their own earlier gains at the expense of Indian peoples, just as abolitionists ignored the oppression of labour in the ostensibly free North and shrank from acknowledging blacks as their social equals. Although there was some truth in such accusations, they neither deterred humanitarians nor prevented the development of a close connection between anti-slavery sentiment and opposition to Indian removal, which duly contributed to the sectional split over that policy. The split was always likely, given the pressure for removal by a southern president, the strong resistance to it by the progressive southern tribes and the political possibilities it presented to all northern enemies of the administration. But the abolitionist connection sharpened the confrontation, driving the Jacksonians to strengthen their claim that they wanted to save the Indians from degradation or extinction in the East and civilize them in the West, a claim which laid removal advocates in their turn open to the charge of hypocrisy.[61]

Abolitionists like William Lloyd Garrison, Lydia Maria Child, the Grimké sisters, Elijah P. Lovejoy and James and Lucretia Mott defended the Indians because their rights had been guaranteed by treaty. These individuals believed that removal, slavery and African colonization alike denied Indians and blacks the civilization to which each could aspire; that they put prejudice before principle, brought America's libertarian creed into disrepute, invited divine retribution and were equally indicative of white greed, cruelty and expansionism, indulged for sectional advantage. Protest petitions opposing removal came to Washington from the same sections of the population as opposed black slavery: New Englanders and easterners generally, Protestant sects, missionaries, colleges and benevolent societies. In addition to the abolitionists proper, a number of prominent individuals who were at various times sympathetic to anti-slavery spoke out against wholesale, unjustly enforced removal. They included Ralph Waldo Emerson, Theodore Frelinghuysen, Daniel Webster, Edward Everett, John Howard Payne, Samuel Houston and Henry Clay.[62] And foreign observers added words of condemnation, albeit they were moved by their own prejudices about America, as well as by genuine humanitarianism. The anti-American Mrs Frances Trollope is a good case in point. Commenting on the treatment of Indians during the 1830s in her *Domestic Manners of the Americans,* she concluded that if the people's character 'may be judged by their conduct in this matter, they are most lamentably deficient in every feeling of honour and integrity'.[63]

Foreign and domestic critics of removal, including, of course, the Indians themselves, correctly forecast its consequences. In their estimation, the removal process would be unfair and destructive, the Indians would be further alienated from the whites and the lands promised in perpetuity in the west would either bear no comparison with those vacated or would eventually be coveted by whites. If fresh removals then ensued, the progress made by the southern Indians would have been disrupted to no purpose. The removing tribes were liable to clash with strange and hostile Indian bands across the Mississippi, while grave problems were bound to occur in connection with the settlement and administration of the new Indian country.[64] In terms of the volume of printed matter on the subject, as Tyler observes, the opponents of removal won the debate.[65] They also had the most impressive arguments. Jackson's critics may have had mixed motives, yet it is worth stressing that the same pecuniary and repressive culture which produced the Indian-haters of this period prompted some real concern for Indian peoples. Unfortunately the altruists shared with their enemies a belief in the superiority of white culture, a conviction that only the private ownership of land realized its full potential and a tendency to blame others for the Indians' difficulties. Thus instead of acknowledging the inconsistencies within Jeffersonian philanthropy, humanitarians reserved their criticism for cynical politicians or grasping frontiersmen.[66] More importantly, they lost the political battle.

On 28 May 1830, the Removal Act was passed after a bitter struggle. It authorized the President to provide unorganized public lands west of the Mississippi for the settlement of eastern Indians willing to move there. Indian emigrants were to be given permanent title to their new land, compensation for improvements in the East, help in moving and protection on arrival. To implement the Act, Congress appropriated $500,000 and it was soon apparent that every device would be employed to secure tribal compliance. The Indian country was defined in 1834 as 'That part of the United States west of the Mississippi, and not within the states of Missouri and Louisiana, or the territory of Arkansas, and, also, that part of the United States east of the Mississippi river, and not within any state to which the Indian title has not been extinguished'. By about the mid 1840s, most of the eastern Indians had been, or were in the process of being, relocated. During Jackson's administration, some 100 million acres of Indian land east of the Mississippi had been secured through nearly seventy treaties, at a cost of approximately 68 million dollars and 32 million acres west of the river.[67]

The President's backing for this programme was of tremendous importance. He was widely popular, a southerner sympathetic to states rights, and at best a paternalist where the Indians were concerned. As an Indian fighter he believed that the tribes respected force and as a nationalist he felt that the United States was so strong that it no longer had to treat 'savages' as equals through the treaty-making relationship. Jackson was convinced that removal would at one and the same time resolve an internal security problem and strengthen the lower Mississippi valley against any possible foreign threat. It can be argued that, faced with choosing between the white majority or enlarging the army to guarantee the integrity of Indian states within the states, the President's only politically feasible option was removal. The inability of past governments to keep whites out of Indian land they really wanted gives weight to this argument. And at least, in peacetime, Jackson did not advocate the extermination of the tribes; that 'solution' was ruled out in a civilized country, however cheerfully some Americans may have looked forward to the Indians' extinction.[68]

Northern leaders were able to agree with southerners about the desirability of Jackson's policy which, as Stephen A. Douglas of Illinois piously declared, 'commends itself alike to the head and heart of every politician and christian'.[69] Indeed, the ostensible concern for legality and civilization which surrounded removal made it infinitely dangerous. Key individuals acquainted with Indian affairs, including Isaac McCoy, Thomas McKenney and Michigan's territorial governor, Lewis Cass, also supported the programme. McCoy admitted that the United States should not have permitted its citizens to ignore Indian land ownership, but felt that the tribes would never 'prosper on small tracts of country, surrounded by people of other colour, other prejudices, and other interests'. Removal was desired by Christians as a means of civilizing the Indians, who could not be allowed to accept or reject the option at will without producing 'a perversion of order and the abolition of all Government'. Although a genuine convert to removal and anxious that the Indians should be guaranteed orderly consolidation and self-rule in the West, McCoy was employed by the federal government as a teacher and explorer. He therefore had good practical reasons for turning his mind away from the drawbacks to removal. Yet his caution did not pay dividends, and the administration found less use for McCoy after 1832.[70] McKenney provides a still more dramatic example of an expendable ally. An able advocate of the civilization programme and a believer in the intellectual equality of

Indians and whites, he may have convinced himself that he had the best interests of the Indians at heart; he was a paternalist in the Jeffersonian tradition. But McKenney's career was even dearer to him and he consequently supported the Monroe-Calhoun proposals for removal and gave his backing to Jackson until, having served his purpose, he was dismissed. He thereupon joined the ranks of the opposition.[71]

Harassed by their enemies, the Indians turned for help to the Supreme Court. However, though not sympathetic to Georgia, the court proved unable to help the Cherokees who brought suit against the state. In *Cherokee Nation v. State of Georgia* (1831) and *Worcester v. Georgia* (1832), the court ruled that the tribes were 'domestic dependent nations' for whose welfare the *federal* government was responsible. While they were not sovereign entities, they enjoyed internal self-government and should not be put at the mercy of the states. Georgia's extension of state law over the Indians was deemed unconstitutional and it was ordered to release the Cherokees' imprisoned missionaries, who had refused to seek a licence from the state. Happily for Jackson, he 'did not have legal authority to use military force to execute the Supreme Court's order' and the court 'had no way to enforce its decree'. The President's northern enemies made much of his inaction, but Jackson was able to ride out the criticism and present himself as a good nationalist in his stern response to the crisis provoked by South Carolina's nullification of the high tariffs of 1828 and 1832. Against the background of this crisis and in response to suggestions from the President and pleas from his enemies, Georgia officials offered pardons to the two missionaries and they accepted them. Politics had defeated the Cherokees; Georgia's general attitude to their presence remained unchanged.[72]

Even if one accepts the claim that in removal the Jacksonians adopted the only Indian policy tolerable to the majority of white Americans, the implementation of the policy provides bleak evidence of growing prejudice and callous injustice. After the War of 1812, there had been renewed interest in offering Indians the option of moving west or taking up individual allotments of land where they resided. The allotment policy had originated in the colonial period and had not provided the answer to 'the Indian problem'. But perhaps just because the Indian take-up rate on allotments proved low following treaties with the southern tribes negotiated between 1817 and 1820, the option was offered to the Choctaws, Creeks and Chickasaws during the 1830s. An embarrassingly large number of Indians then applied for allotments, whereupon white settlers moved prematurely on to tribal land and they, together with speculators, cheated Indians out of their property. Mary Young has estimated that 'speculators acquired 80 to 90 per cent of the land allotted to the southeastern tribesmen'; this amounted to approximately 25 million acres. In the Northwest, whites likewise benefited at the expense of the allotted Indians and the administration took refuge in the argument that it could not interfere with contracts voluntarily entered into. Allotment became just another means of separating Indians from their land and expediting removal.

Equality of opportunity was the only kind of opportunity most Americans envisaged in these years of economic transformation. Accordingly the Indians could be considered to have wasted their allotment opportunities, just as they had wasted their chances to become civilized. That such opportunities were meaningless to the majority of Indians mattered little to the majority of whites. As J. R. Pole observes,

> It fell to a later generation than Jackson's to extend the obligations owed by government to members of every race or heritage, as it had fallen to Jackson's to affirm that these obligations were owed to every social or economic class. Jackson, who never had the slightest concern for racial equality, might have failed to see the line of connection. That difficulty arose from the nature of his vision, not from the nature of the case.

When bribery, fraud and intimidation had not cleared all the Indians from the East by the middle of the 1830s, troops were used to move the Indiana Potawatomis, Cherokees, Creeks and Seminoles, after a war with the Seminoles lasting from 1835 to 1842, in which the Indians' resistance and their friendliness to black fugitives (see Chapter 5) were said to prove their savagery and justify white tactics. The removals were a source of hardship in themselves, particularly the later ones employing force and involving the partly acculturated southern tribes. Travelling long distances over rough terrain in frequently severe weather, the already demoralized emigrants suffered from the government's poor forward planning and the substandard rations and transport provided by the grasping private contractors on whom it relied. Approximately 4,000 Cherokees died on the 'Trail of Tears' across the Mississippi and a private soldier who witnessed the Cherokees' expulsion in 1838 recalled:[73]

> One can never forget the sadness and solemnity of that morning . . . I saw the helpless Cherokees arrested and dragged from their houses, and driven by bayonet into the stockades. And in the chill of a drizzling rain on one October morning I saw them loaded like cattle or sheep into six hundred and forty-five wagons and started towards the west.

In fairness to the Democrats, it must be pointed out that opposition denunciations of the expense of the removal policy encouraged them

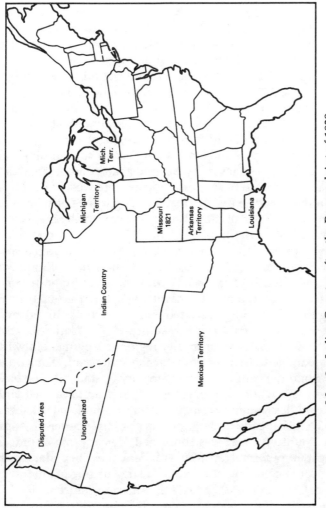

Map 2 Indian Country after the Removal Act of 1830.

Source: Ronald G. Satz, *American Indian Policy in the Jacksonian Era* (Lincoln, NE: University of Nebraska Press, 1975).

to cut corners. Moreover, military and civilian removal agents often struggled to carry out their duties honourably, while government officials improved the procedures for Chickasaw allotment having learned from the problems encountered with the Creeks and Choc-taws.[74] But their combined efforts could not offset the wretchedness of the 'Trail of Tears'.

Many reforms suffer so badly from reluctant and bungling implementation as to cast doubt on their claims to be reforms at all. Prohibition was such a cause in the twentieth century. In the nine-teenth century, removal seems to be another. Coleman, Satz and Prucha have shown that humanitarians and commissioners of Indian Affairs alike from the 1830s remained optimistic about Indian edu-cation and resisted explaining white–Indian differences in terms of race. Individual reformers, including some old-time abolitionists, also tried to expose the faults of the Indian service, highlight the grievances of various Indian peoples and eradicate injustices surrounding Indian trade and annuity payments.[75] The civilization campaign was not simply abandoned once the eastern Indians were west of the Mississ-ippi. None the less, the self-interest and negligence of whites com-bined with the situation of the tribes to render it totally ineffective.

The adjustment of the Indians in the West was a protracted and uneven one, bedevilled as they were by disease, material losses, unfamiliar surroundings, unwelcoming Indian neighbours, white meddling and intensified factionalism. If the great irony in removal from the white standpoint was that it transported groups, thereby preserving the tribal units associated with 'savagery', this advantage was counterbalanced for the northwestern and New York tribes by the fact that they were not given a specific region as a permanent western home, comparable to that set aside for the southern Indians on land that lay beyond the confines of any territory or state. The result was that by the 1840s whites had spread into Iowa and acquired land in Minnesota, while clamour was mounting for the removal of tribes and bands which had already undergone that searing experience. As far as the Indian country proper was concerned, defeat came to proposals for turning it into a formal territory with permanent boundaries where the tribes would come together, enjoy a large degree of autonomy, a delegate in Congress and finally full American citizenship. White northerners and southerners were equally opposed to giving security to Indians in the West if, in the process, the balance between the sections was altered and maturing expansionist objectives were checked. In addition, if northern whites were particularly averse to Indian territories because they would increase the power of the executive and the army, southern whites dreaded the extension of political equality to dark-skinned peoples and feared the loss of the Indian service jobs they dominated in the existing Indian country. The situation there was further complicated by the objections of the Cherokees, Choctaws and Creeks to a 'territorial council based on equal representation that would allow the smaller tribes to outvote them'.

It may fairly be said that the federal government proved both too strong and too weak in Indian matters. On the one hand it did not effectively use its strengthened powers under the 1834 and 1847 Trade and Intercourse Acts to protect the tribes against white intruders and fraudulent traders. On the other hand, government agents, missionaries and the white courts bordering Indian country were allowed to make a nonsense of Jackson's promise of self-rule and sovereignty to the Indians who crossed the Mississippi. It must likewise be said that the Whigs, for all their criticisms of removal, saw no mileage in trying to reverse the Jacksonian programme once they gained power in 1841. Their later backing, when in opposition, to the traders battling the reforming Indian Commissioner, William Medill (1845–9), casts further doubt on the genuineness of Whigs' concern for the Indians.[76] As would be the case many times in the future, partisan advantage rather than principle or sentiment determined politicians' attitudes towards Indian policy. And neither party could secure the enforcement of unpopular Indian legislation. The army may have been given increased power after 1834 to intervene in quarrels between the Indians and may have fulfilled its difficult role in the West rather better than its enemies sometimes admitted, but it still lacked the manpower to carry out its duties under the Trade and Intercourse legislation, just as the contemporary forces of public order lacked the ability to prevent white mobs from harassing white minorities they disliked. Indeed, between 1808 and 1853, the peacetime establishment of the army only rose from 9,991 to 10,417.[77]

IV

Towards Reservations

American Indian policy in the 1830s had combined long-term optimism with short-term planning. The philanthropists, blaming the environment in the East for the comparative failure of the civilization programme, did not question its wisdom but, in order to stay in business, predicted its future success in a new location. And the politicians, more understandably wedded to coping with emergencies of the moment, produced a 'solution' to the crisis in Indian–white

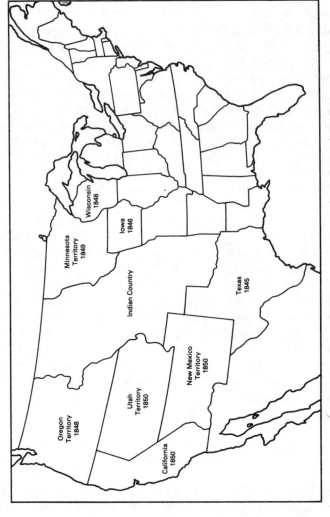

Map 3 Indian Country after the Mexican War of 1846–8.

Source: Ronald G. Satz, *American Indian Policy in the Jacksonian Era* (Lincoln, NE: University of Nebraska Press, 1975).

relations which they themselves flouted: a remedy which depended on spending more money than Congress would authorize on securing a period of stability in the West. What followed from the mid 1840s, in fact, was an era of extraordinary expansion and accompanying anxieties about American defence needs. Between 1845 and 1848, another 1,202,286 square miles were included in the national domain, containing some 209,000 Indians to add to the 191,000 already within American borders.[78] The United States assumed new responsibilities over a wide variety of both sedentary and nomadic tribes in Texas, Oregon, California, New Mexico and Utah. Yet it lacked the new powers needed to cope with them because American citizens remained wedded to frugal and limited government. Uneasiness in Indian service, political and military circles was intensified by the persistent westward movement of whites, leading to bloody clashes between settlers and Indian warriors and demands for the building of a transcontinental railroad through Indian territory. A way out of these difficulties that sidestepped some of them but pleased the white majority was found when it was agreed that the goal of tribal autonomy within Indian country would have to be replaced by a policy of concentrating the tribes on reservations.

By the 1850s, having come to regard the Indian country as a threat to developers and pioneers, whites professed their dismay at finding it too large for Indian needs and not the nursery for civilization that it was intended to be. Such former supporters of removal as Stephen Douglas could now see that an Indian barrier 'has become so ludicrous that we are amazed, that wise and patriotic statesmen ever cherished the thought'.[79] The work of 'uplifting' the natives would go on faster, or begin better in the case of the wild tribes, if the Indians were contained within smaller territories, under closer supervision, and thus unable to harm either the whites or each other. The proposals for reservations, which had originated in colonial times, were made because Indian policy-makers had been overtaken by events, as they were in the Jacksonian period. Like the removal scheme, reservations appeared to be practical and humane; in both programmes, Indian civilization was to be achieved through the segregation, rather than the integration, of the races. Unlike removal, reservations could not be recommended as an economy measure. More agents, farmers, blacksmiths and teachers would be needed for them to work, for the Indians to be made self-sustaining. In many cases reservations required an even more drastic change of lifestyle from the tribes involved than removal had done. And since reservations were frequently surrounded by white settlements, there were more chances of racial conflict in the future.[80]

By 1860, however, the reservation policy had been initiated in California, Washington, Oregon and New Mexico. For contemporaries, the condition of the Indian service and the state of American humanitarianism were not so dire as to encourage expectations of failure, particularly when, again as applied with removal, whites stood to gain substantially in terms of security and land. Thus, as Tyler has noted, the years between 1853 and 1856 alone, when the new policy was getting under way, saw the negotiation of fifty-two treaties which gave the Indian office jurisdiction over some four to six thousand square miles of territory and the United States around 174 million acres of land.[80] If sectional issues and meagre appropriations continued to embarrass the bureau and the results of missionary efforts among the northwestern tribes, the Kansa and the Sioux were disappointing, some enlargement of the BIA's personnel was achieved, while the evangelists' supporters could temper their disappointment with the reflection that church membership had grown in the lands vacated by Indians moved west of the Mississippi.[81] That the fledgeling reservations were agencies for facilitating social control over the Indians, reformers could accept as happily as their opponents. That the reservations sheltered native instead of white civilization, it was left for a later generation to discover.

Antebellum Indian reformers, like politicians concerned with Indian matters, on the whole responded to emergencies and trends only partly of their making and beyond their control. As the United States expanded, the primarily eastern humanitarians were geographically more removed than ever from the objects of their concern. They were united in desiring the civilization and assimilation of the tribes without having devised the means to carry out their goals. It is difficult to know what those means should have been. One may hazard that instruction in white farming techniques, unaccompanied by other attempts to alter native culture, would have succeeded better than the existing programmes. It might have been helpful had the modern objective of bicultural education been envisaged and applied (see Chapter 9), although this has proved a highly controversial policy. Even so, Indian resistance or apathy in the face of white interference would probably have remained. The problems caused by the inadequate funding of the civilization campaign and encountered by the Indians in the West would certainly have endured.

Indian reform also had profound staffing difficulties. Only the missionaries had a secure institutional base before the 1880s and they had a limited appeal to fellow whites, let alone to the tribes. It would have been useful if unsuitable missionaries had been weeded out, or if the number of Indian reformers had been vastly increased while the number of rival reform movements was drastically reduced. It would have been gratifying if there had been no quarrels between missionary groups, or between eastern humanitarians and missionaries in the field; for example, over the permissibility of tolerating black slavery among the Five Civilized Tribes (see Chapter 5). But these conflicts do not account for the poor showing of the Indian reform movement, which was never so faction-torn as such contemporary causes as abolitionism.

It is easy now to see the destructiveness of the drive to wean the individual Indian from the support of his society. Yet white faith in individualism was understandable at a time when it was the energy of devoted individuals that sustained reform, despite the organizational achievements of the anti-slavery and temperance crusades. The philanthropists' commitment to agrarian solutions for Indian problems, given the rural circumstances of the tribes, their affection for the land and the continuing importance of agriculture to the American economy, does not seem so inappropriate as the anti-urban bias of many white reformers would appear when the United States rapidly industrialized in the later nineteenth century. Though their expectation of swift success appears naive in retrospect, such naivety was apparently a necessary feature of the entire reform community in a period when so many material factors conspired against it.

Our verdict on the humanitarians' efforts must be a critical one, just the same. It had not proved possible to persuade white Americans to show as much interest in the fate of the semi-independent first Americans as they did in African Americans, the injustices endured by the slaves seeming clearer, the remedies for them more obvious and blacks' endorsement of the humanitarians more apparent. In tune with the coercive and paternalistic strain in the national reform tradition, neither the Indian office nor the philanthropists felt it was necessary to consult Indian opinion before taking policy decisions and there was certainly no formal machinery for doing so, albeit treaty negotiations and the reports of the field officers were important sources of information about Indian attitudes. And neither the Indian office nor the reformers were yet strong enough to make Indian policy; this was the prerogative of Congress, influenced by the army and guided by the House and Senate Committees on Indian Affairs.[83]

The next great phase of Indian reform in the 1860s would again be initiated by the federal government, though drawing upon its missionary connection, and it would have to reckon with strong hostility to the Indians as a race. For notwithstanding humanitarian endeavour, white prejudice against the Indians as a race had grown steadily under the influence of more widespread frontier clashes and disparaging popular literature and because the early anthropologists were unable to provide a value-free guide to Indian cultures (see Chapter 7). The success of nativism, or organized anti-foreigner feeling, by the 1850s was an ominous indication of how unlikely many Americans were to display tolerance towards non-white minorities. Blacks and Indians, though not identically depicted, had come to serve as 'negative reference points', helping whites to define what they were and what they should not be.[84]

Indian affairs in Canada could offer some comfort to American administrators as they contemplated their own difficulties; but not much. Before confederation, little educational work was done outside Upper and Lower Canada, and what there was fell mainly to the lot of unaided missionaries or the Indians themselves. By 1867, 'the Indian office recognized only one residential school and forty-nine day schools'. As in the United States, Indian annuities and trust funds were manipulated and misused. Traders, chiefly those in liquor, exploited the tribesmen. Whites encroached on native lands and depleted their resources, missionary quarrels undermined their efforts, and though Indian cultures were disparaged, the Indians were very slow to accept the newcomers' customs. Conversely, a truthful American would have to admit that the small, closed, unallotted reservations which were slowly being established offered more hope of rough racial justice than the mixed and confusing American system. Defensive observers from Jefferson onwards might reasonably complain that the Canadians bought the allegiance of the Indians. However, the results of their subsequent cynical frugality were sometimes impressive. Demography and history were still on the side of the Canadians.[85]

3

Assimilationist Pressures Mount: the 1860s to 1920

I

THE IMPACT OF THE CIVIL WAR

War years are not usually good years for reform groups. The pressure is on them to lay aside their campaigns, take up war work instead and generally foster national unity. They may hope to be remembered for good behaviour when hostilities end, but they are just as likely to find a public grown tired of the old crusades and a government grown anxious for retrenchment. The temperance and women's movements were both disrupted by the Civil War and the conflict followed a depression which had already had an adverse effect upon reformer efforts, especially in the North.[1] Indian peoples were particularly unlikely to be viewed sympathetically by whites during a war which saw the southern tribes giving assistance to the Confederacy, the Apaches, Cheyennes, Shoshonis and Sioux terrorizing assorted Indian neighbours, interracial conflicts erupting in Colorado, Minnesota and California, and some of the reservation tribes leaving their supposedly established homes in search of better food resources elsewhere.[2]

None the less, the Civil War underlined a number of weaknesses in the Indian service, which were publicized by individual Indian reformers, among them the Episcopal Bishop of Minnesota, Henry B. Whipple, and the Methodist minister and farmer, John Beeson. The ranks of reform also soon included various abolitionists and Quakers, whose antebellum interest in the native population we have already noted, and a number of organizations, the most prominent of which were the Universal Peace Society and the (privately operated) United States Indian Commission. These groups and individuals were concerned that the withdrawal of troops from the frontier had led to the invasion of Indian land by miners, settlers and dishonest traders. They

71

were aware that annuity payments arrived late and often in unwelcome paper currency. And it was known that corruption among bureau personnel, though it may have been overestimated, was a disagreeable feature of the wartime crisis, while missionary and educational work among the Indians had been badly disrupted.[3]

An uneasy President Lincoln responded to the humanitarians by promising reform 'as soon as the pressing matters of this war is [*sic*] settled' and his Secretary of War, Edwin Stanton, asserted that corruption in Indian affairs would be rooted out when the American people demanded reform, not before – a familiar politician's ploy. The Commissioner of Indian Affairs, William P. Dole, could claim some achievements. He resisted demands for the renewal of army control over the bureau, obtained aid for Indians who had fled from the war-torn Indian Territory to Kansas, and extracted better information and financial returns from his field officers. Yet the Commissioner did not wish to embarrass the Lincoln administration through controversial activities and for most northerners Indian policy remained an unimportant sideshow while the nation fought the first modern war.[4]

As Allan Nevins has pointed out, the North was launched into civil war with a primitive administration, 'only small managerial groups and little skill in cooperative effort'. The old order had been dominated by 'small enterprises, local outlooks, and unrestricted individualism', with the meaning of the word organization 'hardly known'. By 1865, an organized, confident, very different society had emerged.[5] The cost had been great and there had been no time to extend the managerial revolution to the Indian service where, Dole's successor complained, the oversight of about 300,000 Indians was left to a small Washington office, aided by 'fourteen superintendents and some seventy agents'.[6]

In the years immediately after the war, the direction of policy was no more in the hands of this weak bureau than it had been in the antebellum period. The Doolittle Committee and the Indian Peace Commission of 1867 inquired into ways of resolving continuing Indian–white hostilities at the behest of Congress, not the BIA, and each investigation criticized the civilian administration.[7] With three Commissioners of Indian Affairs serving between 1865 and 1869, one of whom was never officially confirmed in the job, and all of whom were appointed for strictly political reasons, any hopes for substantial improvements in the Indian service had to be deferred. Treaties were negotiated with the southern Indians which pleased the government, at least (see Chapter 6). The bureau continued to defend itself against the military, further efforts at house-cleaning were made and a civilization programme on the reservations was envisaged.[8] But Congress and the nation at large, outside the West, gave first priority to reconstructing the South and debating how best to secure freedom for the former slaves.

In the case of blacks and Indians alike, humane whites faced the question: how were the races to live amicably together? Although expansion into new territory might have been justified as a way of extending American freedom, many Americans, dedicated to a continent dominated by the white race, would not have objected to the extermination of the Indian population within this territory. Both Indians and blacks suffered from the conviction of a majority of whites that the minority commitment to racial equality was sustained only by emotion and flew in the face of the facts of national life. That economic progress which had been marked since the 1830s and which resumed in a spectacular fashion after 1865, sharpened the contrasts between the material circumstances of the three races, while in an increasingly democratic and changing country it was comforting for whites to believe in the fixed racial superiority of all their number. The importance of the nation's 'Anglo-Saxon' roots and tradition was emphasized and immigrant groups as well as racial minorities were coerced into conformity with that tradition. The confusion of race and culture, the rudimentary state of anthropology and the arrogance bred by domestic and foreign policy successes had likewise encouraged the growth of racism by the 1860s. Under such circumstances, the admittedly imperfect Bureau of Indian Affairs and the Freedmen's Bureau (established in March 1865) offer welcome evidence of continuing white concern for minorities.

There are, of course, obvious differences between the two bureaux. Employees of the freedmen's agency, unlike the Indian agents, were not in a position to make a sustained profit from their positions. Contemporary hostility towards the short-lived Freedmen's Bureau was greater than that shown to the more isolated representatives of the Indian office.[9] The institution offended against the still strong states rights sentiment of the South and alarmed rural employers by drawing blacks to the towns, where bureau offices were located; it appeared to say to southerners that the past was dead and to promise them a future that they did not want. Its use of military men in a region recovering from war, whose white population felt well able to defend themselves against blacks, was more controversial than troop deployment in western territories, to which the army brought valued business and protection against warlike Indian tribes. If the association of the Freedmen's Bureau with radical Republicans turned the debate about its performance into a violently partisan affair, the parties rather routinely took turns to lambast the Indian Bureau, depending on whether they were in or out of power. Indian agents were likely to be engaged in showing tribesmen how to farm on their own account, while the agents of the Freedmen's Bureau, under President Johnson at least, set the ex-slaves to work for others. Furthermore, Indian service officials at this time struggled to carry out their duties despite lawlessness which they were powerless to check, whereas in the South, as conservative whites quickly showed, the law could be used in numerous ways to 'redefine class and property relations and enhance labor discipline'.[10]

On the other hand, the bureaux' common problems and experiences show just how little most white Americans in the 1860s saw the need for special help for minorities. Neither agency had enough money or staff, so that their clients could not be sure of receiving the attention and services to which they were entitled. Neither found that its connection with missionary workers was an easy one, partly because secular and religious personnel had different priorities, partly because local whites were suspicious of the evangelists' values and objectives and partly because the Protestants involved were fearful of the Catholics, while the interdenominational groups looked suspiciously on the sects working independently in the field. Those who disliked the organizations accused their employees of corruption and trouble-making. Both bureaux experienced conflicts between military and civilian personnel. Both were expected to carry out an unreasonably large range of duties in adverse circumstances. And notwithstanding local white criticisms, Indians and blacks invariably had the most to complain of in the operation of the two agencies.

As one would expect, the white agents generally shared the ethno-centric, elitist assumptions of their race and class and frequently sided with local whites against their 'wards'. Thus, just as BIA agents could interfere in tribal politics, manipulate annuity payments and control trade, the provision of rations and other matters with comparatively little check by Washington, so the Freedmen's Bureau officials could use their roles as mediators between planters and freedmen, and employment agents in the chaotic Reconstruction labour market, to the advantage of whites. This is not to say, however, that all agents behaved in such a fashion, or that acting according to white priorities automatically spelled injustice for non-whites; indeed, without the agents' presence, the lot of blacks and Indians would often have been worse.[11]

The Freedmen's Bureau ultimately failed as an instrument of social change because it was ahead of its time and envisaged better prospects for the freedmen than southern whites were willing to contemplate. Self-help was expected even from the most vulnerable, and postwar labour leaders were concerned to foster 'the virtue, the intelligence

74

and the independence of the working classes' through their own organization and effort.[12] If self-help failed, the failure was regretted but the state was not seen as having any duty to bail out the unfortunate. Accordingly, when 1874 saw the collapse of the Freedmen's Savings Bank, neither the use of the government's name in advertising the bank nor the failure of Congress to question the wisdom of amending its charter in 1870, thereby facilitating speculation, procured any federal help for the cheated depositors. Even the winding-up of the bank was an occasion for greedy mismanagement by the commissioners, agents and attorneys concerned,[13] who displayed an opportunism unpleasantly similar to that in evidence whenever Indians had any such assets to dispose of as land, annuities or *per capita* tribal payouts.

Conversely, the Bureau of Indian Affairs survived because it benefited whites as well as Indians, was spending tribal as well as public money and was concerned with non-citizens. Yet controversy continued to surround the bureau and bedevilled the notable attempt to reform it which emerged in 1869, on the initiative of President Ulysses S. Grant.

II

THE PEACE POLICY

Grant's motives for launching his so-called Peace Policy are not absolutely clear, despite Robert Keller's excellent reconstruction of the policy. The President seems to have been broadly critical of frontier whites, sympathetic to the Indians' problems and in favour of their 'ultimate citizenship'. He was impressed by the Quakers' record of honest and effective dealing with the tribes (exaggerated though this was) and drew on the proposals of such contemporary reformers as Bishop Whipple and his fellow Episcopalian, the Philadelphia merchant, William Welsh. While advocating the use of the army to keep the tribes quiet and prevent them from obstructing white expansion, Grant believed that Indians should be civilized on reservations and that the work of assimilation should be in the hands of civilians. Since corruption became a scandal during his presidency only as he revealed his gullibility, negligence and political incompetence, it is perhaps not so incongruous as it might be supposed, to find Grant in the guise of reformer early in his first term.[14]

The President's campaign for justice, peace and economy in Indian–white relations began with initiatives by the executive and Congress. He appointed the first Indian, Ely S. Parker, to the post of Commissioner of Indian Affairs and in April 1869 was authorized to establish an unpaid, independent Board of Indian Commissioners, whose ten wealthy and philanthropic members were 'to exercise joint control with the Secretary of the Interior over the disbursement of the appropriations made by ... [the April] act'. Grant envisaged that education and conversion would go together and from the 1869 appropriation onwards, federal aid for Indian missions and schools was increased. To assist this work and reduce corruption, nominees of the Society of Friends were appointed to the Central and Northern Superintendencies, embracing Nebraska, Kansas and the Indian Territory, and army officers filled the remaining superintendencies and missions, except in Oregon, where the incumbents were retained.[15] When Congress in 1870 forbade the allocation of civil list posts to army officers, the President opened up the vacated positions to other religious denominations.

Unfortunately, the churches were unprepared, financially or otherwise, for their sudden responsibilities. The evangelical revival of the 1860s may have encouraged conscience-stricken Christians to turn to the reform of Indian policy, but Indian missions were languishing. Like the Indian office before them, the denominations found suitable Indian agents difficult to come by. The job, though it was better paid than that of a minister or missionary, offered 'less money than a third-class clerk could earn in Washington. Church appointees often lacked business or practical skills and their schools were criticized for placing too much emphasis on moral and literary instruction. Uncertainty about whether the new policy would survive was another complicating factor, while disputes quickly erupted over how the agents should be nominated within the various sects and which agencies and superintendencies should go to which churches. There were complaints about the Protestant-oriented government's neglect of Catholic interests when making the allocations. Jewish, Mormon and southern claims were similarly slighted, but the snub proved less damaging. Contention arose over the proper relationship between the nominating bodies and their agents, once they were in the field. Several of the churches concerned failed to set up special machinery to cope with their duties under the policy and liaise with the government. Ineffectiveness was the usual result. Senate confirmation of the agents was a problem and the sects themselves echoed politicians' unease about blurring the traditional line between church and state in America, as they came to receive more funds than customary for their religious and educational efforts and to control, by 1872, 'some nine hundred government employees'. By the beginning of the 1880s, a row had also broken out over whether the group which named the agent should have exclusive rights to undertake missionary work on the reservation. The under-represented Catholics were particularly anxious to secure such rights and a self-interested struggle for religious freedom developed among whites who were engaged in denying that freedom to the tribes.

Since the Peace Policy was essentially a vote of no confidence in the Indian Bureau, created an awkward division of loyalties among its employees and was begun with no detailed operating instructions, it is understandable that the bureau responded to the policy in a rather independent and erratic fashion. Hence the Indian office sometimes acted on its own initiative in recommending and removing agents, taking their part against the nominating sect and appointing the lesser field personnel who had once been named by the agents themselves. Alternatively, it omitted to act at all, thereby failing to show the sort of concern about the new nominees that Indian interests demanded. Offended by bureau intervention and otherwise demoralized, some denominations started to withdraw from the work during the administration of Grant's successor, Rutherford B. Hayes.[16]

Despite these differences and obstacles, various of the sects involved in the Peace Policy tried to co-operate with each other. But events and their enemies conspired against them. Critics were, for example, able to exploit the embarrassments suffered by Quaker agents in Kansas, Nebraska and the Indian Territory. Contrary to their own preferences and in the face of reproaches from their eastern brethren, the Friends were obliged to use force in these areas to repel white intruders, punish murder, keep the peace between opposed groups of Indians and control disgruntled Kiowa, Comanche and Cheyenne warriors. Conscientious agents like Lawrie Tatum and John Miles were predictably miserable, not least because the violent tribes won bigger reservations from the whites than the peaceful Indians. As the Kiowa chief, Satanta, put it philosophically, 'The good Indian, he that listens to the white man, got nothing. The independent Indian was the only one that was rewarded.' The wretched condition of Satanta's amenable neighbours, the Wichitas, seemed to prove his point.

State politicians, the army and Congress were never reconciled to the loss of influence and patronage entailed by Grant's programme. Funding for missionary work, which was always inadequate, felt the effect of the panic of 1873 and denominational appointees were not always incorruptible. Their probity seemed to be officially in doubt when Congress in 1873 provided for five inspectors 'to supervise and report on agents'. The fact that an inspection system had been proposed before 1869, that some of the first inspectors were selected from the churches and that they produced no miracle cure for corruption or other agency evils was small comfort. Even ideal agents continued to be demoralized by Washington mistrust, impossibly long hours, isolation, barren reservations, acquisitive local whites and uncooperative Indians.

Westerners on the whole were never won over to the Peace Policy, albeit there were divisions within western and eastern opinion alike, depending on the politics, religious persuasion, racial attitudes and financial interests of the commentators. The South was also a problem. Although post-Civil War southern opinion on Indian policy was no longer as important as in the prewar days, when decisions about the bureau's responsibilities in the territories were complicated by the South's anxiety over the expansion of slavery, neither ex-Confederates nor Democrats generally could welcome a programme associated with their conqueror, Grant, and similar in its objectives to freedmen's aid. Texans whose main desire in the 1850s had been to get rid of the local Indians and who were still on the receiving end of Kiowa and Comanche raids, were particularly impatient with the claims of eastern philanthropy.[17]

Reformer efforts were further undermined by the disappointing early showing of the Board of Indian Commissioners (BIC), though the board's basic resilience enabled it to survive until 1934. Its powers regarding the expenditure of Indian appropriations, supervision of Indian supplies and oversight of bureau records, were defined between 1869 and 1872; they were simultaneously limited by politicians uneasy about hobbling the Indian office. President Grant charged the board with 'helping the Indians to change their way of life' and in their rejection of *laissez-faire* and undaunted commitment to social service the commissioners resemble the men and women whose work on state investigative and regulatory agencies in the second half of the nineteenth century has recently been assessed by William R. Brock. On the whole, however, they seem to have been rather less successful.

If the board was able to improve 'the methods of letting contracts for Indian supplies and ... advertising for goods', so that more bidders and better goods were forthcoming, it did not exercise the degree of control over bureau accounts and records that was originally envisaged. All the commissioners' vigilance could not root out fraud from the Indian supply business, or prevent aspersions being cast on their own honesty. The board's members were divided among themselves, suspicious of the Interior Department and undermined by being closely associated with the religious appointees, once they came under attack. The operating funds they received from Congress were consistently inadequate. After 1874, the Indian Bureau's power over appointments to the board grew and it remained open to criticism for its aversion to Catholic members. Commissioners faced fluctuating sectional and political opposition that nearly brought about the board's abolition in 1880. And their attempts to institute field inspections or inquiries and to publicize the government's programme among the Indians, though they might sometimes be requested by the Indian office, could either be hindered by differences with agents or made to seem superfluous by the creation of the inspection system, ironically on the prompting of the board itself.[18]

In time, the commissioners claimed credit for laying down 'the basic principles underlying some of the important policies adopted, reforms instituted and legislation ... relating to Indians and their affairs'. Among the measures they urged and eventually saw applied were small reservations; the individual allotment of land in severalty, with appropriate safeguards against the premature alienation of allotments; the discouragement of tribal relations; the abandonment of the annuity system; schools to introduce the English language to every tribe; a judicial tribunal within the Indian Territory; and the assimilation as United States citizens of members of the Five Civilized Tribes.[19] Yet the board was not primarily intended to be a clearing house for reformer ideas and when reforms were obtained one cannot give a precise weight to the commissioners' part in achieving success. Thus, in explaining the ending of the treaty system in 1871, something which the board had urged two years before,[20] the approval of the commissioners has to be set alongside the support of Ely Parker and many humanitarians, the long-maturing political impatience with treaty-making and the desire of the House of Representatives to attain parity in Indian matters with the Senate.[21] A persuasive case is nevertheless made by Henry E. Fritz for the importance of the board's advocacy of allotment during the 1870s.[22]

The appointment of Ely Parker did not usher in a new era of distinguished Indian commissioners, religious control of the agencies was ended by the 1880s and the Board of Indian Commissioners could not secure enough power to fulfil its watchdog function. Grant's Peace Policy must therefore be judged an overall failure. But it had some lasting effects. Keller has shown that measured by their own standards, the policy's agents had achieved considerable success in sustaining and sometimes increasing schools, fostering religious and farming activity and persuading the Indians to settle down, live in houses and adopt white dress. That the success rate was variable relates to the sheer scope of the venture as well as to human, environmental and inherited problems. After all, thirteen mission boards had sent around three hundred agents to seventy different reservations spread across twenty states and territories.[23] The close relationship between the Indian office and the churches persisted, principally in educational efforts on the reservations. Government spending on Indian education, boosted by the first general appropriation for education in 1870 and the operations of the Peace Policy, continued to increase later in the century (see Chapter 8). A new generation of reformers was inspired to take up the assimilationist crusade. And though wars with such tribes as the Modocs, Sioux, Cheyennes, Utes, Apaches, Nez Percés and Bannocks in the course of the Peace Policy made it look like a contradiction in terms, after a struggle lasting from 1876 to 1884 the civilians won the argument with those who wanted Indian affairs to revert to army management, just as they had won it in 1867 and 1868.[24]

Army control was urged, particularly by the army, on the grounds that it would be strong, honest and popular with most whites in areas where most Indians were to be found. Dual control, critics rightly complained, had brought damaging feuds between the military and civilian authorities at many of the Plains agencies. It was suggested, in the words of the Indian Territory's *Star Vindicator*, that 'the army was the only part of the United States Government for which the Indians had the slightest respect'. On the other hand, the army was discredited by its massacre of Piegan Indians in 1870 and damaging evidence of corruption in the War Department emerged in 1876. The Interior Department disliked the thought of losing control of appropriations through transfer and Congress was equally averse to losing patronage. Church groups and humanitarians usually resisted military control. In the 1860s, Republican representatives had supported transfer as part of their battle with a Republican Senate over the direction of Indian policy. By the 1870s, Republicans generally were inclined to oppose transfer because it had Democratic backing, given to try to embarrass the party in office. Despite the considerable literature and strong feeling generated on both sides of the question, political considerations rather than principle determined the civilian triumph. They likewise served to defeat the reformer alternative to transfer, namely the creation of an entirely independent Indian department.[25]

Indian reformers, like American reformers at large, offered simplistic solutions for complex social problems and shied away from questions of power. Corruption in the Indian service, and corruption in the South during Reconstruction, did not arise simply because certain categories of people – missionaries in the one case, northern carpetbaggers in the other – were innately venal. It arose because in each

instance whites collectively perceived great opportunities for exploitation and no effective barrier to their actions. The Indians on the
reservations and in Indian Territory were powerless to prevent white
depredations, in the same way that Democrats were initially powerless to check radical Republican regimes and the blacks were unable to
undermine white power either during or after Reconstruction. Transfer was offered as a panacea; it was defeated through the exertion of
Republican power. Had it been implemented, public opposition to a
large army in peacetime and the fact that army leaders accepted the
need for a civilization programme would have ensured the continuing
participation of civilians in Indian affairs.

III

The Reservations

The administrative unit with which humanitarians were grappling
from the 1860s through the 1880s was the reservation. Reformers
objected when Indians were forced on to reservations, in violation of
their treaties, and whites adjacent to or covetous of the designated
lands often opposed removals. But they took place anyway, the
Osages being moved in 1870; the Modocs, Kaws and Kickapoos in
1873; the Pawnees in 1875; the Poncas and Nez Percés in 1877; the Utes
and Iowas in 1879; and the Otos in 1881. The suffering of tribes which
had been shunted about earlier in the century was not a restraining
factor and humanitarians themselves believed that the first reservations had been too large. Smaller territories, it was urged, could be
more easily defended against intruders; the lands released could be
put to better use by whites and the money realized could be employed
to civilize the Indians.[26]
Not surprisingly, the tribes took a different view, so that it frequently took years to settle them on reservations. In the process,
Indian health suffered. Following the systematic destruction of the
Plains buffalo herds by hunters provided with an eastern market by
the railroads, whites sent the reservation tribes food and clothing
supplies, but these might arrive late or in inadequate quantity and
quality. Peoples adjusting to dietary changes and unused to living in
confined communities were prone to disease and at risk from sani-
tation problems. Tribal disruption and white opposition undermined
the effectiveness of native medicine, while the division of Indian
medicine created within the bureau in 1873 was still poorly staffed and
overstretched a decade later.[27]
As the new programme was implemented, the tribesmen were

reduced to the status of wards. Although treaty terms had long been altered or flouted at white convenience, the ending of treaty-making formally subjected the Indians to government without consent and they were unaffected by the Fourteenth and Fifteenth Amendments, which in 1868 and 1870 extended citizenship to blacks and banned the exclusion of citizens from the suffrage 'on account of race, color, or previous condition of servitude'. In *Elk v. Wilkins* (1884) and *U.S. v. Kagama* (1886) the Supreme Court decreed that an Indian could not make himself a citizen simply by renouncing his tribal allegiance and that the United States had full power over Indians on or off the reservations. It was only at this point that reformers began to press urgently for Indian citizenship rights. Unlike American feminists, they had been content to regard the 1860s as 'the Negro's hour' and there had been no Indian pressure upon them to think otherwise. Most tribesmen tended to be either suspicious of the motives behind citizenship proposals or indifferent to them, until the twentieth century. Hence neither the humanitarians nor the Indians were in a position to stop the Supreme Court after *Kagama* from further asserting the power of Congress over tribal areas.[28]

Congress and the Indian service also affirmed the dependent status of the Indians in a number of ways. General instructions were issued to agents, assuming that all reservation Indians could be treated in the same way, and distinctions between them were blurred by placing several contrasting tribes under the jurisdiction of a single agent.[29] In 1871 tribes were forbidden to make contracts without the consent of the Secretary of the Interior and in 1874 able-bodied Indian men between 18 and 45 years of age were required to 'perform service in return for provisions'.[30] An Indian police service was set up in 1878 and provided employment for members of soldier societies made redundant by the pacification of the tribes. It spread rapidly across the reservations and was soon employing hundreds of tribesmen. Within the Courts of Indian Offences authorized by the Secretary of the Interior in 1883, Indians tried Indians who broke the often repressive rules governing their way of life which were laid down by the bureau, while Indian judges determined the penalties subject to approval by bureau agents.[31] Two years later, reservation Indians were made answerable in United States courts if they committed murder, man-slaughter, rape, assault with intent to kill, arson, burglary and larceny.[32]

Yet though the government tried to produce a uniform, acculturated Indian on the reservation, the actual course of reservation life differed according to the culture of the Indians, the quality of their land and agents, the size and climate of their territory, the legacy of their previous dealings with whites, the role of intermarried whites in the tribe, the restraint of local whites and the presence or absence of luck.

Carlson has shown that encouraging farming efforts were made by the Sioux in the Dakotas; the Oneidas of Wisconsin; the Coeur d'Alenes of Idaho; the Flatheads of Montana; the Warm Springs reservation Indians of Oregon; the Yakimas, and the Spokane and Colville reservation Indians of Washington. In addition, ranching which combined open ranges with individual ownership of cattle had made promising strides among the Indians settled in the western Dakotas.[33] On the other hand, a number of tribes in Minnesota, Michigan, Wisconsin and the Pacific Northwest continued to follow their old pursuits of hunting, gathering, lumbering and fishing, and the Cheyennes, Arapahos, Pine Ridge, Lower Brule and Fort Berthold Indians found the pressures on them to become farmers irksome, because they were variously opposed to agriculture, more interested in ranching, harassed by white horse thieves and cattlemen or undermined by drought, high winds, poor soil and grasshopper plagues.[34] Even on reservations and Indian lands where farming was established, for instance among the Osages, Yakimas and Five Civilized Tribes, much of it was done by mixed bloods, while some Indians continued in their traditional activities, some found off-reservation labour and some, especially older people, still relied on government rations.[35]

Adjustment to new localities could be complicated by many additional factors. The Shoshonis who were allocated the Wind River reservation in Wyoming in 1868 were adversely affected by invading white miners and game hunters, hostile Cheyenne, Arapaho and Sioux raiders, insufficient military protection and the settlement of 938 Arapahos on part of their land.[36] On the Quawpaw reservation, the Indians disliked 'chiefs' being foisted on them by the agent, while the Osages in Indian Territory recovered from the losses caused by a re-survey of their land, but found agricultural efficiency hard to sustain because of the willingness of industrious tribesmen to share their produce with the indolent or unfortunate. Just as white Freedmen's Bureau workers might condemn distracting black kin obligations during Reconstruction, so Indian generosity, time-consuming neighbourliness and wasteful use of federal payouts were deplored by agents on many reservations, for whom the cultural value of Indian practices were less important than their economic implications.[37]

Particular difficulties were experienced by and with the warlike tribes, as one might expect. The absurdity of the policy pursued during the 1870s of concentrating opposed tribes on small reservations, where they were able to continue their old feuds, is vividly shown in Dan Thrapp's account of the consolidation of Apache groups.[38] Among the western Sioux, attempts to reduce their land holdings aggravated resentments caused by enforced education, interfering bureau personnel, drought, blizzards, epidemic diseases and the rations system, and at the Standing Rock reservation, the unreconciled chief, Sitting Bull, found solace in one of the best-known religious revitalization movements of the nineteenth century, the Ghost Dance. Participants, through prayer, music, dance and visions, protested against reservation conditions and looked to a future in which traditional Indian ways could again flourish. For whites, the Dance was both a curiosity and a cause for alarm, and it led directly to the killing of Sitting Bull, 'the most famous Sioux', as well as to the massacre of Big Foot and most of his band of Sioux by the Seventh Cavalry at Wounded Knee Creek, South Dakota, in the bleak winter of 1890.[39] The Cheyennes and Arapahos, who shared a reservation in Indian Territory, were similarly slow to accept the constraints of their new life, despite the successful employment of members of both tribes to do the freighting for their agency, a system that was subsequently adopted at other reservations. And a part of their resistance, too, took the form of responding to the Ghost Dance, as well as continuing to practise the Sun Dance, which survived its eventual prohibition in 1904.[40]

Even when Indian groups responded positively to white demands upon them, they might find themselves the losers in the long run. On the Kiowa and Comanche reservation, neighbouring whites, intermarried whites and white officials who saw the profits to be had from using the Indians' grazing lands came to terms with such like-minded chiefs as the mixed-blood Comanche, Quanah Parker. But though the cattlemen helped the tribes to delay a more damaging opening of the reservation to outsiders, the money gained from leasing was not used to bring the Indians long-term economic benefits, and the outsiders' elevation of Parker to 'head chief' status through his control of lease money and the tribal court was scarcely edifying.[41]

The Five Civilized Tribes were likewise beset by white economic interests. Their story has been compellingly told by H. Craig Miner. At the end of the Civil War, support for the Confederacy by elements of the Five Tribes was used to justify divesting them of land and giving permission for railroads to enter Indian Territory. By the 1870s, railroad and coal corporations were established there; cattle corporations arrived in the 1880s and oil corporations in the 1890s. Leaders of the Five Tribes, who had at first welcomed the corporations, came to regard them with dismay when it became apparent that the tribes would not be able to direct the economic changes to which they had agreed. In fact the accompanying rise of towns, the increased white presence, outbreaks of disease and lawlessness, divisive petitioning and litigation, and capitalist-backed congressional demands from 1866 for the creation of a US territory out of Indian Territory raised the price of 'progress' too high for most of its Indian inhabitants to relish. Unhappily the resources of the Five Tribes, intellectual or otherwise, were not such that they could successfully resist capitalists whose power overawed white citizens, while the Indian department clerks, though they made more effort to protect Indian interests than either Congress or the corporations, were involved in a bureaucracy which was increasingly professional but bafflingly difficult to confront or hold responsible.[42]

Yet if the reservation period was damaging to Indian integrity, this does not mean that it satisfied the advocates of assimilation. The amended provisions system continued to discourage the kind of work ethic of which whites approved, the Indians' customary ways of working hard being impossible on the reservations.[43] Removal of Indians to reservations on a group basis helped to sustain their group identity, as did the limited contacts with whites permitted by the system. The termination of treaty-making did not end the bureau's practice of dealing with Indians as tribes. Negotiations of the established kind continued, with the resulting agreements being ratified by both houses of Congress. And bureau officials, like reformers, continued to see the usefulness of having tribal authorities to deal with, or to see dangers in their premature deposition. The result was that the reservations were no more nurseries of 'civilization' than slave communities had been. Rather, the reservations and slave quarters alike were closed societies, permitting the emergence of distinctive cultures which were neither aboriginal, nor African, nor white. Disenchanted humanitarians would ultimately describe the reservations as prisons and they were admitted by the bureau to have a 'penal' function.[44] Like prisons, the reservations were good at containing their 'inmates', bad at reforming them and very expensive. Certainly the contemporary white, middle-class enthusiasm for reservations may be equated with their enthusiasm for restraining institutions and conventions of every type: asylums for the insane and afflicted, prisons for the dangerous, schools for the unassimilated poor, 'the home' as a safe haven for women and children.[45] On the reservations, however, Indian peoples were not made over and made safe, since whites failed to suppress recognizably non-white attitudes to treaties, competition and individualism, kin ties, the natural world, the pace of life and economic activity.

IV

THE RISE OF NEW REFORM GROUPS

Disappointment with the expense and limited civilizing power of the reservation contributed directly to the rise of new Indian reform organizations and objectives in the last two decades of the nineteenth century. Financial and freedmen's aid issues no longer dominated the political stage, as they had done after the Civil War, while the ending of the major Indian wars would make the West less strident in its demands for military solutions to 'the Indian problem'. The urgent need to assimilate the tribes was apparently underlined by continued white expansion across the continent, resulting from population growth, railroad construction and the search for minerals, land and markets. There was also enough evidence of injustices in the management of Indian affairs, and of progress on the part of some Indians, notably in the area of schooling, to make humanitarians both confident of engaging public concern and convinced that their efforts would be rewarded.

The suffering involved in the removal of the Ponca Indians from Dakota Territory to Indian Territory in 1877 was especially important in stirring up public sympathies, with the speaking engagements to publicize Ponca wrongs undertaken by the *Omaha Daily Herald*'s T. H. Tibbles, along with the Ponca chief Standing Bear and two Omaha Indians, resembling in their impact the tours of ex-slaves in the North and in Britain before the Civil War. And just as the militant ex-slave lecturer, Frederick Douglass, was warned to tell his story with 'a little of the plantation speech', since 'it is not best that you seem too learned', so Standing Bear was advised not to reduce his audience appeal by cutting off his braids or abandoning native costume. Having helped to secure compensation for the Poncas in 1881, the humanitarians were encouraged to fresh efforts and determined to avoid in future the heated exchanges with Indian policy-makers that had marked their campaign.[46]

The controversy generated by the Ponca affair was sustained by the publication of two reformist tracts critical of US Indian policy: George Manypenny's *Our Indian Wards* (1880) and Helen Hunt Jackson's *A Century of Dishonor* (1881). It is difficult to gauge their impact, albeit the anti-slavery movement had demonstrated and the twentieth-century Progressive reform endeavour would confirm the value of carefully timed individual muck-raking tracts. Both books were well written and single-minded. Both were optimistic about Indian assimilation if missionary endeavours were supported and whites were shamed into

86

respecting Indian property and other rights. Mrs Jackson's contribution, though likened in its impact to *Uncle Tom's Cabin*, was more condemned than Manypenny's, on the grounds of its haste, sentimentality and partisanship. None the less, the two together gained great publicity for the reform case, which was then taken further by organized philanthropists ominously inclined to the panaceas which Jackson and Manypenny had shunned.[47]

Reformer efforts to arouse the national conscience were helped by one more important factor and that was the awareness that Indian affairs were allegedly better managed in Canada. As we have seen, American statesmen of the early republican era were anxious that outsiders should not detect a betrayal of republican idealism in the treatment of the country's Indian population. During the subsequent controversy over slavery, it was irksome to Americans to be placed under a moral embargo by Britons who had already moved against the peculiar institution. In the post-Civil War years, it was equally tiresome to watch such disenchanted Indian elements as the eastern Sioux refugees from the Minnesota uprising of 1862 flee across the Canadian border in the expectation of improving their lot. Nor was it pleasant to hear the frequently expressed view that, unlike American tribes, Canadian Indians were allowed to remain on reservations in their original localities, were given the rights of British subjects and were effectively protected in those rights.[48] As Priest and Price have pointed out, American reformers also noted that in Canada the liquor traffic and trade generally were more effectively controlled and Indian administrators served longer than their American counterparts. Indian land was annexed with native consent, and although the sale of land by Indians was closely controlled, while individual allotments were granted extremely sparingly, tribal responsibility was fostered by providing the various groups with detailed accounts of their funds. In addition, the work of the Royal Mounted Police in befriending and controlling the tribesmen and defending them against lawless white men was widely admired. Detailed studies and regular exchanges did not, however, follow from awareness that the two countries faced similar Indian challenges and that Canada, with some initial advantages over the United States (see Chapter 1), had responded to them better. Hence Americans did not learn from the Canadians' retreat from lifting tribal controls on individual Indians, embarked upon in 1857 and questioned as early as 1868.[49]

Moreover, the Canadians could respond to Indian fugitives from America with an improvised heavy-handedness all too familiar south of the border. When Sitting Bull and his followers crossed into Canada in the winter of 1876, Canadian officials did not relish their presence, withheld both material assistance and recognition and waited for the United States to act. No one wanted the Sioux leader to establish a base in Canada for raiding southwards and there were fears about the consequences of newcomers settling on Indian terrain where game was already scarce. Sitting Bull returned to America in desperation in 1881, though when he visited Canada in a Wild West show four years later, Canadians then felt able to applaud his determined resistance to American government policies. In the mean time, assuming that Canadian Indian policy was superior to that of the United States, Canadian administrators were reluctant to admit how hard they, too, found the task of reconciling their mobile western Indians to reservations, agriculture and a rations system.[50]

There were other parallels in Canadian and American Indian matters, from the Indian point of view. Thus, for example, whites invaded Canadian Indian reserves, grazing their cattle there and taking native timber. On the Pacific coast, white and later Japanese fishermen trespassed, with the support of the law, on what had been traditional Indian fishing grounds. The Canadian Pacific Railway cut through Indian territory in the 1870s, bringing permanent white settlement to the great western prairies and plains. Discontented Canadian Indians, like certain American groups, took refuge over the international border, notably after the 1885 Méti (mixed blood) and Indian uprising. Schools continued to rely heavily upon church support, to employ coercive methods and to turn out poorly trained pupils, who were sometimes educated at institutions far from their homes and for whom there was no suitable work on the reservations. Indian health was neglected, epidemic diseases took their familiar toll and Indian numbers declined until the early twentieth century. Traditional authority figures were undercut and tribal factionalism increased as missionaries and agents arbitrarily elevated chiefs and headmen who co-operated with them. As well as giving up huge tracts of land, the tribes were compelled to abandon native names for their children, polygamy, the potlatch (a giving feast), spirit and drum dancing, lip ornaments and other customs of which the missionaries disapproved. As Anglicans and Roman Catholics struggled for converts, they divided the communities in which they worked and vitiated the Christian ideal. And assimilation and protection were the twin aims of government policy in Canada and the United States alike.[51]

Nevertheless, Canada's Indian administration is seen as being more effective than America's because it was fairer. Having clearly asserted sovereignty over the tribes, Canada assumed the power necessary to implement its wishes, kept or exceeded its fairly moderate promises to the Indians, and considered Indian cultural traits, at least to some extent. Hence Indian chiefs were allowed to choose, subject to government confirmation, the denominational teachers for their schools and to retain their own languages. If the independence of the Indian branch from parliamentary pressures made it difficult to sustain political interest and an adequate budget, the system had the merit of simplicity. Under dominion rule after 1867, there was 'only one Indian Act and Indian administration' in Canada.[52] The explanation of Canadian attitudes and actions is more elusive. Perhaps the most plausible is the numbers argument we offered in Chapter 1. The whites in Canada simply did not pose the same threat to the Indians as did their more numerous American counterparts for a long period. By the time that they did, in the later nineteenth century, Indian numbers were still such that they demanded the degree of attention that blacks were accorded as the largest 'minority' in the United States. That the attention given was kindlier owes much to the fact that Canada contained, as Price has stressed, more relatively peaceful societies organized at the band level than did the United States. Such groups were less liable to offer resented forms of opposition to white encroachments than tribal level societies, even though they might also be the most difficult to integrate into 'the homogeneous Native ethnic culture' of the reservation era.

Furthermore, whatever the fortuitous elements in the tolerably good early relations which prevailed between Indians and whites in French Canada (see Chapter 1), these good relations persisted, characterized by a high level of Indian-white intermarriage. And because a solution to Canadian Indian–white differences did not seem so urgent as it did south of the border, administrators were happy not to rush the process of acculturation.[53] Indeed in the inhospitable regions of northern Canada, as Keith Crowe's study makes plain, whites made slow and variable inroads which in many areas had not transformed native life until 1900; in Kutchin and Inuit country, the transformation came even later.[54] It should be noted, however, that in one respect the carefulness of Canadian officials had very harmful results for the original Americans. Under the terms of the Indian Act (passed in 1876 and subsequently added to and amended), the government defined who could legally be regarded as an Indian, membership of a band being the basic requirement. As a result, many people who were Indians biologically or socially were not legally Indians, thus losing access to Indian lands and government services. The intention was also to support patrilineal Indian societies. Consequently, when a woman married she became a member of her husband's band. An Indian woman who had 'Indian status' lost it if her husband lost his, or if she married a person without such a status. A man who married out did not forfeit his status. Having once lost status, a woman could only recover it by marrying a status Indian. Arrangements designed to foster family arrangements on the white pattern actually had the effect of encouraging cohabitation rather than marriage between attracted white men and Indian women, since the latter had no wish to lose their Indian status.[55]

If ability to take the long view usually characterized Canada's Indian administrators, it was emphatically not one of the virtues of two out of three groups of American advocates of Indian reform active in the later nineteenth century. The new organizations got underway with the formation of the Women's National Indian Association (WNIA) in Philadelphia in 1879. Three years later the Indian Rights Association (IRA) was established in the same city, and the Lake Mohonk Conference of Friends of the Indian followed in New York state in 1883. Each group went on from outrage over a particular aspect of Indian affairs – the WNIA over intruders in Indian Territory, the IRA and Mohonk over the difficulties of the Sioux – to fashion enduring associations which combined familiar and novel tactics and aims.

Led by Amelia S. Quinton and enjoying Baptist and other church backing, the WNIA had a central body whose officials and executive board determined the main lines of work to be undertaken, with departments responsible for tasks ranging from missionary work to memorials to government. To inform and stir up the public, the WNIA developed active auxiliaries (fifty-six branches in twenty-seven states by 1885), held 'parlor and public meetings', bombarded the churches, educators, societies, the press and Congress with articles and memorials about 'the unjust and cruel treatment of the Indians', and published a monthly journal which endured until 1951, *The Indian's Friend*. The women stayed in touch with other reformers, monitored the progress of key legislation concerning the Indians, urged the defence of existing treaties and supported contemporary pleas for Indian citizenship and land in severalty. In addition, the WNIA found its own particular niche in the humanitarian effort. Avoiding overt political activity and links with the women's suffrage movement, the association formed part of what has been called social feminism, a type of social activism in which women claimed public implications for their traditional home-oriented exertions. Accordingly, the WNIA concentrated on missionary work, initiating or helping some thirty-two missionary stations between 1884 and 1893. It also gave priority to instruction and charitable work in schools, health care and the building of homes on the reservations. These were activities, it felt, that would 'be needed long after the political work is done'.

The large membership of the organization and its steadily growing and impressive income by the standards of the day – about $3,000 in 1884, some $28,000 by 1895 – indicate that it had effectively tapped into the considerable contemporary desire among American women for respectable involvement in the public sphere. As one might expect with a group of the population inured to slow changes in their own circumstances, the WNIA was prepared to contemplate a process of gradual assimilation for the Indians, in a way that the IRA and Mohonk were not. Otherwise the women were entirely in sympathy with the broad objectives of the reform community, the government and the Indian service.[56] The same might be said of the IRA, but its style was altogether more brisk and dictatorial, its focus more political and its resources less impressive.

The IRA was founded by Herbert Welsh, a nephew of the earlier Indian reformer, William Welsh, and from thirty or forty members it soon evolved a network of branches which, like those of the WNIA, liaised with the parent body but developed considerable independence. The organization was intensely practical from the first, spending its funds on a corresponding secretary in Philadelphia (Welsh), a legal expert (Henry S. Pancoast), and a full-time lobbyist in Washington (Charles C. Painter, succeeded by Francis E. Leupp, who became Commissioner of Indian Affairs between 1905 and 1909). The IRA's main aims were citizenship, lands on an individual basis and education for the Indians. As was the case with Mrs Quinton, Welsh and Painter travelled widely to preach the cause of Indian reform. Fact-finding field trips were made to Indian reservations, so that the IRA was not susceptible to the accusations about armchair philanthropy often levied against eastern humanitarians. On the contrary, the inquiries imbued association officers with enormous faith in their own wisdom and certainly they were able to command better information than most of the legislators they hoped to influence. The material gathered by the association and supplemented by articles from other sources was widely distributed; 44,000 pamphlets were circulated in 1892 alone.

Both the IRA and Mohonk proved, as have American reform movements before and since, including the campaigns for peace, higher education for women and better treatment for the insane and the afflicted, that it was possible to have influence without numbers. But given the IRA's structure and constant efforts to boost membership, its record was disappointing. The association's central body never listed more than a few hundred names, while the combined membership of parent group and branches (numbering twenty-eight in 1887) was only about 1,200 in 1888. Income ranged from $1,700 in 1883 to $11,600 in 1916, the nineteenth-century high point being reached in 1888, just after general severalty legislation had at last been secured. Many of the IRA's members were women from its sister organization in Philadelphia, and most of the association's work was undertaken by Welsh, who had a good deal of his uncle's drive and ego. The specialist standing committees seem to have done little to shape policy and Welsh even held the tireless Painter on a short rein. The Quakers played an important role in the IRA, as befitted a group prominent in the Peace Policy, but Mohonk had the most aggressively Christian emphasis of the three new alliances.[57]

The Lake Mohonk conference met each autumn at the resort hotel, and at the expense, of Albert K. Smiley, who was a Quaker educator and member of the Board of Indian Commissioners. A Washington lobbyist was not retained, since this was regarded as too worldly and partisan a gesture, but those in attendance were often well placed to influence policy decisions, notably Henry L. Dawes of Massachusetts, the Republican chairman of the Senate Committee on Indian Affairs; James Sherman, the chairman of the House Committee on Indian Affairs; and John J. Fitzgerald, his fellow committee member. Indeed, Mohonk was eventually accused of being too much influenced by delegates from the bureau and the Board of Indian Commissioners. Although BIA chiefs William Jones and Francis Leupp were associated with Mohonk's important business committee in 1907 and 1908 respectively, while the conferences attracted General Eliphalet Whittesley and Merrill E. Gates, of the Board of Indian Commissioners, and Thomas J. Morgan, who was Commissioner of Indian Affairs from 1889 to 1893, the charge of direct manipulation by Washington seems to have been unjust. None the less, Mohonk was essentially a moderate, 'establishment' body. After days of formal papers and informal discussions, the planks in its annual platform were decided unanimously each year, whereupon the conference employed its press committee and journalist members to secure widespread publicity for its recommendations or findings. And if the limited guest list might range from only 12 in 1883 to 246 in 1914, the annual report, financed by the delegates, was printed in an edition of several thousands and reached politicians, administrators, editors, colleges and reformers, for whose ideas Mohonk acted as a clearinghouse. Yet with all its advantages, the conference was not ideologically innovative; its commitment to increased appropriations for Indian education of all kinds, allotment of Indian lands in severalty, the erosion of the tribal tie, the inculcation of the Protestant work ethic, the imposition of the Christian religion and family order, and the recognition of Indian citizenship put it safely in the mainstream of

Indian reform as it had been developing during the nineteenth century.[58]

The new Indian reformers, like their predecessors, encompassed active Protestants, including missionaries and clergymen and their wives from a range of sects. Among their number were humanitarians interested in other reform activities such as freedmen's aid, women's rights, pacifism and temperance, as well as journalists and writers, educators, lawyers, businessmen, anthropologists and federal government employees. Geographically the movement was concentrated in the eastern states, though there were some members from the midwest and the West, and politically Republicans were well represented. The reformers were middle-class individuals who did not take up the cause with a view to making money out of it and who welcomed to their gatherings educated and atypical Indian apostles of the white way.[59] Members of the three main Indian reform organizations – and there were many lesser ones – attended and reported each other's meetings, giving credit where credit was due and creating in their proceedings a certain air of self-satisfaction which is only slightly less repellent to the unregenerate than reformer bickering.[60] Since the gap between East and West, Republican and Democrat, and reformer and administrator over the conduct of Indian affairs had narrowed by the 1880s, and the humanitarians aimed at change through legislation, a conciliatory approach to legislators and bureau officials was sensible.[61] Less sensible was their conviction that Indians could be quickly turned into white men.

Like most people, the Indian reformers thought that everyone else should admire what they admired: cleanliness, monogamy and patriliny, diligence, thrift and sobriety, an intensely personal religious commitment and the 'selfishness, which is at the bottom of civilization'. Indian forms of selfishness would not do; an individual had to acquire the *'wants'* of a white man before he could acquire a white man's intelligence and know a white man's duties.[62] Yet why should it be supposed that this could be done swiftly, when many freedmen's aid workers under the influence of Social Darwinism, southern hostility and northern indifference, had concluded that progress among the freedmen, once optimistically proclaimed, would in fact be gradual, leaving equality as a distant goal? One reason for the confidence of the 'friends of the Indian' may be that, like the abolitionists in the 1860s, they sensed that their opportunity had come and could not afford to be diffident. Then, while anthropologists such as Alice Fletcher did attend their meetings, they were sometimes distrusted as antiquarians and certainly did not dominate the gatherings or the shaping of Indian policy (see Chapter 7).[63] It was therefore feasible for humanitarians to ignore or be unaware of the writings of anthropologists such as Lewis H. Morgan, who believed it was impossible for 'savage' or 'barbarous' peoples to skip any of the stages on the way to civilization and argued that most Indian tribes were currently suited to a pastoral, not an agricultural, economy. In any event, the moral negativism of Social Darwinism, which encouraged 'the fittest' merely to congratulate themselves on their good fortune, was unattractive to individuals of a reformist bent.[64]

The reformers were also less racially prejudiced than many of their contemporaries, albeit the same could have been said in the 1860s of the afterwards disillusioned abolitionists. Both groups rejected arguments about the permanent inferiority of non-whites and explained inequality of conditions between the races with reference to the environment. Regarding Indians as culturally rather than racially inferior to themselves, the Indian reformers were more sanguine than even the freedmen's aid workers initially were about the possibility of turning non-whites into white men. And they were not entirely averse to the physical amalgamation of the Indian and white races, although when humanitarians talked of assimilating the tribesmen they usually had political and social integration in mind.[65]

Another reason for the optimism of the 'friends of the Indian' could be that they simply were not much influenced by the anti-slavery endeavour or the cause of the blacks. Undoubtedly the Indian population was less a part of white society and more opposed to assimilation than the freedmen. While leading abolitionists lent their names to the cause of Indian reform in the 1860s, they could not lift it from the doldrums in the 1870s and were mostly not around to involve themselves in the campaign of the 1880s onwards. There were differences in the way blacks and Indians were regarded by the public and, as Gilcreast has shown, the 'friends of the Indian' never matched the anti-slavery movement in organizational and financial terms.[66] The Indian reformers were less divided than the abolitionists about the need for political action and legislation to secure reform and this trait, together with their desire to improve the Indian service by bringing its appointees under civil service rules, makes them in one sense the forerunners of the Progressives rather than the heirs of the anti-slavery crusaders.[67]

Indian reformers also lacked abolitionism's relevance to working men. It was difficult enough for white urban and agrarian interests to make common ground at this time and it would remain so right through the farmers' protest of the 1890s, known as Populism. Most Indians lived in rural areas and were engaged in rural pursuits, whereas labour reformers were seeking 'social harmony within the new world of the factory, not an imaginary arcadia of days gone by'. The land reformers might have looked for just that, yet they dreamed of men enjoying the fruits of their own toil in an agricultural order which was disagreeable to many Indians, while labour was committed to a system of land distribution which gave 'lands to those who have the will and heart to cultivate them'.[68] These aspirations might, if tapped, have fed the clamour for allotment of Indian lands, but the allotment act is seen in retrospect as the most damaging aspect of the programme advanced by the 'friends of the Indian'.

Nevertheless, the Indian reformers tried to link their cause with that of the abolitionists, claimed that Indians and blacks should be assimilated by the same means, employed the same organizational techniques and appealed to the same middle-class constituency 'to right a great national wrong'. They likewise generalized about the objects of their concern as if they were all the same, though the tendency sprang in part from a recognition of universal human rights rather than the racist's inability to see individuality in the members of despised groups.[69] And evangelical Christianity was the inspirational element in both the anti-slavery and Indian aid movements.

In each case, what was involved was an evangelicalism concerned with the conversion and uplifting of the individual, whose adherents were suspicious of corrupt, institutionalized power. But the 'friends of the Indian' were less anti-institutional than some abolitionists, for all their complaints about BIA paternalism. Anticipating the New Freedom Progressives of the Wilsonian era, they wanted the assertion of government power in order to foster individualism and competition. Nor did they echo the sweeping condemnations of neglectful churches and clergy associated with the Garrisonian abolitionists. Such criticisms would have been out of place, given that the sects had provided missionaries for the tribes and worked among them when other whites still remained indifferent. The late-nineteenth-century evangelicals, even more than those of the antebellum period, were concerned with the need for a unified Christian America. As Prucha has demonstrated, they equated Protestantism with Americanism at a time when the industrial revolution, westward expansion and immigration were transforming the nation and threatening national unity. The surrounded Indian population could not be allowed to become another threat or to resist the tide of progress, but must be absorbed with all speed. To this end the churches, though theoretically separate from the state, were to play a vital part in Indian education, albeit the Indian reformers showed signs of the anti-sectarianism that had marked abolitionism and mounted a sustained campaign against government aid for sectarian, especially Catholic, schools (see Chapter 8).[70]

Being human, the 'friends of the Indian' had their disagreements; for instance, about the merits of the Indian Bureau as then constituted compared with an entirely independent agency, and over the native use of peyote in a religious context.[71] Yet their quarrels brought no schisms of the kind that afflicted abolitionism or feminism, and they encountered less damaging opposition. The journal *Council Fire*, founded in 1878, and T. A. Bland's National Indian Defense Association, established in 1885, came to the view that it was vital to gain the Indians' consent to changes in their condition, which changes should only be gradual. During the slow transition to civilization, the tribal unit and the reservation should be retained.[72] Some Christians believed that the Indians had a right to religious freedom and that destroying all native practices did not necessarily advance the work of conversion. Others questioned the overweening merits of American culture or maintained that the Indians were diverse in abilities and resources, so that trying to force them all into family farming was foolish and would fail. Many westerners, whether from prejudice or first-hand experience of what was involved in culture change, continued to doubt whether the Indians could be easily assimilated.[73] However, these were opinions which most whites did not wish to hear. They seemed old-fashioned and negative, besides requiring the sort of patience and restraint on the part of whites that they were unaccustomed to showing. During the 1880s, the reformers' sense that they could influence policy, the government's sense that it could fulfil its traditional if contradictory aims of obtaining Indian land and looking after Indian interests, and the desire of ordinary whites for Indian territory, drowned the combined voices of dissent.

By the beginning of the twentieth century, reformers had contributed to the procuring of more changes in Indian affairs than their past influence had given them any right to expect. In this crucial respect, they were more powerful than their abolitionist counterparts. The 'friends of the Indian' had helped to prolong the Peace Policy, sustain civilian control over Indian affairs, end the treaty system, extend the homestead law to detribalized Indians and drastically reduce government aid for sectarian schools. Their agitation was important in raising the level of educational appropriations and persuading sceptics that education could turn the Indians into patriotic, self-supporting individualists (see Chapter 8). Humanitarians had worked hard to improve Indian health and reduce the abuse of alcohol on the reservations and had assisted efforts to impose an alien code of morality upon the Indians, particularly in matters pertaining to marriage and family life. This meant both trying to change Indian behaviour and attempting to make individual conscience rather than custom determine morality.[74]

Within the limits imposed by slender budgets, the reformers had investigated particular cases of bureau and agency corruption and the ill treatment of individual tribes; according to their own lights, they had sought justice for, among others, the Poncas, the Sioux, the Chippewas and the California Indians.[75] Humanitarians had also taken up the cause of civil service reform and applied it to the Indian Bureau, though since the campaign was founded on false assumptions it yielded disappointing results. The movement made its break-through nationally in 1883, and in the Indian service during the 1890s, but in each case patronage appointments were not completely ended, while the replacement of spoilsmen by civil servants did not restore democracy to America, or eliminate fraud and inefficiency in Indian affairs. Civil service reform was a panacea which, as Prucha points out, gained popularity among Indian reformers when other cherished objectives had been achieved.[76]

Most significantly, the three main reform groups and the BIC had played a key role in securing severalty legislation in 1887. A new chapter in allotting Indian land in severalty had begun after the Civil War, as tribes like the Santee Sioux, Utes and Omahas were allotted to secure them in a specific location against those who had favoured their removal.[77] Treaties negotiated from the 1850s had increasingly pro-vided for allotment for particular categories of Indian. But the cam-paign to transform all reservation Indians into individualistic farmers through allotment developed slowly, the dangers involved being clearly seen in advance by some tribesmen and some whites,[78] just as the drawbacks to removal were anticipated before 1830. Unfortunately the main white opposition came from the maverick Bland and members of the National Indian Defense Association, local whites had gladly profited from the inadequate safeguards furnished for such recently allotted peoples as the Indians of Kansas and the humanitar-ians' ethnocentrism hardened them against the acute defence of tribal autonomy offered by the Five Tribes in Indian Territory during the second half of the nineteenth century.[79]

Repudiating white charges that their governments were corrupt, incompetent and unjust, leaders of the Five Tribes maintained that white demands for a general severalty law were prompted by greed. They pointed out that much of their own land was unsuitable for allotment. They warned that the early experiments with severalty had been a disaster for the tribes and that current proposals would again cheat Indians, especially full bloods, out of much land, although treaty

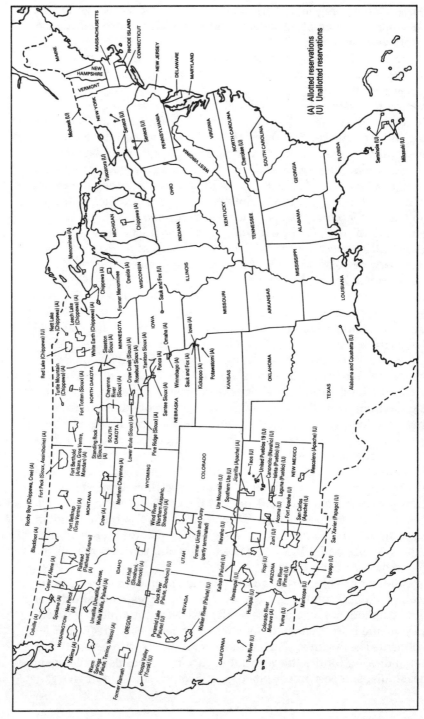

Map 4 Indian reservations today, showing the impact of allotment.

Source: F. P. Prucha, *American Indian Policy in Crisis: Reformers and the American Indian, 1865–1900* (Norman, OK: University of Oklahoma Press, 1976).

(A) Allotted reservations
(U) Unallotted reservations

guarantees should have preserved their group integrity. They accurately predicted that the Indians' aversion to sharing their thoughts with strangers and preference for the politics of personality would put them at a disadvantage in the struggle to retain the tribal domain. Unmoved, white critics merely reaffirmed their faith in the individual Indian's ability to cope in an 'Anglo' world. Indian pleas were dismissed as the outpourings of a selfish elite or discounted as a sign that the tribes were 'wedded to the superstition of the past', were 'possessed of the devil' and might properly be coerced along the path to virtue.[80]

The severalty act proposed in 1886 by Henry Dawes, a comparatively late convert to the severalty cure-all, was passed a year later. As Washburn has shown, the Senator's willingness to accommodate such advocates of forced allotment as the Reverend Dr Lyman Abbott, the editor of the *Christian Union*, was crucial in securing a bill that was highly favourable to whites.[81] Under the Dawes legislation, from which the southwestern tribes especially escaped but which dispensed with tribal consent, the President had discretionary power to have reservations surveyed in whole or part, the surveyed lands to be allotted among the resident Indians (see Map 4). Where the total area permitted and existing treaties did not demand larger allotments, each head of a family could select 160 acres for himself. Unmarried persons over 18 years of age and orphans under 18 were entitled to 80 acres; all other single persons under 18 were to receive 40 acres. Where land was only suitable for grazing, the acreage allotted was to be doubled. When selections had been made and approved by the Secretary of the Interior, fee patents were to be issued and the occupants of the lands became United States citizens. Indeed, all Indians who had abandoned their tribes and adopted the habits of civilized life were to be made citizens. Allotments resulting from the Dawes Act could not be leased, sold or willed for twenty-five years, after which title in fee might be conferred unless it was thought inadvisable. Unallotted lands not kept back for tribal use were to be sold, subject to tribal approval, the proceeds of the sale to be held in trust for the tribes concerned.

After 1887, additional legislation applied allotment to the Sioux, the Chippewas of Minnesota, tribes in Montana, Idaho and Washington, and the Five Civilized Tribes. The Dawes Act was also altered several times. In 1891, primarily in order to protect divorced wives, it was ruled that each individual should receive 80 acres, rather than 160 acres going to the head of a household; and the Secretary of the Interior was empowered to authorize the leasing of allotments made to children, old people and others thought to be incapable of farming. The grounds on which leasing might be permitted were later enlarged.

From 1901, the Secretary was authorized to sell heirship allotments; that is, holdings which were held in trust but where the original allottee had died. In 1906, the Burke Act provided that allottees were not to become citizens until they were deemed legally competent to take care of their own affairs; the trust period could be extended beyond twenty-five years, yet an individual might be declared competent before the twenty-five years were over. A person who was deemed competent could sell his land, which became liable for local and state property taxes. And in 1907, the Commissioner of Indian Affairs was granted the power to sell the allotment of a trust status Indian. This amending legislation perpetuated the basic paradox of the Dawes Act by simultaneously attempting to 'emancipate' the Indians and to provide special protection for them.

The severalty law operated as most whites had hoped and most Indians had feared. An estimated 9,894 fee patents were issued between 1906 and 1916, another 10,956 between 1917 and 1920, and from 1887 to the 1930s, when allotment was halted, the Indians lost 91 million acres, so that their land base dwindled from 139 to 48 million acres. Indians without experience of commercial transactions were persuaded to part with their territory by waiting buyers and often wasted their suddenly acquired assets. Those who retained their land tended to be left in possession of the most arid and undesirable stretches of terrain, entirely unsuitable for homesteading. Much of the alienated land was in the 'surplus' category, but allotments, too, were disposed of with disturbing speed. It has been calculated that between 1900 and 1934 almost a half of Indian allotments had been released on fee patents, the majority of which had been sold or forfeit for non-payment of taxes, while by 1916 over a third of allotted agricultural lands was leased, thus defeating the legislators' ostensible intention of encouraging Indian agriculture.[82] Harassed BIA officials, lacking adequate instruction about how to judge competence, frequently approved the applications of individuals who turned out to be the very opposite. Leasing arrangements proved hard to monitor and illegal contracts soon flourished. The determining of heirs to allotments and the settlement of debates between them over petty amounts of land and money were nightmarish tasks which distracted bureau employees from 'instructing Indians in the methods of land use'.[83]

The allotment process left Indians congregated together, on reservations in all but name, at the same time as it admitted them to citizenship without adequate preparation or on restricted terms that made it meaningless. Indian farming and ranching declined as the sale and lease of Indian land increased, with the result that, as Carlson puts it, the tribesmen lagged 'further behind white farmers in 1930 than they had been in 1900 and 1910'. And humanitarians, having warned against the premature relaxation of the Dawes Act's safeguards for the Indians, proved less than zealous watchdogs once the Act was passed, albeit they seem to have been guilty of fickleness and feebleness rather than malevolence or hypocrisy.[84]

By the early twentieth century, notwithstanding reformer attempts to build up 'self-supporting industries in Indian communities', government efforts to improve irrigation and forest management programmes on Indian lands, and the endeavours of both to stimulate Indian agriculture, some Indians had become the very paupers which the despised reservation system had supposedly produced. At that point, the white demand for Indian artefacts was still limited, the Indians lacked entrepreneurial traditions and capital and national politicians were cautious about making loans to those whose economic situation they expected to be transformed by allotment alone. Most Indians therefore remained, like the Populists whose pleas for local democracy they would have appreciated, isolated country dwellers in a fast-industrializing country. Just when their social isolation was turning white farmers into rebels, Indians as a whole were expected to project themselves into the American mainstream by becoming farmers, the very element that the rest of white society was leaving behind.[85]

As the humanitarians' long crusade for Indian assimilation ran out of inspiration, both they and the white public became convinced that there was no need for further agitation, rather as some abolitionists lost interest in blacks once emancipation was secured and some feminists retired from the half-won battle for equality in 1920. Having promised so much from their proposed reforms, it was impossible for the humanitarians to admit that they had failed to achieve their objectives; and many had grown tired along the way. Attempts begun at Mohonk to link Indian reform with a new, white-aided effort on behalf of the black population were abandoned after a few years.[86] Had reformers entertained realistic expectations, of course, the slow rate of progress could have been presented as perfectly reasonable. As it was, it was best ignored.

With popular backing for the reformers declining from 1887, the Indian Office came into its own, its growth paralleling the general post-Civil War expansion of government agencies. The new importance of the bureau and its greater organizational strength were signified by an enlarged budget and workforce, the central selection of agency personnel, greater involvement in education, the extension of civil service rules to BIA positions and the elaboration of an inspection system, all of which reduced the necessity for missionary, military or Board of Indian Commissioners interference in bureau concerns and enhanced the power of the Commissioner of Indian affairs. Its growth in turn reflected the BIA's expanded responsibilities. Administering the Dawes Act alone created a blizzard of paper work. From the Indian point of view, these developments were not auspicious. The creation of an elaborate and self-confident Indian office bureaucracy made it more difficult for the Indian voice to be heard and strengthened the assimilationist campaign. Awareness that corruption, fraud and inefficiency persisted in the BIA after the 1890s merely brought demands for fresh tinkering with the organization. The hiring of more field and Washington employees which followed and the bringing of more positions under civil service regulations did not foreshadow a new deal for the tribes. The national Progressive reform movement could find no secure place within its ranks and concerns for blacks. Indeed, Progressivism's focus upon purifying politics helped to 'excuse' the disenfranchisement of controversial black voters in the South. When the Progressive ethos influenced Indian reform, it brought a similarly slight benefit to the nation's original inhabitants, changing the tone and outlook rather than the main thrust of the assimilation campaign.

A reform crusade which had stressed that it would remove Indian dependence on government programmes ended up by increasing that dependence and entrenching government paternalism towards the Indians. Even the rundown of services occasioned by the First World War failed to produce a major challenge to federal government power or to erode the white commitment to Indian assimilation, while the President, the Secretary of the Interior, Congress, and the heads of the House and Senate Indian Committees continued to listen sympathetically to their white constituents and to strike down BIA or reformer-backed bills and measures that they did not like.[87] However, just as Indian reform had sustained a momentum of its own during the second half of the nineteenth century, despite being influenced by national trends, so it was able to gather strength again in the 1920s, despite the decline of Progressivism by that time.

4

The Uncertain Road to Self-Determination: the 1920s to the 1960s

I

THE REVIVAL OF REFORM

The 1920s were years of renewed ferment in Indian affairs. During the 1820s and 1830s there had emerged the first concerted humanitarian protests about Indian policy; the 1860s and 1870s had seen the launching of a government-backed reform campaign; and the 1880s and 1890s witnessed a crusade in which humanitarians, Indian service and government were usually at one. In the 1920s, with frugal and *laissez-faire* Republican administrations secure in Washington, the reformers again worked from an adversary position. And although they resolutely looked forward to Indian assimilation and tried to ignore past disappointments, they were noticeably less confident and ethnocentric than their predecessors had been in the nineteenth century.[1]

Economic distress among Indian peoples was one of the most intractable problems facing humanitarians during the decade. The collapse of agricultural prices following wartime expansion and subsequent dislocations in the international economy hit white and Indian farmers alike, as did drought and severe weather between 1919 and 1921. However, since they farmed remote and often indifferent lands with few credit and technical facilities, most Indians had little or nothing to cushion them against losses and they showed no desire to escape their problems by a mass migration to the cities (see Chapter 11).

If the bureau's Forestry Division had improved the administration and protection of Indian timber resources, unsuitable forest lands were still allotted and unallotted timber areas cut too heavily. Local white interests tended to oppose the creation of permanent Indian forests and looted Indian woodlands when they could, while in some areas grazing animals which damaged trees went unchecked by their Indian owners, for whom they provided a readier and more acceptable source of income than timber sales.[2] Indian ranching was undermined by white cattle thieves and squatters, and over-grazing had been apparent on Navajo sheep pastures since about 1910. The 1928 Preston-Engle Report on irrigation projects and irrigated farming on Indian reservations discovered that 68 per cent of the irrigated territory was farmed by whites, and where Indians did control irrigable lands they tended to produce wild hay upon them rather than more profitable crops, not having made the transition to the highly labour intensive form of agriculture which those lands demanded.[3] Indifferent to the fact that land in severalty had left most Indians poor and unassimilated, westerners continued to advocate the opening up of the unallotted reservations and whites as a whole were disinclined to condemn the allotment programme in which they had placed so much faith or from which they had directly benefited.[4]

Nor could reformers take comfort in the condition of reservation government. The justice meted out by Indian judges in the Courts of Indian Offenses was said by BIA employees to be quick, cheap and generally respected, but the courts were too much under bureau control to please either humanitarians or Indians.[5] Moreover, as Graham Taylor has shown, factionalism was frequently rife on the reservations, where unrelated peoples had been forced to live together and intra-group disputes had developed over cultural and economic issues, aggravated or actually provoked by government assimilation policies. In areas like the Northern Plains and the Southwest, these divisions were compounded by the fact that the Indians were traditionally organized only at the band or village level. As a result, early twentieth-century efforts by whites to foster tribal councils or business committees with which they could deal had proved disappointing. The All-Pueblo Council, the first alliance of its kind since the Pueblos' anti-Spanish revolt of 1680, was seen as unduly responsive towards the eastern Pueblos. The Navajo Council appears not to have spoken for the isolated Navajo settlements, despite the bureau's effort to tap local opinion in the 1920s by the creation of community chapters. And the business committees established among the Plains tribes were too dependent on BIA officers to be regarded as genuinely expressive of Indian wishes.[6]

After decades upon decades of hard work on the reservations, the missionaries had no more found the answer to 'the Indian problem' than had bureau personnel. Indeed, the evangelists had not solved their own difficulties. In 1919 there were said to be 46,000 Indians on

forty reservations outside the influence of any church, while missionaries still complained that foreign missions gained more support than
missions to the Indians. They also grumbled that controversial native
practices like peyote consumption could not be contained and that
they did not receive the co-operation from laymen that they would
have liked. Missionaries recognized that the conditions on many
reservations militated against progress of any kind and felt that in any
event their work would take ages 'because the Indian is what he is and
our type of ideal Christian citizenship is such as it is'. Attempts by the
Indian commissioners of the 1920s to bring missionary and bureau
workers closer together seem to have met with little success.[7]

The support of Indian women continued to be regarded as crucial
for the success of white reforms, but their conservatism in some
matters was hard to break down. Whites did not have to worry about
keeping them in the home, for it was difficult to find paid jobs even for
educated Indian girls (see Chapter 8). The percentage of Indian
women 'gainfully employed' in 1930 was the lowest of any population
group in the census.[8] Nor were politics a major distraction. It was not
until 1931, for instance, that eastern Cherokee women voted in
elections for chief.[9] Yet partly as a result of their poverty and lack of
familiarity with white ways of living, Indian women were often
criticized by whites for indifferent home-making. Their unwillingness
to send their children away to school was similarly censured, albeit
one of the main reasons for reluctance was the high death rate at the
boarding schools, which seemed intolerable coming on top of the
already high Indian infant mortality rate. The government field
matrons who had been instructing Indian women since the 1890s
might sometimes command respect, a case in point being Susan
Peters, who worked among the Kiowas in Oklahoma, encouraging the
artistic efforts of the local young people through entrance into the
University of Oklahoma's art classes and sales of their work.[10] This
was the kind of activity for white women in the Indian service and for
women's clubs that their male co-workers could patronizingly
approve, though Indian women were employed as field matrons
where possible.[11] None the less a number of the white matrons were
clearly regarded as tiresome busybodies.[12]

If the condition of Indian women and children was particularly
worrying to white humanitarians, the health, education and welfare of
Indians as a whole gave cause for concern. Indian educational developments are considered elsewhere (see Chapter 9), but it is worth
noting here the dangerous rundown of the Indian medical service
during the First World War and the high incidence of trachoma and
tuberculosis on many reservations. These diseases resulted from a

poor diet, harsh climate and inadequate housing and required long and expensive treatments. Funds squeezed from Congress were sufficient to finance a special, if inept, campaign against trachoma, together with the building of three new hospitals and two new tuberculosis sanitoriums. Unfortunately they did not facilitate the upgrading of salaries that might have enabled the service to attract and keep quality staff or to provide effective preventive medicine, although reorganization was usefully begun in 1926, in co-operation with the US Public Health Service.[13]

During the first part of the 1920s, the Indian difficulties outlined above were only beginning to provoke a constructive public response. Having ceased to be a distinctive menace to white America's safety and aspirations, not least because of their dramatic population decline, the Indians were reduced to the status of just another minority. And like other minorities at that time, they both excited popular animosity and were subjected to strong assimilationist pressures. The best destiny that most whites could envisage for Indians remained their transformation into self-supporting American citizens, indistinguishable from all others. Accordingly, in 1924, there was some support among whites for the Indian Citizenship Act, which conferred citizenship on Indians born in the United States. Although it divided reformers, the legislation was pushed by Progressive politicians anxious to curb the power of the BIA and the Interior Department and from the government's point of view it usefully tidied up the maze of existing laws granting citizenship to tribes and individuals. The willingness of approximately 15,000 Indians to fight for America in the First World War and of Indian women to undertake Red Cross work suggested that they would likewise welcome the Act and it was hoped that citizenship would both mark and encourage their integration into the cultural mainstream. Its impact was in fact minimal.[14]

Politicians also offered assimilation on more threatening terms. The Bursum Bill of 1922 attempted to force the New Mexican Pueblo Indians to cede lands along the Rio Grande to white settlers, while the Indian Omnibus Bill of 1923 envisaged individualizing Indian tribal property, paying Indians the cash value and ending federal direction of Indian affairs. Then there was Interior Secretary Fall's directive of 1922, which opened the resources of Indian reservations created by presidential order rather than by treaty to exploitation by oil companies under the terms of the General Leasing Act of 1920, on the grounds that the United States rather than the Indians owned such lands. The directive was especially alarming to the Navajos, who had some 9 million acres of affected land and newly discovered oil to be exploited.

By the mid 1920s, however, these threats to Indian property rights had galvanized reformers and a number of other factors strengthened both their outrage and their optimism. Congress might have been too mean to support the BIA as a modern, social service agency, comparable to other federal agencies, but it had expanded steadily in terms of appropriations, staff and Indian funds handled; and Commissioner Charles H. Burke (1921–9), for all his support of assimilation, made it clear that the 1924 Citizenship Act did not remove federal authority over unallotted Indians or allotted Indians still in the probationary period laid down by the severalty legislation.[15] The bureau thus remained a formidable worry to the advocates of change.

More encouragingly, successful Progressive campaigns for the expansion of social services showed that white Americans were not entirely devoted to selfish ends in the postwar period, while the decade saw the academic rejection of racial explanations of group difference (see Chapter 7) and elite recognition of the value of cultural diversity.[16] If efforts had been made to obliterate the allegedly alarming features of immigrant culture, there was mounting appreciation of black music and Indian art. In an era which celebrated America's freedom from Victorian shackles of all kinds, nostalgia for a simple rural past, strong community ties and 'folk' culture was ironically pronounced. To a limited extent the Indians were the beneficiaries, as whites living in the Southwest, notably near Santa Fe and Taos, acclaimed the lifestyle and artefacts of Indians who had not been allotted or demoralized by outsiders.[17]

Against this background, new Indian organizations emerged to fight for racial justice (see Chapter 12). They worked alongside white reform groups, which now included more anthropologists (see Chapter 7), and what Downes calls an orgy of muckraking got under way in liberal journals and on the radio and lecture circuit.[18] Public indignation was fed by the coverage given to a number of specific crises on the reservations and by the realization that if the values of rural and small town communities were worth preserving, rural poverty could nevertheless be as oppressive as the urban variety which Progressives had tried to tackle. Agitation by Indian and white reformers helped to block the Omnibus Bill and procure the defeat of the Bursum Bill. A Pueblo Lands Board was created to sort out the conflicting land claims in New Mexico, though they were not finally settled until 1933. Public clamour was equally important in assisting the passage of the Osage Guardianship Act of 1925, which gave protection to the Osages' oil-rich lands in Oklahoma, and in securing the Indian Oil Leasing Act of 1927, which provided for the development of executive order reservations on the same basis as treaty reservations. Under the terms of the Oil Act, reservation boundaries could not be changed except by act of Congress and the tribal councils were to be consulted in future about the expenditure of tribal funds.[19]

It was a harder task to come up with positive proposals for improving the administration of Indian affairs. One favourite suggestion was the turning over to the states of responsibilities for the Indians that were held by the federal government.[20] But many whites, including members of the bureau and the Board of Indian Commissioners, felt that it would be wise to retain federal control over matters relating to Indian property, no matter how incompetent control had proved in the past. They wanted decentralization to encourage Indian involvement in BIA activities, not termination of federal direction. For their part, the state governments, though they were enthusiastic about having taxing powers over Indian lands, showed less interest in assuming responsibility for law and order difficulties on the reservations.[21]

The restless search for solutions is reflected in five reappraisals of Indian policy initiated during the decade. In 1923–4 the Committee of One Hundred advised the Secretary of the Interior, Hubert Work, on a number of issues, at his request. An investigation by the nearly moribund and consequently rather deferential Board of Indian Commissioners followed. Four years later there came the Preston-Engle Report, and the Meriam Report on the whole of Indian policy, again authorized by Work but this time undertaken by the independent Brookings Institution. And between 1928 and 1933 the Senate Committee on Indian Affairs carried out its own survey of reservation conditions.

The best known of these inquiries was the Meriam Report, which built on the work of the ineffectual Committee of One Hundred and took a stance rather similar to that assumed by the journal, *Council Fire*, many years before, and by John Collier and his American Indian Defence Association in the 1920s. In other words, recognizing that some Indians wished to remain Indians, it argued that assimilationist policies must be pursued only with Indian consent and at the Indians' own pace. While they were being converted to white values, the report maintained, Indian peoples were entitled to enjoy religious liberty, federal assistance, detailed consultations and authority over their tribal communities. The report specifically suggested the overhaul of Indian education (see Chapter 9), aid to housing, agriculture and employment, and great caution in the issuing of fee patents, the leasing of Indian lands to whites and the sale of inherited lands. The consolidation of Indian land with bureau aid and the management of tribal property through corporations was suggested. Meriam favoured the decentralization of the Indian service, the recruitment of more and better bureau personnel and the creation of a planning division to develop Indian resources. The consolidation of Indian law and the improvement of law enforcement on the reservations were also urged, together with preference for Indians in bureau jobs and the investigation of Indian claims against the federal government.[22]

Commentators at the end of the 1920s, just as at the end of the Civil War, talked of the need to touch the hearts of the American people; it was not enough merely to blame injustice towards the Indians on the administration.[23] The Meriam Report evidently did move white Americans. Having helped to bring the investigation about, the General Federation of Women's Clubs, the Eastern Association on Indian Affairs, Collier's group, the Indian Rights Association and the Board of Indian Commissioners not surprisingly agreed with most of Meriam's findings. Yet it was apparent that the report's proposals needed more funds than were forthcoming under the Republican ascendancy and on past experience it was over-sanguine in assuming that inferior employees could be removed from the bureau and vastly more Indian involvement in its policies effected.[24]

A partial shake-up in the Indian service, at least, came under President Hoover, a man of Progressive leanings. Commissioner Burke was forced to resign as a result of the Senate survey and years of reformer criticism, whereupon Hoover selected the Quaker banker and president of the Indian Rights Association, Charles Rhoads, to be Commissioner. Rhoads promptly chose as Assistant Commissioner his fellow Quaker and IRA member, Joseph Scattergood, and the commissioners were supported by a liberal Secretary of the Interior, Ray Lyman Wilbur. These men were reformers in the nineteenth-century tradition of assimilationist Indian reform. They opposed government paternalism and favoured allotment, taking advantage of the Meriam Report's ambivalence on the latter point to urge it forcefully, while maintaining that heirship problems must be tackled. Although they advocated corporate control of Indian lands to prevent their dissipation, Rhoads and Scattergood were willing to see such lands taxed and shrank from the policies advocated by their initial supporter but ultimate enemy, John Collier.

An opponent of allotment and the ending of Indians' tax immunity, Collier favoured the creation of powerful tribal councils to govern the existing and former reservations. And he was irked by the Quakers' reliance on simply requesting action from Congress, when years of agitation had shown him that much more forceful tactics were necessary to bring about changes in Indian policy. Collier had a point. Nothing came of the commissioners' hopes for a special court to hear

Indian claims, by-passing the regular Court of Claims. Having aimed at following the Preston-Engle Report's recommendations and freeing the BIA from involvement with Indian irrigation projects, they ended up spending another 5 million dollars on them and retaining control. Expenditure on health, education and welfare was increased and the reorganization of the Indian service into the five divisions of education, health, agricultural extension, forestry and irrigation, each responsible for formulating programmes to be implemented at the local level, was intended to professionalize the service and leave the Commissioner more time for overall policy direction. But the upheaval provoked internal squabbles, as superintendents found themselves caught up in additional red tape, and staffing the new system was not easy.

The rift between Collier and Rhoads also grew wider, with the two men disagreeing over the treatment of Indian boarding-school children, the best way to encourage Indian arts and crafts, the proper level of compensation for the Pueblos and about whether the Commissioner had removed the 'old guard' from the BIA. Prudently, the protagonists sought their own allies in Congress and Collier gained from the Democratic victories in the 1930 elections, which brought more men of his viewpoint to the important House Indian Committee. Collier was willing to concede that some progress had been made under the Quaker regime; for example, in the collection of statistics, the standard of the inspectorial system, co-operation with the states and the scrapping of government charges on the Indians for the construction and maintenance of their irrigation ventures since 1914. His overall attitude to the commissioners remained hostile, none the less, because they had not basically changed the expensive and cumbersome bureau 'system'.[25]

Between 1926 and 1932, the BIA's cost had practically doubled, while the number of Indians it had to take care of remained roughly constant. By the early 1930s, approximately 6,500 regular and over 2,000 extra staff were apparently required for the service of 195,000 Indians. Had the Indians been effectively served, this outlay might not have mattered, but much of the money was said to go on maintaining the bureaucracy and on dealing with individuals of very little Indian blood.[26] Critics noted that Canada, by contrast, defined who was an Indian and had 'an Indian Act ... contained in fifty-four pages', whereas 'a thousand such pages would not contain the Indian law of the United States'. They stressed that the instructions to Indian agents and the Indian school regulations were brief in Canada, overwhelming in the United States. The Canadian regime was said to have the further merits of paying its administrators properly, depending on specialists outside politics and refraining from trying 'to make white men out of the Indians overnight'. The traditional American rejoinder – that Canadians treated the Indians as minors, while American administrators were flexible and progressive – continued to sound somewhat hollow and defensive.[27]

Actually, of course, the differences between Canadian and United States Indian policy and problems were exaggerated by American observers. Paternalism flourished on both sides of the border, even if the government itself was not so intrusive in Canada as it was in the United States. As Keith Crowe points out, the last treaties signed by the northern Canadian Indians in the first three decades of the twentieth century did not avoid the injustices of the nineteenth-century agreements. In other words, the government obtained a very large amount of land for a small outlay. Hunting, fishing and trapping rights were guaranteed, but the rights became difficult to exercise as white economic developments changed the region and strangers divided and regulated the northern lands or concerned themselves with conservation without consulting the local population. Chiefs and councillors were elected according to white direction rather than native practice and 'no Indians or Inuit were policemen, justices of the peace, or magistrates', so that the native people fretted at being treated like children or 'punished for breaking laws which they did not understand'. Medical care was extended by way of missionary, police and trading posts and education was provided through the mission schools, yet support for both was inadequate, so that tuberculosis was endemic and over 80 per cent of Inuit children were not attending school as late as 1944.[28]

In Canada and the United States alike, awareness of past neglect and Indian discontent led to the enlargement of government responsibilities regarding the Indians. And in both countries that awareness was sharpened by knowledge of the suffering caused by the Depression. Of course the Depression took its most dramatic toll upon the whites who had enjoyed prosperity in the 1920s. However, Indians and Inuit who were already poor were badly hit and ill-equipped to cope with the crisis. In Canada, during the 1930s, the prices for furs dropped while those for flour and ammunition rose. As a result, Price observes, the government was obliged to provide relief for about a third of the native population and was driven to launch a special rehabilitation programme for the hard-core unemployed in 1938. In the United States, native peoples were affected by the further decline in agricultural prices, the withdrawal of paying white users from Indian lands and the additional damage caused to over-grazed western lands by blizzards and drought.[29]

II

John Collier and the Indian New Deal

It was left to John Collier to tackle United States Indian problems when he became Commissioner of Indian Affairs, following the election as President of the Democrat Franklin D. Roosevelt, and the resignation of Rhoads and Scattergood in 1933. Collier held the office of Commissioner of Indian Affairs until 1945, longer than any of his predecessors or successors. He was also unusual for the range of his contacts and reform interests, which included social work and adult education in New York and California, and for his crusading involvement in Indian affairs, which had given him a particular interest in the tribes of the Southwest besides a close acquaintance with Washington politics. The Commissioner was fortunate in that when he took up his office he had the backing of the President, the Secretary of the Interior, and many members of the Senate.

Like Roosevelt, Collier seems to have been able to inspire his associates with a sense of the urgency of their tasks and the possibility of their achievement. Like Roosevelt, he was willing to by-pass normal administrative channels and establish new agencies in order to get things done. And like Roosevelt, the Commissioner deplored the social effects of industrialization, took a somewhat romantic view of pre-industrial societies and found that his humane concern to preserve or rebuild community life laid him open to charges of fostering communism and 'un-American' activities.[30] Unlike Roosevelt, Collier was not a pragmatist by instinct. Consequently, just as he had been unremitting in his attacks on the assimilationist policies of Commissioners Burke and Rhoads and rather dismissive of the genuine obstacles they faced, so Collier single mindedly pursued his own approach once he assumed office. In the process, he often simplified substantive criticisms and ironically gave staunch support to the bureau staff whose 'old guard' he had once denounced, but had by no means entirely replaced.

Unlike many of his predecessors, and again like Roosevelt, Collier wanted to achieve reform on many fronts simultaneously. The humanitarians of the 1880s and 1890s had seen allotment, education and citizenship as the key components of their assimilation programme, but they had tended to press these objectives one at a time and to vacillate about their order of importance. For Collier in the 1930s, the economic, the cultural and the political vitality of Indian peoples were equally important and inextricably linked. Yet in both the general and Indian New Deals, individual successes came in the early years, when conditions seemed to demand action and Congress was ready to provide it, while overall success proved elusive. In neither case was executive narrowness the cause of failure. To assist his efforts the Commissioner put together a special Indian Bureau 'brain trust', paralleling Roosevelt's larger body and 'black cabinet'. Hence Collier sought advice from anthropologists (see Chapter 7), social scientists and those who worked with minorities in other countries. The Board of Indian Commissioners, which was too sympathetic towards past bureau policies for his liking, was abolished.

In addition to helping to settle the Pueblo lands issue and obtain additional lands for the Navajos, Collier was able to hire more part-time doctors, dentists and nurses for the Indian health service and to secure the creation in 1935 of an Indian Arts and Crafts Board. On a modest budget, the board tried to promote the marketing of Indian goods, improve methods of production and protect their authenticity through a government trademark. It enjoyed some success, although the public was still unused to paying realistic prices for Indian goods, and there was tension between modernizers and those who wanted to retain the old methods, however hard on the Indians. Not surprisingly, when relief programmes provided the artists with quick alternative funds, they sometimes preferred not to continue with their time-consuming crafts. The number of Indians working for the Indian service was increased and in this area the United States was already ahead of Canada. By the end of June 1934, there were 1,785 Indians among the 5,325 individuals holding classified positions within the service, and in time the percentage of Indians that it employed was raised from thirty to sixty-five.[31]

Showing that his old lobbying flair had not deserted him and that in official circles there was much temporary good will, at least, towards the Indians, the Commissioner was able to find assistance for them through a variety of regular New Deal agencies, including the Federal Emergency Relief Administration, the Civil Works Administration, the Public Works Administration, the Resettlement Administration, and (following Commissioner Rhoads's initiative) the Civilian Conservation Corps. These and other New Deal organizations, in conjunction with such government agencies as the Department of Agriculture and the Forest Service, helped Indians to build roads, bridges, fences, wells, dams, reservoirs and look-out towers and to control crop pests. Their assistance was valuable in improving sheep breeding, cattle raising and forestry, in reducing over-grazing by the purchase of surplus animals and in repairing reservation buildings. Employment was found for Indian artists, while new schools, hospitals, homes, farm buildings and sewerage plants were constructed and money was provided for food, clothing, supplies, additional land purchases and a variety of self-help projects.[32]

Federal–state co-operation to improve Indian health, education and welfare facilities had been urged since the 1920s by reformers as well as members of the Indian service and Congress and in 1934 the Johnson–O'Malley Act was passed. This measure channelled money to the states so that, through appropriate agencies, they could provide or improve 'education, medical attention, agricultural assistance, and social welfare' for the Indians.[33] Without this assistance, at a time when state resources were uniquely strained, the dream of co-operation and decentralization would not have been realized. The education funded under the Act and during the Collier years generally (see Chapter 9), reflecting reformer demands of the 1920s and the thinking of Progressive educators, stressed the instruction of children in their own communities, in skills that would be useful there and by teachers who would take account of Indian cultures. The emphasis on the reservations seemed sensible when there were few jobs elsewhere and besides suiting white self-interest and Indian wishes the programme accorded with the American tradition of local control of education.

The Indian courts were made more responsive to Indian opinion by providing for the election of judges, who had previously been chosen by the reservation superintendents. And instead of operating according to the superintendent's direction, these bodies were modelled on the state courts. Although Collier had no wish to antagonize the missionaries, he determinedly encouraged native religious practices along with other forms of native cultural expression. Obsolete espionage and gag laws affecting the Indians were repealed in 1934 and the codification of Indian law, talked about by reformers since the second half of the nineteenth century, was finally undertaken, resulting in 1942 in the publication by the Interior Department of Felix Cohen's *Handbook of Federal Indian Law*. But the most important part of the Indians' 'new day' was the Wheeler-Howard, or Indian Reorganization, Act of 1934.

The legislation arose out of Collier's concern that allotment had neither profited nor assimilated the Indians, some 90,000 of whom were without land by the 1930s. In its original form, the Act proposed to confer local self-government on Indian communities. It provided for the repeal of the Dawes Act, the consolidation of allotted lands under tribal control, the extension of restrictions on the alienation of allotted territory, and the purchase of additional lands. The future sale of communal property to non-Indians was forbidden. A Court of Indian Affairs was to be established to deal with controversies arising in the chartered communities and provision was made for job training, education and the encouragement of traditional Indian cultures.

For all its commitment to Indian self-determination, the Act strengthened bureau control over Indian land and community resources and suggested that the gap between Collier and his predecessors was not so wide as has sometimes been supposed. Advocates of assimilation and critics of BIA paternalism were dismayed. Anthropologists and reformers saw difficulties ahead and said so. Missionaries and traders felt threatened by the prospect of greater tribal independence and protested. The Commissioner had sounded out Indian opinion before the Bill was formulated and had decided to go ahead in the face of considerable criticism. Once the Act had been produced, Indian congresses were called to consider its terms, but misinformation about it had spread rapidly. Collier made modifications in the Bill to meet objections that the legislation perpetuated a disagreeable reservation system, penalized acculturated and successfully allotted Indians and threatened existing treaty rights or outstanding tribal claims. Yet white objections led to the adoption of additional amendments before the Act was finally approved by Congress, and some of the Indians found the end product hard to recognize. Since the tribes were given the right to vote on the revised legislation of 1934, these crossed wires proved very unfortunate.

The Wheeler-Howard Act that became law in June 1934 nevertheless bore some resemblance to the bureau proposal. Moneys were still provided for the purchase of additional lands ($2 million a year); to facilitate loans to the tribal corporations (a revolving credit fund of $10 million); to help organize the chartered corporations ($250,000 annually); and to finance scholarships for Indian students seeking college and vocational education ($250,000 annually). The allotment laws were revoked, the restoration of surplus reservation land to tribal control was permitted and restricted trust lands could be exchanged for shares in tribal corporations. Indians employed by the bureau could be exempted from civil service qualifications. Constitutions and by-laws adopted by a majority of the adult members of any tribe were to provide for its self-government and might contain a bill of rights. The charters of incorporation, once adopted, gave tribes the right to stop the sale or leasing of land without their consent, bring lawsuits and negotiate with the state and federal governments for public services. In addition, tribes were empowered to foster economic developments with the aid of the credit fund, regulate their councils and monitor federal appropriation requests on their behalf. And at long last 'Indians' were clearly defined: either as persons of one half or more Indian blood, or as persons of Indian descent who were members of a recognized tribe subject to federal jurisdiction when the Act was passed, together with their descendants who were living on the reservation at that time. The Act was seen as bringing America into line with 'the Canadian system under which the Indians of that country have increased their land-holdings while ours have steadily lost them.'

However, the Indian court scheme was scrapped and the tribal governments did not acquire the power of municipalities. It was no longer compulsory for allotted Indians to transfer their land titles to the new corporations, existing practices of inheritance were retained and the Secretary of the Interior was authorized to instigate conservation measures on Indian terrain and review many of the powers of the tribal councils. Any tribe that wished to remain under direct bureau control and exempt itself from the legislation could do so if this was the wish of the majority expressed in a referendum. The Commissioner hailed this proviso as a 'rare and unusual privilege'. But the need to hold prompt referendums forced the Indian office to proceed with tribal organization more quickly than was desirable. Moreover, since a proposal to allow the incorporation of groups smaller than the tribe was omitted, at Collier's own prompting, the Act chose to ignore the fact that the tribe was not the basic organizational unit for all Indian peoples.[34]

Figures concerning the Indian response to Wheeler-Howard vary, but the mixed nature of that response is apparent in all of them. According to the statistics used by Philp, '181 tribes which contained a population of 129,750 approved of the I.R.A. [Indian Reorganization Act], while 86,365 repudiated it', the opponents being contained in 77 tribes.[35]

Collier bravely claimed that the Indian vote cast, in relation to the total of eligible Indian votes, 'has been larger at these tribal referendums than is the white vote at Presidential Elections'. Although he had actually hoped for a better immediate response, the Interior Department subsequently came to terms with additional tribes. Despite the strangeness of the whole process, in the course of the New Deal 93 tribes adopted constitutions and 73 established charters of incorporation.[36]

For a number of tribes, including the Mescalero and Jicarilla Apaches of New Mexico, the Flatheads and Northern Cheyennes of Montana and the Chippewas of Wisconsin, Wheeler-Howard brought money which was used to improve farming and housing, start community enterprises and reduce white exploitation. Many loans also went to individuals, who used them to buy seed, livestock and machinery and maintained an excellent repayment rate. At reservations in Minnesota, North and South Dakota, Arizona and Montana, especially, surplus land was restored to good effect. By 1941, Congress had spent $5.5 million for 400,000 acres of land and had returned nearly a million acres of ceded surplus land to the tribes. When the terms of the Wheeler-Howard Act were extended to Oklahoma Indians and Alaska natives by special legislation in 1936, the many acculturated Indians in Oklahoma and the many whites with a vested interest in the exploitative status quo guaranteed that there would be a cautious response from the state. None the less, in Oklahoma loans were used to acquire land, start new ventures, care for the indigent and help out individuals, while in Alaska, where the forces of localism were very strong, Wheeler-Howard funds were acceptable for the purchase of boats and the repair of equipment.[37] The amount of grazing land controlled by the Indians increased by 15 per cent between 1936 and 1940, as a result of purchases under the Wheeler-Howard Act and the transfer of leases from whites. With the aid of money from the credit fund, the number of cattle, sheep and horses on Indian ranges was more than doubled in roughly the same period and their average value per head was increased by $6.50. By 1940, the Indians owned approximately 40 per cent of the livestock on Indian lands, and as Taylor suggests, the 'rebuilding of tribal herds in the Northern Plains constituted a major accomplishment of the Indian New Deal'.[38]

A useful part of this success story was played by the already existing Division of Extension and Industry, which made a point of encouraging Indian involvement in manageable local schemes, unlike some of the more ambitious, region-wide New Deal endeavours.[39] Home extension work and the formation of youth clubs were given high priority, in the belief 'that in all subsistence farm programs for any race, unless the women and children contribute their help, the program will fail'. In 4-H clubs young people aged between 10 and 21 years undertook agricultural or home economics activities under the supervision of an agency worker, agricultural expert, or local leader. Club projects doubled between 1932 and 1939, the number of clubs rose from 294 in 1934 to 478 in 1939 and parents were indirectly educated in the process. Local Indian women were said to be 'excellent co-operators' in the home extension programme, once they understood its importance. Sometimes in alliance with representatives from the General Federation of Women's Clubs, they concerned themselves with nutrition, food production, conservation and storage, the care of children, clothes, yards and the home generally, the production of better bedding and furniture, community welfare and recreation. Loans were given so that the participants could buy cookstoves, pressure cookers, bedding, tables and other household necessities and the drying and canning of meats, fruits and vegetables increased.

The Extension Division took a close interest in co-operative livestock associations on the reservations. These had numbered 53 with 2,217 cattle owners in 1935; by 1938 there were 126 co-operatives with a membership of 5,244 and by 1950 the figure seems to have risen to 150. Communal enterprise was further encouraged by the building of chapter houses which served as 'social and civic centers where community life flourishes', as well as centres for the farm and other work of the division. By 1938, 333 such houses were in existence. In its agricultural activities, the division placed emphasis upon soil conservation and the restoration of soil fertility, showing farmers how to terrace their farms where necessary and trying to improve yields. The number of families planting gardens increased by 14 per cent between 1932 and 1939, cereal production rose by 30 per cent and forage crops harvested by 8 per cent. These gratifying improvements must have owed something to the fact that the qualifications of those employed by the division had been greatly improved during the decade.

Even allowing for the built-in cheerfulness of reports to paymasters from those looking to stay in business, the work of the division really does seem to show that group life as Collier envisaged it could still flourish on the reservations, notwithstanding external pressures. Inevitably a unit which relied on white technical expertise can be criticized for working according to past assumptions that whites knew best. The white settlement houses that tried to improve the lot of white immigrants and black migrants to the North could be attacked as similarly patronizing and extension workers among poor white farmers were often regarded with suspicion by individuals who did not want to be improved in their own best interest. But just as investment dollars were more acceptable to southerners during Reconstruction than missionaries and carpetbaggers, so economic assistance was generally more tolerable to black slum dwellers, white dirt farmers and Indians on the reservations than lectures on their customs or interference in their politics. After all, the settlement house or extension worker was closely involved in the daily lives of his 'clients' and working with people is always more acceptable than working for them.

The Extension Division showed its concern to help rather than direct Indian communities by stressing the vital role of voluntary local leaders, who heavily outnumbered its white employees. It was noted that Indian initiative and management skills had been fostered by the livestock associations, and one superintendent claimed in 1938 that 'the Indians had actually learned more about credit and doing business on a business basis during the past two years than probably in any 25 years prior thereto'.[40] Yet in private correspondence with the Commissioner the head of the Extension Division conceded that he was entangled in red tape and hampered by suspicious white officials.[41]

The economic policies of the Indian New Deal were, in fact, generally hard to implement. The new tribal enterprises left bureau personnel with fewer means of extracting results than formerly and it was admitted that the projects did not 'even give maximum employment to Indians in their operation'.[42] When new lands were purchased for the Indians, they and BIA employees differed about their proper use and Assistant Commissioner Zimmerman acknowledged that there was opposition to land acquisition 'in almost every State'. Indian land policies might have been reoriented towards resource protection and away from resource disposal, but public opinion had not kept pace with the change. By the end of the New Deal, though the Indians had acquired through Wheeler-Howard and other means something above 4 million extra acres of land, this amount was over 5 million acres short of what was needed, while regions where the Indians had been allotted and new land was badly needed were not the prime beneficiaries, since little public domain could be recovered in those areas.

The bureau tried to operate as wide a range of projects as possible, to counteract the argument of politicians that since many Indians had opposed the Wheeler-Howard Act, the appropriations it envisaged could be safely reduced. They were reduced anyway. The land purchase fund was cut by over 50 per cent after 1937 and the credit, educational and tribal organizational funds were savaged in 1935. Even without budget cuts, the bureau and the tribes lacked the means to buy back all or most of the heirship lands and the land destined to pass to heirs. Moreover, they lacked the arguments to persuade the heirs to sell their property, or the allotted Indians to surrender their allotments to tribal management. The reluctance of the allottees was not a simple matter. Some had become as assimilated as whites had hoped, and objected to what they thought was a plot to put the clock back. Some feared that they might lose their economic security and others were just hostile to interference by either local or distant authorities.

Many of the criticisms levied against the Collier regime were similar to those directed against the New Deal as a whole. There was confusion in the field as officials felt their way forward, dealing with new people and agencies as well as old enemies, and everywhere there were complaints about haste, lack of clear planning, poor administration and bureaucracy. No planning organization of the kind proposed in the Meriam Report was established and it was probably not desired by the different divisions, whose directors talked piously about co-ordination but valued their autonomy, however much officials in Washington might urge the need for specific projects which touched Indian life in a direct way and which made sense 'in geographical rather than in divisional terms'.

The assistance provided by the bureau and regular New Deal agencies alike during the 1930s often had little lasting effect or was unevenly spread, so that some Indians were getting 'more assistance than is good for them. Others of course . . . like those in Oklahoma . . . are getting very inadequate aid.' Administrators worried about the need to awaken the recipients of aid to their responsibility for maintaining projects that had been freely constructed for their benefit. In addition, reservation Indians were being encouraged to leave the land and take employment on relief programmes, without thinking of the long-term consequences. Indians were thus helped to survive, but Indian poverty, underemployment, unemployment and dependency could not be permanently reduced by temporary assistance. New and permanent reservation jobs had to be created before Collier's hopes for Indian communities could be realized. Furthermore, through economic aid and the creation of tribal councils, whites may ironically have given the tribes the strength to oppose aspects of the Indian New Deal that they disliked.[43]

The Navajos are a good case in point. The existence among them of strong local headmen and a council, the tribe's vital culture and its clear social and economic needs encouraged the Commissioner to hope that the Navajos' response to the Wheeler-Howard Act would be a positive one. It was not. The tribe rejected the Act by 8,214 votes to 7,795, and the conflict which ensued, detailed by Kelly and Parman, demonstrated the difficulty of achieving new beginnings in Indian affairs.[44]

Collier's objectives of stock reduction, soil conservation, land acquisition, local education, a consolidated administration and vigorous self-government for the Navajos were well intentioned, but all aroused suspicion. Stock reduction during the New Deal left white farmers uncomprehending and angry, but the Navajos' animals determined their social status, formed the focus for the activities of the extended family and were central to their entire culture in a very special way.[45] Tempers flared when more than one cut in the herds proved necessary and the operation was carried out in the interests of the powerful owners, rather as the general New Deal farm legislation benefited the large producers. The result was that many small owners were driven from subsistence on to relief and the bureau was never able to provide enough economic alternatives to offset the impact of its controversial policy.[46] The coercion involved in the programme was also resented and its efficiency was not helped by the tensions that developed between Soil Conservation Service workers and Indian service personnel, as the latter shrank from assuming full responsibility for the unpopular measures.[47]

Navajo annoyance with the federal government was sustained for various other reasons. There was anxiety about the tribe's new educational programme (see Chapter 9), resentment that old administrators were dispersed before the new tribal government was established at Window Rock, Arizona, and bitterness after whites were able to block government efforts to provide the eastern Navajos with additional land. It is perhaps not surprising that the tribe felt it was not worth accepting the Wheeler-Howard Act from an administration which had already failed them. Their large numbers, pronounced individualism, earlier escape from allotment, and faith in their existing institutions and treaty rights made the Navajos determined to resist legislation from which they felt they had little to gain. In their resistance, they were encouraged by traders and missionaries.[48]

The opposition to Collier was led by the pro-assimilationist Navajo politician, Jacob C. Morgan, who was just the sort of educated and converted Indian that white reformers had been extolling for decades. As a result of the Commissioner's economic policies and efforts to manipulate the tribal council, Morgan's influence grew and he became its chairman in 1938. As he built up his power, Morgan co-operated with other critics of the BIA, including the assimilationists in the American Indian Federation (see Chapter 12). Once he became chairman, Morgan's opposition to the administration declined and no one of comparable stature took up the fight. None the less, the emergence of the Navajo Indian Rights Association led by Dashne Cheschillege in 1940 kept the protests against stock reduction alive. The Indian service consequently suffered additional unfavourable publicity, with anxious inquiries coming from Mrs Roosevelt, an effective appeal to the Navajos for co-operation coming from the President and yet more explanations and assurances coming from Collier.[49]

The best and worst of the Commissioner and the bureau are to be seen in this controversy. It does seem clear that the problem of soil erosion needed urgent attention and that without prompting the Navajos would not have taken it up. When the tribe was left to administer stock controls entirely independently after 1947, through a system of grazing permits, further range deterioration took place.[50] Collier did initially try to *persuade* the Navajos into his way of thinking, and though he obviously wanted success with them because they were the nation's largest tribe, his genuine concern for their welfare is evident in the many documents relating to the Navajos in his official files. Moreover, the council did not buckle under pressure and was making itself felt by the 1940s. Indeed, the Commissioner at least believed that observing the tribe at work was 'watching the processes of democracy right down at the root of things'.[51] On the other hand, Collier never fully appreciated the Navajos' distaste for the economic innovations of the 1930s and his threats and justifications made the Commissioner seem more like his embattled predecessors than the herald of a 'new day'. There was some validity in BIA complaints that the stock issue was manipulated by different groups of Navajos for their own ends, but such grumbles appeared to deny the validity of the factional disagreements that Collier acknowledged were an unavoidable feature of democracy.[52] The fact that the administration continued to chivvy white friends and opponents, notably the sometimes critical Oliver La Farge and his American Association on Indian Affairs, did not do the Commissioner any good with the Indian groups who felt his wrath.[53]

Collier's difficulties with Indian spokesmen and white employees were not confined to the Navajo jurisdiction. It was recognized by the BIA that either the Indian service or the councils could assume the lead in Indian affairs as appropriate and that complaints against bureau employees were normally to be channelled through the superintendents, as in the past.[54] The likelihood of these still powerful officials taking an advanced line was limited, since, as one bureau observer put it, the 'cultural tone at too many of our Agencies is about as inspiring as dinner time in a boarding house. The spiritual atmosphere is that of a "service club" meeting in a western "Main Street".'[55] Rather more importantly, administrators fretted about 'whether harm had been done in giving to the Indian democratic forms without a knowledge of democratic processes' and about the prospect of irresponsible Indians getting on to the councils and dominating tribal affairs in a tyrannical fashion. The election of those with little Indian blood who knew 'how to handle whites' might theoretically have benefited the generally older and less well educated full bloods, who did not. In practice, the full bloods might simply come to regard council operations with suspicion.

Hence bureau files detail the divisions that earlier bureau policies had helped to produce and the 1930s did nothing to end. They relate the continuing quarrels between mixed and full bloods, the activities of individuals who were regarded as political trouble-makers and the animosities between opposed tribes concentrated on a single reservation. There are also indications in the records that the development of councils gave encouragement to the old conflict between Indians who wanted the *per capita* distribution of funds and white administrators who feared the reckless dissipation of tribal resources.

Real efforts were made to see that the different factions were adequately represented on the councils. Yet when bureau staff commented bracingly on how 'interesting and assuring' it was to see younger members of the Menominee council disputing the proper running of its affairs, and on the habit of certain elements in the tribe of attacking either their superintendent or their mill manager, one cannot but detect the sharp uneasiness about Indian self-government which undercut the radical aspects of the Collier programme.[56] Furthermore, as Taylor has shown, the Indian office was generally reluctant to work with the small communities that were the basic social unit among many Indian peoples. The Canadian government had always done so, but in the United States it was argued that the large-scale organization made possible through *tribal* councils was economically essential. This attitude naturally did not gratify Indians who had expected a free hand to run their own affairs, in traditional contexts. They found instead that the bureau had retained guardianship over their property and impelled them into alien political groupings where they were in complete control only of comparatively unimportant issues, often concerning personalities. And so the BIA interfered where and when it thought proper, the tribes protested and the Commissioner's enemies rejoiced. For they were able to show that despite his defence of the tribes as diverse 'sovereign nations' and despite the efforts of the lawyers concerned, the tribal constitutions devised in the 1930s were overly standardized, while the Indians were still in thrall to government paternalism.[57]

Even in the matter of religious liberty, where Collier was particularly anxious to make a break with the past, Indian traditionalism undermined his efforts and whites exploited his discomfort. The use in ceremonials of the image-producing cactus bean, peyote, was the chief cause of trouble. The cult had spread from Mexico to the United States in the last quarter of the nineteenth century and claimed about 13,300 adherents by 1919. The peyote-using Native American Church, like the Ghost Dance but unlike the entirely traditional Sun Dance, combined elements of Christianity with native practices. As had been the case with the similarly persecuted pan-Indian Ghost and Sun Dances, the peyote church was strongest among the Plains tribes, for whom all three religions can be seen as a form of resistance to white pressures and a reaffirmation of faith in the power of Indian ways in a threatening world.[58]

123

Matters came to a head over peyote at the Taos pueblo in 1936, when the new council leader, Antonio Mirabel, launched a crusade to eliminate the cult. Members of the Native American Church at Taos petitioned Collier for religious freedom. They stated that they had long professed but been hounded in their faith, harmed no one and simply wanted the right to carry on their activities. A difficult choice thus faced the Commissioner: he could either infringe Indian political autonomy or deny the Taos protesters the liberty of conscience that other Americans enjoyed. In the Taos case, where Mirabel was backed by Collier's former mentor, Mabel Dodge Luhan, the rights of the peyotists were upheld. Mirabel was removed and an effort was made through the All-Pueblo Council to secure the cult against persecution, though not before the controversy had aggravated existing tensions generated by BIA efforts at land improvements and administrative reform among the Pueblos. In the case of the Navajos, where Morgan opposed peyote, Collier wanted to avoid another quarrel with the council and so reluctantly accepted the cult's prohibition. Unhappily, the matter provoked disagreements in white and Indian communities alike and could not easily be settled.

Accordingly Indians wrote to the bureau making contradictory claims about peyote. Some correspondents stressed that the bean was employed in a religious context, not as a selfish form of drug addiction. And it allegedly had a good influence on the behaviour of users who, for example, shunned alcohol and were 'the most dependable in their relations with white people and farther advanced in their material welfare than those who do not practise this faith and are users of intoxicating liquor'. Others maintained that peyote was an un-Christian, expensive habit which injured the health, weakened the mind and will, and so worked against educational, political and economic progress. In the words of Adelbert Thunder Hawk, secretary to the Rosebud (Sioux) Council of South Dakota, the cult threatened to send 'the Sioux people back to paganism'.

As far as whites were concerned, the debate about peyote precipitated hearings in Congress and a proposal to outlaw its interstate transportation. In the course of the discussions, Collier expressed opinions strikingly at odds with the official bureau line on peyote summed up in 1929, and defended them against a background of largely hostile state opinion, which had produced anti-peyote legislation in the Dakotas, Idaho, Montana, Nebraska, Iowa, Wyoming, New Mexico, Colorado and Utah. The Commissioner's view was that 'peyote is not habit-forming ... [or] deleterious' and though he was careful to point out that he could not interfere with state laws against peyote, he urged that the Indians be given 'entire freedom' to sort out the subject of the peyote church. Collier won the broad support of anthropologists for his stance (see Chapter 7) but he drew the fire of assorted assimilationists, including missionaries and reform organizations such as the Women's Christian Temperance Union.[59] Since these elements opposed other aspects of the Indian New Deal, the peyote dispute, like the publicity about the Navajos, brought the Commissioner much political anxiety.

Rather in the manner of nineteenth-century feminists who simplistically blamed their defeats on the liquor and other interests ranged against them, the Indian office under Collier tended to hold selfish white economic interests responsible for its difficulties. This, too, was an over-simplification. While undoubtedly many westerners were opposed to proposals for extending the Indians' land base, much of the hostility was fuelled by the genuine conservatism that shackled the New Deal as a whole. Congressmen denounced as divisive and un-American expenditures which singled out certain groups for special treatment. They found it hard to shake off the animosity towards the bureau which Collier himself had helped to stir up in the 1920s and which their own investigations of reservation conditions had confirmed. They were encouraged by the protests of acculturated Indians against Wheeler-Howard to believe that assimilation policies might yet succeed and that the Act created undesirable nations within the nation.

The objections to the Commissioner's activities that surfaced in the House Committee on Indian Affairs, its Committee on Appropriations and the Senate Committee on Indian Affairs, were also fostered by the knowledge that Collier had made 'advanced' friends, notably in the Jewish liberal elite and the American Civil Liberties Union (ACLU), and alienated 'sound' citizens, including members of the disbanded Board of Indian Commissioners, threatened church groups and the veteran Indian Rights Association. The Commissioner tried to devalue the association's criticisms by suggesting that it 'was in the process of losing any prestige it ever had'. He established his own journal, *Indians at Work*, to offset the blasts contained in the association publication, *Indian Truth*. None the less, the organization's opposition was damaging. Efforts from 1937 to repeal the Wheeler-Howard Act, or exempt certain tribes from it, were defeated with reformer assistance. But by the late 1930s, like his ally Roosevelt, Collier was on the defensive. And one result of defensiveness, Taylor points out, was the self-defeating caution with which the credit facilities provided under Wheeler-Howard were extended.[60]

The more one looks at the Commissioner's political difficulties, the more it seems as if the odium attached to the bureau offset the advantages that the Indians gained from reformer activism in the 1920s and from having an institutional ally ready to lobby on their behalf during the Depression. Their position, in the end, was much like that of American blacks, although Indian peoples did not invariably encounter the discrimination experienced by blacks, while the western congressmen were not such powerful opponents of change on race matters as the southern Democrats. The President expressed an interest in both minorities, but gave neither priority. His advisers and the liberal public and politicians generally were preoccupied with the national economic emergency and neither blacks nor Indians were strong enough politically to force whites to give the needed attention to their problems. Political caution led Roosevelt to refuse action on black civil rights, and if he acknowledged Collier's difficulties and intervened on behalf of the Wheeler-Howard Act and in the Navajo dispute, he played little part in Indian policy. Black leaders found a valuable ally in the courageous and humane Eleanor Roosevelt and Indian petitioners likewise appreciated the possible advantages to be gained from an appeal to her.[61] Parman observes that a Navajo delegation which saw the First Lady was helped to obtain an irrigation project, the first positive result of years of lobbying in Washington.[62] It was therefore understandable that Cheschillege and his allies should write to Mrs Roosevelt, sending her 'a bunch of grass and wild flowers that is growing on our reservation now', as proof 'that we have food range and that our herds should not be reduced', and ending with a plea that 'you will help us all you can'. But the fact was that the First Lady gave less time to Indian matters than to blacks and was apparently anxious to avoid controversies that would embarrass the administration in her dealings with either race.[63]

Despite the partial or total success of parts of his programme, Collier's 'new day' for the Indians was not an overall success. The Commissioner had not tried to end bureau direction of Indian affairs, create a bureau dictatorship, or drive the Indians 'back to the blanket', as critics charged, so that he cannot be blamed for failing to achieve any of these things! He was, D'Arcy McNickle reminds us, in favour of acculturation, of 'people accommodating to each other'.[64] Yet Collier had hoped to 'get the Indian Service down to human and local terms' and to enlist the 'active, intelligent participation of the Indians'; and as we have seen, the Commissioner won only limited Indian support.[65] Contemplating the unfinished tasks of the service, Collier noted that the special court to hear Indian claims had still not been created and that while social scientists had helped in the work of modernizing and more actively implementing bureau policies, there was 'a permanent and desperate danger of relapse into unproductive institutionalism'.[66]

Furthermore, the taste for wage work which the New Deal programmes had fostered subsequently drove an increasing number of
Indians away from those traditional communities that the Commissioner had romanticized and tried to strengthen.

On the other hand, urban job opportunities, reservation poverty
and growing Indian numbers would probably have accelerated the
drift to the cities (see Chapter 11) without the stimulus of the New
Deal; this was certainly what happened in Canada. With hindsight it
seems that Collier acted prudently in preserving the bureau and under
his administration it was more responsive to Indian pressures than it
had ever been. If there was less progress in training Indian leaders
under Wheeler-Howard than had been hoped, and Indians of all kinds
found it hard to adjust to the councils, electoral districts, secret ballots
and American-style officials introduced by the Act, the councils
survived and in the long run the Indians' ability to manage their own
affairs was enhanced. Finally, because the New Deal as a whole gave
priority to economic issues, the Commissioner was able to make more
headway than might otherwise have been the case in trying to
compensate Indian peoples for past territorial losses. For the first time
in its history, the bureau was not concerned with parting the Indians
from their 'surplus' land or obliterating their culture. For the first time
in its history, the bureau came close to making rather than merely
administering Indian policy.

III

THE SECOND WORLD WAR AND THE POSTWAR ASSIMILATION CRUSADE

The coming of the Second World War was a disaster for the Indian
service. To make room for administrators directly concerned with the
war, the bureau, minus Collier and a few advisers, was moved to
Chicago. As a result, vital contacts with legislators and other Wash-
ington-based organizations were lost. In Philp's words, the BIA also
'experienced the greatest loss of personnel in its history when over 800
regular employees left for military service or transferred to agencies
more directly connected with the war'. Wartime requirements were
made the excuse for further cuts in the bureau budget and the
termination of those emergency programmes which had accounted for
the main increase in BIA outlays during the 1930s.[67] In addition, the
relocation of some Japanese-Americans on tribal land took up time
that the bureau could not spare and aroused understandable Indian
resentment. If BIA officials thereby gained the opportunity of study-

127

ing the impact of shock and social change on the Japanese concerned, just as they were interested in examining the impact of change on Indian peoples, the affected Colorado River Indians saw simply another injustice and threat to their lands. The threat was not a permanent one but relocation proved a distraction and a nuisance.[68]

Military service and war work drew about half the able-bodied Indian men from the reservations and Indians who remained felt the loss of talented people and the impact of reduced federal funds. Among the Navajos, for example, Civilian Conservation Corps projects were ended, the schools lost needed teachers and fuel shortages aggravated existing transport difficulties.[69] Further south, the superintendent of the Sells Agency in Arizona reported that the conflict had brought neglect and demoralization for the Papagos. When it ended, there were a mere three bureau employees to help develop the reservation's resources, medical facilities were available for only a few and less than half the children of school age were being educated.[70]

The BIA tried to make the best of things by collating and publicizing Indian contributions to the war effort as 'skilled and fearless' soldiers, industrial workers, food producers and purchasers of war bonds.[71] But there were dangers as well as merits in this focus. The Indian response to the draft had, in fact, been mixed;[72] and as a result of stressing wartime developments, the idea had spread 'that if the Indians can do so well in civilian and military war service, there may after the war remain no need for supervision'.[73] In northern Canada, where American military personnel moved in to build roads and air bases, the crisis brought a better awareness of 'the existence and problems of the northern native people' and the assumption of 'a new responsibility' for them on the part of 'the federal and prairie governments'.[74] In the United States, where politicians worried about overspending and developers again eyed Indian resources acquisitively, it led to the emasculation of the Wheeler-Howard Act and stimulated fresh efforts by assimilationists to end the special relationship between the national government and the tribes.

Collier's enemies had forced his resignation by 1945, although he continued to fight for Indian reform and, like the Indian protest organizations of recent times (see Chapter 12), he looked for an inter-American solution to Indian problems. After Collier's departure, Commissioners of Indian Affairs came and went again with great regularity, as in the past, a fairly clear indication of the difficulties involved in the office and the uncertain status of the bureau. William Brophy, who was Commissioner between 1945 and 1947, and his successors, John R. Nichols (1949–50) and Dillon S. Myer (1950–3), found themselves struggling with the unenviable task of helping the run-down reservations while being sniped at from every side.

The most important reservation crisis concerned the Navajos. Discharged servicemen and war workers returned home to find that there were few jobs and no solutions to the tribe's historic problems. Because the attention of politicians had been focused on the Navajos by the New Deal, it was not too difficult to secure a special session of Congress in November 1947 to consider their circumstances. Reformers and bureau officials promptly made a good case for assistance, pointing out that 'the plight of the Navajos has been used by the anti-American foreign press in an effort to derogate the treatment received by minority groups in the United States' and that the Indian service spent on each Navajo half of the average *per capita* expenditure of the federal government on each citizen. The bureau then came forward with proposals for developing the Navajos' output of timber products and minerals, helping them to find off-reservation employment, improving the marketing of arts and crafts, constructing roads, establishing small community industries, investigating their coal deposits, repairing schools and hospitals and expanding their irrigation and soil conservation programmes.

Progress was held up, however, in part by the desire of some politicians to see the extension of state civil and criminal laws and court jurisdiction over the Navajo and Hopi reservations, in part by the refusal of New Mexico and Arizona, alone among American states, to extend old age assistance or aid to dependent childen and the blind to reservation Indians. The attitude of these two states, which also denied Indians the vote, was essentially that they would not help those already 'supported' by the federal government. Under the circumstances, although the BIA and the Justice Department backed the Indians' successful bid for enfranchisement, while Social Security was extended to them in 1950, the time for dramatically increasing state powers over the Navajos and Hopis did not seem to have come.[75]

The Navajo–Hopi Long Range Rehabilitation Act which was finally secured in 1950 aimed at raising the standard of living of the two tribes to parity with that of their neighbours, something that the New Deal had not aspired to do. It provided for the expenditure of $88,570,000 over ten years on the projects outlined by the bureau, while the Navajos were authorized to adopt a constitution and the tribal council was given control over tribal funds and future income.[76] Indicating that Collier's blend of paternalism and concern for Indian wishes was still a feature of Washington thinking, President Truman emphasized the importance of Indian involvement in the rehabilitation programme and of respect for Navajo and Hopi religion and social customs, 'in accordance with this Nation's long-established laws and traditions'.[77] Truman's assurances seem to have come in response to the strongly expressed determination of the Navajo council to have its amendments to the rehabilitation scheme adopted and to enjoy 'the fullest possible exercise of powers and responsibilities in the administration of their affairs as the Secretary of the Interior may now approve'.[78] The council which Collier had manipulated and many Navajos had mistrusted was at last an effective force. In the years after the Second World War, the religious concerns which had preoccupied Morgan were replaced by economic and educational demands and with the aid of federal funds and private developers the Navajos were able to make considerable progress.[79]

The Alaska natives were another group which caused the BIA and reformers anxiety in various ways during the late 1940s and revealed the growing public desire for the decentralization of Indian affairs. In the course of a debate about the extinguishing of native claims to the public domain in return for land grants and protection of certain existing land and water rights, pressure mounted, as in the Navajo case, for shifting power from the BIA to the whites on the spot. The native population was suspicious of a distant government which had been slow to protect them and had by 1944–5 pushed them towards the restricting reservations that they opposed in the 1930s. Having been used to independent village life, they certainly did not want bureau officials running their communities. Moreover, reformer critics of the BIA, including Harold Ickes, Indian activist Ruth Bronson, and Associate Solicitor at the Interior Department, Felix Cohen, complained in an all too familiar fashion that the Alaska natives had not been sufficiently consulted, that their timber, fishing and mineral rights were not safeguarded and that the entire attempt to settle land title was just another land grab in which the Interior Department had unpleasantly combined 'overtones of benevolence with the stark fact of racial expropriation'.[80]

Despite the determination of the interested parties, the Alaska land question remained unresolved until the Alaska Native Claims Settlement Act was passed in 1971. Indian claims generally were assisted by the creation in 1946, after two decades of agitation, of an Indian Claims Commission. Originally intended to last for ten years, the commission operated until 1978, after which outstanding cases were referred to the Court of Claims. As Collier had predicted, the commission did not bring riches to the Indians who had pressed for it.[81] The making of awards proceeded slowly and in time millions of dollars were spent by the Indians on lawyers' fees. None the less, $534 million were awarded between 1951 and 1974, and the commission brought hope and a partial redress of grievances to some of those whose land had been obtained by whites in the past at unrealistically low prices. From the point of view of many whites, however, settling the old treaty claims was simply a necessary preliminary to the assimilation of the Indians.[82]

In such a climate, it is hard to see how the bureau could have both pleased its Indian clients and protected its own position. Brophy was sympathetic to tribal needs and wishes, having served as a special attorney from the Pueblo Indians between 1934 and 1942.[83] He was aware that the 'revival of the idea that Indian property is public property is a reflection of an underlying feeling that Indian property is there for the taking' and he was determined to 'vigorously oppose any attempts to raid Indian resources'.[84] But the abolition of the bureau, the transfer of its powers to other federal agencies and the distribution of tribal funds had been advocated by the Senate Indian Investigating Subcommittee in 1943, and while Congress had not approved the proposal, Collier and his successors lived in fear of similar propositions.[85] They did, at least, offer a delaying defence against them.

To begin with, the bureau co-operated in demands for its reorganization in the interests of decentralization. As early as 1940 Collier had envisaged that some shake-up would be necessary and in 1946 field jurisdictions were consolidated under six district offices located at Juneau, Minneapolis, Billings, Portland, Phoenix and Oklahoma City. Each district office outside Alaska controlled several states and the duties of the Commissioner's office, district offices and field jurisdictions were carefully defined.[86] Congress was unhappy with the result, for financial reasons as much as anything else, and by 1948 the bureau was involved in a headquarters reorganization. The large number of divisions under the control of the Commissioner, though all concerned with vital services, could scarcely have pleased the advocates of limited government.[87] By 1949, yet another reorganization was effected. It retained the district offices, which had already been transformed into regional offices and were now designated as area offices. Some independent field units reporting directly to the Commissioner were permitted, and the headquarters organization was revised.[88] Even then, arrangements were not entirely satisfactory. Work-loads and administrative procedures varied between the eleven area offices (including Alaska) and the number of independent offices was seen as excessive. The wearying effect of these reforms on bureau officials and the irritated uncertainty they produced in the Indians may be readily appreciated.[89]

Apart from trying to put their own house in order, BIA spokesmen publicized the enormity of the problems still facing the Indians and the huge amounts of money that would be necessary to solve them, whether the federal government or the states attempted to do so. The land base remained inadequate and unequally distributed, with perhaps as many as 100,000 Indians being totally landless, and some 9 million acres out of the 17 million acres of allotments having passed from the original owners to heirs who could not divide them and were generally driven to leasing. Demands for the issuing of fee patents and the removal of restrictions against the alienation of allotments within the trust period meant that in 1948 the rate of Indian land disposition was greater than the rate of acquisition. Resource management, preventive medicine, the treatment of endemic diseases, dental care, school and credit facilities were still unsatisfactory on most reservations.[90]

Unfortunately for the bureau, its emphasis on the grim aspects of reservation life suggested to many conservatives that the states could hardly do a worse job of managing Indian affairs and the BIA, reformers and Indian groups could not immediately make common cause against the new assimilation campaign. The Association of American Indian Affairs and the National Congress of American Indians, an important pan-Indian lobby formed in 1944 (see Chapter 12), both opposed the 'emancipation' of the Indians from the bureau, but the General Federation of Women's Clubs, which had long been involved in Indian work and did not wish to be rendered powerless by hostility to prevailing opinion, contented itself with approving the withdrawal of federal supervision over the tribes, 'providing such plans contemplate fulfillment of federal obligation toward Indians, and . . . that they place proper emphasis on protection of Indian lands, concern as to the readiness of the Indians for release, the ability and willingness of states to assume Indian burdens, and adequate safeguards for Indian welfare and future prospects'.[91]

Undermined by budget cuts, reformer differences and conflicting evidence coming in from the field about the desirability or feasibility of 'emancipation', the bureau shifted from opposition to a stance akin to the federation's.[92] This accommodating position was outlined in a *Policy Statement* of 1947, produced by the Secretary of the Interior and building on suggestions made by William Zimmerman, the Acting Commissioner of Indian Affairs during Brophy's absences due to sickness. The statement listed a group of some 53,000 Indians (see Table 4.1, List A) who might be immediately released from federal 'subsidy and supervision in whole or in large part under some form of corporate organisation suited to the present economic conditions of the group and the nature and status of their holdings'. It was predicted that tribes comprising about 73,000 individuals (see Table 4.1, List B)

TABLE 4.1   Tribes grouped according to supposed readiness for 'emancipation', 1947

List A Reservation	State	List B Reservation	State	List C Reservation	State
Flathead	Montana	Blackfeet	Montana	Cheyenne and Arapaho	Oklahoma
Hoopa Valley	California	Cherokee	North Carolina		
Klamath	Oregon	Cheyenne River	South Dakota	Choctaw	Mississippi
Menominee	Wisconsin	Colville (subject to restoration of ceded lands)	Washington	Colorado River	Arizona
Mission	California			Consolidated Ute	Colorado
New York	New York			Crow Creek	South Dakota
Osage	Oklahoma			Five Tribes	Oklahoma
Potawatomi	Kansas	Consolidated Chippewa	Minnesota	Fort Apache	Arizona
Sacramento	California			Fort Berthold	North Dakota
Turtle Mountain (conditionally)	North Dakota	Crow	Montana	Fort Hall	Idaho
		Fort Belknap	Montana	Hopi	Arizona
		Fort Peck	Montana	Jicarilla	New Mexico
		Fort Totten	North Dakota	Kiowa	Oklahoma
		Grand Ronde-Siletz	Oregon	Mescalero	New Mexico
		Great Lakes	Wisconsin	Navajo	Arizona and New Mexico
		Northern Idaho	Idaho		
		Quapaw (in part Wyandot Seneca)	Oklahoma	Pawnee	Oklahoma
				Pima	Arizona
				Pine Ridge	South Dakota
				Quapaw (in part)	Oklahoma
		Taholah Tulalip (consolidation in part)	Washington	Red Lake	Minnesota
				Rocky Boy	Montana
				Rosebud	South Dakota
		Tomah	Wisconsin	San Carlos	Arizona
		Umatilla	Oregon	Sells	Arizona
		Warm Springs	Oregon	Seminole	Florida
		Wind River (Shoshoni only)	Wyoming	Shawnee	Oklahoma
				Sisseton	South Dakota
		Winnebago	Nebraska	Standing Rock	North Dakota
				Taholah Tulalip (in part)	Washington
				Tonge River	Montana
				Truxton Canyon	Arizona
				Uintah and Ouray	Utah
				United Pueblos	New Mexico
				Western Shoshoni	Nevada
				Wind River (Arapaho only)	Wyoming
				Yakima	Washington

Source: Taken, without most of the lists' marginal notes, from *Policy Statement*, 25 March 1947 (see note 93)

would be in that position in five or ten years' time, while a further group (see Table 4.1, List C) would require federal 'aid and protection' for perhaps ten to fifteen years. Indians could renounce their tribal or federal status, provided that in the case of the removal of trust restrictions on property held for them by the United States, they relinquished claims on the federal government for further services. Other federal agencies, together with state and local authorities, were to be encouraged to assume extra responsibilities in the areas of education, welfare, and law and order before the federal government withdrew its services. And assurances were given that there would be no abandonment of government trusteeship until it could be seen that the release of lands would not result in the wholesale losses that followed the Dawes Act of 1887. The fact that the lists had been prepared without the knowledge and agreement of those who appeared on them in fact rendered all assurances valueless.[93]

Each year between 1949 and 1953, similar commitments were made by the BIA to what became popularly known as 'termination'. On each occasion it was stressed that the bureau would only terminate its responsibilities for the Indians after paying due regard to their wishes and circumstances, implementing preparatory reservation development programmes, respecting existing treaty and property rights and guaranteeing basic services to the Indians from some source. But hostile politicians and advocates of tribal sovereignty alike found it difficult to believe bureau protestations that it was reducing its role. The magnitude of the appropriations it requested to carry out its transfer programme seemed to indicate the opposite. So, too, did the very large number of tribes on the BIA's list for whom termination was considered to be a fairly distant prospect, and the emphasis in its literature upon the difficulties involved in 'orderly withdrawal'.

Indicative of the bureau's dilemma were the spirited debates during the early 1950s about the BIA involvement in reservation law enforcement and about whether it was denying Indians the attorneys of their own choice. Commissioner Myer might argue that he merely wanted to prevent the tribes from 'being victimised by unscrupulous attorneys' and that the Indians exercised their rights 'frequently and vigorously . . . as the files of the Bureau will amply testify'. Yet to the tribes, and to such allies as the ACLU, Ickes, Collier and Cohen, who had now left the Interior Department and was able to express himself more forthrightly than ever, the bureau, headed by a man who had no previous experience in Indian affairs, was providing an example of 'Colonialism: U.S. Style'. In fact BIA spokesmen recognized that the existing tribal councils were 'usually lacking in adequate responsibility in handling economic matters, and often lack the confidence of Indians themselves'. What they failed to do was to acknowledge their share of responsibility for this state of affairs and to suggest constructive remedies. For their part, many tribes continued to complain about bureau interference with their funds, lands and elections and to press for more control over the BIA. They also wanted aid of all kinds: complete 'emancipation' was not their goal.[94]

As the patience of Congress started to run out and the bureau's own organization had been geared up to action on the state level, it is not surprising that BIA officials began termination negotiations in a piecemeal fashion, selecting tribes in California, Oregon and western

Washington, where it was thought that Indian resources and co-operation, plus state approval, would bring success.[95] In addition, Commissioner Myer co-operated willingly with efforts to extend state control over Indian schooling, health, and law and order matters and he condoned the leasing of Indian land and the negotiation of private Indian loans that undermined the tribes' economic viability.[96] Although President Eisenhower required Myer's resignation in March 1953, like-minded, generally western, politicians were suitably encouraged by such 'progress' and in July 1953 the House Concurrent Resolution 108 stated that the policy of Congress was to 'free Indians from federal control and supervision, end their wardship, and make them subject to the same laws and entitled to the same privileges as other citizens'.[97] To this end, Congress proposed the immediate termination of federal services and administration for the tribes of California, Florida, New York and Texas, together with five of the tribes proposed for termination in 1947. Shortly afterwards, Public Law 83–280 provided for the delegation of reservation jurisdiction to Alaska, Wisconsin (the Menominees apart), California, Minnesota (excluding the Red Lake reservation), Nebraska and Oregon (except for the Warm Springs reservation). Other states had the option of assuming civil and criminal jurisdiction over the tribes in the future and, with varying degrees of effectiveness and consultation of the Indians concerned, Nevada, North Dakota, South Dakota and Washington responded to the opportunity.

In the period from 1941 to 1953, the Indian Bureau had been the scapegoat for all the diverse interests that were dissatisfied with Indian policy and had certainly been as much of a hindrance as a help to the tribes. Indians had shown their willingness to act with other Americans during the Second World War and were moving in considerable numbers to the cities, partly in response to the government's relocation programme (see Chapter 11). The federal prohibition against supplying liquor to Indians was repealed in 1953 and its sale on reservations was allowed on a local option basis. Indians were also permitted to purchase firearms and, except on their trust property, they paid state and federal taxes just like non-Indians, something the bureau had long pointed out.[98] It was, then, perhaps little wonder that many American citizens, and especially those who saw economic opportunity in the offing or lived in areas where the Indians were not so numerous as to arouse prejudice, believed that with a little more effort than the bureau was evidently making, assimilation could be achieved.

The options posed were continuing wardship or individual freedom. At this time, whites did not regard self-determination through the tribe as a serious alternative and misunderstood the degree to which Indians remained different as a result of past agreements and present choice, rather than bureau coercion.[99] In view of the very recent creation of tribal governments and their various difficulties, reviewed above, such an attitude was as predictable as it was regrettable. After all, if the assimilation of minorities was seen as a necessity in a diverse nation and as the best option for white ethnics, which they themselves did not seriously dispute until the 1960s, why should it not be offered to the first Americans? The Canadian government, similarly pressed to solve its 'Indian problem', launched a comparable programme as late as 1969. Unfortunately, policy-makers in the United States were as vague about how termination would achieve assimilation as their predecessors had been about allotment. Indeed in some ways the two processes were very similar.

The termination policy was not implemented with the care and safeguards that Zimmerman had proposed and that reformers had originally suggested with regard to allotment, but was hastily applied to peoples who were in very different stages of readiness for 'emancipation' and who regarded it very differently. Termination did not end vast outlays of federal funds, any more than allotment had done. California, Nevada and Wisconsin memorialized Congress to continue federal direction of Indian services and the legislatures of New Mexico, Arizona, North Dakota and Montana requested additional federal aid for them.[100] After the United States Public Health Service took over full responsibility for Indian health care in 1954, its budget soared. Since health costs are clearly related to the circumstances of the citizens served, and Indian peoples are generally poorer and worse housed, and have larger families, than most whites, this situation is unlikely to change for the foreseeable future. Federal expenditure on adult education and the public schooling of Indian children likewise increased during the decade (see Chapter 9).

Far from becoming simpler to administer as a result of termination, Indian affairs merely acquired an additional level of complexity, rather as the Indian office bureaucracy had expanded to cope with the problems created by allotment. Far from forcing assimilation, termination, like allotment, perpetuated Indian distinctiveness. Even where termination brought the loss of tribal self-government and property, the Indian sense of separateness was preserved because Indian peoples continued to live together, united, as after 1887, by a heightened resentment of outsiders and a harsher experience of poverty. And as had been the case with the Dawes Act, though not with Wheeler-Howard, Indians' consent to a major change in their circumstances was dispensed with; between 1953 and 1958, termination was mandatory.[101]

All this is not to say that the bureau staff acted heartlessly in the 1950s, that termination touched more than a small minority of Indians, or that its results were identical from tribe to tribe. What is apparent, however, is that there was lack of strength at the top levels of the BIA. Just as the Allotment Act might have been very different if Senator Dawes had been a stronger character, so assimilationist pressures from Congress might have been moderated had the well-intentioned Commissioner Glenn Emmons (1953–61), appointed by President Eisenhower after consultation with the Indians, made them his first concern. Instead, he contented himself with genuine gains in the areas of health, education and urban employment.[102] As a result, in 1954 the bureau submitted proposals to comply with Resolution 108 and by 1955 Bills had been passed to terminate the Menominees in Wisconsin, the Klamaths in western Oregon, four groups of Paiutes on the Uintah and Ouray reservation in Utah and the Alabama-Coushattas in Texas. Other similar Acts followed, for example for the Wyandots, Peorias, Ottawas and Poncas. Between 1954 and 1960, 'sixty-one tribes, groups, communities, *rancherias*, or allotments were terminated',[103] and in Barsh and Henderson's judgement, 'instead of allotting tribal lands and subjecting them to state governance after a "trust" period, individual termination acts allotted tribal capital and subjected it to state governance after a transition period of one or two years'.[104]

The view from the BIA is predictably rather different. Feeling harassed by his superiors, Emmons adopted tactics which involved a blend of blarney and threats akin to that favoured by his predecessors. On the one hand, he maintained a fierce opposition to 'solutions' along the lines of the Omnibus Bill of the 1920s and to a swift abandonment of its responsibilities by the bureau.[105] On the other hand, he told the tribes that unless they produced termination programmes and thus prepared for the future, an impatient Congress might secure these dire developments when he was not around to fight against them.[106] According to the Commissioner, he had won the right for the tribes to keep their lands in common if they so wished,[107] and he was proud of having consulted the council leaders of every tribe in the United States and of having 'the greatest catalog of information regarding every tribe in the country that has ever been gathered in the history of the Bureau'.[108] But the conferences held by the BIA with the Indians revealed much that should have given it pause.

Tribal delegations which included women, whose importance in community work Emmons recognized, made it plain that they were worried about the pressure coming for termination from off-reservation Indians looking to benefit from *per capita* payouts.[109] They were concerned about dissipating their capital assets, or losing their land, water, hunting and fishing rights. And if a group like the Osages managed to make their opposition to termination quickly effective, the Sauk and Fox, the Nez Percés, the Fort Hall Indians and the Cherokees indicated that they were confused and disturbed about the policy. Individuals would say, 'Are they going to take our hospitals away from us . . . certain lands that we now own are going to be sold out from under us.' There was also Indian testimony to the effect that 'the Klamaths were very disappointed and sorry that they went out of Government supervision' and that the termination of the Menominees had been a mistake.[110]

The bureau's own employees indicated that the programme presented them with real difficulties. In California, it was reported that county and state as well as tribal personnel were uncertain about the implications of termination and that the various bands and groups were not organized for the range of activities they would have to carry out under the new order. In Tawa, Iowa, it was acknowledged that the Sauk and Fox Indians objected to termination because they feared injustice from local whites and because it would involve costs they could not meet, breach their treaties and destroy tribal integrity. Officials on the spot agreed with them. There were indications of divided counsels among the Minnesota Sioux and the superintendent at the Menominee agency in Neopit, Wisconsin, reported in 1954 that 'the Menominees, or at least their leaders, are violently opposed to withdrawal and have repeatedly stated at meetings "The Government and Congress want withdrawal, now let them do it as we don't want any part of it", which means that studied efforts are made to discredit or stop any attempts on the part of the Bureau or Bureau employees' to effect termination.

Elsewhere, BIA officials conceded that the Indian people were only 'partially prepared' for 'the transition from the trust status of property' and that although it had been hoped that resource development programmes would be devised for the reservations as a whole, only a few had been produced. Meanwhile, industry was reluctant to come to the reservations because of fears about government restrictions, a poor infrastructure, an unskilled labour supply and the isolation of Indian communities, while bureau personnel remained slow to share responsibilities with the Indians for fear of costly mistakes.[111] Having resigned itself to what it believed was inevitable, after a painful struggle, the BIA did not feel it could reverse its position. And so there were the customary reassurances and philosophical reflections on the discomfort implicit in change.

The positive argument for termination was said to be 'that the Indians are thereby exempted from certain disabilities under special Indian statutes, that integrated community services are frequently better services through consolidation than those afforded by the Bureau, and that achieving status in the community by removing the onus of being a minority in trusteeship portends acceptance for greater employment opportunities and security'.[112] In the case of the Menominees, since the tribe had petitioned for the extension of state law and order and appeared to wish to take over its own affairs, the role of bureau coercion and haste could be played down without too much embarrassment and the point made that 'we have never been under the illusion that these readjustment programmes would be painless'. In the case of the Klamaths, it was stressed that continuing federal supervision had been 'producing a very serious and deterimental sociological effect on the people' and in 1961 the bureau felt able to report fairly optimistically on progress with respect to the Klamaths, Menominees, and Ute mixed bloods of Utah.

None the less, by that time the BIA was obliged to admit that the tribes had objected to the speed of the federal withdrawal, that 'there has been a virtual breakdown of communication with the Indians on this subject' and that termination 'has become a kind of scare-word to many of the Indian people'. Commissioner Emmons issued a plaintive reminder that neither he nor the bureau staff had formulated Resolution 108.[113] But because the BIA was a constant, while public opinion changed and politicians promptly adjusted, the bureau naturally received much of the blame for termination once the greater tolerance for ethnic diversity which developed in the 1960s made its impact upon Indian affairs. The Association on American Indian Affairs, the Indian Rights Association and the National Congress of American Indians were united in condemning the programme. Various liberal journals added their criticisms and in 1966 a report by a private Commission on the Rights, Liberties, and Responsibilities of the American Indian, initiated in 1957, painted a very different picture of termination's effects than did the BIA.

Former Commissioner Brophy and Sophie D. Aberle, its compilers, showed how termination failed to clarify the remaining federal responsibilities towards the Indians, who were frequently saddled with inadequate local services and threatened water rights, impoverished by new state charges and baffled by new state regulations regarding such matters as registering to vote, hunting and fishing and obtaining welfare. During the transition to independence, or in groups where resources were still held in common, Indians were obliged to deal with unfamiliar private trustees who treated them with a familiar paternalism. The Paiutes consented to termination but, being ill-prepared for it, were demoralized in consequence, while the Klamaths speedily disposed of a large part of their rich land. The decision of a majority of the Klamaths to accept a *per capita* distribution of tribal assets can, of course, be described as their choice, and in fairness to the bureau, it had always opposed such distributions. Moreover, the few hundred Klamaths who rejected termination were allowed to organize as a trusteeship under state law. Yet the tribe had not been readied to handle its own affairs, which may explain the majority's decision and the subsequent inability of many Klamaths to manage the cash they received. As far as the Menominees were concerned, a new county and tribal corporation were set up and it was hoped that their property would be safeguarded and their existing prosperity enhanced. However, the prosperity of the tribe was in comparison to other tribes rather than to the whites of Wisconsin. The impact on the Menominees of local and state taxes, the ending of federal support and a speedy and massive community restructuring was dire. Poverty, unemployment and resentment were the immediate results of termination.[114]

By 1968, dissatisfaction with the programme was such that Congress ruled that existing transfers of jurisdiction could be reversed if the tribe and state concerned agreed, while future transfers could only take place after tribal plebiscites. In 1975, legislation was introduced to allow tribes to retrocede without state consent.[115] During the same year, Congress restored the Menominees to federal control, after extensive hearings in which it was admitted that termination had inhibited tribes from taking on certain responsibilities for fear that they would thereby show themselves ready for this fate, and that the complete collapse of Menominee Enterprises Inc. had only been averted by emergency federal and state aid. Such aid, by its very nature, had not tackled 'the basic causes of Menominee poverty: our lack of diversified industry, our dearth of economic opportunities, our negligible investment capital, and our inadequate tax base'.[116] The Canadian government, too, felt obliged to retreat from its effort at termination, for similar reasons.

From the 1960s onwards, the policy of the federal government has been to direct assistance to the reservations and to help the tribes to achieve self-determination without termination. As we shall see in Part Two, increasingly skilful Indian organizations and groups, helped by a period of national prosperity and responsiveness to minority interests, have won court victories, economic aid and an input into their own education which would have been unthinkable in the 1950s and which have strengthened their ability to resist future white coercion.[117] Would it therefore be fair to say that the assimilation crusade has failed outright, merely failed for the time being, or achieved some successes? Even if it is decided that the assimilationist efforts of Congress and the bureau have failed, are there factors which may yet revive their old objectives, or is assimilation for any large subgroup, simply an impossibility in a democracy?

Apart from the allotment and termination policies and the missionary pressures that we have noted in Part One, the best hopes for forcing assimilation were thought to be education, the imposition of Anglo family and sexual mores on Indian communities and the drawing of Indians from the reservations into the larger society. These efforts are assessed in Chapter 8, 9, 10 and 11. Where Indian independence seemed to have been assured by treaty, whites worked to subvert it by manipulating economic, political, judicial and racial factors to their advantage. This process is traced in Chapters 5 and 6, which detail the struggle between the Five Civilized Tribes, their black population and the intruding whites. The respectability long given to assimilationist pressures by anthropologists who knew Indian societies well and might have been able to challenge the prevailing wisdom of their day is discussed in Chapter 7. In Part One, I have tried to show that while some individuals were assimilated, whole groups were integrated and certain groups were destroyed, the Indian peoples as a whole were not assimilated. In Part Two, the same point is made.

By the 1960s and 1970s, Native Americans continued to be distinguished from the majority of Americans by their pride in Indian values and the Indian heritage. They were distinguished also by their poverty, paucity of supporting economic institutions and entrepreneurial traditions, large families, low median age, limited educational attainments and rewards from education, small middle class, peculiar relationship with the federal government, tribal organizations and special rights.[118] Thus as Price has pointed out, Indians differ from whites before the law in a number of ways. They are, for example, protected in their right to wear traditional clothing and long hair and may select their tribal leaders according to 'kinship and religious criteria'. The separation of church and state is not insisted upon in tribal governments, and tribes have the right to 'discriminate against non-Indians and hire Indians for tribal jobs'. Conversely, the states may not discriminate against them because of the tax-exempt status of their lands, or exclude them from participating on school boards and in school board elections because they do not 'own property within the school district'.[119]

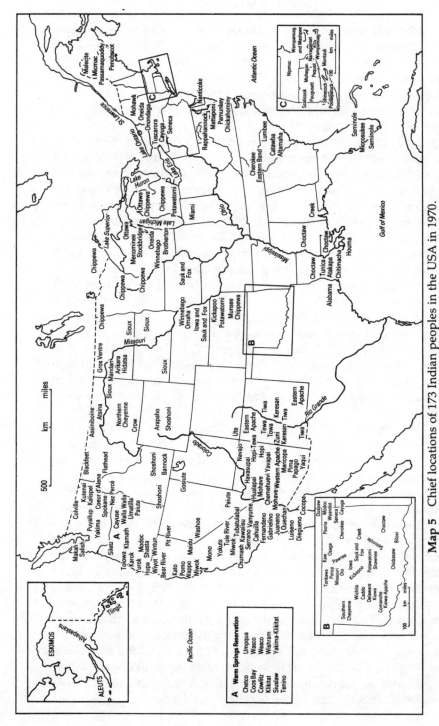

Map 5 Chief locations of 173 Indian peoples in the USA in 1970.

Source: S. Thernstrom (ed.), *Harvard Encyclopedia of Ethnic Groups* (Cambridge, Mass. and London: Belknap Press of Harvard University Press, 1980; 1981 edn); adapted from Theodore W. Taylor, *The States and their Indian Citizens* (Washington, DC, Bureau of Indian Affairs, 1972).

If assimilation is taken to mean the dispersal of the members of minority groups through the majority population, their adoption of majority customs and their acquisition of a similar lifestyle and statistical profile, then it has to be admitted that a great many minorities, and especially the non-white groups, have yet to be assimilated. Colour, class and particularly poverty, nationality reinforced by geographical concentration, language, religion and other distinguishing marks still survive as viable bases for ethnicity.[120] As is argued in the concluding Chapter 12, American Indians, like other minorities, have found political advantages in organizing themselves on the basis of race that they are unlikely to surrender, even if the *ideology* of racism against which they have campaigned may no longer serve its old purpose in a late capitalist country like the United States, which has 'substituted the free market for direct forms of discrimination'.[121] Many minority groups, and not just the Indians, are conscious of distinctiveness because they have suffered from wildly fluctuating government policies towards them.[122] The Irish as well as the Indians, Thomas Sowell reminds us, have learned that 'the political route to economic advancement' is a very uncertain one. In the process, they have been made to feel their peculiar circumstances.[123]

There may perhaps be a temptation to exaggerate the distinctiveness of ethnic group cultures. The attachment to land and religion, the dislike of bureaucracy and the suspicion of progress associated with Indian peoples may likewise be noticed among both southerners and many inhabitants of farm regions and small towns.[124] Similarly, the present-mindedness and desire for recognition within the local group, which are remarked upon in Indian communities, are to be found in many working-class cultures.[125] Nor should we ignore the differences between and within the minorities themselves. As far as Indians are concerned, those 'living in Chicago, New York or Detroit earn more than twice as much as Indians living on the reservations'.[126] And it can be argued that there is something artificial or commercialized about the ethnicity of the white ethnics, since its original material and institutional underpinnings have been greatly eroded with time.[127] Growing prosperity and confidence may have allowed white ethnics to take open pride in a past which was once a hindrance to them; but for some prosperous practitioners, ethnicity is only a weekend diversion, not a central fact of life.[128] We may also speculate that educational and transport improvements, socioeconomic mobility and the promotion of national consumption patterns through the media could again erode the ethnicity which it had become fashionable to celebrate by the 1960s.

Moreover, if equality in America no longer has to mean identity,[129] there may be dangers for Indians and other minorities in the ethnic resurgence. After a period of group assertion resulting in gains, there is a risk of backlash; and this risk will be magnified in difficult or complacent times. The signs of a backlash are apparent; the times are auspicious. Liberals calling themselves 'new conservatives' have joined old-style conservatives in criticizing what they have come to regard as the misguided and unduly costly liberal approaches to social problems during the 1960s.[130] The effects of the educational reforms, among others, have been deplored, and as Diane Ravitch has observed, bilingual instruction was never popular with the general public. Like affirmative action programmes, it raised a debate about 'the nature of equal opportunity and the question of compensatory justice' which it was difficult to conclude to national satisfaction.[131] Whereas Indian respect for the environment was praised and sentimentalized when ecological issues were looming large in American politics, there is evidence that Americans of and after what Tom Wolfe called the 'me decade' (the 1970s) may have come to terms with waste, pollution and the other social problems of their age in a less helpful and sympathetic fashion.[132] And there are indications that the continuing influx into the United States of large numbers of immigrants from Mexico, Cuba, Haiti, Central America and South East Asia is once more making established Americans less friendly towards celebrations of ethnicity, because of the economic and sometimes diplomatic tensions that the newcomers create.

It is quite possible that sympathy with ethnicity will decline while the drawbacks attached to it, at least for non-whites,[133] will remain. Even now, those who want to achieve status in American society must conform to the norms of the 'dominant Anglo-Bourgeois core culture'.[134] Even now, Americans are more sympathetic to 'harmless' cultural 'survivals' among ethnic groups than they are to altering the rules of society to the benefit of such groups. In general, American Indians have valued other things more highly than status. We should not therefore underestimate the desire of many Indians to change those aspects of their distinctiveness that are rooted in poverty and powerlessness. Nor should we ignore the fact that their combination of colour and lower-class status still makes most Indians vulnerable to arguments that assimilation could be in their own best interests. The small size of the Indian population – there are about 1.2 million Native Americans, compared to approximately 2 million Asians, 15 million Mexican Americans and 27 million blacks – means that the task may seem manageable to the large numbers of whites who have not yet conceded that assimilation, if it is to be achieved without an uncivilized degree of coercion, can only be accomplished on a voluntary basis.

PART TWO

The Case Studies

5

Slavery, Red and Black

Slavery has been practised in most civilizations throughout history and survives to the present in some parts of the world. It should therefore come as no surprise to learn, as the pioneering work of Almon Lauber demonstrated, that the institution was to be found among the Native Americans even before the coming of the white men encouraged its expansion and elaborate justification in the New World. Its stronghold in what is now the United States was the Pacific Northwest, although it also existed elsewhere, notably among the Iroquois. Yet while reliable figures are unobtainable, the numbers involved do not appear to have been large. The ownership of as many as ten slaves by a household was uncommon. Considerable numbers might be captured – for example, 300 or 400 at a time in the Iroquois raids on Ohio country – but the mortality rate among them was high since they were reduced to a shameful and hapless condition. In Indian societies where clan membership was vital for acceptance, excluded slaves were, as Theda Perdue points out with regard to the Cherokees, anomalies who simply strengthened the group consciousness of their owners.

The terms 'prisoner' and 'slave' were often interchangeable in the writings of early white commentators on Indian bondage, which increases the difficulty of estimating its extent, and the Indians of the Pacific Northwest evolved a distinctive kind of debt slavery for their own people. However, it seems clear that the enforced tribal adoption of captives did not necessarily entail their enslavement and not all prisoners became slaves. Captives were taken to restore depleted tribal populations and replace fallen kinsmen. Slavery generally resulted from warfare, supplemented by extensive slave trafficking and increasingly by organized slave raids. Those seized appear to have largely escaped the stigma of 'innate' inferiority and automatic servitude for life; they might hope, indeed, to be redeemed for ransom by their relatives. And slavery among Indians further differed from the system which developed in the southern states in that slaves, who were commonly women and children, had no special economic function which might simultaneously increase their value to owners and make their emancipation more difficult.[1]

Early white settlers in various parts of North America were quick to see the utility of Indian servitude. Faced with enormous opportunities which they could not exploit unaided and short of labour to perform immediate tasks, the immigrants enslaved the natives who opposed them and acquired additional bondsmen through the slave trade. Indian tribes supplied the traders by means of raids or the sale of runaways, receiving guns, ammunition and other coveted goods in return. During an era before large-scale plantation agriculture, the slaves taken were used as guides and interpreters, household servants, carriers of burdens, hunters, fishermen and farm labourers. White traders, with the aid of Indian slaves, extended their control of the interior and Indian enslavement helped to clear areas for white settlements.[2]

Efforts made by the distant Spanish authorities after 1543 to terminate Indian slavery in their American possessions were unsuccessful, and while some anxiety about the fate of Christian Indian bondsmen was shown by the French Jesuit missionaries, French pronouncements against trading in Indian slaves and holding Christians in slavery were likewise ineffective. In the English colonies, too, greed and prejudice restrained any widespread revulsion against Indian slavery, though according to Lauber there is no evidence that the English in the metropolis knew of its existence. More plausibly, Gary B. Nash notes that the rapid growth of the Indian slave trade caused shock and consternation in London.[3] The news of Indian servitude was conveyed there by merchants as well as missionaries appealing for support from the civil and religious authorities; and by prominent individuals like John Eliot, Morgan Godwyn, George Fox and John Wesley, publicizing it to the small reading public of their day as a state which, at the very least, threatened to cut men off from the 'means of grace'.[4]

Such commentators were, none the less, more concerned to censure slaveholders than to discuss their slaves and frequently avoided condemnation of slavery itself. Their protests may have strengthened the main anti-slavery movement from the end of the eighteenth century, but settlers determinedly sustained Indian slavery, despite the security considerations which seem to have led Virginia, South Carolina, Rhode Island and New York to forbid the importation of native bondsmen, or ban the system altogether.[5] If black slavery became increasingly important in the English colonies by the middle of the eighteenth century, blacks were valued over Indians not because the cultural attributes of the tribes were held in greater esteem but because their large numbers, unfamiliarity with America, greater suitability for agricultural work, distant capture and consequent lack of resentful local connections made Africans more viable subjects for enslavement. Indian and black slavery was covered by a common body of legislation, the treatment endured by each set of slaves was much the same and the justifications of their condition were similar.[6]

Consequently, all the colonies still had a few Indian slaves by the Revolutionary period and Missouri as late as the 1830s.[7] In the Southwest, Indian slaves were traded and provided household labour for whites until the 1860s. The holding of Indian slaves by other Indians also continued in the Pacific Northwest during the nineteenth century, being most prevalent in the Columbia River region.[8] Meanwhile, long before this time, the southern Indians were beginning to exploit the existence of black slaves for their own benefit. It will be the purpose of this chapter and the next to examine why and how they did so and to assess both the impact of the peculiar institution on Indian–black relations and the general nature of that relationship.

I

THE ORIGINS AND DEVELOPMENT OF
BLACK SLAVERY AMONG THE FIVE TRIBES

Adoption of black slavery by the southern tribes came as a result of white example and pressure in the colonial period. Blacks fled into tribal territory to escape bondage to whites and were brought in by white traders, officials and settlers. As the number of intermarried whites and mixed bloods increased in the eighteenth century, so did the number of black slaves. By the early years of the American republic, when game and traditional hunting grounds had dwindled and the Indians were exhorted to farm as part of the government's civilization programme, the mixed bloods especially could see the value of black slaves for agricultural labour, housework and personal services. White traders were happy to deal with their Indian contacts for black as well as Indian slaves. Tribes like the Chickasaws, Creeks and Cherokees, who had traded in Indian slaves, proved willing to switch to dealing in blacks and to stealing black slaves from their enemies, while blacks who would once have been traded back to the whites, under treaty agreements in the case of the Creeks and Cherokees, might instead be kept by the Indians.

There was some variation, however, in the immediate response of the southern Indians to slaveholding opportunities, notwithstanding the similarity of their material cultures, their comparable polities and the close affinity between the languages of the Choctaws and Chicka-saws, and the Creeks and Seminoles. As members of a notoriously warlike tribe, with a fairly clear sexual division of labour which allotted to women the agricultural tasks, Chickasaw men and women alike could see excitement and advantage in the traffic. By contrast, the Seminoles' small numbers, isolation and fierce opposition to removal from Florida made them attract and welcome black runaways from enslavement by southern whites. Many of the fugitives they emanci-pated; some they continued to hold as slaves. The martial and more numerous Creeks were similarly criticized by their white neighbours for harbouring black runaways; but Daniel Littlefield has shown that they had no need, and hence apparently no wish, to receive the blacks as allies or, until the Revolutionary War, as slaves.

The numbers of slaves and slaveowners in the Five Tribes before removal also varied considerably, albeit they were a minority in each nation. By 1837, there were 1,156 black slaves and five or six thousand Indians in the Chickasaw nation. Mixed bloods were the major owners, but there was some full-blood possession of blacks. The Choctaws never had as many slaves or masters, though their mixed-blood owners were comparably important and a few individuals each owned a considerable number of bondsmen. Censuses taken in 1831 revealed 521 slaves (or 248, the figures are discrepant) in a population of over 19,500. By about 1811 there were more black slaves than whites in Cherokee territory and by 1825 there were 1,227 slaves out of a total population of 15,160. A census of the Cherokees still in the East in 1835 reported 1,592 slaves and revealed that twenty citizens held 20 or more slaves, with two of them owning 100 and 110 respectively. Over 80 per cent of the Indian slaveholders possessed less than 10 slaves and mixed-blood owners were again prominent, as they were among the Creeks, whose Upper Towns supported a population of 14,142 in 1832, including 445 slaves, and whose Lower Towns contained 8,552 people, including 457 slaves. Most of the Creek slaveholders held fewer than 10 blacks. In Florida, probably for fear of arousing the covetousness of white or Indian outsiders, the Seminoles declined to disclose the number of blacks in their midst. The total may have been anything between 800 and 1,000 to some 5,000 Seminoles by the early 1820s, of whom perhaps 200 were slaves.[9]

Despite the minority status of the black slaves and their Indian owners, they had a profound effect on the culture and foreign relations of the Five Tribes. Communal Indian agriculture was under-mined and the value of Indian landholdings was enhanced in the eyes of the whites. The fact that the Cherokees, Chickasaws and Choctaws were operating successful plantations by the nineteenth century, that

Indians were in fact among the bigger slaveowners in Georgia during the 1820s and 1830s, made whites covet their land and press for Indian removal. The ownership of slaves and the use of them as an article of trade enhanced the power of the mixed bloods, particularly in the Cherokee, Choctaw and Chickasaw nations. Black bondsmen allowed them to enjoy the fruits of a new economic order whose emphasis on sustained manual labour was alien to their way of life, while their wealth and command of English gave them the advantage over other Indians in tribal politics and the increased dealings with whites which slavery entailed.[10]

The slaves themselves, because they both spoke English and learned Indian languages, served to strengthen Indian links with the larger society and acted as intermediaries between Indian and white cultures. This was especially true of Creek, Seminole and Chickasaw slaves.[11] In addition, as English speakers, interpreters and slaves to be pitied, blacks attracted the attention of missionaries, something which improved and yet complicated their position. Missionaries improved the blacks' lot by offering them the prospect of a rudimentary education and membership of a faith to which they might already have been introduced. They complicated it because, as representatives of the white way of life, missionaries eventually received some of the blame for removal, and where they were not particularly welcomed by the Indians in the first place, their black converts were poorly regarded. Hence slavemasters among the Creeks, who 'furnished an uninviting field' to evangelists, 'bitterly persecuted' slaves won to Christianity, though it is not clear whether this treatment sprang from a dislike of any manifestation of white power, a fear that missionaries were inclined to abolitionism, or a more specific cruelty on the part of Indian slaveowners.[12]

The relationship between the Five Tribes, and between the Indians and their white neighbours, was strained as a result of black slavery, with difficulties being most pronounced for the Creeks and Seminoles. The whites lost slaves to the Creeks, who in turn lost blacks to the Seminoles in Florida, developments which the whites and Creeks resented. The Creeks likewise objected to white attempts – made on the grounds that the Creeks and Seminoles had originally been one people – to hold them responsible for slaves who fled from white masters into Florida. At the end of the Red Sticks War of 1813–14, in which the Creeks offered their last serious resistance to American encroachments, the Red Stick Creeks were not above seeking the aid of black fugitives (and British renegades) in an abortive attempt to stave off defeat. But the subsequent flight of the Red Sticks to Florida formalized and widened the Creek–Seminole rift and in 1821, by the

Treaty of Indian Springs, the Creeks were obliged to give up more land in Georgia and pay for the blacks who had absconded or been seized by the British during the recent war.[13] For their part, the Seminoles paid for their complaisant reception of blacks, first when the lax Spanish were ousted from Florida by security-conscious Americans and secondly when whites tried to contain the threat they feared from a mixed race community by confining the Seminoles to a reservation after 1823 and extracting from them a promise to return black runaways. Unhappily, since Florida's governor took the part of whites in all disputes over blacks, while whites continued to pour into the region, racial tensions persisted and pressure for Indian removal grew until, in 1832, partial Seminole consent was given to move West and there reunite with the Creeks.[14]

Information about day-to-day contacts between Indians and blacks before removal is scarcer than it is for the years in the West, but there seem to have been some differences from tribe to tribe. Within the Cherokee nation, slaves were used to look after cattle, horses, sheep, pigs and goats, to grow cotton, indigo, tobacco, corn, wheat, oats, potatoes and fruit and to work in private houses as well as such small ventures as taverns, mills and ferries. The slaveowners treated their blacks as property and emulated the plantation society of the South, as far as they could, but not so severely as to provoke their bondsmen to abscond.[15] Creek slaves, too, were regarded as property, raised crops, tended animals and carried out a range of other jobs. But they appear to have enjoyed rather more freedom in a community which was still not greatly affected by white customs. The blacks were allowed to acquire personal property, to rear fowl and produce their own food and to enjoy freedom of movement.[16]

Even better were the conditions experienced by the Seminole blacks. The runaways settled in separate communities, Spanish slaveowners in Florida were willing to let their slaves purchase their freedom and Seminole chiefs who bought black slaves permitted them to live in their own villages on payment of a tribute of grain or livestock. Given control over their own time to a unique degree, they cultivated fields and owned crops and livestock, while dressing, eating and living very much like their Indian hosts. The various groups of blacks intermarried with each other and there was some mixing with the Seminoles, the children of the latter unions being free. It is not directly known what blacks made of these circumstances. However, their behaviour in fleeing to Florida and later resisting removal from the region suggests that they recognized their good fortune. Their relative immunity from sale, economic exploitation and harsh punishment seems to have more than compensated for the personal and community comforts some southern slaves must have sacrificed in joining a poor, scattered and embattled tribe.[17]

There were other factors which should have made it possible for those of African and southern Indian background to coexist agreeably in the early nineteenth century. As Perdue has pointed out, kin relationships were carefully respected in both cultures. In both, there was a widespread dependence upon subsistence agriculture and a determination to live harmoniously with nature.[18] Possibly because of these affinities, some amalgamation of the races took place in all the southern tribes and there was no elaborate justification of the peculiar institution as a positive good.[19] Yet self-interest not sentiment appears to have governed the connection of the southern tribes with their blacks, just as it determined Indian–black relations on the Texas frontier. There, as Kenneth Porter's researches demonstrate, the local Indians' treatment of blacks varied according to whether, like the Comanches, they associated them with the alien life of whites and sedentary Indians, or whether, as sometimes happened with women, children and co-operative captives, a use could be found for them within the tribe concerned. It is Porter's contention that Texas Indians did not feel 'any hostility for the negro on a racial basis'. The response of the southern Indians, whose contacts with blacks and whites were more extensive, was different; it was similarly calculating. Thus if the Five Tribes did not originally think of themselves or strangers in terms of race, their laws indicate that their attitudes changed with circumstances and that they eventually came to do so. A record of these laws exists for the Creeks and Cherokees prior to removal and in the West for the Choctaws and Chickasaws as well. Only the Seminoles did not produce a slave code, an omission explained by their failure, as the least acculturated of the Five Tribes, to adopt a written constitution before the Civil War.

The proceedings of the Creek Council survive from 1818, and the laws of the Lower Creeks, particularly from 1825, suggest that the Indian attitudes to blacks were less than benign. A black who killed an Indian suffered death, whereas an Indian killing a slave had to compensate his owner. Intermarriage between the races was stigmatized, and the slaves were forbidden to own property. But it is difficult to discover how far these laws were enforced and how the Upper Creeks treated their blacks, though their greater distance from the large concentration of blacks in Seminole country and their greater freedom from coercion by neighbouring whites may explain the Upper Creeks' apparently larger tolerance towards slaves.[20]

The Cherokees east of the Mississippi left written laws from as early as 1808, established a national council in 1817, a supreme court in 1822 and a constitution in 1827, institutions which survived removal, so that there is more formal evidence of developing attitudes to slavery among the Cherokees than exists for the remaining southern Indians. Whereas Cherokee owners at first permitted their slaves to attend school and tolerated miscegenation, in the 1820s they moved to punish black–Indian intermarriage; to prevent livestock ownership by slaves; to discourage black runaways from seeking freedom or an improvement of their lot in the Cherokee nation by forbidding them to own property or stay without a permit; to bar blacks from any role in tribal government; and to provide for the whipping of blacks found guilty of misdemeanours – having no money, they could not pay the fines levied from Indian malefactors. Slave patrols were also active from the 1820s. Assessing the impact of such developments, and the reasons behind them, is not an entirely straightforward matter.

According to Cotterill, the Cherokees alone of the southern Indians had any aversion to 'zambos' (the product of black fathers and Indian mothers), and Halliburton maintains that they 'were exhibiting a strong color consciousness' as early as the 1740s. This prejudice may have resulted from the Cherokees' pride in their own position as the biggest and best-known tribe of southern Indians and from their growing association with southern whites and adoption of aspects of white civilization. The Cherokees may also have been anxious to prevent neighbouring whites from pursuing their fugitive slaves into the tribal domain and to reassure them that they were 'sound' about the peculiar institution. There is some missionary evidence that Cherokee masters were lax about applying the laws, but evangelists may simply have been trying to present Indian society favourably to their eastern financial backers, who were often critical of slavery. What is clear, as Perdue has noted, is that the Cherokees' slave laws were not so elaborate as those of the southern states, frequently penalized the masters rather than the slaves and punished women who engaged in interracial sex – an anathema to southern whites – less severely than men. The Cherokee government was still not as geared up to interfere in citizens' affairs as the southern state governments were where slavery was concerned.[21]

II

Black Slaves During and After Removal

When whites forced removal west of the Mississippi on the southern Indians, the slaveholders were blamed by conservative tribesmen for embroiling them in white affairs and contributing to their dispossession. The slaveholders were then favourably placed or treated during the removal process, which aggravated these factional divisions among the Five Tribes and so added to their difficulties in Indian Territory. Cherokee, Choctaw and Chickasaw slaveowners were able to sell eastern assets accumulated with the aid of blacks. Choctaw and Chickasaw masters received land grants in the East, which they sold to buy slaves, and subsequently moved their blacks westwards aided by a *per capita* allowance from the government. Certain Indians purchased slaves to trade to other migrants on their arrival in the West and with slave labour new plantations were begun and the economic suffering caused by removal was eased, albeit there were individuals who never recouped their fortunes. Furthermore, black services made the actual migration more bearable for the Indians then it would otherwise have been.[22]

Although the Creeks were able to benefit from slave labour in the West, they did not have as many blacks to take with them as the Chickasaws, Cherokees and Seminoles, while Creeks who wished to remain in the East were harassed by white speculators who wanted their lands and used black slaves to hunt out the Indian owners of unsold allotments and pressure them into selling.[23] A number of the Creeks who stubbornly remained in Alabama were even reduced to slavery themselves, from which state not all were ransomed by their western brethren: a supremely galling fate for people who had taken pride in the fact that 'We have never been slaves.'[24] The position of the Seminoles was yet more complicated. Between 1835 and 1842, Indians and blacks in Florida fought together against removal, with whites arguing that the blacks had 'a controlling influence over their masters' and that the war was 'a negro, not an Indian' conflict. Such comments reflect white fears and do less than justice to Indian resistance. Just the same, the Seminoles did rely on trusted black allies and were reluctant to surrender them, whether because of friendship, kin ties, or fear of weakening the tribe, and hundreds of plantation slaves fled to Florida during the war. Some of the plantation blacks may have joined the Seminoles in pure relief, since Florida masters had a reputation for cruelty; some showed by their prompt surrender to American troops that they had regretted their decision when conditions proved tough. But, in the end, many recent black runaways in addition to established Indian blacks and free blacks won the right to emigrate to Indian Territory with the Seminoles. So, too, did blacks taken from Creek mercenaries; the Indians had fought in the war for the whites on the understanding that they could keep the blacks they captured and their dispossession was the cause of much future friction between Seminoles and Creeks. Perhaps five hundred blacks in all went with the Indians across the Mississippi.[25]

Once in the West, as Littlefield has pointed out, the blacks became less a source of strength to the Seminoles than a source of anxiety and race relations worsened. Indians who had surrendered and removed from Florida expected protection for their slave property in the Indian Territory; blacks expected freedom. When blacks were restored to Seminole owners or seized and sold into slavery by disgruntled Creeks, and unscrupulous white traders provided a ready market for captives or kidnapped blacks who came their way, some slaves were driven to join the prominent Seminole, Coacoochee or Wild Cat, in his attempt to found a colony on the Mexican side of the Rio Grande in 1849–50, to the dismay of Arkansas, Creek and Cherokee slaveholders. For their part, the Seminoles were driven to oppose that union with the Creeks which the US government was determined to force upon them, being finally granted an independent terrain in the West in 1856.[26]

After removal, from the late 1830s through the 1850s, the Creeks, Cherokees, Choctaws and Chickasaws evolved more elaborate and severe slave codes. The Creeks set out to curb slave violence, miscegenetion, the harbouring of runaway blacks and the emancipation of slaves. They taxed free blacks, restricted the slaves' freedom of movement and forbade them to carry weapons, engage in business, or 'preach to an Indian congregation'. The free time in which they had once raised food and made clothes for themselves was ended and in March 1861 an edict was even passed to enslave free blacks, who were required 'legally to choose their owners' or 'be sold to the highest bidder', whites excluded.[27] The Chickasaws laid it down that the council should not emancipate slaves without owner consent and compensation,[28] and the Choctaws passed an identical law, besides acting to prevent blacks from obtaining education, property, or public office, and subjecting them to a special criminal code. In the 1840s the Choctaws moved to exclude free blacks from annuity benefits and in the 1850s the Chickasaws sought to expel theirs.[29] Among the Cherokees, the pre-removal ban on black political rights was upheld, Indian–black intermarriage was prohibited, property ownership by slaves was disallowed and legislation elaborated the power of slave patrols, provided for the punishment of slave violence, forbade free blacks and slaves to carry arms, made it illegal to trade with slaves or teach them to read and write, prohibited the introduction of liquor into the nation by slaves and free blacks, banned free blacks 'not of Cherokee blood' from acquiring improvements in Cherokee territory and tried to oblige blacks not emancipated by Cherokee citizens to quit the nation, those remaining to be answerable to their masters.[30]

There are many factors behind this spate of legislation. It was evidently thought necessary to strengthen the institution of slavery after the upheaval of removal and in the lawless conditions that prevailed in Indian Territory. Slaveowners in the Cherokee nation had been disturbed by slave uprisings in 1841 and 1842 and a threatened revolt in 1846, while Creek masters had been dismayed by the absconding of some two hundred slaves in 1842. Southerners dominated the BIA posts in Indian Territory and may have reinforced the fears and racial prejudices of mixed-blood slaveholders in the Cherokee, Choctaw and Chickasaw nations. Given the close ties between the Choctaws and Chickasaws in the West from 1837 to 1856, when the latter adopted an independent constitution, one would expect them to have devised similar rules regarding their slaves; after all, Choctaws and Chickasaws married each other, settled on each other's land and owned blacks who were linked by marriage. The Creeks may have been influenced by knowledge of the laws adopted by the Choctaws, Chickasaws and Cherokees, besides being concerned to show Cherokee blacks that flight to Creek country would not improve their position, and the more tolerant Seminoles that they meant to preserve the institution of slavery. As abolition gained ground in America and missionaries from the anti-slavery North increased their activities in Indian Territory, the harsher laws may also have been designed as a reassurance to whites in the bordering slave states of Texas, Arkansas and Missouri, and an indication to would-be abolitionists that their cause was hopeless in the Territory. Finally, there was a desire to discourage southern black runaways from entering Indian country, either because the free black community was seen as too large and dangerous or in order to cut down the disturbances connected with the white pursuit of such runaways, which was common long before it was legalized under the terms of the US fugitive slave law in 1854.[31]

Unfortunately, we cannot determine the exact role played by white pressures, Indian prejudices, security and material considerations in stiffening the slave laws, though we shall see later that the abolitionist threat was exaggerated, and it can be established that, with the exception of the Cherokee edicts, the Indian codes did not match their southern counterparts in severity and complexity while the official enforcement machinery was less relied upon to give them effect. Nor can we generalize about the legislation's impact on the fate of the free black community in Indian Territory, about which comparatively little is known. It is nevertheless plain that if the Cherokee free black element dwindled, free blacks were not frightened into leaving Indian country *en masse*. Indeed, they appear to have continued to live much like, if generally apart from, the non-slaveholding Indians and their

159

numbers were still augmented both by runaways and emancipated slaves, for Indian masters did not entirely cease to liberate their bondsmen in the West. Accordingly, records from 1866 relating to male and female Creek free blacks at the outbreak of the Civil War indicate that they often possessed considerable property, whatever the slave code may have stipulated. Cow Tom, for instance, a leader of Canadian Town blacks, who was 'considered quite well off, and had everything comfortable about him', claimed, in broadly corroborated testimony, to have lost 10 horses, 11 oxen, 75 cows and calves, 60 steers, 110 hogs, 50 bushels of corn, house and kitchen furniture, harnesses and farming implements in the course of the war.[32] As far as slaves and masters are concerned, it seems fair to say that while the new laws signalled that slavery in Indian Territory was becoming more like that in the South, the two systems differed in some respects right up to the 1860s and in neither region did uniform conditions prevail.

Let us look first at the similarities between Indian and southern slavery. Overseers were used on Indian plantations which produced a surplus and these were concentrated along rich, river-bottom land. Slaveowning made possible the production of corn, cotton and cattle for export and slaves were hired out and employed in domestic service and a wide variety of enterprises, as well as on the land. The Cherokees, Choctaws and Chickasaws had a contemporary reputation as severe masters, mainly because of the importance in these nations of mixed-blood slaveholders; in fact, it was reported that Chickasaw slaves frequently left their masters and had to be recovered, either from neighbouring Choctaws or, for ransom, from the Shawnees and Delawares.[33] But it is important to note that slave circumstances in all the Five Tribes varied with the qualities of individual masters and over time, with kind and brutish masters to be found in each nation, as the twentieth-century slave narratives make plain.[34] The break-up of families through sales was common; so, too, was the sexual abuse of female slaves by their masters and the pairing of slaves without formal marriage ceremonies. Many slaves were ignorant of their antecedents. They might be given their masters' names, unusual names, or a single name only, while elderly bondsmen were called 'aunt' and 'uncle' and might be treated as aged retainers. Even among the fairly independent Seminole blacks, 'quaint names may be found ... such as: Slavery Pompey, Human Carolina, Pinchie Cudjoe, Caesar Bowlegs, and many others. Cicero, Cato and other good old Roman names may be found in abundance.' The final roll of Seminole freedmen, years after slavery was abolished, contains references to Pompey, Venus, Minerva, Scipio and Samby.[35]

Slaves were possessed by a minority of Indians, just as they were owned by a minority of southerners. In 1860, approximately one Indian in fifty owned slaves in the Territory, as opposed to one in four southerners, and most owners in each area held comparatively few slaves. There were anywhere between a few hundred and a thousand blacks in the Seminole nation in 1860; 2,349 Choctaw slaves; 975 among the Chickasaws; over 2,500 Cherokee slaves; and 1,651 Creek bondsmen.[36] However, the political influence of the large slaveowners was crucial in both the South and Indian Territory, although the positions of the Indian full bloods and southern poor whites were not strictly equivalent; the Upper Creek full bloods, for example, exercised considerable power.

As a sign of their value, particularly by the 1850s, Territory slaves sold for as much as $1,000 and $1,500, albeit $700 to $800 was nearer the norm; these figures are not too out of line with slave prices in the South. In both regions, attempts were made to restrict the slaves' religious activities, though with owner permission slaves were allowed to attend mission church services in all the Five Tribes, much as southern slaves were welcome to the white man's religion on the master's terms. Moreover, southern and Indian blacks conducted their own brush arbour meetings, with local blacks preaching. In both regions, slavetraders and auctions operated, while bondsmen resisted, ran away and were punished. And racial segregation had not hardened into its post-Civil War mould: children of Territory slaves fraternized with those of whites and Indians, rather as children crossed the colour line in the slave South.

We should, nevertheless, notice certain differences between the two slave systems: differences which indicate that there existed, at least temporarily, some common ground between Indians and blacks, no matter how much whites might try to encourage in the Five Tribes the growth of their own brand of racial exclusiveness. Thus if Indians had adopted commercial farming through the use of black slavery, the Five Tribes did not use gang labour on the southern scale. Nor was the profitability of slavery as important to the Tribes. Transport and agricultural methods remained comparatively primitive in Indian country, although economic diversification was facilitated by slavery and there were some sophisticated producers. Because the Territory was situated to the north of the main cotton belt, commercial cotton production was less important than it had been before removal,[37] and leaving the minority of wealthy planters out of the picture, there was on the whole less contrast between the lifestyles of masters and slaves than prevailed in the southern states. In a developing area, where land and wild game were plentiful, material conditions were often such that the Indian bondsmen them-

161

selves liked to claim 'dat us niggers . . . didn't have to work so hard as dey did in de old states'.

The slaves of the Creeks and Seminoles especially enjoyed perks which were not entirely withdrawn amid the tensions of the 1850s. Creek bondsmen might accumulate property and buy freedom. They might never see their owners until harvest time, they were known to have been buried in the same graveyards as their masters and Littlefield suggests that the light horse police did not enforce the slave code. Neither Seminole nor Creek slaves were driven by overseers and Seminole slaves continued to live in separate communities after removal, hiring their own preachers and working at their own pace. Considerable Indian–black intermarriage took place in these two tribes and it persisted in the Cherokee, Choctaw and Chickasaw nations, notwithstanding Creek, Choctaw and Cherokee prohibitions.[38]

In terms of those classic tests of harmonious race relations – flexibility about social intercourse, social rising and intermarriage – the Indian Territory was an ethnocentric community before the Civil War, not a racist society as was the South. It was more akin to eighteenth-century than to nineteenth-century American slave communities. Yet blacks were one of the principal means of acculturating the Five Tribes during the antebellum years, outnumbering the white agents, travellers, traders, missionaries and soldiers to be encountered in Indian Territory, whose civilization they in some senses represented. Indian numbers in each tribe declined between the 1830s and 1860s, under the stress of removal; the number of whites increased in the same period, but they constituted no more than 5 per cent of the population in any of the five nations; whereas blacks, who had likewise grown in numbers, constituted 10 per cent of the Creek population, 14 per cent of the Choctaws, 15 per cent of the Cherokees and 18 per cent of the Chickasaws. (It is impossible to give an accurate estimate of the black percentage of the Seminole population.)[39]

The impact of blacks on Indian culture was greatest prior to removal but throughout the antebellum period they helped to widen the gulf between mixed bloods and full bloods, to strengthen and centralize Indian government, to undermine traditional attitudes to property and its disposal and, because they undertook what had been women's work, to subvert the ancient tribal divisions of labour. This, of course, is not to say that acculturation was a one-way process. Even in Indian Territory, the slaves' lives were to a large extent determined by their masters. The blacks' prospects of shaping an entirely independent Afro-American culture consequently suffered and the slave narratives make it obvious that the dress, language, marriage customs, food and leisure pursuits of the blacks were influenced by Indian practices.[40]

III

ABOLITION AND CIVIL WAR

Although the circumstances of blacks in the Five Civilized Tribes were generally worsening by the 1840s, the last decade before the Civil War was particularly demoralizing because of the mounting if misplaced fear of abolitionists in Indian Territory. Whereas the representatives of the American Board of Commissioners for Foreign Missions working with the Cherokees and Choctaws, and evangelists elsewhere in the Territory, actually felt obliged to tolerate slavery and its practitioners and to hire black slave labour at their missions, while Indian country was not troubled by an underground railroad, Indian slaveowners saw the missionaries as subversives, because of their willingness to educate and convert the blacks. Accordingly, in the 1830s and 1850s the Choctaw Council ruled that abolitionists should be expelled from tribal territory and the Creeks in the 1850s prohibited their schools from employing as teachers 'any holder of abolition principles'. But it was the slaveowning Cherokees, backed by southern officials and citizens of neighbouring Arkansas, who felt most strongly on the subject and with more cause than the other Five Tribes, since the missionary Charles Cutler Torrey and the Cherokee (Northern) Baptist mission led by the Reverends Evan and John B. Jones were actively opposed to slavery.

The Cherokees defended their right to own slaves, in emulation of whites; warned that anti-slavery agitation meant 'Brother . . . arrayed against brother'; and worried about a 'secret abolition organization' in their midst. In fact the organization alluded to, the Keetoowah Society of Pin Indians, though undoubtedly critical of the mixed-blood elite, supportive of Chief Ross (a major slaveholder!) and opposed to leaving the Union on the issue of slavery, was only a counterpart to similarly secret, but secessionist, groups among the more affluent slaveowners, known as the Blue Lodge and the Knights of the Golden Circle. More than a traditional alliance, it was probably less than an abolitionist association in the American sense; indeed, no such associations seem to have existed in Indian Territory, where slavery failed to excite opposition from the tribes on moral grounds and was never under serious threat. Loyalist sentiments were summed up in an 1864 petition to President Lincoln, which argued that the slavemasters, not the abolitionists, constituted the Cherokees' disturbing minority and criticized them for their attitude to the tribal government and support for southern traitors. Both sides to the dispute were right in seeing the debate over slavery as dangerously disruptive. It contributed to the withdrawal of American Board missionaries from the Choctaws and Cherokees between 1859 and 1860 and the Cherokee nation was drawn into the Civil War partly because of the peculiar institution. In the course of the conflict the Unionist element freed its slaves and its adversaries, led by Stand Watie, ignored the 1863 emancipation edict, despite the provision of heavy fines for non-compliance. The split of the Creeks into pro-North and pro-South factions was more straight-forwardly along traditional lines, with slaveholders and non-slaveholders in both factions.

Quite apart from their commitment to slavery and expectation that it would be abolished by the Lincoln government, it was hard for the Five Tribes to decide on the best course to follow when the Civil War came. They did not wish to jeopardize the investments and moneys held for them by the federal governemnt, but the Union had left Indian Territory without protection by the spring of 1861. By contrast, the Confederacy sought their support and guaranteed security for their borders and their slaves. Since the Five Tribes were southern, had received their agents and superintendent from the South and feared trouble from neighbouring Arkansas and Texas if they stayed aloof, it is little wonder that they yielded to the Confederate envoys. The Cherokees, Choctaws and Chickasaws, who were the closest neighbours of Arkansas and Texas, felt especially vulnerable, while the more removed Creeks and Seminoles were less responsive. None the less, between June and October 1861 the South secured agree-ments with all Five Tribes, though loyalist elements in each continued to operate.[41]

During the war, bitterness between old tribal factions intensified and 'Northern' Indians would kill their 'Southern' brethren when they got the chance. The slaveowners took their valuable investments south or left them behind as they entered Confederate service, with those thus abandoned or sympathetic to the Union either remaining true to their owners' families or heading north to what they hoped would be a safe refuge in Kansas. On the journey there, at the mercy of slave patrollers and bushwackers, many of the blacks recalled 'almost indescribable' suffering. On arrival, the refugees were downcast by the very cold weather, work proved scarce, except what was provided by the army, and they could earn practically no wages. Plantation agriculture in Indian Territory was predictably disrupted and the chaotic conditions made possible some of the slave revolts that had long been feared. Loyal blacks were terrorized by 'mixed bands of Indians and whites, in the Rebel Service' and the Union soldiers operating in the area often proved to be light-fingered opportunists rather than true emancipators.[42] Conditions having become so difficult for Territory blacks and Indians alike by 1865, the prospects for postwar reconstruction did not look good.

Black slavery among the southern tribes had grown out of the commerce in Indian slaves, fostered by white traders. In time it developed an economic usefulness and encouraged cleavages in Indian society which the aboriginal institution had not involved. The acceptance of black bondage opened Indian societies to white pro- and anti-slavery influences, and the anxieties they produced, together with post-removal difficulties, caused relations between Indians and blacks to deteriorate even among the rather easygoing Creeks and Seminoles. Through the bridgehead of black slavery, white customs were transported into the land of the Five Tribes, first in the South and then in the West. One cannot prove that the integrity of these Indians would have been preserved without the institution, for whites had many ways of trying to make them adjust; yet it seems probable that they would have been allowed to change more slowly had they been free of black bondsmen. Certainly slavery came to epitomize the disturbing white way to conservative elements in the Five Tribes and black emancipation after the Civil War merely added to the Indian divisions which would eventually facilitate the ending of tribal government in Indian Territory.

6

Red, Black and White:
Reconstruction and Beyond

The reconstruction process for blacks in the southern states and for the inhabitants of Indian Territory was in some respects similar, even if many Americans regarded Indians and freedmen quite differently and chose to treat freedmen differently in the two regions. In each case, the desire to effect social and political change among defeated peoples produced resentment, an increase of racial tension and a defence of the old ways, albeit less successful among the Five Tribes than among the whites of the South. And reformers concerned with both blacks and Indians displayed a common commitment to the assimilation of non-whites into the ways of the majority. Specifically this meant advocating homesteads, citizenship rights, the provision of instruction in Christianity and of secular education, especially vocational training.

These years of rebuilding, in the South and the Territory alike, saw a disturbing level of political corruption and lawlessness, which was made the excuse for the end of Reconstruction in Dixie and, conversely, the end of tribal government in Indian country. It was the Republicans who pressed for the extension and clarification of black rights in the South and West and in the eyes of contemporary whites the same party was also responsible for the major reforms in Indian policy. Yet from the Indian perspective these alleged reforms were so disastrous as to make many of the politically active among the tribes into Democrats, once their own political systems had been destroyed. Both southern blacks and the Indian population of Indian country had occasion to realize the growing reluctance of the federal government, when in pursuit of economy and 'normality', to intervene and fulfil its legal responsibilities in response to a whole range of petitions and pressures from embattled and embarrassing minorities. And the postwar years saw blacks pulling away from their former masters in both regions. In the South, economic contacts were reduced and freedmen took the opportunity to strengthen the distinctive culture

166

they had developed in slavery. In Indian Territory, before the Civil War, the blacks had helped informally to acculturate the Indians, primarily because of their close contacts with them and their understanding of the white man's language and agriculture. After the war, many Indian freedmen allied themselves with intruder blacks and whites to try to bring the Indians' supposed autonomy to an end. Blacks in Indian Territory tried to fashion their own communities, partly from choice and partly in response to Indian and white pressures for racial segregation.

Furthermore, on the face of it, the way of life of the inhabitants of the South and Indian Territory seems to have been very similar: namely simple, hard and agricultural, yet with the old isolation broken down by railroad expansion and growing exploitation of natural, particularly mineral, resources. But on closer examination we can see that conditions for all the inhabitants of Indian Territory were better and afforded better prospects than were widely available in the South during the second half of the nineteenth century. This was partly because of the opportunity, extended even to blacks, of using and then owning considerable tracts of land, though as we shall see, the allotment legislation applied to Indian land holdings was fraught with many dangers.

I

THE POLITICAL ASPECTS OF RECONSTRUCTION

When the Civil War had ended, representatives of the federal government and the Five Civilized Tribes met at Fort Smith on 8 September 1865. The government wished to see the long-term integration of Indian Territory into the United States and the short-term relocation of Kansas and Plains Indians on western land in the Territory, owned, but not then occupied, by the Five Tribes. Indian involvement in the war was used by the federal authorities to justify treating the Five Tribes as conquered nations, regardless of their divisions and difficulties over that conflict. After a treaty of surrender, admitting guilt, had been signed by the Indians at Fort Smith, Arkansas, separate compacts were negotiated with each of the Five Tribes in 1866.

The 1866 agreements required the following five concessions. (1) The emancipation of the blacks and their admission into the tribes as citizens. (Only the Chickasaws failed to comply, and these demands will be our chief concern in the ensuing chapter.) (2) The compensation of loyal Indians and freedmen on terms determined by the government. Scarce resources, as well as tribal-US differences, made

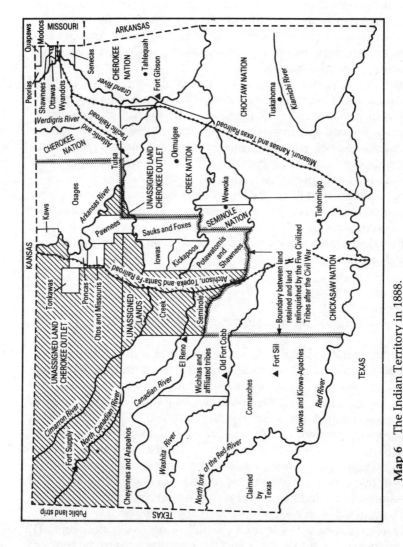

Map 6 The Indian Territory in 1888.

Source: F. P. Prucha, *American Indian Policy in Crisis: Reformers and the American Indian, 1865–1900* (Norman, OK: University of Oklahoma Press, 1976).

this a slow business.[1] (3) The cession of the desired western lands in Indian Territory. In response the Creeks gave up their western terrain; the Seminoles surrendered all their land, receiving in return, and for a higher price per acre, a reduced domain in the territory just bought from the Creeks; the Choctaws and Chickasaws ceded the so-called Leased District; the Cherokees sold the Neutral Lands and the Cherokee Strip and consented to the settlement of any Indian tribes in the Cherokee Outlet; and additional Indian groups could be settled on other Choctaw, Chickasaw and Cherokee lands. (4) Railroad rights of way. (5) A commitment to the organization of the Indian country into a territory with a general council composed of delegates from each of the Indian tribes. This clause proved difficult to implement because of tribal differences.

The Seminoles, the smallest of the Five Tribes, numbered approximately two or three thousand after the Civil War, not counting their eight hundred or so freedmen. In view of their previously fairly close relationship with the blacks among them, it might not seem remarkable that the Seminoles were the first to reach agreement with the government, apparently accepting their freedmen as equals in political and civil (including educational) rights without objection. The Indians' poverty, lack of a half-breed elite, small numbers and consequently limited bargaining leverage may also explain the speedy settlement and it should be noted that the two interpreters in the delegation to Washington were of Negro blood. In fact the treaty, which increased tribal members by about a third at a time when the national domain was being reduced by some nine-tenths, aroused considerable resentment among the pro-southern Seminoles and was described by their representative, E. B. Grayson, as being 'of the most unjust and oppressive character to the Seminole people – got up as was plainly seen by interested parties to accomplish their speculative schemes upon the Nation, regardless of the interests or true welfare of the people'. A decade later the matter continued to rankle, though a Seminole deputation to the capital managed to secure '$10,000 from the General Government as an act of equity for the shameful manner in which they were speculated upon by the treaty of 1866'.[2]

None the less, resentments about blacks do not appear to have been critical among the Seminoles. Their agent, George A. Reynolds, commented as early as 1869 that the freedmen were enjoying 'equal rights in the soils and annuities' of the tribe and 'hold office and sit in their councils'.[3] Following the pattern set in prewar days, the blacks had their own towns (two out of the total of fourteen), and they were now entitled to send six members from these towns to represent them in the National Council. Moreover, the black population contributed a number of members (two for each of their towns or bands) to the Seminole law enforcement agency, a body which was known as the light horse police.[4] Reynolds's report confirmed the evidence of General John B. Sanborn, who was sent at the prompting of the Republican party to report on the treatment of the free slaves in Indian Territory. The Freedmen's Bureau records in Washington for the Arkansas District which covered the Territory are very slight, so that Sanborn's account of conditions there becomes crucial. And since his judgement on the Seminoles was favourable, when three of the tribes – the Choctaws, Chickasaws and Cherokees – came in for heavy criticism, we may take it to be a more accurate statement of affairs than his subsequent, generalized praise for the progress being made towards racial readjustment by the Indians, possibly designed to procure his prompt release from what was proving a tiresome inquiry.[5]

The most important step for the black Seminoles, as for all the freedmen, was their resettlement on tribal land: on the unfamiliar terrain the Indians were obliged to accept at the end of the Civil War. There being no special allocation of territory to the ex-slaves, they put down roots where they could, and this sometimes meant living with former masters and Indian associates. However, following the prewar tendency of the Indians and blacks to maintain their own communities, separate black settlements grew up on Turkey Creek, at Bruner (or Noble) Town on Salt Creek, and at Lima. When, at the end of the nineteenth century, in response to the demands of white reformers and would-be settlers, black and white, the Seminole land was divided into allotments among the individual members of the tribe, the black members, who comprised in 1907 some 996 out of a total population of 3,127, received their share on the same basis as the Indians. In other words, they obtained an average allotment of 120 acres with a 40-acre homestead. Often, like the Indians, they were awarded the land they were living on at the time of the division.[6]

This partition was opposed during the 1880s and 1890s by Seminole leaders, including the mixed-blood chief, John Brown, who still smarted under the treaty of 1866 and who feared the consequences of new negotiations. Yet because no Indian protests impressed the white policy-makers, the Seminoles opted for prompt negotiations with the Dawes Commission with a view to obtaining favourable treatment. As it turned out, Indians and freedmen alike were cheated out of their allotments 'by cold hearted land gobblers who've left all thoughts of fair dealing behind'.[7]

The postwar period did not develop so straightforwardly among the Creek Indians who, like the Seminoles, had reputedly enjoyed fair relations with their slaves and were said by Sanborn in 1866 to look kindly on their freedmen.[8] The Southern Creek delegation to Fort Smith opposed the adoption of the freedmen, but they were eventually defeated by the Northern Creeks, who were possibly stiffened up by a black interpreter and were certainly supported by the white negotiators. Citizenship was consequently conferred on all individuals legally entitled to be living in the Creek nation, provided, in the case of refugees, that they had returned within a year of the ratification of the 1866 treaty. This status was to bestow a share in national funds and land. The blacks tended to settle in the Arkansas-Verdigris valley, where the old plantations had been, showing both a profound neighbourhood attachment and a loyalty to the families for whom they had once worked, as well as a sense that there was initially little alternative. There they quickly developed their own towns – Arkansas, Canadian and North Fork – all of which were north of Muskogee. The full bloods preferred to live in the hilly western terrain, while the mixed bloods were concentrated in the North Fork Town region.[9]

From the first, the interpretation of the 1866 agreement caused difficulties, with the full-blood chief Samuel Checote unsuccessfully attempting to exclude the freedmen from a payout of tribal moneys[10] and other Creek politicians, though not averse to bidding for the black vote, proving reluctant to admit to citizenship freedmen who had returned to Creek territory after the stipulated twelve-month time limit. The numbers of the freedmen – 1,774 out of a tribal total of 10,141 immediately after the Civil War – and their geographical concentration made them difficult either to coerce or ignore with ease. They were able to elect members of their race to the National Council on the same terms as the Indian towns: that is, one representative from each to the House of Kings and, to the House of Warriors, one member plus an extra member for every 200 people. Because of the growth of the black population, both by natural means and as a result of an influx of so-called 'state Negroes', who flooded into Indian Territory from the South, in the hope of improving their lot, the number of black representatives was eventually considerable, as the election returns for the House of Warriors and the House of Kings reveal.[11] In addition to producing members of the National Council, the Creek freedmen were nominated for other important governmental positions, serving in the light horse and as attorneys and judges and providing a secretary to the chief under Ward Coachman (1876–9).[12]

As in most societies, the politically active controlled more than was healthy, especially in a system where there was no secret ballot. Thus the boards certifying elections often contained the names of individuals who were also standing for election, although this practice was not confined exclusively to the coloured towns. Furthermore, the records of the Creek National Council and of the national elections contain evidence of a number of disputed elections involving these towns and their candidates and of minors and non-citizens of towns apparently voting, as well as of outbreaks of violence at election time.[13]

For the most part, the black voters allied with the full bloods, perhaps predictably, considering that former slaveowners were generally half bloods. But the alliance was by no means simple, given the fluidity of postwar Indian politics and the opportunism of the freedmen.[14] During the 1870s, Creek blacks had attended the inter-tribal councils called to resist illegal encroachments on Indian lands. By contrast, towards the end of the century, that interest in obtaining land and opportunity for advancement which had always dictated their voting habits led blacks to welcome the expansion of cattle ranching and, in particular, allotment as their best security in a changing world, albeit every Creek political party then actively opposed the Dawes Commission.[15] The freedmen did not appear to be grateful for the fact that the Creeks had not prevented the coloured towns from swelling their numbers by admitting the 'state Negroes'. Rather, they merely gained confidence from having grown from a sixth to something under a half of the tribe between 1867 and 1895.[16] And Ned Thompson, who had served on the Creek Council, probably expressed a common black view when he commented that, while he had nothing against the Indians, they and not the government had broken their treaties and proved simply incapable of keeping intruders out.[17]

When the Dawes Commission eventually completed its work it had rejected some of the doubtful black aspirants to Creek status but others had clearly 'got by' its investigators, so that blacks still comprised around 37 per cent of Creek citizens. On average, the successful blacks obtained, like the Indians themselves, 160 acres of land with a 40-acre homestead, usually where they were living.[18] Relations between Indians and blacks not surprisingly deteriorated as the Creek government was wound up during the administration of Pleasant Porter and arguments erupted between them over the disposition of allotments from the tribal 'surplus' and over the best way to project, in Oklahoma, the voice of the former voters of the Indian Territory. A similar debate took place in the Choctaw nation in the early twentieth century. The Indians, being wooed by the anti-black Democrats, felt that the freedmen would inevitably incline to the Republicans whose national leadership had helped their cause in the Territory. It may consequently have been a chilly comfort to some Creeks that, after

Creek blacks were permited to sell everything except their 40-acre homestead, in 1904, they were promptly robbed of land by acquisitive whites.[19]

Among the Cherokees, the fate of the freedmen aroused even more protracted contention. The treaty-makers in 1866 set aside a separate district of Cherokee country – the Canadian – for the freedmen and for free blacks who had lived in the Cherokee nation before 1 June 1861. Those wishing to locate there were given two years to do so. By the terms of articles IX and X of the 1866 treaty, the ex-slaves of the tribe, the free blacks who were in the country when the Civil War began and were residents in 1866, or returned within six months, together with their descendants, were to be accorded equality with native Cherokees.[20] The tribe adopted its freedmen and they, having declined to confine themselves to the Canadian District (a mere seventy were recorded there in 1880), congregated together, notably on river-bottom land in Illinois District, near Fort Gibson. Yet a number of Cherokees, like the Creeks, believed that the federal government should have removed the ex-slaves from their nation altogether and the conservative full-blood supporters of the National party held that the tribe's reduced property belonged exclusively to Cherokees by blood. Hence a dispute developed about whether the rights conferred on the blacks were civil and political only, while antipathy between blacks and Cherokees seems to have contributed to keeping black service on the council to a minimum without deterring Indian politicians from appealing to the black voter. Still more disturbing was the debate over which persons were entitled to be regarded as members of the nation according to article IX, with the Cherokee authorities adopting a tough line towards blacks who returned to the nation after the allotted six months or whose claims to a Cherokee connection they disputed.[21]

The Cherokees were the biggest of the Five Tribes and the freedmen did not constitute such a large and therefore threatening minority among them as was the case with the other southern Indians. (There were 2,000 to 2,500 Cherokee blacks compared with around 17,000 Indians in the 1860s). Cherokee resentments seem rather to have been based on an unwillingness to give the black population more than the letter of the law, as they saw it, to the benefit of intruders and at the unwarranted prompting of United States officials. The integrity of the Cherokee nation was believed to be at issue and suggestions that blacks were being mistreated by the Indians were dismissed as 'a new cord to the Territorial Harp of a thousand strings' whose sweet music appealed to all who wanted, for pecuniary reasons, to create a United States Territory out of Indian Territory. Conversely, the freedmen not unreasonably felt themselves to be the victims of a harsh legalism inspired by race prejudice; they had a fair point in complaining that the terms of the 1866 agreement were not sufficiently widely publicized and that six months did not give refugees long enough to return from the southern part of Indian Territory or the southern states.[22]

At first the tribal council tried to cope by authorizing the enumeration of the blacks and the referral of citizenship cases first to the nation's Supreme Court and then to special and costly citizenship commissions. The agents to the Cherokees usually sympathized with black claims, as did a United States inspector commissioned to look into them in 1875. Interlopers were therefore not removed, which caused resentment among successive tribal leaders, who, though they wanted the race question settled, felt that their treatment of freedmen and intruder blacks was already more generous than that of the South. What the tribe regarded as black assertiveness led the council to classify as intruders those blacks who tried to claim citizenship on the grounds of marriage to Cherokee citizens.[23] The blacks, on the other hand, complained of persecution and dispossession, despite blood ties to the Cherokees and deserving efforts in Indian Territory, and they took their case to the local agents, the Indian Commissioner, congressmen and the President of the United States, sometimes with the aid of lawyers who made black misery a most profitable business.[24]

Blacks were successful in obtaining a ruling from the Court of Claims that they were entitled to share in the common property of the tribe and the proceeds from it when distributed *per capita*; and they won financial disbursements based on this principle and on federal censuses of the blacks, whose validity the Cherokees disputed.[25] The blacks joined hands with those who wanted to colonize the Cherokee Outlet at the end of the 1870s, and with J. Milton Turner's Freedmen's Oklahoma Association, which shortly afterwards tried to promote the settlement of freedmen from Indian Territory and the United States in the 'unassigned' lands yielded by the Creeks and Seminoles in 1866, an enterprise which aroused considerable white interest.[26] But their real chance came when the Cherokees were obliged to treat with the Dawes Commission, the last of the Five Tribes to do so.

The commission took over consideration of black claims, the removal of intruders was delayed and the Cherokees' demand that the blacks be awarded a less generous land allotment than the Indians was rejected. The tribal roll was finally adjusted, after litigation, Cherokee allegations of fraud and notarized testimony on behalf of claimants, as well as expensive searches for testimony against them, which were resisted by the Cherokee Freedmen Protective Association. This roll contained 4,919 freedmen out of a total of 41,835 Cherokee citizens.

Indians and blacks were both awarded, on average, a 110-acre allotment with a 40-acre homestead. Many freedmen who benefited were
able to improve their standard of living as a result, while remaining
on the property they had long occupied, and the fact that they
obtained some of the most fertile and valuable sections, including
oil-bearing lands, did nothing to reconcile a people always resentful of
the scale of the concessions they had been forced to make to the blacks.
It scarcely helped that when restrictions on black allottees were lifted
in 1904, the freedmen were speedily swindled by just the kind of white
speculators who had once fostered their cause. The Cherokees, by
refusing to accept their late-returning freedmen, had brought down
far worse consequences upon themselves. In helping the Cherokee
blacks from the 1880s, the far from disinterested federal government
secured a deal for them that they could have won unaided, and in the
process, United States officials advanced their major objective of
destroying Cherokee autonomy.[27]

The working out of the reconstruction treaties among the Choctaws
and Chickasaws was in some ways even more difficult than in the
Cherokee nation. These two tribes were, after all, said to be particularly hostile to blacks, they were predominantly pro-Confederacy
and were obliged to make a joint treaty with the United States,
although they had separated from each other in 1855–6. In return for
ceding the Leased District, the Choctaws and Chickasaws were to
receive $300,000, once they had adopted laws giving equal rights to
the ex-slaves and their descendants, and accorded them 40 acres of
land if the country was allotted. Two years were allowed for compliance, failing which the funds were to be used for the benefit of
freedmen who would leave tribal territory within 90 days; they were
also to afford assistance to blacks removing elsewhere during the
two-year adjustment period. As a reflection of the ability of the
mixed-blood delegation in Washington, which had demanded compensated emancipation as a bargaining counter, the Choctaws and
Chickasaws did not have to give their ex-slaves a share in annuities or
other moneys.[28]

At first there was some Choctaw support for adopting the freedmen, who were needed as labourers and might, it was feared, become
a magnet for discontented 'state Negroes' if they were removed to the
Leased District. In addition, it was recognized that generosity to the
blacks would predispose the United States to look favourably on the
tribe's 'unsettled claims and demands'. However, the dismay caused
by lawless black communities in the Red River valley, the difficulties
involved in regulating the wages and employment of the freedmen
and the knowledge that they comprised between 12 and 15 per cent of

the tribal population in 1867 prompted removal sentiment. Differences among the Choctaw leadership may have helped the federal government, but the government was, in any event, sympathetic to the blacks and determined to see them adopted as the Indians' equals. Accordingly it ignored Choctaw requests for the removal of the freedmen from the tribe and tried to force adoption by dividing $200,000 of the promised $300,000 between the Choctaws and Chickasaws.

The Choctaw freedmen, for their part, may initially have chosen to live with or near their former masters and may have worked for them of necessity, but the two races increasingly came to live apart, with the blacks concentrated in the Skullyville region, otherwise a full-blood area. Although the freedmen were allowed to cultivate the land, the amounts involved per individual were often nearer 20 than the hoped-for 40 acres. Blacks did not have any legal rights in the public domain and came under the criminal jurisdiction only of the federal district court at Fort Smith. Whilst some dismayed blacks petitioned the government for removal, by 1869–70 their demands for equal rights and the allotment of land in the Choctaw nation to all comers were being encouraged, to Indian disgust, by whites who hoped that the blacks' plight could be used to open the nation to white settlement.[29]

Efforts to block white encroachments through the Okmulgee Council, provided for by the treaties of 1866, were abortive.[30] So, too, were Choctaw attempts to settle the status of their blacks in conjunction with the Chickasaws (see pp. 177–8).[31] Backed by blacks and whites from outside Indian Territory, the Choctaw blacks kept up their pressure for equal rights for themselves and intermarried blacks, arguing that their labour had made the nation what it was and complaining that the Indians still regarded them as property.[32] Tired of the matter, in 1883 the Choctaws adopted the freedmen resident within the tribe when the preliminary reconstruction treaty was signed (September 1865), receiving in return $52,125 as their share of the balance of the Leased District payment. The registration and enrolment of blacks followed and whenever possible the registrars rejected those who had been owned in slavery by non-citizens; had arrived after the treaty agreement; had a claim dependent on intermarriage with Choctaw freedmen; or could be identified as 'state Negroes'. Blacks who wished to remove were to be compensated with $100 each, as laid down in 1866. It is not clear how many elected to do so; it is clear that they were a minority of the blacks, possessing substantially less property than individuals registering to stay, and sometimes none at all, albeit the possession of small numbers of stock was fairly common. The blacks who remained were, with white assistance, allowed to exercise the vote and their land holdings went undisturbed under Choctaw rule, notwithstanding the tribe's desire to limit them to 40 acres, its successful exclusion of blacks from office holding and its denial of intermarried status to non-citizen blacks who married Choctaw freedmen.[33]

Choctaw endeavours to prevent black and white immigration after 1866 and to limit the rights of their freedmen laid them open to the charge of chauvinism.[34] Yet their efforts were entirely understandable from the Indian point of view, since by the 1890s it was estimated that the Choctaws made up only about a quarter of their nation, 'a smaller proportion than that of any other Indian tribe except the Chickasaws, who made up only 9 per cent of the inhabitants of their country'.[35] None the less, with the coming of the Dawes Commission the Choctaws' once united opposition to allotment and political change crumbled, and they co-operated with the pro-black envoys in the hope of avoiding harsh treatment. The subsequent enrolment of the freedmen precipitated the usual expensive and bitter conflicts, with the Indians striving to limit black gains, the blacks' organizations striving to maximize them and black claims being considered well after the 1897 agreement to allot them 40 acres, and its 1902 confirmation.[36] The final tribal roll listed 5,994 freedmen, as against 7,076 full bloods, 18,981 Choctaws of various blood categories and 1,639 Mississippi Choctaws.[37]

The Choctaw and Chickasaw freedmen urged and obtained removal of all restrictions from their allotments in 1908 and thereupon suffered from gross exploitation by sharks of all kind. Such was the last, unsavoury episode in this long-running racial conflict and the blacks shared their sad fate with the Creek, Seminole and Cherokee freedmen. Throughout the tussle, all three races had been motivated by material self-interest and group loyalties. In the case of Indians and blacks these motives are to be seen particularly starkly at work in Choctaw politics from the 1890s onwards, when black voters gave their backing to the Indian politicians who offered them most, and even tribal leaders like the full blood, Green McCurtain, who contemptuously referred to blacks as following the man with corn in his sack, appealed to the black electors.[38]

At the opposite pole from the relatively tolerant Seminoles, and still more determined to resist the adoption of the freedmen than their Choctaw neighbours, were the Chickasaws. Consequently their fight was both against the United States government and, for a time, against the Choctaws, among whom some Chickasaw blacks took refuge after the war, because their owners were reluctant to accept emancipation and the ex-slaves feared violence at their hands.[39] Since there were also Choctaw freedmen living among the Chickasaws, the task of sorting out who belonged to whom was a difficult one and, predictably, the Choctaws found it impossible, once they had adopted their own blacks, to persuade the Chickasaws to extend tribal rights to this group of black settlers in their midst.[40] The small size of the Chickasaw tribe, the invasion of tribal territory by a tide of black and white intruders, and the comparatively large number of former slaves among them – there were about 2,000 in a population of 4,000 to 5,000 after the war – do much to account for the Indians' fear of fostering the aspirations of blacks within or adjacent to the nation.[41]

From 1866 onwards, the Chickasaws periodically asked for the removal of the blacks, since the legislature declined to adopt them and it was feared that they would 'be the wedge with which our country will be rent asunder and opened up to the whites'. Tribal law officials could not cope with the poor and often lawless 'state Negroes' from Louisiana and Texas, but their efforts to do so alarmed the federal officials who should have removed the interlopers. Negotiations with the Choctaws having got nowhere, it was unfortunate that the government in Washington failed to act on the Chickasaws' one offer before 1883 to adopt their freedmen on the same terms as the Choctaws. Out on their own after 1883, the Chickasaws continued to oppose adoption because it would 'result in great injury to them . . . as a people' and they made no official census of the freedmen. But though some blacks had once considered relocation, they soon set their sights on citizenship, while Chickasaw intransigence on the freedmen question and resistance to all efforts to make them modify tribal ways alienated whites.[42] Thus the Dawes Commission report of 1894 condemned the tribe's exclusion of the 'Peaceable, law-abiding and hard-working' freedmen from educational, legal and land rights.[43] Aware of their danger, as the Choctaws entered into negotiations with the Dawes team and their own blacks had come to outnumber them, the Chickasaws reluctantly followed suit, in order to put a limit on possible concessions.

A bitter struggle followed concerning which blacks were to be placed on the tribal roll before land allotment and the Chickasaws belatedly co-operated with the Choctaws to get many false claimants excluded. In 1906 the tribe was obliged to accept 4,670 blacks, 3,670 more than it was hoping for; at this point there were 5,684 Indians of various blood degrees. Chickasaws were, however, pleased with the fact that they were able to confine the land allotted to each black to 40 acres, the same amount as was granted by the Choctaws but much less than the acreage permitted by the Cherokees, Creeks and Seminoles.[44]

There was further comfort to be derived from the exclusion for enrolment of children born to Chickasaw freedmen after 31 October 1899 and from the successful conclusion of a struggle waged between 1905 and 1911 for compensation for the land the tribe had been obliged to yield for the blacks' allotments.[45]

Given these various unharmonious dealings, it is no surprise to find the Chickasaws' National party spokesman and ex-chief, William L. Byrd, complaining to an interviewer in 1906, as white competition developed for Indian votes, that the Republican party had 'confiscated our lands for homesteads for the negroes, thus thrusting upon us an undesirable African citizenship'. What neither he nor the self-interested American authorities acknowledged was that the Chicka-saw freedmen had been harshly consigned to an unjust insecurity since the Civil War and that among those blacks whose claims for enrolment were rejected were many with Chickasaw blood.[46]

II

Social Developments after the Civil War

Seminole records are not particularly illuminating about the lifestyle of the Seminole freedmen. As far as can be judged, they had a similar diet to their Indian neighbours, including a corn gruel called sofkey.[47] A few fought for the United States in the Seminole-Negro Indian Scouts in the Indian fighting either side of the Rio Grande in the 1870s and early 1880s.[48] But the majority seem to have cultivated the land, and with some success, for they were reported to be the most progressive members of the tribe.[49] Ex-slaves might nevertheless lead varied lives and the interpreter Coody Johnson served as the secretary to Chief Hulputta Micco, besides representing 'both blacks and Indians in civil and criminal cases'.[50] More information is available for the other Civilized Tribes, yet a comparable picture emerges. For the blacks, as for people generally in developing communities, the work experience was the dominating one of their lives. Most freedmen, like most Indians, earned their living from the land. The crops grown were corn, wheat, cotton, rice, fruit and vegetables. For each race, the standard housing was a log hut, women made the clothes and food usually consisted of beef, pork and deer, chickens, turkeys, fish and squirrels, since wild game was plentiful, and a variety of corn dishes. Habit and mutual affection resulted in some freedmen being employed by ex-masters in all four tribes,[51] and there were many blacks who, out of insecurity or perceiving opportunity, tried several jobs. This might involve employment on other men's ranches and farms, ferry and sawmill work, mail carrying, stagecoach driving, hotel and store keeping, teaching, preaching, herb doctoring and blacksmithing.

Despite the difficulties accompanying political reconstruction in these four nations, they contained a minority of successful and affluent blacks. If the Choctaws denied their freedmen the opportunity of profiting from timber resources on the public domain they cultivated and blacks only slowly got a stake in the country, while the Chickasaw freedmen found it difficult to secure their land improvements and to obtain permits to hire labour,[52] the tribes' agent, George Olmsted, was probably not far from the truth in the early 1870s when he declared of the blacks that 'those of them with energy to labor for themselves and their families live as well as the Indians, and are better able to take care of themselves than the majority of their race in the Southern States'.[53]

In addition, the freedmen worked in the towns which grew in Indian Territory during the later nineteenth century, finding openings as construction workers, labourers, porters and waiters, cleaners, laundresses and prostitutes. What is more, they managed to run their own small businesses, which included saloons and dance-halls, boarding houses, restaurants and barbers' shops.[54] Few Indians settled in the white towns; blacks and whites rather than Indians were the entrepreneurs and 'modernizers' of the Territory. Over twenty all-black towns were also founded in Indian Territory and Oklahoma Territory, which was formed from the Unassigned Lands and other unoccupied portions of Indian country and opened to settlement in 1889. Their promoters promised splendid communities; the reality often seems to have been closer to Khrushchev's similarly heralded but daunting 'agro-towns' of the 1950s. The settlements were planted just when many small towns elsewhere were being undermined by the emergence of national transport networks, markets and large-scale enterprises. Black businesses suffered a high failure rate, the towns' economies were not sufficiently diversified and their existence encouraged local white justifications of racial segregation. Even so, their inhabitants found opportunity in the new communities, maintained a sympathetic, albeit somewhat patronizing, attitude towards the Indian population and enjoyed themselves in Emancipation Day picnics and games, concerts, debates and fraternal organizations.[55]

The social and educational contacts of the three races in the Territory after the Civil War involved some separation and some mixing, in part dictated by pioneer conditions, but they had moved towards that separation which characterized race relations in the United States as a whole by the end of the nineteenth century. On the one hand, notwithstanding the considerable degree of segregation prevailing between Indians and blacks, individuals of each race provided services for and befriended one another, practised polygamy, drank, traded liquor and sometimes worked together. They attended each other's doctors, churches, camp meetings, picnics and stomp dances and were finally buried in common graveyards. Nor were white contacts with Indians and blacks limited to economic exchanges. Hence the whites and Indians were said to like to hear the blacks sing and pray, the blacks and whites to see the Indians dance and play ball. Miscegenation continued, most noticeably in the Creek and Seminole nations, and primarily between tribal members and men, both blacks and whites, who hoped to benefit materially from a tribal connection. Territory children hunted and played together, regardless of colour; and Indians and blacks were swindled together by grasping traders, for instance at the *per capita* payouts of tribal funds.[56] They both enforced the law together, serving as light-horsemen in the Creek and Seminole nations, and broke the law together, joining forces in the criminal bands which roamed Indian Territory and in order to resist Chief Checote's rule over the Creeks, rather as Indians and blacks had allied in the Lowry band to fight white supremacy in North Carolina during Reconstruction.[57] Blacks and Indians alike suffered from the fact that jurisdiction over offences in the Territory was shared between tribal courts and the US district courts (initially in Arkansas, from the 1880s inside the Indian Territory), with US marshals increasingly asserting themselves because the Indians' laws and facilities for dealing with crime could not cope with the Territory's growing and mixed population. And whatever disagreements the Indians may have had with the ex-slaves, the lynching of blacks was never a feature of Indian Territory.[58]

On the other hand, the political differences among Indians, blacks and whites were aggravated by a number of factors. Some full-blood Indians continued to question the value of a Christian presence in Indian Territory, whereas the underfunded and frequently changing missionaries were normally tolerated or welcomed by the mixed bloods, not least because of their educational labours and increasing use of Indian languages and teachers. Indian–black contacts were also reduced by the postwar evangelists' habit of establishing separate Indian and black churches, which by the end of the nineteenth century had become the focus for separate communities. The Indians objected to the growing number of ambitious whites illegally in their country, and if the black troops stationed in the West removed intruders and helped protect the Five Tribes from their warlike Indian neighbours, they sympathized with the would-be settlers and intermarried with the local freedmen, thereby adding to Indian unease.[59] While miscegenation did persist, with Indian–black amalgamation taking place even among the Chickasaws, the Creeks, Cherokees and Choctaws tried to limit the rights of intermarried whites in their nations and were officially opposed to black–Indian intermarriage.[60]

In the area of education, the separation of Indians and blacks was the Indians' principal aim and whites were eventually able to advance the case for Oklahoma statehood by publicizing the inadequacy of the instruction provided for blacks and their own lack of facilities in Oklahoma Territory. They had a case, but not all their strictures about the tribal educational systems were fair. Missionaries were allowed to teach the blacks, and having first provided for Indian children, the Creeks, Seminoles and Cherokees established schools for the freedmen as early as the 1870s. What is more, there is evidence of Indian–black mixing in Seminole and Creek institutions long after the numbers of black intruders became alarming and might have been expected to bring it to an end.[61] However, even when the Cherokees had adopted their freedmen, it took four years for black neighbourhood schools to be set up and these did not accept 'state Negroes'; the tribe regarded its conduct as generous.[62] The Chickasaws did not feel obligated in any way to educate their blacks, who had to rely on missionary assistance and the federal government which, in a punitive gesture, cut off assistance after the Chickasaws had refused to adopt the freedmen.[63] As a result, though their experiences were clearly varied, most blacks acquired little formal instruction and the position of the Choctaw and Chickasaw blacks, as well as of the whites, was therefore improved after the end of tribal government. Yet the price was high for the blacks, namely the legal enforcement of segregated education. Moreover, many of the deficiencies of black schools in Indian Territory – including the inadequate provision for older pupils, corrupt administrators who were appointed for political not scholastic reasons, the failure to deliver much-vaunted vocational training, a short school term and no means to enforce attendance, and indifferent and poorly paid teachers bent on imparting the values of the nationally dominant culture – can be observed throughout the American educational system in the second half of the nineteenth century.[64]

Whites were inclined to blame blacks for the lawlessness in Indian Territory and used conditions that were common in other frontier regions as an argument for ending the Indians' independence. Although the federal government's handling of the freedmen issue had helped to encourage the influx of 'state Negroes' from the late 1870s, whites living in the Territory regarded the newcomers with dismay and their prejudices were fed by white migrants from the

South, after the creation of Oklahoma Territory.[65] While blacks were never more than 10 per cent of Oklahoma's population in the 1890s, anti-black demonstrations occurred in both Territories and the 'state Negroes' aroused greater Indian resentment, albeit it varied in intensity within the Five Tribes. The result was that blacks were expelled from numerous biracial settlements and compelled to develop their own. Freedmen in the Indian Territory, after initially welcoming 'state Negroes', came to despise their poverty and resent the white backlash they provoked.[66] And the use of blacks as strikebreakers in the mines did not help race relations, particularly where, as in the Choctaw nation in 1899, they brought the smallpox with them.[67] Racial friction mounted throughout the Southwest after 1910, but notably so in the new state of Oklahoma, established in 1907 after the allotment of the Five Tribes and the winding up of their governments. The exploitation of rich economic resources was at stake and acquisitive whites frustrated any possible black bid for a real share in them by disfranchising the blacks, extending segregation and excluding them from many towns after sundown. In desperation, some blacks were driven to look for better prospects elsewhere: in Liberia, the Gold Coast, Canada and the northern United States.[68]

The Indian population was felt by whites to be politically incompetent and unfit to possess vast land resources, although Indians and whites were on better terms in Indian Territory than in some parts of the West and mixed bloods were a majority in all the Five Tribes when the final tribal rolls were taken.[69] The eventual loss of numerical supremacy by the Indians in Indian Territory helped the whites achieve their objective of absorbing the Territory into the United States, to which end they had manipulated its racial, educational, economic and law and order problems. Having expressed concern for the Indian freedmen in the early postwar period, whites were, by the early twentieth century, willing to appeal to Indian prejudice against blacks and give way to their own. As a belated acknowledgement of the historic white preference for Indians over blacks in theory, if not in practice, the Indian population was classified as white in the Oklahoma constitution, which recognized only the black and white races.[70] White politicians promised Five Tribe Indians that they would be a major force in Oklahoma politics and could rely on their white friends to put blacks in their place. The 'Billups Booze Bill' even conceded prohibition, in deference to Indian wishes. But the whites had not achieved their objective of bringing the tribes into conformity with their own society, for traditional Indian ideas and customs survived and Indian distinctiveness persisted into the twentieth century.[71]

III

Twentieth-Century Developments

Against this sombre background, the three races in Oklahoma worked out their destinies and after the disputes of the recent past it was not easy for Indians and blacks to come together. Some Indians seem to have resented any tendency or actions which equated them with another non-white race simply on account of colour. If they were to be linked with any other group, the preferred connection was with whites. Hence Joseph Bruner, head of the American Indian Federation during the 1930s, claimed to have received complaints about the hiring of a black nurse at the Sequoyah Orphan Training School at Tahlequah, Oklahoma. He himself protested 'against the appointment of negroes in any capacity in the Indian Service' and stressed that Indians and blacks were separated in Oklahoma.[72] In the face of such self-consciousness, the old informal exchanges between Indians and blacks in religious matters came under strain. An investigator of 'A Negro Peyote Cult' in the 1930s reported that her Indian informant 'seemed to resent the fact that negroes were taking up "the old Indian religion"' and suggested that 'the older Indians were more friendly toward the coloured people than the younger Indians'.[73] The two races also had different priorities in the area of education. The blacks were initially anxious to improve their separate institutions, including the university at Langston, though they eventually attacked segregation on the ground that the expense of a dual system meant that it could not be adequate at all levels. For their part Indians were concerned to assert their legal right both to attend Oklahoma's educational facilities with whites and to retain special schools when this seemed appropriate.[74]

The Indian–black connection was not entirely sour, any more than it had been in the nineteenth century. In the 1930s, it was noted that black agricultural workers were moving on to Indian-owned land 'with the consent of the Indians' and that certain 'of the Indians show a disposition to mingle socially with the Negroes'.[75] Oral history testimony suggests that the twentieth-century descendants of Five Tribe freedmen continued to have access to remaining tribal facilities and some moneys and that good relations between members of all three races in Oklahoma were not uncommon. Yet a 1970 study of blacks and Indians in Seminole County, the former tribal homeland of the Seminoles, concluded that intermarriage between the two had become unacceptable some time in the twentieth century because 'many Indians desire identity with only "true" Indians'. The Seminoles' attitude might have been encouraged by whites' glorification of the state's Indian past, despite their callous dispossession of the tribes and tendency to concentrate, in press reporting, on negative aspects of black and Indian life.[76]

Problems of this sort were not confined to Oklahoma. As Walter L. Williams and his collaborators point out,[77] during the first half of the nineteenth century whites in the South abandoned their efforts to divide and rule the two non-white races. After Indian removal, security considerations no longer dictated such a strategy. Instead, whites tended to place Indians in the 'coloured' category. Because the Indians who successfully resisted removal tended to be the least 'progressive' elements of their respective tribes, the remnants of the southern tribes were already disinclined to mix with whites. Their reluctance was increased by the whites' new tactic and contacts with blacks were reduced to demonstrate the Indians' distinctiveness. White pressure on the Indians' remaining land holdings was unremitting. However, with the exception of the North Carolina Cherokees and Lumbees, who during the Civil War were pressured to perform military labour alongside black slaves, the war and its aftermath did not affect the southern Indians as it did the tribes of the Indian Territory.

As segregation hardened in the South, whites renewed their efforts to make Indians a separate social group from blacks and from themselves. They sometimes banned Indian–white marriages, as well as those between blacks and whites. Marriage between Indians and whites usually led to the whites merging into the Indian settlements; Indian marriages with blacks forced them into the black neighbourhoods. In response, the Indians might accept a legal status between whites and blacks, but were also driven to a variety of stratagems. These included carrying group membership cards, striving for recognition from the states and the federal government, attempting to acquire land, campaigning for admission to their own, white or bureau schools, depending on which was the most feasible, accepting missionary assistance and forming separate religious organizations. Outside awareness of the problems of the remaining southern Indians was created by a number of scholarly investigations. None the less, the difficulty remained that several of the southern Indian groups had mingled with blacks, if only in the eighteenth and nineteenth centuries, and were so racially mixed as to make official recognition of their status as Indians an uncertain business.

Keeping to themselves for fear of the consequences has certainly helped to preserve the southern Indians' sense of identity and, in some cases, their languages, but it has tended to smother whatever sympathy they may have felt for the local blacks, as fellow victims of white discrimination. Meanwhile blacks possessing or anxious to claim Indian ancestry have avoided occupational and other associations with the black community proper, which has regarded the mixed bloods' claims with tolerant contempt. Determined not to be Negro, as Brewton Berry puts it, the mixed-blood blacks would probably prefer to be accepted as white, but since they cannot achieve this objective, they have settled for being Indian.[78]

During the 1930s, news of these awkward tripartite systems of race relations disturbed reformers and officials concerned with Indian policy, who recognized the not always benign power that state authorities could exercise over the small groups of disorganized eastern Indians. But no obvious solution emerged and in response to news that the states were seeking to classify mixed Indian communities as black and that Indians were keeping their children from school rather than have them instructed at black institutions, bureau officials could only exclaim over all the difficulties concerned and offer cautious recommendations: federal educational aid for backward rural communities, and the discrete establishment of separate Rural Resettlement Administration projects for Indians at Pembroke, North Carolina.[79]

With the existence of Indian–black contacts thus kept before them, Indian administrators continued to compare the fate of the two non-white races, as nineteenth-century reformers had done (see Chapters 2 and 3). So, too, did other interested observers of Indian affairs. To those anxious or sceptical about Indian progress or federal efforts at assistance, it was useful to point out that Indian poverty, ill health or alleged criminality were no worse than that prevailing among many poor blacks and immigrants. In a state such as Oklahoma, it could be shown that grafters were keen to rob Indians and blacks alike of their heritage.[80] And both races were supposed to find their salvation in the same way: that is, by their constituent individuals cultivating the work ethic, something which, after receiving freedom and civil rights, blacks had been obliged to do, but which Indians reputedly had not, partly because of the reservation system and their 'enslavement' to the BIA.[81]

On the other hand, Indians were admitted to have some advantages over blacks. Their education was not as controversial as that of blacks and their attainments were sometimes said to be greater. Although Indians might suffer from loneliness and other pressures when they moved to the cities (see Chapter 11), it was suggested that they encountered less discrimination there than blacks. Because their problems were less rooted in the 'social prejudice' of whites, an

optimist like John Collier could maintain that it would be 'comparatively easy', if Congress were willing, 'to put an end to the wrongs
against the Indian[s]'.[82]

Indians themselves compared their position with that of the black
population, yet they were in no way united about the use, if any, to
which their findings could be put. At the second convention of the
National Congress of American Indians in 1945 it was pointed out that
the 'Indians in the North occupy the same racial positions that the
Negroes do in the South'.[83] It was felt that the answer was to organize
politically to obtain redress, and as we shall argue in Chapter 12, this
course was followed with real success; but there was both appreciation
and dislike of the tactics followed by blacks in their similar, if earlier,
campaign. While groups of southern Indians have improved their
position through agitation, benefiting from the preceding black civil
rights movement and learning new forms of community organizing,
there have been mixed feelings about the loss of separate Indian
schools, which were a focus for local activities and a mark of Indian
distinctiveness. More generally, members of the older generation
have been diffident about getting involved in unfamiliar community
projects or Anglo politics and have often shrunk from violence or
feared the white backlash it produced; whereas younger, urban
Indians have been inclined to emulate black 'direct action' tactics.[84]

Indian activists might, nevertheless, feel that as comparative latecomers to the city, their needs in urban areas were subordinated to
those of the larger black settlements which had been making their
protests felt over a longer period of time.[85] It was likewise thought that
Native American Studies were granted less importance by educators
than Black Studies programmes.[86] Moreover, it was not apparent that
Indians always understood enough about the meaning of 'black
power' to want to sympathize with its ideology, and where they did, a
belief in their own special past and present might quickly assert itself:
'Indians are trying to protect their identity from a lot of things that are
happening and perhaps Blacks are trying to find one.'[87] There was a
belief that Indians had always fought for control of their own affairs,
whether literally or through non-co-operation with whites, so that
they were not as desperate as certain black militants.[88] By the 1960s,
whites, especially in the media, had grown accustomed to demands
for 'black power' and expected similar assertions of 'red power': yet to
some Indian commentators, the slogan remained essentially a white
creation, which sprang from an inadequate understanding of Indian
life and organizations, though on occasion it could bring useful
publicity to Indian affairs.[89]

Even where race has not been a factor, coalitions between minorities have been notoriously difficult to build. Their success has depended on their power to enlist the support of elements within the majority and such elements have tended to be liberal and of limited influence. The component parts of minority alliances have feared loss of identity, the alienation of their hard-core supporters and discrediting by extreme actions undertaken by individual members. In the case of the Indians, co-operation with blacks has been hampered not only by the lack of historic ties outside Oklahoma and parts of the South, but also by the racial prejudice whose erratic manifestations we have been observing in the last two chapters. As a black contributor (with Indian blood) sadly noted in *Wassaja* in 1977, 'I've yet to meet a Black who has expressed the pure hatred about Native-Americans that I have encountered among some Native-Americans towards Blacks.' She felt that this sentiment 'prevails all over', notwithstanding the frequent intermingling of red and black. Its existence demonstrated that the 'old divide and conquer game', begun by whites in the colonial period and abandoned by southerners for a while after Indian removal, continued to enjoy a degree of success in the later part of the twentieth century.[90]

7

American Indians and American Anthropologists

In recent years the anthropologist has been added, by some Native American spokesmen, to their list of enemies masquerading as friends: the federal government and the Bureau of Indian Affairs, the churches in general and missionaries in particular, traders and reservation developers and assorted white charitable organizations. It is a development which the profession has noted with dismay.

As obnoxious as all intrusive visitors to quiet parts, anthropologists are also allegedly suspect because they derive a living out of their Indian 'observations' and the academic controversies they provoke, thereby advancing their careers rather than Indian interests. Scholars may appear to be verifying theories to which they are already committed, or may neglect to see that their eventual findings are made available to the community which has been studied. To the anthropologist, critics argue, people are objects like chessmen, available for experimentation and manipulation. It is further maintained that many Indians have become resistant to anthropologists' supposedly expert abstractions about how they should behave, or about their inescapable cultural heritage, with the result that practical solutions to the problems of poverty and local self-determination in modern America have become harder to find.[1]

Are these strictures fair? They are certainly not new, having been frequently applied to social or cultural anthropologists by black African spokesmen. They may help to explain the recurring complaints of field workers about the dearth of candid informants, at the same time as they reflect the natural transference of hostility aroused by unfriendly strangers to individuals with more kindly intentions. And as anthropologists have been consulted by policy-makers, it is understandable that those affected should exaggerate the closeness of the connection. Yet it should be borne in mind that Indians themselves have provided recruits for the profession of anthropology, that Indians have used and teased anthropologists working among them and that criticisms of the discipline have neither been constant nor uniform among Indian peoples. Moreover if, as David Marden notes, Indians were until recently interpreted to the American government 'by observers whose primary interests were not in the Indians themselves, but in some other tasks', this was not necessarily the fault of anthropologists.[2] Perhaps we can establish whether American anthropologists have anything more than a fashionable case to answer by way of a brief survey of some of their main contributions to the study of the native population. For the question of whether scholars should also be activists has not and never will be settled to general satisfaction and their scholarship must always be the main basis for judging their worth.

I

EARLY AMERICAN ANTHROPOLOGY

In the account that follows, space limitations rule out an attempt to trace the general historical development of anthropology and the differences which have emerged between its practitioners, particularly in Britain and the United States during the twentieth century. None the less, the individual authorities looked at here will be placed in the context of an evolving discipline, and some key terms must be defined before we proceed any further:

1   *Ethnology*: the science of races, their relation to one another and their characteristics. When ethnological societies were being founded – Paris (1839), London (1841), New York (1842) – the 'primary goal lay in tracing historic relations by comparison of human physiques, languages and customs' (Voget, p. 108). The term might be seen as involving an interest 'primarily in the past history of peoples without written records, and ... therefore closely allied with archaeology' (Mair, pp. 8–9).

2   *Ethnography*: the description (rather than theoretical analysis) of a people's mode of life, through the accumulation of data 'by direct inquiry and observation' (Mair, p. 9).

3   *Anthropology*: the whole science of man. The aims of the anthropological societies being established in Paris (1859), London (1863), Berlin (1869), Vienna (1870), Stockholm (1873) and Washington (1879), were to enlarge the scope of ethnology in the light of new developments in geology, palaeontology, prehistory and anthropometry (anatomical measurement, or the measurement of 'body and skeletal relationships between conventionalized points', and

190

the development of 'indices which express these relationships to effect intergroup comparisons' – Voget, pp. 13, 861). In time, the demands imposed by trying to study the anatomical, physiological, psychological, social and cultural features and circumstances of men led to the emergence of specialisms such as social and cultural anthropology and their various spin-offs.

Social anthropology, dominant in Britain, emphasizes the importance of social structure.

Cultural anthropology, particularly strong in the United States, emphasizes cultural facts and, sometimes, the personality of a people who share a particular culture (Mair, pp. 9–12; Voget, pp. 535–8).[3]

The earliest European works on what we would now call anthropology were prompted or produced by travellers who from the late fifteenth century commented on the peoples of newly discovered lands. Although the classical and medieval worlds had produced a rich tradition concerning wild men beyond the pale of civilization, in the age of exploration travel literature provided ostensibly 'hard' evidence for Western speculations about the origins, physical attributes, languages, artefacts and religious beliefs of peoples encountered overseas.[4] In the United States, information about the Indians, the chief focus of American anthropology when it emerged, was provided by travellers, traders and missionaries and in the collections of Indian orations and stories of returned white captives for which a keen public appetite soon developed. Indian lore attracted the interest of the American Philosophical and Antiquarian Societies and of the nation's leading men decades before the formalization of ethnological inquiries from the 1840s, encouraged by the foundation in 1846 of the Smithsonian Institution for the 'increase and diffusion of knowledge among men'.[5] Ancient native earthworks in the eastern half of the continent were being investigated from the early nineteenth century and the study of Indian languages began even sooner.[6] These undertakings reflect a preoccupation with Native American origins and antiquity and from the first the ethnologists found controversy their natural condition, for the Indians were made use of, as well as studied, to demonstrate the venerable heritage of a raw and struggling state.

Thus, for example, a lively debate developed over whether the Indians were descended from the ten lost tribes of Israel or other Hebrew migrants, as opposed to the Welsh, Scandinavians, Chinese, or Egyptians, via the lost continents of Mu in the Pacific or Atlantis in the Atlantic;[7] and believers in the European or Asiatic antecedents of the Indians lined up against those who thought them to be as indigenous as the bison.[8] Nor did ethnologists agree about whether there was a time break between prehistoric and living Indian cultures, or about such vexed issues as the possibility of progress and the significance of evolutionary theory; the unity of the human species; and the equality of the different races of man.

Until well into the nineteenth century, a theory of progress seemed more in tune with American experience than the argument of some European thinkers that the Indians had descended, or rather degenerated, 'from civilized man'. But it was not always easy for individuals judging from the standards of their own culture, and with more information to utilize than most of their contemporaries, to believe in the progressive qualities of 'primitive' peoples.[9] A conviction that the Indians were static, backward-looking groups was entertained even by evolutionists, a number of whom equated progress with evolution, though they produced no culture-free criteria for measuring progressive change.[10] The main pitfall was the tendency of evolutionists to contrast the benefits of civilization, the apex of social evolution, with the drawbacks of 'savagery'. And this trap could ensnare those who avoided the conviction that whites alone, supposedly representing the summit of organic evolution, were or could be fully civilized. It in turn led some men of science to argue that civilization should be substituted for savagery with all speed, albeit there is a wonderful optimism in assuming that those who had not progressed as they should have could be forced to do so by those who had achieved civilization. Considering the vagueness often shown about how progress was or might be made from one stage of social development to another, the optimism is the more remarkable.[11]

The ethnologist Henry Rowe Schoolcraft, who worked as an agent among the Chippewa Indians at St Marie from 1822 and as superintendent of Indian affairs for Michigan from 1836, remarked on the conservative, retrospective cast of the Indian mind[12] and concluded that societies based on hunting could never progress if left to their own devices. He therefore urged the adoption of reservations for Indians, as well as their religious and secular education. Because of his background and staunch religious beliefs, Schoolcraft's conclusions were predictable, despite the fact that the Algonquian and Iroquois peoples he studied were partly horticulturalists, rather than pure nomads.[13] The ethnologist and anthropologist Lewis Henry Morgan, though a firm believer in progress and aided in his work by an Indian informant, Ely S. Parker, was similarly ambivalent about the dynamism of the tribes he studied and, like Schoolcraft, he advocated education of the Indians as the best means to their salvation.[14] Nor

192

was the ethnologist John Wesley Powell prone to doubt that the imposition of white civilization upon Native Americans would be beneficial.[15] Comparable views about the unprogressive nature of Indian cultures and their consequent likely fate if left alone were entertained by other major anthropologists, with supporting evidence apparently supplied by the orations of leading Indians, who appeared as defenders of an ideal past or, at the very least, of the status quo.[16]

So far as the equality of man and the unity of the human species are concerned, anthropological inquiry during the eighteenth century had been dominated by biblical and enlightenment beliefs in unity. These had stressed the descent of all men from the Creation (monogenesis); the similarity of men's bodies; and the importance of the environment in shaping men's biological and mental structure.[17] By the early nineteenth century, however, racial assumptions had become increasingly important, stimulated by a variety of factors, including the desire to justify slavery and dismay about the 1791 black revolt in St Domingue, which appeared to throw doubt on the rationality and goodness of 'natural' man. Regarding these assumptions, men of science were neither consistent nor united; but they were long preoccupied with them. For when the work of Darwin eventually destroyed the polygenist explanation of human inequality – that is, the argument that mankind consisted of several species, separately created – the doctrines of Social Darwinism, by their stress on human conflict and the survival of the fittest, gave fresh stimulus to debates about race differences.

Students of culture, including Morgan, often emphasized cultural likenesses not racial contrasts, asserting the psychic unity of man. Morgan, Bieder remarks, was actually willing to advocate inter-marriage between whites and 'respectable' Indians, 'the best blood of their race'. Conversely, biologists or physical anthropologists like Samuel Morton accepted the diversity of men, although in his early work on the Indians Morton stopped short of asserting that the races constituted distinct species. Both he and Josiah Nott, his collaborator on *Types of Mankind* (1854), had a low opinion of the cranial attributes and inherent character of the Indians, whom they put just above 'the Ethiopian' in their fivefold classification of the world's races.[18] Such estimates of the position of Indians in the racial hierarchy were ostensibly 'rectified' by the Civil War anthropometrical investigation of a cross-section of the American population undertaken by the US Sanitary Commission.[19]

Serious nineteenth-century investigators of race aimed to steer a course between the 'poets and romanticists' on the one hand, and the 'traducers and vilifiers' on the other: to present 'the Indian as he is, not as he might be'.[20] Just the same, under the impact of evolutionary teaching, prominent scientific spokesmen placed even greater emphasis on the existence of profound racial inequalities and the interdependence of race and culture during the post-Civil War years than they had earlier in the century. Notable in this context are the anthropologist, Daniel Brinton; the historian and anthropologist, Adolph Bandelier; the ethnologist, Cyrus Thomas; and the chief ethnologist with the Bureau of American Ethnology from 1893 to 1903, W. J. McGee. Brinton, for instance, believed in a hierarchy of higher and lower races, with the American Indian coming above the African in terms of physical characteristics, but with neither race able to build complex or durable social organizations because of the 'limitations of the racial mind'; while Thomas, McGee and Bandelier were scathing about Indian creeds and beliefs, which were said to produce 'slavish cringing before natural phenomena', a reliance upon the voices of nature 'which stifle the silent throbs of conscience [and] . . . are no guide to the heart, no support for the mind'.[21]

It is very much more difficult to move from a brief summary of some of the attitudes of the pioneer ethnologists to an evaluation of whether or not these scholars acted upon their beliefs; to an estimate of whether they desired or achieved practical influence either among their white contemporaries or the Indians themselves. Indeed, until the twentieth century the scarcity of Indian documents on the subject makes it extremely difficult to gauge the response of Native Americans to the investigators who came among them. Bieder constructs a convincing case for early ethnology as at once an expression of contemporary white concern for the improvability of man and a handy explanation for the course of American development.[22] Yet this is not to say that scientific observers were always conscious of the role they were playing or that their views were invariably applauded by other Americans.

Hence various anthropologists plunged into public controversy when they tried to refute both the biblical story of creation and attacks on black slavery which involved an environmentalist rather than a racial explanation of the 'deficiencies' of slaves. Their activities may have repelled as well as attracted adherents, just as was the case in Britain in the 1860s, when the President of the Anthropological Society of London, Dr James Hunt, tried to find a practical application for the racist views of himself and his followers.[23] Certainly historians disagree about the pre-Civil War application of American scientific judgements on race. On the one hand, it has been urged that slavery was regarded as a moral, not a scientific, issue, while plenty of practical and political arguments for dispossessing nomadic peoples and for the westward expansion already existed. The considerable support among American anthropologists for polygenesis and for the contention that non-white 'species' were innately inferior to the white, made scientists' findings useless to the anti-slavery movement, which repudiated, without itself being free of, race prejudice. Their views were equally unacceptable to southerners who based their defence of slavery on the literal truth of biblical teaching. On the other hand, Fredrickson and Horsman have demonstrated that the scientific theories had rather wider circulation than Stanton accorded them.[24] And they undoubtedly did nothing helpful for the image of American Indians in the first half of the nineteenth century.

Had ethnologists of an activist bent initially chosen to oppose government policies – which they did not – they would have been embarrassed by a number of factors. As we have seen, these policies were frequently popular and ostensibly dedicated to the assimilation and civilization of the Indians, which made them difficult to criticize. Denunciations consequently tended to be left to enemies of the party in power, Indian haters and religious groups jealous of their hold over the tribes. The ethnologists valued the ethnographic information gathered by government-backed exploring expeditions and they themselves collected such data, so playing a crucial part, as Goetz-mann has shown, in the 'winning of the American West'. This victory in turn facilitated the ethnologists' ultimate objective of destroying Indian hunting cultures, though a sop to the tribes was proffered in the short term when the explorations suggested that parts of the West were unfit for white habitation and might accordingly be regarded as 'Indian country'.[25] Furthermore, the attention of the early students of mankind usually had to be focused on earning a living.

The developing science of ethnology could claim few professionals and many self-taught dilettanti, as was to be expected. Albert Gallatin, the founder of the American Ethnological Society, spent the principal part of his career in politics and finance, while Morton and Nott were successful doctors. Samuel Stanhope Smith was a professor of moral philosophy, James Hall a jurist and banker and Ephraim Squier a journalist. For many years after his marriage, Morgan was obliged to lay aside his Indian studies to make money, while Brinton began work as a military surgeon and editor of the *Medical and Surgical Reporter*. In addition, the influential Morton and Brinton never ventured into the field, there is some evidence that Bandelier found this aspect of his work rather trying and the first four heads of the Bureau of Ethnology, founded in 1879, were 'all self-educated in anthropology'.[26] If they escaped criticism as armchair experts and undertook field investigations, the pioneers might be reproved for their ruthlessness in obtaining information, albeit their convictions about the phenomenally destructive encroachment of white civilization on native cultures provide an excuse of sorts.[27]

There were, none the less, individuals whose sympathy with the Indians was not nullified by the restraints of contemporary theory and who could admit to making mistakes. Thus Schoolcraft, in addition to his efforts as an agent, visited Washington and wrote and lectured with a view to changing popular misconceptions about the Indians. He was also willing to concede that the reservation by which he had set so much store left much to be desired in practice.[28] And Morgan effectively organized a defence of the Seneca Indians against the attempt of the Ogden Land Company in New York to secure their land for far below the market price. Later in the century, he was prepared to risk defending Sitting Bull and the Sioux in the hysterical aftermath of the Custer massacre. Morgan was described in the *American Indian Magazine* in 1917 as 'indeed a faithful friend of the race'.[29] It was, unfortunately, very hard to alter public indifference or hostility towards Indians when appeals for justice were preceded by scholarly affirmations of Indian inferiority and when 'friends of the Indian' like Schoolcraft and Morgan so obviously favoured the assimilationist programme supported by less broad-minded whites.

In the years after the Civil War, as anthropology became stronger and more respectable, Powell lobbied in Congress and elsewhere for the application of its findings to government policy respecting the Native Americans, while Morgan pressed for the establishment of an Indian Department, separated from the existing unsatisfactory institutions concerned with Indian policy.[30] The erudite studies of native cultures by Alice Fletcher were inspired by an initial philanthropic interest in Indian welfare which she never lost. A Harvard fellow and ethnologist, Fletcher was best known for her studies of Indian music and of the Omahas. She was notable for her generosity to the Indians among whom she worked and her sympathetic temperament as well as professional interest led naturally to an involvement with the postwar Indian reform movement; an involvement which could not be an easy one, given the reformers' general lack of anthropological insight.[31]

As a prominent woman scholar, Fletcher was made welcome at the meetings of the Lake Mohonk Conference and she was an honorary member of the Women's National Indian Association. But in Mohonk meetings she was exposed to the feeling that there had always been a gulf between ethnologists and administrators of Indian affairs, because the scientists were seen as impractical at best, and at worst interested in preserving 'savagery' for their professional perusal, rather as missionaries were felt selfishly to attach more importance to Indian converts than to Indian progress.[32] Not surprisingly, Fletcher clashed at Mohonk with the aggressively assimilationist educator, Richard Henry Pratt of Carlisle Indian School, over the value of Indian industries practised in the home. To Fletcher, the fact that they were a link with the 'primitive' past was less important than their ability to provide work, enjoyment and income, especially for the old.[33] However, in her support for the allotment of Indian land, Fletcher was congenial to most Mohonk attenders. From her point of view, allotment would secure the Indians against further removals from their homes while hastening their assimilation and she happily became a seasoned allotting agent.[34] Fletcher's attitude to allotment was shared by her fellow scientists.[35]

Notwithstanding the controversial support of James Mooney and later anthropologists for the Indians' religious use of the peyote root,[36] it would seem that the tension between them and the Indian Bureau was no larger than that which existed between the BIA and other outside groups which tried to bring pressure to bear on its policies. In fact there is much evidence of co-operation between the fledgeling profession and the government. Prior to the Civil War, the secretary of the Smithsonian Institution had sought government backing for research into Indian cultures before they were destroyed. From 1867, John Wesley Powell conducted a number of expeditions to the Rocky Mountain West, first with university and then with congressional support, which engaged both in exploration and the gathering of ethnographic data. After 1873, he directed his staff to collect materials ranging from Indian vocabularies to artefacts for deposit in the US National Museum and Powell's successful efforts to consolidate government surveys of the West in one geological survey resulted in the creation of a Bureau of Ethnology in the Smithsonian to receive the findings of the survey. (The word 'American' was added to the bureau's title in 1894.) Through the bureau, under the direction of Powell, the government subsequently gave support to field surveys among the Indians, concerned with their present as well as past circumstances. Surveys were further stimulated by the desire of American museums, and especially the National Museum, to enlarge their holdings.

It must be admitted that the results of some of this early fieldwork, though vital for the anthropologists' compilation of bibliographies and information on Indian languages and land cessions and for the professionalization of their subject, have since been dismissed as unduly descriptive.[37] Yet it is unreasonable to expect much more before the growth of concern among twentieth-century anthropologists to apply the techniques of ethnology to modern societies; before the emergence of 'applied anthropology' as a subject in its own right. In the meanwhile, from Schoolcraft onwards, the ethnologists offered a public increasingly interested in wild, heroic and picturesque natives some insight into 'the Indian mind' and lifestyle, as well as into the Indian 'fate'.[38] Schoolcraft's investigations of the stories, poems and spiritual concerns of the Indians threw light on their character and social organization. Morgan, like Schoolcraft, spent time among the Indians he wrote about and learned their language in order to produce his account of the political system of the Iroquois. In a period when westerners often presented Indians as savage and humanitarians portrayed them as degraded, he praised the 'civil institutions', 'domestic affections', 'religious enthusiasm' and general character of the Iroquois.[39]

The introductions to Indian languages by Gallatin and Powell were ground-breaking contributions to the subject, as were, in their respective areas, McGee's monograph on the Seri Indians, Thomas's work on the Mississippi Valley mound builders, Bandelier's findings on the Indians and history of the Southwest and Brinton's scholarship on the Florida peninsula and broad survey of 'The American Race', which included the first classification of Native American languages. And although these observers were not flattering in their comments upon the Indians' stage in human progress, they were at pains to show that the Indians' mastery over their environment had helped Europeans to survive in America; that the position of Indian women was better than whites supposed; that Indian parents were fond of their children; that if Indian languages were primitive, then English had only just emerged from a barbaric condition; and that the 'injurious effect of the Indian shamans on their nations was not greater than has been in many instances that of the Christian priesthood on European communities'.[40]

II

THE DEVELOPMENT OF MODERN ANTHROPOLOGY

It was not until the Indian researches of Franz Boas began to appear, however, that the nineteenth-century preoccupation with evolution and conviction that race determined culture were really challenged within the science of anthropology. A fieldworker among the Eskimos of the Cumberland Peninsula (1883–4) and subsequently among the Indians of the Northwest and Mexico, Boas fought for a discipline committed to the essential unity of man. He proved himself capable of approaching the Indians he studied, and their languages, without the condescension that had usually afflicted even the best-intentioned of his predecessors.[41] The Indian's voice is also to be found in Boas's work. If his comparative neglect of social and economic organization and the fact that he did not live among the Indians as a 'participant observer' are now criticized, the importance of his habit of collecting innumerable 'texts' or statements from native informants is acknowledged.[42] An extraordinarily versatile scholar, whose interests included anthropometry, linguistics, ethnography and photography, Boas played an active part in establishing anthropology in the American Association for the Advancement of Science; in a reinvigorated American Ethnological Society; and in the foundation of an American Anthropological Association in which untrained amateurs enjoyed little say. Increasingly, anthropologists had either university or museum connections.[43]

Boas protested against white racism and tried to put pressure on white authorities to improve the social conditions of the Indians he investigated, while his pupil, Frank G. Speck, together with later anthropologists, helped to draw attention to the existence of eastern Indians and to assist the Nanticokes to obtain a corporate charter from the state of Delaware. Yet Boas and his followers remained aloof from the 'friends of the Indian' and pan-Indian movements of their day, partly for fear of compromising their claims to scholarly objectivity. By the 1920s, anthropologists provided no members for the still active Indian Rights Association;[44] and the profession had produced no Indian defence organization of its own. None the less, Alanson B. Skinner (a white) and J. N. B. Hewitt, Dr Charles Eastman, Arthur C. Parker, Sherman Coolidge and Francis La Flesche (all Indians), were among the academics who joined the first modern pan-Indian association, the Society of American Indians (SAI), formed in 1911, while Parker and La Flesche had been the first Indians to be included on Mohonk's influential business committee.[45]

La Flesche, Hewitt and Skinner were occasional attenders at SAI meetings; none of them is listed as an active member of the society in or after 1914. As participants, they collectively indicated a support for Indian assimilation balanced by a keen interest in the differences between Indians and whites that would have made them very acceptable to the progress-minded SAI.[46] Parker alone gave regular and vital service to the society. A Seneca Indian who worked for the Museum of Natural History in New York city, he acted as the SAI's secretary, the editor of its journal and eventually its president. Whilst he was anxious not to seem destructively critical of the BIA, Parker favoured much that policy-makers had long resisted, did not then support, or could not produce: an Indian junior college, an adequate education system which would reduce Indian illiteracy, a defined legal status and codification of Indian law, the speedy handling of Indian claims and better explanation to Indians of government policy affecting them.[47] In the later stages of the society's career, when its *American Indian Magazine* was using more material from white anthropologists, the organization showed a growing acceptance of the difficulties involved in political action and tended to focus, as anthropologists had always been accused of doing, on 'Indians of the past at the expense of topics of more immediate concern'.[48]

It would be wrong, of course, to suggest that the Indian service remained untouched by reformer pressures during the commissionerships of Robert Valentine (1909–12) and Cato Sells (1913–21). But their combined efforts to improve its rectitude, economy and efficiency, which included the appointment of personnel with sociological and social work training and experience,[49] did not result in a positive willingness in the BIA to look for ways of using anthropological expertise. And because the American colonial presence was regarded as so impermanent, American anthropologists – unlike their British counterparts – did not have good prospects of exerting influence overseas, albeit a few worked in the Philippines between 1906 and 1910, until local opposition forced the termination of their efforts.[50] Just the same, when the embattled Commissioner of Indian Affairs between 1921 and 1929, Charles Burke, responded to criticisms of Indian policy by setting up an advisory Committee of One Hundred, the committee was headed by Arthur Parker and included several other anthropologists. Moreover, the impact of scientific opinion is shown in the committee's advocacy of an open-minded investigation of the effects of peyote consumption and in its support for Indian arts, crafts, ceremonies, rites and customs which were not illegal or harmful to the Indians' welfare and progress.

Anthropologists like Herbert Spinden and Oliver La Farge, who worked for the Eastern Association on Indian Affairs, were involved in the fight to save Pueblo Indian lands provoked by the 1922 Bursum Bill and La Farge was eventually an adviser to Commissioner Rhoads (1929–33). The American Anthropological Association, the anthropology division of the American Association for the Advancement of Science, the American Ethnological Society and the Bureau of American Ethnology likewise protested against the treatment of the Pueblos, but anthropologists were not consulted in the drawing up of the 1928 Meriam Report on the Indian service. This omission was apparently the result of their still limited activism, of the desire of the report's backers to avoid bias by shunning those who had previously investigated Indian affairs and of the lingering association of men of science with the 'glass case policy' of presenting Indians as museum specimens, a policy condemned by Meriam.[51]

Such strictures are not entirely unfair. As Joan Chandler has pointed out, American anthropologists in the 1920s remained anxious to record Indian ways that they thought were fast vanishing, only really turning to accounts of Indian life as it was, and of culture change, in the 1940s. Consequently studies of folklore, ceremonial, kinship and taxonomy attracted more attention than, say, the impact on Indian groups of wage work; the variable responses of Indians to money-making opportunities; the practical effect of federal policies; and the results of technological change in or near Indian communities. Fieldwork continued to be difficult, so that investigators might be obliged to take whatever informants they could find, regardless of suitability or reliability; or they might be tempted to go where others had already broken the ground. Academic, money and time pressures all conspired to keep the field anthropologist's eyes fixed on the difficult job in hand rather than the relationship of the Indians being investigated to the wider world.[52]

The breakthrough in relating anthropology to Indian policy finally came during the 1930s. By that time, scholars on both sides of the Atlantic had become more than formerly convinced of the need to examine the alterations produced by ethnic contact and to ensure that the distinctive ways and needs of indigenous peoples were respected in the process. In Britain, this kind of work was undertaken at the International Institute of African Languages and Culture. In the United States, anthropologists were deputed by the Social Science Research Council to study acculturation, which was said to include 'those phenomena which result when groups of individuals having different cultures come into continuous first-hand contact, with subsequent changes in the original patterns of either group or both groups'.[53] Among other things, scholars emphasized the 'psychological impact of acculturation', the 'acceptance, modification, or rejection of culture traits'.[54] At the American Association for the Advancement of Science meeting in 1930, the chairman of the anthropology section declared that members of her profession must relate their knowledge 'to present-day problems ... We can aid the government officer, the social worker, the missionary, the teacher ... A great amount of material has been collected; it now becomes our duty to make it available to those who can apply it.'[55] President Franklin D. Roosevelt's Commissioner of Indian Affairs, John Collier, proved ready to respond to this optimistic spirit.

III

THE RISE OF APPLIED ANTHROPOLOGY

The American Anthropological Association made no comment on Collier's most important measure, the 1934 Indian Reorganization Act (I.R.A.), which was designed to facilitate a measure of tribal self-determination. But in December of that year, the Commissioner consulted a gathering of anthropologists at Pittsburgh on how, generally, their involvement might be secured by the Indian service and what, specifically, were the best means of establishing or restoring the tribal constitutions and councils required by the I.R.A. As a result, Dr William Duncan Strong was seconded from the Bureau of American Ethnology to advise the Commissioner about 'how to use tribal institutions as vehicles for social change'. An Applied Anthropology Unit was formed by the Indian Bureau in 1935, and Collier sought anthropologists' recommendations on such matters as the selection of field workers.[56]

Was the new association anything more than a predictable marriage of convenience? After all, a number of anthropologists, by their condemnation of land allotment, were saying what reforming administrators wanted to hear, just as Alice Fletcher's support for allotment had made her acceptable in an era when it was generally favoured.[57] And anthropologists were not the only 'experts' whose advice was solicited by Collier, while their consultation was a source of annoyance to the Commissioner's enemies, in the same way that there was suspicion of the President's more famous 'Brain Trust'. The answer would seem to be that the connection was an important one, though not extraordinary in the context of the 1930s or able to unite the academically separated anthropologists and social workers recruited by Collier in practical work among the Indians.[58] There is something very refreshing in the frank recognition by the bureau of the merits of the profession it had so long suspected.[59] It was, nevertheless, easier to make than to act upon Collier's pledge of future co-operation.

Anthropologists were asked by the Commissioner to survey reservation conditions and report on the problems likely to accompany the ending of allotment and the implementation of the I.R.A. Where the anthropological verdict was that no change in the status quo was desirable – as, for instance, was concluded regarding the Oklahoma Comanches – this was reported, despite running contrary to Washington expectations. Attention was paid to both eastern and western groups and the advice given was realistic. Yet the impact of the Applied Anthropology Unit was limited, because by the time it had carried out its investigations (1936–8), the implementation of the I.R.A. was already well advanced.[60]

Although Collier did not uncritically believe that anthropologists, regardless of their particular orientation, would be helpful to the Indian service,[61] H. Scudder Mekeel, the field representative in charge of applied anthropology, Boas, A. L. Kroeber of Berkeley and Ales Hrdlicka of the Smithsonian were all supportive of the Commissioner during the 1930s debate on the Indians' right to use peyote, explaining its consumption in religious and social terms and condemning the legislation then proposed to prevent the distribution of peyote.[62] In addition, anthropologists were used during the decade in the BIA's education branch, investigating the deficiencies of the Navajo and other school systems and producing texts for the teaching of Indian languages and cultures in schools. Anthropologists were employed by the Soil Conservation Service and the Bureau of Agricultural Economics of the US Department of Agriculture to study Indian rural life and were detailed to help Indian farmers come to grips with the methods of white agriculturalists. They also investigated the economic and social progress of urban Indians. Since their findings urged the need to recognize the continuing vitality of Indian ways, however, they excited the hostility of those who opposed what they saw as the 'back to the blanket' thrust of the Indian New Deal.[63]

It was argued with disarming modesty by anthropologists themselves that their insights and skills had contributed to a sensitive awareness of Indian distinctiveness in the Roosevelt era, had thus ensured the willing Indian involvement in the Second World War and would expedite the integration of nationality groups in the United States once the war was ended.[64] But the funds allocated for applied anthropology were inadequate for the implementation of Mekeel's ideal of employing 'in each division of the [Indian] Service . . . a man with proper anthropological training who could assist in making the technical services of each division more effective in terms of actual Indian life'.[65]

There were other problems. After the first Pan-American Conference on Indian life at Patzcuaro in Mexico, in the spring of 1940, had endorsed the value of applied anthropology, a National Indian Institute was set up in the United States. It received Rockefeller funds and was charged with 'promoting the cooperation of learned societies in the fields of Indian administration, developing research projects, and publishing bibliographies on Indian matters'.[66] The institute, directed by Collier, began an Indian Personality Study through the University of Chicago's Committee on Human Development. Between 1941 and 1946 bureau funds were channelled into the project, which was extended and wound up by the Society for Applied Anthropology. One reason for this shift of responsibility, notwithstanding the optimism of anthropologists and the Commissioner, seems to have been that the scientists found it difficult to make those suggestions about Indian administration that were part of the project's purpose. Nor could they make them at the kind of speed required by harassed administrators.[67]

The studies undertaken by the institute covered eleven contrasting communities among the Hopi, Navajo, Papago, Sioux and New Mexico Pueblos and were described as historical, cultural, environmental and personality investigations. The role of the Society for Applied Anthropology was to relate the assembled data to bureau organization, methods and goals in the above areas and as a whole, to see how the objectives of the Indian New Deal could be more effectively implemented. Whilst Collier put up a spirited defence of the studies, perhaps for political reasons, Chandler has established that the personality tests were less than scientific and the relation of personality patterns to culture was not clarified. Furthermore, the inquiries provided no detailed evaluation of BIA programmes, albeit they drew attention to the bureau's failure to recruit staff 'for career service within tribal areas'; to the scarcity of locally engendered and integrated programmes for the Indians; and to the continuing failure of administrators to consider the 'cultural factors of Indian life'. Accordingly Laura Thompson's conclusions for the society, published in 1951, recommended the decentralization of bureau services, particularly in the areas of education and medicine, and the creation of community organizations built on tribal ways and personality 'types'.[68]

By the 1940s, anthropological methods and ideas had been used by administrators in industry, politics and philanthropic agencies for over a decade and a society and journal had come into being for the advancement of applied anthropology.[69] The Second World War, while interrupting some studies by anthropologists, resulted in the employment of many to advise on matters ranging from the relocation of the Japanese to reading languages regarded as important to the conduct of the war effort. Yet anthropologists were unable to make a full evaluation of Collier's programmes before these were abandoned. They were unable as a group to prevent the swing back to assimilation policies or to quell clamour for the termination of the BIA's special relationship with the Indians during the 1950s, something which is not too surprising. 'Applied anthropologists', like most academic consultants, found it difficult to determine their exact role and to operate as critics of those who employed them, especially within a cumbersome bureaucracy like the bureau. They were working in a relatively new field and lacked the power that can come with numbers.

It was one thing to make expert information or general advice available to administrators and to help train those administrators. This was done not just within the Indian service but also by scientists working for the Department of State, notably on the Point Four development aid programme outlined by President Truman in his 1949 inaugural address. Anthropologists acted in a similar capacity with regard to the trust territories of Micronesia in the Pacific, when they passed to American direction after the Second World War.[70] It was another, much more difficult and controversial task to move from recognizing the customs and interests likely to be affected by and opposed to change, to showing how it could actually be achieved, to advising on policy. Overseas, at least, notwithstanding the intellectual constraints imposed by the Cold War objectives of successive US governments, American aid was frequently welcome and the problems of applying it fell primarily to foreign governments. At home, there was much less chance of escaping the vagaries of public opinion and the pressure of unrealistic national expectations about how quickly changes of any kind could be realized.

The danger, therefore, for anthropologists concerned with Indian matters was of resuming their pre-Collier reputation as a merely critical, negative or complicating influence. Certainly, until the changed political climate of the 1960s, they lost ground in government circles. To be effective, they needed to be equally at home in white and Indian society, but they had no automatic *entrée* into the latter and risked losing effectiveness in the former unless they preserved a careful neutrality. All of which meant that it was inadvisable to press a specific course on either side. It has been suggested that the anthropologists' best hope lay in underlining 'the right of minorities by self-choice to achieve their own life-style'. And although Indian pressure groups, combined with those of other ethnic minorities, did more to bring acceptance of that right, anthropologists have played their part since the Second World War. In pursuit of this end, it has been helpful that a number of scholars, in their work on the complexities of culture change, have stressed the importance and durability of a culture 'core', or inner 'covert' culture, which was immensely difficult to transform.[71]

In the years after 1946, while anthropologists were not consulted about the creation of the Indian Claims Commission, they were called before it as expert witnesses and worked with Indian groups to help them regain land and exercise their legal rights. A good case in point would be the assistance the anthropologist John J. Bodine was able to give to the Taos Indians in their successful struggle to recover the Blue Lake, which they had lost without negotiation or compensation in 1906, his contribution being essentially to demonstrate the importance of the shrine 'to the correct functioning of Taos religion' and to underline the uniqueness of the Taos claim.[72] Anthropologists were among those who protested against termination and Dr Nancy Lurie of the Milwaukee Public Museum, after thoroughly studying its application to the Menominees, decided that the policy had 'no rationality', besides being obviously unpopular with the Indians and dire in its effects upon them. Her conclusion, in line with those reached by other 'action' anthropologists,[73] was that the Menominees should be enabled to 'tell us what they have decided upon as in their best interest' and that we should 'then support them in accomplishing it'.[74]

Another critic of termination was Philleo Nash, a specialist in applied anthropology from Wisconsin, who worked with such early opponents of the policy as the National Congress of American Indians and the Association on American Indian Affairs. Together with anthropologist James E. Officer of the University of Arizona, Nash was a member of the Kennedy Task Force on Indian Affairs, which in 1961 recommended that the 'federal government switch its emphasis from "termination of Federal supervision and benefits to spurring the development of Indian-owned resources"'.[75] In 1961, Nash became Indian Commissioner and Officer served as Associate Commissioner; but five years later opponents either impatient with the degree of innovation he had been able to achieve or critical of his stand on termination secured Nash's removal from office, whereupon he resumed his academic career and subsequently volunteered his services to the Menominees who were fighting termination.[76]

For most American anthropologists, the opportunity of combining the roles of scholar and influential activist did not arise, yet there were some openings. Although the Bureau of American Ethnology, long short of money and appreciation, was merged with the US National Museum's Department of Anthropology to constitute the Smithsonian's Office of Anthropology, Congress maintained its own research unit and anthropologists were employed by the State Department and the Bureau of Indian Affairs. Medical anthropology emerged as a separate field after the Second World War and anthropologists, as Voget notes, were able to advise on the reconciling of 'traditional' and 'modern' approaches to disease. On the other hand, after the retirement from the Indian education service of Willard Beatty, they were never as closely involved again in trying to provide the materials and insights necessary to produce cross-cultural instruction, notwithstanding the encouragement of the American Anthropological Association and the preparation by scholars of some useful texts for the purpose.[77]

In 1967, the association, prompted by a fear that members of the profession were being used in an unreasonable fashion to advance US political objectives in Chile, declared its opposition to government censorship or covert use of anthropological inquiry and to involving anthropologists, except during wartime, in activities unconnected with their normal teaching, research and 'public service functions'.[78] Such a move was wise, since following the increased activity of pan-Indian political groups in the course of the decade anthropologists working in the United States found themselves condemned both for their association with policies they actually did little to effect and for their assumption of expertise without involvement. Just because anthropologists strove to penetrate the 'inner core' of Indian cultures, their presence as investigators became more unacceptable in an era of heightened ethnic and political consciousness among Indians. Even though anthropology played an important part in the university Indian Studies programmes which were then being established, there was some feeling that, while the subject might enlarge a student's understanding of his or her own society, its disciples had been disagreeably associated with removing Indian artefacts and offending Indian religious sensibilities. Partly on account of this last grievance, it was thought that tribal elders could teach other Indians better, whatever their lack of formal qualifications acceptable to whites.[79] Owing to these difficulties and the fact that applied anthropology still suggested to some professionals an unacademic neglect of theory and objectivity alike, it was comparatively little taught in graduate schools as late as the 1960s.[80]

Yet, in fairness, it must be acknowledged that at least since the Second World War, but especially from the 1960s, anthropologists have shown in their major works a clear awareness of contemporary Indian difficulties, of the necessity for change to follow the existing values of the community concerned and of their own role in providing a public critique of government policy. This awareness in turn indicates that the problems inherent in studying semi-assimilated tribes have made present-day scholars less confident than their predecessors and more sensitive to the destructive implications of 'progress'.[81] It would seem that anthropologists, whatever their own unsolved methodological difficulties, are now allowing their 'objects' rather than their theories to take the centre of the stage. Thus, for instance, works published in the Holt Rinehart & Winston series, 'Case Studies in Cultural Anthropology', sensitively explore the complexities of still adapting and enduring Indian cultures, while Edward Spicer provides an exemplary account of 'American Indians', past and present, in the *Harvard Encyclopedia of American Ethnic Groups*.[82] Anthropological research has always increased available knowledge about Indian cultures. But its practitioners are now playing a larger and less culture-bound part than was possible in the infancy of their subject in instructing uninformed whites about Native American cultures, as well as about some of the trials involved in seeking to implement the goal of cultural pluralism.

8

Indian Education: Goals and Illusions

White educational efforts on behalf of American Indians began early, as part of a religious concern to spread literacy and hence understanding of the Scriptures among the heathen, thus justifying European settlement among them. In time they became part of a broader effort to control disaffected or unruly elements of the population and so promote order in a rapidly growing society.

I

THE RELIGIOUS ORIGINS OF INDIAN EDUCATION

During the colonial period, much of the work of instructing youngsters fell upon parents, preachers and masters of apprentices. Government played an important part only in New England, whose towns were required to maintain elementary and secondary schools; and even there, payments were expected from parents. Throughout the colonies, only the affluent could afford the private tutors, schools and colleges from which members of the leadership class generally emerged after courses of instruction in which classical and religious subjects dominated. Yet the sectarian piety which produced so many colleges also prompted the foundation of pauper schools and efforts to reach the black and Indian populations.

From the first, these efforts were both an intended compensation for white disruption of non-white ways and a device for fostering the assimilation or Americanization of so-called savages. As the anthropologist, Lewis Henry Morgan, would remark, 'If the Indian puts forth his hand for knowledge, he asks for the only blessing which we can give him in exchange for his birthright, which is worthy of his acceptance.'[1] Equally, educational endeavours were always vulnerable to the disillusionment which racial hostilities, inadequate finances and slow progress easily bred, as well as plagued by discussions about how schools among the Indians could be made self-sustaining and whether the tribes should be civilized before they were Christianized.[2]

In Virginia, plans were made for an Indian college at Henrico and an East India Company school, but missionary hopes were dashed by the Indian massacre of 1622. Schooling and conversion alike demanded enormous changes in the lives of the affected Indians, who were able to educate the whites in the ways of the wilderness without making comparable demands on them and preferred the newcomers' material goods to their culture.[3] In New England, the Puritans' exacting social code made conversion a difficult process until, as Lawrence Cremin has observed, white preachers learned how to appeal to Indian tribesmen with the aid of native intermediaries. Their successes encouraged the creation in 1649 of the London-based Society for Propagation of the Gospel in New England. During the next few decades the society raised thousands of pounds and used the moneys to pay clergy and schoolmasters for the Indians and to buy them 'clothing, building materials, and tools'. It financed the printing of books – including the Bible – in Algonquian and facilitated the construction of an Indian College at Harvard in the 1650s. The society also helped to maintain fourteen 'praying towns' in the Bay Colony, where converts lived a settled agricultural existence.

However, outside Massachusetts and the islands of Martha's Vineyard and Nantucket, there were few conversions to either civility or religion. Racial hostilities culminating in King Philip's War of 1675 disrupted missionary work, creating white suspicion and Indian doubt about the value of the praying towns. If, as Tanis has shown, these communities then contained some 11,000 Christian Indians, had supported schools for twenty years and largely relied on Indian preachers and teachers, only four of them survived the conflict. Whilst the white missionary, John Eliot, might have been genuinely concerned to offer the Indians a variety of educational experiences, the Puritan authorities seem to have been primarily concerned that the Indians should learn to obey white laws. And even in Massachusetts, only a handful of Indians attended the common schools or went to Harvard.[4]

New educational efforts followed when, in 1701, the Society for the Propagation of the Gospel in Foreign Parts (SPG) was created in England to uphold orthodox religion and convert the heathen in the colonies. From its inception to 1783, it founded approximately 170 far-flung missions, employed over eighty teachers and distributed a mass of religious and educational literature, some of it in Indian languages. The society's envoys were often far from welcome: Dissenters disliked them, local worthies were suspicious, local Indians hostile. Colonial conditions could be harsh and ambitious instructions drawn up at a safe distance from the New World were consequently carried out with difficulty. Early missions to the Yamassee and other Indians of South Carolina and to the Mohawks of New York yielded meagre results yet, following the SPG's example, the Society in Scotland for Propagating Christian Knowledge assisted the efforts of the New England educator of the Indians, Eleazar Wheelock, whose most famous pupil, the Mohegan, Samson Occom, undertook a successful fund-raising tour of England and Scotland in the 1760s.

Judged overall, these and other pioneering activities failed. Patronized and coerced, required to undertake irksome and sometimes unintelligible tasks and finally offered no secure place in the white world if they wanted it, the lot of the small number of educated Indians was an unenviable one. Though the ability of a few of them to mediate between two worlds was vital to the whites' early educational efforts and though, as Margaret Szasz has shown, Wheelock even took the bold step of instructing some girl students at his Moor's Indian Charity School, the majority of Indians were reached only by the 'informal education of day-by-day existence'.[5]

When missionary operations were resumed after Independence, they were sustained both by old white assumptions about the superiority of the Christian religion and by a new vision of their national scope. Better transport and the growing prosperity of the United States meant that the missionaries were no longer obliged to confine their ministrations to tribes adjacent to white settlements and had more funds at their disposal,[6] while by the nineteenth century secular reformers were likewise convinced of the need for enlarged educational provision as the young republic was transformed by immigration, urbanization, industrialization and the advance of democracy. According to white educators, tax-supported schools at the elementary and secondary levels would afford a means of helping religious instruction to keep pace with population growth, of reaffirming the place of the church in education which the separation of church and state had destroyed and of providing that moral discipline which urban parents were allegedly ceasing to exert upon their children. They would bridge the growing gulf between the classes and ethnic groups and fit the young of town and frontier alike for the new political and economic opportunities which were developing in society. If those who most needed this education could not see its advantages or accept such priorities, then there must be what Michael B. Katz has called 'reform by imposition'.

Now of course the educational work undertaken among the Indians was for a long time largely concerned with the problems created by a poor, rural environment and with elementary instruction, while the schools established among them were initially private, philanthropic ventures. But they too were affected by contemporary optimism about the transforming power of education and felt the growing importance in that process of the state, once primarily associated – outside New England – with providing for the children of paupers or granting land for the endowment of public schools.[7] They too became the raw material for an educational experiment about whose form and objectives they were little consulted and which their apathy or opposition failed to prevent. Moreover, those active in pushing for educational reform among the Indians were frequently lay 'experts', as Katz found with his pre-Civil War Massachusetts educationalists.[8] Hence political appointees in the Bureau of Indian Affairs, the various commentators on Indian culture and the missionaries' eastern patrons, as well as missionaries themselves, saw education as a key to 'improving' the natives, at the same time as they recognized that Indians 'could not be made to appreciate the offers of education and Christianity by one portion of the [white] community, while others [on the frontier] were arrayed against them in arms'.[9]

It was therefore comparatively easy for the Indian administrator, Thomas L. McKenney, to lead a variety of well-intentioned eastern groups into a petition campaign which resulted in the passage of the Indian Civilization Fund Act of 1819, whereby Congress was to lay out ten thousand dollars annually to finance teaching among the Indians. By 1830, as Herman Viola notes, 'the system boasted fifty-two schools and an enrollment of 1,512 students'.[10] This was not an impressive number, but there were many practical obstacles in the way of success. Although missionaries declared themselves encouraged by the Indians' desire for their ministrations and the benefits which flowed from instruction,[11] in the period up to the 1830s, the Indians in fact proved far from amenable.[12] Holding a gloomy view of what schools involved, many Indian parents felt that they were bestowing a favour on teachers by allowing their children to attend. Even more than their white counterparts in the city and remote areas, such parents did not seek to break down resistance among their offspring or enforce attendance, valuing the company of children at home and their practical contribution to the household.[13] To those accustomed to despise agricultural labour or – as in the case of the southern Indians – to associate it with black slaves, the use of pupils as labourers at school seemed to be reducing them to a state of servitude,[14] notwithstanding white arguments that the labour extracted instilled desirable work habits and skills in the Indian youngsters. Some adults, particularly among the mixed bloods who gradually welcomed the teachers and provided their students, might hope that education would equip their children to survive in an obviously stronger white world. But parents disliked having their infants educated far from home in boarding schools, finding them strange both in ways and assumptions when they returned home and so being tempted to join in the local ridicule meted out to the vacationing students.[15]

Furthermore, the tribes had their own educational 'machinery' and techniques. Through subgroups called sodalities, Indians instructed the uninitiated in tribal lore, medicinal skills and religious secrets, usually through ceremonies, dances and dramas. Much instruction in adult skills was, nevertheless, carried out at the individual level, exclusively so in tribes like the Navajo, which lacked sodalities, and unsupervised observation was also vital to learning. Despite some evidence of punitive treatment of the young, Indian parents were generally more unwilling to discipline their children than their white counterparts, relying upon relatives, ridicule, or invocations of the supernatural to produce essential correction.[16] Whatever the reasons for this trait – ranging from fear of stunting the child's development to respect for infant connections with the spirit world – it brought the Indians into conflict with white educators. Calvinist attitudes to child-rearing might have been changing,[17] yet in Indian schools discipline continued on the whole to be strict.

Small wonder, then, that Indian children played truant or learned little when placed in institutions which sought to regulate their days in an unprecedented fashion, instructing them in an alien language and religious faith and keeping them indoors for long hours when they would normally have been outside or at play. Memorization was an essential feature of education in red and white culture, but the Indian mission children were asked to memorize hymns and passages from Scripture which they frequently did not understand and which contradicted all their own learned traditions. Incomprehension was compounded by the fact that pupils of every degree of attainment were at first taught together and discomfort was created by the stern emphasis upon cleanliness, white naming practices, modes of dressing, eating and manual labour. Just when the academy was coming under attack by white reformers because it separated impressionable children from steadying parental support, the academy and the manual labour boarding school were being urged for Indian pupils partly in order to destroy hostile home influences and enforce attendance. To make matters worse, since academies did not exist outside the southern tribes before removal, children frequently had to be sent east if they aspired to further education.

It would be wrong, however, to imply that pedagogical problems were confined to Indian schools, that feelings of dismay were confined to Native American students, or that their teachers were invariably as callous as they were culture-bound. White working-class parents, essentially in the position of the full bloods, objected to paying for educational changes in which they could see little benefit or whose authors they suspected, along with the moral values they strove to impose on youngsters said to display 'the inherited stupidity of centuries of ignorant ancestors'. White schools were plagued by poor attendance and unruly pupils, and white reformers, though sure of the proper ends of education, disagreed about the proper means to achieve them. They failed in their attempts to change the total educational environment of both the Indian and the white masses and because they expected too much from schooling they were pre-ordained to fail.

The teachers none the less often applied the best that white pedagogy had to offer in their Indian schools, including a broadening curriculum, instruction for both sexes, graded classes, better material conditions than might be found in the pupils' homes, relatively advanced training for the professions and guidance in practical subjects. Despite the stress on the English language, some missionaries – notably the Baptists and those of the American Board of Commissioners for Foreign Missions – translated the texts they used into native languages, taught in the local tongue and used native converts as instructors. The level of education in the leading Indian schools – for example, Cornwall Academy in Connecticut, the Choctaw Academy in Kentucky and Spencer Academy in the Choctaw nation – was superior to that available in rural regions to poor whites.[18]

II

QUASI-AUTONOMY:
FROM REMOVAL TO THE CIVIL WAR

When the press of whites into Indian country led to the removal of the eastern Indians across the Mississippi during the 1830s, humanitarians and administrators looked forward optimistically to the educational gains that the transplanted tribes would make in the West, free from contacts with unsavoury whites. In the course of removal, large treaty annuities were accordingly earmarked for education. But in the short term, of course, a policy officially justified as advancing the cause of civilization ironically involved the destruction of schools built up with the aid of the Civilization Fund. It forced migration upon the Baptist missionaries working among the Miamis, Shawnees, Potawatomis and Ottawas in the Northwest. The sect's evangelists also accompanied three of the Five Civilized Tribes to the West, in the process abandoning schools in former Choctaw, Chickasaw and Creek country. A still greater wrench was experienced by the Presbyterian missionaries of the American Board, who by 1830, using government and Indian funds, had been operating eleven schools reaching 260 children among the Choctaws.[19]

Once the tribes were in the West, missionaries renewed their efforts with varying degrees of success, against an initial background of physical hardship and scarcity, intensified tribal factionalism caused by disputes over the terms and consequences of removal, and increased Indian hostility towards evangelists as agents of the government responsible for the removal programme. The Seminoles, because of their poverty and isolation from white influences, had not sustained schools at all in Florida, though they sent some children to the Choctaw Academy. The tribe found it equally difficult to do so in the West, even by 1860. Nevertheless, a school was opened with government aid in 1844, and in 1849 a mission school had been established through the efforts of a Presbyterian, the Reverend John Lilley, and his wife Mary Ann. Ten years later they were teaching 22 children, but through remembering that the tribal population was then 2,253, some idea of the small scale of their venture and the large scope of the field can be gained. By the 1840s, mission and tribal schools were functioning in the remaining Five Tribes, predictably in view of their partial pre-removal adaptation to white civilization, sedentary habits and powerful mixed-blood elements. And if the new institutions did not reach the majority of school-age Indians and instructed pupils primarily in English, the educational systems of these tribes had some notable features.

Thus, for example, the Cherokees, Creeks and Choctaws were able to employ a body of vernacular literature in their schools. The mixed-blood Cherokee, Sequoyah, having worked out a system of characters representing the various sounds of the Cherokee language in the 1820s, the tribe was already publishing books and a newspaper before removal, while missionaries among the Creeks and Choctaws helped them to devise written versions of their languages, which were then put to good use in the education process. The Choctaws and Cherokees struggled to make higher education available to their children and native superintendents were employed by the Creeks. Moreover, the Cherokee public schools were primarily staffed by Cherokee teachers and by 1859 had an enrolment of over 1,500. There could be no doubt that the southern Indians were educable and that education helped them to strengthen their own group identity as well as to adapt to white civilization.

In the Southwest, where the United States acquired vast territories after the Mexican War (1846–8), it was difficult to give priority to schooling before peace and American jurisdiction had been securely established there, while the tribes of the central and northern Plains were disturbed by the need for new or further relocations as a result of wars and white demands. Among the nomadic Comanches, for instance, the Penetethkas were in 1855 persuaded to settle on a reservation provided in Texas, where a school was begun. Yet local white hostility, the lure of old ways and the outbreak of the Civil War destroyed the enterprise. As far as the Indians of the Southwest are concerned, Dale notes that 'almost no educational work was done prior to 1870, and very little for ten years after that date'. The early educational endeavours in the Columbia River region (1830s–50s) seem to have been similarly negligible in effect, and attempts to operate a day school for Indian boys at the mission to the Flathead Indians were abandoned after a year, in 1857, as premature, despite the strong missionary interest in the tribe. On the other hand, a certain success was enjoyed with mission-run elementary schools among the Santee Sioux, newly confined to a reservation during the 1850s, and then prospering despite an enforced move to Nebraska in 1866. For its part, notwithstanding much initial opposition from Indian men to acquiring 'female' skills, the government managed to set up some of the manual labour schools by which it hoped to transform 'savages' into farmers. Indeed, by the 1860s all but two of the agencies of the Central Superintendancy – which encompassed a large part of modern Wyoming, Nebraska and Kansas – supported such institutions.

III

THE POST-CIVIL WAR DRIVE FOR ASSIMILATION

Just when schools had been re-established or begun, however, Civil War intervened. Lasting for four years (1861–5), the war was for the southern Indians a tragedy comparable to removal, in the course of which tribal schools were abandoned and either fell into decay or were occupied for other purposes as their patrons struggled for survival. The few schools which existed among the 'wild' tribes were similarly prone to interruption in the disturbed wartime conditions.[20] But interest in Indian education steadily grew after the Civil War, for a variety of reasons. The inadequacy of educational provision for the Indians could not be doubted by whites, whatever the tribal objections might be to schools. As railroads forged westward through past and present tribal lands and with them went more settlers, the forces of civilization and 'savagery' came into the kind of close contact which had precipitated removal in the 1830s, yet at a time when the injustice and destructiveness of Indian removals were being more strongly highlighted by humanitarians and the enormous cost of military operations against the western Indians was being called into question. It was hoped that the education of Indians on secure reservations would destroy 'savagery', ease racial friction and thereby cut government costs in the long run. And the success of Freedmen's Bureau and freedmen's aid society schools in the post-Civil War South had shown that educational advance was possible in the most daunting circumstances,[21] albeit with eager black co-operation and involvement, described by W. E. B. DuBois as 'a mass demand for popular education unequalled by any other group in world history'.

It must be admitted, even so, that we would not now applaud the later nineteenth-century tendency of middle-class educators, influenced by class snobbery as well as racial and cultural prejudices, to equate the needs and prospects of Indians, blacks and immigrants. Reformers felt that both the red and black races might be taught effectively by whites, who could deal directly with individuals from each race as if they had no sense of group identity. The Indians were merely the worst off of the minorities in the degree to which they were denied the opportunity to exercise that entrenched American educational principle, local control, still hallowed though everywhere under attack during the nineteenth century. Because the home environments in which blacks and Indians lived were held by whites to be the cause of the 'inferiority' of the two races, educators assumed that they would gratefully abandon their values and institutions when prompted to do so by their 'superiors'. The same assumption was made about the immigrants who crowded into America's cities and it reveals the general failure of the reforming elite to appreciate the complexities involved in social change. Not least among the benefits of schools for minorities, it was believed, was their ability to act as agents of Amercianization: such institutions were pre-eminently fitted to inculcate patriotism, diligence, cleanliness, self-discipline and the desire for respectability. For their part the Italians, Germans, Poles, Czechoslovakians, French and Norwegians in America saw some benefits in education but resisted attempts to prevent them from teaching their own languages and religious precepts in their own schools, something which the isolated Indian peoples were only able to protest by the traditional methods of withholding their children and deriding educated tribesmen. Indian education was also affected by national trends in other ways. Thus, for example, the strongly anti-Catholic campaign against sectarian schools among the Indians, which gathered pace from the 1880s, paralleled the renewed attack on Catholic instruction in American schools, comparable in its vehemence to that which had driven Irish Catholic parents to keep their children away from the common schools before the Civil War.

None the less, educators did make some distinctions between the assorted dangerous classes and consequently the educational provision for them was not absolutely unvarying. Having once – and alone – been excluded from schooling and having then been instructed in the South by humanitarians who wanted to equip them for citizenship and to compete for social benefits, blacks, like immigrants, were subsequently schooled for a special position as 'raw labour' in the changing economic order. Indian education, by contrast, though it was similarly shaped by economic factors, was at least different from that of blacks in that some experts could be found to testify that the Indians' 'brain power is fully equal . . . to the whites'; hence they were not immediately consigned to education for place rather than opportunity. But English-speaking blacks and white immigrants alike were better positioned to fight for quality education than were the more isolated, alienated and loosely organized Indians, with the exception of the semi-autonomous Five Civilized Tribes, who ran their own, elite-dominated educational systems.[22]

Before the 1880s, the primacy of the missionary societies in Indian education was not seriously challenged. Indeed, President Grant's Peace Policy, inaugurated in 1869 (see Chapter 3), enhanced their opportunities in this field beyond their capabilities. Adopting assimilation as their goal, the missionaries at the same time – if to different degrees – believed that the Indians should be taught and learn from texts in their native languages as well as English, and by Indian teachers where they were available. Pressure on mission schools receiving government aid unfortunately resulted in the vernacular being confined to Bible instruction in those institutions by the late 1880s. The moral lessons of education continued to be most valued in mission schools; conversion was the main objective and there was consequently an anxious search for suitable employees and concern about corrupting contacts between Indians and unsympathetic local whites.

Industrial training – specifically agricultural work for boys and housework for girls – was emphasized and children were generally said to learn well, although at least ten years 'of arduous work for each child' might be necessary to enable educators to secure their influence over pupils. More attention than formerly was paid to the mature Indians. Their experiences with freedmen's aid had shown missionaries what could be achieved with adults, and evangelists working among the Indians likewise hoped to educate both old and young. Considerable time had to be spent on informing patrons, usually in glowing terms, about the progress of the missionaries' schools, but while Indian parents were carefully cultivated, the Indian verdict on schooling is hard to find, just as the reaction of white parents and pupils to education is a scarce commodity. It would have been useful to have the response of George Enos, a student at the Presbyterian Board of Home Missions' Tucson Indian Training School in Arizona, to this description of his average day, sent to an interested easterner:

> He rises at half past five in the morning, eats his breakfast at six after which we have devotional exercises in the dining-room. Then he marches in line to his dormitory and makes his bed ... After his bed is made he is assigned some other work until eight o'clock. Then he has a short period of play before schooltime, and goes to school in the forenoon. With a little over an hour at noon for dinner and play he works in the afternoon either at cleaning up the yard, cutting wood or watching the cows at the ranch. At four o'clock his work is done and he has an hour to play before supper. After supper he has half an hour to play, then we have devotional exercise, and after that three quarters of an hour to study the lessons for the next day, after which comes half an hour more playtime and then he goes to bed, repeating his prayer in concert with the other boys.

The missionaries hoped to 'fit [the Indians] for family and home life ... The home is the unit of society and the church.' With this in mind, the physical welfare of their pupils was entrusted to matrons and field matrons were employed to advise Indian women in 'home-making'; the first government field matron was appointed in 1891. There is some evidence that the Indians 'respond[ed] quickly' to field matrons, but this is what whites wanted to believe. Their appointment was meant to prevent the home-making instruction provided for female students in schools from being undermined by uncomprehending mothers. It indicates, too, the strength of nineteenth-century, middle-class convictions about women's special responsibilities for child nurture and the encouragement of all finer feelings and of the white prediction that, once shown ways of improving their lot, Indian women would prove readier converts than men. After all, it was a commonplace of white observers that Indian women were mere drudges, callously exploited by their husbands and enjoying limited political leverage in many tribes. Whereas Indian men were often profoundly averse to white views of the proper sexual division of labour, which imposed 'women's work' upon them, it was not unreasonable to hope that Indian women, especially in tribes where they exerted little influence, might accept the change and then go on to persuade their husbands and children towards the white way. It was merely one of the many ironies of the campaign for Indian education that undue elevation of the mother's role in child nurture, which distorted the fabric of Indian societies, was, as Joseph Kett reminds us, actually designed by white reformers to strengthen 'social cohesion' in an age of 'rampant individualism'.

Missionaries sustained both day and boarding schools. After 1870 these establishments might be operated according to a contract with the Bureau of Indian Affairs, which paid a *per capita* fee for students while the denominations provided teachers and buildings. By the 1870s, not least in order to cope with the children of the newly pacified western tribes and to take account of reformer thinking about the Indians' home environment, federally supported off-reservation boarding schools were also being planned. Yet for reasons shortly to be examined, the off-reservation schools did not fulfil educators' hopes, whereas the contract schools proliferated in a way that had not been anticipated, taking some 25 per cent of the government's educational aid by the 1890s. The expansion of the system was aided by a vigorous effort on the part of the Catholic Church to reassert itself in the field of Indian education, following the exclusion of its members from the Board of Indian Commissioners (until 1902) and disappointment over the number of agencies it was allotted under Grant's Peace Policy. Hence as late as 1900, Prucha records, twenty-five Catholic boarding schools on Indian reservations received contract support, with an average attendance of 2,078 students and at a cost to the church of around $150,000 annually; albeit by that time the government had withdrawn its support from some contract schools and purchased others, in response to anti-Catholic pressures from Protestant and lay educators. In addition, Catholics ran fifteen other boarding schools and thirteen day schools for Indians.[23] Notwithstanding this kind of outlay on teachers and plant, the missionaries' efforts enjoyed very limited success when measured against the unreasonable contemporary expectation about what the school alone could accomplish. But the debate about missionary schooling and the desirability of its religious bias helped to make educational improvement one of the main preoccupations of well-meaning whites until the end of the nineteenth century.[24]

Although the federal government's involvement in black schooling via the Freedmen's Bureau had been abandoned by the end of 1870, its role in education generally increased following the Civil War, with the creation of a national office of education in 1867, a commitment to general appropriations for Indian schools from 1870 and the assumption of responsibility for instructing the native children of Alaska after 1885. Congress failed to allocate more than $130,000 a year for Indian schooling before 1880, but by that time the government was being pressed by the Board of Indian Commissioners, the Women's National Indian Association, the Indian Rights Association and the Lake Mohonk Conference on the Indian to devise a general educational system not chiefly dependent on missionary groups. To this end, it would need to increase appropriations; to establish a permanent fund for Indian education out of the proceeds from the sale of Indian lands; to introduce 'the English language in every tribe'; to provide more schools of every type, but particularly industrial schools; and to appoint 'a government inspector for Indian schools'.[25] The reformers' case was helped by the mounting public clamour for the allotment of tempting reservation lands on an individual basis; education, it was hoped, would help the Indians compete in the competitive white world which was encroaching upon them.

In 1882, Congress agreed to the appointment of an inspector of Indian schools and empowered him to draw up a comprehensive programme for Indian education. When Thomas Morgan became Commissioner of Indian Affairs at the end of the decade, he inherited an enlarged budget, a stronger superintendency of Indian schools, with the power to appoint and dismiss teachers, and government-financed day schools which stressed the teaching of agricultural skills, using English as the medium of instruction.[26] Henceforth the importance of missionary schools was to be played down and the leadership in Indian education passed to the government. A firm believer that the main agencies for Americanization were the public schools, wherein 'race distinctions gave way to national characteristics', Morgan argued that these schools could do for the Indians what they had done for blacks in the South. He did not acknowledge the inadequate funding of black schools, which were heavily reliant upon philanthropic assistance. Morgan reaffirmed the established emphasis upon vocational training in Indian schools, while attaching new importance to the standardization of instruction methods, texts and curricula and to improving the quality and security of teachers in Indian institutions, partly by increasing the number of civil service appointments in the Indian service. The Commissioner also urged the need for teaching in English, coeducation, compulsory attendance and advanced education for potential native leaders.[27]

As with many well-intentioned programmes imposed from above, Indian educational reform enjoyed little success, except as a means of advancing uniformity in instruction and the powers and centralization of the Indian office. Between 1881 and 1887 the number of Indian schools rose from 106 to 221 and the pupils from 4,221 to 14,333, yet Indian educational facilities still reached only a fraction of Indian children of school age, while very few were educated in white public schools until after the turn of the century. Even when a new national reform movement – Progressivism – developed early in the twentieth century and its supporters came to influence Indian affairs, too much was expected from schooling and the 'experts' it utilized.[28]

This is not to say, however, that there were no white critics of the Indian educational programme. Western interests opposed what they feared were becoming increasingly expensive policies for tribal schooling and doubted whether Indians as a whole could be taught, rather as many southern whites had doubted the educability of the freedmen.[29] The atypical reformers associated with the journal *Council Fire* feared that by the time the schools had done their work, most of the Indians would have been reduced to penury, as a result of the premature destruction of the tribe and the reservation. Army officer Richard Henry Pratt, the founder at Carlisle in Pennsylvania of the best known off-reservation boarding school, believed that land allotment would not aid assimilation, because Indian holdings would be grouped together, so that their owners and Indian schools would remain apart from white society. He was equally perceptive in arguing that the encouragement of Indians to concentrate on farming as an occupation narrowed the scope of educational efforts. Indian educators genuinely worried about which schools and methods were most likely to advance their assimilationist goals, as well as about the charges of their critics. And a few individuals, such as the Indian Rights Association's agent and eventual Indian Commissioner (1905–9), Francis Leupp, were starting to question the educational philosophy which sought to 'kill the Indian' to save the man, albeit the result might be an undesirable tendency to conclude that Indians, if different from whites, were inferior to them, and should be schooled with that assumption in mind.[30]

Several factors contributed to the Indians' continuing resistance to schooling and the educators' poor performance. As Jacqueline Fear observes, no attempt was made to consider whether Indian children had any unique qualities which should be taken into account in the classroom.[31] Not least because of the greater Indian resistance to white-controlled education and the Native Americans' diverse languages, there was less effort made to train Indian teachers than there was to produce black instructors and until Benjamin Harrison's presidency (1889–93), appointments were largely determined by political considerations and an easy-going nepotism. Government reservation schools were less well funded than the off-reservation boarding schools, but Indian parents disliked sending their children far afield and objected to recruiters' sometimes forcible removal of their offspring to the off-reservation institutions, if necessary with the aid of the Indian police, who were also used to restore runaways.

Indian anxiety was further aroused by the schools' resort to corporal punishment (officially prohibited in the 1890s) and by the imprisonment of recalcitrant pupils in school jails (not abolished until 1927). It was sustained by the high death rate among boarding and returned students (though in fairness it should be noted that the general Indian infant mortality rate was high); by the practice of cutting off the braids of Indian youths; and by attempts to compel school attendance and instruction in English by the 1890s. In areas where tribal government was weak or non-existent, the machinery for passing on complaints about Indian schools and what went on in them was entirely in the hands of self-interested whites.[31] There were instances when Indian requests did reach Washington and did have an effect, as witness the Comanches' success in getting their own boarding school opened at Fort Sill in 1892 and effective tribal requests for contract schools in 1904. But such instances were the exception, not the rule. Moreover, inspection of schools, though formalized from the 1880s, was never as frequent as would have been desirable and was undertaken by individuals basically in sympathy with their goals and methods.[32]

The one thing the schools could have offered that might have made them acceptable – a usable skill – was provided for only a handful of students. In other words, they could not impart to the tribes the technology which had led to the ascendancy of white civilization. Instead, teachers remained wedded to the Jeffersonian dream of turning them into yeoman farmers and educated citizens. Unfortunately, while the Indian education programme theoretically equipped tribesmen to farm on their own account, with agricultural instruction in schools from 1870, the lands whites had left them with were frequently unsuitable for farming of any kind, certainly for small family farms. And even after the implementation of the Dawes Act had made it essential, there was just not enough instruction in agricultural methods or useful trades in Indian schools, notwithstanding the national campaign to improve rural education which gained momentum between 1890 and 1914 and was distinguished, as Ann Keppel has shown, by its attempt to break down barriers between the classroom and the world beyond.[33]

Every type of Indian school had its problems. By 1900, the number of off-reservation boarding schools had risen to twenty-five. Among these foundations, only Virginia's Hampton Institute, established by

General Samuel Chapman Armstrong, accepted black and Indian students, and the 'wild' state of the latter initially led to the two races being taught separately; thereafter, Indians and blacks at Hampton remained socially distinct. In Armstrong's judgement, though he had not sought out Indian pupils, Indians and blacks were in equal need of special education for a special place in society. But Pratt of Carlisle feared that joint educational ventures would pass on to red men some of the greater prejudice which whites felt towards blacks. Opposed to 'exclusively race schools', Pratt maintained that all races should ideally be instructed together in the public schools and equipped to compete in an American, not an ethnic, environment. Carlisle was successful in obtaining and retaining its pupils, without resort to unpleasant coercion, and in maintaining good relations with the local community, among whom students, with their consent, lived out for months at a time, in order to increase their contacts with the white world. The students – 1,024 in 1900 – devoted at least half their day to industrial training, in the hope that they would acquire skills at least equivalent to those of white working men, yet they were paid for their labours and managed to accumulate some savings.

On the other hand, one must acknowledge that most of the boarding schools were not as viable as Carlisle. The majority of their students came ill-prepared and found it a struggle to graduate in five years or at all. Hopes that the big training schools would help Indians to gain access to white public schools and colleges were thus for the most part disappointed and until 1921 Haskell Institute alone among government foundations offered instruction beyond eighth grade.[34] The impressive record of the post-1865 black colleges, despite the often conflicting aims and attitudes of white and black educators and students in the South, suggests that more could have been attempted and that higher education for Indians was sacrificed in the late-nineteenth-century crusade to establish the common school. As Hazel Hertzberg has shown, the boarding schools brought together pupils from different tribes to create a de-tribalized elite whose members refrained from criticizing the schools that had educated them and absorbed some white values, without ever abandoning their links with their own cultures. What they failed to do was to transform their graduates' prospects of obtaining a broad range of off-reservation jobs or work in the East. Since, with the exception of Carlisle and Hampton, the schools were located near large populations of Indians, the students' temptation was either to run away or to return legitimately to the adjacent reservation, if possible in the service of the BIA, which gave priority to Indians from 1882 onwards. Should they then revert to tribal ways, critics preferred to blame the expensive schools that had produced them rather than the limited resources of Indian settlements and the remaining reservations. The whole process was aided by the way the outing system was operated in the West. There, Trennert and Hoxie have established, Pratt's ideal of work as an educational experience facilitating assimilation was corrupted because the boarding schools used outing to provide cheap labour for their local communities, while Indian service bureaucrats, who had come to believe that Indians were only partly assimilable and destined to remain on the reservations, rationalized the educators' decision.[35]

The local schools and reservation boarding schools frequently operated much further below capacity and white ambitions than their off-reservation counterparts.[36] Day schools were established among the Navajo from 1869, but by 1878 it was reported that 'not a solitary Navajo can either read or write', mainly because their mobile way of life and suspicion of education resulted in highly irregular attendance. When the government attempted to compel attendance in 1887, the Navajo offered strong and effective resistance. The peace treaties made with the Plains tribes in the late 1860s, which had pledged them to compel their children to attend school, are more an indication of white hopes of encouraging civilization as the whites understood it than of a genuine commitment on the part of the Indians. Furthermore, Congress was reluctant to provide the funds to make white hopes a reality. Consequently, so Hagan notes of the Comanches, as 'late as 1879 only about 65 of a reservation population of 500 school-age children were enrolled'. The unwillingness of the Comanche, Kiowa and Kiowa-Apache parents to send their children to school meant that they could not fill even the places made available in 1885 for only a quarter of their children, due to government parsimony. By the 1890s the facilities for the Comanches and related tribes were still incapable of meeting the needs of all their students, while rivalry between the mission schools and government day schools did not help the educational process. None the less, the government schools survived allotment and the official ending of the tribal era, not least because of local white opposition – encountered throughout the West – to admitting Indian children to the public schools.[37]

Elsewhere, outside the Five Civilized Tribes and one or two exceptional tribes like the Santee Sioux, there is a comparable story of government schools being slowly established from the 1870s and persisting after severalty. There is the same struggle against local white prejudice and preoccupation with institutional minutiae.[38] There is the same indifference to missionary complaints that the government schools were turning out 'polished heathens',[39] the same reluctant Indian attendance and erosion of the instructional functions of tribal elders, with whites resorting both to coercion and eventually schooling in the home community to try to break down resistance and increase the influence of educated Indians on their uneducated brethren. Local institutions also appealed to the government because they reduced the cost of transporting students to school. Within the Five Tribes, educational provision was complicated by the freedmen question, as we have seen (above, Chapter 6), and the Indians' efforts to run their own educational systems failed to meet white approval, partly because

> They had been led to believe that only book learning should be carried on in their schools; that manual labor was fit only for the Negroes and white renters.

In fact, vocational instruction had its advocates and opponents among the Indians of Indian Territory, just as it did among blacks and whites in the United States.[40]

It would, however, be unreasonable to expect late-nineteenth-century educators to be too dismayed by the results of their efforts at a time when it was considered quite acceptable for urban white children to leave school at between 12 and 14 years and when 95 per cent of pupils attending rural schools had no further education. Before 1890, the earning losses and time involved in a high school education made it the preserve of sections of the native-born, white middle class. Blacks, immigrants and working-class whites were trained to serve, not compete with, the children of better-off Americans, while women were still warned not to strain their constitutions with too much learning in adolescence. Under such circumstances, we should not anticipate any profound departure from prevailing paternalism in Indian education.[41]

IV

EARLY-TWENTIETH-CENTURY TRENDS

When urban America and technological change advanced and most Indians and blacks remained in predominantly rural regions, each group became part of that 'rural problem' in education that worried Progressive reformers. Each minority was regarded as 'backward' for economic as well as racial reasons. Accordingly, influenced by Progressive thinking which elevated efficiency and professionalism, educators campaigned for more agricultural instruction by qualified persons at Indian schools and for Indian adults, while curricula were further standardized and teachers were more carefully trained and rated, moved less frequently and obliged to co-operate with their superintendents in the preparation and improvement of lessons. There was a renewed drive to place Indian children in public schools, especially after 1914, when government schools closed their doors to children of less than a quarter Indian blood, unless they lacked school facilities, or their parents lacked funds, or they were unfit. In 1900 only 246 pupils were reported to be attending public schools as against 22,124 in government schools and 4,081 in other institutions, whereas in 1920 the public schools claimed 30,858, government schools, 25,396, and the remainder 5,546.

On the other hand, Indian schools and teachers were lost during the retrenchment occasioned by the First World War and the expansion of public school education proceeded slowly in the Southwest. In Oklahoma, the Five Tribes mourned the loss of their tribal schools and worried about the prospects of the full bloods under the new order. They were right to do so; as late as the 1930s the school drop-out and retardation rate was reported to be highest among the full-blood children, in part because of their faulty English and the lack of rapport between them and their teachers, who were apt to judge their silence to be a sign of stubbornness or deficiency. Many reservation day and boarding schools had no more than three grades. Industrial and agricultural training was an expensive business if done properly and it often remained inadequate or non-existent in Indian and white schools alike, notwithstanding the extension to both of government support for such training. And greater uniformity in the content and methods of Indian education was bought at the price of making it less responsive than ever to local Indian needs, regardless of the pleas of Indian school supervisors in 1911 for more attention to be paid to the rights of employees and pupils at the schools and to building up better contacts between the schools and their surrounding communities.[42] Letters from the Indian office to individual institutions suggested balancing conventional academic subjects with the teaching of, say, Indian myths and legends or geography related to home circumstances. But sample exam papers show questions weighted towards the concerns of whites. Thus the 1911 history and civics papers for Albuquerque Indian School for the third to eighth grades contained out of sixty-four questions only three specifically involving Indian history: one of them on Indian relations with the French and English, one on Penn's relations with the Indians and one on Pocahontas.[43]

The Indian members of the first pan-Indian political association, the Society of American Indians (SAI), did not object to the standardization drive or to Indian instruction in the public schools and neither did their white associates. Yet they were frustrated by the lack of response to their call for higher education for Indians able and willing to benefit from it. Hopes for an Indian junior college came to nothing and so, until 1926, did the SAI's proposal for reorganizing the Indian school system under a powerful superintendent of education.[44] The combatant and uncompromising Pratt supported Indian demands for higher education but opposed the idea of a separate Indian college. Undeterred by the fact that off-reservation schools were out of favour, he continued to campaign for these foundations as a means of 'Americanizing and assimilating and abolishing race differences for the Indians', thereby coming into conflict with black organizations and institutions which saw his work as undermining theirs. He was also at odds with the 'shifting, ignorant, remote' BIA bureaucracy which controlled Indian property and perpetuated the reservations and with those SAI members who stressed the Indian's 'alleged peculiar qualities'. Pratt looked forward to the day when 'no Indian societies of any sort will be at all necessary or even thought of' and rejoiced that the Freedmen's Bureau had been short-lived.[45]

Indian educators had additional causes for concern, most notably the recurring complaints that the end products of Indian schools and the prospects for their graduates were disappointing. The grumbles are not a uniquely American phenomenon. Britons abroad feared, disliked and ridiculed the educated natives they had set out to create and were sometimes obliged to employ, while imperialists generally, and not merely educators dealing with Indian 'colonies', have found it hard to rise above arguments about relevance and cost effectiveness when discussing the schooling of 'inferiors'. Acting on the assumption that no solution had been found to the problem of the 'returned student' – estimated at 35,000 in 1913 – the Board of Indian Commissioners asked for the advice of reservation superintendents, hoping to come up with some new explanations and ideas. But though there was general agreement about the need for the 'improvement of reservation life and environment and remunerative employment', a number of respondents were pessimistic about what could be achieved through exploiting existing opportunities, establishing community centres and increasing the numbers of field matrons and of similar advisers for boys. They therefore advocated sending students to be more swiftly acculturated in shops, offices and farms away from their reservations.

Such advice led to the appointment of a mixed-blood Carlisle graduate, Charles E. Dagenett, to promote off-reservation Indian opportunities and his records afford us some interesting native and white accounts of Indian education and the expectations it produced. Clearly in 1914 many whites felt that the Indian schools had failed to turn out 'finished workmen', or even individuals interested in 'steady, laborious work'. Most of the girls married and if education had more effect on their home life than anything else, it was hard to gauge even there, especially if they acquired 'non-progressive' husbands. Parents still tried to undercut what their children had learned so that, in the words of William Peterson of the Fort Apache Indian School at Whiteriver, Arizona, 'we cannot hope for very much result until the school boys become the dominating power on the reservation'. Some students, as of old, were said to 'feel themselves above ordinary labor such as they are fitted to do', albeit not all who aspired to more than manual work were advised to think again. Ironically the entire project was denounced by Pratt, who mistrusted Dagenett, as distracting Indians' attention from their homes and allotments, in exchange for periodic peonage.[46] Comparable comments on the consequences of early–twentieth-century schooling emerge from interviews with Arizona Indians conducted during the 1960s. Informants recalled being punished for speaking their own tongue and struggling to acquire English. They remembered better food than was available at home and days divided between book and practical work. They recollected parental fears that they would get sick and die. They spoke, too, of being homesick at distant schools and of running away; of girls leaving to marry early; and of punishments which included boys being dressed as girls to shame them. But two informants offered wry comments which are especially significant: that what was chiefly learned was how 'to go to school'; and that 'Whatever I learned, I did not use it.'[47]

In his magazine, *Wassaja*, a damning endorsement of this kind of judgement was given by Carlos Montezuma, a Yavapai Apache, a successful doctor and the product of a Chicago public school, Illinois State University and Chicago Medical College, who practised first at Carlisle and then in Chicago. Dedicated to obtaining freedom for the Indian by abolishing the Indian Bureau, allowing Indian children access to the public schools and higher education and giving Indian adults all the freedoms of whites, Montezuma asserted that the graduates of Indian schools were not equipped for employment except in special circumstances – and particularly by the bureau – where the deficiencies of their education were overlooked.[48] To the extent that his assertion was true (for Montezuma was a man of unusually strong views) one reason may have been the close regimentation of pupils from dawn to dusk at the boarding schools, on or outside the reservations. Apart from the experiments with outing, they afforded no opportunities for the development of those powers of initiative and self-help which education was supposed to inculcate. Indian students were especially ill-prepared to compete for jobs in an urban environment.

Montezuma's private papers, containing correspondence with a wide variety of well-known and obscure figures, provide from all concerned a similarly gloomy picture of Indian education. Thus Pratt, despite receiving grateful letters from former pupils and commenting proudly on a number who were 'hoeing their own row among our people and doing well', complained to Montezuma that 'Except you, Indians don't seem to care, even my most valued graduates.' There is evidence that Indians with schooling found themselves criticized, even by other Indians, because of 'the standing collar and the strut, and lack of respect for parents', or isolated because they were 'a little more educated' than their peers. And for them, there was a restless search for roles in which they could emulate Montezuma and be not 'marginal men' but individuals at home in two worlds.[49]

9

Indian Education in the Twentieth Century

If the steady aim of Indian education up to the First World War had been the assimilation of the Indians into white civilization, we have seen that opinions had varied about the best means to achieve this end. In the twentieth century, the overall aim became the improvement of the quality of Indian education, which was given even higher priority by the Indian Bureau and was to be made available to all Indian children, while taking account of different Indian cultures and preferences. Yet it soon proved equally difficult to find the machinery by which this new objective could be realized, partly because of a reversion in the late 1940s and 1950s towards the old assimilation crusade, which affected all aspects of Indian policy.

I

Transition Era: the 1920s

After the First World War, when 23,000 Indian children of school age were said to be without facilities, circumstances at first looked inauspicious for Indian reform. The conflict had divided and weakened the Progressive movement and a period of political reaction had set in at all levels of government. However, even if revisionists are right and American education was and is, in Katz's words, 'bureaucratic, racist, and class-biased', the school did seem to act as a limited agent for social change at this time and was certainly seen as such by the middle-class activists who chiefly battled for and benefited from better educational provision. They accordingly played their part when, as had been the case in the second half of the nineteenth century, a scandal caught popular fancy and helped to create a climate conducive to investigation and alteration in Indian affairs generally. The Bursum Bill of 1922, designed to legalize white settlement on Pueblo lands, became the equivalent, in the revulsion it produced against white rapacity, of the disastrous removal of the Poncas to Indian Territory in the 1870s.[1] Among those who protested the Bursum measure was the General Federation of Women's Clubs and the forceful Mrs Stella Atwood of the Federation's Californian branch sustained a regular correspondence on this and a variety of matters with the Commissioner of Indian Affairs, Charles Henry Burke (1921–9). Her letters give today's reader a good deal more pleasure than they can have given the Commissioner and Atwood's determination 'to keep on' until satisfied, buttressed as it was by a similar resolve on the part of other humanitarians, meant that Burke could not give free rein to his conservative instincts.[2]

The Commissioner approved of all types of Indian schools and had even favoured the continuation of Carlisle which, following Pratt's retirement and a period of corrupt management, was shut in 1918 to make way for an army hospital. After about the fourth grade, Burke held that Indian children, just like white children, might safely venture further afield to complete their instruction and improve their educational prospects. He valued public schooling as a means of mixing the races and enabling the Indians to learn English quickly. In Indian schools, the Commissioner hoped to see no one employed who was not up to the standard of the local state teachers. He believed that the government should provide 'such vocational instruction as may fit Indian boys to adopt and follow some pursuit which will enable them to be self-supporting and to train Indian girls in home economics in order that the standard of the Indian home may be raised through their influence'. Yet Burke acknowledged that, to date, Indian education had not enabled many of its graduates to make 'good from an economic point of view'.[3] With this in mind, and in line with the long American tradition of providing 'social institutions for youth' to inculcate morality, usefulness and awareness of civic responsibilities,[4] the Commissioner welcomed the organization of clubs among the Indian youngsters. Modelled on the agricultural clubs for white boys and girls so popular from the early part of the century, they claimed 'a total membership of nearly 2,000' in 1925.

As far as Burke's overall programme was concerned, progress was invariably tempered by disappointment. The movement of Indian pupils into public schools accelerated during the decade and appropriations for the enrolment of Indian children in such schools increased from $200,000 annually in 1920 to $400,000 in 1929. By 1925, the Commissioner claimed that state school districts were co-operating 'much more willingly' than they had formerly done and between 1920 and 1924 attendance at public schools rose from 30,858 to 34,834, while the number of pupils attending government establishments fell from 25,396 to 23,589. In order to facilitate transfer to the public schools, the course of study at government institutions was revised in 1922 to bring it closer to that pursued in the public sector. But since the aim after 1920 was to oblige all children under federal control to attend school, new day and boarding schools were built for the Indians in areas where they were still vital, notably the Southwest. The appointment in 1926 of a general superintendent, aided by nine district superintendents, to supervise Indian schools and vocational training was meant to improve the entire system of Indian education.

On the other hand, despite the existence of a number of Indian reform organizations in the 1920s (see Chapter 12), it remained difficult for Indians to make their wishes known in Washington and the short-lived Committee of One Hundred (1923–4), which recommended the spending of more money on better personnel, improving existing facilities and extending scholarships to high schools and colleges for ambitious Indians, required something that Burke was not good at getting from parsimonious Congresses. In fact, the Commissioner often simply used scarce funds as an excuse to his critics, rather than mounting an unremitting campaign to obtain more. As a result, he and his employees devoted much time to highlighting aggravated evils for which no solutions were in sight.[5] The state of Indian higher education is a good case in point. Burke hoped to enable Indian students to compete 'both academically and industrially . . . with those of other nationalities' and he took pride in the fact that, by December 1924, 'the course of instruction in day schools in Indian reservations has been increased to six grades; in reservation boarding schools to eight grades; and [in] certain large government schools four grades will be added representing high school work'.[6] By 1930, nine additional Indian schools had joined Haskell (Kansas) in providing high school instruction for 2,500 to 3,000 students. In a decade when the high school was increasingly valued by whites as an avenue to better, more respectable jobs, this emphasis was to be expected. Yet the standard of the Indian schools did not correspond with that of white high schools and their work was consequently impeded by the scarcity and high turnover of teachers.[7]

The Meriam Report, produced after two years' research in 1928, at the request of the Department of the Interior, gave further cause for alarm. Although Warren K. Moorehead of the Board of Indian Commissioners felt that the education sections of the report contained nothing new and had failed to take account of the educational policies of the Canadian government, reported on approvingly in 1915 by the board's secretary, they provided a valuable summary of the state of Indian schooling and offered some clear recommendations.[8] They were largely the work of W. Carson Ryan, an educator who had already been involved in a number of similar inquiries and was an expert in vocational instruction.

The bureau boarding schools, viewed suspiciously since the 1890s, were damned by the report, which found their inhabitants ill-fed, over-crowded, unhealthy, poorly taught, unduly regimented and still obliged to contribute too much labour in order to maintain their institutions. It was therefore proposed that Congress should contrive an extra appropriation of 1 million dollars to improve the variety and amount of food provided in the boarding schools. It was urged that military discipline should be abandoned and that child labour should be reduced and not extracted in violation of the state laws. The report recommended that purchasing methods be overhauled so as to ensure the provision of proper clothing for pupils and that extra money should be spent to equip the dormitories adequately. The boarding schools could not be abolished at a time when 27 per cent of Indian children attended them, but it was believed that more community day schools should be established, so that young students were first educated at home – Burke's ideal. It was suggested that the uniform curriculum imposed in Indian schools should be relaxed to take account of tribal interests and differences, a proposal which seemed less daring than it might have done in the early 1920s, when missionaries, agents, some acculturated Indians and the Commissioner alike remained hostile to Indian ceremonials as immoral and disruptive of steady work and learning.[9] Meriam also called for more money to be spent on medical personnel, teacher salaries and housing and advised that instruction should be more realistically related to existing job opportunities and reservation needs.[10]

The Meriam Report reflected, via Ryan, the theories of the Progressive educational reformers, which had been gaining currency since the beginning of the century and were given a fillip in 1919 by the foundation of the Progressive Education Association. Accordingly it wished to see Indian instruction as a functional system, which the young and adults alike would recognize as being related to the world they lived in and which would make them socially useful members of that world. However, the Progressives' desire to foster group consciousness underestimated that which already existed among both immigrants and Indians and it was to some extent at odds with their desire to release the 'uniquely creative potentialities' of each individual. The report's recoil from excessive discipline reflected the accelerated move away from Victorian morality in American society generally during the 1920s and took place against a background of protests on black campuses about the severe regulation of dress, social relationships and leisure activities by college staff. Meriam's tone was harsh and the Board of Indian Commissioners complained that it was unfair to measure Indian schools 'by the standards of the best schools and colleges for white boys and girls'. The fairest comparison might have been between Indian institutions and those of rural, southern and especially black districts, where sparse equipment, ungraded classes, poor teachers and dim prospects of acquiring a high school education were likewise commonplace. But in a decade of enlarged expenditure on education and increased enrolments for every level of instruction, dismay at the broadly unsatisfactory nature of Indian schooling was understandable.[11]

Prospects for implementing the report improved when in 1929 the Quaker reformers Charles Rhoads and Joseph Scattergood became Commissioner and Assistant Commissioner of Indian Affairs. The two commissioners and the Secretary of the Interior, Ray Lyman Wilbur, looked forward to the assimilation of 'the least American element in the population' through education, hoping to foster public schooling, scholarship aid for higher education, and practical instruction on the reservations to train Indians for jobs within and beyond their own communities.[12] Action was taken to increase funds for the boarding schools, so that the food and clothing they provided at last became adequate, and the reduction of child labour and school congestion was set in train. Moreover in response to denunciations of brutality at the boarding schools, Rhoads looked at the effects of his predecessor's efforts to moderate the punishments meted out. Yet by deciding to allow superintendents continuing discretion, even with regard to flogging, the Commissioner alienated humanitarians just as Ryan took over as Director of Indian Education in 1930.[13]

Criticism was temporarily appeased when Ryan outlined his objectives and set about implementing them with rather more vigour than his superiors had shown. He was aided by the fact that education had been upgraded as one of the five major divisions in a reorganized Indian service, and throughout his period of office (1930–6) the director put the problems of Indian schooling in a broad perspective, taking account of prevailing educational theory, the educational practices of other countries and the rest of the United States, and the views of the man on the spot. As a good Progressive he was particularly impressed by the Alaskan situation, where appropriate vocational instruction was provided and the schools functioned in relation to the Indians' homes and communities.

Ryan aimed to phase out the boarding schools, which could not serve a community purpose so effectively as local day schools. Wherever possible the public schools were to be utilized, and assisted

235

by contracts made between the federal government and the states, rather than the individual school districts dealt with in the past. It was hoped that the partnership would improve educational facilities in poor rural areas for Indians and whites alike, while removing white resentment against Indians who received services when they did not pay taxes. In a further retreat from a uniform course of study in Indian schools, teachers were to be encouraged to put together their own readers and introduce their students to English and learning generally through incidents and subjects related to their cultures, their own daily lives. This might, in government schools, mean the abandonment of a range of strictly 'academic' disciplines such as algebra and ancient history or, in public schools, involve exposure to a curriculum which at least took account of state conditions and preferences. And in a fresh attempt to make instruction functional, Ryan urged the appointment of a director of vocational guidance to study and develop vocational education in the schools and help with job placement. Indeed, he recognized that his plans, especially the shift away from the boarding schools, required the appointment of a number of new staff to determine which boarding schools should survive; to act as visiting social workers for the Indians, liaising between their schools and homes; to visit all schools enrolling Indians and work directly with the state commissioners or superintendents of education; and to improve the quality of vocational instruction among boys.[14] Home economics teaching was felt to be adequate already. In fact there was said to be better provision in this subject for Indian than for white schools.[15]

As is ever the case, the gap between the reformer's theory and actual achievements remained considerable. So far as public schooling is concerned, measurable progress was made. State supervisors for Indian education were appointed in Oklahoma in 1931 and then in Arizona, South Dakota, Washington, Wisconsin, Nebraska and Michigan. The appropriation for Indian student enrolment had been raised to $600,000 by 1933, at which time there were about 56,000 such students in the public schools, with the federal government, paying tuition for some 44,000 of them.[16] Letters from the regions in the director's files nevertheless bear witness to the difficulties both races experienced in adjusting to the teaching of Indians in the public schools and conflicting reports came in from certain areas.

In Oklahoma, for instance, there was some Indian support for public school education and Indian attendance rose rapidly between 1930 and 1931. But the increased expenditure on public schooling remained inadequate, insufficient attention was paid to the difficulties of the mixed-blood communities and there was, contrary to bracing official pronouncements, at least a degree of white opposition to biracial education, on the grounds that Indian children were dirty, unhealthy and slow learners.[17] Whites in Harlem, Montana, made the same kind of objections, provoking the following dignified response from the local tribal council:[18]

> in all our pride of race and in justice to our children we, the Indians of Fort Belknap reservation, do not wish to force our association upon the honorable citizens of Harlem, but as a part of the school district No. 12 ask that advanced grades with high school facilities be built on the reservation. Failing this, it is suggested and under consideration that we have our reservation withdrawn from this county and annexed by another where the Indian will be recognised as an honorable American citizen.

Racial opposition to Indian children was reported from Nebraska, aggravating the dilemmas created by Indian opposition to schooling, indifferent local authorities and inadequate funds for such special practical needs of Indian children as meals and transport. It was likewise strong in the South (see Chapter 6) and in Nevada, resulting in the segregation of Indian students in certain of the state's public schools and the Indians refusing to attend institutions in which they were disliked. In California and Wisconsin, the poverty of the Indians seemed to cause most difficulty.[19]

Although Ryan did not publicly accept that there was much prejudice against the Indians, he regretted the 'real cultural loss' involved when Indians joined the public school system, so that these reports must have given him pause. Conversely, the state of many Indian schools commented on by inspectors seemed to make recourse to the public sector imperative. A haunting image is conjured up of one primary school, as vivid as that recalled by Hamlin Garland in *Son of the Middle Border* and probably as traumatic in its impact on the inmates:

> Dark, shades drawn half way down on dark day, no cords on shades to pull them down if they rolled up high; no green plant of any kind . . . no pets; no decorations; rooms barren and gloomy; air most impure and foul; temperature probably below 65, but no thermometer in rooms . . . no weight-height charts, one room had an old one from year before, no records for this year on it; *thick mud* in chunks and piles on the floors. The mud out-of-doors could not be prevented at the time, but there was no real effort made to keep it out of the rooms.

Poor teachers, pupils drilled rather than taught, inadequate equipment and ill-clothed, infrequently attending children with poor prospects remained an embarrassment, despite the closure of twelve unsatisfactory boarding schools and the creation of new day schools, some of which utilized Indian instructors and provided services for the localities in which they were situated.[20] Unfortunately, the communities which benefited from the business brought by boarding schools in their midst objected to their demise and graft had not been eliminated from their expenditures.[21]

Indian education as a whole suffered from the tension which developed between the administration's 800 or so new educational appointments and the old guard in the Indian school system.[22] Long-serving personnel might be encouraged to upgrade themselves by attending special summer school courses and local normal schools; it was harder to ensure that they questioned entrenched attitudes and assumptions. And notwithstanding Rhoads's best efforts, friction also persisted between missionary educators and Indian service personnel. Even so, under the guidance of new teachers for the school vocational subjects, the quality of vocational instruction was improved and more closely related to Indian reservations and home conditions, and adult education was tackled in conjunction with school housekeepers, 'State and school agricultural agents and home demonstration agents'. The director of the new placement service and his two Indian assistants managed to find 1,000 permanent jobs for clients before being frustrated by the Depression and, for the first time, serious attention was given to higher education. This was a controversial area of activity. As Richardson notes, vocational and higher education 'were supplemental' rather than antagonistic and Progressive educators wanted to develop both practical skills and intellectual potential in the classroom. But certain whites felt that, unlike the Japanese 'and other brown races', the Indians were opposed to acquiring white civilization and were unlikely to want or attain professional jobs. Not surprisingly, some Indian leaders responded by stressing the importance of 'a liberal education' and further training, fearing that an undue emphasis on vocational instruction and their special racial needs would consign them to an inferior status in American society. By 1933 over 160 advanced Indian students had received reimbursable loans from federal and tribal funds and five scholarships were made available to Indians at the University of Michigan: scarcely enough to satisfy those who saw higher education as essential for the creation of Indian leaders, but a beginning.[23]

II

AN INDIAN NEW DEAL IN EDUCATION?

The appointment of John Collier as Commissioner of Indian Affairs (1933-45) gratified the many reformers who had been discontented with the gap between what Rhoads and Scattergood had promised and what they had managed to obtain from Congress and put into effect. The new Commissioner was also sympathetic towards the ideas of Progressive education, brought to the Indian Service by Ryan, whom he first retained in office, and by the bureau's Director of Education from 1936 to 1952, Willard Walcott Beatty. The president of the Progressive Education Association, Beatty was well known for introducing Progressive ideas, including 'individualized' teaching and learning, in the prosperous suburban districts of Bronxville, New York, and Winnetka, Illinois.[24] As one would expect, therefore, except for the novel assistance from New Deal agencies, the policies pursued in Indian education were essentially a continuation of those already set in motion by Ryan and urged by reformers in the 1920s.

Public school provision for Indian students was assisted by the Johnson O'Malley Act of 1934 (JOM), which was similar to the Swing-Johnson Bill defeated late in Hoover's presidency and which, with an addition in 1936, made federal funds available to the states 'and other political units' for improving Indian education. By 1941, California, Washington, Minnesota and Arizona had negotiated contracts with the government. Two years later there were nearly 37,000 pupils attending the public schools, more than at the government institutions, and approximately 1.25 million dollars were being paid for their tuition. Between 1933 and 1943, sixteen boarding schools were closed and, with the aid of a New Deal agency, the Public Works Administration, nearly one hundred day schools were constructed, designed to serve as community centres. The pupils enrolled in these community day schools rose from 6,836 to 21,559 in the same period, their numbers exceeding those attending boarding schools. Higher, vocational and trade school education was aided by clause II of the amended Indian Reorganization Act of 1934 (I.R.A.), which provided for an annual expenditure of up to $250,000 for the children of Indians organized under the Act who desired such education.

The federal and tribal funds for higher education, extended on various terms – some reimbursable, some not, and some in exchange for services in government schools – were more generous than they had been in any other decade and were supplemented by scholarships offered by a number of colleges, organizations and clubs. In 1937, over 600 Indian students were said to be receiving educational loans. Vocational instruction relevant to the circumstances of different Indian communities was pursued at Indian day and secondary schools and was supplemented by the Indian branch of the New Deal's Civilian Conservation Corps, which helped some 85,000 Indians. As was appropriate in a period of high urban unemployment, vocational education for the most part meant instruction in farming skills for boys; the emphasis continued to be on 'home-making' as far as girls were concerned.

Beatty himself was very concerned to stimulate the use of bilingual textbooks and dictionaries, not least in order to reduce Indian illiteracy. The missionaries in the nineteenth century had, of course, considered Indian languages in the same light and their successors still did. Bureau teachers were encouraged to attend summer training courses in native languages and the teaching of English to non-English speakers. Instruction was also available in arts and crafts, rural life, vocational subjects, Progressive education methods and anthropology. Universities and colleges gave credit for many of the courses attended and the periodical, *Indian Education*, was published every two months to try to reach teachers as a whole and keep them in touch with the theoretical and practical developments in their field.[25]

The hope that education would prove to be among the least controversial and most successful aspects of Collier's programme was, however, disappointed. During the 1930s, because of the Depression and concern about mounting BIA costs, the education budget declined from $11,224,000 in 1932 to $10,523,475 by 1940, also declining as a proportion of the overall bureau budget. In consequence, there was not enough money to ensure school facilities for all Indian children. Indeed some 8,000 were said to lack facilities in 1940 and 12,000 to be out of school in 1943, albeit pupils frequently remained at home by their own or their parents' design.[26]

In a number of areas the community schools with Indian teachers were wanted by the Indians themselves and in some, notably Oklahoma, they achieved good results.[27] There was less progress among the Navajos, for whom nearly half the community schools had been built. The day schools provided poor food and then no clothing allowance, following a budget miscalculation. They were served by bad roads and were not so well supplied as the boarding schools, while their imaginative construction in the style of Navajo hogans did not compensate for the maintenance difficulties they involved. And since many Navajos still lived the migratory lives dictated by sheep rearing on poor terrain, attendance was low.[28] Moreover an acculturated element among the Navajos expressed some suspicion that their children were being taught Navajo songs and dances to the neglect of reading, writing and arithmetic. They wanted 'the white man's offer of education'.[29] In fact, the Commissioner was bombarded with conflicting advice and his complex intentions were easily misunderstood. While Collier had been at pains to state that Indians were 'entitled to the fullest educational privileges, not in sequestered institutions but in the schools and colleges which serve us all', a view which was shared by his Cherokee higher education guidance officer, Ruth Bronson, he and other well-meaning whites saw no contradiction in promoting 'the study of Indian civilisation' to prevent Indian children from being educated 'out of their . . . heritage' and so given a negative self-image which hindered the learning process. This last point was and would remain contentious – did the whites or the Indians have an image problem? – and the assimilationist American Indian Federation preferred to concentrate on fears that the Commissioner's policy fostered the 'art of living', not learning, while a down-to-earth Navajo correspondent like William Collins advised Collier simply to provide day schools 'where our children can learn to read[,] write and speak the white man's tongue[.] That's all the schooling the Indian needs or can handle. After that he will take care of himself like our fathers always have.'[30]

By 1944, the Commissioner had to admit that among some of the southwestern Indian groups he knew best and admired most, bureau efforts had failed once more: 'After two lifetimes of government schooling enterprise, eighty per cent of the Navajos and perhaps seventy per cent of the Pueblos neither speak nor read English.' Even Progressive educational methods had not been able to bridge the gap between the school and tightly knit Indian families and communities, and the Society of Applied Anthropology was called in to help decide why, just as anthropologists had been used to investigate disappointing educational programmes in South Dakota and California. The investigators accurately noted the lack of co-ordination between educational and other efforts on the reservation. They commented that the schools were too much the product of government initiative, lacked suitable personnel and failed to take sufficient account of the Navajos' own 'social organisation' and values. But no immediate solutions were found and the bureau's community schools remained at best a partial success during Collier's tenure of office.[31]

The record of other types of Indian schools was equally mixed. Notwithstanding efforts to relax discipline and introduce new subjects and teaching methods, many institutions remained unadventurous, poorly staffed, indifferent to Indian complaints and unattractive to those they were intended to serve.[32] As Progressive educators generally fell into disarray,[33] it was not to be expected that their ideas would transform the bureau system, and the Commissioner's reduction of missionary activity in government schools by two executive orders of 1934 brought him into conflict with the evangelists and their supporters, who feared that missionary schools might be in jeopardy and objected to the closure of boarding schools where their representatives were active.[34] Some comfort was to be derived from the successful encouragement of Indian arts and crafts in a number of institutions, of which the Santa Fe boarding school was the best known. White interest in such products had grown steadily from the early twentieth century, when even a crusty agent like Charles Burton at the Moqui Training School in Arizona, who spent much of his time fulminating against intrusive anthropologists, distracting Indian customs and meddling missionaries, and was ready to contemplate flattening the Hopis' First Mesa to force the inhabitants to live safely on level ground, recognized that Indians made true works of art, whose production might be regularized through education.[35] With the assistance of an Arts and Crafts Board founded in 1935, income from this source for students and their parents had greatly increased by 1942. Yet output was of necessity constrained by traditional methods of production; by the Second World War, as in 1933, only a 'limited number of individuals . . . [could] make a living' from the work.[36]

The anxieties produced by the Indian schools might have mattered less if the efforts to improve the public school, advanced and adult education of Indian peoples had enjoyed more success. In 1935 Collier was pleased with the high level of Indian service spending on tuition, food, clothing and books for Indians in public schools.[37] Unfortunately, vocational instruction in the public schools bore no comparison to that provided in the Indian boarding schools, while time had not overcome the hostile response of whites in some areas to Indian children attending the state institutions, or the anxieties of Indian parents about what their children might learn from white youngsters. The state authorities which benefited under JOM resisted attempts by the bureau to direct them or the moneys given, often neglecting their Indian pupils, or failing to take students of less than a quarter Indian blood, for whom tuition was not paid, but who were excluded from the reservation schools. And while the children of all minorities found their cultures slighted in the public schools before the 1960s, the indifference of these institutions to Indian needs and traditions was in sorry contrast to the brave, if faltering, move towards bicultural education under way in the government schools.[38]

In the realm of higher education, the need for the I.R.A. assistance was unquestioned.[39] A mere 385 Indian students were attending college in 1932, although the intelligence tests which had once been said to prove their inferiority to whites were, in the course of the decade, tending to show Indians to be on a par with the rest of the population, a judgement which men like Ryan strongly endorsed.[40] The bureau, under Ryan and Beatty alike, preferred to encourage the attendance of Indians at existing institutions in their states rather than establishing 'segregated schools'.[41] It was, however, difficult and daunting to break into essentially unwelcoming white colleges and remembering the sterling pioneer work of the black and women's colleges one cannot but question the wisdom of the Indian educators whose respect for the Indians' capabilities, greater than that showed by their predecessors for the potential of women and blacks, may ironically have worked against them in this instance. The Indians who did graduate from college – and the majority of entrants did not – tended to be mixed bloods, who were thereby still further detached from traditional Indian communities by long absences and Anglo studies.[42]

Finally, if special schools for the afflicted were unlikely in the difficult conditions of the Depression and only slight attention was paid to the setting up of nursery schools,[43] the relative stagnation of adult education as late as 1941 was disappointing. The white Indian aid organizations attached considerable importance to working with adults and the community schools tried to draw them into their activities.[44] But without funds and personnel exclusively set aside for its own use, adult education remained reliant on the work that could be obtained from Indian service workers employed in other fields.[45]

III

RETRENCHMENT AND REAPPRAISALS: THE 1940S AND 1950S

All of these aspects of educational activity were adversely affected by American involvement in the Second World War. As had been the case during the 1914–18 war, schools were run down and closed and the staff working in education decreased while the number of children out of school rose.[46] Furthermore, as Margaret Szasz points out, the crisis led to the abandonment of bilingual pamphlets, ended efforts to increase the number of Indian teachers through teacher apprenticeships and caused a reduction in the summer training schools.[47] If the war made additional Indian converts to the practical value of education and increased tribal concern about its provision and deficiencies, those deficiencies could only be more marked when the struggle ended. Thus Randolph McCurtain, the Oklahoma Choctaw who handled federal scholarship funds for Indian youths, reported after the war that scholarship aid remained inadequate and that most Indian students were too poor to aspire to college.[48] And while a 1945 report on Navajo education indicated that the old community school ideals still survived, Commissioner William A. Brophy (1945–8) admitted that the day schools were expensive and under-used, but unlikely to have boarding facilities added to them by an economy-minded government.[49]

The 1946 Navajo Special Education Program instead responded to the crisis by sending students to existing on-reservation boarding schools or by dispatching them to board at Indian schools in California, Utah and Oklahoma. Since the Navajo Council was reminding the government of its failures to honour pledges about education made in the 1868 treaty with the tribe, the aim was to find school places for Navajo children above all else.[50] The programme's emphasis was on English teaching and vocational training designed to fit youngsters and adults for jobs off the over-populated reservation. Those trained under it had some success in finding work, which seemed to justify the departure from the reservation orientation of the New Deal, and Beatty himself uneasily accepted the need for a retreat from the policies of the 1930s.[51] Given the postwar desire among assimilationist politicians to terminate the federal government's special relationship with the Indians, the director would have found it very difficult to do otherwise.

By the end of the 1940s, notwithstanding its goal of closing all government schools and making education 'the responsibility of the states', the bureau was still painfully aware of its heavy educational commitments to Indians in areas such as Alaska and Mississippi, with special problems, and to the Navajos, Papagos, Apaches, Sioux and other largely non-English-speaking Indian groups. The best it could do in terms of its overall goal was often just to adjust the curricula in Indian service schools to provide the training necessary for employment beyond the reservations, meanwhile accepting inadequate facilities without too much fuss. The missionaries likewise struggled to keep their enterprises going, not always effectively. Hence the Tucson Indian Training School despite opening its doors to non-Indians, improving its facilities and publicizing its success in producing graduates who were employed in government service and as 'leaders of their people', found it could not compete with the local public schools and was obliged to close down in 1960.[52]

As had been the case in the early twentieth century, educators devoted their major energies to increasing school enrolment, preferably in the public schools. Beatty's successor, Hildegarde Thompson (1952–65), was dismayed to find that 20,000 Indian children remained out of school in 1953, about 14,000 of them on the Navajo reservation. Dramatic inroads into this figure were made either by transferring pupils to the public schools, a move favoured by the National Congress of American Indians founded in 1944, or by sending more to federal boarding schools. By 1964 some 60 per cent of Indian students were attending public school and by 1965 a little over 90 per cent school enrolment had been achieved, the main breakthrough coming in the 1960s.

As attendance was being pushed up, JOM payments were supplemented (and sometimes supplanted) during the 1950s by 'federally impacted area legislation' (P.L. 874). Under its terms, from 1958, JOM funds were to be employed for special needs such as lunches, fees, books and transport, while P.L. 874 monies were to pay for the basic support of Indian children. Whether JOM payments were used properly was hard to determine until the end of the 1960s, in the absence of adequate accounting and feedback from the Indians supposed to be benefiting. Financial assistance in educating Indian children of low-income families, or attending schools with a high proportion of children from such families, was made available to the public schools by the Elementary and Secondary Education Act of 1965. Like P.L. 874, this Act was administered by the US Office of Education, on bureau advice. It supported, among other things, curriculum development, kindergarten provision, the payment of teacher aides and in-service training. By the mid to late 1960s, Szasz records, $505,900,000 was being appropriated under impacted area legislation, $11,552,000 under JOM, and $9,000,000 under the 1965 measure.[53] But statistics, as ever, tell only part of the story.

While the Indian office was cheerfully proclaiming that the Indians in California and south-central Oregon were educationally prepared to sever their connection with the federal government,[54] Indians and white officials feared the educational consequences of termination.[55] The experiences of the Paiutes in Utah, the Menominees in Wisconsin and a number of Indian groups whose instruction was transferred to state or local control in 1952, soon proved the doubters right. Forced into public schools which took no account of their cultural background and special needs, many Indian children fell behind their grade level and then dropped out of school disenchanted and ill-educated, necessitating from 1960 a special system of summer schools for Indian youngsters designed to reawaken their interest and help them recover lost ground.[56] An additional problem was posed by Indians who relocated in the cities during the 1950s, with federal encouragement and some assistance. Again, the difficulty was frankly recognized in the beginning by the bureau and the Indians themselves. Accordingly educational loans and grants were urged to facilitate relocation, as well as a 'very strong' adult education programme to prepare the Indians concerned 'for social, political, and citizenship responsibilities'.[57] By 1957, Commissioner Emmons (1953–61) was able to report that adult education classes, designed especially to reduce illiteracy, were being provided at some one hundred reservation locations, and that members of the 18 to 35 year age group were being enrolled at private or state vocational schools, tuition and subsistence being provided for the students and their families. Yet as the Commissioner acknowledged, the $3.5 million expended annually for this purpose was insufficient.[58]

There was an increase in the number of students going on to higher education during the 1950s, but bureau officials admitted the money available for it from all sources remained inadequate.[59] Consequently, Thompson's encouragement of post high-school education by limiting the amount of time spent at most federal boarding schools on vocational instruction was a hazardous, albeit well-intentioned step. It was also one which put additional strain on those schools, including Chilocco boarding school in Oklahoma and the Institute of American Indian Arts (opened in 1962 in the old Santa Fe boarding school), which continued to offer vocational courses.[60]

IV

New Challenges and New Hopes:
The 1960s and 1970s

If the 1940s and 1950s had been marked by retrenchment and attempts to reduce federal responsibility for Indian affairs, the 1960s and 1970s were to be significant for the intensification of Indian pressures on policy, together with the proliferation of programmes designed to aid Indian groups and enhance their direction of their own affairs. They were also notable for frequent changes in the overall direction of Indian education, so that the benefits of new blood and ideas were sometimes offset by the confusion and insecurity which are the normal by-products of change in a complex system.

Indian education was assisted by the Economic Opportunity Act of 1964, which set up the Office of Economic Opportunity (OEO). It was OEO money, for instance, which went towards kindergarten facilities, not offered in government schools until 1967. The office likewise helped in 1966 to fund on the Navajo reservation the Rough Rock Demonstration School, the first school to run under Indian direction and control, and in 1968 to finance the Navajo Community College. Opening in 1969, and until 1972 operating from accommodation provided by the Indian boarding school at Many Farms, the college was the first Indian controlled two-year college. It accepted students between the ages of 18 and 35, whatever their previous education, and like the Rough Rock school and the community schools of the 1930s, its emphasis was upon tribal as well as white history and culture. In 1970, 80 per cent of its 530 students were Navajos, 10 per cent were Indians from other tribes and 10 per cent were non-Indians. Efforts to train bureau personnel in teaching English as a second language, already begun by Thompson, were given a boost by the Bilingual Education Act of 1968 and the bureau was generally kept alert by the creation of several new organizations and the publication of critical inquiries into Indian education.[61]

The 1960s saw the formation of a policy advice body for bureau schools, the National Indian Education Advisory Committee (1967); the foundation of President Johnson's National Council on Indian Opportunity (1968), which established its own Indian Education Sub-Committee in 1970; and the setting up of the National Indian Education Association (1969), through which Indians strove to keep the government in touch with Indian reactions to education measures and to advise Indians about legislation, fund applications, programmes, innovations and organizations in the field. Among the reports on education, perhaps the most publicized, damning and resented in bureau circles was that produced by Senator Robert Kennedy's special subcommittee on Indian education in 1969. As others had done before it, the report stressed the need to teach Indian history, culture and languages, besides urging the expansion of existing programmes and funding.[62]

In fairness, it might be argued that the willingness of private foundations and corporations to assist Indian education projects already indicated a new concern on the part of whites as well as Indians. The whole of the secondary and especially the college sector of American education was being transformed during the 1960s. As Nasaw reminds us, enrolments soared and the community college system greatly expanded, as did the intake of black, Hispanic and women students, and those 'from families of low socioeconomic status'. But the spending of more money, a characteristic liberal response to social evils in the 1960s, involved its own particular dangers. For just as disillusionment set in when expensive poverty programmes did not eradicate black poverty, though in the process generating considerable waste, so some of the most innovative Indian school projects, not least those on the Navajo reservation, were vulnerable to criticism on account of both their cost and their curricula. In particular, critics complained, as an earlier generation had complained of the community schools, that Indian culture was advanced at the expense of 'academic' subjects; this accusation was also levelled in due course at the Deganiwidah-Quetzalcoatl University established in the early 1970s for Indians and Chicanos near Davis in California, albeit its community support and work with tribal elders were praised by supporters. Moreover, insufficient recognition was given throughout the education system to the difficulty of offsetting the effects of years spent in poverty and 'ability groupings' simply by the provision of new courses, scholarships and similar opportunities for 'underachievers'.[63]

Despite some uneasiness about what might result from Indians' control of their schools, the bureau attempted to relate the curricula in its own boarding schools to Indian and Eskimo beliefs and ways and set up all-Indian school boards for each of them. These boards represented the main tribes who provided students for the schools, though attempts were made in Nevada and (successfully) in the Pacific Northwest to bring the schools under local control. The daunting business of involving parents who had hitherto enjoyed little say in their children's education was facilitated after 1971 by the Coalition of Indian Controlled School Boards, which gave information and assistance to Indian school boards and organizations concerned with education.[64] For certain parents, at least, the question of who educated their children was less important than ensuring that they were given 'quality education'. And for certain Indians, this was evidently felt to be unlikely to occur when teachers failed to take account of the Indians' frequent aversion to competition in the Anglo manner and their way of learning through watching, and impossible at bureau schools where, fairly or not, it was alleged that the students were not pushed, while the teachers were substandard, uncomfortable with their pupils and 'just interested in getting through the day'.[65] A number of familiar headaches were admitted by the teachers themselves. Thus an instructor at Fort Wingate elementary school on the Navajo reservation, who had been trained to teach English as a second language and had taken an introductory course on Navajo culture, conceded that he taught 'American culture', that Navajo teaching materials were scarce and that the teaching aides were not always well qualified. Nor were relations with the student counsellors close. Hardly surprisingly, perhaps, some children simply went 'to school for . . . board and room', learned slowly and ran away.[66]

Where Indian control of instruction was impossible, a degree of progress might be made towards the goal of cultural pluralism in education by persuading public schools and colleges to recognize the Indians' ancient traditions and present needs through amending textbooks and enlarging their curricula. Universities in California, New Mexico, Utah, Arizona, Oklahoma, Minnesota and Michigan responded positively to demands for Indian Studies and the teaching of courses concerning Indians within existing college departments also increased.[67] There were growing pains, too. Black students and educators who had pressed for Afro-American Studies argued, once they had won their case, about the proper purpose and content of such programmes, about who should control and be admitted to them.[68] Similar debates took place among Indian college youths, though with their own special twist. Was there any point trying to teach languages that might soon be extinct? Did not reservation Indians already know what was being taught in the Indian Studies classes, though they might prove useful to urban Indians? Should not those who needed them be taught these things at the elementary rather than the university level? Were whites to be admitted to the courses or would that make it impossible for sacred subjects to be discussed? Could a balance be struck between the contributions of Indian elders and oral tradition on the one hand and professional scholars and educators on the other, perhaps by opening programmes to Indian communities as well as university students? Would students from different tribes be able to get along and how could desirable links with the reservations be kept if courses were held away from them? And should their main purpose, and that of education generally, be to persuade Indian students of the need to 'return home and help their tribal leaders and people'? The answers to these questions were not easily found. They had to be worked out through trial and error by those involved who, as Washburn, Gregory and Strickland have pointed out, simultaneously struggled to stimulate the production of necessary teaching materials; to reconcile the interests of ethnic and non-ethnic students; to disarm critics of the separatist and political orientation of Indian Studies; and to prevent them from becoming merely 'an academic Wild West Show'.[69]

The move towards Indian self-determination in educational matters was taken further by the 1972 Indian Education Act, which fostered the establishment of Indian controlled schools by specifically allocating funds to schools that were not local educational institutions and made Indian participation in the setting up and direction of P.L. 874 programmes compulsory. The finance was provided for the mounting of courses involving Indian cultures and languages, with preference being given to Indian schools and groups, while grants were allotted for adult education courses and for training teachers for bureau schools. At the same time, an Office of Indian Education was set up to administer these funds in the US Office of Education, to be run by a Deputy Commissioner for Indian Education, who was to be chosen from nominees put forward by a new, President-appointed, all-Indian National Advisory Council on Indian Education. One of the great advantages of the legislation was the aid it extended to terminated and state recognized Indians and it was passed not only in response to the demands of concerned congressmen following the Kennedy investigation but also because of pressures from Indian groups. These pressures subsequently shaped the 1975 Indian Self-Determination and Education Assistance Act, which generally provided for maximum participation in government programmes by those concerned, and specifically for direct contracting with Indians who received JOM moneys and full bureau review of their expenditure, the lack of which had caused anxiety since the 1930s.[70]

Even when changing political and economic circumstances by the middle of the 1970s resulted in inadequate funding for Indian education programmes, their centrality and basic direction was not questioned. This may be seen from the passage in 1976 of amendments to the Vocational Education Act, which authorized awards for the purpose to Indian tribes and organizations, and in the approval in 1978 of legislation which afforded backing for the planning, development, operation and improvement of tribally controlled community colleges and more equitable support for the Navajo Community College. The same year saw the passage of a measure to help implement the Self-Determination Act through, among other things, making an input by Indian parents on local school boards obligatory and the report of the American Indian Policy Review Commission, set up in 1975, recommended the control of education by the tribe rather than the state or local government, as well as provision 'for the study of Indian history, culture, language, academic skills and career training without assimilation'.

However, the bureau, Indian and public response to educational innovation continued, as always, to be variable. On the one hand, the JOM system seemed to be working well in areas like Oklahoma, while college enrolment had risen steadily from the 1960s, with students attending both Indian and non-Indian institutions, including Haskell (which in 1965 became Haskell Junior College) and the tribally controlled community colleges at the Pine Ridge, Rosebud and Navajo reservations. By 1976, approximately 16,000 students in higher education were receiving some $33 million in assistance, with help for the first time being given to a limited number of graduate, married and urban Indians, and real progress was being made in producing graduates in the fields of law, medicine and educational administration, where Indian leaders had long been needed but were scarce.

On the other hand, there was some tribal uneasiness that the Self-Determination Act might be termination in a new guise, the BIA was still unable to provide adequate special education, bilingual teaching and local instruction for Indians under its authority and there was an unresolved contradiction between the officially respectable policy of Indian self-determination in education and the assimilationist pressures still applied in the public schools.[71] Moreover, the bureau knew little about the Indian students going to college: how they prepared for the experience, how they fared, how they could be helped to stay the course. Only 3.5 per cent of Indian men had completed college in 1977, as opposed to 12 per cent of all American men, with low grades being a problem and only perhaps 10 per cent of all Indian freshmen eventually graduating. As 1970–1 interviews with Papago students at the University of Arizona made plain, there was urgent need for more and better information and counselling services at high schools and colleges, as well as for remedial courses, especially to help freshmen struggling with culture shock and the realization that they had been poorly taught at school. It was far less obvious how students with family responsibilities could cope with the economic pressures on them; how those with few university graduates in their tribe could avoid an inferiority complex about advanced education and resist the temptation 'to stop after the first defeat'; and how the desire to keep Indian culture and compete in the Anglo world might be reconciled.[72]

We have yet to see if a fair chance will be given to the new campaign for an 'alternative' education system, geared to Indians as in the 1930s but this time more securely shaped by the Indians themselves. Although the will to achieve change exists, its achievement will take decades. It is, therefore, vulnerable both to overall shifts in the economic or political climate, and to that impatient American desire, noted by an observer contemplating reform of the Indian service in 1929, 'to do in a day the job of a generation' and to offer education as 'the panacea for almost all shortcomings'.[73]

10

Indian Women in Fancy and Fact

According to McKenney and Hall, the compilers in 1836 of an influential *History of the Indian Tribes of North America*, the 'men are free, and the women are slaves'. This verdict summed up the attitude of white men in the nineteenth century towards Indian women. It also helped to justify the efforts made, during that century, to persuade Indians of the merits of the family farm, where Indian men would take on the bulk of agricultural work, Indian women would concentrate on 'home-making' and 'surplus' common lands could be sold off to white settlers. Since Indian women were presumed to have most to gain from such changes, they increasingly attracted the attention of white reformers. Yet the view of Indian women as unfortunate drudges or subordinates did not dominate in the colonial and early national eras, when its social usefulness to whites had not been fully worked out, albeit in all three periods white pronouncements were shaped by the intellectual preoccupations and social circumstances of whites and primarily made by men whose main concern was the threat posed by Indian men.[1]

I

EARLY CONTACTS:
THE PUSH AND PULL FACTORS

The colonial settlers were keenly interested in the appearance of Native Americans. And while they commented disapprovingly on the semi-nakedness of both sexes, they took the opportunity to observe the 'handsome lymbes, slender armes, and pretty handes' of Indian women and to dwell upon 'their faces plump and round' and their bodies 'as soft and smooth as mole-skin'.[2] Given the general lack of aversion among whites to what they saw, despite the fact that Indians frequently looked very different from Europeans, one might anticipate that cohabitation between the races would have been common. But it was not. Indian men on the whole seem to have preferred the colour and looks of their own women and, Axtell has noted, the rape which was sometimes held to follow the natives' capture of white women apparently seldom occurred among the eastern tribes, since it would either have violated their 'religious ethic of strict warrior continence', or transgressed incest taboos where captives were intended to replace lost daughters, sisters or cousins. So far as can be determined, captives were encouraged, not obliged, to marry and they might come to love their Indian families. However, Slotkin points out that many colonial leaders dreaded that a marriage of Indian and white cultures would be effected by such contacts, while other settlers feared for the captives because they believed that the Indians were generally lewd and unrestrained in their sexual relationships.[3]

This conviction, expressed from the sixteenth century, was particularly marked in New England, where Puritans emphasized the need to control lust through 'patriarchal authority in marriage'. Both Puritan and Indian cultures stressed human sexuality. Yet whereas the Puritans sought to regulate it and make divorce very difficult, lest authority and order should break down in the wilderness, the Indians' free sexual expression from an early age ensured the survival of their numerically small and vulnerable groupings.[4] Indian marriages required neither legal nor religious sanction and divorce, though not necessarily common, was easy, all of which was the opposite of Puritan practice. What whites were slow to acknowledge was that while young women might 'take undue liberty before marriage', they were 'when married, chaist', as William Penn said of the Delawares; and outsiders were equally unlikely to concede that separation or divorce without difficulties compensated Indian women for the generally stern treatment of adultery on their part.[5] This in turn has been explained by Alice Schlegel as a means of discouraging the introduction of illegitimate children into the father's descent group, in patrilineal societies, and of averting disruption of 'the in-law bond between husband and brother', in matrilineal societies.[6]

Instead, the colonists were inclined to believe that Indian attitudes to divorce were simply a further proof of their immorality, just as Indian cruelty was revealed by the punishments for adultery, which in the case of a woman might range from casting off, beating or disfiguring the culprit to exposing her in a public place 'as the victim of all men who chose to be present'. (Male adulterers might also be punished, though seldom so severely as women, and members of either sex might escape lightly by hiding or if their relatives were stronger than those of the injured party.[7]) Lack of knowledge about Indian customs further led the first settlers to exaggerate the degree to which the tribes sustained polygamy,[8] from which misunderstanding part of the subsequent white view of the degradation of Indian women was formed.

Nevertheless, if all these factors, together with lack of opportunity and the souring impact of intermittent warfare, served to inhibit Indian–white cohabitation, they did not prevent it entirely. Accordingly the records of Virginia, the Carolinas, New York and New England indicate an element of racial intermixture, although there is dispute about the degree of success enjoyed by the colonial whites who encouraged intermarriage as a means of civilizing the tribes and improving race relations.[9] Most usual were the liaisons formed by white men with Indian women for diplomatic or trading purposes. The best-known diplomatic marriage, in 1614, between English settler John Rolfe and Pocahontas, the daughter of the Indian chief Powhatan, caused Rolfe much doubt. He confessed that her 'education hath bin rude, her manners barbarous' and he feared that his countrymen might think him lascivious or relapsing into savagery.[10] As it was designed to do, the marriage helped to secure peace between Indians and whites in Virginia; Pocahontas herself did not survive it long, dying in England in 1617.[11] Such interracial attachments increased during the eighteenth century, as more whites pushed into Indian lands and the Indians showed growing interest in white trade goods.

John Ewers has shown that the French Canadian fur traders working the Upper Missouri were attracted to the women of the Mandan and Arikara, that marriages between white men and Indian women were taking place by the last quarter of the century and that hundreds of such women were linked with whites in the heyday of the trade in that region.[12] While physical appeal, the scarcity of white women and the usefulness of Indian women as guides, interpreters and 'entry cards' into Indian society may explain the matches from the white point of view, Indian women, according to Ewers, took a strictly practical view of their white partners. It seems likely that only better material conditions could have compensated them for the weakening or severing of their ties with Indian society and the risks involved in what were frequently short-term relationships, though for their part Indian men might positively value marriages which gave them a kinship link to the trader and his source of manufactured products.[13] Among the southern Indians, similar Indian–white contacts were being made, with the Scot, Lachlan McGillivray, marrying into the upper Creek nation, his fellow countryman, James Colbert, into the Chickasaw tribe, and the whites, John Pitchlynn, the Folsoms and the Leflores, into the Choctaw nation, looking to gain thereby a position in Indian society which they could not otherwise have enjoyed, including the right to use Indian land.[14]

As racial attitudes hardened in the new republic and Massachusetts, Rhode Island and Maine prohibited intermarriage between Indians and whites, regardless of the fact that they no longer faced an Indian threat,[15] it is not surprising that Indian–white matches stood their best chance of success if the whites involved remained in or connected with Indian country. Perhaps because they were both useful and malleable, the female offspring of these matches appear to have been regarded in the most favourable light by whites and not all of them seem to have found the strains resulting from their unusual backgrounds to be intolerable.[16] Moreover, a number of the intermarried women of the Upper Missouri introduced aspects of white material culture to their own people, as well as becoming individually acculturated, while the Shoshoni woman, Sacajawea, who was married to a French Canadian trader-interpreter, acted as guide and interpreter to the Lewis and Clark expedition in the far Northwest in 1804–6, helping whites to gain access to the Indian groups encountered on the trip, besides caring for her baby and foraging, cooking, nursing and tending to clothes for the party.[17]

II

MATRILINY OR MATRIARCHY?
INDIAN WOMEN AND THE FAMILY

In the course of sexual and other close contacts with Indian peoples, white settlers were baffled by the matrilineal societies they encountered,[18] that is, societies in which descent and relationship were reckoned through the mother and property passed through the female line. Although they do not seem to have concluded from their experiences that matriliny and matriarchy, or female domination of the family, should be equated, they *were* confused in the nineteenth century by a number of commentators, who regarded both as the primitive, universal predecessors of those patriarchal systems towards which the world, especially the Western world, was evolving when they wrote. Since women in matrilineal groups were not controlled by their husbands in the approved Victorian manner, such a confusion was understandable.[19] Modern scholars think differently about matriliny. In his entertaining study of kinship and marriage, Robin Fox includes as one of his basic 'principles' governing the subject the statement that 'The men usually exercise control'. No matter what the economic organization of society or the influence of woman, 'the sheer physiological facts of her existence make her role secondary to that of the male in the decision-making process at any level higher than the purely domestic'.[20] Even feminists today cannot find evidence of the existence of vanished matriarchies, acknowledging that individuals who have done so have taken the founding myths for the actual histories of past societies.[21] None the less, a valuable debate is going on about the varieties and significance of matrilineal groupings and about the status of women generally in pre-industrial societies.[22]

The following broad conclusions and questions have emerged. Matriliny and patriliny alike could develop in the distant past, no matter that matriliny might have been a form of social organization particularly suited to promiscuous eras, when the only parent known for certain was the mother.[23] The adoption of matriliny probably resulted when men had to spend long periods of time away from home in 'hunting or warfare or religious activity'; patriliny may have ensued when the principal food resource was game, 'non-migratory and scattered, which ... [made] it advantageous for men to remain in and exploit the territory in which they were born and which they ... [knew] intimately'.[24] It now seems plausible that matrilineal systems tended to flourish when the household was of productive, but not unduly marked, importance. In other words, the more limited the value of the property women produced or owned, before the growth of craft specialization, the less likely it was for dominant male figures to emerge in matrilineal societies, or for matriliny itself to be challenged.[25] The main exceptions to this rule among Indian peoples were the Iroquois and the southeastern tribes, as we shall see. Matriliny was further assisted by, and indeed often grew out of, matrilocal residence: a situation where a man who married joined his wife's household and the organization of the domestic group consequently complemented that of the descent group, as is the case in patrilineal communities, rather than the domestic group being controlled by either brothers or husbands, which is the normal arrangement in matrilineal units. We know, too, that acquisitive whites and anxious missionaries, in the Southeast and elsewhere, responded to matriliny by pressuring tribal authorities to enact 'new regulations regarding land ... that emphasised the position of men as the head of the family' and entitled widows to dower rights and children to inherit their fathers' estates.[26]

In addition, it has been established that Indian societies have not imbued 'divinity only with male qualities'. Yet it is still necessary to ask, with Hoch-Smith and Spring, whether 'the symbolic image of woman' is equated, in conflicting ways, with her sexual function.[27] A linked consideration here is how far we may apply to American Indian peoples the Western pejorative association of women with natural forces and with the materialistic and particularistic concerns of the domestic sphere, whereas men are associated with concern for culture and the conquest of the wild, with larger social issues and the more respected public domain.[28] Or is it more accurate to see the roles of the sexes in Indian societies as genuinely flexible and complementary? Finally, we must try to decide whether women's status in the pre-capitalist era was enhanced not just because of matriliny and the fact that the household was a productive unit, but also because of the vital nature of the contribution made by women as food gatherers and horticulturalists, a contribution relatively little disrupted by child bearing.[29] An answer to these questions will be sought by looking first at the role of Indian women in the family and sexual matters, and then at their involvement in work, religion and political affairs.

Women in Indian, as in all societies, enjoyed a kind of power which came from their exclusive ability to bear children. From puberty to middle age, this power was literally manifested at menstruation. While Native American groups were less inclined than, say, Oceanic peoples to make biological differences between the sexes the crucial definition of gender,[30] they generally respected the power of menstruating women by requiring their segregation for the duration of the monthly period. The Indians' asumption was that a menstruating woman could harm the men of her group by a glance or touch, thereby depriving them of their own special accomplishments and possibly bringing calamity on the entire community. In Ruth Underhill's words, 'Fear of such consequences was the reason why women were so often excluded from ceremonies, a blanket prohibition being the safest rule . . . It was why, in many areas, women could not become shamans, at least until after the menopause.' Rules about how the separation should be conducted varied from area to area and so did belief in its importance. Segregation seems to have been most pronounced among the hunting peoples, where anything which interfered with man's food-providing ability would have been very damaging. The fact that women contributed to the subsistence of such societies seems to have mattered little when the primary economic activity was thought to be threatened.[31]

Menstrual segregation was denounced by white missionaries as degrading to women, despite the fact that Western attitudes to menstruating women were similarly fashioned by revulsion and myth.[32] Their strictures were too simple. The monthly seclusion could be seen by women as a welcome rest. It was justified as a protection for both men and women and was reinforced by codes of differing levels of strictness concerning sexual separation during and after pregnancy. As Schlegel suggests, the restrictions placed on menstruating women were similar to those imposed upon 'men in a state of spiritual tension or danger, such as before warfare or the hunt, after homicide, or during ceremonial periods'.[33] And they did not seem peculiar to peoples whose economies and social organization segregated the sexes for much of the time.

A high degree of separation between men and women has characterized peasant societies until the present day, but nineteenth-century white observers deplored the absence among American Indians of the fond, conjugal family which they associated with progress. Domestic closeness, in the ideal Victorian family, was ensured by removing the women from work outside the home, though in fact the very separation of home and work under industrialization imposed a new barrier between the sexes, while marriages of convenience in which property considerations dominated were still common in the nineteenth century. Disregarding these inconvenient facts, the ethnologist Morgan disapproved of the arranged matches to be noted among the Iroquois, which, incidentally, were to be found in other tribes. What he admired were unions 'founded upon the affections' and he regretted that the Indians sustained 'but little sociality' between the sexes 'as this term is understood in polished society'.[34]

The relationship between Indian parents and their children also interested whites and in some Indian societies the mothers' marked influence over their children is a measure of their importance. The Iroquois provide the most striking example of such a society. Judith K. Brown points out that the agricultural activities in which they were prominent could be effectively combined with child rearing. Accordingly, among the prerogatives of Iroquois women were the arrangement and 'monitoring' of marriages; the custody of children, as a rule, when parents separated; and the spacing of the births of children. Women often had the right to decide the names for their offspring and to pick the children to assume names which 'might culminate in high administrative titles of community or nation'.[35] Female isolation in matrilocal communities where men were away for long periods might likewise enhance the influence of women in their primary area of responsibility. Among the Mescalero Apaches, for instance, mothers cared for their children with the aid of female kin, providing enduring households which could absorb adopted captives and in which women instructed 'younger members in traditional behaviour patterns, kinship, and language forms'.[36]

But if Indian women gained by working with their young children around them, in a manner denied to many white mothers, and enjoyed a very close relationship with their unweaned infants, the men of even matrilocal tribes were not prevented from forming responsibilities towards their offspring, or from teaching their sons adult duties.[37] Nor should it be forgotten that the special bonds between mothers and children were of short duration, not least because youngsters of both sexes were introduced to the world of work at an early age. Whites may ironically have played a part here in reinforcing traditional practices. Despite the nineteenth-century elevation of the childhood state, whites disliked Indian indulgence of their children. They therefore invariably urged the importance of the work ethic upon Indian peoples, were happy to see Indian children working when at school and, unless they lived in urban comfort, were likely to condone the employment of their own youthful offspring.[38]

Whites were similarly inclined to depreciate the absence, in Indian societies, of that public chivalry towards women which was expected in their own polite circles and to rejoice, like the Indian administrator Thomas McKenney, that with the advance of Christianity and school-ing, 'The female character is elevated, and duly respected'.[39] The outspokenness of Indian women on sexual matters gave offence to outsiders, while the lack of privacy in sexual relations and the continued practice of polygamy and sexual violence were additional sources of displeasure.[40] Yet Indian societies, like all human societies, could combine the abstemious and the indulgent with regard to sex and might authorize the most draconian punishments for sexual offences without finding many occasions to implement them. Little allowance was made for the fact that Indian–white warfare, by upsetting the balance of the sexes, may have strengthened polygamy, or for the fact that plural marriages often involved sisters or other relations, who might be glad not to be separated. Native American communities did not produce the conditions that drove large numbers of white women into organized prostitution, or make the invidious distinctions between wives and concubines to be found in 'civilized' society, while the fact that Indian families were generally smaller than those of whites did much to alleviate the lot of the supposedly over-burdened Indian wife. And whereas the termination of nose-slitting, and the reduction of forced marriages, wife-selling and the neglect of girl children in hard times were benefits brought by Anglo intervention, the lot of plural wives abandoned by husbands conver-ted to monogamy was frequently unenviable.[41]

Moreover, there were Indian groups who, notwithstanding their frankness about adult or infant sexuality, were as modest as Victorians could have wished in their attitudes to bodily exposure. Hence Navajo women were voluminously attired and the same was true of the Sioux women affectionately remembered by Elaine Goodale Eastman, who taught in their schools during the 1880s. Commenting on one of their dances, she observed that their 'dress was, as always, completely unrevealing ... and their attitudes modest. We were expected to frown upon all "heathen spectacles", but could not help knowing that the modern round dance in which men and women publicly embrace was a shocking thing in the eyes of our ceremonious Dakotas.' The Sioux women, though enjoying no privacy, even managed to suckle their children without displaying the breast.[42]

III

THE MATERIAL LOT OF WOMEN

The lack of public courtesies between the sexes which whites deplored was nowhere more evident, to their mind, than in the division of labour in Indian societies. We have already suggested that the early colonists had not stressed the physical work done by Indian women in quite such stark terms as nineteenth-century commentators.[43] This relative unconcern was understandable when the lives of the majority of white women in the colonies were dominated by hard labour and at a time when the demarcation lines between men's and women's vocations and between commodity production by men and production for the household by women were not as clear as they would later become. Whites were able to recognize the economic contribution of Indian women to native society, albeit the tasks in which Indian men engaged were underestimated. And the newcomers also appreciated the deference shown by Indian women to their husbands.[44]

Once the balance of power tipped in favour of the whites, their numbers grew and middle-class moralists extolled the importance of women as the guardians of the nation's children, morals and cultural heritage,[45] so policy-makers, missionaries and a range of commentators saw value in trying to persuade more Indian men to take up farming and more Indian women to 'confine themselves to domestic duties and the cares of the house and the family'.[46] In asking Indian women to concentrate on 'home-making', whites were at least demanding a smaller change from them than they expected from Indian men and they had before them the example of the partial withdrawal of black women from wage work after the abolition of slavery. But black women, having been forced into agricultural labour, were readier when economic and family circumstances permitted to withdraw from the fields, much to the alarm of the white southerners.[47] In Indian societies, intervention by outsiders, made on the grounds that Indian women were 'beasts of burden',[48] was both unwelcome and ignored the testimony of a number of whites that Indian women were neither unhappy nor downtrodden.[49] However, such a state of affairs could always be credited to the ignorance or innate conservatism of 'primitive' groups, while nineteenth-century humanitarians felt they had to show that the Indians could be 'improved' in ways acceptable to whites because so many of their contemporaries were arguing that Native Americans could not progress and were bound for extinction.[50] Consequently, most white observers interpreted the varied material circumstances of Indian women in a way that best suited their own interests.

Among the Iroquois, the high status of women clearly owed a good deal to a prosperous environment, which they were crucial in exploiting. The bulk of the confederacy's food came from agriculture, in which women were dominant. They planted and cultivated the fields, after the ground had been prepared by men; both sexes joined in the harvest. Women gathered foods to supplement these staple crops and they were not only the producers and collectors of food but also the owners of the means of its production. Although there is some dispute about the nature of Iroquois land and implement tenure, Brown maintains that, if communally owned, the land was held by the women, and they certainly controlled access to the implements and seeds and stored and distributed the food of the tribe and the household, even when it was obtained by men. Such control was facilitated by matrilocality.[51]

A similar situation prevailed in the major southeastern tribes before large-scale encroachments by whites. Hunting and agriculture-gathering, the work of men and women respectively (though men helped on the public farms), were equally important to subsistence and the strength women derived from their economic role was buttressed by matriliny and matrilocality. Whites who thought that this division of labour was unfair to Indian women did so in part because it was not understood that men would build houses, clear the ground for cultivation and make agricultural implements. When whites tried to convert southern Indian men to the merits of agriculture in the white fashion, the first response came, ironically, from their women. Mary Young has shown that Cherokee women 'took to cultivating cotton themselves', as well as demanding spinning wheels, cards and looms, the provision of which through Indian agents was opposed by some hunters, who feared that the implements might make their wives 'oppressively independent'.[52]

It is nevertheless dangerous to generalize, from the above observations, about all matrilineal Indian societies. The western Pueblo peoples were matrilineal in descent and matrilocal in residence and far from exploiting abundance were engaged in a constant struggle for survival in the arid Southwest, while both agriculture and sheep herding were undertaken by men. Yet the crops, houses and most of the household authority belonged to the women, despite their reliance on men's economic activities, a situation productive of a certain tension between the sexes. Eggan suggests that in these societies matrilocal residence and matrilineal descent developed because of the importance of women in the transition to agriculture and the need for their co-operation in corn-grinding. Disagreement exists about when this pattern emerged in the western settlements and when a bilateral system evolved among the eastern Pueblos, but bilateralism may have resulted from the growing involvement of men in agriculture.[53] The Navajos' social organization was similarly complex. Whereas they traced descent through the mother, residence might be matrilocal or patrilocal and matrilocality, while being practised by the majority of the tribe, was more usually a feature of the livestock than of the farming regions. But regardless of the residence pattern involved, women were supreme in their homes, owned property independently of their husbands and supplemented their income through weaving. Craft skills have always contributed to the wealth and status of individual Indian women, a fact which was not fully appreciated by whites until the twentieth century, when widespread respect developed for the skills of the potter, Maria Martinez of San Ildefonso Pueblo, and for other women artists.[54]

The Plains Indians, sometimes taken by whites as representative of all Indian groups, were generally presented by them as being the most exploitative of female labour.[55] They did not seek to explain what they saw as being part of a complicated social response by these tribes to the ecology of their region. Dividing the Plains peoples into High and Prairie Plains groups, Eggan notes that in the case of the former, descent was bilateral and residence variable. What appears to have given overall primacy to men here was the vital economic contribution to group survival of the buffalo hunter. Where matriliny and matrilocality existed, for example among the Crows, they did not seem able to enhance the position of women when the material basis for female power that horticultural labour provided was lacking. The ecology of the tribes of the Prairie Plains, living in semi-permanent earth lodge villages and relying on agriculture as well as game hunting, afforded more opportunities for women. It was they who cultivated the crops, which were consumed, stored, or traded with the High Plains peoples. Yet once again there is diversity as regards living and kinship arrangements, with the Omahas and some of their neighbours adopting patrilocality, 'an organization that facilitated both hunting and defence against enemy attacks'.[56]

In the judgement of whites, the final indignity suffered by Indian women in material affairs was their treatment in widowhood. The period of mourning required from them was longer than that expected from bereaved men and, to make matters worse, they could find themselves impoverished by the giving away of their property. To the widows, things looked rather different. They chose poverty and self-mutilation as a means of showing the greatest possible honour to their departed husbands; the disposal of goods was in their hands, albeit their freedom of manoeuvre was limited by tribal expectations.[57] Just the same, there was no one pattern of behaviour regarding Indian widows. Male relatives would often come to their assistance and in matrilineal groups widows were certainly not deprived of their belongings. Indeed, neither widowhood nor divorce automatically spelled destitution for Indian women.

Furthermore, despite the female disabilities whites deplored, we should note that there existed in Indian societies a class of men who aspired to be women and for whom institutional provision existed. The male berdache, found among most North American Indian groups though most fully documented for the Plains Indians of the Siouan language category, is literally a male prostitute. But in Native American practice, the significant attributes of the berdache were as much social as sexual; and while the reasons for becoming a berdache were varied, ranging from a vision to captive status, the most common would seem to have been a preference for the occupational tasks of women.

As Harriet Whitehead has shown, a berdache was seen as more than 'a mere woman', being able to fulfil the work of both a man and a woman. Just because he was a man, he might be thought capable of doing women's tasks 'better than actual women'. On the other hand, the division of labour in Indian communities according to sex, which whites deplored, was less rigid than that prevailing in many white societies. In Whitehead's words, the duties of men and women 'did not generate the consistent inequalities in power and influence associated with full prestige differentiation ... In as much as women's activities generated wealth and influence comparable to that of men, men appeared who were willing to take up these activities.' Sexual crossing by women was less common and not institutionalized; it was less easy to ignore the responsibilities which followed from female physiology, especially menstruation. An interesting account by John Ewers of the extraordinary women who were accepted as warriors by the Crows and Blackfeet makes it clear that they rose to prominence because of their unusual height and strength and that they did not repudiate female dress and tasks.[58]

IV

Women in Religion and Politics

Since the sexual attributes of Indian women constrained them more than men, we might expect that their religious powers and limitations would relate more directly to their sexuality or ascribed status and less to individual 'grace' than those of men. This is largely true, although the association has not deprived female deities of importance, which might be good or evil: witches could be either men or women, there was no exclusive 'criminalization' of women in this respect, such as occurred in Europe. There was, even so, a tendency to represent women in mythology as either all good or all evil, something which accords with the dichotomy noted recently by Hoch-Smith and Spring in their broad study of women in ritual and symbolic roles.

The fertility of the earth was widely associated with the supernatural in female form: woman was, as ever, a nurturing force. Among horticultural peoples, corn was variously seen as a gift from the mother-creator, mother corn, the spirit of corn, corn maidens or corn women. The strong position of Navaho women in Navaho religion is shown by the existence of several important female deities, including Changing Woman, the wife of the Sun and giver of corn, and Spider Woman, who taught people how to weave. By common consent a woman could destroy the efficacy of the hunter, who was further threatened by a number of malevolent female spirits; conversely she was recognized by the eastern Pueblos as the Mother of Game. For the eastern Eskimos, the 'owner' of the sea mammals on which they depended was a female spirit. As the source of all living things, Mother Earth was revered, if not to the same degree as 'in the Old World when agriculture took the place of hunting'.[59] Yet the contrast with Christianity, in which 'the figure of God was purely patriarchal', could not have been stronger and in Indian creation myths male and female sexuality were of equivalent importance.[60]

The significance of female deities or spirits to Indian groups does not, however, alter the fact that the major part in Indian ceremonials was played by men, largely as a consequence of fears about the malevolent power of menstruating women. Because of these anxieties, women were frequently confined to providing food and spectators for ceremonies, while in rites that involved female roles, the parts were played by men. The role of women none the less varied from region to region.[61]

Among the Iroquois, women helped to organize the religious festivals and to select the 'keepers of the faith'. They sang in the rituals of the society of women planters and in their own curing societies and could become clairvoyants. Women walked over the cornfields at night to protect the fields from vermin and to ensure plant growth and performed dances for the corn, beans, squash and wild fruits. In the longhouse Dance of the Dead, the march was executed by women to music provided by the men. Whereas Pueblo men have exercised primary responsibility for religious ritual, Hopi men required support from their households to carry out their ceremonial duties, women officially threw 'water on the men at certain ceremonies, as rain magic' and their three women's societies mounted three women's cere-monies.[62]

If medicine men and shamans were normally men, women (especially after menopause) might experience dreams and trances and occasionally act as shamans, as in the instance of the Shasta of California.[63] And while Plains cultures could be male-dominated in some ways, men and women might be admitted jointly to religious societies. Women could sponsor ceremonials if they had the prestige and means and could belong to their own special societies.[64] The Arapahos' Buffalo Lodge was a women's organization and their Seven Old Women, though not comprising a lodge, 'corresponded in a measure to the highest of the men's age societies'. Its members, like the Seven Old Men, had supernatural powers epitomized by their medicine bags and they taught the women of their tribe craft skills.[65]

Because the public aspects of religion among Indian groups were largely controlled by men, one would anticipate that politics, the other main aspect of public life, would be a masculine preserve. Such was the case, but with the same exceptions to male domination that we have noted for sexual, economic and religious affairs. In other words, there were some differences between the agrarian and the hunting, between the less warlike and more warlike tribes. If we accept that being 'able to give and receive items of food and items of social exchange is the material basis for exercising political power',[66] it is not surprising to find that in Indian communities where women inherited wealth, produced a large part of the food resources (particularly if these were destined for exchange as well as use) and had 'marketable' craft skills, they were more likely to be regarded as 'social adults' than they were in societies where they lacked these assets. Matrilineal societies in which brothers rather than husbands were the controlling males, or in which neither male group dominated, were also likely to be helpful to women by extending the decision-making power outside 'the smallest societal unit' and reducing the 'concentration of authority over women'.[67]

Among the Iroquois, the production by women of the major food source allowed them to influence male activities – 'the hunt, the warpath, and the Council' – by supplying or withholding the necessary food supplies. As Brown suggests, female control of the stored wealth of the tribe further enhanced the position of matrons who controlled the households and work groups. These women were able to propose and depose council elders, affect the deliberations of the council through their representatives and, on occasions, influence decisions for war and peace. Molly Brant, the Iroquois consort of the British Indian Superintendent from 1755 to 1774, Sir William Johnson, was credited with real power in Iroquois politics.[68] Outside this group, the economic importance of women and matrilocal residence have produced less significant political consequences. The women of the Hopis, who are dominated neither by husbands nor brothers, 'participate freely and actively in the greater social life' and 'have a voice . . . in the settlement of land disputes' at the clan level, but the community's political actors, like the priests, are men. Mina Lansa is said to have become the first Hopi woman kikmongwi, or village leader, in 1960.[69] Divided kin responsibilities among Navaho men likewise help to enlarge the social freedom of Navaho women, yet while older men and women have traditionally been deferred to, the principal local authority figures are 'headmen'.[70]

Government was in the hands of men in the southeastern tribes, despite the importance of women in agriculture and the clan organization, and the *relatively* unwarlike nature of these groups. This is not to say that the women did not exercise an indirect influence on political decisions, as they did among the Iroquois, though to a lesser extent. Thus Gibson points out that the women of the slave-owning Chickasaws, who were a warlike people, 'could be expected to urge their men to more fury, more raids, and more slaves, which changed their status from laborers to overseers of slave laborers' and O'Donnell observes that many southern Indian women 'attended the tribal councils and spoke their minds'.[71]

The Indians of southern New England in the early seventeenth century did not accord their horticulturalist women political power, but Salisbury records that a few women were able to achieve band leadership. Two centuries later, when the Sioux assembled in a big council, Elaine Eastman noted that the 'intelligent interest' of the ostensibly 'disfranchised' women 'was apparent to one who heard the matter debated in family groups from end to end of the reservation'.[72] And throughout North America, Indian women were accorded a large say, kindly or otherwise, in the treatment of prisoners taken in war.[73] Nevertheless, the military and age societies, tribal councils and chiefs of the Plains tribes were masculine, as one would expect where social life was dominated by masculine concerns, though the degree to which government was formally institutionalized in the tribes varied considerably.[74]

However, if the public sphere was largely man's sphere in Indian, as in all other, communities, no elaborate ideology evolved which projected men as the civilizing, and women as the natural, forces in the world. Men's government weighed less heavily on Indian women than it did on their white (especially married) counterparts. Indian societies were not authoritarian class societies, supporting correspondingly autocratic family structures.[75] Depending on their own political preferences, whites praised or deplored the Indians' limited government based on consent of the people and valuing leaders for their self-denial, appropriateness and personal achievements, instead of their inherited position.[76] Whites even recognized that women might occasionally rise to the rank of chief and fight as fiercely as their menfolk.[77] Yet these non-domestic activities were endangered by the pressures of white reformers, whose campaign to change Indian women had mixed results.

President Van Buren's Commissioner of Indian Affairs, T. Hartley Crawford, emphasized the importance of educating Indian girls as well as boys, but in order that they would exercise a benign influence over their husbands and children and become 'good and industrious housewives', rather than to broaden their own horizons. The Creek chief Ward Coachman might stress the need for a girls' high school among his people in the 1870s and contemporaries might applaud on the grounds that 'woman everywhere is the most important element in the educational systems of the day'; yet this judgement was truer of white than Indian societies and most tribes had to accept whatever they could get in the way of schooling.[78] The steady efforts of whites to replace women farmers by men were largely successful, but the transposition of roles and the allotment of Indian plots of land to male householders (wherever possible) did not make Indian agriculture more profitable in the white sense.[79] Nor did occupational changes swiftly persuade Indian women to abandon traditional ways of housekeeping. Their proud conservatism led to the door often being slammed on field matrons, Indian or white, who tried to acquaint them with white methods of health and home care, notwithstanding the ultimate acceptance by Indian women of the benefit of such innovations as hospital delivery in the case of difficult births.[80]

After Indian peoples were enfranchised in the twentieth century, and many adopted political systems based on white practice from the 1930s, Indian women technically had a voice in government in a way that many had not under native government. But since white women, though enfranchised earlier, have played only a small part in politics as actors rather than voters, it would be unreasonable to expect Indian women to have transformed their customary political influence into anything more startling. Wilma Mankiller, the current chief of the Cherokee nation, is no more typical of Indian politics than Margaret Thatcher is of the British political scene. Furthermore, as we shall see in the next chapter, when Indians responded to government prompting and moved into the cities, the position of women was frequently unenviable, not least because the defensive social life that developed around the bars was an essentially masculine one.

Just the same, there are some signs that whites were not entirely wrong when they predicted that Indian women would prove better allies and adapt better to the new ways than Indian men. In areas where prejudice against employing Indians exists, Indian women may seem less threatening and alien to whites. This, at least, is the finding of Joseph Westermeyer's study of Indian sex roles in Minnesota.[81] Indian women have also proved willing to take advantage of the educational opportunities opening up since the 1930s, which no longer aimed to prepare them simply for domestic work of one kind or another. In their interest in making up lost ground, they have resembled young black, and white, American women; though on the other hand we must note such counter pressures as the continuing tendency towards early marriage and large families among Indian peoples and the traditional emphases of the bicultural education that has made headway since the 1960s.[82] Finally, Indian women have been active in the urban community organizations and twentieth-century pan-Indian political movements, protests and legal struggles detailed in Chapters 11 and 12. They have had good reason to become involved, for if their employment prospects may sometimes be superior to those of Indian men, they have not been helped to a comparable degree by the relocation programmes, while the Bureau of Indian Affairs employs fewer Indian women than men, and those few are usually confined to clerical jobs. The very fact that women's leaders remain liable to head separate women's alliances reaffirms the difficulty of transforming the public sphere from a masculine sphere to one in which the two sexes participate equally and together.[83]

The adaptability of Indian women has not, of course, indicated that they have been glad to quit their 'primitive slavery' for the freedom whites offered. We have tried to show that Indian women, particularly where agriculture was important, had opportunities to create wealth and prestige by their own efforts that whites underestimated. These opportunities were strengthened in the various matrilineal and matri-

268

local societies, which enabled women to work together and receive wealth through inheritance. We have argued that though women were more constrained by their sexual attributes than men and more limited in their religious and political roles, the dichotomy between the sexes was not as marked in Indian cultures as it was in more elaborately stratified white communities. If matriarchy was not the norm among Native Americans, then neither was masculine tyranny.

White law may have succeeded in stressing 'the nuclear rather than the matrilineal extended family relationship', even in groups as slow to change as the Navajos.[84] Yet Indian women have not been remodelled *en masse* according to white middle-class ideals and whites should perhaps be grateful that their efforts to modernize Indian societies via Indian women met with only limited success. After all, when similar attempts have been made and eventually abandoned by white colonists or foreign elites in other parts of the world, the backlash from native men anxious to reassert their authority has often produced a more severe traditionalism and exploitation of native women, from the Western point of view. And when well-meaning whites have denounced the modern matrifocal black family as 'pathological' and advocated remedial action, the results have largely been harmful, albeit the black 'matriarchy' is seen as stemming from the vulnerability of black men since slavery times and from inept welfare laws, rather than from 'savage' conservatism.[85]

11

Urban Indians since the Second World War

Until well on into the twentieth century, the majority of whites concerned with Indian affairs assumed that the native population was ideally suited to, and most likely to follow, a subsistence farming life. The decision to encourage relocation of Indians in the cities after the Second World War was an admission that first the allotment of land and then efforts to bring work to the remaining reservations had failed to provide many with an adequate standard of living, either on the land or as wage labourers. Allotment and the reservations, whatever their limitations, had also dissuaded Native Americans from emulating blacks in a Great Migration to the cities.

I

THE MOVEMENT TO THE CITIES

Between 1910 and 1930, though the numbers of Indians living in cities approximately doubled, they still comprised a mere 9.9 per cent of the total Indian population. At a time when the United States was becoming an urban nation, and when the proportion of blacks in urban areas rose from 27.4 per cent to 43.7 per cent, the majority of Indians lived in rural communities, with only 65 per cent of men and 15.4 per cent of women gainfully employed in 1930. At that date, the employment figures were 73.4 per cent for native-born whites, 88.4 per cent for foreign-born whites and 80.2 per cent for black men, with the statistics for the corresponding groups of women being 20.5 per cent, 18.8 per cent and 38.9 per cent.[1]

It was not until the Second World War that large numbers of Indians began migrating to the cities, but as early as 1905, in an attempt to promote off-reservation employment for Indians, BIA Commissioner Leupp appointed a mixed blood, Charles E. Dagenett, to recruit and assist workers and some of the paid work they undertook was in urban areas.[2] The correspondence of Dagenett's office with educated Indians and white administrators on the reservations indicates the complex difficulties inherent in the project. Certain Indian groups disliked contacts with whites, preferring to labour in their own communities, and the white prejudice against Indians reported throughout the Northwest was likely to make racial mixing at the workplace difficult. In the case of women, while domestic service jobs could be secured for them in the towns, Indians themselves might think 'it a disgrace for the girls to work as servants'. Whereas one superintendent reported that he had tried to obtain openings through the employment bureaux of the YMCAs and wrote approvingly of the 'discipline of the cities', others worried about undermining reservation agriculture and placing the Indians in an unfavourable environment. And clearly the liaison between Dagenett and local superintendents, when job opportunities did materialize, was not always effective.[3]

The Indian service's awareness of the need to enlarge these opportunities was intensified as the reservation population expanded and bureau efforts appeared to be endorsed in 1928 by the Meriam Report. Although it was critical of almost all aspects of Indian administration, the report commented optimistically on the treatment and prospects of the approximately 10,000 Indians estimated to be living in towns, mostly close to the western reservations.[4] White reformers, for their part, were interested in seeing that individuals obliged to work off the reservations obtained suitable employment and fair wages and were not lured away into 'protracted Fairs, Rodeos, Celebrations, etc.'[5] Given the continuing assimilationist thrust of the federal Indian policy and the difficulty of forcing adequate funds from Congress for reservation development, it was highly desirable that urban prospects should be presented in the best light. Yet as Sorkin notes, contemporaries knew that urban Indians suffered from discrimination, poor housing and a dearth of social services, which makes Meriam's recommendation that no special bureau assistance should be provided for them particularly unfortunate.[6] When conditions deteriorated even further in the Depression, many Indians reacted as sensible migrants have always done to hardship in the 'promised land': they returned home. While John Collier remained Commissioner, Indian schools endeavoured to equip their pupils for work in their native communities, both because of the difficult national economic situation and because of Collier's admiration for Indian community values. This experiment did not last long. The historic scarcity of reservation jobs was not swiftly remedied and may explain why large numbers of Indians joined the armed forces after 1941 or sought employment in war industries.

271

Starved of funds during the war and facing one of the periodic public demands that the government should get out of 'the Indian business' and 'emancipate' the Indians, the BIA took advantage of this renewed migration to launch its first major programme to relocate the Indian population. Ironically, the successful employment of Japanese interned as a result of the war, some of them on Indian land, was seen as a promising precedent for the project. Commissioner Myer (1950–3) had, in fact, headed the War Relocation Authority, which until 1946 was in charge of Japanese evacuation, and he urged voluntary groups in the cities to offer migrating Indians the same sort of aid they had extended to Japanese American evacuees and refugees from Europe. They could, he maintained, help with jobs, housing and recreation and put pressure on state and local authorities to discharge their duties. Unfortunately, the Japanese internees provoked a degree of belated interest and sympathy in employers and other whites which Indian migrants did not generally encounter. Moreover, after initial divisions about whether to resist internment, Japanese Americans showed a degree of solidarity and organizational flair in coping with consequent relocation that the diverse Indian groups affected by urbanization could not muster,[7] and as Walter Woehlke pointed out, glib talk about Indians relocating ignored the problems attendant upon the process in the past and present alike. His anxieties proved well founded. If the relocation policy was being urged in 1945, the obstacles to Indian migration were removed only slowly and with difficulty.[8]

The skeletal nature of the Indian Bureau's early placement service limited its effectiveness, as did the knowledge that many Indians employed in the defence industries had been laid off in peacetime, necessitating their return to the reservations. The Navajos and Hopis who received special assistance to find off-reservation work were reluctant to leave home permanently because of the educational, health and housing problems that beset them and the BIA had to convince those who quit the reservations that they could go back and would not have forfeited their tribal rights.[9] Undeterred by these problems, the Indian service in 1950 extended the placement service to all bureau areas and offices were established in several cities to facilitate the Indians' resettlement. Twenty years later, offices were still operating in Chicago, Cleveland, Dallas, Denver, Los Angeles, Oakland, San Francisco, San Jose (California), Oklahoma City and Tulsa.[10] The first applicants were placed in February 1952 and by the late 1960s more than 60,000 Indians were said to have been assisted.

After applying to the local employment officer and undergoing aptitude testing by the state employment service, the prospective migrant was advised about job seeking and urban conditions, given medical assistance if necessary, travel expenses, health insurance and aid towards housing costs. Such material aid might continue for three years and additional counselling and job placement help might be extended for a year after relocation.[11] In order to stimulate applications, and in answer to a long-felt need, the Indian Vocational Training Act was passed in 1956. The legislation established an Adult Vocational Training Programme, with participants instructed at urban centres or near reservations and eligible for support while studying, as well as for the same benefits as individuals who were directly relocated. The numbers of Indians in the two categories turned out to be roughly the same and there was a further, smaller class of migrants who received urban on-the-job training under the terms of the 1956 legislation. Most of the recipients of all three kinds of vocational instruction settled in the cities. Bureau efforts were supplemented from the 1960s by the extension to urban Indians of poverty and manpower programmes designed for the American population at large. In 1973, these were consolidated by the Comprehensive Employment and Training Act (CETA). Three years later, urban Indians received some $20 million of CETA funds. The total number of participants was then 20,000, of whom about 7,000 subsequently obtained unsubsidized employment. One advantage of CETA was its availability to long-term Indian residents of towns and cities.[12]

Indians were alarmed as well as interested by the prospect of urbanization. Some feared that white prejudice would operate against them[13] and since relocation was expanded during the 1950s, when the hated 'termination' policy was being launched, it was perhaps inevitable that the two should be linked in Indian minds and that compulsory involvement in each should be feared.[14] In fairness, however, it must be pointed out that bureau spokesmen stressed that relocation would be entirely voluntary.[15] Movement to the cities was urged because, even with the full exploitation of reservation resources, the Indian standard of living would remain 'pitifully low'.[16] The Indian service frankly acknowledged the hard tasks it faced:[17]

> determining the skills of employable Indians; proper registration with State Employment Services; relocation of families; housing facilities; and acceptance of the Indian in the community where he may locate.

And Commissioner Emmons (1953–61), aware that bad stories sometimes filtered back from relocation areas, stressed that the bureau helped migrants who failed the first time around, assisted the wives involved as well as the husbands and chose cities with excellent employment opportunities for the programme.[18]

It was hoped that more industry could be persuaded to move to the reservations, something which various Indian groups would have preferred. Relocation close to home was seen as the next best thing by doubters. Neither objective was realized during the policy's formative years. Some of the anxieties might have been stilled had tribal councils been fully involved in reviewing relocation applications, although the councils themselves seldom satisfied all groups on the reservations. The fact that 'younger adults' were regarded as the most appropriate migrants was eventually to prove a further source of contention, since the reservations therefore tended to become the refuges of the very young and the old. There was also unease about both the amount of training and the amount of assistance given, and rightly so, for it was made plain that the aid extended could not match that provided on the reservations, or the savings designed to accrue to the government from the programme would be lost.[19]

By 1960, Commissioner Emmons was claiming that two-thirds of those concerned had made a successful transition to city life,[20] but in the first years of relocation the return rate may have been as high as 75 per cent; 50 per cent is possibly an accurate estimate of the rate in later years. While these figures attracted damaging publicity and may seem damning, they partly reflect the fact that many Indians, having always hoped for employment in or near their home communities, went back to them whenever reservation prospects had or were claimed to have improved. A number of studies have, none the less, suggested that the projects enhanced the employment and earning prospects of migrants. In 1949, the median income of reservation Indian men was 80 per cent of that of urban Indian men, whereas in 1969 it had declined to 57 per cent; and by 1969, the median income of black males and urban Indian males was nearly the same. Between 1950 and 1970, the unemployment level for non-reservation Indian men declined by almost 40 per cent (from 15.1 per cent to 9.4 per cent). Furthermore, the numbers of Indian skilled and semi-skilled workers and professionals increased considerably. Between 1946 and 1970, Indian males employed in professional and technical posts rose from 2.2 per cent to 9.2 per cent, as against a rise from 1.8 per cent to 5.7 per cent for black males; by 1970, 11.4 per cent of the Indians holding such posts were to be found in urban regions and 6.8 per cent throughout the country as a whole.

In the light of these figures, it is not surprising that the years from 1950 to 1970 saw a dramatic urban migration by American Indians. By 1970, over 45 per cent of their total lived in towns or cities. Almost half live in great metropolitan areas adjacent to Indian settlements: Tulsa, Oklahoma City, Phoenix, Tucson, Albuquerque, Minneapolis,

Seattle, Tacoma and Buffalo. Yet as Stanley and Thomas indicated in 1978, there are large Indian populations in cities far from these settlements, including Los Angeles (*c.* 30,000), San Francisco (*c.* 20,000), Chicago (*c.* 8,000), Detroit (*c.* 5,000) and Dallas/Fort Worth (*c.* 7,000). They made the additional point that, with urban sprawl, the towns and cities are reaching the reservations.

What relocation has obviously not achieved is a real reduction of reservation unemployment and some commentators have been cautious in recommending a further expansion of the programme for fear that its growth might either aggravate reservation difficulties or reduce the economic opportunities of the established urban Indians. Sorkin, though favouring the growth of relocation efforts, warns that their efficiency seems to have declined over time, especially since the shift of emphasis, after 1972, to placing Indians on or near the reservations.[21] The diversity of American cities and Indian urban settlers has ensured that economic success has been variable, with the 1970 unemployment rate for Indian males ranging from 3.8 per cent in Dallas and 4.3 per cent in Chicago to 18 per cent in Seattle. The highest level of Indian urban unemployment was then in Minnesota, Washington and Oregon.[22] We do not yet know the relative importance in explaining these differences of local economic factors, the efficiency of the placement services, the suitability of the migrants and discrimination against the Indians concerned.[23] Moreover, we need to discover more about Indian on-the-job experiences. Statistics may show that the Indian middle class has grown, for example, along with the numbers of craftsmen and foremen, but Indians remain concentrated in the lowest paying positions. Although Indians interviewed about whether their occupational gains in the cities were not offset by the loss of BIA services felt that they were still better off,[24] by the late 1970s, 47 per cent of urban Indian families headed by women lived in poverty and so did 26 per cent of urban Indians.[25]

Poverty is undoubtedly increased by the fact that many Indians, including women, turn to day labouring as a form of employment which allows them some of that freedom to control their own time which has always been a feature of reservation life. This benefit is bought dearly, because the wage rates for such work are low, it dries up during hard times and it carries none of the fringe benefits that go with permanent employment.[26] At the moment it is only possible, following Stanley and Thomas, to roughly categorize three main types of Indian city dwellers, and the day labourers fit into the large, fluid groups to be found in the cities, who still maintain regular contacts with their home communities, whatever the distances involved.[27] Forming rather more stable groups are the Indians in the working-class suburbs, generally employed as skilled labourers; and the small professional elements, which include the personnel who work for the BIA.

II

ADJUSTMENT IN THE CITIES

The significant feature of American urban life for all the Indian migrants is change; in return for economic benefits, they are obliged to forfeit, at least temporarily, crucial aspects of their traditional environment. Urban areas are valued for the jobs, credit and shopping facilities they provide and for the opportunities they give Indians to meet individuals from other tribes, to escape small community restraints, to have adventures. As one might expect, the migrants do not always remain there.

It would seem that Indians established in small towns and large cities alike decide to return home for interconnected economic, social and cultural reasons. As was true in the early twentieth century, those who have received training which makes them exceptional in Indian communities are angry or discouraged when employers do not find their qualifications acceptable. Training for semi-skilled jobs has sometimes proved no advantage and there has been reasonable resentment of Anglos or other ethnic group workers who have received higher wages than Indians for the same work. In most cases, the leverage of Indian workers is not increased by union membership. Economic discrimination might be justified, from the white point of view, because Indian workers have tended to possess less education and industrial experience than prospective white employees and to show less initiative. The qualities admired in many Indian cultures – 'present-mindedness', concern for nature, reflectiveness, opposition to self-aggrandizement – do not facilitate success in urban, capitalist America. Indian migrants, unlike most, may move in search of economic gain without aspiring to social mobility. But since even conservative whites, averse to social contacts with Indians, appear to favour Indian employment, education and adaptation to the larger society, it is unfortunate that urban employment experiences can prove swiftly embittering.

If previous employment, vocational training, family experience of wage work, competence in English and the stability frequently given by marriage help some Indian migrants to succeed in the cities, settlers from all backgrounds will journey back to the reservations to visit relatives and take part in important religious or cultural occasions. A

276

proportion of the women who have relocated leave the cities when they get married, albeit this is not the case with all groups. Thus more women than men have migrated from Papago communities, gravitating towards the domestic work for which there is a steady demand; once in the cities, fewer women than men have returned and more Papago women have settled permanently in non-Indian locations. Deteriorating health can drive Indians of both sexes back to the reservations to seek free medical assistance in more sympathetic surroundings than the cities provide and the decision to head homewards may equally be prompted by bad housing, loneliness, white prejudice, the high Indian arrest rate, the 'artificiality' of reservation towns and the commercialization of Indian culture in the border towns.

Certain categories among the Indian migrants have been liable to find difficulties in obtaining work and settling down in the cities, just as the same categories did among many immigrant groups; they include families with large numbers of children, those with minimal education or sense of purpose, and individuals with a drink problem or an arrest record on arrival. Military service, whatever it might have done in terms of acquainting Indians with the wider world and their rights as citizens, does not seem to contribute to later economic success in the cities. Further research is needed before we can account for the widely differing rates of return from the cities shown by various Indian peoples. Martin, for instance, establishes a contrasting level of adaptability between the Navajo, Choctaw and Sioux in one southwestern city, but he does not explain the contrasts.[28]

Although urban life is usually seen as exercising a broadening and modernizing influence over rural migrants to the city, its transforming power over Indians has been limited. They, like other minorities, do not generally possess sufficient educational advantages to exploit urban economic opportunities to the full, while their *de facto* segregation and pride in their own cultures have worked to prevent Indians' assimilation in the cities. Indian integration into Anglo society is, however, obviously greater than on the reservations. Outmarriage is one area where this is very apparent. In 1968, Price found that, with regard to Indians interviewed in Los Angeles, 64 per cent of marriages in the generation of the respondents' parents were within the tribe, whereas approximately 39 per cent of the marriages in the respondents' own generation were within the tribe. Intermarriage between Indians and whites may well result in the adoption of white mores and Indians, on the evidence of a Seattle study, seem more ready for amalgamation to take place.[29]

Indeed, by 1970 over a third of Indian men in the United States were said to have white wives, as opposed, for example, to 2.1 per cent of black men. It is noticeable that there is far greater willingness among Indians to contemplate liaisons with whites than with blacks. It is not clear how far this state of affairs simply reflects Indian reluctance to incur the disabilities attached to being black in white-dominated society and how far it reveals a mutual aversion between red and black, a subject we have discussed in Chapters 5 and 6. Yet dislike of marrying or living alongside blacks clearly exists both among Indians, like the Lumbees, who have had firsthand experience of the disadvantages entailed, and among groups like the Nez Percé, who have not. Indian attitudes to marrying outside their tribe or group and about the possibility of friendships with outsiders nevertheless vary considerably, so that generalizations on this subject are dangerous.[30]

Coming to the cities at a time when the economic opportunities for the unskilled were drying up and the problems of urban government were becoming critical, Indian migrants have been obliged to develop institutions which will ease urban adjustment. There is no such thing as a single Indian lifestyle in the cities for which they can cater and most Indians, like most Americans, abjure civic activism; just the same, these institutions do provide Indians with an alternative to a BIA office, and they offer a pluralist approach to Indian problems. That is to say, they seek Indian political integration by pressing for the rights of Indians as American citizens, while at the same time offering a place where Indians can meet Indians and confirm their 'Indianness'. By the late 1970s, eighty or so urban Indian centres supplemented the social contacts Indians made with each other in houses, bars, clubs and churches and at dances and pow-wows. The best known are probably to be found in Los Angeles, Oakland, San Francisco, Minneapolis and Chicago. Although they are not always pan-Indian in scope, the centres facilitate intertribal contacts which would be uncongenial or unlikely in a reservation setting, mediate between Indians and federal, state and local authorities, and try to make each side aware of the needs and services that exist in a particular city in such areas as health, education and welfare. Long-range planning is, unhappily, rendered difficult by the dearth of permanent funding, which in turn demoralizes staff and involves them in time-consuming applications to local, state and federal bodies.[31]

The fact that whites will usually not belong to such organizations, whereas Indians may join predominantly white associations, means that, socially, they act to slow down Indian acculturation, if one accepts that acculturation is a two-way process, an interaction between Indians and whites, not an accommodation by the former to the latter. They may do so even in a city where each race favours social interaction and the Indian clubs or centres are involved with the larger community as well as 'sectarian' concerns. Whites and Indians are known to fraternize at pow-wows, whose features range from religious ceremony and dancing to drinking and general socializing. But gatherings of this kind, whether religious and tribal, local and social, or white-sponsored and commercial as at Flagstaff (Arizona), Gallup (New Mexico) and Sheridan (Wyoming), do not have the political functions or formal basis of the Indian clubs and, as Laxon points out, they may generate some tension between the races when held in urban areas.[32]

Indian housing patterns similarly serve to impede the coming together of Indians and whites. Because of their smaller numbers and later arrival in the cities and because of more tolerant white attitudes towards them, urban Indians as a whole are not crowded into established and self-contained ghettoes, as are many blacks. Certainly Indian numbers are not normally sufficient to support *tribal* ghettoes. They are therefore less likely than blacks to conform to Lieberson's maxim that groups 'highly segregated in their residential patterns are found to also deviate from the general patterns of the social system'.[33] Yet if the Indian population of Seattle, for instance, is 'well dispersed throughout the entire city', Minneapolis Indians are concentrated in a midtown district which is known as the 'Red Ghetto', and there are comparable concentrations of Indians in Baltimore, Los Angeles and Chicago.[34] Moreover, most urban Indians live in the poorer, central parts of town, adjacent to members of other disadvantaged ethnic groups. Like their neighbours, they have difficulty in finding fair landlords and low rent accommodation. They may likewise move repeatedly to remain close to friends, or to escape from conflicts with landlords.

Indians settling in the cities are, however, likely to be peculiarly ill-informed about housing availability, problems and laws, despite the efforts of Indian centres and relocation officials. Lacking substantial BIA assistance in this area, seldom accommodated in public housing units and slow to complain of housing code violations for fear of faring still worse, Indian migrants may have to struggle with the extra difficulties posed by poverty, large families and their generous habit of taking in fresh arrivals from the reservations. As a result, Sorkin reminds us, '19 per cent of all urban Indians live in moderately or severely overcrowded housing, while only 7 per cent of the total urban US population lives under such substandard conditions'. Indian migrants hoping to escape from reservation discontents may, in other words, encounter housing as bad as or worse than that they left behind, with the additional drawbacks of unappealing surroundings and competition with strangers for scarce facilities.[35]

One escape from a grim environment, disappointed expectations or other forms of stress, for Indians and Americans at large, has always been heavy drinking. But Indian drunkenness in the cities presents a number of special problems for analysts, for the Indians involved and for Indian spokesmen. In the first place, it produces an Indian arrest rate for alcohol-related crimes that is far higher than the national average and contributes to a high rate of Indian penal confinement. Alcoholism also causes an Indian death rate of cirrhosis of the liver that is about three times that of the population as a whole and appears to be a factor in dismissal from jobs and the large number of suicides among Indian groups.[36]

Whites have customarily supposed that Indians could not drink and undoubtedly for those aboriginal cultures in which liquor was unknown its introduction, after provoking varied responses, eventually caused problems. On the other hand, modern research has demonstrated that neither Indians nor any other ethnic group have a physiological incapacity to cope with alcohol.[37] Rather, the historical context in which Indian drinking patterns have developed is important. As Price has argued, Indians frequently first learned from whites that drinking 'excused' excessive behaviour and the special regulations whites evolved to try to control Indian drinking both encouraged the exploitation of the tribes by unscrupulous liquor traders and precluded Indian regulation of alcohol abuse.[38]

At the present time it is none the less true that, though Indians may resent white comment on their liquor consumption, they do not necessarily regard heavy drinking in the same way as whites. They may rightly point out that white alcoholism is often concealed in private homes, while Indian drinking bouts generally occur in bars, where rowdy behaviour is more liable to lead to brushes with police conditioned by stereotypes about the Indian drinker. Yet several studies suggest that bars provide Indians with a venue for meeting other Indians that is more attractive than BIA offices or even Indian centres. More importantly, buying or accepting drinks provides Indian men with the opportunity of reaffirming Indian attitudes about appropriate male behaviour and the primacy of social obligations towards others, while for groups which value personal reticence and attach importance to the supernatural, sustained drinking helps to remove inhibitions and induce a prized, dreamlike state. In Nancy Lurie's judgement, it has become a protest, 'an established means of asserting and validating Indianness'.[39]

The social factors influencing Indian drinking in the cities (and, indeed, on the reservations) appear to be much more similar to those which shape the alcohol consumption of Americans as a whole. And if it is not known why some urban Indian groups are more prone to heavy drinking than others, it seems clear that dependence on alcohol is reduced when Indians are well prepared for a move to the city, have realistic expectations and are economically secure when there, and when they are married. Indian women, like women in many cultures, usually drink less than their menfolk and urge them to avoid immoderate drinking, not least because of the economic strain and loneliness imposed on them by the primarily masculine Indian bar culture.[40] It remains hard to decide just how drinking patterns have been affected by the fact that in 1953 Congress lifted the ban on off-reservation liquor sales to Indians and authorized reservation dwellers to decide whether their local communities should be wet or dry, though participants in an oral history project studied by the writer regretted the relaxation of the liquor law and one respondent felt that drinking close to the towns and cities was a particular problem.[41] The banning of alcohol by many tribal councils makes it likely that it will remain so.[42]

Whatever the causes of Indian alcoholism, by the late 1960s the Indian Health Service had come to regard it as a serious health hazard and in the 1970s the service received Office of Economic Opportunity and National Institute of Mental Health funds for treatment projects. These were supplemented by moneys from the National Institute on Alcohol Abuse and Alcoholism, to be used both for the treatment of alcoholics and the training of people to operate the programmes. Unfortunately, while millions of dollars have been forthcoming from such sources, they have not been commensurate with the size of the problem and states have been reluctant to allocate funds for Indians, thereby underlining once again the dilemmas created for urban Indians by the federal government's limited definition of its reponsibilities towards them. Furthermore, since Indians are reluctant to attend urban alcoholism clinics with or run by whites, there is need for additional Indian facilities which will take account of Indian attitudes to drinking. This may mean avoiding Anglo demands for total abstinence, putting the focus on youth and involving ex-alcoholics in rehabilitation projects. To date, however, a prison rather than a clinic is the most likely destination for the majority of unrestrained Indian drinkers.[43]

Urban Indians may receive inadequate medical treatment for reasons other than suspicion of white-run services. In addition to the usual uncertainty about what health care is available and where, which affects most migrants to the cities, Indians may be deterred

from seeking aid by poverty, inadequate English, modesty, a preference for Indian medical practices and the knowledge that if they put
off treatment until a visit to the reservation, they can obtain free health
care. The refusal of the Indian Health Service to deal with non-
reservation Indians led, in such cities as Seattle, San Francisco, Los
Angeles, Chicago and Minneapolis, to the establishment of private
clinics, supported by donations and staff willing to work without pay.
These clinics, attracting Indian professionals, have aggravated the
'brain drain' from the reservations.[44] More helpfully, they have
received some federal funding since the passage of the Indian Health
Care Improvement Act of 1976. Money has also been given under the
Act to assist urban Indian groups in providing 'outreach and referral
services'. Federal funding has in turn helped Indian health centres to
raise additional finance, and in 1980 the Indian Health Service committed itself to special funding for the tribal and urban Indians in greatest
need. But because the level of funding remains inadequate, so too
does urban Indian antenatal care, dental treatment and preventive
medicine, and the rate of deaths, accidents, gastrointestinal and
respiratory diseases, otitis media and stress-related illnesses remains
alarmingly high.[45]

The situation of urban Indians with regard to other social services is
much the same. Initial ignorance about how the system works is
compounded by dismay at finding only Anglo advisers at the various
agencies. Individuals arriving from the reservations without the
documentation necessary to obtain welfare may be deterred from
reapplying. Relations between services catering to the general public
and agencies dealing specifically with Indians could be improved and
the difficulty the former experience in recruiting Indian social workers
may relate to the fact that they prefer employment with exclusively
Indian organizations. This is not to say that relatively few urban
Indians receive welfare payments. On the contrary, as they have
become better acquainted with the welfare system and fulfilled the
residence requirements, the numbers on welfare have risen steadily.
Aid to Families with Dependent Children has proved an especially
important programme for Indians in the city.[46]

Despite such assistance, the large size of many Indian families and
repeated parental moves produce casualties. In response, white caseworkers have increasingly tended to place in care the Indian children
whom they deem neglected. Indian permissiveness with their children from the white point of view and their reliance upon the watchful
guidance of relatives when they are themselves absent from home
may explain numerous cases of apparent neglect or abandonment.
Even so, severe strain may be placed on Indian marriages by the

erosion of traditional sex roles in the urban environment and the anxiety of social agencies is understandable, as is the resentment of Indians whose children are frequently put in white foster homes and so cut off from Indian culture.[47] Again, mutual tensions might be eased if there were more Indian caseworkers to be involved in the problem.

An alternative to fostering for children who persistently play truant, begin to drink early, or otherwise fall foul of the city authorities, is to send them to Indian boarding schools away from the source of their troubles.[48] But this scarcely does anything to improve the image of a category of schools which has always been controversial and expensive and the problem of truancy is not, of course, confined to urban Indian children. Revisionist historians have argued that, for the most part, America's city schools have failed to provide a decent education for the consequently alienated children of the poor. Prematurely 'streamed' according to biased views of their ability and destined place in society, these children, it is urged, have been consigned to inadequately funded schools and cheated of both adequate vocational instruction and conventional liberal education.[49]

Although Indian parents sometimes believe that urban schools are better than those on or near the reservations,[50] their children have the disadvantage of being just another minority in the city public schools, and a small one at that.[51] Like other children of the poor, urban Indian youngsters have a high drop-out rate from high school, which may be accounted for by factors ranging from lack of parental interest to student knowledge that they will not usually be rewarded, as whites are, with jobs commensurate with their qualifications. Some pupils, following Indian custom, will be slow to assert themselves in the classroom, while the difficulties posed by poor English and frequently changing teachers, who know little of Indian cultures, can deter even interested students. Nor does the acknowledgement in the classroom of cultural differences between whites and Indians itself guarantee a better relationship between teachers and pupils. As Judith Kleinfeld has pointed out, a heavy-handed cultural relativist may simply reinforce the sense that Indian children have of being somehow peculiar, unable to meet white standards. A patronizing or romantic emphasis on traditional culture may unhappily result in human problems, which are shared with other students, being defined as inescapable Indian problems.[52] Indeed, the emphasis may ironically have little relevance to the dilemmas of the urban Indian, which relate as much to recent arrival in a decaying environment as to cultural considerations.

Conversely, it can be argued plausibly that courses in Indian languages and culture are most useful for city dwellers, since while Indian urbanites are better off than the white ethnics in that many of their members retain touch with a land base and a larger part of their ancient linguistic, kin and religious ties, these ties are undermined by wage work and outmarriage in the cities, as well as by the whole style of city living. For that 20 per cent or so of Indians who have no tribal or band affiliation, schools provide one of the few means of access to an Indian past. It is therefore encouraging to anyone interested in bicultural education to discover efforts to sustain it in public and 'free' schools alike, partly with assistance under Part B of the 1972 Indian Education Act (Title IV of Public Law 92–318).[53]

Yet though some attractive materials for bicultural Indian education have been produced,[54] the enterprise remains politically controversial and hence vulnerable. And it will be interesting in the years to come to see whether bicultural instruction can impart pride in an identifiable urban pan-Indian culture, able to draw strength from the present and recent past as well as from the infinitely varied strands of Indian history. Courses on contemporary Indian issues of the kind now available do not really suffice. At the moment, the 'free' or 'survival' schools engaged in this endeavour, some of which are supported by the American Indian Movement (AIM), appear to have been valuable in their stress on Indian language teaching and employment of Native American teachers (who are in short supply). Because there are so few 'alternative' schools and they are so new, evaluation of them is difficult. Leaving aside the question of what they have to offer in terms of transmitting Indian culture, old or new, there is evidence to suggest that they appeal to Indian students and hence improve pupil attendance and performance.[55] But just as Progressive or vocational schools proved costly and controversial alternatives to 'conventional' education earlier in the century (see Chapter 8), so the 'free' schools of today are hampered by suspicions that they neglect academic subjects and employ underqualified staff, while they are clearly expensive to establish. Worse still, if they fail to win accreditation from state educational offices, as has been the case with certain AIM schools, their students are placed in a vulnerable legal position.

III

PROSPECTS FOR THE FUTURE

There is now a considerable amount of material available on Indian motives for moving to and leaving the city, on the impact of the BIA relocation programme, the problems faced by urban Indians and the services available to them from various sources. What we lack is adequate information about the effectiveness of different aid programmes and detailed Indian views about the best way to improve their situation. Urban protest groups have been formed to put the Indians' case, as is noted in Chapter 12, but they have been hampered by inadequate funds, a radical image and sometimes strained relations with older, tribally oriented Indian organizations, as well as with whites. Thus a study of Seattle found that whites there, though admitting Indians had real grievances, were not prepared to agitate with them for some redress.[56] For their part, urban Indian pressure groups, unlike the early pan-Indian associations, have usually opposed the admission of white members and recoiled from cooperation with blacks or other disadvantaged elements of the population. And if a measure of financial stability came to these organizations and the Indian centres with the passage in 1974 of the Native Americans Program Act, whose object was to support Indians in defining and meeting their own needs and priorities and which led to the establishment of the Office of Native American Programs, Indian associations continue to proliferate and compete with each other in an often wasteful manner.[57]

With the BIA still playing a limited role in assisting urban Indians, they may be driven to bitter disputes with distant reservation leaders about the use of tribal moneys, or to demand a voice on tribal councils so that their interests will not be ignored. The newer Indian organizations have given support to such demands, albeit the resultant efforts to register urban Indians to vote in tribal elections have been wearing and difficult.[58] Yet it may well be argued that the dual allegiance of many Indians prevents their total disorientation in an alien city world and should be preserved. Alternatively, the difficulties encountered by Indian migrants to the cities and their slow acculturation might lead to the conclusion that relocation programmes should be abandoned and every effort made instead to develop the reservations. Deplorable as the alternating white neglect and exploitation of the reservations have been, however, any implication that Indians cannot succeed in the cities would uphold the unacceptable negative stereotypes about Native Americans. Rather more useful would seem to be the consolidation of all existing programmes involving urban Indians within the BIA; the improvement of its training for relocatees so as to enhance their job prospects and consequently their hopes of adjustment; and the extension of aid to migrants for longer than is now the case. If a massive expansion of bureau operation in the cities is thought to be impractical, when other urban dwellers suffer severe difficulties without special help, an increase in the funding levels for existing projects is not and nor is the extension to the cities of the Indian Health Service.[59]

Even if none of these things is done, Indian citizens, like their fellow Americans, will doubtless continue to move to and from towns and cities, as it suits them, finding there a freedom that is not always possible in BIA-dominated communities and leaving historians and bureaucrats to debate the merits of formal relocation.[60]

12

Indian Political Protest Groups

From the colonial period onwards, as we have argued in Part One, white commentators were both critical of the limited powers, scope and unity of Indian polities and prepared to treat loosely organized Indian peoples as nations for bargaining purposes.[1] But by the nineteenth century, as they grew conscious of their mounting strength, whites came to argue, in John C. Calhoun's words, that the Indians 'neither are, in fact, nor ought to be, considered independent nations. Our views of their interest, not their own, ought to govern them.'[2] Acting upon this assumption, white policy-makers removed the eastern Indians west of the Mississippi, ended formal treaty-making with the tribes and strove to undermine traditional sources of authority among them by such means as the appointment of Indian police and Courts of Indian Offenses. It was not until the later part of the century, when whites realized that the allotment programme had reduced many Indians to poverty without assimilating them, that bureaucrats and reformers began actively to encourage the emergence of new Indian leaders who could advise Indians being admitted to citizenship under the terms of the 1887 Dawes severalty Act about the political system of the white world and the possibilities of the Indian race.[3]

I

EARLY-TWENTIETH-CENTURY PROTEST

Before the formation of the Society of American Indians (SAI) in 1911, Indian individuals might find a connection with the realm of white politics through membership of delegations to Washington and lobbying there on their own account. The experience could be disillusioning. Exposure to delays, demands for bribes and the priority given to political considerations in the capital left even so staunch an advocate of assimilation as the mixed-blood Sioux doctor, Charles Eastman, frustrated and disenchanted. He recalled:[4]

I came to Washington with a great respect for our public men and institutions. Although I had had some disillusioning experiences with the lower type of political henchmen on the reservations, I reasoned that it was because they were almost beyond the pale of civilization and clothed with supreme authority over a helpless and ignorant people, that they dared do the things they did. Under the very eye of the law and of society, I thought, this could scarcely be tolerated. I was confident that a fair hearing would be granted, and our wrongs corrected without undue delay. I had overmuch faith in the civilized ideal, and I was again disappointed.

Alternatively, from the 1880s Indians were at liberty to attend the meetings of the white 'friends of the Indian': primarily those held at Mohonk, in New York state, and by the Indian Rights Association (IRA).

If we judge from the public statements of the Indian participants, we must conclude that they endorsed the white reformers' stress on the destruction of the reservation, assimilation, individualism, self-help, education and citizenship.[5] Had this not been the case, it is unlikely that they would have been admitted.[6] On the other hand, the white organizations had rather small memberships,[7] so that ideally they could not afford to be at odds either with each other or the people they were endeavouring to help. As a result, the foundation of the SAI was warmly welcomed at Mohonk, which had received visits from some of the Indians involved, notably Eastman, Francis La Flesche, Arthur Parker, Charles Dagenett, Carlos Montezuma, John Oskison and Henry Roe Cloud.[8] The IRA was similarly enthusiastic about the society's advent, seeing it as evidence 'that the Indians have competent leaders', while the Board of Indian Commissioners, as well as the educator, Richard Pratt, and the journal of his Carlisle school, *The Red Man*, were sympathetically interested in the venture.[9] However, Indian activists did not reciprocate by uncritically supporting the conduct of the white organizations. They were among the dissidents who by 1912–13 felt that the Mohonk conferences had lost force and independence[10] and a couple of years later Eastman censured these assemblies for concealing rather than resolving genuine differences of opinion.[11] The IRA was criticized as a complaining committee, a label which the SAI was anxious to avoid.[12]

The Society of American Indians, in form, leadership and aims, resembled the white reform associations and the emerging black movements of the Progressive era. Its most energetic members – though this has been true of prominent social reformers in America at any time – were middle class, well educated, conscious of their attainments and responsibilities to those less favoured than themselves and proud of their respectability. Women as well as men attended society proceedings, yet since Indian women generally played a less active role in public life than men, it is not surprising to find that few became officers of the SAI. Among the exceptions were Estaiene M. De Peltquestangue and Marie L. Baldwin, both Chippewas, who in 1915 became vice president responsible for membership and treasurer respectively, and Gertrude L. Bonnin, a Sioux author, who a year later was made secretary.[13]

The proper role of whites in the organization was a source of concern, as it subsequently became in the initially white-led National Association for the Advancement of Colored People (NAACP). Much of the point of a race movement was lost if it was dominated by outsiders, but the positive backing of representatives of the majority culture was necessary where legislative changes were sought. The solution was the one which has prevailed among minority alliances to the present day: whites were admitted to 'associate' status.[14] Among the Indian 'actives', Hertzberg has established, there were men and women who worked for the government, in education, medicine, the law and the church; among the 'associates', there were employees of the Indian service, clerics, academics and individuals concerned with other Indian aid groups.[15] The existence of a class of Indian associates bore witness to society hopes of attracting Indian members from outside the United States. By 1913 it claimed them in Europe, Mexico, Canada and the Canal Zone, aiming for a hemispheric influence just as American blacks were starting to do.[16]

In the majority of reform organizations it proves difficult to work out and sustain a viable relationship between a central office and local workers, between vigorous leaders and slumbering members, reluctant after a while even to pay their subscriptions. In addition to these customary difficulties, the SAI was faced with the awesome task of trying to represent a host of contrasting and unconnected Indian peoples. At the 1911 conference it was proposed to meet this problem by establishing a body in which all the tribes were represented, but the project never got off the ground.[17] It would have to wait for realization until the creation of the National Congress of American Indians (NCAI) in 1944. A single issue as pressing as allotment had been in the 1880s might have brought the tribes together. Yet by 1911, some Indians had accepted allotment, some had never experienced it and some had limited experience of the great 'reform'. Various Indian peoples no longer had tribal governments in any more than name and many, of course, only possessed such governments in the opinion of whites. We should not, therefore, be too critical of the society's willingness to settle for a membership of individuals who primarily represented themselves, included no tribal officials or delegates and even in the optimistic days of 1913 were drawn from under thirty tribes.

SAI members were more divided over where they should meet, with one element advocating the urban university campuses which were chosen as likely to ensure maximum white attention and support, and another in favour of reservation gatherings.[18] The annual conferences did move further west, but the shift was not enough to make the society a grassroots operation.[19] Its headquarters were in Washington (albeit this is usual for national reform groups) and local activities appear to have been strictly limited.[20] Unable to tap tribal funds, the SAI was dependent on individual subscriptions of $2, supplemented by donations, for its ability to publish a quarterly journal, circulate propaganda literature, lobby and petition for alterations in Indian administration and laws and help individuals. The officers of the society all worked without pay at first, the secretary-treasurer only receiving office expenses, yet eventually the press of business resulted in this full-time official being paid $2,000 a year plus expenses, which could scarcely be spared.[21] Keeping up enrolments and gifts was hence essential – and hard. The first conference was convened with only 56 'actives', after a disappointing response to thousands of appeals.[22] Matters then improved for a while. A peak of 200 'actives' was reached at the 1913 annual conference, drawn primarily from Oklahoma, Montana, South Dakota, Nebraska and New York, with about 400 white 'associates' in attendance.

By 1916, familiarity, failures and wartime distractions had taken their toll: some twenty to thirty delegates turned up and the need for money was admitted. All conventions were said to be badly hit in that year, however, and proposals for state societies were unveiled. They were never realized. In 1918, again putting on a brave front, the society claimed some new recruits and asserted that its membership, though small, was impressively representative. In fact, the more numerous 'associates' were threatening to vitiate its aim of securing 'a united expression of Indian opinion on the great questions affecting the welfare of the race'.[23] Many Indians still had neither experience of pan-Indian meetings nor funds to attend them[24] and the emphemeral nature of pan-Indian ventures was acknowledged by contemporaries, including the SAI itself.[25]

Objectives are not easy to clarify among strong-minded individualists. Nevertheless, the SAI was more successful in this area than any other and it struggled to sustain a non-partisan, non-sectarian approach so as to avoid unnecessary distractions.[26] The vital overall aims were to encourage Indian leadership, promote self-help and, somewhat paradoxically, to foster the assimilation of Indians while exhorting them to pride of race. If nineteenth-century ideas about evolution were being modified by men of science, supporters of the society were unabashed in their belief that the Indian race could advance 'by the laws of evolution'.[27] Society spokesmen urged the importance of public school and further education, as well as the need for better teachers, standardized curricula and more effective supervision in Indian schools.[28] They favoured the abolition of the reservations and the BIA and the distribution on an individual basis of tribal property.[29] Because Indians needed to know and be assured of their civil rights in order to become assimilated, the SAI worked for the codification of laws governing Indians with a view to clarifying their status and for an Indian Court of Claims open to all petitioners without special enabling legislation.[30] The government was pressed to enforce the laws against the liquor traffic on the reservations, to enact laws against the use of peyote and to improve Indian health care, and while Indian involvement in the war effort was supported, the society condemned segregated military units.[31] Indian pride and social contacts were to be encouraged by the celebration of American Indian Days, which would also educate whites and offset the exploitative Wild West shows.[32] Miscegenation won approval and at a time when there was a high degree of faith in the value of social surveys as the basis of social engineering, we find the society advocating the compilation of a survey of Indian communities.[33]

After any such brief review of SAI aims, one is struck by the absence of innovative economic content, a criticism that could be made of the white Indian aid organizations by this time and of the NAACP. The liberating power of individual hard work was overestimated, the daunting power of the Anglo environment was underrated and no contribution was made to tackling the problems and opportunities of the stubbornly surviving reservations. Moreover, progress towards society goals ranged from slow to nil. Individual Indians were helped to settle legal claims, but the SAI did not have the funds to provide a comprehensive legal aid service and feared becoming bogged down with special cases. The same dilemma faced the better-off white reformers and ultimately confronted the NCAI. The society did try to reach its constituents by setting up Indian community centres, yet the initiative failed, partly because of limited resources and inability to secure government support.[34] Educational improvements, the clarification of Indian status, Indian citizenship, the opening up of the US Court of Claims to all American Indian tribes and bands, and desegregation of the armed forces, though achieved in the decades after the SAI's demise, were advocated by other reformers, as well as by far from disinterested politicians.[35] State legislation outlawing peyote was similarly supported by missionaries and the BIA as well as the SAI, and was ineffective. Finally, the American Indian Days held in

Wisconsin, Connecticut and New York, if satisfactory in themselves, were scarcely sufficient to transform entrenched white opinion about Indians and would have been more valuable in areas with larger Indian populations.[36]

Like all the reform groups of the Progressive era, the Society of American Indians relied heavily on moral exhortation which must have seemed a little chilly to the poor and powerless who were aware of its existence.[37] By 1919, it was torn by disputes over whether the BIA should be abolished or reformed, certain of the Indian 'actives' were plainly resentful of the white 'associates' and Indian service representatives, the society's journal was vainly bidding for popular support and Carlos Montezuma had for some time been using his rival paper, *Wassaja*, to express his intermittent doubts about the SAI's efficacy and independence. But while the society was moribund, due to the 'scheming of the Indian Bureau', in Richard Pratt's view, it had demonstrated that Indians possessed leaders willing to work within and bring pressure to bear on the white political system: free, in other words, of that 'parochial' outlook with which whites had traditionally associated them and able to function in two worlds.[38]

It was, none the less, difficult for Indian activists to make headway in the 1920s. White awareness of the potential of Indian voters had only really begun to grow during Woodrow Wilson's administration (1913–21)[39] and although BIA officials liked to claim in the debate leading up to the Indian Citizenship Act of 1924 that many Indians had already accustomed themselves to American politics and were 'well represented in Congress by members of their own race', this was far from being the case.[40] Oklahoma Indians did have a number of spokesmen there and Charles Curtis, a Kaw Indian from Kansas and eventually Herbert Hoover's Vice President (1929–33), was a member of the Senate. Naturally it was better to have such political representatives than none at all, and like the black congressmen in due course, they concerned themselves with the affairs of their own race.[41] Yet neither group could devote itself exclusively to race affairs. Indian political leaders had non-Indian constituents to consider and were expected to demonstrate that members of minorities were like other American citizens rather than preoccupied with special interests. Thus the presence on the political scene of 'assimilated' Indian politicians from Oklahoma helped to secure the modification of protective restrictions on Indian allottees and did nothing to ensure that the conduct of the state's Indian affairs during the 1920s was in the interests of the Indians.[42] Fayette A. McKenzie, a white sociologist and 'associate' of the SAI, was right in 1912 to sound a warning note about the gains to be made from minority politics. Pointing out that even in Oklahoma, which had some 40 per cent of the 40,000 Indian voters in the country, the Indian population was only 4.5 per cent of the total population of the state, McKenzie claimed that 'the Indian does not have the numbers which will enable him to force his rights through the ballot-box. His strength and power will come through his intelligence.'[43]

From the mid 1920s to the 1930s, the National Council of American Indians tried to continue the work the SAI had begun. Founded in Washington, DC, by two former society members, Gertrude and R. T. Bonnin, the council attempted to interest Indians in voting, to assist individual Indians who petitioned in Washington for redress of grievances and to represent tribal concerns. It publicized its activities in a newsletter and worked closely with the white reformers, but the Bonnins were ultimately defeated by the enormity of their objectives.[44] Somewhat less ambitious were the various local Indian associations. The Oklahoma Society of Indians, formed in 1924, pressed the Oklahoma delegation in Congress to expedite action on assorted pieces of legislation and looked to the journal, *The American Indian*, for publicity,[45] while Oklahoma's non-partisan Tushkahoma League, founded in 1927 and with members from some twenty-eight tribes, struggled to get out the Indian vote and worked for the election of men friendly to Indian interests. *The American Indian*, which deplored the dearth of Indian leaders, regularly exhorted its readers to use their votes.[46] In New York, a predominantly Indian Society for the Propagation of Indian Welfare had meanwhile been initiated to improve race relations in the state and obtain better education facilities, health provision and law enforcement for the state's reservation Indians.[47] And the Alaska Native Brotherhood (ANB), established in 1912, continued to operate after the First World War, as did its complementary Sisterhood.

The leading members of the ANB were well educated, influenced by Christian teaching, in favour of Indian assimilation and predictably praised by whites.[48] Apart from its respectable image, the brotherhood had the two great advantages of a clear purpose and adequate finances. Having established itself as the negotiating agent with local white industry and administrators, the ANB could charge fairly high membership dues ($12 annually after a $10 initiation fee). It was in turn able to establish community centres in a way that the SAI would like to have done. Other practical objectives were added, including the formation of fishermen's unions. Politically, both in tactics and aims, the brotherhood was in the mainstream of Indian reform. It opposed segregated schooling and reservations and struggled to establish Indian voting rights. Its methods were protest, boycotts and court action.[49] The BIA was denounced as a wasteful restraint upon Indian independence and it was argued that the American government would not be free of its slaves 'until the American Indian is given every right of citizenship guaranteed him by the constitution of the United States'.[50] The biggest achievement of the Alaska organizations at this stage of their history was probably their contribution to the development of leadership skills and group pride. Their major drawback, in the eyes of some Indians, may have been their strongly Christian temper and adaptation to white ways.[51]

The club movement which spread so rapidly in predominantly middle-class white communities in the second half of the nineteenth century had also made an impact on Indian life by the 1920s. The Grand Council Fire of American Indians, established in 1923 in Chicago, provided social functions for its members and let the Indian office know its priorities for action. These were in line with white reformer thinking during the decade, notably in stressing the importance of education and job training, the value of Indian cultures and the need for justice, not charity.[52] And encouraged by the National Federation of Women's Clubs, so long concerned with Indian welfare, a National Society of Indian Women was formed in the 1920s, with a comparable concern for self-improvement.[53] Its appearance was appropriate at a time when white American women had received the vote and were involved in the myriad of activities which made up 'social feminism'. Yet Indian women were no more likely than the leaders of the SAI to venture into radical projects. Hence the Cherokee-Creek singer Tsianina, who organized the Chicago First Daughters of America Club, and attached importance to educational opportunities, directed her energies towards the improvement of Indian–white understanding, and providing clothes for needy Indians.[54]

II

Activism in the 1930s

By the end of the 1920s, these Indian associations, together with their white counterparts, had helped to persuade the government of the need for major changes in Indian administration. When John Collier's Indian New Deal was implemented in the 1930s, however, it became apparent that reform involved strengthening the Bureau of Indian Affairs even as the Indians' control over their own communities was ostensibly being enhanced via the 1934 Wheeler-Howard Act (see Chapter 4). In consequence, as Hauptman has shown, a new organization called the American Indian Federation (AIF) came to represent a variety of discontented Indian elements, some with historic griev-ances against the BIA and some specifically opposed to New Deal measures.[55] Founded in 1934 and surviving until about 1945, the AIF contained traditionalists and supporters of assimilation, members and critics of the Native American Church, and its two best-known spokesmen were its president, Joseph Bruner, a Creek full blood from Oklahoma, and Alice Lee Jemison, a forceful Seneca Indian journalist who acted as its Washington representative.[56] Like other contempo-rary reform groups, the federation was officially non-partisan and non sectarian, appointed national officials and district presidents, main-tained Washington headquarters, held an annual conference, lobbied and issued publicity material.

Even before Collier was appointed, Jemison was denouncing the Indian Bureau in a manner reminiscent of the SAI in its later days and advocating the appointment as Commissioner of Joseph Latimer, a New York lawyer and Carlos Montezuma's former adviser, who favoured legislative protection for Indian lands but no other controls over the Indians.[57] Jemison argued that no race ever progressed through its cultural contributions alone. She belived that to 'condemn all members of a race to slavery to protect their cultural contributions is outrageous' and declared that this was what the Wheeler-Howard Act entailed. Her solution to the problem was the one favoured by the SAI:[58]

> Give the Indians their freedom and then as individuals each will find his own level and his own medium of expression and the cultural contributions will be far more outstanding than they have been to date. Race pride will take care of that.

Jemison noted that the descendants of emancipated slaves had 'schools, churches, hospitals and homes for the old, crippled and blind', concluding that 'if we Indians were turned loose and allowed to manage our own affairs we could do the same'.[59] As a good propagan-dist, she did not choose to notice here that the black institutions she extolled were the result of social segregation in many ways more pernicious than the geographical segregation sustained by the reser-vations and the bureau.

Striking a responsive chord in missionary hearts, the federation depicted the Commissioner's tolerance of Indian religious practices as 'Christ-mocking'. Collier's support for Indian community organi-zation and employment of foreign advisers and 'radicals' in the Indian service was interpreted as an unpatriotic drive to foster 'Russian communistic life in the United States'. Critics of official policy were said to be 'subject to vindictive treatment' and everything was done to 'segregate the Indian, keep him an Indian, not an American Citizen'. Priority was allegedly given to educating Indians in bureau, rather than state, schools. Legislation was proposed on white rather than Indian initiative and to make matters worse the expenditure and waste involved in Collier's programme were vast. Despite this expenditure, many Indian children remained out of school, many Indians remained in abject poverty and government backing for Indian arts and crafts was ineffective. The referendums through which Indian peoples could accept or exempt themselves from the operations of the Wheeler-Howard Act were dismissed as comparable only 'to the "free" elections under the dictator Hitler', because the Indians voting were 'a subject people, with no knowledge of its consequences'.[60]

While the federation could never entirely decide whether Indians were incompetent slaves under bureau rule or quite capable of handling their affairs immediately, its charges were damaging and the Indian service records for the 1930s bear witness to the time that had to be spent on refuting the federation's attacks before various committees. Legal action against Bruner and his associates was even contemplated.[61] Some AIF complaints could not simply be dismissed: bureau schools were still numerous, Indian schooling, employment assistance and programme funding inadequate, Indian claims a daunting tangle. Many Indian groups did find the elections under Wheeler-Howard baffling, dislike the new tribal councils the legislation established and discover that BIA bureaucracy was more elaborate than ever during the 1930s. The toleration for Indian religions, coming so soon after the pro-missionary policy of Collier's predecessor, was predictably resented by religious interests and the Christian members of the federation, and the equation of Indian community building with communism, though misguided, was perhaps understandable in the 'red decade'.

The federation never attracted a mass following, any more than the SAI had done, though it claimed members from California, Oregon, North and South Dakota, New York, North Carolina, Idaho, Arizona, New Mexico and especially Oklahoma. Its supporters were criticized as 'individuals with personal grievances', who had little Indian blood, had mostly forgotten their heritage and were not authorized to speak for their respective tribes. Furthermore, they were allegedly motivated by greed. Bruner was said to collect payments due to Indians for a commission and AIF took money from its members on the understanding that it would persuade Congress to enact a bill paying them $3,000 as a final settlement of any claims they might have on the United States. The so-called 'Settlement Bill' was not passed, but the proposal was considered by the Senate Committee on Indian Affairs and the hearing allowed white and Indian grievances against the BIA to be aired. In response, the Indian service suggested that its main opposition was to the federation's financial manoeuvres; exception was not taken to AIF hopes of abolishing the bureau, since BIA staff looked forward to the day when Indians could 'stand alone without the assistance of a special agency', and Collier stated that he simply feared alliances like AIF might undermine more sincere adversaries. These protestations seem a trifle disingenuous. The Commissioner was quite ready to cross such sincere Indian adversaries when it suited him, as witness the way he ignored the Alaska Native Brotherhood's opposition to the reservations being proposed for Alaska as part of the New Deal. The day when Indians could 'stand alone' appeared to tribally oriented and pro-assimilation Indians alike to be very distant, and the 4,664 federation members who wanted action on the Settlement Bill were not a negligible force, albeit the issue alienated AIF's traditionalist wing.[62]

Collier's best way of discrediting the federation was the argument that it had become a front for a pro-German, 'Jew-baiting, anti-government' operation, in league with right-wing splinter groups, including the James True Associates and the Silver Shirts of America. It seems safe to assume that anti-Semitism was confined to a tiny fraction of AIF's leadership, which, in common with many whites, disliked the liberal, Jewish sympathies of the New Deal,[63] though it was not helpful that Indians of California Inc., an aid organization originating in 1910, was discredited on the same grounds.[64] But for all its exaggerations and its failure to secure the removal of Collier, the repudiation of Wheeler-Howard and the abolition of the BIA, the American Indian Federation was not totally without effect. It was one of a number of voices which helped to discredit the Indian New Deal and prepare the way for the post-Second World War drive to 'terminate the federal–Indian relationship'.[65] Less negatively, it helped to make the point that the diverse Indian community was insufficiently consulted about the direction of Indian affairs and it may have contributed to the growth of political awareness among Indians apparent in the 1930s, for example in Oklahoma.[66] The BIA was consequently obliged to explain – not very convincingly – why it was that Indians were still denied the suffrage in certain areas, while AIF and the California Indian Rights Association encouraged them to 'VOTE FOR YOUR FRIENDS' in 1940. For federation members this meant Republican, to get rid of Collier and the Democratic New Deal, and for the Californians it meant Democrat, to keep benefits gained under the Democratic administration.[67]

III

Protest Organizations Since the Second World War

Experience of service in the Second World War was also a factor in stimulating Indian interest in American politics. Returned veterans, alienated by the contrast between America's overseas idealism and domestic injustice, helped to galvanize existing minority protest groups and to found, in 1944, the first permanent, national, political, pan-Indian movement: the National Congress of American Indians (NCAI). It remains the only nationally registered Indian lobby.

From the first, the NCAI realized the ambition of the Society of American Indians to be open to groups and tribes as well as individuals. The former SAI leader, Arthur C. Parker, was included on its first executive council, together with a number of past and present tribal chairmen. Its purpose was

> to secure to ourselves and our descendants the rights and benefits to which we are entitled under the laws of the United States, the several States thereof, and the Territory of Alaska; to enlighten the public toward a better understanding of the Indian race; to preserve Indian cultural values; to seek an equitable adjustment of tribal affairs; to secure and to preserve rights under Indian treaties with the United States, and otherwise to promote the common welfare of the American Indians.

At the first convention in Denver, there were Indian delegates from twenty-seven states, representing more than fifty Indian tribes, groups and associations. A year later the NCAI claimed members from nearly all of the tribes in the United States, yet it secured somewhat less impressive attendances at its conferences. By 1955, at least half the delegates were women and it was obligatory to have at least one woman on the executive board. The NCAI's newsletter was designed to keep supporters informed on Indian matters and it hoped to stay in touch with their opinions through polls.

The organization's early objectives included the creation of a special and well-inclined commission to hear and settle Indian claims against the United States. It was concerned to suggest improvements in the administration of Indian affairs; with the provision of legal assistance to members of the association; and with the monitoring and, if necessary, smothering of legislation affecting Indians in Washington. In order to achieve legislative success, it was thought essential to interest Indians in voting, organizing politically at every level for their protection and influencing the congressional delegations from all states with Indian populations. The NCAI wanted to persuade the BIA to increase its employment of Indians and to make sure that Indian veterans enjoyed full benefits under the G.I. Bill of Rights. Priority was given to the improvement of the Indian health service and of educational facilities, particularly in the public schools. And twenty-five years after the decline of the SAI, the idea of mounting an American Indian Day surfaced again.

Whites welcomed the formation of the NCAI as a means of hastening Indian assimilation, but its aim was to preserve the Indians' right to choose their lifestyle. This catholic approach, together with its desire to become a truly national body, in turn meant that the congress had to grapple with internal dissension frequently avoided by more exclusive organizations. On the grounds of their divided loyalties, there was hostility towards Indian Office personnel in the NCAI, just as there had been in the SAI, and accordingly they were excluded from the council. The older Indian sometimes felt a gulf between himself and the young, educated Indian. In time, discontented elements came to see the congress as being too dominated by prosperous and acculturated members, a complaint which has commonly surfaced in minority protest alliances. On the other hand, membership dues were set low to attract poorer individuals and groups and, contrary to white assumptions, the supporters of bodies like the NCAI, whatever their regional and class differences, had more in common with each other than with outsiders. Indian leaders would eventually be at pains to stress the latter point, though not until after factionalism had spawned a number of rivals to the congress.

There are difficulties involved in assessing the NCAI's early effectiveness, partly because many of its goals were shared by other Indian aid organizations; while an Indian Claims Commission was established in 1946, for example, it had been demanded by a variety of groups. Educational opportunities were secured under the G.I. Bill of Rights, but it would have been difficult to exclude Indians and foolish to block an obvious road towards assimilation, when this was again being seen as the main purpose of Indian policy. Other G.I. Bill benefits proved much harder to secure. Improvements in the Indian Health Service followed chiefly from transferring it to the Public Health Service, which was the result of medical rather than Indian politics. The congress was, however, instrumental in securing a guarantee that in the postwar Indian service cuts, Indian employees would receive preference for retention.[68] It was also particularly consistent, albeit backed up by part of the white reform community, in opposing the BIA's plans for relocating reservation Indians in the cities, terminating its responsibilities for the Indians and transferring those duties to the states in which Indians resided. The NCAI's campaign helped to increase Indian voter registration in the 1950s. It ran workshops to encourage Indian leaders from every type of background and offered individual assistance together with help in establishing work projects in Indian communities. And it drew up a 'Point Four Program for Indians', which aimed at the development and training of reservation resources and manpower under the auspices of reservation planning commissions.

NCAI's effectiveness continued to be impeded by an inadequate dues income and the demands on it of non-members, whose appeals it felt it could not automatically reject. The $30,000 it could hope to spend annually by the late 1950s was not enough. Needing to obtain outside money, as well as a hearing in political circles, the congress accordingly avoided direct action protests, preferring the 'responsible presentation of . . . grievances before proper Congressional and Interior Department authorities and the courts'. Its reward was 'coming to be recognized by the committees of Congress as the responsible Indian voice on matters affecting their welfare'.[69] Yet even as the pressurized BIA retreated from termination, different voices were beginning to make themselves heard and the NCAI itself changed in response to circumstances which were at once more auspicious and more challenging for its leadership.

By the 1960s, impatience with the pace of change and with the NCAI's methods and composition was expressed by younger Indians and those whose acquaintance with city life had enlarged their understanding of white society. Among the groups which have arisen out of this discontent are the National Indian Youth Council (NIYC), founded in 1961, and the American Indian Movement (AIM) which developed in 1968. With a base in Minneapolis, as well as autonomous chapters concentrated in the Midwest, AIM attracted a young, urban-reared and tribally mixed membership and a number of its spokesmen were suspect in the eyes of older Indian leaders because of their unconventional, even criminal, backgrounds and militant tactics. In return, AIM publicists have been strongly critical of existing tribal government and leadership. Notwithstanding the notable bitterness of AIM attacks, Indian activists of all kinds and connections showed, and still show, anxiety about the efficacy of tribal governments. Some have seen them as the creatures of the Bureau of Indian Affairs, federally sponsored governments set up under the Wheeler-Howard Act and destructive of ancient forms of authority. Others have resented what they have seen as the domination by 'progressive' elements and representation only of reservation opinion while organized or urban Indians were neglected. These differences in outlook are reflected in the Indian press, a sharp contrast existing between, say, *Akwesasne Notes*, with its pro-traditionalist and crusading style, and a more upbeat and broad coverage newspaper like the *Navajo Times TODAY*.

The shock troops of Indian nationalism, AIM spokesmen came to public attention by a series of demonstrations: the brief Mount Rushmore protest in June 1971, the 'trail of Broken Treaties' march on Washington in 1972, the occupation of the village of Wounded Knee, South Dakota, in 1973, designed to highlight the problems of the Oglala Sioux and other Indians. But the movement has suffered from its brushes with the law, and while it has certainly attracted enormous and quite favourable publicity, so that leaders like Dennis Banks (Chippewa), Clyde and Vernon Bellecourt and Russell Means (Oglala Sioux) became nationally known in a manner impossible for the earlier SAI spokesmen, the wide media coverage had certain unfortunate effects. It concealed the existence of such moderate AIM activists as the Chippewa George Mitchell and John Trudell, a Santee Sioux protest organizer and a navy veteran. It alarmed some Indians and whites, who feared a resultant white conservative 'backlash'. Sensationalist reporting served to obscure the organizers' key demands, which included: examination and enforcement of US Indian treaty promises, notably those made in the 1868 Fort Laramie treaty with the Sioux; the replacement of white-style by genuinely Indian forms of government on the reservations; and an independent, Indian-dominated Bureau of Indian Affairs. Furthermore, differences within the AIM itself over money, leadership positions, objectives and methods disillusioned some followers.

The NIYC made its headquarters in New Mexico rather than Washington, yet since its objectives were not exclusively political, this did not matter; it was more important to be close to the large centres of Indian population. Its members, like those of AIM, are frequently young and urban and intermittently at odds with the NCAI in terms of priorities and style. But though committed to militant tactics, the council has proved less controversial than AIM and has enjoyed steadier growth, claiming a membership of 2,000 by 1970. In a manner reminiscent of the NCAI, it has undertaken research on key issues and publicized its findings and activities through talks, pamphlets and an annual report. It has also supported diverse local and short-term projects, in a way that the NCAI has not, recognizing the Indian tendency – noted by Deloria and others – to coalesce round issues of immediate and personal concern, ignoring calls for unity for unity's sake. After establishing chapters in universities, the council has been involved in setting up Indian Studies programmes and counselling students. It has assisted community schools, Indians seeking off-reservation work and ex-offenders; demonstrations to uphold native fishing rights threatened by commercial and sporting interests; and voter registration campaigns. Through the courts, it has been concerned to fight white exploitation of Indian economic resources, denial of Indian civil rights and job discrimination against Indians. The council has tried to help Indians excluded from or disenchanted with existing tribal governments to gain a greater say in their affairs. Rather like the NCAI, the organization has provided information about 'backlash' legislation proposed in Congress in response to Indian successes; and it has endeavoured, in co-operation with staff deployed under the Comprehensive Employment and Training Act (1973), to encourage the development of technology appropriate to Indian communities, 'ranging from low-cost solar greenhouse retrofits for family food and space-heating needs to a variety of water and energy conservation techniques'.

Council spokesmen have secured contributions both from non-Indians and Indian organizations and individuals, partly by mail fund-raising appeals. They have profited from whites' increased response to minority pressures, at least in monetary terms, from the mid 1960s. But NIYC has regarded itself most emphatically as a body which was responsible to Indian communities, 'that is groups of people rather than individually selected leaders . . . sometimes selected by the press'; it did not see itself as responsible to the rest of society or the press. There was some feeling that the NCAI was too 'leader' oriented, tended to be drawn into partisan politics and was neglectful of Indian youth, though the council stressed that, its title to the contrary, it had members of all ages. In trying to forge a distinctively Indian organization, NIYC rejected suggestions that its members were youthful 'militants': they preferred to think of themselves as warriors, whose object was not to stir up trouble but to 'give courage to the other people'. Nor was there enthusiasm for acknowledging any debt to the black and other vocal groups of the 1960s, although one of the council's first leaders, Clyde Warrior, had used the example of black and Hispanic protest to encourage Indian action.[70]

Such reluctance was understandable. As Nancy Lurie has pointed out, the black civil rights movement, at least, was concerned with rights due to all blacks, whereas Indian activism revolved around special rights.[71] Much as it may suit white politicians to dismiss Indian organizations as representative of just another selfish interest group, there are obvious differences between Indian protesters and the rest, which their spokesmen have sensibly exploited: the treaty legacy and claims to sovereignty, the reservations, the distinctive relationship with the Bureau of Indian Affairs, the dual involvement in tribal and white politics. And we have noted in Chapter 6 the existence of a degree of antipathy between Indians and blacks which makes their political collaboration in the fight against white neglect or exploitation unlikely, given the normal difficulties in the way of reform coalitions and the competition between their component elements for scarce public resources.

Of course one could argue that interest in the rights of all Indians prompted the NCAI campaign to get out the Indian vote at non-Indian elections and has resulted in the application to Indians of the national civil rights legislation and the passage of the Indian Bill of Rights of 1968, which extended to the reservations the rights guaranteed in the first ten amendments to the Constitution. On the other hand, these developments have aroused suspicion among many Indians, who regard them as just another encroachment on reservation autonomy, feel too disenchanted with white politics to go to the polls, or think that the importance of voting in American elections has been exaggerated. In this vein, NIYC's Jerry Wilkinson maintained that Indians had their own ways of voting:[72]

> they've voted against the economic system by dropping out of school, they've voted against the economic system by staying on the reservations, they don't go out and punch a time clock, they stay at home. So maybe Indians have been voting all the time.

The fact remains, however, that for the growing numbers of urban Indians, there are many similarities between their economic and social circumstances and those of other ghetto dwellers. A diminution in public expressions of red–black aversion is already apparent, perhaps from a realization of this fact and from knowledge that black as well as Indian activists, on and off the reservations, have increasingly emphasized the importance of community projects and controls. Conversely, the influx into the Southwest of white Americans inclined to treat Indians as they had once, in the North, treated blacks, may make complete harmony impossible. We shall have to wait and see. Individual contacts between Indians and blacks will no doubt continue to take place in a harmonious fashion, as they have always done.

In the mean time, urban Indian discontents have been channelled through a variety of city community centres and had so far affected the NCAI by 1971 as to precipitate the establishment of a more conservative National Tribal Chairmen's Association (NTCA), soon representing leaders of some two hundred authorized tribal governments. Given the circumstances of its formation, it was fairly predictable that the NCTA would come to be regarded by radicals as the puppet of the Bureau of Indian Affairs, whereas to its members it held out hope of giving 'a more unified voice' to the tribes and reflecting the opinions of 'grass-roots constituents' on the reservations. When the national organizations and tribal governments failed to do so, pressure groups sprang up to fight on particular issues and many of the campaigns of traditionalists to preserve their resources and culture have recently been detailed by Peter Matthiessen in *Indian Country*. He also brings out the part played in such struggles by women and one can find additional examples. We may note, for instance, the work of the Oklahomans for Indian Opportunity, under the direction of the Comanche, LaDonna Harris, which has helped Indians both highly conscious of their Indianness yet without the reservation base to be found in some states. And we should recognize the valiant struggle of Menominee women like Ada Deer and Silvia Wilber against termination and for the survival of the tribe, the activism of Indian women during the 'Red Power' demonstrations of the 1970s, and their leadership roles, indicated by Malcolm McFee and Dorothy Miller, in the fields of child welfare, education, health care and family maintenance.

As these assorted groups and associations formed, the NCAI endured, never openly alienated, despite differences, from the newcomers and itself changing with the times and managing to remain the most respected Indian pressure group. It has continued to try to force the federal government to fulfil its responsibilities towards the Native Americans. This has involved lobbying against hostile legislation supported by state interests, launching media campaigns to re-educate whites about Indian cultures and history and agitating for Indian voting and social security rights, for better health care, more spending on Indian education, professional and vocational training, the development of employment opportunities within Indian communities and the adjudication of land or resource disputes in the interests of the tribes. NCAI efforts to reconstruct legally recognized tribes and units in the East and the cities, which would have access to funds unavailable to private citizens, have met with a good response and similar objectives have been embraced by the Coalition of Eastern Native Americans.

If, then, there can be no doubt about the vitality and diversity of pan-Indian endeavours, there can equally be no doubt that all organizations in the field face certain stubborn problems. Although every state has some Indians and urbanization has involved many more Indians with the American political process, over half the Indian population remains settled in areas away from the eye and understanding of the white public and disillusionment quickly follows when voters in a minority group recognize how little real power they have. In 1978, the NCAI still spoke for only 154 of the nation's federally recognized tribes and groups and was supported by about 3,000 individual members.

Indian associations have been right to press their case through the courts, not least because they possess rights enshrined in treaties which survive to the present. But the white reaction to victories has often been hostile, leading to new proposals for termination.[73] Indian demonstrations contributed to the setting up of the Indian-dominated American Indian Policy Review Commission in the summer of 1975, the findings of whose eleven taskforces were presented to Congress in 1977. Unfortunately and ironically, since the commission was suspect to both radicals and traditionalists, who felt excluded from it, Indian militancy had likewise helped to create an environment in which whites would react suspiciously to the commission's proposals. Among the most controversial recommendations were those for full tribal jurisdiction over taxation, the trial of offenders and natural resources in Indian territories, and for an independent BIA. Yet as Prucha observes, the commission's recommendations were so varied, required such extensive funding and were so hastily produced, considering the inquiry's scope, that its ultimate impact was limited.[74]

None of the Indian associations has been able to resolve the dilemma posed by the existence of the BIA. None of them has agitated for its abolition, as did the SAI in its later days. While it exists, it protects the special status which most Indians want to retain and so many whites resent. As it exists, it is at once ineffective in carrying out its main task and an effective barrier both to the sovereignty radicals covet and to more aid being given by the other federal agencies which help minorities. The number of Indians on the payroll is higher than ever, thanks in large part to the efforts of Indian protest groups, but they have not yet been able to reduce the BIA bureaucracy or end its dependence on the committees of the Indian section of the Bureau of the Budget and the Department of the Interior, departments with many other, and often conflicting, interests. Neither the activists nor anyone else, as we have argued in Chapters 9 and 11, have been able to produce inexpensive programmes for self-determination, though the shift away from the direct federal administration of reservations towards contracting with them regarding reservation programmes is to be welcomed.[75]

In their irritation with this dilemma, Indian leaders have looked outward for a solution, as have black spokesmen in the United States. Thus friendly relations have been cultivated with Indian organizations in Canada and Latin America, which have developed a similar interest in hemispheric co-operation. Part of the intention has been to secure UN recognition for the integrity of the various tribal cultures, although differences have surfaced about what degree of independence should be recognized. Unfortunately, while the UN may be the talking-chamber of the 'emerging' nations, many of the countries there represented themselves operate oppressive or neglectful Indian policies, which makes the procuring of a UN initiative more than usually hard to predict.[76] In the short term, clearly, activists will be pressed for practical solutions to local or regional difficulties. Yet here, too, the path is strewn with obstacles. Apart from considerations of cost, reservation leaders and traditionalists disagree about just what constitutes progress and how desirable it is.[77]

There are, in fact, no simple courses before Indian political protest groups and, given the diversity of Indian peoples and the low value that they still attach to unity as whites understand it, we should welcome the range of existing associations. Like the similarly antagonistic moderate and militant black protest groups, they have many material objectives in common.[78] The Indian organizations here described, in common with other minority movements, need outside sponsorship and a favourable political climate to be able to realize their full potential. In common with other minority associations, they have difficulty in sustaining membership support and building durable leadership out of the work of charismatic and eventually exhausted individuals. But pan-Indian political groups have been less riven by class problems than many American protest alliances and have an invaluable, if eroded, linguistic and territorial base for their nationalism. Their efforts have strengthened the prospects for Indian self-determination in the political, economic, educational and religious spheres.[79] And they have helped to make Indian peoples more 'visible' to whites without losing a distinctive Indian style and focus.

Notes and References

The following abbreviations and terms are used in references to primary sources:

AHS: Arizona Historical Society manuscript collections, Tucson, Arizona

BIC files: Board of Indian Commissioners reference files, records relating to the Bureau of Indian Affairs, RG 75, National Archives, Washington, DC

BIC Newspaper Clippings: Board of Indian Commissioners newspaper clippings, records relating to the Bureau of Indian Affairs, RG 75, National Archives, Washington, DC

Bureau of Indian Affairs: post-1945 records read at the Bureau of Indian Affairs, Washington, DC (held at Washington National Records Center, Suitland, Maryland)

DD for New Mexico: Doris Duke Indian Oral History Collection, University of New Mexico Library, Albuquerque, New Mexico

DD for Oklahoma: Doris Duke Indian Oral History Collection, Western History Collections, University of Oklahoma Library, Norman, Oklahoma

IPP: Indian Pioneer Papers, Western History Collections, University of Oklahoma Library, Norman, Oklahoma

OHS: Indian Archives Division of the Oklahoma Historical Society, Oklahoma City

WHC: Western History Collections, University of Oklahoma Library, Norman, Oklahoma

INTRODUCTION

1 See Wilbur R. Jacobs, 'The fatal confrontation: early native-white relations on the frontiers of Australia, New Guinea, and America – a comparative study', *Pacific Historical Review*, vol. 40, 1971, pp. 289–90, 297; Joan Mary Chandler, 'Anthropologists and U.S. Indians, 1928–1960' (PhD dissertation, University of Texas at Austin, 1972), p. 69; A. Grenfell Price, *White Settlers and Native Peoples. An Historical Study of Racial Contacts between English-speaking Whites and Aboriginal Peoples in the United States, Canada, Australia and New Zealand* (Melbourne, Georgian House, and Cambridge, Cambridge University Press, 1950), p. 8.

2 See, for instance, James Stuart Olson, *The Ethnic Dimension in American History* (New York, St Martin's Press, 1979), pp. 47–51, 192–5.

3 See, for instance, Grenfell Price, p. 192.

4 See, on Bantu adaptability, Roger Bastide, *African Civilizations in the New World* (New York, Harper & Row, 1971), p. 106; and Daniel C. Littlefield, *Rice and Slaves. Ethnicity and the Slave Trade in Colonial South Carolina* (Baton Rouge, La, and London, Louisiana State University Press, 1981), pp. 13–16, 158–9.

5　Quoted in Angie Debo, *And Still the Waters Run* (Princeton, NJ, Princeton University Press, 1970 reprint of 1940 edn), pp. 13–14.

6　See Ralph Linton (ed.), *Acculturation in Seven American Indian Tribes* (New York, Appleton-Century, 1940); Ralph Linton, *The Study of Man. An Introduction* (New York, Appleton-Century-Crofts, 1964 edn.), p. 340; Evon Vogt, 'The acculturation of American Indians', *Annals of the American Academy of Political and Social Science* (hereafter *Annals*), vol. 311, May 1957, pp. 137–46; Edward H. Spicer (ed.), *Perspectives in American Indian Culture Change* (Chicago, University of Chicago Press, 1966 edn), pp. 517–44.

7　Chandler, p. 69.

8　This view is strongly stated by Grenfell Price, p. 2 and *passim*.

9　See Diane Ravitch, *The Troubled Crusade. American Education, 1945–1980* (New York, Basic Books, 1983), pp. 148–9.

10　Carl N. Degler, 'Remaking American history', *Journal of American History*, vol. 67, no. 1, June 1980, p. 18.

CHAPTER 1

1　Winthrop D. Jordan, *White over Black. American Attitudes towards the Negro, 1550–1812* (Chapel Hill, NC, University of North Carolina Press, 1968), ch. II, especially p. 80; Carl N. Degler, 'Slavery and the genesis of American race prejudice', *Comparative Studies in History and Society*, vol. XI, October 1959, pp. 49–66; Oscar Handlin and Mary F. Handlin, 'Origins of the southern labor system', *William and Mary Quarterly*, vol. VII, April 1950, pp. 199–222.

2　James Axtell, *The European and the Indian. Essays in the Ethnohistory of Colonial North America* (New York, Oxford University Press, 1981), pp. 85 and 378, for an ambivalent view; Richard Slotkin, *Regeneration through Violence. The Mythology of the American Frontier* (Middleton, Conn., Wesleyan University Press, 1973), pp. 68–9; Richard Drinnon, *Facing West. The Metaphysics of Indian-Hating and Empire-Building* (Minneapolis, Minn., University of Minnesota Press, 1980), pp. 19–20, 48–55, 99, 236, 240, 358–64, 474–6, 505–6; Wilbur R. Jacobs, *Dispossessing the American Indian. Indians and Whites on the Colonial Frontier* (New York, Scribner, 1972), pp. 1–5 and *passim*.

3　Bernard W. Sheehan, *Savagism and Civility. Indians and Englishmen in Colonial Virginia* (Cambridge, Cambridge University Press, 1980), pp. 48–9; Karen Ordahl Kupperman, *Settling with the Indians. The Meeting of English and Indian Cultures in America, 1580–1640* (London, Dent, 1980), pp. 35–7; Wesley Frank Craven, *White, Red and Black. The Seventeenth-Century Virginian* (Charlottesville, Va, University Press of Virginia, 1971), p. 41; Alden T. Vaughan, 'From white man to redskin: changing Anglo-American perceptions of the American Indian', *American Historical Review*, vol. 87, no. 4, October 1982, pp. 917–53.

4　Compare Vaughan, 'From white man to redskin', pp. 939–53, especially p. 948, and Reginald Horsman, *Race and Manifest Destiny. The Origins of American Racial Anglo-Saxonism* (Cambridge, Mass., Harvard University Press, 1981), pp. 1–6 and *passim*.

5　See, for instance, Slotkin, p. 51; Drinnon, *Facing West*; Kupperman, p. 27; Roy Harvey Pearce, '"The ruines of mankind": The Indian and the

Puritan mind', *Journal of the History of Ideas*, vol. XIII, 1952, pp. 203, 209–10; Wesley Frank Craven, 'Indian policy in early Virginia', *William and Mary Quarterly*, vol. I, 1944, pp. 71–2; and Alden T. Vaughan, *New England Frontier. Puritans and Indians, 1620–1675* (Boston, Mass., Little, Brown, 1965), pp. vii–viii and *passim*.

6　On the different perception of blacks and Indians see, for instance, Jordan, pp. 89–91 and ch. I. See also H. C. Porter, *The Inconstant Savage. England and the North American Indian, 1500–1660* (London, Duckworth, 1979), on English attitudes.

7　Christine Bolt, 'Red, black and white in nineteenth-century America', in A. C. Hepburn (ed.), *Minorities in History* (London, Edward Arnold, 1978), especially pp. 116–19.

8　Kupperman, pp. 121–2, 141, 189–95.

9　ibid., ch. 2.

10　Sheehan, *Savagism and Civility*, p. 94.

11　Kupperman, ch. 3, especially pp. 47–55; Sheehan, *Savagism and Civility*, pp. 96–7.

12　Sheehan, *Savagism and Civility*, pp. 91–3.

13　ibid., pp. 98–110, quotations from pp. 99 and 108; Kupperman, ch. 5; James Axtell, 'The scholastic philosophy of the wilderness', in *The School upon a Hill. Education and Society in Colonial New England* (New Haven, Conn., and London, Yale University Press, 1974), ch. 7 (especially pp. 247–65).

14　Kupperman, ch. 4; Vaughan, *New England Frontier*, p. 19.

15　Kupperman, pp. 120–1; Gary B. Nash, 'The image of the Indian in the southern colonial mind', in Edward Dudley and Maximillian E. Novak (eds), *The Wild Man Within. An Image in Western Thought from the Renaissance to Romanticism* (Pittsburgh, Pa, University of Pittsburgh Press, 1972), pp. 74–8.

16　See Axtell, 'The scholastic philosophy', pp. 276–7, quotation from p. 276; Axtell, *The European and the Indian*, ch. 7; Sheehan, *Savagism and Civility*, pp. 110–15; Kupperman, p. 118; Jacobs, *Dispossessing*, pp. 112–15; Dwight W. Hoover, *The Red and the Black* (Chicago, Rand, McNally, 1976), p. 42.

17　Richard S. Dunn and Mary Maples Dunn (eds), *The Papers of William Penn*, vol. Two, *1680–1684* (Philadelphia, Pa, University of Pennsylvania Press, 1982), pp. 39, 54, 64, 98–101, 418, 435, 441, 448–54, 458–9, 573, 607–10 and *passim*; Joseph E. Ilick, *Colonial Pennsylvania. A History* (New York, Scribner, 1976), pp. 26–8, 165–70, ch. 8; Stephen B. Weeks, *Southern Quakers and Slavery. A Study in Institutional History* (Baltimore, Md, Johns Hopkins University Press, 1896), pp. 173, 384–5; Rayner Wickersham Kelsey, *Friends and the Indians, 1655–1917* (Philadelphia, Pa, Associated Executive Committee of Friends on Indian Affairs, 1917), pp. 57–8; Olson, *Ethnic Dimension*, p. 11; Gary B. Nash, 'Red, white and black: the origins of racism in colonial America', in Gary B. Nash and Richard Weiss (eds), *The Great Fear. Race in the Mind of America* (New York, Holt, Rinehart & Winston, 1970), pp. 8–9; Thomas E. Drake, 'William Penn's experiment in race relations', *The Pennsylvania Magazine of History and Biography*, vol. LXVIII, no. 4, October 1944, pp. 377–83.

18　Vaughan, 'From white man to redskin', pp. 936–7; see also Neal Salisbury, *Manitou and Providence. Indians, Europeans, and the Making of New England, 1500–1643* (New York, Oxford University Press, 1982), p. 187; D. W. Hoover, *The Red and the Black*, pp. 21–2.

19 See Vaughan, 'From white man to redskin', p. 950; Nash, 'The image of the Indian', pp. 73–9; Margaret T. Hodgen, *Early Anthropology in the Sixteenth and Seventeenth Centuries* (Philadelphia, Pa, University of Pennsylvania Press, 1964), pp. 196–201; and D. W. Hoover, *The Red and the Black*, pp. 67–79.

20 See Francis Paul Prucha, *American Indian Policy in the Formative Years* (Lincoln, Nebr., University of Nebraska Press, 1962; 1970 edn) for a partial defence of government policy in this period.

21 See Francis Jennings, *The Invasion of America. Indians, Colonialism and the Cant of Conquest* (Chapel Hill, NC, University of North Carolina Press, 1976 edn), pp. 73–85; Sheehan, *Savagism and Civility*, pp. 144, 172–6; Drinnon, pp. 49 ff; Slotkin, pp. 78 ff.; Jacobs, *Dispossessing*, pp. 12, 102, 110–11.

22 Sheehan, *Savagism and Civility*, p. 116; and see his ch. 5 generally.

23 See Neal Salisbury, 'Red Puritans. The "praying Indians" of Massachusetts Bay and John Eliot', *William and Mary Quarterly*, vol. 31, 1974, pp. 27–54, especially p. 29.

24 Sheehan, *Savagism and Civility*, pp. 165–6; Axtell, *The European and the Indian*, pp. 84–5.

25 Jacobs, *Dispossessing*, p. 15.

26 See, for instance, Jacobs, *Dispossessing*, pp. 116–19; Axtell, *The European and the Indian*, chs 3, 9 and 10; Sheehan, *Savagism and Civility*, pp. 177–8; Jacobs, *Dispossessing*, p. 117; Salisbury, *Manitou and Providence*, p. 189.

27 See Jacobs, *Dispossessing*, p. 166.

28 Sheehan, *Savagism and Civility*, pp. 141, 154, 164; Nash, 'Red, white and black', p. 8; Jacobs, *Dispossessing*, p. 7.

29 Salisbury, *Manitou and Providence*, Introduction; for an opposite viewpoint, see Axtell, 'The scholastic philosophy', p. 251.

30 Axtell, *The European and the Indian*, p. 140; Sheehan, *Savagism and Civility*, p. 94.

31 Axtell, *The European and the Indian*, pp. 133–5; Nancy Oestreich Lurie, 'Indian cultural adjustment to European civilization', in James Morton Smith (ed.), *Seventeenth-Century America. Essays in Colonial History* (Chapel Hill, NC, University of North Carolina Press, 1959); pp. 33, 37–9, 43–4, 51, 58, 60; Carolyn Thomas Foreman, *Indians Abroad, 1493–1938* (Norman, Okla, University of Oklahoma Press, 1943); Nash, 'The image of the Indian', pp. 78–95; Jean-Jacques Rousseau, *Discourse upon the Origin and Foundation of the Inequality among Mankind* (London, 1761; originally 1755), p. 254; Sheehan, *Savagism and Civility*, p. 15; Francis Parkman, *The Jesuits in North America in the Seventeenth Century* (Boston, Mass., Little, Brown, 1893), pp. 204, 400; Cornelius J. Jaenen, 'Amerindian views of French culture in the seventeenth century', *Canadian Historical Review*, vol. 55, no. 3, September 1974, pp. 261–74.

32 Calvin Martin, *Keepers of the Game. Indian-Animal Relationships and the Fur Trade* (Berkeley, Calif., University of California Press, 1978; 1982 edn), p. 153; Kupperman, pp. 57–8; R. S. Cotterill, *The Southern Indians. The Story of the Civilized Tribes before Removal* (Norman, Okla, University of Oklahoma Press, 1971 edn), p. 15; Jennings, pp. 66, 85–6.

33 Axtell, *The European and the Indian*, p. 254; George F. G. Stanley, *New France. The Last Phase, 1744–1760* (London, Oxford University Press, and Toronto, McClelland & Stewart, 1968), pp. 28–9, 39.

34 Wilbur R. Jacobs, 'The fatal confrontation', pp. 293–4; Kupperman, p. 57;

Sheehan, *Savagism and Civility*, p. 137; E. E. Rich, *The Fur Trade and the Northwest to 1857* (Toronto, McClelland & Stewart, 1968), pp. 9, 13; Allen W. Trelease, in 'The Iroquois and the western fur trade: a problem in interpretation', *Mississippi Valley Historical Review*, vol. 49, 1962–3, p. 45, doubts the middleman argument and suggests that their own trade always remained more important to the Iroquois; for this reason, he argues, they tried to obtain new hunting grounds from the Hurons. But see Bruce Trigger, 'The French presence in Huronia: the structure of Franco-Huron relations in the first half of the seventeenth century', *Canadian Historical Review*, vol. XLIX, June 1968, p. 131.

35 W. Neil Franklin, 'Pennsylvania-Virginia rivalry for the Indian trade of the Ohio Valley', *Mississippi Valley Historical Review*, vol. 20, March 1934, pp. 463–80; Rich, p. 136.

36 R. David Edmunds, 'Old Briton', in R. David Edmunds (ed.), *American Indian Leaders. Studies in Diversity* (Lincoln, Nebr., University of Nebraska Press, 1980), pp. 1–8.

37 Axtell, *The European and the Indian*, pp. 261, 264–5; Jacobs, *Dispossessing*, p. 10; Charles M. Johnston (ed.), *The Valley of the Six Nations* (Toronto, University of Toronto Press, 1964), pp. xxxiii ff.; Trelease, p. 51; Cotterill, *The Southern Indians*, pp. 17 ff; Theda Perdue, *Slavery and the Evolution of Cherokee Society, 1540–1866* (Knoxville, Tenn., University of Tennessee Press, 1979), pp. 26, 29–31; Charles M. Hudson (ed.), *Four Centuries of Southern Indians* (Athens, Ga, University of Georgia Press, 1975), Intro-duction, p. 6.

38 Kupperman, pp. 173, 182; Salisbury, *Manitou and Providence*, p. 189.

39 Sheehan, *Savagism and Civility*, pp. 102 ff.

40 Axtell, *The European and the Indian*, pp. 256–62; Rich, p. 102; John K. Mahon, 'Anglo-American methods of Indian warfare, 1676–1794', *Mississippi Valley Historical Review*, vol. 45, 1958–9, p. 255.

41 Jennings, p. 85; Axtell, *The European and the Indian*, pp. 25–6; Rich, p. 102.

42 Salisbury, *Manitou and Providence*, p. 9; Rich, p. 296.

43 Perdue, *Slavery and the Evolution of Cherokee Society*, pp. 32–5; quotation from Robert F. Berkhofer, Jr, 'The political context of a new Indian history', *Pacific Historical Review*, vol. 40, August 1971, p. 379; Martin, pp. 10–11, 152–3; Jennings, pp. 102 ff; Sheehan, *Savagism and Civility*, pp. 137–9.

44 Jennings, pp. 67–8, 85–7ff.

45 ibid., p. 87; Rich, pp. 252–3; Jacobs, 'The fatal confrontation', pp. 306–7.

46 Martin, ch. 6 and *passim*.

47 Lewis O. Saum, *The Fur Trader and the Indian* (Seattle, Wash., University of Washington Press, 1965), pp. 27–8, 40, 46, 206–10, 236–44, and ch. 7.

48 Jennings, pp. 88–91; Salisbury, *Manitou and Providence*, pp. 186–7, 202, 238–9.

49 Henry F. Dobyns, 'Estimating Aboriginal American population. An appraisal of techniques with a new hemispheric estimate', *Current Anthropology*, vol. 7, October 1966, pp. 395–416, and the commentary on pp. 417 ff; Kupperman, pp. 81–5; Salisbury, *Manitou and Providence*, pp. 187, 227; Martin, pp. 179–82; Sheehan, *Savagism and Civility*, pp. 100–1; Jennings, pp. 62–3, 65–7; Jacobs, 'The fatal confrontation', pp. 283–4, 296; Jacobs, *Dispossessing*, pp. 6, 152, 154–5, 160–1; Cotterill, *The Southern Indians*, p. 17; W. J. Eccles, *France in America* (New York, Harper & Row, 1972; 1973 edn), pp. 121–2; Gary M. Walton and James F.

Shepherd, *The Economic Rise of Early America* (Cambridge, Cambridge University Press, 1979), pp. 39–40, 50, 150–1.

50 Sheehan, *Savagism and Civility*, pp. 141–2, 179–80; Axtell, *The European and the Indian*, p. 249; Cotterill, *The Southern Indians*, p. 26.

51 Kupperman, pp. 5–6; Axtell, *The European and the Indian*, p. 248; Salisbury, *Manitou and Providence*, pp. 7–8, 190–2, 209–10, 215–16; Alfred W. Crosby, 'Virgin soil epidemics as a factor in the Aboriginal depopulation of America', *William and Mary Quarterly*, vol. 33, 1976, pp. 289–99; Grenfell Price, *White Settlers and Native Peoples*, pp. 6, 19–20.

52 A. L. Kroeber, *Anthropology* (New York, Harcourt, Brace & World, 1923; 1948 edn), pp. 182 ff.

53 Kupperman, pp. 6, 31–2, 111, 115; Axtell, *The European and the Indian*, pp. 251–2.

54 Kenneth F. Kiple and Virginia Himmelsteib King, *Another Dimension to the Black Diaspora. Diet, Disease and Racism* (Cambridge, Cambridge University Press, 1981), pp. 11, 23, 31, 35, 67, 139, 142, 144.

55 Jennings, pp. 72–3.

56 See Eric Foner's interesting discussion of non-white peasant groups in different parts of the world in *Nothing But Freedom. Emancipation and its Legacy* (Baton Rouge, La, and London, Louisiana State University Press, 1983), pp. 30 ff. and *passim*.

57 P. Richard Metcalf, 'Who should rule at home? Native American politics and Indian–White relations', *Journal of American History*, vol. LXI, no. 3, December 1974, pp. 652–3.

58 ibid., pp. 654–7; see also Salisbury, *Manitou and Providence*, pp. 215, 226, 229.

59 Salisbury, *Manitou and Providence*, pp. 231–5, quotation, p. 232; Sheehan, *Savagism and Civility*, pp. 155–7.

60 Kupperman, pp. 49–50; Salisbury, *Manitou and Providence*, pp. 187–8.

61 D. W. Hoover, *The Red and the Black*, p. 19.

62 Morton H. Fried, *The Notion of Tribe* (Menlo Park, Calif., Cummings, 1975), Preface, p. 98, and *passim*.

63 Gary Clayton Anderson, *Kinsmen of Another Kind. Dakota–White Relations in the Upper Mississippi Valley, 1650–1852* (Lincoln, Nebr., University of Nebraska Press, 1984).

64 Cotterill, *The Southern Indians*, p. 12; Berkhofer, 'The political context', pp. 363–80; Jennings, pp. 110–11, 113–18 ⎟

65 See Robert F. Berkhofer, Jr, 'Native Americans', in John Higham (ed.), *Ethnic Leadership in America* (Baltimore, Md, Johns Hopkins University Press, 1978), pp. 121–2.

66 Jennings, p. 51.

67 See Howard Peckham, *Pontiac and the Indian Uprising* (Princeton, NJ, Princeton University Press, 1947).

68 Grenfell Price, pp. 27–8; Salisbury, *Manitou and Providence*, p. 227; S. Lyman Tyler, *A History of Indian Policy* (Washington, DC, Dept of the Interior, Bureau of Indian Affairs, 1973), p. 29; F. W. Hodge (ed.), *Handbook of American Indians North of Mexico* (New York, Rowman & Littlefield, 1971), pt two, p. 25.

69 Wilcomb E. Washburn, 'The moral and legal justifications for dispossessing the Indians', in Smith (ed.), *Seventeenth-Century America*, pp. 15–18 ff.

70 Reginald Horsman, *Expansion and American Indian Policy, 1783–1812*

(Lansing, Mich., Michigan State University Press, 1967), p. 15; Prucha, *American Indian Policy*, ch. 1.

71 Parkman, p. 31.

72 Nash, 'Red, white and black', p. 13.

73 Alvin M. Josephy, Jr, *The Indian Heritage of America* (Harmondsworth, Penguin, 1968), pp. 288–9; Walton and Shepherd, p. 32; Grenfell Price, pp. 25–6.

74 Eccles, p. 141.

75 Stanley L. Robe, 'Wild men and Spain's brave new world', in Dudley and Novak (eds), *The Wild Man Within*, pp. 39–46, 52.

76 Olson, pp. 11–15; Thomas F. Gossett, *Race: The History of an Idea in America* (New York, Schocken Books, 1970), pp. 13–14.

77 Josephy, *Heritage*, pp. 290–6, 299–300; Walton and Shepherd, p. 33; Grenfell Price, pp. 25–7, 194–5; S. F. Cook, *The Indian Versus the Spanish Mission*, Vol. III (Berkeley, Calif., University of California Press, 1943), pp. 113–28; Edward H. Spicer, *Cycles of Conquest. The Impact of Spain, Mexico, and the United States on the Indians of the Southwest, 1533–1960* (Tucson, Ariz., University of Arizona Press, 1962); Robert Heizer and Alan F. Almquist, *The Other Californians* (Berkeley, Calif., University of California Press, 1971), pp. 1–138.

78 Jack D. L. Holmes, 'Spanish policy toward the southern Indians in the 1790s', in Hudson (ed.), *Four Centuries*, pp. 68 ff.

79 Jacobs, *Dispossessing*, pp. 125, 153.

80 Robe, p. 48.

81 Eccles, pp. 11, 146; Jennings, pp. 96–7; Diamond Jenness, *The Indians of Canada* (Ottawa, National Museum of Canada, Bulletin 65, Anthropological Series no. 15, 1967 edn), p. 259.

82 Eccles, p. 13; Grenfell Price, pp. 59, 64.

83 Gustave Lanctot, *Canada and the American Revolution* (Cambridge, Mass., Harvard University Press, 1967), p. 3; Eccles, pp. 8, 66, 158 ff.; though James W. Covington, 'Relations between the eastern Timucuan Indians and the French and Spanish, 1564–1567', in Hudson (ed.), *Four Centuries*, p. 24, notes that hostilities broke out between the French, Spanish and Timucuan Indians in Florida sooner than they did between whites and Indians in Virginia and New England.

84 Tyler, *A History of Indian Policy*, p. 18; on the vexed question of Indian population figures see also Dobyns, and Josephy, *Heritage*, pp. 61–2.

85 Eccles, p. 176; Saum, pp. 75, 86; Rich, pp. 103–4; Stanley, *New France*, pp. 28–9, 39, 85, 258; Jenness, pp. 251–8.

86 See, for instance, Stanley, *New France*, p. 49.

87 Saum, pp. 71 ff.

88 Jaenen, pp. 277, 290.

89 Eccles, pp. 57–8, 78, 168–9, 180; Grenfell Price, pp. 63–4.

90 Gossett, p. 24.

91 Vaughan, 'From white man to redskin', p. 950; Slotkin, pp. 203–4, 266–7, 315–16, 333–4; John Hopkins Kennedy, *Jesuit and Savage in New France* (New Haven, Conn., Yale University Press, 1950), ch. 10.

92 Parkman, pp. 417–18.

93 Jaenen, pp. 268–9; Parkman, pp. 201–3.

94 Axtell, *The European and the Indian*, pp. 69 ff.; Parkman, pp. 225, 451; Slotkin, pp. 26–7, 124; Tyler, *A History of Indian Policy*, p. 26.

95 Jordan, pp. 210–11.

96 Stanley, *New France*, p. 83; Parkman, p. 227.
97 Eccles, p. 25; Parkman, pp. 225, 452; Axtell, *The European and the Indian*, pp. 71–6.
98 Parkman, p. 451; Axtell, *The European and the Indian*, pp. 76, 80.
99 Trigger, pp. 119, 121, 133–4.
100 Axtell, *The European and the Indian*, p. 72; Grenfell Price, p. 65.
101 Eccles, pp. 39–40 ff., 46, 77.
102 Eccles, pp. 158, 171.
103 Hodge, pt one, pp. 385–6, 619, 926; pt two, pp. 29, 69, 231, 409; Jacobs, *Dispossessing*, pp. 154–5; Salisbury, *Manitou and Providence*, p. 238; Cotterill, *The Southern Indians*, pp. 30–6; Nash, 'The image of the Indian', p. 74; Alfred Tamarin, *We Have Not Vanished. Eastern Indians of the United States* (Chicago, Follett, 1974), pp. 14, 16, 18–20 and *passim*.

CHAPTER 2

1 See James H. O'Donnell III, *Southern Indians in the American Revolution* (Knoxville, Tenn., University of Tennessee Press, 1973); Barbara Graymont, *The Iroquois in the American Revolution* (Syracuse, NY, Syracuse University Press, 1972); William T. Hagan, *American Indians* (Chicago, University of Chicago Press, 1961), pp. 31–9.
2 Cotterill, *The Southern Indians*, pp. 57–60; Holmes, 'Spanish policy', pp. 66, 77; Horsman, *Expansion and American Indian Policy*, chs I and II; Prucha, *American Indian Policy*, ch. II; *The Federalist Papers*, 5th printing (New York, Mentor Books, 1961), pp. 44, 161, 163, 165, 268–9; Allan Nevins, *The American States during and after the Revolution, 1775–1789* (New York, Augustus M. Kelley, 1969; reprint of 1924 edn) pp. 544–6, 600, 607, 625, 658–9 and Ch. 13.
3 James Hugo Johnston, *Race Relations in Virginia and Miscegenation in the South, 1776–1860* (Amherst, Mass., University of Massachusetts Press, 1970), pp. 272–92; Jordan, *White over Black*, p. 169; Almon Wheeler Lauber, *Indian Slavery in Colonial Times within the Present Limits of the United States* (New York, Columbia University, 1913), pp. 107, 287; Lorenzo Johnston Greene, *The Negro in Colonial New England, 1620–1776* (Port Washington, NY, Kennikat Press, 1969), pp. 160–3, 198–201; Sidney Kaplan, 'The "domestic insurrections" of the Declaration of Independence', *Journal of Negro History*, vol. 61, July 1976, pp. 243–55; Benjamin Quarles, *The Negro in the American Revolution* (Chapel Hill, NC, University of North Carolina Press, 1961), pp. 19, 21, 52, 125; A. M. Davis, 'The employment of Indian auxiliaries in the American War', *English Historical Review*, vol. 2, 1887, pp. 709–28; D. W. Hoover, *The Red and the Black*, pp. 49–50; William S. Willis, '"Divide and rule": red, white and black in the Southeast', *Journal of Negro History*, vol. 48, 1963, pp. 157–76.
4 Maldwyn A. Jones, *American Immigration* (Chicago, University of Chicago Press, 1960), p. 40.
5 Horsman, *Race and Manifest Destiny*, ch. 1; Vaughan, 'From white man to redskin', pp. 944–7.
6 Duncan MacLeod, *Slavery, Race and the American Revolution* (Cambridge, Cambridge University Press, 1974), p. 183 and *passim*.
7 Nevins, ch. 10, especially pp. 420 and 467; Prucha, *American Indian Policy*, pp. 36–9.

8 Grenfell Price, *White Settlers and Native Peoples*, pp. 70, 84; Tyler, *A History of Indian Policy*, p. 36.
9 Horsman, *Expansion and American Indian Policy*, pp. 55, 171 and *passim*.
10 Rusel Lawrence Barsh and James Youngblood Henderson, *The Road. Indian Tribes and Political Liberty* (Berkeley, Calif., University of California Press, 1980), pp. 32–3.
11 C. M. Johnston (ed.), *The Valley of the Six Nations*, p. xxxiv; Cotterill, *The Southern Indians*, p. 58; Michael D. Green, 'Alexander McGillivray', in Edmunds (ed.), *American Indian Leaders*, pp. 44–5.
12 Cotterill, *The Southern Indians*, p. 34.
13 James H. O'Donnell III, '*Joseph Brant*', in Edmunds (ed.), *American Indian Leaders*, pp. 29, 33, 36; C. M. Johnston (ed.), *The Valley of the Six Nations*, pp. xxxix, xliv–xlv; Grenfell Price, p. 68. The British, in fairness, seem to have denied Brant's claims in order to prevent his alienating some of the recently granted land.
14 Walton and Shepherd, *The Economic Rise of Early America*, pp. 178–87.
15 ibid., pp. 171–2.
16 Eric Foner, 'Abolitionism and the labor movement in antebellum America', in Christine Bolt and Seymour Drescher (eds), *Anti-Slavery, Religion and Reform* (Folkestone, Dawson and Hamden, Conn., Archon, 1980), pp. 254–71, quotation from p. 262.
17 Eric Foner, *Tom Paine and Revolutionary America* (London, Oxford University Press, 1976), quotation from p. 94, see also pp. 249–51, 228–9; MacLeod, p. 69.
18 Henry Adams, *History of the United States of America during the Administrations of Jefferson and Madison* (abridged and edited by Ernest Samuels; Chicago, University of Chicago Press, 1967, from 1921 edn), p. 129.
19 Jordan, p. 90.
20 Foner, *Tom Paine*, pp. 88–9.
21 ibid., pp. 101–3.
22 See Prucha, *American Indian Policy*, pp. 40 ff.; Horsman, *Expansion and American Indian Policy*, p. 83, chs IV, VI; Tyler, *A History of Indian Policy*, p. 41.
23 Prucha, *American Indian Policy*, pp. 151–5, 215; Drinnon, *Facing West*, pp. 74, 76, 99; Frederick M. Binder, *The Color Problem in Early National America as Viewed by John Adams, Jefferson and Jackson* (The Hague, Moulton, 1968).
24 Jordan, ch. XII; Bernard W. Sheehan, *Seeds of Extinction. Jeffersonian Philanthropy and the American Indian* (Chapel Hill, NC, University of North Carolina Press, 1973), chs I and III; Drinnon, chs VIII and IX; Horsman, *Expansion and American Indian Policy*, ch. VII and *passim*; Ronald Takaki, *Iron Cages, Race and Culture in 19th-Century America* (London, Athlone, 1980), ch. III.
25 Drinnon, pp. 86, 88; Sheehan, *Seeds of Extinction*, p. 152.
26 Takaki, pp. 40 ff., 64–5; Jordan, pp. 462 ff.
27 Max Beloff, *Thomas Jefferson and American Democracy* (Harmondsworth, Penguin, 1972), pp. 60–1.
28 Drinnon, pp. 82, 95–8; Takaki, pp. 55, 62; Sheehan, *Seeds of Extinction*, pp. 191, 209–10.
29 Drinnon, pp. 84–5; Takaki, p. 59.
30 Horsman, *Expansion and American Indian Policy*, pp. 112, 157; Arthur H. De Rosier, Jr, 'Myths and realities in Indian westward removal. The Choctaw

example', in Hudson (ed.), *Four Centuries*, p. 86; Drinnon, pp. 86–8; Takaki, pp. 60–2; Cotterill, *The Southern Indians*, pp. 139–41, 150, 153; George Dewey Harmon, *Sixty Years of Indian Affairs. Political, Economic and Diplomatic, 1789–1850* (Chapel Hill, NC, University of North Carolina Press, 1941), pp. 158–9; Sheehan, *Seeds of Extinction*, ch. IV, pp. 141–2, and chs VI and VIII.

31 Drinnon, pp. 84–5; Sheehan, *Seeds of Extinction*, p. 246; Beloff, p. 148 (source of quotation).

32 Arrell M. Gibson, *The American Indian. Prehistory to the Present* (Lexington, Mass., D. C. Heath, 1980), pp. 312 ff. Horsman, *Expansion and American Indian Policy*, p. 114; Takaki, p. 56; Beloff, pp. 148–9; Sheehan, *Seeds of Extinction*, pp. 224–6, 247–8.

33 On the dangers of this tendency in Jeffersonian democracy, see Beloff, p. 185.

34 Drinnon, p. 199.

35 G. A. Shultz, *An Indian Canaan. Isaac McCoy and the Vision of an Indian State* (Norman, Okla, University of Oklahoma Press, 1972), p. 33; and Calvin Colton (ed.), *The Works of Henry Clay*, Vol. 7 (New York, Putnam, 1904), p. 655.

36 See, for instance, E. L. Fox, *The American Colonization Society, 1817–1840* (Baltimore, Md, Johns Hopkins University Press, 1919); Louis Filler, *The Crusade Against Slavery, 1830–1860* (New York, Harper Torchbooks, 1963), pp. 20–2; August Meier and Elliott Rudwick, 'The role of blacks in the abolitionist movement', in John Bracey, Jr, August Meier and Elliott Rudwick, *Blacks in the Abolitionist Movement* (Belmont, Calif., Wadsworth, 1917), pp. 108–11; Leon F. Litwack, *North of Slavery. The Negro in the Free States, 1790–1860* (Chicago, University of Chicago Press, 1965), pp. 20–9 and *passim*.

37 See Robert H. Keller, Jr, *American Protestantism and United States Indian Policy, 1869–82* (Lincoln, Nebr., University of Nebraska Press, 1983), pp. 146–7.

38 Metcalf, 'Who should rule at home?', pp. 657–61.

39 See Cotterill, *The Southern Indians*, pp. 189 ff., 224–5, and chs IV–VI, VIII, IX; Martin Zanger, 'Red Bird', pp. 64–87, and Green, 'Alexander McGillivray', pp. 41–63, in Edmunds (ed.), *American Indian Leaders*; R. S. Cotterill, 'Federal Indian management in the South, 1789–1825', *Mississippi Valley Historical Review*, vol. 20, 1933–4, pp. 333–51, especially p. 346; De Rosier, 'Myths and Realities', pp. 88–9; Metcalf, pp. 661–4; Mary E. Young, 'Indian removal and land allotment: the Civilized Tribes and Jacksonian justice', reprinted in Edward Pessen (ed.), *New Perspectives on Jacksonian Parties and Politics* (Boston, Mass., Allyn & Bacon, 1970), pp. 240–57; and Henry T. Malone, *Cherokees of the Old South. A People in Transition* (Athens, Ga, University of Georgia Press, 1956), pp. 74–90.

40 Robert T. Handy, *A Christian America. Protestant Hopes and Historical Realities* (New York, Oxford University Press, 1971), quotation from p. 210.

41 See James D. Essig, *The Bonds of Wickedness. American Evangelicals against Slavery, 1770–1808* (Philadelphia, Pa, Temple University Press, 1982); Donald\G. Mathews, 'Religion and slavery: the case of the American South', in Bolt and Drescher (eds), *Anti-Slavery, Religion and Reform*, pp. 208–32; W. P. Harrison, *The Gospel among the Slaves. A Short Account of Missionary Operations among the African Slaves of the Southern States* (Nash-

ville, Tenn., Publishing House of the M. E. Church, South, 1893), pp. 149–50.

42 See R. Pierce Beaver, *Church, State and the American Indians* (St Louis, Mo, Concordia, 1966), ch. 1; Henry Warner Bowden, *American Indians and Christian Missions. Studies in Cultural Conflict* (Chicago, University of Chicago Press, 1981), ch. 6; Sheehan, *Seeds of Extinction*, pp. 120–30; Robert H. Keller, Jr, 'Christian Indian missions and the American frontier', *American Indian Journal*, vol. 5, April 1979, pp. 19–29; Robert H. Keller, Jr, 'Church joins state to civilize Indians, 1776–1869', *American Indian Journal*, vol. 5, July 1979, pp. 7–16; Robert F. Berkhofer, Jr, *Salvation and the Savage* (Louisville, Ky, University of Kentucky Press, 1965), ch. 3; Lawrence F. Schmeckebier, *The Office of Indian Affairs. Its History, Activities and Organization* (Baltimore, Md, Johns Hopkins University Press, 1927; reprinted New York, AMS Press, 1972), p. 40; Schultz, pp. 34–5; Schultz suggests that the beneficiaries from the Civilization Fund put in 'much more than they received'.

43 Sheehan, *Seeds of Extinction*, p. 126.

44 Schultz, pp. 32–3, 42, 57–8; Carl Coke Rister, *Baptist Missions among the American Indians* (Atlanta, Ga, Home Mission Board, Southern Baptist Convention, 1944), pt II, especially pp. 42, 44–5, 48–9.

45 Rister, pp. 28, 31–2, 42, 48, 55; Isaac McCoy, *History of Baptist Indian Missions* (Washington, DC, and New York, 1840), pp. 555, 575–6; Oliver Wendell Elsbree, *The Rise of the Missionary Spirit in America* (Williamsport, Pa, the Williamsport Printing and Binding Company, 1928), pp. 74–5; Lydia Maria Child, *The First Settlers of New-England* (Boston, Mass, Munroe & Francis, 1829), pp. 277, 282; Isaac McCoy, *The Annual Register of Indian Affairs within the Indian (or Western) Territory*, Vol. 1 (J. Meeker, Shawanoe Mission, 1835), pp. 34–5.

46 See Sheehan, *Seeds of Extinction*, chs V and IX; Schultz, pp. 50–1; Anthony F. C. Wallace, 'New religions among the Delaware Indians, 1600–1900', *Southwestern Journal of Anthropology*, vol. 12, Spring 1956, pp. 1–21; Cotterill, *The Southern Indians*, pp. 226–9; Keller, 'Christian Indian missions'; Berkhofer, *Salvation and the Savage*, pp. 101–6; Horsman, *Race and Manifest Destiny*, pp. 200–1.

47 See Bowden, *American Indians and Christian Missions*, ch. 6.

48 See, for instance, Eugene Genovese, *Roll, Jordan, Roll. The World that the Slaves Made* (New York, Pantheon, 1974), pp. 168–284; Lawrence W. Levine, *Black Culture and Black Consciousness. Afro-American Folk Brought from Slavery to Freedom* (New York, Oxford University Press, 1977), pp. 1–80.

49 Mathews, 'Religion and slavery', pp. 216, 220–9; and see also Elsbree, p. 62.

50 See C. M. Johnston (ed.), *The Valley of the Six Nations*, pp. lxxix–lxxxviii, 232–68; quotation from p. 268.

51 Rich, *The Fur Trade*, p. 256.

52 Joseph Tuckerman, *A Discourse, Preached Before the Society for Propagating the Gospel Among the Indians and Others in North America, November 1, 1821* (Cambridge, Mass., Hilliard & Metcalf, 1821), pp. 15–16.

53 Prucha, *American Indian Policy*, pp. 88 ff; Royal B. Way, 'The United States factory system for trading with the Indians, 1796–1822', *Mississippi Valley Historical Review*, vol. 6, June 1919–March 1920, pp. 228–30, 234–5.

54 William M. Neil, 'The territorial governor as Indian superintendent in the

trans-Mississippi West', *Mississippi Valley Historical Review*, vol. 43, September 1956, pp. 213–37; Tyler, *A History of Indian Policy*, pp. 46–7; Ronald N. Satz, *American Indian Policy in the Jacksonian Era* (Lincoln, Nebr., University of Nebraska Press, 1975), pp. 152–3, 155; Prucha, *American Indian Policy*, ch. IV; Francis Paul Prucha, *Broadax and Bayonet. The Role of the United States Army in the Development of the Northwest, 1815–1860* (Lincoln, Nebr., University of Nebraska Press, 1973 edn), pp. 67 ff. and *passim*.
55 See Glyndon G. Van Deusen, *The Jacksonian Era, 1828–1848* (New York, Harper Torchbooks, 1963), pp. 34–5.
56 ibid., p. 36.
57 Lynn L. Marshall, 'Opposing Democratic and Whig concepts of party organisation', in Pessen (ed.), *New Perspectives*, pp. 38–65.
58 Satz, pp. 164 ff.
59 Prucha, *American Indian Policy*, pp. 260–1, 270; Satz, ch. 7 and *passim*; see also De Rosier, 'Myths and realities', pp. 92–5, on two contrasting Choctaw agents.
60 Horsman, *Race and Manifest Destiny*, pp. 194 ff.; Takaki, pp. 77–8, ch. V; Michael Paul Rogin, *Fathers and Children. Andrew Jackson and the Subjugation of the American Indian* (New York, Knopf, 1975), p. 165; Van Deusen, pp. 48–9, quotation from p. 49; Satz, pp. 3–4; Marvin Meyers, *The Jacksonian Persuasion. Politics and Belief* (Stanford, NJ, Stanford University Press, 1968 edn), pp. 134–5; Barsh and Henderson, pp. 45–9; Sheehan, *Seeds of Extinction*, pp. 256–60, 265; Young, 'Indian removal', pp. 243–5. Young, 'Indian removal', p. 241, gives nearly 60,000 Cherokees, Creeks, Choctaws and Chickasaws, living on a 25 million acre domain, whereas Takaki, p. 78, estimates the Five Tribes at some 70,000.
61 Horsman, *Race and Manifest Destiny*, pp. 203 ff.; Satz, pp. 26, 43, 55–6.
62 See 'William Penn' [pseud. Jeremiah Evarts), *Essays on the Present Crisis in the Condition of the American Indian* (Philadelphia, Pa, Thomas Kite, 1830), pp. 86–90; Colton (ed.), pp. 649–51; *Speech of Mr Frelinghuysen . . .* April 6, 1830 (Washington, DC, 1830), pp. 6–17, 22, 25–6, 28; Prucha, *American Indian Policy*, p. 243; Schultz, pp. 130–2; Louis Ruchames (ed.), *The Letters of William Lloyd Garrison*, Vol. IV (Cambridge, Mass., Harvard University Press, 1975), pp. 120–1; Wendell Phillips and Francis Jackson Garrison, *William Lloyd Garrison, 1805–79*, Vol. 1 (New York, Century, 1885–9), pp. 56, 182–3, 232; Gerda Lerner, *The Grimké Sisters from South Carolina. Pioneers for Women's Rights and Abolition* (New York, Schocken Books, 1973), pp. 92, 270–1; Child, *The First Settlers*, pp. 263–4, 277, 281–2; Lydia Maria Child, *Letters of Lydia Maria Child* (Boston, Mass., 1883), p. 220; Lydia Maria Child, *Letters from New York* (London, 1843), pp. 280–2; Isaac McCoy, *The Annual Register*, Vol. 3 (J. G. Pratt, 1837), p. 69.
63 Frances Trollope, *Domestic Manners of the Americans*, 5th edn (London, Richard Bentley, 1839), p. 175.
64 See, for instance, 'William Penn', *Essays*, pp. 96–100; Satz, pp. 26–7, suggests that the protagonists in the removal debate disagreed about the nature of the western territory but that there were some fears that it might be a wasteland; this is denied by Francis Paul Prucha, 'Indian removal and the Great American Desert', *Indiana Magazine of History*, vol. 59, December 1963, p. 321.
65 Tyler, *A History of Indian Policy*, p. 58.
66 See, for instance, Sheehan, *Seeds of Extinction*, pp. 268–70.

67 Satz, p. 97; Alban W. Hoopes, *Indian Affairs and their Administration. With Special Reference for the Far West, 1849–1860* (New York, Kraus Reprint Co., 1972; originally 1932), p. 8.
68 Satz, ch. 1; Takaki, ch. V; Rogin, *Fathers and Children*; Francis Paul Prucha, 'Andrew Jackson's Indian policy: a reassessment', *Journal of American History*, vol. LVI, December 1969, pp. 527–39; James W. Silver, 'A counter-proposal to the Indian removal policy of Andrew Jackson', *Journal of Mississippi History*, vol. 4, October 1942, pp. 207–15; Horsman, *Race and Manifest Destiny*, pp. 201–2.
69 Robert W. Johannsen (ed.), *The Letters of Stephen A. Douglas* (Urbana, Ill., University of Illinois Press, 1961), p. 29.
70 Schultz, pp. 61–3, 95–8, 128, 138, ch. VII: *Address to Philanthropists in the United States, Generally, and to Christians in Particular, on the Condition and Prospects of the American Indians* (Neosho River, I. T., 1831), pp. 7–8; McCoy, *History of Baptist Missions*, pp. 33, 35, 38–41, 380, 383, 496, 583.
71 See Drinnon, ch. XIV: Herman J. Viola, *Thomas L. McKenney. Architect of America's Early Indian Policy, 1816–1830* (Chicago, Swallow, 1974); Francis Paul Prucha, 'Thomas L. McKenney and the New York Indian Board', *Mississippi Valley Historical Review*, vol. 48, March 1962, pp. 635–55; Thomas L. McKenney, *Memoirs, Official and Personal* (Lincoln, Nebr., University of Nebraska Press, 1973; reprint of 1846); Herman J. Viola, 'Thomas L. McKenney, 1824–30', in Robert M. Kvasnicka and Herman J. Viola (eds), *The Commissioners of Indian Affairs, 1824–1977* (Lincoln, Nebr., University of Nebraska Press, 1979), pp. 1–7.
72 Satz, pp. 44–9; Joe Burke, 'The Cherokee cases. A study in law, politics, and morality', *Stanford Law Review*, vol. 21, February 1969, pp. 500–31; Barsh and Henderson, ch. 5.
73 Schultz, pp. 184–5; Satz, chs 3 and 4; Arthur H. De Rosier, Jr, *The Removal of the Choctaw Indians* (Knoxville, Tenn., University of Tennessee Press, 1970), p. 125; Takaki, p. 100; J. R. Pole, *The Pursuit of Equality in American History* (Berkeley, Calif., University of California Press, 1978), pp. 129–47, quotation, p. 146; Young, 'Indian removal', p. 255; Mary E. Young, 'The Creek frauds. A study in conscience and corruption', *Mississippi Valley Historical Review*, vol. 42, December 1955, pp. 411–37; Mary E. Young, *Redskins, Ruffleshirts and Rednecks. Indian Allotments in Alabama and Mississippi, 1830–1860* (Norman, Okla., University of Oklahoma Press, 1961); Jay P. Kinney, *A Continent Lost – A Civilization Won. Indian Land Tenure in America* (Baltimore, Md, Johns Hopkins University Press, 1937); Paul W. Gates, 'Indian allotments preceding the Dawes Act', in John G. Clark (ed.), *The Frontier Challenge. Responses to the Trans-Mississippi West* (Lawrence, Kans, University of Kansas Press, 1971), pp. 141–70.
74 Young, 'Indian removal', pp. 254–5; Satz, pp. 53, 86, 108–9.
75 Robert A. Trennert, Jr, *Alternative to Extinction. Federal Indian Policy and the Beginnings of the Reservation System, 1846–51* (Philadelphia, Pa, Temple University Press, 1975), pp. 41–2; Kvasnicka and Viola, *The Commissioners*, *passim*; Michael C. Coleman, 'Not race, but grace: Presbyterian missionaries and American Indians, 1837–1893', *Journal of American History*, vol. 67, no. 1, June 1980, pp. 41–60, esp. 42–9; Francis Paul Prucha, 'American Indian policy in the 1840s. Visions of reform', in J. G. Clark (ed.), *The Frontier Challenge*, pp. 82–98, 104; Satz, ch. 9; Hoopes, *Indian Affairs and their Administration*, p. 238; Christine Bolt, 'The anti-slavery origins of concern for the American Indians', in Bolt and Drescher (eds), *Anti-Slavery*,

319

Religion and Reform, p. 243; Henry E. Fritz, *The Movement for Indian Assimilation, 1860–90* (Philadelphia, Pa, University of Pennsylvania Press, 1963), pp. 34–5; Robert Winston Mardock, *The Reformers and the American Indian* (Columbia, Ma., University of Missouri Press, 1971), pp. 8–11.

76   Satz, pp. 50–2, 86–7, 112–15, 143–5, 149–50, 215–21, 224, 233–4, 246–7 ff., chs 5 and 8 generally; De Rosier, 'Myths and realities', pp. 89–91; Horsman, *Race and Manifest Destiny*, pp. 203–4; Prucha, *American Indian Policy*, pp. 261–9; Annie H. Abel, 'The history of events resulting in Indian consolidation west of the Mississippi', *American Historical Association, Annual Report for the Year 1906*, 1, 1908, pp. 233–450; Annie H. Abel, 'Proposals for an Indian state, 1778–1878', *American Historical Association, Annual Report for the Year 1907*, 1, 1908, pp. 87–104; Trennert, *Alternative to Extinction*, pp. 29–32, chs 2, 6; Robert A. Trennert, Jr, 'William Medill, 1845–49', in Kvasnicka and Viola (eds), *The Commissioners*, pp. 29–39.

77   See Robert M. Utley, *Frontiersman in Blue. The United States Army and the Indian, 1848–1865* (New York, Macmillan, 1967); Prucha, *Broadax and Bayonet*; Pole, p. 151; Hoopes, *Indian Affairs and their Administration*, pp. 3–4.

78   Hoopes, *Indian Affairs and their Administration*, pp. 1, 3.

79   Johannsen (ed.), *The Letters of Stephen A. Douglas*, p. 270.

80   Trennert, *Alternative to Extinction*, pp. 30–1, 193 ff. and *passim*; Hoopes, *Indian Affairs and their Administration*, pp. 50–1, 129; Kvasnicka and Viola (eds), pp. 34, 44, 62, 71, 83; Alban W. Hoopes, 'Thomas S. Twiss, Indian agent on the Upper Platte, 1855–61', *Mississippi Valley Historical Review*, vol. 20, 1933–4, pp. 359–64.

81   Tyler, *A History of Indian Policy*, p. 74.

82   Clifford Drury, *Marcus and Narcissa Whitman, and the Opening of Old Oregon* (Glendale, Calif., Arthur H. Clark, 1972, 2 vols); Alvin M. Josephy, Jr, *The Nez Percé Indians and the Opening of the Northwest* (New Haven, Conn, Yale University Press, 1965); William E. Unrau, *The Kansa Indians. A History of the Wind People, 1673–1873* (Norman, Okla, University of Oklahoma Press, 1971); Roy W. Meyer, *History of the Santee Sioux. United States Indian Policy on Trial* (Lincoln, Nebr., University of Nebraska Press, 1967); Trennert, *Alternative to Extinction*, pp. 134–6; Hoopes, *Indian Affairs and their Administration*, p. 80; see W. C. Barclay, *History of Methodist Missions: Missionary Motivation and Expansion*, Vol. 1 (New York, Board of Missions and Church Extension of the Methodist Church, 1949), pp. 234, 237, 244.

83   On the limited role of the Indian office by the 1860s, see Paul Stuart, *The Indian Office. Growth and Development of an American Institution* (Ann Arbor, Mich., University Microfilms International, V.M.I. Research Press, 1979), p. 152.

84   Horsman, *Race and Manifest Destiny*, pp. 205–7, chs 7–8; D. W. Hoover, *The Red and the Black*, ch. 4; Robert F. Berkhofer, Jr, *The White Man's Indian. Images of the American Indian from Columbus to the Present* (New York, Knopf, 1978), pts two and three; Ronald G. Walters, *American Reformers, 1815–1860* (New York, Hill & Wang, 1978), quotation from p. 194.

85   Grenfell Price, pp. 68–71; Rich, pp. 252–3, 255–6; E. Palmer Patterson, *The Canadian Indian. A History Since 1500* (Don Mills, Ontario, Collier-MacMillan, 1972), pp. 111 ff.; George Dewey Harmon, 'The Indian trust funds, 1797–1865', *Mississippi Valley Historical Review*, vol. 21, 1934–5, pp. 23–30.

CHAPTER 3

1 See George M. Fredrickson, *The Inner Civil War. Northern Intellectuals and the Crisis of the Union* (New York, Harper & Row, 1965), pp. 113–29; Eleanor Flexner, *Century of Struggle. The Woman's Rights Movement in the United States* (Cambridge, Mass., Belknap Press of Harvard University Press, 1973), p. 108; Filler, *The Crusade Against Slavery*, pp. 253–4; Barbara Leslie Epstein, *The Politics of Domesticity. Women, Evangelism and Temperance in Nineteenth-Century America* (Middletown, Conn., Wesleyan University Press, 1981), p. 93.

2 Edmund Jefferson Danziger, Jr, *Indians and Bureaucrats. Administering the Reservation Policy during the Civil War* (Urbana, Ill., University of Illinois Press, 1974), pp. 198–200 and *passim*.

3 Mardock, *The Reformers and the American Indian*, chs 1 and 3; Fritz, *The Movement for Indian Assimilation*, pp. 34–55; Danziger, pp. 36, 79–80, 162 ff.; Harry Kelsey, 'William P. Dole, 1861–65', in Kvasnicka and Viola (eds), *The Commissioners*, pp. 92–4, 95; Francis Paul Prucha, *American Indian Policy in Crisis. Christian Reformers and the Indian, 1865–1900* (Norman, Okla., University of Oklahoma Press, 1976), ch. 1.

4 Mardock, p. 13; Schmeckebier, *Office of Indian Affairs*, p. 47; Kelsey, 'William P. Dole', pp. 91–2, 95–6; Danziger, pp. 132–3, 164, 175, 186 ff., 199, 202–3; Harry Kelsey, 'William P. Dole and Mr. Lincoln's Indian Policy', *Journal of the West*, vol. 10, July 1971, pp. 484–92.

5 Allan Nevins, '1861: a primitive administration' and '1863: organization for war', in William R. Brock (ed.), *The Civil War* (New York, Harper & Row, 1969), pp. 132–46, quotations from pp. 133 and 146.

6 Gary L. Roberts, 'Dennis Nelson Cooley, 1865–66', in Kvasnicka and Viola (eds), *The Commissioners*, p. 105.

7 See Donald C. Chaput, 'Generals, Indian agents, politicians: the Doolittle survey of 1865', *Western Historical Quarterly*, vol. 3, July 1972, pp. 107–20; Stuart, *The Indian Office*, pp. 18, 30, 56–9; Fritz, *Assimilation*, pp. 62–6; Mardock, ch. 2, and pp. 30–1, 35, 37; Keller, *American Protestantism*, pp. 9–10.

8 See essays on Commissioners Cooley, Bogy and Taylor in Kvasnicka and Viola (eds), *The Commissioners*, pp. 99–122.

9 For a balanced modern account of the Freedmen's Bureau see Martin Abbott, *The Freedmen's Bureau in South Carolina, 1865–1872* (Chapel Hill, NC, University of North Carolina Press, 1967).

10 Foner, *Nothing But Freedom*, pp. 60 ff.

11 For a sympathetic account of Indian agents, see William E. Unrau, 'The civilian as Indian agent: villain or victim?', *Western Historical Quarterly*, vol. 3, no. 4, October 1972, pp. 405–20; on the Freedmen's Bureau, see Abbott, chs VIII and IX; Robert C. Morris, *Reading, 'Riting and Reconstruction. The Education of Freedmen in the South, 1861–1870* (Chicago, University of Chicago Press, 1981), pp. 13, 15, 43 ff., 59 ff., 226.

12 David Montgomery, *Beyond Equality. Labor and the Radical Republicans, 1862–1872* (New York, Vintage Books, 1972 edn), p. 177.

13 Carl R. Osthaus, *Freedmen, Philanthropy, and Fraud. A History of the Freedman's Savings Bank* (Urbana, Ill., University of Illinois Press, 1976), especially ch. 7.

14 See Keller, *American Protestantism*, ch. 1; Mardock, ch. 4; John Y. Simon (ed.), *The Papers of Ulysses S. Grant*, Vol. 1, *1837–61* (Carbondale, Ill.,

Southern Illinois University Press, 1967), pp. 296, 310; Grant, U. S., *Personal Memoirs of U. S. Grant. In Two Volumes* (London, 1885–6), Vol. I, pp. 204–5, Vol. II, p. 551; *A Compilation of the Messages and Papers of the Presidents, 1789–1897. Published by Authority of Congress by James D. Richardson, a Representative from the State of Tennessee*, Vol. VII (Washington, DC, Government Printing Office, 1898), p. 8; Prucha, *Crisis*, pp. 51–2.

15   Keller, *American Protestantism*, pp. 17–18, 28; Stuart, *The Indian Office*, p. 32; Fritz, *Assimilation*, ch. IV; Schmeckebier, pp. 56–7; Prucha, *Crisis*, pp. 31 ff.

16   Keller, *American Protestantism*, pp. 12, 196 ff., 237, and chs 2, 3, 7 and 9, quotation from p. 168; Loring B. Priest, *Uncle Sam's Stepchildren. The Reformation of United States Indian Policy, 1865–1887* (Lincoln, Nebr., University of Nebraska Press, 1975; reprint of 1942 edn), pp. 28–31, 39–40; Fritz, *Assimilation*, ch. IV; Stuart, *The Indian Office*, pp. 30–40; Mardock, pp. 48, 71, 74, 81–3; Peter J. Rahill, *The Catholic Indian Missions and Grant's Peace Policy, 1870–1884* (Washington, DC, Catholic University Press, 1953); Prucha, *Crisis*, pp. 55 ff.

17   Fritz, *Assimilation*, chs V, VI and VII; Keller, *American Protestantism*, pp. 44–5, 47–9, 52, 56, 67 ff., 71, 73, 94, 98 ff., 114, chs 6 and 7, pp. 146–7, 278–9; Lawrie Tatum, *Our Red Brothers and the Peace Policy of President Ulysses S. Grant* (Lincoln, Nebr., University of Nebraska Press, 1970; originally 1899), pp. 29–30; see also pp. xiv–xv, 56, 161, 165–6; Priest, pp. 31 ff.; Mardock, pp. 67–73, 88 ff., 98, 111, 113, 115 ff., 144 ff., ch. 6; Stuart, *The Indian Office*, pp. 77 ff., John Fahey, *The Flathead Indians* (Norman, Okla., University of Oklahoma Press, 1974), pp. 178–86.

18   Keller, pp. 73, 79, 81–4, 194–6, 202 and ch. 4; Prucha, *Crisis*, pp. 33 ff.; Stuart, *The Indian Office*, pp. 60–2, 64 and ch. V; William R. Brock, *Investigation and Responsibility: Public Responsibility in the United States, 1865–1900* (Cambridge, Cambridge University Press, 1984); *Summary, Work and Recommendations of Board of Indian Commissioners from Annual Reports, 1868–1915* (hereafter *Summary*) (1 April 1916), pp. 5, 8; Board of Indian Commissioners reference files (hereafter BIC files), entry 1395, tray 106, Bureau of Indian Affairs (hereafter BIA) records, RG 75, National Archives, Washington, DC; Priest, pp. 45–6 and ch. 4; Roy W. Meyer, 'Ezra A. Hayt, 1877–80', in Kvasnicka and Viola (eds), *The Commissioners*, pp. 155–66; Henry E. Fritz, 'The Board of Indian Commissioners and ethnocentric reform, 1878–1893', in Jane F. Smith and Robert M. Kvasnicka (eds), *Indian–White Relations. A Persistent Paradox* (Washington, DC, Howard University Press, 1976), pp. 57–61, 67; Mardock, pp. 105–6.

19   *Summary*, pp. 3–6.

20   *Summary*, p. 4.

21   Schmeckebier, pp. 56, 58, 64–5; Mardock, p. 105; Priest, ch. 8; Prucha, *Crisis*, pp. 64 ff.; Henry G. Waltmann, 'Ely Samuel Parker, 1869–71', in Kvasnicka and Viola (eds), *The Commissioners*, pp. 128–9.

22   Fritz, 'The Board of Indian Commissioners', in Smith and Kvasnicka, pp. 61–5.

23   Fritz, *Assimilation*, ch. VII; Keller, *American Protestantism*, p. 209, and Appendix 2, 'Church Performance'.

24   Keller, *American Protestantism*, chs 10 and 11; Mardock, pp. 130–1.

25   *Star Vindicator*, vol. 4, no. 9, 7 April 1877, in Choctaw Miscellaneous Papers, Miscellaneous Box, Western History Collections, University of Oklahoma Library (hereafter WHC); Priest, ch. 2; Prucha, *Crisis*, ch. 3;

322

Keller, *American Protestantism*, pp. 191 ff., 306; Mardock, pp. 33, 42–4, 81–2, 131, 140–1, 159 ff.; Keller, *American Protestantism*, pp. 31–2.

26 Keller, *American Protestantism*, p. 153; Prucha, *Crisis*, pp. 109–10, 129–30, 170 ff.; Mardock, pp. 96–7, 164; Priest, ch. 1; Prucha, *Crisis*, chs 4 and 13; Fahey, pp. 161–5; William T. Hagan, 'The reservation policy: too little and too late', in Smith and Kvasnicka (eds), *Indian–White Relations*, pp. 158–63.

27 Keller, *American Protestantism*, p. 298; Schmeckebier, pp. 227–9, quotation from p. 228; Virginia Allen, 'The white man's road. The physical and psychological impact of relocation on the Southern Plains Indians', *Journal of the History of Medicine*, vol. 30, April 1975, pp. 148–63; Virginia Allen, 'Agency physicians to the Southern Plains Indians, 1868–1900', *Bulletin of the History of Medicine*, vol. 49, Fall 1975, pp. 318–30.

28 Barsh and Henderson, *The Road*, ch. 6, pp. 69, 82, 88–9, 94–5; Prucha, *Crisis*, pp. 70–1; Mardock, pp. 36, 81, 83–4, 217; Priest, pp. 105, 175–6; Everett Arthur Gilcreast, 'Richard Henry Pratt and American Indian policy, 1877–1906. A study of the assimilation movement' (Ph.D dissertation, Yale University, 1967; Ann Arbor, Mich., University Microfilms, 1976), pp. 191–2.

29 William T. Hagan, *United States–Comanche Relations. The Reservation Years* (New Haven, Conn., and London, Yale University Press, 1976), p. xiv.

30 Barsh and Henderson, p. 62; Fritz, *Assimilation*, p. 161 (quotation).

31 See William T. Hagan, *Indian Police and Judges. Experiments in Acculturation and Controls* (New Haven, Conn., Yale University Press, 1966); Prucha, *Crisis*, pp. 201 ff., 209 ff.

32 Schmeckebier, pp. 76–7.

33 See Leonard A. Carlson, *Indians, Bureaucrats and Land. The Dawes Act and the Decline of Indian Farming* (Westport, Conn., Greenwood Press, 1981), ch. 5.

34 Keller, *American Protestantism*, pp. 160 ff.; Stuart, *The Indian Office*, p. 103; Tatum, p. 199; Donald J. Berthrong, *The Cheyenne and Arapaho Ordeal. Reservation and Agency Life in the Indian Territory, 1875–1907* (Norman, Okla., University of Oklahoma Press, 1976).

35 Carlson, pp. 120, 129.

36 Peter M. Wright, 'Washakie', in Edmunds (ed.), *American Indian Leaders*, pp. 144 ff.; Tatum, p. 14.

37 Stuart, *The Indian Office*, p. 113; Carlson, pp. 104 ff., 121; Tatum, pp. 249 ff.; and Jacqueline Jones, *Labor of Love, Labor of Sorrow. Black Women, Work and the Family from Slavery to the Present* (New York, Basic Books, 1985), pp. 65–6.

38 See Dan Thrapp, *The Conquest of Apacheria* (Norman, Okla., University of Oklahoma Press, 1967).

39 Herbert T. Hoover, 'Sitting Bull', pp. 164 ff., in Edmunds (ed.), *American Indian Leaders*.

40 Virginia Cole Trenholm, *The Arapahoes, Our People* (Norman, Okla., University of Oklahoma Press, 1970), chs 11 and 12, and pp. 226, 228–34; Berthrong, *Cheyenne and Arapaho*, pp. 79–80.

41 William T. Hagan, 'Kowas, Comanches, and cattlemen, 1867–1906: a case study of the failure of U.S. reservation policy', *Pacific Historical Review*, vol. 40, August 1971, pp. 333–55; Hagan, *United States–Comanche Relations*, ch. 6 ff.; and William T. Hagan, 'Quanah Parker', in Edmunds (ed.), *American Indian Leaders*, pp. 175–91.

42   H. Craig Miner, *Tribal Sovereignty and Industrial Civilization in Indian Territory, 1865–1907* (Columbia, Mo., University of Missouri Press, 1976), pp. 64 ff., 72, 88–9, 96, 107, 117, 155 ff., 182–5, ch. VII and X and *passim*.

43   Keller, *American Protestantism*, p. 152.

44   Barsh and Henderson, pp. 63, 86.

45   On this subject, see Takaki, *Iron Cages*, *passim*.

46   Mardock, ch. 10; Fritz, *Assimilation*, pp. 185 ff.; Leon F. Litwack, 'The emancipation of the Negro abolitionist', in Bracey, Meier and Rudwick, *Blacks in the Abolitionist Movement*, p. 72; J. Stanley Clark, 'Ponca publicity', *Mississippi Valley Historical Review*, vol. 29, March 1943, pp. 496–514, especially pp. 504 and 507; Earl W. Hayter, 'The Ponca removal', *North Dakota Historical Quarterly*, vol. VI, no. 4, July 1932, pp. 262–75; Prucha, *Crisis*, pp. 65 ff., 76–9.

47   George W. Manypenny, *Our Indian Wards* (Cincinnati, Ohio, Robert Clarke, 1880), pp. vii–xxv, 194–8, 203–16, 342 ff. and *passim*; Helen Hunt Jackson, *A Century of Dishonor. The Early Crusade for Indian Reform* (ed. Andrew F. Rolle; New York, Harper Torchbooks, 1965 reprint of 1881 edn), 'Author's Note', chs I, X, pp. 64, 95, 184–5, 294 and *passim*; Mardock, pp. 185–6; Theodore Roosevelt, *The Winning of the West*, Vol. 1 (New York, Putnam, 1889), pp. 70, 81, 86 ff., 331 ff.; Vol. II, pp. 142 ff.; Vol. III, pp. 34 ff, 280 ff., and Vol. IV, ch. 11.

48   See, for instance, *Lands in Severalty to Indians. The Question, Is He a Citizen Under the Fourteenth Constitutional Amendment, Discussed. Speech of Hon. Joseph E. Brown, of Georgia, in the Senate of the United States, January 24, 1881* (Washington, DC, 1881), pp. 8–9, box 48, Cherokee Nation Papers, WHC.

49   Priest, pp. 167 ff.; Grenfell Price, *White Settlers and Native Peoples*, pp. 83–6.

50   Gary Pennanen, 'Sitting Bull. Indian without a country', *Canadian Historical Review*, vol. LI, no. 2, June 1970, pp. 123–4, 126, 131–3, 139–40; Hoover, 'Sitting Bull', pp. 160–2, 164; George F. G. Stanley, *The Birth of Western Canada. A History of the Riel Rebellions* (Toronto, University of Toronto Press, 1963 edn), pp. 194–226, 228–42, 269–94.

51   Grenfell Price, p. 82; Patterson, *The Canadian Indian*, pp. 123 ff.; John A. Price, *Native Studies. American and Canadian Indians* (Toronto, McGraw-Hill Ryerson, 1978), pp. ix, 99, 106–7; George Woodcock, *Peoples of the Coast. The Indians of the Pacific Northwest* (Bloomington, Ind., and London, Indiana University Press, 1977), pp. 27–8, 203–5; Keith J. Crowe, *A History of the Original Peoples of Northern Canada* (Montreal and London, Arctic Institute of North America and McGill-Queen's University Press, 1974), pp. 127–9, 148–9.

52   Priest, pp. 172–4; Patterson, pp. 139–40; Grenfell Price, pp. 81, 84–6, 88–9.

53   John A. Price, pp. ix, 15–16, 42–5 (quotation from pp. 42–3), 219, 220–1; Grenfell Price, p. 83.

54   K. J. Crowe, *Original Peoples of Northern Canada*, pp. 90 ff., ch. 6, p. 129 and *passim*.

55   Patterson, p. 141; John A. Price, pp. 83–4.

56   See *Annual Meeting and Report of the Women's National Indian Association . . . 1883* (hereafter *WNIA* plus date), pp. 510–13; *WNIA*, 1884, front cover and pp. 3–6, 8, 54, 57–8, 60; *WNIA*, 1885, pp. 13, 26, 32; *Address of the President of the Women's National Indian Association* (Philadelphia, Pa, 1885), p. 2;

Sketches of Delightful Work (Philadelphia, Pa, 1893); *Report of Missions, 1911* (Philadelphia, Pa, 1912); A. S. Quinton, *Indians and Their Helpers* (no details), p. 6; Helen M. Wanken, ' "Woman's sphere" and Indian reform. The Women's National Indian Association, 1879–1901' (PhD dissertation, Marquette University, 1981); see also William O'Neill, *Everyone Was Brave. The Rise and Fall of Feminism in America* (Chicago, Quadandle, 1969) on social feminism; and on the reform societies, Prucha, *Crisis*, especially ch. 5; Mardock, especially chs 10–12; Fritz, *Assimilation*, ch. IX; Priest, especially ch. 7; Gilcreast, especially ch. IV; and L. E. Burgess, 'The Lake Mohonk conferences on the Indian, 1883–1916' (PhD dissertation, Claremont Graduate School, 1972), especially p. 58; Francis Paul Prucha (ed.), *Americanizing the American Indians. Writings by Friends of the Indian, 1880–1900* (Cambridge, Mass., Harvard University Press, 1973). I draw and build here on my ch. 3 in Alec Barbrook and Christine Bolt, *Power and Progress in American Life* (Oxford, Martin Robertson, 1980).

57 See *First Annual Report of the Executive Committee of the Indian Rights Association, for the Year Ending . . . 1883* (Philadelphia, Pa, Indian Rights Association, 1884; hereafter *IRA* plus date), pp. 5, 9, 19; *IRA*, 1884, pp. 7, 9–10, 12–13, 20–2, 37–42; *IRA*, 1892, pp. 4, 9; for accounts of field work see *IRA*, 1913, pp. 6–40, and *Brief Statement of the Nature and Purpose of the Indian Rights Association with a Summary of its Work in the Year 1892* (IRA Tracts, 2nd series, no. 6), pp. 1–2; on the work of the Washington agent see *Why the Work of the Indian Rights Association Should Be Supported* (IRA Tracts, 2nd series, no. 24, 1895); Gilcreast, pp. 173 ff.; Prucha, *Crisis*, pp. 149 ff.; and William T. Hagan, *The Indian Rights Association. The Herbert Welsh Years, 1882–1904* (Tucson, Ariz., University of Arizona Press, 1985).

58 See *Proceedings of the Sixth Annual Meeting of the Lake Mohonk Conference of Friends of the Indian . . . 1888* (Lake Mohonk Conference, New York, 1888; hereafter *LMC* plus date), pp. 44–8, 97–9 on Mohonk's aversion to a lobbyist but careful concern for desired legislation, p. 11 on Mohonk's role in harmonizing the activities of other Indian reform groups; *LMC*, 1890, pp. 110–11, notes the establishment of a standing committee of seven to pursue Mohonk objectives between the sessions of the conference; Burgess, pp. 17, 21, 71–2, 83–4, 131–2, 142, 160–3, 184, 189, 215–16, 256, 296, 299–300 and appendices; and *LMC*, 1883, for its general aims.

59 *WNIA*, 1885, pp. 39, 42–7; Quinton, *Indians and Their Helpers*; *IRA*, 1885, p. 10, and 1887, pp. 65–7, for an indication of its membership; Burgess, pp. 422–7 on the Mohonk Conference membership, and p. 198 and *passim.* on Indian visitors to Mohonk.

60 *IRA*, 1885, p. 13; *IRA*, 1891, pp. 1–10; *WNIA*, 1884, p. 8; Burgess, pp. 57–9, 73, 186–7, 270.

61 *LMC*, 1909, p. 86; 1892, pp. 15–16; 1912, p. 48; 1913, p. 195; *IRA*, 1884, p. 23; 1900, p. 7.

62 *LMC*, 1896, p. 11; quotation from D. S. Otis, *The Dawes Act and the Allotment of Indian Lands* (ed. Francis Paul Prucha; Norman, Okla, University of Oklahoma Press, 1973 edn; originally 1934), p. 10.

63 See *LMC*, 1903, pp. 51, 60, 73, 79–80, 105; 1911, p. 230 for a taste of the reformer debate about the role of anthropology.

64 See Glenn C. Altschuler, *Race, Ethnicity, and Class in American Thought, 1865–1919* (Arlington Heights, Ill., Harlan Davidson, 1982), pp. 82–4.

65 *LMC*, 1886, pp. 9–10, and 1906, pp. 75–6; Burgess, p. 136; Prucha, *Americanizing*, pp. 260–71; Priest, p. 147.

66 Gilcreast, pp. 179–80; Priest, pp. 58, 174–6, and Prucha, *Crisis*, p. 26, suggest respectively that the two movements drew little from each other, and that the old abolitionist leaders were not a major force in the post-Civil War Indian reform movement; however, Mardock, in *The Reformers and the American Indian*, stresses the connection; and see my 'The anti-slavery origins of concern for the American Indians', in Bolt and Drescher (eds), *Anti-Slavery, Religion and Reform*, especially pp. 243–8.

67 On the desire to take politics out of the Indian service and to reform the Indian Bureau see Mohonk platforms of 1891, 1901, 1903 and 1916; the proceedings of the 1904 Mohonk conference; and *IRA*, 1887, pp. 8–13; 1888, pp. 32–8; Burgess, p. 357.

68 Montgomery, pp. 178, 417, 445. Henry George, though interested in the contacts between 'savagery' and civilization and applauding the 'independent power' of the individual in 'savage' societies, was not concerned with Indian peoples as such; see his *Progress and Poverty* (London, Kegan, Paul, Trench, 1883), pp. 201–2, 346–7, 355.

69 J. P. Dunn, *Massacres of the Mountains* (London, 1886), p. 716; Elaine Goodale Eastman, *Pratt. The Red Man's Moses* (Norman, Okla, University of Oklahoma Press, 1935), pp. 66, 69–70; Richard Henry Pratt, *Battlefield and Classroom. Four Decades with the American Indian, 1867–1904* (ed. Robert Utley; New Haven, Conn., and London, Yale University Press, 1964), pp. 213–14; Prucha, *Americanizing*, pp. 36, 46; *LMC*, 1886, pp. 9–10, 42; *Report of Hon. Theodore Roosevelt, etc.* (IRA, 1893), p. 14; Quinton, *Indians and Their Helpers*; A. S. Quinton, *Constitution and By-Laws of the Indian Rights Association* (Philadelphia, Pa, 1883); *IRA*, 1885, p. 10; 1887, pp. 65–7.

70 Prucha, *Crisis*, pp. 152, 158 ff., and on the sectarian education issue see *A Response to Senator Pettigrew* (IRA Tracts, 2nd series, no. 4, 1897); *IRA*, 1912, pp. 14–19; *Shall Public Funds be Expended for the Support of Sectarian Indian Schools?*, pp. 23–4, 65–7, 78–9, 269.

71 For the debate on peyote, see *IRA*, 1917, pp. 67–8; *Peyote – An Insidious Evil* (IRA Tracts, 2nd series, no. 114, 1918); Burgess, pp. 333–7, 346, 348–52.

72 Prucha, *Crisis*, pp. 88 ff., 165–7; Priest, pp. 60–1, 86, 239–40; Gilcreast, pp. 162 ff.; Mardock, pp. 116–17, 134–7, 156; Fritz, *Assimilation*, pp. 203–4.

73 Keller, *American Protestantism*, pp. 154 ff., 186, 295.

74 *IRA*, 1912, p. 80; *The Alaska Situation* (IRA Tracts, 2nd series, no. 93, 1914); *Address of the President of the Women's National Indian Association*, op. cit., pp. 6–7; Burgess, pp. 246, 311; Lawrence C. Kelly, *The Navajo Indians and Federal Indian Policy, 1900–1935* (Tucson, Ariz., University of Arizona Press, 1968), p. 12.

75 See *IRA*, 1891, pp. 11–23; IRA Tracts, 2nd series, no. 55 (1901); no. 58 (1901); no. 61 (1902); no. 68 (1904); *IRA* 1903, pp. 4–16; 1904, pp. 21–2; 1905, p. 29; 1906, p. 16; *LMC*, 1891, pp. 109–11; 1908, pp. 8, 76; 1910, pp. 28–32; Burgess, pp. 127–8, 140–2, 191–5, 309; Prucha, *Crisis*, ch. 6 pp. 12, 218 ff.

76 Prucha, *Crisis*, ch. 12; Burgess, p. 16; Donald J. Parman, 'Francis Ellington Leupp, 1905–1909', in Kvasnicka and Viola (eds), *The Commissioners*, p. 231.

77 Burgess, pp. 23, 50, 74; Fritz, *Assimilation*, p. 211; Fritz, 'The Board of Indian Commissioners', in Smith and Kvasnicka, pp. 67 ff.; Stuart, *The Indian Office*, pp. 121–2; Robert M. Kvasnicka, 'George W. Manypenny, 1853–1857', in Kvasnicka and Viola (eds), *The Commissioners*, pp. 64–5; Priest, pp. 189–90.

78 Prucha, *Crisis*, p. 231 and ch. 8 generally; Fritz, *Assimilation*, pp. 207 ff.; Gates, 'Indian allotments preceding the Dawes Act', in Clark, *The Frontier Challenge*; Manypenny, pp. 119–21.
79 Priest, chs 14–15; Gilcreast, ch. V, especially pp. 212–14; Wilcomb E. Washburn (ed.), *The Assault on Indian Tribalism. The General Allotment Law (Dawes Act) of 1887* (Philadelphia, Pa, Lippincott, 1975), pp. 8 ff.; Kvasnicka and Viola (eds), *The Commissioners*, pp. 64, 66.
80 See (all in WHC) articles in *South McAlester Capital*, 12 July 1894, *The Indian Citizen*, 12 July 1894, *The Indian Chieftain*, 18 October 1894, *The Purcell Register*, 19 October 1894, *The Indian Citizen*, 25 July 1895, *The Indian Citizen*, 8 October 1896, *The Purcell Register*, 22 October 1896, *The Indian Citizen*, 8 October 1903, 26 November 1903, *The Wapanucka Press*, 28 July 1904, *The Blue County Democrat*, 26 August 1904, in the Green McCurtain Collection; in *The Star Vindicator*, 19 October 1878, and 16 November 1878, in Garvin Collection; in *The New State Tribune*, 6 September 1906, in Choctaw Miscellaneous Papers; report of an International Convention, I.T., 27–8 May 1879, in Cherokee Documents Box; Acts of Choctaw Nation, Vol. 12 (1896), no. 1; articles in *The Purcell Register*, 26 June 1891, *The Chelsea Commercial*, 14 April 1905, *Muskogee Democrat*, 3 August 1905, 5 December 1905, in Pleasant Porter Collection; article in *The Oklahoma War-Chief*, 15 July 1886, in Samuel Checote Collection; letter from Principal Chief Isparhecher in Creek Documents; article in *The South McAlester Capital*, 13 January 1898, in Creek Miscellaneous Papers; letter from Frank J. Boudinot in Miscellaneous Seminole–Creek Documents; letter from E. B. Townsend on the Shawnees, 6 April 1883, pp. 2–6, Miscellaneous Indian Documents; article in *The Cherokee Advocate*, 16 January 1875, in John Jumper Collection; article in *The Indian Journal*, 16 June 1887, *The Muskogee Phoenix*, 31 May 1894, in John F. Brown Collection; articles in *The Cherokee Advocate*, 19 January 1881, *The Indian Chieftain*, 11 November 1897, in Bushyhead Collection; letter 81 on Indian politics in box 20 of Cherokee Nation Papers, article no. 87 in box 47, ibid., no. 6 in box 48, ibid., Mr Naked Head's Speech, 18 May 1897, in box 127, ibid., *Appeal of the Delegates of the Chickasaw, Creek and Cherokee Nations to the President of the United States* (1887), pp. 4–6, ibid.; Miner, pp. 44–6, 116–17, 155, 187.
81 Washburn (ed.), *The Assault on Indian Tribalism*, pp. 24–5.
82 Priest, pp. 211, 218; *IRA*, 1887, p. 36; Tyler, *A History of Indian Policy*, p. 110; Gilcreast, pp. 231–2; Otis, pp. 107–31, 149–50, 487; Harold E. Fey and D'Arcy McNickle, *Indians and Other Americans. Two Ways of Life Meet* (New York, Harper & Brothers, 1959), p. 75; Carlson, pp. 9 ff.; Graham D. Taylor, *The New Deal and American Indian Tribalism. The Administration of the Indian Reorganization Act* (Lincoln, Nebr., University of Nebraska Press, 1980), pp. 4–6; Stuart, *The Indian Office*, p. 25.
83 Stuart, *The Indian Office*, pp. 122–3.
84 Kvasnicka and Viola (eds), pp. 226–7, 234, 248–9; Priest, ch. 18 and pp. 218–22, 224, 228, 252; Gilcreast, pp. 211, 234–6, 245–51, ch. v, appendix B, and pp. 402–4; Washburn (ed.), *The Assault on Indian Tribalism*, pp. 28 ff.; Carlson, pp. 14, 16, 22 ff., and ch. 7; Taylor, pp. 6–7; Prucha, *Crisis*, ch. 13; Fritz, *Assimilation*, pp. 210–13; though see the Board of Indian Commissioners' *Summary*, pp. 25–7, for condemnation of indiscriminate leasing. And see M. Gidley, *With One Sky Above Us. Life on an Indian Reservation at the Turn of the Century. Photographs by E. H. Latham* (New York, Putnam, and Exeter, Windward/Webb Bower, 1979).

85 *The Indian Craftsman*, vol. 2 (5), January 1910, pp. 9–16; reports of the Indian Industries League for 1907, 1909–10 and 1915; Burgess, pp. 185, 202–4, 244; Carlson, pp. 177–9; Parman, 'Leupp', p. 231; Lawrence C. Kelly, 'Cato Sells, 1913–21', in Kvasnicka and Viola (eds), *The Commissioners*, pp. 245–7; Robert H. Wiebe, *The Search for Order, 1877–1920* (New York, Hill & Wang, 1968 edn), pp. 61–2; James Turner, 'Understanding the Populists', *Journal of American History*, vol. 67, 1980–1, pp. 370 ff.

86 *LMC*, 1907, p. 184; F. E. Partington, *The Story of Mohonk* (Fulton, NY, Morrill Press, 1911), p. 29; Burgess, pp. 175, 254, 268, 293, 311, 321, 331; *The Red Man*, vol. 5 (5), January 1913, pp. 209–10; Priest, pp. 249–50. Though in Appendix V, pp. 428 ff., Burgess gives H. C. Phillip's list of unfinished work, compiled in 1916.

87 Stuart, *The Indian Office*, pp. 48–54, ch. X and *passim*; see also Paul Stuart, 'United States Indian Policy: from the Dawes Act to the American Indian Policy Review Commission', *Social Service Review*, vol. LI, September 1977, pp. 451–63; W. David Baird, 'William A. Jones, 1897–1904', in Kvasnicka and Viola (eds.) *The Commissioners*, pp. 217–18; Carlson, pp. 172–3; Priest, pp. 214–15; Kvasnicka and Viola (eds), pp. 207–8, 226, 236–8; Board of Indian Commissioners' *Summary*, pp. 20–38, especially p. 30; and Kenneth O'Reilly, 'Progressive Era and New Era American Indian policy. The gospel of self-support', *Journal of Historical Studies*, vol. 5, Fall 1981, pp. 35–56. Prucha, *The Great Father*, vol. II, pp. 759–63 ff., stresses continuity.

CHAPTER 4

1 See complaints about the tendency to ignore the past in Warren King Moorehead, *An Analysis of the Problem of Indian Administration, Published by the Institute for Government Research*, pp. 8–9, 12–13, 23, in BIC files, tray 116. See also, on some of the issues covered by this chapter, Sandra L. Cadwalader and Vine Deloria, Jr (eds), *The Aggressions of Civilization. Federal Indian Policy since the 1880s* (Philadelphia, Pa, Temple University Press, 1984).

2 J. P. Kinney, 'The administration of Indian forests', paper presented before Washington Section, Society of American Foresters, 24 April, 1930, tray 113 in BIC files; Schmeckebier, *The Office of Indian Affairs*, p. 188; Diane T. Putney, 'Robert Grosvenor Valentine, 1909–12', in Kvasnicka and Viola (eds), *The Commissioners*, p. 239.

3 Kelly, 'Cato Sells', in Kvasnicka and Viola (eds), *The Commissioners*, pp. 245–7; and Lawrence C. Kelly, 'Charles Henry Burke, 1921–1929', ibid., p. 257; and 'Charles James Rhoads, 1929–33', ibid., pp. 265–6; Carlson, *Indians, Bureaucrats and Land*, pp. 135–41; and Kelly, *The Navajo Indians*, ch. 6.

4 See article in the *Denver Post* (Colo), 31 March 1912, on the desirability of allotting Indian lands in New Mexico, in tray 104, BIC files; and in BIC Newspaper Clippings, entry 1397, RG 75, records relating to the Bureau of Indian Affairs, National Archives, Washington DC, see articles expressing hostility to reservations in *Washington Post*, 2.10.1929 and 3.17.1929; in *Saturday Evening Post*, 8 June 1929; in *Portland Oregonian*, 28 November 1929. And see Kelly, 'Rhoads', p. 266; Carlson, p. 144;

Barsh and Henderson, *The Road*, p. 96; and Tyler, *A History of Indian Policy*, p. 109.

5 See letters of 29 December 1924, 30 December 1924, 5 January 1925, from superintendents in North Dakota and Oklahoma, in Courts and Judges Folder in BIC files.

6 The best discussion of this problem, from which this paragraph has drawn, is in Taylor, *The New Deal and American Indian Tribalism*, pp. 45 ff. and 69 ff.; on the Navajo and Pueblo councils, see Kelly, *The Navajo Indians*, ch. 11. See also Donald L. Parman, *The Navajos and the New Deal* (New Haven, Conn., and London, Yale University Press, 1976), pp. 13–14; Parman notes that about half of the chapters died out during the 1930s when government backing was withdrawn; and see Kenneth R. Philp, *John Collier's Crusade for Indian Reform, 1920–1954* (Tucson, Ariz., University of Arizona Press, 1977), pp. 65 ff. and 105 ff.

7 See letters of Rt Rev. Hugh L. Burleson, to Malcolm McDowell, 19 March 1925, of McDowell to Burleson, 16 March 1925, of Rev. Royal H. Balcom to McDowell, 17 February 1925, from H. M. Bowman (no details), and of McDowell to Rev. W. A. Petzoldt to McDowell, 29 January 1925, on missionary work, all in tray 118, BIC files; circular letter (54093) about co-operation between missionary and lay workers from Commissioner Charles J. Rhoads 'to the superintendents and all employees of the Indian Service', 21 May 1931, in ibid.; and on peyote, article by Gertrude Seymour, and 'Extracts of letters from Catholic missionaries in regard to the prevalence at the present time of the "mescal habit" among the Indians', tray 119, in ibid.; and see also, on mission work, article by Rudolf Hertz in YMCA Bulletin, Haskell Institute, January and February 1925, in BIC Newspaper Clippings; on missionary work and the impact of peyote, G. E. Lindquist 'Where are the unevangelized Indians?', in ibid. And see Bowden, . . . *Christian Missions*, ch. 7.

8 Carlson, p. 156.

9 See unidentified newspaper report of September 1931 in BIC Newspaper Clippings.

10 John A. Price, *Native Studies*, p. 128.

11 See article by Francis E. Leupp, 'Women in the Indian Service', in tray 116, BIC files; and similar article by O. H. Lipps, in Office File of General Superintendent (Peairs), entry 722, RG 75; Hagan, *U.S. – Comanche Relations*, p. 222.

12 Moorehead, *An Analysis*, pp. 15–16, 20–1.

13 See Kelly, 'Burke', pp. 253–5; Schmeckebier, pp. 231–6; and article on Indian health by the Bureau's Chief Medical Director, in *U.S. Daily*, 13 March 1929, BIC Newspaper Clippings; Kelly, *The Navajo Indians*, pp. 181–7.

14 See Gary C. Stein, 'The Indian Citizenship Act of 1924', *New Mexico Historical Review*, vol. 47, July 1972, pp. 257–74. Stein points out that the Indians' war service could already lead to citizenship before 1924.

15 Kelly, 'Burke', p. 256; Carlson, p. 173; Schmeckebier, pp. 513 ff.

16 See Otis Graham, Jr, *Encore for Reform. The Old Progressives and the New Deal* (New York, Oxford University Press, 1967); and on reform generally in the 1920s, see Clark Chambers, *Seedtime of Reform. American Social Service and Social Action, 1918–1933* (Minneapolis, Minn., University of Minnesota Press, 1963); and see, for suggestions that there should be more tolerance for Indian customs, religion included, report on the work

of the Committee of 100 in *The Native American*, vol. XXIV, no. 2, tray 109, BIC files; and articles from *New York Times*, 9 November 1924, 'Giving the Indians a chance', and *Christian Science Monitor*, 18 March 1931, in BIC Newspaper Clippings.

17   Oliver La Farge, 'An art that is really American', in *Washington Post*, 26 April 1931; and similar article, 'The art of the American Indian', in *Christian Science Monitor*, 31 August 1931, in BIC Newspaper Clippings. And see Taylor, pp. 11–12.

18   Randolph C. Downes, 'A crusade for Indian reform, 1922–34', *Mississippi Valley Historical Review*, vol. 32, December 1945, pp. 331–45, especially pp. 337–8; and see Lawrence C. Kelly, *The Assault on Assimilation. John Collier and the Origins of Indian Policy Reform* (Albuquerque, N. Mex., University of New Mexico Press, 1977).

19   See 'The red man in need', *Washington News*, 29 September 1932, BIC Newspaper Clippings, complaining that the Indians were not being paid what the Pueblo Lands Board had awarded them; Commissioner Rhoads opposed the award as excessive and the matter was not settled until John Collier was Commissioner. And in the board's files, tray 106, see the undated typescript noting the board's concern for a number of specific crises on the reservations. See also Parman, *The Navajos and the New Deal*, pp. 14, 16, though Parman notes that no oil was discovered on Navajo land outside the treaty reservation and additional exploration was being discouraged because of national over-production; Philp, *John Collier's Crusade for Indian Reform*, chs 2 and 4, and pp. 104–5, 111, 118, 197–8; and Kelly, *The Navajo Indians*, pp. 58 ff., 99–100, 191, and *passim*.

20   See, for instance, report of the Committee of One Hundred, 1923, tray 109, in BIC files; and report of the Board in *U.S. Daily*, 27 November 1931, in BIC Newspaper Clippings,

21   See Annual Report of the Eastern Association on Indian Affairs, 1928, p. 4, tray 110, in BIC files; and 'Secretary Work Letter', p. 4, tray 109, in ibid.; and article in *New York Times*, 15 December 1929, in BIC Newspaper Clippings.

22   See Lewis Meriam (ed.), *The Problem of Indian Administration* (Baltimore, Md, Johns Hopkins University Press, 1928); and on the work of the American Indian Defense Association, *American Indian Life*, bulletin 8, May 1927, bulletin 16, July 1930, and bulletin 18, July 1931, in tray 105, BIC files. And see Tyler, *A History of Indian Policy*, pp. 113–15.

23   See article in *Christian Science Monitor*, 20 August 1930, 'Justice for the American Indian', in BIC Newspaper Clippings.

24   See, for instance, in BIC files: *American Indian Life*, bulletin no. 8, and bulletin no. 16, p. 28, tray 105; Moorehead, *An Analysis*, p. 1; Annual Report for 1929 of the Eastern Association on Indian Affairs, pp. 3–5, tray 110; and Mrs Joseph Lindon Smith of the General Federation of Women's Clubs, 'A bulletin on the Meriam Report' (tray 113); and in BIC Newspaper Clippings, see article in *U.S. Daily*, 30 January 1929, 'Indian Commissioners answer criticisms of Institute of Government Research', and 'Progress in Indian affairs', by M. K. Sniffen, IRA Tracts, 2nd Series, no. 138, Philadelphia, Pa, 1931. See also Kelly, *The Navajo Indians*, pp. 142–5.

25   See in BIC files: *American Indian Life*, bulletin no. 8, bulletin no. 16, pp. 6–8, 29, 42 and bulletin no. 18, pp. 30–1, tray 105; and 'The Indian Bureau's record', by Collier, in *The Nation*, 5 October 1938, tray 105. See articles in *Washington News*, 30 December 1929, 'Indian Commissioner

asks policy change in administration', and *Washington News*, 6 September 1932, 'Normal civil rights sought for Indians'; article by Ruby A. Black, 'A new deal for the red man', 2 April 1930; articles in *Washington News*, 13 August 1930, 'Americanizing the Indian', and 1 October 1932, (no title); and article in *Daily Oklahoman*, 10 March 1932: all in BIC Newspaper Clippings. See also Tyler, *A History of Indian Policy*, p. 113; and Philp, *John Collier's Crusade for Indian Reform*, ch. 5.

26 See in BIC Newspaper Clippings, Max Stern, 'Indians look to Roosevelt', *Washington Daily News*, 27 January 1933, and articles by Alice Lee Jemison on the Indian service in the *Washington Star*; see also Kelly, *The Navajo Indians*, pp. 148 ff.

27 Moorehead, *An Analysis*, pp. 17–18; in BIC Newspaper Clippings, an article in the *New York Times*, 12.2.28; and in BIC files, tray 108, 'Canada Indians ask to vote', in *The Word Carrier*, Santee, Nebraska, November–December 1912.

28 See K. J. Crowe, *Original Peoples of Northern Canada*, pp. 128, 156–7, 161–6, 173; and for a typical reformer statement that Indian–white relations were harmonious in Canada, see ACLU pamphlet, August 1932, 'Indian primer', 7–8, Reference File of John Collier, 1939–45, entry 179–80, RG 75.

29 K. J. Crowe, *Original Peoples of Northern Canada*, pp. 114–15, 172; Grenfell Price, *White Settlers and Native Peoples*, p. 87; Taylor, pp. 119–20; Parman, *The Navajos and the New Deal*, pp. 22–4.

30 For an account of the congressional hostility to the Roosevelts' concern with helping and resettling some of America's distressed farm and industrial workers, see, for instance, Joseph P. Lash, *Eleanor and Franklin* (New York, Norton, 1971), ch. 37. And on Collier's philosophy, see Stephen J. Kunitz, 'The social philosophy of John Collier', *Ethnohistory*, vol. 18, Summer 1971, pp. 213–19; and John Collier, *From Every Zenith* (Denver, Colo, Sage Books, 1963).

31 Tyler, *A History of Indian Policy*, p. 128; and Kenneth R. Philp, 'John Collier, 1933–45', in Kvasnicka and Viola (eds), *The Commissioners*, p. 277. And on arts and crafts problems, see the 1934 report on the Navajo situation, and the letter of William Zimmerman to Adolph Green, 21 August 1937, in Arts and Crafts File, Office Records of Assistant Commissioner William Zimmerman, Correspondence 1935–48, box A–M, entry 190, RG 75; see also letter from George F. Miller, the Santa Fe School, 6 January 1933, to W. Carson Ryan, in Office Files of Chief of Education Division, W. Carson Ryan, entry 723, RG 75.

32 See Philp, *John Collier's Crusade for Indian Reform*, pp. 120–6.

33 Tyler, *A History of Indian Policy*, p. 123.

34 See Taylor, ch. 3 and pp. 102–3; Kelly, *The Navajo Indians*, pp. 163–6; Philp, *John Collier's Crusade for Indian Reform*, ch. 7; Barsh and Henderson, pp. 107 ff; 'Department of the Interior, Memorandum for Press', 6 February 1935, containing statement by Collier, in box 6, Office Files of Chief of Education Division; for an account of one of the conferences held to explain Wheeler-Howard, see clipping from *Rapid City Journal*, 5 March 1934, box 1, ibid.; and for the Canadian comparison, see 'Is the proposed new programme as embodied in the Wheeler-Howard Bill, desirable and feasible?' p. 7, by Allan G. Harper, 24 May 1934, box 1, in ibid. The introduction of blood quantum as a test of Indianness ran counter to Indian emphasis on descent.

35 Philp, *John Collier's Crusade for Indian Reform*, p. 163.
36 Ibid., pp. 163–4; Taylor, p. 59; Office File of Commissioner John Collier, box 14, P–R: Collier note of 13 October 1936.
37 Philp, *John Collier's Crusade for Indian Reform*, pp. 168–70, 176, 183–4, 186; Taylor, pp. 34–6; and see on the Oklahoma situation, letter of 29 April 1935 from the field representative to the editor of the Tulsa *World*, box 6, Office Files of Chief of Education Division.
38 Taylor, pp. 125–6.
39 ibid., pp. 134 ff.
40 See Annual Reports of the Division of Extension and Industry, entry 785, RG 75; letters in General Federation of Women's Clubs file in Office File of Commissioner John Collier, praising the home extension work. Mrs Atwood of the Federation, in the 1920s, took pride in working 'for the Indians and not with them', because they were 'a primitive people'. See Atwood to Commissioner Burke, 21 September 1921, in the Personal and Semi-Official Files, 1921–32, of John Collier, entry 177, RG 75.
41 Cooley to Collier, 17 August 1943, in box M–P, Correspondence 1935–48, in Office Records of Assistant Commissioner William Zimmerman.
42 See, for instance, Harold W. Foght, Superintendent, Cherokee Indian Agency, NC, 17 March 1937, in ibid.; and memorandum to Zimmerman from Heacock, 25 April 1945, on 'Staff meeting discussion on failure of tribal enterprises', and memorandum from Willard W. Beatty to Zimmerman, 29 March 1945, in box D–M, Memoranda, in ibid.
43 See Zimmerman to Alida C. Bowler, Superintendent, Carson Agency, Stewart, Nevada, 2 July 1937, in ibid., Box M–P, Correspondence; 'Policy statement', p. 2, in Office File of Assistant Commissioner John H. Provinse, 1946–50, 'Policy statements', Indian Service File, B–P, entry 192, RG 75; and memorandum of 1 April 1946 on land policy in Office Records of Assistant Commissioner William Zimmerman, Memoranda, D–M. On land use problems, Joe Jennings to Zimmerman, 28 August 1939, Zimmerman Correspondence, box A–M; on the problem of getting co-ordination, see memorandum from John Herrick to W. Woehlke, 6 January 1940, in Subject Correspondence Files of John Herrick, 1936–41, box 1, entry 195, RG 75; and in ibid., memorandum from Herrick to Dr Sophie D. Aberle, Superintendent, United Pueblos Agency, 1939, and Collier to Messrs Beatty, Cooley, Jennings, Murphy, Townsend, etc., 27 December 1937; and in box 7, memorandum from Herrick to Collier, 6 November 1936. See Herrick to Mr Murphy, 28 May 1940, Staff Memos File, 1940–1, box 16, S–T, Office File of Commissioner John Collier. And also Taylor, pp. 123–5, 132; Parman, *The Navajos and the New Deal*, p. 63, and Philp, *John Collier's Crusade for Indian Reform*, pp. 176, 198.
44 See Kelly, *The Navajo Indians*, and Parman, *The Navajos and the New Deal*, on the reasons why the Navajos were accorded such importance, and on their economic needs by the 1930s.
45 Kelly, *The Navajo Indians*, pp. 66–7.
46 Kelly, *The Navajo Indians*, pp. 159–60, 162–3; and Parman, *The Navajos and The New Deal*, pp. 293–4.
47 Parman, *The Navajos and The New Deal*, pp. 46, 63–4; and on the staff tensions involved in implementing the stock reduction programme, see letter of 4 December 1935 from W. G. McGinnies, Acting District Manager, Central Navajo Agency, to Hugh G. Calkins, Regional Conserva-

tor, Soil Conservation Service, in box 16, S–T, Office File of Commissioner John Collier.

48 Parman, *The Navajos and the New Deal*, pp. 67–9, 74, 77, 157–8; Kelly, *The Navajo Indians*, pp. 168–70.

49 See correspondence in Office File of Commissioner John Collier, box 9; and in ibid., box 10, N, Navajo Stock Reduction (1) File, Mrs Roosevelt to Secretary of the Interior Ickes, 17 July 1941; letter from Ickes of 13 August 1941; President Roosevelt 'to the Navajo People', 6/19/41; Collier to Mrs Roosevelt, 1 July 1941. See also Parman, *The Navajos and The New Deal*, pp. 69 ff., 131, 192, 232, 263.

50 Kelly, *The Navajo Indians*, pp. 196–7; Parman, *The Navajos and The New Deal*, pp. 288–9, 293–5.

51 See memorandum for Secretary Ickes, 6 December 1940, in Office File of Commissioner John Collier, box 13, P, and Collier's address to the Navajo Tribal Council, July 1943, p. 18, in ibid., box 6, H–L; see also Parman, *The Navajos and the New Deal*, pp. 263, 291, 295.

52 See Miscellaneous File, Office File of Commissioner John Collier, box 7, L–M, for a summary of Navajo complaints; compare Collier's 1930s stand with his attack on Bureau defensiveness in a letter of 26 July 1925 to Dr Edgar L. Hewett of Santa Fe, in Reference File of John Collier. And see memorandum for the Commissioner from Navajo Service, Window Rock, Arizona, 9 October 1941, in Office File of Commissioner John Collier, box 11, N–P; and in ibid., box 6, H–L, letter from Collier to Mr Raymond Armsby, Indian Defense Association of Central and Northern California, 16 July 1941; and memorandum on stock reduction from H. E. Holman, Field Service, Window Rock, Arizona, 21 March 1938, in Miscellaneous File, box 7, L–M. See also letter from Zimmerman, 7–7–37(7) in Navajo File, 1937–43, Zimmerman Correspondence, box M–P, deploring efforts of an 'unrepresentative' group of Navajos to see the President; Parman, *The Navajos and the New Deal*, pp. 77 ff., 191–2, 291; and Taylor, pp. 61–2.

53 F. W. La Rouche to Oliver La Farge, 17 October 1938, La Farge File, in Office File of Commissioner John Collier, box H–L; and see, in ibid., the careful correspondence with the Association, box 1, A–B, as well as La Farge's critical comments on BIA mistakes in box 6, H–L, 29 August 1938 and 10 October 1938.

54 See 'Proposed circular on complaints', 6/17/36, box 7, Subject Correspondence Files of John Collier.

55 Memorandum to the Commissioner from Herrick, 30 August 1939, 'Postscript to two months in the field', in ibid.

56 See letters in the Osage File, in Zimmerman Correspondence, box 3, P–W; and in Standing Rock File, letter to Hon. John Moses, Governor of North Dakota, 1 May 1941; in Box A–M see 'Proceedings of Conference of Indian Field Service Employees, Denver, Colorado, April 3–7, 1939; minutes of the Intermountain Superintendents' Council Meeting held at Salt Lake City, 21–2 June 1940; letters from Frank O. Jones, 9 April and 13 April 1938 in Jones File; and the correspondence in the Klamath File. See also 'Indian opinion on the Indian Reorganisation Act', 'The new day for the Indians: a survey of the working of the Indian Reorganisation act of 1934', pp. 44–5, in Office File of Commissioner John Collier, box 6, H–L. For a full discussion of Indian factionalism during the New Deal, see Taylor, ch. 4; see also pp. 107–8,

57 Taylor, p. 37, and chs 5 and 6; Barsh and Henderson, pp. 119–22.

58 See John A. Price, *Native Studies*, pp. 41, 111; and see Joseph J. Jorgenson, *The Sun Dance, Power for the Powerless* (Chicago, University of Chicago Press, 1972).

59 See the voluminous correspondence and reports in the Peyote 1925–1940 File, Office File of Commissioner John Collier, box 12, P; all quotations are drawn from documents contained in it; see also Collier to the Rev. A. Lockwood, Synod of the Province of the Pacific, Portland, Oregon, in box 14, P–R; 'Legislation forbidding peyote', 9 April 1937, Subject Correspondence Files of John Herrick, box 7. Taylor, p. 47; Parman, *The Navajos and the New Deal*, p. 71; Philp, *John Collier's Crusade for Indian Reform*, pp. 193–7; and the Collier documents quoted in note 51.

60 See Collier's 'Memorandum for Press', 6 February 1935, op. cit., p. 9; Indian Rights Association File, Philadelphia 1940–1, Office File of Commissioner John Collier, box 6, H–L; see also box 14, P–R, Propaganda, Adverse, Miscellaneous File, and file on Religious Freedom; Philp, *John Collier's Crusade for Indian Reform*, pp. 154, 170, 173–6, 198, 202–4, 211–12; Kelly, *The Navajo Indians*, p. 156; Taylor, pp. 110–11, 113–14, 142–3.

61 Nancy J. Weiss, *Farewell to the Party of Lincoln. Black Politics in the Age of FDR* (Princeton, NJ, Princeton University Press, 1983), especially pp. 35–40, and ch. VI; Philp, *John Collier's Crusade for Indian Reform*, pp. 211, 193; Parman, *The Navajos and the New Deal*, p. 29; Kelly, *The Navajo Indians*, p. 165.

62 Parman, *The Navajos and the New Deal*, pp. 279–80.

63 See letter to Our Friend, Mrs Roosevelt, White House, Washington, DC, 20 June 1941, from Aztec, New Mexico, from Dashne Cheschillege *et al.*, in Office File of Commissioner John Collier, box 10, N; and in ibid., clip from *Albuquerque Journal*, 6/4/37. See also Weiss, p. 131.

64 See D'Arcy McNickle, 'Commentary', in Smith and Kvasnicka (eds), *Indian-White Relations*, p. 255.

65 See John Collier, Commissioner, to the Service Employees at Kansas, 21 May 1934, box I, Office Files of Education Division.

66 See 'The unfinished tasks of the Indian Service', in Miscellaneous File, B–P, Office File of Assistant Commissioner Provinse.

67 See Philp, *John Collier's Crusade for Indian Reform*, p. 205.

68 See documents on the Japanese relocation in Office File of Commissioner John Collier, box 17, T–W; and Japanese Relocation Project File, in Office Records of Assistant Commissioner William Zimmerman, box 3, P–W, corr.

69 Parman, *The Navajos and the New Deal*, pp. 264–89.

70 See letter of Morris Burge to William Brophy, 27 March 1946, in Office Records of Assistant Commissioner William Zimmerman, D–M, Kemos.

71 See article in *The American Indian*, vol. IV, no. 2, 1947, p. 2, in Office File of Joseph C. McCaskill; 'Indians in World War II', memorandum sent by Jack Durham to Commissioner Myer, 12 July 1950, Desk Files of Commissioner Dillon Myer, 1950–3, Bureau of Indian Affairs, Washington, DC; Collier to Dr A. Grenfell Price, 12 October 1944, Reference File of John Collier; and National Defense File in Subject Correspondence Files of John Herrick, box 3.

72 See Parman, *The Navajos and the New Deal*, p. 282.

73 See F. W. La Rouche to Collier, Window Rock, Arizona, 1 December 1943, p. 3, in Office File of Commissioner John Collier, box 11, N–P.

74 K. J. Crowe, *Caught . . . Original Peoples of Northern Canada*, pp. 175–6.

75 See 'Summary of social and economic conditions, Navajo Indian Reservation – Arizona – N.M. – Utah – and outline of plan for resource development', in Office Records of Assistant Commissioner William Zimmerman, Memoranda, box 2; 'Shall we save the Navajo?' New Mexico Association on Indian Affairs, Santa Fe, 1947, p. 1, in Office File of Assistant Commissioner Provinse, B–P; and see 'Statement by the President, December 2, 1947', 'Report to the President on conditions of the Navajo Indians for release 2 December 1947', 'Summary of Navajo developments, February 1, 1950', and 'Statement by the President, April 19, 1950', 'Statement by Secretary of the Interior J. A. Krug before the Subcommittee on Indian Affairs of the House Public Lands Committee, April 18, 1944', Allan G. Harper to Ruth Kirk, from Window Rock, Arizona, 5 November 1949, and Paul Fickinger to Nicols, from Regional Office no. 2, Billings, Montana, in Desk Files of Commissioner William A. Brophy and Commissioner John R. Nichols, 1945–50, Bureau of Indian Affairs, Washington DC.
76 Kelly, *The Navajo Indians*, pp. 198–9.
77 'Statement by the President', op. cit.
78 Letter from the Navajo Tribal Council, 19 March 1948, to Hon. John Taber, Chairman, Appropriations Committee, House of Representatives, in Desk Files of Commissioners Brophy and Nichols.
79 Notes on the meeting of the Navajo Tribal Delegation, 13 May 1946, meeting on peyote, p. 56, in ibid., indicating some Navajo irritation with the debate about peyote, and keen interest in educational and economic issues; Kelly, *The Navajo Indians*, p. 199.
80 See memorandum from Provinse to Assistant Secretary Warne, 21 December 1948 on 'Alaska native rights', letter from Secretary of Interior J. A. Krug, to Senator Butler, and statement by Assistant Secretary William E. Warne before the Senate Committee on Interior and Insular Affairs . . . 24 February 1948, draft of letter by the Assistant Secretary for rewriting by Mr Warne, to Mr Ickes, 2/9/50, memorandum to Secretary J. A. Krug . . . 14 May 1949 . . . re 'Action of the Advisory Committee on Indian Affairs on the proposed Alaska legislation', signed Ruth M. Bronson, and memorandum for Oliver La Farge . . . re proposed Interior Dept Bill to extinguish land titles of Alaska natives, from Felix Cohen . . . 28 April 1949, in Desk Files of Commissioners Brophy and Nichols; 'Our national honor and the Indians of Alaska' by Ruth Muskrat Bronson, in *The American Indian*, vol. IV, no. 2, 1947, pp. 14–18, and NCAI Washington Bulletin, vol. 1, no. 4, June–July 1947, p. 1, in Office File of Joseph C. McCaskill, 1939–46, entry 191, RG 75; and Taylor, pp. 34, 67.
81 See 'The unfinished tasks of the Indian Service', p. 3, in Miscellaneous File, Office File of Assistant Commissioner Provinse, B–P.
82 Barsh and Henderson, pp. 125, 256; William A. Brophy and Sophie D. Aberle (compilers), *The Indian, America's Unfinished Business. Report of the Commission on the Rights, Liberties, and Responsibilities of the American Indian* (Norman, Okla, University of Oklahoma Press, 1968 edn), p. 29; and Nancy Oestreich Lurie, 'The Indian Claims Commission', *Annals*, vol. 436, March 1978, pp. 97–110.
83 See S. Lyman Tyler, 'William A. Brophy, 1945–48', in Kvasnicka and Viola (eds), *The Commissioners*, p. 283; and on Brophy's concern for Indian attitudes, Brophy to Mrs O. A. Rosborough of the General Federation of Women's Clubs, 13 June 1946, Desk Files of Brophy and Nichols.

84 Address of Brophy at the sixty-third annual meeting of the IRA, 17 January 1946, reported in *Indian Truth* vol. 23, no. 1, January–February 1946, pp. 1–2, in Desk Files of Commissioners Brophy and Nichols.
85 Philp, *John Collier's Crusade for Indian Reform*, p. 208.
86 'Organisation of the Office of Indian Affairs', 12 June 1946, Office Records of Assistant Commissioner William Zimmerman, Memoranda, D–M; and Collier's circular no. 3370, 23 September 1940, ibid., M–W.
87 See 'Speeding up legislation', memorandum from Walter V. Woehlke to Commissioner Brophy, 7 August 1945, in Office File of Assistant Commissioner Provinse, B–P; memorandum from Zimmerman to Assistant Secretary Warne, 1 December 1948 on 'Indian Office reorganisation', and memorandum from Zimmerman on 'Reorganisation of the Washington office', to Mrs J. Atwood Maulding, Division of Personnel Supervision and Management, in Office Records of Assistant Commissioner William Zimmerman, M–W; and postwar planning circular devised by Collier, 10–23–43, in Desk Files of Commissioners Brophy and Nichols.
88 Order no. 2535, 'Subject: reorganisation of the Bureau of Indian Affairs', 13 September 1949, in Office File of Assistant Commissioner Provinse, B–P; Princeton University on the Field Services of the Department of the Interior, 1950, document 84734, on the Bureau of Indian Affairs, pp. 1–5 and *passim*, in the Desk Files of Commissioner Dillon Myer.
89 See E. Morgan Pryse, Portland, Oregon, to Nichols, 19 August 1949, reply by Nichols, September 1949, and memorandum to Nichols from Willard W. Beatty, in Desk Files of Commissioners Brophy and Nichols.
90 See 'Statement presented by William Zimmerman, Jr, Acting Commissioner of Indian Affairs before the Senate Committee on Interior and Insular Affairs ... 3 February 1949', in Desk Files of Commissioners Brophy and Nichols; memorandum to Commissioner Brophy from H. M. Critchfield, Director of Lands; 'Roe Clouds' fee patent proposals', 14 September 1945, and memorandum of 31 August 1945 on proposed legislation to authorize 'the exchange or sale of restricted, allotted and tribal lands for the purpose of consolidating Indian owned lands', in Emancipation File, Office File of Assistant Commissioner John H. Province, B–P; and in ibid., 'Are we giving our Indians a square deal?'
91 See comments by Alice Henderson Rossin, Vice President of the Association on American Indian Affairs, *The American Indian*, vol. IV, no. 2, 1947, p. 28; NCAI Washington Bulletin, vol. 1, no. 4, June–July 1947, p. 3, in Office File of Joseph C. McCaskill; Mrs John J. Kirk, State Chairman of Indian Welfare, New Mexico Federation of Women's Clubs, to the Resolutions Committee of the General Federation of Women's Clubs, in Office File of Assistant Commissioner Provinse, B–P; Associate Solicitor Cohen to Assistant Commissioner Provinse, 3 April 1947, pp. 1–2, in ibid.; and in Desk Files of Commissioners Brophy and Nichols, letter to Commissioner from James B. Ring, 20 October 1949, suggested news item about the role of Indians in Indian affairs, and draft of proposed study of personnel practices within the Indian Bureau, no. 72637.
92 See memorandum, 'Liquidation of agencies', in Office Records of Assistant Commissioner William Zimmerman, box M–W, and 'Report for Law Division Office of Indian Affairs for fiscal year ending June 30 1946', p. 10, in Memoranda, D–M; and in Correspondence, A–M, Samuel H. Thompson to Zimmerman, 29 September 1943; memorandum to F. H. Daiker from J. R. Venning, Chief, Law and Order Section, 3 December 1943, in

Office File of Fred H. Daiker, 1929–43, entry 194, RG 75; reports from the Portland, Sacramento and Minneapolis area offices for very different views about 'emancipation' measures, and Indian reactions to them, in Desk Files of Commissioner Dillon Myer; and letter of 10/13/44 in Wardship Committee file, Office File of Joseph C. McCaskill.

93 Policy Statement, 25 March 1947, in Office File of Assistant Commissioner John H. Provinse, B-P; and 'The withdrawal of federal supervision of the American Indian', paper presented at the National Conference of Social Work, San Francisco, California, 15 April 1947, by John H. Provinse, and revised February 1949, in ibid., P–S.

94 See, for instance, Statement by Dr R. Nichols ... at the Governor's Conference on Indian Affairs, St Paul, Minnesota, 14 March 1950, pp. 3–4, in Desk Files of Commissioners Brophy and Nichols; and circular no. 3704, 15 August 1949, 'Reservation programmes', in ibid.; D. McNickle to Wathen, 5 July 1949 and note by Beatty, 12 July 1949, in ibid.; and in Desk Files of Commissioner Dillon Myer: Attorneys, Contracts/Miscellaneous File, quotation from letter of Myer to Roswell P. Barnes of the Federal Council of the Churches in Christ in America, New York, 16 January 1951; correspondence in Felix Cohen/Miscellaneous Problems File, especially note by Myer, March 1951, in reply to article by Cohen: 'Comments on "Colonialism; U.S. Style"', quotation from p. 4; Attorneys Contracts – James E. Curry File; Summary of Area Directors' Conference, 12–16 May 1952, especially p. 14; Myer to Andrew S. Wing, 29 October 1952, replying to criticisms by Collier; Oscar L. Chapman, Secretary of the Interior, to Hon. J. Hardin Peterson, Chairman, Committee on Public Lands, House of Representatives, 25 July 1950; document 84734, on the Bureau of Indian Affairs, pp. 6–15, quotation from pp. 6–7; Summary of Proceedings, Conference of Area Directors, Bureau of Indian Affairs, 20–2 June 1950, Washington, DC: D'Arcy McNickle, p. 21, suggested that 'there should be a tribal relations officer in each Area Office. This is of top priority'; Proceedings of Meeting of the Montana Inter-Tribal Policy Board, Helena, Montana, 26–7 November 1951; Myer to La Farge, 11 March 1952; R. M. Bronson to Myer, 20 September 1950 and Myer to Bronson, 27 September 1950; Myer to Mrs James B. Patton, 8 November 1951; memorandum to the Secretary of the Interior from the Commissioner, 'Information requested by Mr Charles W. Eliot in letter of November 5, 1951'; article by Ickes in *Washington Post*, 17 September 1950; Cohen on 2/1/52: 'Memorandum on Bill authorizing the Indian Bureau to seize, search, arrest and shoot Indians', and reply by Myer, 'Statement by Commissioner of Indian Affairs Dillon S. Myer concerning Felix S. Cohen's memorandum on S.2543'; 'Proposed item on Indian affairs for inclusion in the President's State of the Union Message'; address by Dillon S. Myer, Commissioner of Indian Affairs, at the Eighth Annual Convention of the National Congress of American Indians, St Paul, Minnesota, 25 July 1951.

95 'Indian Bureau moving to end federal supervision', in Desk Files of Commissioner Dillon Myer.

96 Patricia K. Ourada, 'Dillon Seymour Myer, 1950–53', in Kvasnicka and Viola (eds), *The Commissioners*, p. 297.

97 Brophy and Aberle, p. 22.

98 See, for instance, Nathan R. Margold to the Secretary of the Interior on 'Indians not taxed', 7 November 1940, Office File of Assistant Commissioner Provinse, P–S; and see Brophy and Aberle, pp. 22–3.

99 See ibid., p. 23, and Barsh and Henderson, pp. 126, 129. See also Lary W. Burt, *Tribalism in Crisis. Federal Indian Policy, 1953–61* (Albuquerque, N. Mex., University of New Mexico Press, 1982).

100 See Brophy and Aberle, p. 132.

101 See radio broadcast, 13 September 1958, by Fred A. Seaton, Secretary of the Interior, at Window Rock, Arizona, p. 2, promising that no termination plan would be adopted unless the tribe or group concerned had shown it understood and supported the programme: file no. 111, 1957 (077), Bureau of Indian Affairs, Washington DC.

102 See Patricia Ourada, 'Glenn L. Emmons, 1953–61', in Kvasnicka and Viola (eds), *The Commissioners*, pp. 303–4; and talk by Glenn L. Emmons, Commissioner of Indian Affairs, at a panel discussion held by the Indian Law Committee of the Federal Bar Association, Chicago, Illinois, 1960, file no. 111, 1957 (077), pp. 3–6, Bureau of Indian Affairs.

103 Brophy and Aberle, p. 187.

104 Barsh and Henderson, p. 132.

105 See, for instance, minutes, Tribal Council Conference, second session, Omaha, Nebraska, 23–5 July 1956, pp. 13–14 in 68A–2045, Bureau of Indian Affairs, and talk by Glenn L. Emmons . . . 1960, op. cit., p. 2.

106 Comments of Emmons, Bureau of Indian Affairs, Washington DC, 68A–2045, at Conference with Cheyenne River Tribal Representatives, Omaha, July 1956, p. 17, and records of Bureau-Tribal Conference, with Fort Hall Indians at Boise, Idaho, September 1956, pp. 32–3.

107 See talk by Glenn Emmons . . . 1960, op. cit., p. 2.

108 See Conference of Commissioner of Indian Affairs with Oklahoma, Kansas and Mississippi Tribes, 11, 12, 13 December 1956, p. 131, in Bureau of Indian Affairs, Washington DC.

109 See, in ibid., Aberdeen Area Bureau-Tribal Conference, Omaha, Nebraska, July 1956, p. 11.

110 See, in ibid., the reports of the Bureau-Tribal conferences of 1956, 68A–2045; and 68A–4937 (077), Report of a survey of possibilities of withdrawal of federal supervision and services in affairs of the Sac and Fox Indians of Tama, Iowa, report no. 1, 1951, p. 23, file 5993.

111 See, in ibid., Tri-Area Resources Conference, Phoenix, Arizona, 27, 28 and 29 January 1958, Implementation of Commissioner's memorandum of 12 April 1956, on programming for Indian social and economic improvement, pp. 5–6, E. J. Utz, Assistant Commissioner of Resources, p. 17; field trip report, Sacramento Area Office, 16 May to 5 June 1958, file no. 10140, 66A 641; on the Sac and Fox Indians, file 5993, op. cit.; withdrawal programming report for Pipestone Communities, Sioux, Minnesota, file no. 17136, 1952, letter of Emmons to Hon. Hubert Humphrey about the Upper Sioux Indian community at Grante Falls; reports of General Accounting Office to the Congress on Programming activities. Condensation of Comptroller General's report on termination of federal supervision over Indian Affairs (March 1961), file no. 111, 1957, IC (077), p. 3; letter to the Commissioner of Indian Affairs from Raymond H. Bitney, Superintendent, Menominee Agency, Neopit, Wisconsin, 10 December 1954, File 71344, 1954, Menominee (077).

112 See, in ibid., W. Barton Greenwood, Acting Commissioner, to William O. Roberts, Area Director, Muskogee, Oklahoma, 5 October 1953, in file no. 17131, 1952, Muskogee Area (077).

113 See, in ibid., *Termination of Federal Trusteeship of the Klamath Tribe of*

Oregon, Termination of Federal Trusteeship of Menominee Indians of Wisconsin, and *Termination of Federal Trusteeship of the Ute Mixed Bloods of Utah* in 64A–528; and in the same file, remarks of John Crow, Acting Commissioner of Indian Affairs, at a joint meeting of the Muskogee Chamber of Commerce and the Civic Club of Muskogee, Oklahoma, 6 July 1961, p. 4; talk by Glenn L. Emmons ... 1960, p. 1, op. cit.; and in 68A–4937, chronology of events relating to termination of federal supervision of the Menominee Indian Reservation, Wisconsin, by Melvin L. Robertson, Superintendent, and memorandum to the Secretary of the Interior from Commissioner Emmons, 23 May 1955, Orme Lewis, Assistant Secretary of the Interior, to Senator Watkins, 22 July 1953, and Martin P. Mangan, Chief, Branch of Tribal Programmes, 20 October 1958, to Peter Weil, American Society for Public Administration, Chicago.

114 Brophy and Aberle, pp. 188–213. See also Susan Hood, 'Termination of the Klamath Tribe in Oregon', *Ethnohistory*, vol. 19, Fall 1972, pp. 379–92; and Nicholas C. Peroff, *Menominee Drums. Tribal Termination and Restoration, 1954–1974* (Norman, Okla, University of Oklahoma Press, 1982).

115 Barsh and Henderson, p. 132.

116 *Menominee Restoration Act*. Hearings Before the Subcommittee on Indian Affairs of the Committee on Insular Affairs, House of Representatives, Ninety-Third Congress, First Session, on H.R. 7421 ... Serial No. 993–20 (U.S. Government Printing Office, Washington DC, 1973), pp. 294 and 397.

117 The best account of white policy from this point is to be found in Francis Paul Prucha, *The Great Father. The United States Government and the Indians* (Lincoln, Nebr., University of Nebraska Press, 2 vols, 1984), chs 43–7; see also Sar A. Levitan and Barbara Hetrick, *Big Brother's Indian Programs – With Reservations* (New York, McGraw-Hill, 1971), especially ch. 7 on prospects for self-determination.

118 See Thomas Sowell, *Markets and Minorities* (Oxford, Blackwell, 1981), pp. 8, 11, 16; and see Thomas Sowell, *Ethnic America. A History* (New York, Basic Books, 1981), ch. 1.

119 John A. Price, *Native Studies*, pp. 246–7.

120 Olson, *Ethnic Dimension*, p. 436.

121 See Christopher Lasch, *The Culture of Narcissism. American Life in an Age of Diminishing Expectations* (London, Sphere Books, 1982), pp. 115–16.

122 Sowell, *Markets and Minorities*, pp. 104–5.

123 ibid., pp. 106–7.

124 See Fred Hobson, *Tell About the South. The Southern Rage to Explain* (Baton Rouge, La, Louisiana State University Press, 1983), p. 13.

125 Pole, *The Pursuit of Equality in American History*, p. 334.

126 Sowell, *Markets and Minorities*, p. 13; Sowell, *Ethnic America*, pp. 4–5.

127 See S. Steinberg, *The Ethnic Myth. Race, Ethnicity and Class in America* (New York, Atheneum, 1981), p. 74.

128 See Richard Polenberg, *One Nation Divisible. Class, Race and Ethnicity in the United States since 1938* (Harmondsworth, Penguin, 1980), pp. 246–8.

129 For a discussion of the changing views of equality in recent American history, and for a use of this phrase in connection with the struggle for female emancipation, see Pole, *The Pursuit of Equality in American History*.

130 See, for instance, Peter Steinfels, *The Neoconservatives. The Men Who Are Changing America's Politics* (New York, Simon & Schuster, 1980 edn).

131 Ravitch, *The Troubled Crusade*, p. 280.

132 See Lasch, *The Culture of Narcissism*; and Tom Wolfe, *Mauve Gloves and Madmen, Clutter and Vine* (Toronto, New York and London, Bantam, 1977), pp. 111–47.

133 James H. Dorman, 'Ethnicity in contemporary America', *Journal of American Studies*, vol. 15, no. 3, December 1981, pp. 330–9, quotation from p. 338.

134 Sowell, *Ethnic America*, p. 5, points out, however, that 'a black ethnic group like the West Indians earns more than a predominantly white ethnic group like the Puerto Ricans, and the Japanese earn more than whites in general'.

CHAPTER 5

1 See Lauber, *Indian Slavery in Colonial Times*, ch. 1; J. B. Davis, 'Slavery in the Cherokee nation', *Chronicles of Oklahoma*, vol. XI, no. 4, December 1931, p. 1056; L. Bloom, 'Role of the Indian in the race relations complex of the South', *Social Forces*, vol. 19, December 1940, pp. 268–9; L. R. Bailey, *Indian Slave Trade in the Southwest* (Los Angeles, Calif., Westernlore Press, 1973 edn); Philip Drucker, *Cultures of the North Pacific Coast* (San Francisco, Calif., Chandler, 1965), pp. 51–2, 55, 63, 75–6, 105, 142, 169–70; Elizabeth Colson, *The Makah Indians* (Manchester, Manchester University Press, 1953), pp. 4, 15, 80, 202, 204, 208–9, 213; Hodge, *Handbook of American Indians*, pt two, pp. 597–600; Wendall H. Oswalt, *This Land Was Theirs* (New York, Wiley, 1973 edn), pp. 318, 362, 368, 374, 379, 381, 545; Louise Phelps Kellogg (ed.), *Early Narratives of the Northwest, 1634–1699* (New York, Barnes & Noble, 1959 edn), pp. 51, 241, 243, 292, 359; Elsie F. Dennis, 'Indian slavery in the Pacific Northwest', *Oregon Historical Quarterly* vol. 31, March 1930, pp. 69–81, June 1930, pp. 181–95, September 1930, pp. 185–96; H. F. Hunt, 'Slavery among the Indians of Northwest America', *Washington Historical Quarterly*, vol. 9, October 1918, pp. 277–83; Perdue, *Slavery and the Evolution of Cherokee Society*, pp. 16–18 and also pp. 4–8, 12, 15.

2 See G. Forbes, 'The part played by the enslavement of the Indians in the removal of the tribes to Oklahoma', *Chronicles of Oklahoma*, vol. XVI, no. 2, June 1938, pp. 167–70.

3 Lauber, pp. 35–6, 303, and chs II and III; L. R. Bailey, *Indian Slave Trade*, Introduction and *passim*; Gary B. Nash, *Red, White and Black. The Peoples of Early America* (Englewood Cliffs, NJ, Prentice-Hall, 1974), p. 114.

4 George Fox, *Gospel Family-Order, Being a Short Discourse Concerning the Ordering of Families, Both of Whites, Blacks and Indians* (1776, no details), pp. 14–16; George Fox, *A Collection of Many Select and Christian Epistles, Letters and Testimonies* (London, 1698), epistles 153, 293, 340 and 355, pp. 117, 326–7, 401, 426–8; John Wesley, *Thoughts upon Slavery* (London, 1774), p. 35; John Eliot quoted in Lauber, p. 305, and see also pp. 264–75; Morgan Godwyn, *The Negro's and Indians's Advocate, Suing for their Admission into the Church* (London, 1680); Cotton Mather, *The Life and Death of the Reverend Mr. John Eliot* (London, 1694 edn), pp. 78, 88, 112.

5 MacLeod, *Slavery, Race and the American Revolution*, pp. 110–11; Lauber, ch. VIII. Wesley Frank Craven, in *White, Red and Black*, pp. 75, 104, suggests that the legal sanction for Indian slavery lasted only a few years and was removed for security reasons, but this does not seem to have

been the case; see especially Helen T. Catterall, *Judicial Cases Concerning American Slavery and the Negro*, Vol. I (New York, Negro Universities Press, 1968), pp. 61–71.

6 For an indication of the similar treatment of the two races generally, under English law, see John Codman Hurd, *The Law of Freedom and Bondage*, Vol. 1 (New York, Negro Universities Press, 1968 edn), pp. 164–5, 169–71, 177–8, 188; in the colonies, pp. 204–5, 215–16 and *passim*. For the complex 'legalization' of Indian slavery in the English colonies, see Lauber, pp. 211–15, and on the similar treatment by whites of Indian and black slaves see ibid., ch. XI, and John H. Russell, *The Free Negro in Virginia* (Baltimore, Md, Johns Hopkins University Press, 1913), pp. 127–8.

7 C. Crowe, 'Indians and blacks in white America', in Hudson (ed.), *Four Centuries*, pp. 161–2.

8 L. R. Bailey, *Indian Slave Trade*, pp. xii–xvi, 19–25, 30, 34–5, 41, 45–7, 53–4, 75, 80–2, 86–9, 100–2, 113, 136, 143–4, 146, 176–87; Woodcock, *Peoples of the Coast*, pp. 26–7.

9 *On early black slavery among the Chickasaws, see*:   Arrell M. Gibson, *The Chickasaws* (Norman, Okla, University of Oklahoma Press, 1971), pp. 28–9, 40–2, 65, 140–2; Neeley Belle Jackson, 'Political and economic history of the Negro in Indian Territory' (MA dissertation, University of Oklahoma, 1960), p. 7; James H. Malone, *The Chickasaw Nation. A Short Sketch of a Noble People* (Louisville, Ky, J. P. Morton, 1922), p. 417; Wyatt F. Jeltz, 'The relation of the Negroes and Choctaw and Chickasaw Indians', *Journal of Negro History*, vol. 33, January 1948, pp. 24–32.

  For the Cherokees, see: Perdue, *Slavery and the Evolution of Cherokee Society*, pp. 37 ff.; R. Halliburton, Jr, *Red over Black. Black Slavery among the Cherokee Indians* (Westport, Conn., Greenwood Press, 1977), pp. 5–9, 13–16, 39, 40–3, 46, 52, 55, suggests that there were 1,217 slaves before removal; Marion L. Starkey, *The Cherokee Nation* (New York, Russell & Russell, 1972 edn), pp. 17–19, 56, 175–6, 244; C. K. Whipple, *Relation of the American Board of Commissioners for Foreign Missions to Slavery* (Boston, Mass., R. F. Wallcut, 1861), p. 55; J. B. Davis, 'Slavery in the Cherokee Nation', pp. 1062, 1065, suggests there were 1,277 black slaves in 1825; Grant Foreman, *The Five Civilized Tribes* (Norman, Okla, University of Oklahoma Press, 1972 edn), pp. 355–6, 366, suggests there were 1,377 slaves; Morris L. Wardell, *A Political History of the Cherokee Nation, 1838–1907* (Norman, Okla, University of Oklahoma Press, 1977 edn), p. 5.

  For the Choctaws, see: Jeltz, 'Relation of the Negroes and Choctaw and Chickasaw Indians'; M. Thomas Bailey, *Reconstruction in Indian Territory. A Story of Avarice, Discrimination and Opportunism* (Port Washington, NY, Kennikat Press, 1972), p. 22; W. David Baird, *Peter Pitchlynn. Chief of the Choctaws* (Norman, Okla, University of Oklahoma Press, 1972), p. 45, on black slave ownership in 1831; most Choctaws (and Chickasaws) seem to have owned under 10 slaves each, though Pitchlynn and his father owned 60 in 1831 and Leflore owned 32; Sam Colbert was said to have owned 100 in Indian Territory. See also Edwin C. McReynolds, *Oklahoma. A History of the Sooner State* (Norman, Okla, University of Oklahoma Press, 1972 edn), p. 168; Whipple, pp. 55, 182, on origins of black slavery among the Choctaws, and the smaller number of slaves among them, in 1845; Angie Debo, *The Rise and Fall of the Choctaw Republic* (Norman, Okla, University of Oklahoma Press, 1972 edn), p. 69, suggests there were 19,554 Choctaws in 1831 including 248 Negro slaves.

For the Creeks, see: Daniel F. Littlefield, Jr, *Africans and Creeks. From the Colonial Period to the Civil War* (Westport, Conn., Greenwood Press, 1979), ch. 2; Angie Debo, *The Road to Disappearance* (Norman, Okla, University of Oklahoma Press, 1979 edn), pp. 30–1, 38–9, 44, 48, 50, 52, 56, 60, 63, 68–9, 83, 86, 95, 99; N. B. Jackson, '... the Negro in I.T.', p. 11; Donald E. Green, *The Creek People* (Phoenix, Ariz., Indian Tribal Series, 1973), p. 57.

For the Seminoles, see: 'Biographical sketch of Seminoles', in the *Daily Oklahoman*, 1 January 1922, in Seminole Miscellaneous Papers, WHC; Edwin C. McReynolds, *The Seminoles* (Norman, Okla, University of Oklahoma Press, 1972 edn), pp. 48, 73–5, 87, 89–91, 94–100; Kenneth Wiggins Porter, 'Florida slaves and free Negroes in the Seminole War, 1835–1842', in Bruce A. Glasrud and Alan M. Smith (eds), *Promises to Keep* (Chicago, Rand McNally, 1972), pp. 114–15; Nash, *Red, White and Black*; J. H. Johnston, *Race Relations in Virginia and Miscegenation in the South*, pp. 281–2, 286 ff.; testimonies in *Federal Writers' Project, Slave Narratives* (Vol. 17) (St Clair Shores, Mich., Somerset Publishers, 1976), with Frank Berry, p. 28, and Neil Coker, pp. 83–4; Charles Herron Fairbanks, *The Florida Seminole People* (Phoenix, Ariz., Indian Tribal Series, 1973), p. 14; Rembert Wallace Patrick, *Florida Fiasco. Rampant Rebels on the Georgia–Florida Border, 1810–15* (Athens, Ga, University of Georgia Press, 1954), *passim*.

10   See Perdue, *Slavery and the Evolution of Cherokee Society*, pp. 56–7, 59–60.

11   See, for instance, Littlefield, *Africans and Creeks*, pp. 41, 44–5; Gibson, *The Chickasaws*, pp. 40–1.

12   On expulsion of Creek missionaries see McCoy, *History of Baptist Indian Missions*, pp. 507–12; and see account of the difficulties of missionary work among the Creeks in Indian Pioneer Papers (hereafter IPP) in WHC, no. 7062, 9 August 1937, Vol. XIII, pp. 8–9; and Rister, *Baptist Missions Among the American Indians*, pp. 66–8, 81, 83. See also Littlefield, *Africans and Creeks*, ch. 4; Perdue, *Slavery and the Evolution of Cherokee Society*, p. 112.

13   Littlefield, *Africans and Creeks*, ch. 3.

14   See McReynolds, *The Seminoles*, and Fairbanks, *The Florida Seminole People*.

15   Perdue, *Slavery and the Evolution of Cherokee Society*, pp. 58, 79, 97, and *passim*; Halliburton, pp. 16 ff.

16   Littlefield, *Africans and Creeks*, pp. 44–9.

17   Ibid., pp. 40 ff., and sources cited in note 9.

18   Perdue, *Slavery and the Evolution of Cherokee Society*, pp. 42–3.

19   Ibid., pp. 85, 92; Halliburton, p. 38; Littlefield, *Africans and Creeks*, p. 151; J. H. Johnston, *Race Relations in Virginia and Miscegenation in the South*, p. 290; and as an indication of the amalgamation that had taken place between Indians and Choctaws in slavery days, see Freedman Registration from the Three Districts Choctaw Nation, entry 605, RG 75.

20   Kenneth Wiggins Porter, 'Negroes and Indians on the Texas frontier, 1831–1876', *Journal of Negro History*, vol. XLI, no. 3, July 1956, pp. 185–214, and no. 4, October 1956, pp. 285–94, 307–10; Littlefield, *Africans and Creeks*, pp. 84–8.

21   J. B. Davis, 'Slavery in the Cherokee nation', pp. 1064–7; Starkey, pp. 18–19; Perdue, *Slavery and the Evolution of Cherokee Society*, pp. 36, 56–60, 98; J. H. Johnston, *Race Relations in Virginia and Miscegenation in the South*, pp. 282–4; Cotterill, *The Southern Indians*, pp. 202, 224; Halliburton, pp. 34 ff., 141–2; William G. McLoughlin, 'Red Indians, black slavery and

white racism: America's slaveholding Indians', *American Quarterly*, vol. XXVI, no. 4, October 1974, pp. 367–85.

22 Gibson, *The Chickasaws*, pp. 176–8, 190; Debo, *Rise and Fall*, pp. 59–60; Baird, *Peter Pitchlynn*, pp. 46, 49, 51; McReynolds, *Oklahoma*, p. 171; Littlefield, *Africans and Creeks*, pp. 135–6; Halliburton, pp. 58, 61 ff.; Perdue, *Slavery and the Evolution of Cherokee Society*, pp. 71 ff.

23 Young, *Redskins, Ruffleshirts and Rednecks*, p. 75.

24 Debo, *Road to Disappearance*, pp. 102–3; G. Foreman, *The Five Civilized Tribes*, pp. 174–5; *Creek Indians Memorial of the Headman and Warriors of the Creek Nation of Indians*, 6 February 1832, p. 7, in Grayson Family Collection, WHC.

25 McReynolds, *The Seminoles*, pp. 105–7, 115–16, 120, 131, 150–1, 183 and chs 10–15; Porter, 'Florida slaves and free Negroes', pp. 115–28.

26 Daniel F. Littlefield, Jr, *Africans and Seminoles: From Removal to Emancipation* (Westport, Conn., Greenwood Press, 1977), pp. 74, 78–9, 81, 142–3, 180–9, 193, 200–1, 203; McReynolds, *The Seminoles*, pp. 211, 244–6, 251, 253, 259–63, 269, 272–4, 278–81; McReynolds, *Oklahoma*, p. 188; Kenneth Wiggins Porter, 'The Seminole in Mexico, 1850–61', *Hispanic American Historical Review*, vol. XXXI, February 1951, pp. 1–36; Daniel F. Littlefield, Jr, and Mary Ann Littlefield, 'The Beams family: free blacks in Indian Territory', *Journal of Negro History*, vol. 61, January 1976, pp. 16–35; G. Foreman, *The Five Civilized Tribes*, pp. 226–7, 231 ff., 242–3, ch. 19; Littlefield, *Africans and Creeks*, ch. 9.

27 See *Record Book of Sam Checote*, pp. 5, 9, 12, 13, 16–17, 20–1, 27–30, # 32467–a, section X, Indian Archives Division of the Oklahoma Historical Society (hereafter OHS), Oklahoma City.

28 Gibson, *The Chickasaws*, pp. 226, 257.

29 N. B. Jackson, ' . . . the Negro in I.T.', pp. 40–2; Whipple, pp. 46, 91–2; and on black slave membership of mission churches among the Five Tribes, see *The Annual Register of Indian Affairs Within the Indian (or Western) Territory*, published by Isaac McCoy, no. 1 (1835), pp. 6, 11, 14; no. 3 (1837), pp. 11, 16, 19. See also *The Constitution of the Choctaw Nation, Adopted January, 1857* (Fort Smith, Ark., 1857), p. 17, Inventory of Choctaw Records, # 18299, OHS; Jeltz, pp. 31–2.

30 Halliburton, pp. 50–1, 55–6, 63–5, 68–9, ch. 6, 107–9; J. B. Davis, 'Slavery in the Cherokee nation', pp. 1066–8; Whipple, p. 148.

31 Littlefield, *Africans and Creeks*, pp. 14, 38, 181, 256; G. Foreman, *The Five Civilized Tribes*, p. 171; Rister, pp. 84–5; Inventory of Choctaw Records, Citizenship, # 13631, p. 4, OHS; Perdue, *Slavery and the Evolution of Cherokee Society*, pp. 73 ff.; Halliburton, pp. 82, 106–7; Halliburton, p. 82, argues for one Cherokee slave revolt, in 1842; Wardell, p. 119, and Gary E. Moulton, *John Ross, Cherokee Chief* (Athens, Ga, University of Georgia Press, 1978), p. 134, suggest, respectively, that there were revolts in 1841 and 1842, one large and one small; and that there was just one small revolt in 1842; Perdue (pp. 163–4) thinks there was probably a slave-rising scare in 1841, not an actual revolt – see also pp. 82–3. See Jno Candy to Stand Watie, 10 April 1846, box 12, no. 19, Cherokee Nation Papers, WHC, on lawlessness connected with Cherokee slaves.

32 See 'Records Relating to Loyal Creek Claims under Treaty of 1866', entry 687, RG 75, especially no. 160. On the continuation of slave emancipation – for instance, John Coheia (Gopher John) and Uncle Warren, the head of a small black community, obtained their freedom – see sources in note 35.

See also Halliburton, p. 117; and Littlefield, *Africans and Creeks*, pp. 143, 184–5.

33 N. B. Jackson, '. . . the Negro in I.T.', p. 44; G. Foreman, *The Five Civilized Tribes*, p. 106; testimony in IPP, WHC, of Daniel Webster Burton, no. 7147, 11 November, 1937, Vol. XIII, pp. 394–8, and of B. C. Franklin, 4 February 1938, Vol. XXXII, p. 21.

34 *For master-slave relations see, on the Chickasaws:* in *Federal Writers' Project, Slave Narratives*, Vol. 6, *Oklahoma and Mississippi Narratives* (1976), testimony of Mary Grayson, p. 121, and of Mary Lindsay, pp. 178–80, whose mother was a slave to a rich Chickasaw called Sobe Love, who owned 100 slaves and 4–5 pieces of bottom land; of Emma Thompson Hampton, no. 12968, 15 February 1938, IPP, Vol. XXVIII, pp. 57, 62; of Joe Graham, no. 5868, 18 May 1937, IPP, Vol. 35, p. 150; of Anna Colbert, no. 6049, 25 May 1937, Vol. XIX, pp. 78–9; of Will Nail, no. 7453, 9 September 1937, IPP, Vol. LXVI, p. 56, and no. 13713, 21 April 1938, ibid., p. 67; of Elizabeth Kemp Mead, no. 5203, 2 April 1937, IPP, Vol. 61, p. 423; and of Kizzie Love, no. 9034, 14 October, 1937, IPP, Vol. 55, pp. 391–4. See Gibson, *The Chickasaws*, pp. 188, 260, for description of blacks at the time of removal and estimate of the number of Chickasaw slaves and slaveowners in 1861; and also G. Foreman, *The Five Civilized Tribes*, pp. 106, 115.

See, on the Choctaws: interviews with Peter Hudson, 20 July 1967, T. 284 B, Vol. 26, p. 5 in Doris Duke Indian Oral History Collection (hereafter DD for Oklahoma), University of Oklahoma; see also # 5781, Choctaw Slavery, case 3, drawer 1, inventory X, OHS; Baird, *Peter Pitchlynn*, pp. 83–5; the testimonies of Peter Hudson, op. cit., p. 13; of Polly Colbert and Lucinda Davis, *Federal Writers' Project, Slave Narratives*, Vol. 6, pp. 33–8, 55; and in IPP, of Cora Pritchard, no. 10200, 11 March 1938, Vol. LXXIII, pp. 95–9; of Charley Moor Brown, no. 6219, 14 June 1937, Vol. XII, pp. 22–4; of Polly Ann Colbert, no. 7953, 21 October 1937, Vol. XIX; of Jack Campbell, no. 6449, 24 June 1937, Vol. XV, p. 233; of Wesley McCoy, no. 12086, 9 November 1937, Vol. 57, pp. 38–9; of Irena Blocker, no. 7462, 10 September 1937, Vol. 8, pp. 509–10; of Jefferson L. Cole, no. 13315, 17 March 1938, Vol. XIX, pp. 173–83; of Adeline Collins, no. 4872, 16 July 1937, in ibid., pp. 345–6; of Edmond Flint, no. 6524, 19 June 1937, Vol. XXX, pp. 309–10, 315; of B. C. Franklin, 4 February 1938, Vol. XXXII, p. 21; of Zadoc John Harrison, no. 12776, 24 January 1938, Vol. XXXIX, pp. 408–9; of Charlotte Kursch, no. 5971, 25 May 1937, Vol. LI, pp. 453–6; of William Leslie Smedley, no. 5387, 22 April 1937, Vol. LXXXIV, pp. 213–14; pp. 95–9; of Jane Davis Ward, no. 5399, 19 April 1937, Vol. XCV, p. 145.

See, on the Cherokees: Moulton, pp. 31, 155; Perdue, *Slavery and the Evolution of Cherokee Society*, ch. 6; Halliburton, ch. 5 and *passim*; G. Foreman, *The Five Civilized Tribes*, pp. 418–19; Wardell, p. 17; see testimony of John Armstrong, 9 July 1968, T. 292, Vol. 10, p. 2, in DD; interviews in IPP with Dick Ratcliff, no. 5680, 11 May 1937, Vol. LIX, pp. 265–8; with Moses Lorrian, no. 6652, 13 July 1937, Vol. 55, pp. 220–1, 224, 226–7; with Sam Venn, no. 5963, 26 May 1937, Vol. XCIII, pp. 245–6, 248–9; with Gilbert Vann, no. 6284, 14 June 1937, Vol. XCIII, p. 239; with Eliza Hardwick, no. 6897, 26 July 1937, Vol. 38, pp. 322–3; with Martha Phillips, no. 13704, Vol. LXXI, pp. 256–7; with William Lee Starr, no. 7282, 28 August 1937, Vol. LXXXVII, pp. 133–4; with Burl Taylor, no. 5192, 18 March 1937, Vol. LXXXIX, p. 162; with Walker Gott, no. 12457, 14 December 1937, Vol. 35, pp. 72, 76; with Glover C. Hanna, no. 7130, 12 August 1937, Vol. 38, pp. 207–8; with Henry Henderson, no. 12314, 26 November 1937, Vol. 41, p. 104; Jno. Nick to Stand Watie, 10 September 1856, box 12, folder 3, Cherokee Nation Papers, WHC; and Charles E. Watie to Stand Watie, 7 September 1847, box 40, in ibid.; J. B. Ogden to Stand Watie, 19 July 1852, box 40, in ibid.; J. A. Bell to Watie, 14 March 1855, box 12, no. 75, in ibid.; folders 120 and 125, box 41, in ibid.; box 53, no. 12, unprocessed papers, undated paper concerning the estate of Major John Ridge, in ibid.; *Holdenville Times*, vol. 11, no. 17, 17 August 1906, Cherokee Miscellaneous Papers, WHC; see details of ownership dispute concerning two slaves in box 41, series IV, Vol. X, no. 84, Cherokee Nation Papers, and see also nos 120 and 125 in ibid., and J. W. Washburne to Stand Watie, 28 June 1854, box 12, no. 69, and J. B. Ogden to Stand Watie, 19 July 1852, box 40.

See, on the Creeks: Debo, *Road to Disappearance*, pp. 110, 115–16; G. Foreman, *The Five Civilized Tribes*, pp. 174, 194; N. B. Jackson, '. . . the Negro in I.T.', pp. 46–7; narratives in IPP of Tony Carolina, 15 September 1937, Vol. XVI, p. 86; of Louis Rentie, no. 7306, 23 August 1937, Vol. LXXV, pp. 252–3; account gathered by J. S. Buchanan, no. 6831, 9 July 1937, Vol. CXI, pp. 419–26; of Richard Franklin, no. 12788, 26 January 1938, Vol. XXXII, pp. 38–40; of John Harrison, no. 5145, Vol. XXXIX, pp. 324–7; of Don Cook, no. 7450, 9 August 1937, Vol. XX, p. 172; of Ned Thompson, no. 7395, 10 August 1937, Vol. XC, pp. 386, 388, 391; of Theodoric Burgess, no. 5511, 20 April 1937, Vol. XIII, pp. 234–5; of Lewis E. Lucky, no. 6417, 24 June 1937, Vol. LVI, p. 167; of Lemuel Jackson, 24 June 1937, Vol. XLVII, pp. 114–15; of Alex Blackston, no. 7826, 14 October 1937, Vol. 8, p. 298; of Ben F. Bruner, no. 12836, 24 January 1938, Vol. XII, p. 306; of Alex Haynes, no. 5884, 21 May 1937, Vol. 40, pp. 298–9; and *Federal Writers' Project, Slave Narratives*, Vol. 6, testimony of P. Banks, pp. 8 ff.; of Lucinda Davis, p. 55; of Nellie Johnson, pp. 155, 157, 158–9; and of Mary Grayson, p. 115; and letter from Mary Ann Lilley, Seminole Mission, 30 November 1853 and *The Autobiography of Mary Ann Lilley*, pp. 24, 32–3, in section X, Seminole Records, OHS.

35 On Seminole slaves, especially their names, see: testimonies, in DD for Oklahoma, of Dave McIntosh, T. 211, Vol. 45, pp. 23, 28: and Primus Dean, T. 280, Vol. 43, pp. 1, 3, 21; *The Autobiography of Mary Ann Lilley*, op. cit., pp. 47–8; Final Roll of Seminole Freedmen, pp. 38–54, in section X, Seminole Records, OHS; *Daily Oklahoman*, 1 January 1922, op. cit.
36 Littlefield, *Africans and Creeks*, pp. 154, 256–8; Halliburton, p. 117.
37 Perdue, *Slavery and the Evolution of Cherokee Society*, p. 99; on slave prices in the South, see Kenneth M. Stampp, *The Peculiar Institution. Negro Slavery in the American South* (London, Eyre & Spottiswoode, 1964), pp. 392–3.
38 Littlefield, *Africans and Creeks*, pp. 138 ff., 151, 154; Seminole sources cited in note 35; see also those cited in note 34.
39 Littlefield, *Africans and Creeks*, p. 258.
40 See slave narratives cited in notes 34 and 35; also Perdue, *Slavery and the Evolution of Cherokee Society*, passim; Littlefield, *Africans and Creeks*, passim; and see Theda Perdue, *Nations Remembered: An Oral History of the Five Civilized Tribes, 1865–1907* (Westport, Conn., Greenwood Press, 1980), on the strength of aspects of the Five Tribes cultures, even long after removal.

41 Cherokee Nation Papers, WHC: Memorial of the Cherokee Citizens to the Government of the U.S., box 40, folder 3; in ibid., letter from A. M. Wilson and A. J. Washbourne to Stand Watie, 18 May 1861; petition regarding the Joneses in box 44, folder 18; An Act Emancipating the Slaves in the Cherokee Nation, box 53, folder 31; Cherokee petition to President Lincoln from Fort Gibson, 20 January 1864, box 55, folder 36; petition about abolitionism in box 140, Law and Order/Intruders File; Halliburton, pp. 143–4 and chs 7–9; Wardell, pp. 118–41; *Record Book of Sam Checote*, op. cit., no. 96; Debo, *Road to Disappearance*, p. 127; G. Foreman, *The Five Civilized Tribes*, pp. 83, 215; *Extracts from the Autobiography of Charles Cutler Torrey*, in IPP, Vol. CX, pp. 206–7, 212–13, 215–16, 237 ff.; interviews with John Harrison, op. cit., p. 327, and Edmund Flint, op. cit., pp. 315–16, IPP; Whipple, pp. 27, 38, 41, 56, 95, 136–7, 160–1, 190, 235–41; M. T. Bailey, *Reconstruction*, pp. 23–4; Perdue, *Slavery and the Evolution of Cherokee Society*, pp. 124–9, in discussing the anti-slavery issue, concludes that the Keetowahs were genuinely abolitionist; see also pp. 135, 138, 130–1. And see Littlefield, *Africans and Creeks*, pp. 235 ff.

42 See testimonies in IPP of Mrs Raymond Gordon, 31 March 1937, Vol. XXXV, pp. 30–1; of Squire Hall, no. 6972, 27 July 1937, Vol. XXXVII, pp. 288–90; of Edgar A. Moore, no. 7073, 22 July 1937, Vol. LXIV, pp. 241–2; of O. L. Blanche, no. 6154, Vol. VIII, pp. 417–19; of Theodoric Burgess, op. cit., pp. 235–7; of Chaney McNair, no. 5680, 11 May 1937, Vol. 59, pp. 267–271; of Gilbert Vann, no. 6284, 14 June 1937, Vol. XCIII, p. 239; of Ben Bruner, op. cit., p. 306; of Ellen Bruner, no. 12740, 19 January 1938, Vol. XII, p. 309; of Joe Graham, no. 5868, 18 May 1937, Vol. 35, pp. 74, 77–8; of Eliza Hardwick, no. 6897, 26 July 1937, Vol. 38, pp. 324–5; of Don Cook, no. 7450, 9 August 1937, Vol. XX, p. 173; of Henry Henderson, no. 12314, 26 November 1937, Vol. 41, p. 104; of Charlotte Kursch, op. cit., p. 453; of Moses Lorrian, op. cit., pp. 227–9; of Mrs Ben Smith, no. 4054, 14 May 1937, Vol. LXXXIV, p. 337; of Thomas David Moore, no. 8302, 24 August 1937, Vol. LXIV, pp. 371–2; of William S. Pierson, no. 5205, Vol. LXXI, p. 408; of Burl Taylor, no. 5192, 18 March, 1937, Vol. LXXXIX, p. 162; of John Ward, no. 8580, 20 September 1937, Vol. XVC, p. 173; of Rachael Ward, no. 5028, 2 March 1937, Vol. XVC, p. 223; of Eliza Washington, no. 13122, 28 February 1938, Vol. XVC, p. 358; of Sarah Wilson, no. 5102, 22 February 1937, Vol. XCIX, p. 254; in DD for Oklahoma see narrative of Dave McIntosh, T. 210, Vol. 45, pp. 23–4; and in *Federal Writers' Project, Slave Narratives*, Vol. 6, see interviews with P. Banks, pp. 9–10; with Polly Colbert, p. 37; with Mary Grayson, p. 117; 'Records Relating to Loyal Creek Claims under Treaty of 1866', op. cit., nos 8, 9, 11, 15, 16, 26, 31, 36, 37, 72, 93, 117, 123, 146, 160, 162, 168, 186, 200, 222, 225, 227, 230, 567.

CHAPTER 6

1 See, for instance, entries 687 and 688, RG 75; Creek National Records, OHS, petition to National Council, 19 October 1892 from Sambo Barnett, and covering letter; article by William Nicolson, 'A tour of Indian agencies in Kansas and the Indian Territory in 1870', *Kansas Historical Quarterly*, vol. 3, 1934, p. 378; and Debo, *Road to Disappearance* pp. 189–90, 376, on the protracted struggle to settle Loyal Creek claims under the treaty of 1866.

2 Memorandum on the treaty by E. B. Grayson for Col. C. B. Johnson, Washington, 10 May 1867, Miscellaneous Seminole-Creek Documents, WHC; letter to the editor from J. S. Murrow in *The Vindicator*, Atoka, Choctaw Nation, 27 March 1875, vol. 1, no. 1, John Jumper Collection, WHC; N. B. Jackson, '... the Negro in Indian Territory', p. 85; O. E. Hatcher, 'The development of legal controls in racial segregation in the public schools of Oklahoma, 1865–1952' (D. Ed thesis, University of Oklahoma, 1954), p. 60.

3 Commissioner of Indian Affairs *Report* for 1869, p. 416.

4 See 'Biographical sketch of Seminoles', op. cit.; interview with black Seminole, Dave McIntosh, 28 September 1967, T. 211, Vol. 45, pp. 15–16, in DD for Oklahoma, and with Billy Spencer, Seminole full-blood, 1 May 1967, T.48, Vol. 52, pp. 3–4, in ibid.

5 Commissioner of Indian Affairs *Report* for 1866, pp. ix, 284.

6 Interview with Dave McIntosh, 10 October 1967, T. 210, Vol. 45, pp. 26–7, DD for Oklahoma – the informant still lived on his father's allotment; see also interview with McIntosh in Vol. 45, pp. 28–9, in ibid. Population figures from Debo, *And Still the Waters Run*, p. 47.

7 See letters of and about John Brown in *Indian Journal*, vol. 11, no. 36, 16 June 1887; vol. 7, no. 15, 31 May 1894; the *David Progress*, vol. 2, no. 44, 30 July 1896; *South McAlester Capital*, vol. 12, no. 2, 1 December 1904; all in John F. Brown Collection, WHC; *Daily Oklahoman*, 1 January 1922, op. cit.; letter from Violet P. Crain to the Secretary of Interior, 5 May 1906, from Earlsboro, Oklahoma Territory, # 39519 – A, Seminole Nation – Miscellaneous, section X, OHS.

8 Quoted in M. T. Bailey, *Reconstruction in Indian Territory*, p. 48.

9 Commissioner of Indian Affairs *Report* for 1865, p. 373; article in *Holdenville Times*, 17 August 1906, Cherokee Miscellaneous Papers, Miscellaneous Box, WHC; Debo, *Road to Disappearance*, pp. 161, 167, 168–71, 174, 177–8; M. T. Bailey, *Reconstruction*, pp. 75–6; interview with Ned Thompson, 10 August 1937, IPP, Vol. XC; and on blacks who stayed on with their Creek masters after emancipation see *Federal Writers' Project, Slave Narratives*, Vol. 6, interview with Lucinda Davis, p. 63; with Nellie Johnson, p. 159, in ibid.; and, in IPP, interview with Creek freedman, Richard Franklin, no. 12788, 26 January 1938, Vol. XXXII, pp. 38–9; with John Harrison, descendant of Creek slave, no. 5145, vol. XXXIX, p. 329; with Ada Smith, no. 12012, 10 September 1937, Vol. LXXXIV, p. 294; and with Edgar A. Moore, no. 7073, 22 January 1937, Vol. LXIV, pp. 241–2.

10 See O. A. Lambert's 'Historical sketch of Col. Samuel Checote', included in Samuel Checote Collection, Minor C–2, pt II, WHC.

11 Debo, *Road to Disappearance*, pp. 181, 191, 220–1, 237, 248; message of Ward Coachman to Muskogee Nation, Ward Coachman Papers, entry no. 112, Minor Collections, WHC. In 1871, for instance, two of the three Negro towns sent three members each to the House of Warriors – see Creek National Council record # 29327-a, OHS; by 1897 (see Letter of 12 August to Isparhecher from Paro Bruno) a member of the House of Kings from Canadian Colored Town was asking for nine instead of eight representatives in the House of Warriors because of the 1600 members of his community listed by the Dawes census, Creek Elections, file # 29611, OHS.

12 See Union Party nomination for office, 26 November 1891, Okmulgee, Creek National Council, # 32992, OHS; N.B. Jackson, '... the Negro in

I.T.', p. 125; Debo, *Road to Disappearance*, pp. 202, 221–3, 249; and account by Henry S. Myers of his father, a Creek freedman, interpreter for Isparhecher during the Green Peach War, member of the Creek Light Horse and then of the Council, interview no. 12474, Vol. LXV, pp. 778–9, IPP.

13 See certification of election in North Fork Colored Town, 5 December 1879, in which Simon Brown was both elected and an election judge, # 32604, Creek National Council; election of Eli Jacobs, 6 September 1887, for Arkansas Colored Town, election certified by board of which he was a member, # 32936, no. 316, in ibid.; same state of affairs indicated in election of Simon Rentie, # 32943, no. 404; and of David Dixon, elected for Canadian Colored Town, 1 September 1891, # 32999, no. 577. For a similar state of affairs in an Indian town, see election return for Euchee town, November 1875, of Jackson Barnette, # 32534, all in OHS.

14 See investigation, 9 December 1879 of a disputed election in three towns, including Arkansas Colored, # 32609, Creek National Council; evidence of disputed election at Canadian Colored, necessitating a new election, # 32647; disputed election of Canadian Colored, September 1883, # 32751, no. 4; letter from J. M. Perryman to Samuel Checote, 3 September 1883, on disturbance at Arkansas Colored, Creek National Elections, # 29382, all in OHS; and Debo, *Road to Disappearance*, pp. 192–5, 202, 247–8, 282, and chs 7 and 8.

15 See in IPP Louis Rentie's interview, no. 7306, 23 August 1937, Vol. LXXV, pp. 254–5, and interview with Marshall W. F. Jones, no. 5358, 19 April 1937, Vol. LXIX, pp. 409–13.

16 Debo, *Road to Disappearance*, pp. 332–3, 353.

17 Interview with Ned Thompson, op. cit., pp. 395–6.

18 Interviews in IPP with Lemuel Jackson, 24 June 1937, Vol. XLVII, p. 119, and Lewis E. Lucky, no. 6417, 24 June 1937, Vol. LVI, p. 173; Debo, *Road to Disappearance*, pp. 369–70; for a white view sympathetic to the full-blood Creeks though not to the Negroes, see interview in IPP with Minda Greer Hardin, 25 March 1937, Vol. XXXVIII, p. 261; on location under allotment see testimony in DD, for Oklahoma, Vol. 22, T. 315–1, 7 October 1968, on Creek freedmen round Gibson Station and the Verdigris bottom.

19 See Pleasant Porter Collection, WHC: article in *Holdenville Times*, 10 October 1903, vol. 8, no. 25, box 3; articles in *Claremore Messenger*, 4 September 1903, vol. 9, no. 25, *Okemah Independent*, 14 October 1904, vol. 1, no. 6, *Vinita Republican*, 1 September 1905, vol. 4, no. 28 (editorial), *Tahlequah Arrow*, 12 November 1904, *Chelsea Commercial*, 14 April 1905, vol. II, no. 31, all box 4; and *New State Tribune*, 18 October 1906, *Vinita Leader*, 30 August 1906, vol. XII, no. 27, *Indian Republican*, 21 September 1906, vol. 16, no. 24, *Claremore Messenger*, 2 November 1906, vol. 12, no. 45, all box 5. See also article in the *Indian Citizen*, 23 August 1906, vol. 21, no. 15, box S–Z, Cherokee Miscellaneous Papers, WHC; and article in *Holdenville Times*, 17 August 1906, in ibid.; and articles in *Muskogee Times-Democrat*, 28 June 1906, vol. 12, no. 244, *Kingston Messenger*, 3 August 1906, vol. 5, no. 1, letter 'To the Choctaw People', 7 August 1906, *Muskogee Times-Democrat*, 5 August 1906, vol. 12, no. 283, *Indian Citizen*, 30 August 1906, vol. 21, no. 16; *Byars Banner*, 7 September 1906, vol. 3, no. 19 – all in box 5, Green McCurtain Collection, WHC; and in *Indian Citizen*, 23 August 1906, vol. 21, no. 15 and *New State Tribune*, 6 September 1906, in Choctaw Miscellaneous Papers, box 2, WHC.

20 M. T. Bailey, *Reconstruction*, p. 179; Wardell, *Political History of the Cherokee Nation*, ch. XI, esp. pp. 224–6; and for Indian resentment of the treaty, see interview in IPP with E. F. Venn, 10 March 1938, no. 13177, Vol. XCIII p. 217. The best treatment of the Cherokee blacks is Daniel F. Littlefield, Jr, *The Cherokee Freedmen. From Emancipation to American Citizenship* (Westport, Conn., Greenwood Press, 1978).

21 Wardell, pp. 335–6, 342, 347; N. B. Jackson, '. . . the Negro in I.T.', pp. 169–72; articles in *Sallisaw Star*, 7 and 13 February, 20 February, 29 May, 5 June, 17 July 1903, in Gaston Litton, *Cherokee Papers, 1901–25*, OHS.

22 N. B. Jackson, '. . . the Negro in I.T.', p. 157; Wardell, chs XIII–XIV; Littlefield, *The Cherokee Freedmen*, pp. 28, 36–7, 46; interviews in IPP with Miss E. J. Ross, no. 334, 10 January 1938, Vol. CVIII, p. 334, and Chaney McNair, no. 5680, 11 May 1937, vol. 59, p. 271; speech of W. P. Ross to House Committee on Territories, reported in *Cherokee Advocate*, 21 February 1874, in Litton, *Cherokee Papers, 1815–74*, pp. 305–11, OHS; on the debate about severalty and territorialization, see documents in boxes 20, 47, 48, Cherokee Nation Papers, WHC.

23 See letter of W. A. Phillips to Hon. H. M. Teller, Secretary of Interior, 5 November 1883, pp. 3–4, in entry 577, RG 75, box 2, Letters Received Relating to Cherokee Citizenship, and compare with letter from E. C. Watkins, US Indian Inspector, 15 February 1876, pp. 10–14, 27, in entry 577; and letters of W. A. Phillips to Secretary of the Interior, 13 September 1875, and G. W. Ingalls to Commissioner of Indian Affairs, 23 August 1875, in ibid. For an example of intruder ingenuity, see Census Schedule of Cooweescowee District, Cherokee Nation, Census Roll 1880, WHC. See also letters of Charles Thompson to Acting US Indian Agent at Union Agency, 16 February 1876, and to S. W. Marston, the agent there, on 30 August 1877, in entry 577; Thompson to the Commissioner of Indian Affairs, 28 February 1877 in ibid.; letter in *Cherokee Advocate*, 9 December 1871, box 62, Cherokee Nation Papers, WHC; Wardell, p. 229, 233–4; and *Brief on Behalf of the Cherokee Nation on the Question Touching New Jurisdiction* (Washington DC, 3 May 1879), box 125, Cherokee Nation Papers, for a defence of Cherokee jurisdiction in citizenship cases, a summary of the various categories of illegal black settlers, and an indication of the 1878 commission's cost; according to a report on *Intruders and Disputed Citizenship in the Indian Territory*, entry 577, box 2, B404–80 to 23899–87, Letters Relating to Cherokee Citizenship, p. 1, the commission tried 467 cases, 93 favourably, 308 adversely, dismissing 43 and continuing 23, and before its establishment the National Council was alleged sometimes to have acted 'arbitrarily and unjustly'. See Littlefield, *The Cherokee Freedmen*, p. 101, for slightly different figures.

24 See in entry 577, letters from William Hudson, Lewis Carter, Henry Clay and Phillip Duncan, 31 March 1880; from G. Lynch, 22 January 1880; from Moses A. Sorril (?), 8 April 1880; from attorney D. C. Trim, 3 July 1878 and 24 May 1881; and on blacks denied adoption because of a name change, see interviews no. 6897, 26 July 1937, vol. 38, p. 322, and no. 6652, 13 July 1937, vol. 55, p. 229, in IPP. See letter of J. Milton Turner, 2 June 1883, to Hon. James H. McLean, St Louis, Mo., in entry 604, Letters Relating to Choctaw and Other Freedmen, 1878–84, RG 75; and in entry 577, petition of Cherokee colored people to the President, 20 February 1878; Louis Carter to the Indian Commissioner, 18 July 1878; and attorney W. Boudinot to Secretary of the Interior, 30 January 1879.

25 See article in *Claremore Progress*, vol. 3, no. 25, 27 July 1895, box 111, Cherokee Nation Papers; Wallace Rolls, entry 583, RG 75; *Report* of Commissioner of Indian Affairs, 1891, p. 103; N. B. Jackson, '. . . the Negro in I.T.', pp. 161–5; Wardell, pp. 235–9; Littlefield, *The Cherokee Freedmen*, pp. 140 ff, ch. 8; interviews in IPP, no. 5030, and no. 12412.

26 See letter of William P. Adair and Daniel H. Ross, Cherokee delegates to Washington, 8 July 1879, complaining about E. C. Boudinot's activities in stimulating a 'negro *"exodus"* pointed in the direction of the Indian Territory', box 125, Cherokee Nation Papers; also Boudinot's letters in box 3, ibid., especially those of 26 June 1879 to J. M. Bell, no. 67; and 13 January 1881, no. 75.

27 See Reports on Appraisements of Improvements, Cherokee Intruders, box 1, entry 411, RG 75; Citizenship Claims, 1901, file, and Commission on Citizenship, 1905, file, box 131, Cherokee Nation Papers; article in the *Wagoner Record*, vol. 9, no. 7, 15 November 1900, box 135, ibid.; article in *Tulsa Democrat*, vol. 7, no. 46, 15 November 1901, box 61, ibid.; articles in *Webbers Fall Monitor*, vol. 2, no. 1, 29 March 1901, *Tulsa Democrat*, vol. 7, no. 34, 23 August 1901, *Cherokee Advocate*, vol. 25, no. 15, 13 April 1901, box 135, ibid.; 'Cherokee prepare to push claims for land given Negroes', in Cherokee Freedmen file, no. 3, inventory X, OHS; interviews 5064, Vol. LXXI, p. 191, no. 12314, Vol. 41, p. 105 and no. 13628, Vol. XXXV, pp. 91–2 in IPP; interview 268A, Part 1, vol. 16, p. 11, DD for Oklahoma; N. B. Jackson, '. . . the Negro in I.T.', pp. 166–8; Wardell, ch. XV, esp. p. 331; Littlefield, *The Cherokee Freedmen*, ch. 9, esp. pp. 237–8.

28 Gibson, *The Chickasaws*, ch. 11 and p. 279; Debo, *Rise and Fall of the Choctaw Republic*, ch. IV.

29 Debo, *Rise and Fall*, pp. 99–109, 163–6; Baird, *Peter Pitchlynn*, pp. 186–9; James D. Morrison, 'Social history of the Choctaw, 1865–1907' (PhD dissertation, University of Oklahoma, 1951), p. 32; *Address by P. B. Pitchlynn, Principal Chief of the Choctaw Nation, and Winchester Colbert, Governor of the Chickasaw Nation to the Choctaws and Chickasaws, etc.*, (Washington, DC, Joseph L. Pearson, 1866), pp. 56, # 7067, Inventory of Chickasaw Records, Foreign Relations, OHS; *Report* of the Commissioner of Indian Affairs, 1866, pp. 283–5; in IPP, interviews no. 1245, Vol. LI, p. 26; no. 5971, Vol. 61, p. 455, no. 7453, Vol. LXVI, pp. 57–8; in DD for Oklahoma, interview with Peter Hudson, p. 421, T.285 B.; in *Federal Writers' Project, Slave Narratives*, Vol. 6, interview with Polly Colbert, pp. 33, 37; 'Exhibit B', protest of Choctaw and Chickasaw freedmen, in Miscellaneous Records Concerning the Five Civilized Tribes 1901–23, entry 632, RG 75; *Report of P. B. Pitchlynn*, etc. (Washington, DC, Cunningham & McIntosh, 1870), pp. 3, 18, 20, # 17653, Choctaw-Federal Relations files, OHS; Pitchlynn to Henry (?) Harris, Washington, 1870, Choctaw Freedmen file, inventory X, OHS; *Acts of the Choctaw Nation*, Vol. 2, 1872–4, WHC.

30 See letter of William Bryant, principal chief of Choctaw Nation, 1 November 1870, # 17715, Foreign Relations files of the Choctaw, OHS; message of I. L. Garvin, principal chief of the Choctaw Nation, reported in the *Star Vindicator*, vol. 5, no. 36, 19 October 1878, in Garvin Collection, Minor Archives G–25, WHC; and in ibid., Garvin's message reported in the *Star Vindicator*, vol. 5, no. 40, 16 November 1878; also editorial on the 1874 bill in *Cherokee Advocate*, Vol. 5, no. 7, 27 June 1874, in Choctaw Miscellaneous Papers, WHC; and nos 88, 90, 93 in vol. 2, *Acts of Choctaw Nation*, WHC.

31 *Acts of Choctaw Nation*, Vol. 1, 1869–71, message of 30 September 1869, WHC; Vol. 3, 1875–6–9, no. 21; Vol. 4, 1877–9–80, no. 33 and no. 86; message of B. F. Overton reprinted in *Oklahoma Star*, Vol. 3, no. 36, 28 September 1876, Chicksaw Papers, WHC.

32 See freedmen petitions from Skullyville County, 1881; Boggy Depot, 1881; Atoka County, 1883; and 1884 in entry 604; and, in ibid., letter from Sisson to Secretary of Interior, 5 October 1880; letter of J. Milton Turner to Hon. James McLean, 2 June 1883; and speech on the Deficiency Appropriation Bill . . . 1 March 1883.

33 *Acts of Choctaw Nation*, WHC, Vol. 3, 1875–6–9, nos 103, 117, 127; Vol. 6, 1883–4, nos 2, 48; Vol. 7, 1885–6, nos 46, 47; Vol. 8, 1887–8, no. 122; Choctaw Federal Relations file, # 17677, report of Choctaw delegates to Washington to the Commissioner of Indian Affairs, 13 January 1887, OHS; letter from Secretary of Interior Teller to the Commissioner, February 1884, entry 604; Green McCurtain reported in *Indian Journal*, vol. 11, no. 4, 21 October 1886, pp. 283–4, Choctaw Papers, 1872–1937, WHC; *Report* of Commissioner of Indian Affairs for 1887, p. 114; entry 605, RG 75, Freedmen registration from the Three Districts Choctaw Nation: No. of Persons who shall elect to leave the Nation (completed in July 1865); Debo, *Rise and Fall*, pp. 105–9; Daniel F. Littlefield, Jr, *The Chickasaw Freedmen* (Westport, Conn., Greenwood Press, 1980), pp. 71–2.

34 Debo, *Rise and Fall*, pp. 197–203; *Acts of Choctaw Nation*, WHC, Vol. 10, 1890–1, no. 135; Vol. 12, 1896, no. 37.

35 Debo, *Rise and Fall*, p. 222.

36 Ibid., p. 276; Report of the Dawes Commission, 20 November 1894, reprinted in Francis Paul Prucha (ed.), *Documents of United States Indian Policy* (Lincoln, Nebr., University of Nebraska Press, 1975), p. 194; *Acts of Choctaw Nation*, WHC, Vol. 13, 1897, no. 43; Vol. 18, 1901, no. 6; Vol. 23, 1906, no. 13; Vol. 25, 1909–10, no. 16; article in *Welch Watchman*, vol. 6, no. 19, 7 February 1907, in Choctaw Miscellaneous Papers, box 2, WHC; and, in ibid., *An Agreement Between the Dawes Commission and the Choctaw Commission*, in *Daily Capital*, vol. 1, no. 112, 22 December 1896, box 1, WHC, article in *Ardmore Statesman*, vol. 4, no. 12, 19 March 1910, box 2, WHC, and, in box 3, WHC, Protest of the Choctaw Indians Against Re-opening the Choctaw and Chickasaw Tribal Rolls, 13 October 1908, file 6596; and in Choctaw Papers, 1872–1937, article in *Indian Citizen*, vol. 11, no. 18, 27 August 1896; letter of Crew and Cantwell, 19 November 1910, St Louis, in Miscellaneous Records Concerning the Five Civilized Tribes, and in ibid., *Statement of Hon. Douglas H. Johnston, Governor of the Chickasaw Nation . . . 1922*; and in OHS, Choctaw-Citizenship, # 136331, Report of Census Commission . . . 1899, p. 4; Choctaw Records, # 13688, Papers Relating to Enrolment of Citizens of Choctaw and Chickasaw Nations, pp. 7, 9, 12, 17–18; Choctaw Records – Citizenship, # 13689, undated Protest of the Choctaw Indians Against Re-opening the Choctaw and Chickasaw Tribal Rolls.

37 See Littlefield, *The Chickasaw Freedmen*, pp. 222–4; Debo, *Rise and Fall*, p. 276.

38 See interview with Wesley McCoy, no. 12086, 9 November 1937, Vol. 57, pp. 392–3, IPP; editorial in *South McAlester Capital*, vol. 9, no. 46, 2 October 1902, Chickasaw Miscellaneous Papers, WHC; circular, 'To the Choctaw Freedmen' in Choctaw Freedmen, case 2, drawer 4, inventory X, OHS: and, in WHC, editorial Choctaw Miscellaneous Papers, box 1, in the *Marietta Monitor*, vol. 3, no. 47, 19 August 1898; article in the *South*

McAlester Capital, 21 June 1900, in G. W. Dukes Collection, WHC; letter of Green McCurtain, reported in the *Wynnewood New Era*, vol. 1, no. 48, 18 June 1903, box 3, Green McCurtain Collection, WHC; and article reporting McCurtain's views in the *Indian Citizen*, vol. 11, no. 23, 8 October 1896, box 1, in ibid.; editorial on McCurtain in the *Indian Citizen*, vol. 13, no. 18, 25 August 1898, box 2; report on his third annual message, *Indian Citizen*, vol. 13, no. 25, 13 October 1898, in ibid.; article in *Indian Journal*, no. 41, 17 October 1902, box 3; article on the message of Green McCurtain in the *Atoka News*, vol. 1, no. 36, 5 October 1905, box 5.

39 See interview with William Nail, no. 13713, 21 April 1938, Vol. LXVI, p. 68, IPP; but for evidence of Chickasaw ex-slaves working for and then near their former masters, see interview with Kizzie Love, no. 9034, 14 October 1937, Vol. 55, p. 395, IPP.

40 Debo, *Rise and Fall*, pp. 107–8; and Report of Census Commission appointed to accompany Dawes and enrol Choctaw Citizens, 1899, # 13631, p. 4, Choctaw-Citizenship records, OHS.

41 Gibson, *The Chickasaws*, pp. 291–2; Littlefield, *The Chickasaw Freedmen*, pp. 30, 43 ff.

42 Gibson, *The Chickasaws*, pp. 291–2; N. B. Jackson, '. . . the Negro in I.T.', pp. 101–3; and Littlefield, *The Chickasaw Freedmen*, chs 3 and 6; message of Chief Burney in *Cherokee Advocate*, vol. 4, no. 26, 24 September 1878, in Chickasaw Papers, WHC; proclamation of Burney, 25 April 1879, Chickasaw-Tribal Officers-Governor file, # 12940, OHS; message of Chief Overton, in *Oklahoma Star*, vol. 3, no. 36, 28 September 1876, Chickasaw Papers, WHC; message from Chickasaw governor to Hon. J. G. Wright, US Indian Inspector, Muskogee, I.T., 7 November 1888, Chickasaw Citizenship records, # 4770, OHS, Governor Wolf's message reported in *Indian Champion*, 10 May 1884, in the Chickasaw Papers, WHC.

43 From Report of the Dawes Commission, 20 November 1894, in Prucha, *Documents of United States Indian Policy*, p. 194. And see Littlefield, *The Chickasaw Freedmen*, chs 7–8, on Dawes and allotment.

44 Gibson, *The Chickasaws*, pp. 303–7; Chickasaw Citizenship records, OHS, complaint of governor to Tams Bixby, acting chairman of Dawes Commission, 12/6/1898, and report of Chickasaw Commission on enrolments, November 1898, # 4772; and article in *Indian Citizen*, 15 September 1898, in section X, 12946–A, OHS. There were, in 1906, 635 intermarried whites, and the freedmen roll was adjusted to 4,662.

45 See complaint about taking a census of freedmen children, lest it was to be a preliminary to the enrolment of freedmen children, in Memorial to the Secretary of the Interior, 20 September 1906, in Chickasaw Citizenship records, # 4973, OHS; and see relevant Memorial, # 7181, in ibid.; and message of D. H. Johnston in 1924, indicating that some but not all the desired compensation had been paid for the Negro allotments, in # 12946-A, pp. 202, 204, Some Messages and Papers on Hon Douglas H. Johnston, OHS.

46 Interview reported in *Vinita Leader*, vol. 12, no. 24, 9 August 1906, in Byrd Collection, WHC. And see Littlefield, *The Chickasaw Freedmen*, pp. 208–11.

47 Interview with Primus Dean, 28 June 1968, T. 28, vol. 43, pp. 15–16, DD for Oklahoma.

48 See Kenneth Wiggins Porter, 'The Seminole Negro-Indian Scouts, 1870–1881', *Southwestern Historical Quarterly*, vol. 55, January 1952, pp. 358–77.

49 N. B. Jackson, '. . . the Negro in I. T.', pp. 121, 124.

50 Interview with Dave McIntosh, 28 September 1967, T. 211, Vol. 45, pp. 24–5, DD for Oklahoma; with Carrie Marshall Pitman, no. 12642, 12 April 1938, Vol. LXXI, pp. 503–4; IPP: article in *South McAlister Capital*, vol. 12, no. 2, 1 December 1904, in John F. Brown Collection, WHC; also report of the *Daily Oklahoman*, vol. 34, no. 329, 5 December 1926, Section C, in Seminole Miscellaneous Papers, WHC; A. Hoffman, 'Oklahoma's Black Panther', *The War Chief*, vol. 6, no. 2, September 1972, pp. 1, 3–8.

51 See interviews in IPP with 'Aunt' Martha Jackson (Choctaw black), 1 September 1937, Vol. XLVII, pp. 122, 128; with Elizabeth Kemp Mead (Chickasaw), no. 5203, 2 April 1937, Vol. LXI, p. 425, who recalled her old slave, 'Aunt Tena'; with Zadoc John Harrison (white and Choctaw), no. 12776, 24 January 1938, Vol. XXXIX, p. 409, remembering a family slave; with Edgar A. Moore (Creek and Choctaw), no. 7073, 22 July 1937, Vol. LXIV, p. 242; with Emma J. Sixkiller (Cherokee), no. 6468, 29 June 1937, Vol. LXXXIV, pp. 54–5; with Stella Evelyn Carseloway Crouch (Cherokee), no. 12738, 20–1 January 1938, Vol. XXII, p. 132; with Charlotte Kursch, no. 5971, 25 May 1937, Vol. LI, pp. 455–6; with Joseph Bruner (Creek), 28 February 1938, Vol. XII, p. 323; with James M. Thompson, no. 9127, 3 November 1937, Vol. XC, pp. 331–2; with Will Nail, no. 7453, 9 September 1937, Vol. LXVI, p. 57; and in *Federal Writers' Project, Slave Narratives*, vol. 6, interview with Annie Hawkins, p. 133.

52 Littlefield, *The Chickasaw Freedmen*, pp. 81–3.

53 *See, on the Creeks*: interviews with Vinnie Jones, T. 382–1, Vol. 30, DD for Oklahoma; J. W. Tyner, 5 March 1969, p. 7, ibid; also in DD, Martha Tiger, T. 593, 15 January 1970, Vol. 30, p. 16; Ethel McIntosh, 10 June 1970, T. 591–2, Vol. 29, pp. 1–2; in *Federal Writers' Project, Slave Narratives*, Vol. 6, *Oklahoma and Mississippi Narratives*, interviews with P. Banks, p. 6 ff., and Mary Grayson, p. 122; and in IPP, interviews with John Dill, Vol. XXIV, p. 365; with Travis Carrol Ely, no. 13319, 19 March 1938, Vol. XXVIII, p. 26; with Daniel Barnett, no. 13729, 23 April 1938, Vol. V, p. 369; with Robert Love, no. 5218, 13 April 1937, Vol. 55, p. 405; with Lewis E. Lucky, no. 6417, 24 June 1937, Vol. LVI, p. 168; with Henry S. Myers, no. 12474, 15 December 1937, pp. 580–2; with Louis Rentie, no. 7306, 23 August 1937, p. 251; with Lemuel Jackson, 24 June 1937, Vol. XLVII, pp. 113–15, 118; with Ann Underwood, no. 0410, 16 June 1937, Vol. XCIII p. 3; with John Black, no. 13166, 10 March 1938, vol. 8, p. 222; for comment on Colonel Alex Blackston, no. 7826, 14 October 1937, pp. 298–9; Debo, *Road to Disappearance*, pp. 238, 290; N. B. Jackson, '. . . the Negro in I. T.', pp. 222–3.

See, on the Cherokees: Littlefield, *The Cherokee Freedmen*, pp. 51, 60, 69; N. B. Jackson, '. . . the Negro in I.T.', pp. 152–5; interviews in IPP with Charlie Bowlin, no. 7608, 21 September 1937, Vol. X, p. 27; with Phillis Pettit, no. 5064, 22 February 1937, Vol. LXXI, p. 191; with Gilbert Vann, no. 6284, 14 June 1937, Vol. XCIII, pp. 240, 243; with Miss J. E. Ross, no. 334, 10 January 1938, Vol. CVIII, p. 334; with Anderson Bean, no. 5030, 22 February 1937, Vol. VI, p. 149; with Burl Taylor, no. 5192, 18 March 1937, Vol. LXXXIX, p. 164; with Henry Henderson, no. 12314, 26 November 1937, Vol. 41, pp. 105, 107; with J. J. Cape, no. 10163, 4 May 1938, Vol. XV, pp. 323–5; with Johnson Thompson, no. 5023, Vol. XC, pp. 372–3; interview with Frank Warren, 13 December 1968, T–359–1, Vol. 21, p. 13, in DD for Oklahoma; Fort Smith *Elevator*, 12 August 1892, in Cherokee Freedmen records, case 1, drawer 3, inventory X, OHS.

See, on the Choctaws and Chickasaws: Acts of Choctaw Nation, Vol. 4, no. 33, WHC; Letters Received Relating to Choctaw and Other Freedmen, 1878–84, entry 604; Littlefield, *The Chickasaw Freedmen*, p. 80; 1838 Census Roll, Choctaw Nation, for Cedar County, unmarked box in WHC; and interviews in IPP with Anna Colbert, no. 6049, 25 May 1937, Vol. XIX, p. 79; with Joe Graham, no. 5868, 18 May 1937, p. 150; with Kizzie Love, no. 9034, 14 October 1937, Vol. 55, p. 394; with Amanda Kimball, no. 4639, 26 June 1937, Vol. LI, pp. 59–64; with Charley Moor Brown, no. 6219, 14 June 1937, Vol. XII, p. 24; with Adeline Collins, no. 4872, 16 July 1937, Vol. XIX, p. 347; with Birthet Harper, no. 1011, Vol. XXXIX, p. 115; with Charlotte Kursch, op. cit., p. 456; with Jim Hutton, no. 7539, 16 September 1937, Vol. XLVI, p. 217; with Louis James, no. 13123, 2 March 1938, Vol. XLVII, pp. 300–1; with Will Nail, op. cit., p. 57; with Molly Graham, S–149, 21 May 1972, Vol. XXXV, p. 159; with William Bernard Dwiggins, no. 4065, 17 May 1937, Vol. 26, p. 386; with Henry Clay Kilgore, no. 12454, 10 December 1937, Vol. LI, p. 26; with Dixie Smith, no. 4613, 25 June 1937, Vol. LXXXIV, pp. 436, 439–42; with Col. John W. Hunter, no. 12721, 23 November 1937, Vol. XLVI, p. 59; with Jack Campbell, no. 6449, 24 June 1937, Vol. XV, p. 234; with O. L. Blanche, no. 6154, Vol. VIII, p. 421–2; with Frank Russell, no. 9351, 26 December 1937, Vol. LXXIX, pp. 213–15; with Irena Blocker, no. 7462, 10 September 1937, Vol. 8, pp. 510–11; with Daniel Webster Burton, no. 7147, 11 November 1937, Vol. XIII, p. 398; with B. C. Franklin, 4 February 1932, Vol. XXXII, pp. 21–2.

54 Littlefield, *The Chickasaw Freedmen*, p. 83.

55 See Norman L. Crockett, *The Black Towns* (Lawrence, Kans, Regents Press of Kansas, 1979), pp. 22, 29–40, 64–5, chs 2–3, pp. 110–11, 115–16, 136–66, 178–87; William Loren Katz, *The Black West* (New York, Doubleday, 1973), pp. 250–1, 313–17.

56 See interviews in IPP with Henry Clay Kilgore, op. cit., p. 27; with Molly Graham, op. cit., p. 160; with W. A. Stalworth, no. 12511, 27 December 1937, Vol. LXXXVI, p. 467; with Charlie Bowlin, op. cit., p. 31; with J. J. Cape, op. cit., p. 323 and *passim*; with Daniel Barnett, no. 13729, 23 April 1938, Vol. V, p. 369; with Irena Blocker, op. cit., p. 511; with Garrett Garrison, no. 13614, 15 April 1938, Vol. XXXIII, p. 243; with Gilbert Vann, no. 6284, 14 June 1937, Vol. XCII, p. 242; with W. Fox Chambers, no. 4379, 11 June 1937, Vol. XVII, p. 126; with Carl R. Sherwood, no. 6831, 9 July 1937, Vol. CXI; with J. B. Nichols, no. 13316, 18 March 1938, Vol. LXVII, p. 32; with Fannie Birdwell, no. 8360, 28 August 1937, Vol. 8, p. 172; with Travis C. Ely, op. cit., pp. 24, 26; with Robert Love, op. cit., pp. 411–12; with Lewis E. Lucky, op. cit., p. 172; with Joe Graham, op. cit.; with Lemuel Jackson, op. cit., p. 117; with Alex Blackston, op. cit., pp. 299–300; with Charley Moor Brown, op. cit., p. 25; with V. V. Cape, no. 10163, 4 March 1938, Vol. XVI, p. 323; with Hessie Hunt, no. 6721, 22 November 1937, Vol. XLVI, pp. 7–8. And interviews in DD for Oklahoma with Walter Billingsley, T. 259, 14 May 1968, Vol. 43; with Peter Hudson, T.285, 20 July 1967, Vol. 26, p. 1; with Hepsey Scott Lewis, T. 524, 10 October 1969, Vol. 29, pp. 22–3; with Mrs E. F. Kelley, T. 102, 17 July 1967, Vol. 44; with Vinnie Jones, T. 382–1, 5 March 1969, Vol. 30, p. 3; with John Armstrong, T. 268–3, 31 May 1968, Vol. 10, p. 9.

57 See W. McKee Evans, *To Die Game: The Story of the Lowry Band, Indian Guerrillas of Reconstruction* (Baton Rouge, La, Louisiana State University Press, 1971), pp. 253–4 and *passim*.

58 See, on law and order questions, articles in *Indian Chieftain*, Vol. 12, no. 43, 17 February 1898, in John F. Brown Collection, WHC; and *Cherokee Advocate*, Vol. 7, no. 45, 23 March 1883, Samuel Checote Collection, WHC; interviews in IPP with J. W. Bradfield, 24 March 1937, Vol. X, pp. 211–12; with Asbury Brannan, no. 13635, 18 April 1938, Vol. X, p. 323; with Winifred M. Clark, 'Early day Negro settlers', S–149, 12 October 1938, Vol. CIII, pp. 476–8; with R. P. Hammer, no. 9344, 23 November 1937, Vol. XXXVIII, p. 12; and with J. Wallace McMurtrey, no. 13083, 24 February 1938, Vol. 59, pp. 250–1. And see also the Creek Records in OHS in Foreign Relations files, especially # 30540, 30551, 30556, 30558, 30582; and # 30431, 30432, 30503, 30508; annual message of D. W. Bushyhead in *Indian Journal*, 11 November 1880, box IV, Bushyhead Collection, WHC; Perdue, *Nations Remembered*, pp. 21, 41–2, N. B. Jackson, '. . . the Negro in I.T.', pp. 133 ff., 143; Littlefield, *The Cherokee Freedmen*, pp. 40 ff., 66–8; Littlefield, *The Chickasaw Freedmen*, pp. 46–7, 94–104.

59 Probably only a minority of blacks and Indians were churchgoers. See interviews in IPP with Molly Graham, op. cit.; with C. T. Talliaferro, no. 4268, 2 June 1937, Vol. LXXXIX, p. 99; with Mack Handon, no. 7281, 27 August 1937, Vol. 41, p. 383; articles in John Jumper Collection, WHC and John F. Brown Collection, WHC on Christian influences among the Seminoles, and Adair *Memorial* in box 125, Cherokee Nation Papers, WHC; and letter from H. Smith of the Interior Department, 3 August 1895, to the Commissioner of Indian Affairs, in Reports on Appraisements of Improvements, Cherokee Intruders, box 1, entry 411, RG 75; Littlefield, *The Chickasaw Freedmen*, pp. 45, 144; W. L. Katz, *The Black West* p. 290, ch. 8, pp. 245–7; W. Sherman Savage, *Blacks in the West* (New York, Greenwood, 1977 edn), pp. 54, 59; William H. Leckie, *The Buffalo Soldiers. A Narrative of the Negro Cavalry in the West* (Norman, Okla, University of Oklahoma Press, 1967), pp. 25–8, 245 ff.

60 See Nicolson, p. 358; Michael F. Doran, 'Population statistics of nineteenth-century Indian Territory', *Chronicles of Oklahoma*, vol. 53, Winter 1975–6, pp. 498–501; Debo, *Road to Disappearance*, pp. 140, 188, 285 ff.; Debo, *And Still the Waters Run*, pp. 11, 17, 47; Debo, *Rise and Fall*, pp. 109, 276; Littlefield, *The Cherokee Freedmen*, p. 254; Crockett, p. 100; Littlefield, *The Chickasaw Freedmen*, pp. 45–6, 92, 94, 96–7; Gibson, *The Chickasaws*, pp. 306–7; interviews in DD for Oklahoma with Peter Hudson, 20 July 1967, T 285 A, p. 9, B, p. 1, and Mrs. E. F. Kelly, op. cit; letter from John W. Rhodes in entry 577; message of Samuel Checote, 30 October 1882, and 'Biographical sketch' in Samuel Checote Collection, WHC; letters of 31 March 1880 and 8 April 1880, box 2, Letters Received Relating to Cherokee Citizenship, B404–80 to 23899–87, entry 577; interview in *Federal Writers' Project, Slave Narratives*, Vol. 6, with Nellie Johnson, p. 159; article on Pleasant Porter from *St Louis Post Dispatch*, 17 September 1899, in box 1, Pleasant Porter Collection, WHC; article in *Tulsa Democrat*, vol. 9, no. 3, 18 September 1903, box 3, in ibid.; article in *Indian Journal*, 22 February 1901, Creek Miscellaneous Papers, WHC; newspaper clipping on Brown in the John F. Brown Collection, WHC; article by G. E. Lindquist, Seminole file, section X, OHS; N. B. Jackson, '. . . the Negro in I. T.', pp. 121–2.

61 Hatcher, pp. 60–1; Crockett, p. 28; interviews in IPP with Jim Hulton, op. cit., p. 217; and with Carrie Marshall Pitman, op. cit., p. 505; and in DD for Oklahoma, with Vinnie Jones, T. 382–1, 5 March 1969, Vol. 30, p. 2;

with Billy Spencer, T. 48, 1 May 1967, Vol. 52, p. 6; with Charlie Johnson, T. 337, 21 November 1968, Vol. 51, pp. 6–8.

62   Morrison, pp. 72–3; M. T. Bailey, *Reconstruction*, p. 152; *Acts of Choctaw Nation*, Vol. X, no. 94; Inventory of Choctaw Records, # 18348, Acts and Resolutions Passed at the Regular Term of the General Council of the Choctaw Nation, pp. 11–12, OHS; Choctaw Schools, # 20059, Inventory of Choctaw Records, OHS; a copy from Chief's Message, # 22245, Choctaw-Schools, Miscellaneous, OHS; 'To the Choctaw Freedmen', in Choctaw Freedmen, case 2, drawer 4, inventory X, OHS; *Indian Citizen*, vol. 6, no. 24, 17 October 1891, and *Vindicator*, vol. 1, no. 12, 12 June 1875, Choctaw Papers, 1872–1937, WHC; *Indian Citizen*, Vol. II, no. 23, 8 October 1896, and vol. 15, no. 5, 11 October 1900, boxes 1 and 3, Green McCurtain Collection, WHC; letter to Green McCurtain, 7 March 1879, Gilbert Dukes Papers, OHS.

63   M. T. Bailey, *Reconstruction*, pp. 147–9; Littlefield, *The Chickasaw Freedmen*; quotation from letter of 7 November 1888, Tishomingo, Chickasaw Nation, # 4770, inventory of Chickasaw Records, OHS.

64   Choctaw-Schools, Miscellaneous, # 22190, p. 3, OHS; letter to Gilbert Dukes, 29 August 1901 from Mrs Mary E. Holmes, Gilbert Dukes Papers, OHS; message of I. L. Garvin to the Choctaw National Council summarized in *Indian Journal*, vol. 4, no. 10, 13 November 1879, Garvin Collection, Minor Archives G1–25, WHC; message of Green McCurtain, reported in *Indian Citizen*, vol. 20, no. 7, 29 June 1905, Green McCurtain Collection, box 5, WHC; interviews in IPP with Emma Thompson Hampton, no. 12968, 15 February 1938, Vol. XXXVIII, pp. 59–61; with E. H. Rishel, no. 4519, 22 June 1939, Vol. LXXVI, pp. 303–9; with Phillis Petit, Louis Rentie, Jim Fulton, Polly Colbert, B. C. Franklin, op. cit.; with Sarah Wilson, no. 5102, 22 February 1937, Vol. XCIX, p. 255; interviews in DD for Oklahoma with Dave McIntosh and Vinnie Jones, op. cit.; interviews in *Federal Writers' Project, Slave Narratives*, Vol. 6, with P. Banks, p. 11, and Mary Grayson, p. 122; Littlefield, *The Chickasaw Freedman*, pp. 116, 124, 122, 131, 220–1; Littlefield, *The Cherokee Freedmen*, pp. 55, 58, 251–3; Debo, *Rise and Fall*, p. 237; Debo, *And Still the Waters Run*, pp. 67–8.

65   See interviews in IPP with J. B. Nichols, no. 13316, 18 March 1938, Vol. LXVII, p. 73; with Bill Gilliam, no. 9941, 10 February 1938, Vol. XXXIV, p. 74; with Bird Wilson, no. 8281, 16 August 1937, Vol. XCIX, p. 108; with Henry Clay, no. 4449, Vol. XVIII, p. 273; with Isaac Jackson, no. 12940, Vol. XLVII, pp. 78–9.

66   Crockett, pp. 23–6, 28, 39–40, 93, 99–101; Jeltz, p. 35; A. E. Strickland, 'Toward the Promised Land: the exodus to Kansas and afterward', *Missouri Historical Review*, vol. LXIX, no. 4, July 1975, pp. 404–5, 407; W. Katz, p. 252; Arthur Lincoln Tolson, 'The Negro in Oklahoma Territory 1889–1907: a study in racial discrimination' (PhD dissertation, University of Oklahoma, 1966), pp. 34, 39, 59; Kaye Moulton Teall, *Black History in Oklahoma. A Resource Book* (Oklahoma City, Okla, Oklahoma City Public Schools, 1971); articles in the *Holdenville Times* vol. 5, no. 48, 29 August 1901, in box 2, Pleasant Porter Collection, WHC; and interviews in IPP with John W. Dean, no. 4623, 22 June 1937, Vol. XXIV, p. 37; with Minnie Jones Himes, no. 1377, 13 May 1937, Vol. XLII, pp. 435–6; with Jim Carr, no. 4027, Vol. XVI, pp. 127–8; with Sarah McConnell, no. 7123, 11 August 1937, pp. 266–70; with De Leslaine R. Davis, 11 October 1937, Vol. XXIII,

pp. 217–18; with Nora De Baum Eades, no. 4824, 13 July 1937, Vol. XXVII, p. 7; with C. T. Talliaferro, op. cit., p. 99; with Winifred M. Clark, no. 13918, 20 September 1938, pp. 470–1; with Paul Gregg, no. 9153, 13 November 1937, Vol. XXXVI, p. 76.

67 Article entitled 'Real medicine men', p. 3, *Eufaula Fallins*, December 1975, section X, Newspapers, OHS.

68 A. E. Strickland, 'Toward the Promised Land', pp. 409–10, 411–12; Crockett, pp. 78, 97–8, 168 ff; 'Our opportunity to work among the Negroes', by Mrs G. A. Morrison, inventory no. 420, Minor Collections M–15, WHC; interviews in IPP with Andrew Edwards, no. 4772, 10 July 1937, Vol. XXVII, p. 153; with Adelia Thompson Greenley, no. 10553, 22 April 1938, Vol. XXXVI, pp. 51–2; with Alice Curry, no. 9472, 17 December 1937, Vol. XXII, p. 466; with G. D. Duncan, no. 12657, 10 January 1937, Vol. 26, p. 101; with C. T. Talliaferro, op. cit., p. 99; with Isaac Jackson, op. cit., pp. 79–83; with J. C. Crowell, no. 9196, 15 November 1937, Vol. XXII, pp. 180 ff; with Jay C. Trimble, no. 9565, 30 December 1937, Vol. XCII, pp. 81–5.

69 Debo, *And Still the Waters Run*, pp. 11, 17; Debo, *Rise and Fall*, p. 276; Nannie Alderson and Helena Huntington Smith, *A Bride Goes West* (Lincoln, Nebr., University of Nebraska Press, 1975), pp. 133, 189.

70 For a black reaction, see Crockett, p. 101.

71 See Perdue, *Nations Remembered*, pp. 44–65, 67 ff., 82–115, 124, 128–9; Rennard Strickland, *The Indians in Oklahoma* (Norman, Okla, University of Oklahoma Press, 1980).

72 See memorandum for Division Chiefs, 7 April 1936, by William Zimmerman, Acting Commissioner, Subject Correspondence Files of John Herrick, 1936–41, box 7; however, the papers of four black women nurses in the Indian Service were retained for further consideration.

73 See report of article by Mrs Maurice G. Smith from the *Journal of the Washington Academy of Sciences*, in Office File of John Collier, box 12, Peyote 1925–1940 File.

74 Hatcher, pp. 105–27; and see Wanda Faye Sharp, 'The Black Dispatch. A sociological analysis' (MA thesis, University of Oklahoma, 1951), pp. 23–4, 29.

75 See newspaper article of 1 May 1931 from the *Daily Oklahoman* in box 6, Office Files of W. Carson Ryan.

76 See in DD for Oklahoma, testimony of Dr Ross Underwood, 18 February 1969, T. 506, Vol. 21; interviews with Leslie James, 23 April 1969, T. 457, Vol. 26, p. 2; with Ned Lusty, 28 November 1969, T–547–1(A), Vol. 51, p. 5; with Bentley Beams, 23 April 1969, T. 437, Vol. 26, p. 8; Debo, *And Still the Waters Run*, pp. 292–3; David R. Timmons, 'Elements of prejudice toward Negroes and Indians as found in daily newspapers of Seminole County, Oklahoma, 1950–1959' (MA thesis, University of Oklahoma, 1970), pp. 6–8, and chs 2–4.

77 The next two paragraphs draw on Walter L. Williams (ed.), *Southeastern Indians Since the Removal Era* (Athens, Ga, University of Georgia Press, 1979), pp. 34–43, 49–56, 79–84, 90–100, 107, 114–15, 118, 127, 131–4, 142–9, 154–67, 176–84, 193–202.

78 See Brewton Berry, *Almost White* (New York, Macmillan, 1963), pp. 32–3, 53–4, 63, 68–9, 90–1, 161; John H. Peterson, Jr, 'Louisiana Choctaw life at the end of the nineteenth century', in Hudson (ed.), *Four Centuries*, p. 109.

79 See Berry, pp. 116–17; article in *Christian Science Monitor*, 28 August 1931,

in BIC Newspaper Clippings; Eastern Indian Survey, in BIC files, tray 110; memoranda from John Herrick to Mr McNickle, 9 May 1938, and Ward Shepherd to the Commissioner, 10 October 1940, box 8, Subject Correspondence Files of John Herrick; and memorandum to Mr Herrick, 21 October 1939; on General Form of Reservation Handbooks, and memorandum to Mr Stewart, 1 May 1936, box 7, ibid.; correspondence in Office Records of Assistant Commissioner William Zimmerman, Memoranda, 1944–50, D–M; in Office Files of W. Carson Ryan, note to John Collier of 30 April 1934, box 5, and in ibid., box 7, memorandum on the Catawba Indians, Rock Hill, South Carolina, 'The Indians of Louisiana in 1931', by Roy Nash, Special Commissioner, pp. 11–12, box 4, and 'Probable identity of the "Croatan" Indians', by Dr J. R. Swanton, 1933, box 2. Charles M. Hudson, 'Indians and blacks in white America', in Hudson (ed.), *Four Centuries*, notes that the Lumberton Indians of North Carolina became Croatans by act of the North Carolina legislature in 1885, in the belief that they were descended from the white settlers of a lost colony (Roanoke) and local Indians; intermarriage with blacks was thereafter prohibited 'to avoid "debasing white blood" any further'!

80 See letter of W. Carson Ryan to a Mr Montet, no date (1930s) in box 1 of Office Files of W. Carson Ryan; article by F. W. Seymour, 'Some notes about the Indian', May 1929, in BIC Newspaper Clippings, and article from *Muskogee Times Democrat*, 12 October 1925(?), in ibid.; Moorehead, *An Analysis*, p. 15.

81 Article of 2/12/29, *Washington Post*, in BIC Newspaper Clippings; from *Washington Star*, 5 July 1931, in ibid.; *Washington News*, 12 February 1931, in ibid.; letter in *Portland Oregonian*, 5 May 1931, from Louis F. Paul, executive committee of the Alaska Native Brotherhood, in ibid; article in *The Sherman Bulletin*, Vol. XVII, no. 27, 6 April 1924, in ibid.; from *New York Evening Post*, 12 October 1929, tray 116, BIC files; articles by George P. Donehoo, 'The real Indian of the past and the real Indian of the present', *The Red Man*, tray 113, in ibid.; talk by Alice Lee Jemison, 27 July 1938, p. 2, in Jemison file, box 6, Office File of John Collier; article by John Collier, 'Are we making red slaves?', *Survey Graphic*, 1 January 1927, in Reference File of John Collier, 1939–45; and in ibid., article by Collier, 'Has the Indian more cause for complaint than the Negro?', 30 December 1930.

82 See letter of 4 October 1932 to Mr Millington from J. E. Molinray(?), forwarded to W. Carson Ryan, box 6, Office Files of W. Carson Ryan; W. Carson Ryan, 'Cooperation in Indian education', p. 16, box 1, ibid.; Collier, 'Are we making red slaves?', op. cit.; article from the *Epworth Herald*, 21 January 1933, BIC Newspaper Clippings.

83 Proceedings of the First Convention of the National Congress of American Indians, Denver 1944, pp. 3, 12; Annual Convention of the National Congress of American Indians . . . 1945, pp. 8 ff., 35, 37–8, 83 ff., in section X, Indian Organisations, OHS.

84 See Williams, pp. 204–6, and pp. 45, 64–7, 101, 106, 118, 136–8, 149–50, 166, 186–7; interview in DD for Oklahoma with Bentley Beams, op. cit., pp. 9–10, and Noah Fish, T–536–1, 7 November 1969, vol. 51, p. 6.

85 *Oklahoma County Cherokee Community Organisation Newsletter*, vol. 11, no. 12, December 1974, in section X, Newspapers, OHS.

86 See Tape 635, May 1970, discussion of students with Indian Leaders and Commissioner Bruce, May 1970, pp. 15–16, Doris Duke Collection, University of New Mexico, Albuquerque (hereafter DD for New Mexico).

87 See Tape 501, p. 25, in ibid., Mr Jerry Wilkinson of the National Indian Youth Council speaking.
88 ibid., pp. 26–7; and Vine Deloria, *Custer Died for Your Sins* (New York, Collier-Macmillan, 1969), pp. 3–4, 8.
89 See Tape 270, p. 5, interview with anonymous Navajo woman, transcribed December 1969, in Miscellaneous (current Indian Affairs) section, in DD for New Mexico.
90 See article by Tessie Belue, 'The black and the red: a result of divide and conquer?', *Wassaja*, vol. 5, no. 8, November–December 1977, p. 3, in section X, Newspapers, OHS.

CHAPTER 7

1 Deloria, *Custer Died for Your Sins*, ch. 4; see also P. Collier, 'The red man's burden', in T. R. Frazier (ed.), *The Underside of American History. Other Readings*, Vol. 2 (New York, Harcourt, Brace, Jovanovich, 1971, 2 vols), p. 335; Eileen Maynard, 'The growing negative image of the anthropologist among American Indians', *Human Organization*, vol. 33, no. 4, Winter 1974, pp. 402–3.
2 See David L. Marden, 'Anthropologists and federal Indian policy prior to 1940', *Indian Historian*, vol. 5, Winter 1972, p. 19; June Helm (ed.), *Pioneers of American Anthroplogy. The Uses of Biography* (Washington, DC, University of Washington Press, 1966), pp. 55, 165, 190; Maynard, 'The growing negative image of the anthropologist'.
3 See, reflecting American and British perspectives respectively, Fred W. Voget, *A History of Ethnology* (New York, Holt, Rinehart & Winston, 1975), and Lucy Mair, *An Introduction to Social Anthropology*, 2nd edn (Oxford, Clarendon Press, 1975).
4 See Dudley and Novak (eds), *The Wild Man Within.*
5 See Neil M. Judd, *The Bureau of American Ethnology. A Partial History* (Norman, Okla, University of Oklahoma Press, 1967), p. 7. On Indian autobiographies as a source, see Arnold Krupat, *For Those Who Came After. A Study of Native American Autobiographies* (Berkeley, Calif., University of California Press, 1985).
6 Robert F. Spencer, Jesse D. Jennings, *et al.*, *The Native Americans. Prehistory and Ethnology of the North American Indians* (New York, Harper & Row, 1965), p. 15; Don D. Fowler and Catherine S. Fowler, 'John Wesley Powell, anthropologist', *Utah Historical Quarterly*, vol. 37, Spring 1969, pp. 155–8.
7 For an introduction to the debate on American Indian origins, see Lee Eldridge Huddleston, 'Origins of the American Indians. A Study of European concepts of the origins of the American Indians, 1492–1729' (PhD dissertation, University of Texas, 1967).
8 Thomas L. McKenney and James Hall, *History of the Indian Tribes of North America, etc.*, Vol. 3 (Philadelphia, Pa, 1836, 3 vols), p. 3; H. R. Hays, *From Ape to Angel. An Informal History of Social Anthropology* (London, Methuen, 1959), pp. 38, 66; F. Eggan, *The American Indian. Perspectives for the Study of Social Change* (London, Weidenfeld & Nicolson, 1966), p. 4; and W. Stanton, *The Leopard's Spots. Scientific Attitudes Toward Race in America, 1815–59* (Chicago, University of Chicago Press, 1960), *passim.*
9 Statesman Thomas Jefferson, diplomat and archaeologist Ephraim

359

Squier, professor and minister Samuel Stanhope Smith, and author James Hall, for example, rejected degeneration theory, while contributor to the American Philosophical Society, Benjamin Smith Barton, and ethnologist Henry Rowe Schoolcraft favoured it; see Hays, pp. 70, 78–9; McKenney and Hall, Vol. 3, p. 46; Stanton, p. 34; Robert Eugene Bieder, 'The American Indian and the development of anthropological thought: the United States, 1780–1851' (PhD dissertation, University of Minnesota, 1972), pp. 4, 6–11, 49, 51–9, 102, 289, 291, 356–8.

10 Marvin Harris, *The Rise of Anthropological Theory. A History of Theories of Culture* (London, Routledge & Kegan Paul, 1968), pp. 37–8.

11 Bieder, pp. 203, 396–7.

12 Henry Rowe Schoolcraft, *Indian Legends from Algic Researches ... etc.* (ed. Mentor L. Williams; Lansing, Mich., Michigan State University Press, 1956), p. 22.

13 Gossett, *Race*, pp. 246–8; Bieder, pp. 289 ff., 365, 369, 371, 378.

14 Philip Borden, 'Found cumbering the soil. Manifest destiny and the Indian in the nineteenth century', in Gary B. Nash and Richard Weiss (eds), *The Great Fear*, p. 93; Bieder, pp. 379–80; Lewis Henry Morgan, *League of the Iroquois* (New York, Corinth Books, 1962 edn; originally 1851), p. 445 and *passim*; and Lewis Henry Morgan, 'The Indian question', *The Nation*, vol. XXVII, 28 November 1878, p. 332.

15 Powell quoted in P. Collier article, 'The red man's burden', in Frazier (ed.) p. 340.

16 For the views of James Hall, Samuel Morton, Josiah Nott and his journalist collaborator, Henry Hotz, see Hall, Vol. 3, pp. 12, 45, and Stanton, pp. 35, 175. For a defensive statement by an Indian spokesman, see Jack D. Forbes (ed.), *The Indian in America's Past* (New York, Prentice-Hall, 1964), pp. 56–60, 64–5, 67–9; Bieder, p. 106.

17 Stanton, p. 11.

18 Hays, p. 276; on Squier's ambivalence towards polygenism, see Bieder, pp. 358–9; and see ibid., p. 400; Stanton, pp. 32, 34; Ronald P. Rohner (ed.), *The Ethnography of Franz Boas* (Chicago, University of Chicago Press, 1969), p. xii. Morgan also flirted with the polygenist position, notwithstanding his broad sympathy with the Indians. See Reginald Horsman, 'Scientific racism and the American Indian in the mid-nineteenth century', *American Quarterly*, vol. XXVII, no. 2, May 1975, pp. 152–68.

19 Gossett, p. 237; John S. Haller, *Outcasts from Evolution. Scientific Attitudes of Racial Inferiority, 1859–1900* (New York, McGraw-Hill, 1975 edn), pp. 20–9.

20 Cyrus Thomas and M. J. McGee, *The Indian of North America in Historic Times*, Vol. II of G. C. Lee (ed.), *The History of North America* (Philadelphia, Pa, and London, 1903), p. viii.

21 George W. Stocking, *Race, Culture and Evolution. Essays in the History of Anthropology* (New York, Free Press, 1968), pp. 123–4; see pp. 97–120; Voget, pp. 190–1; Harris, p. 138; Carl Resek, *Lewis Henry Morgan. American Scholar* (Chicago, University of Chicago Press, 1960), p. 63; Haller, pp. 115–17; Daniel Garrison Brinton, *The American Race. A Linguistic Classification and Ethnographic Description of the Native Tribes of North and South America* (New York, 1891), pp. 40, 42; Daniel Garrison Brinton, *Races and Peoples. Lectures on the Science of Ethnography* (New York, 1890), p. 295; Thomas and McGee, pp. 4, 17–18, 424–5; A. F. Bandelier, *Final Report of Investigations Among the Indians of the Southwestern United States,*

Carried on Mainly in the Years from 1880 to 1885 (Papers of the Archaeological Institute of America, American Series, III, Cambridge, Mass., 1890), pt 1, pp. 26–7, 40–1.

22 Bieder, pp. 414–22.

23 See D. A. Lorimer, *Colour, Class and the Victorians* (Leicester, Leicester University Press, 1978), ch. 7.

24 Stanton, ch. 19 and p. 194; George M. Fredrickson, *The Black Image in the White Mind. The Debate on Afro-American Character and Destiny, 1817–1914* (New York, Harper & Row, 1971), pp. 84–90; Horsman, *Race and Manifest Destiny*, ch. 8.

25 Prucha, *American Indian Policy*, pp. 239, 243–4; William Goetzmann, *Exploration and Empire. The Explorer and the Scientist in the Winning of the American West* (New York, Knopf, 1966); Fowler and Fowler, p. 156; Horsman, *Race and Manifest Destiny*, chs 6, 10.

26 Charles H. Lange and C. L. Riley (eds), *The Southwestern Journals of Adolph F. Bandelier, 1880–1882* (Albuquerque, N. Mex., University of New Mexico Press, 1966), pp. 58–9; and Helm (ed.), pp. 209–10; though see also Bandelier's enthusiastic comments in L. A. White (ed.), *Pioneers of American Anthropology. The Bandelier–Morgan Letters, 1873–1883*, Vol. 2 (Albuquerque, N. Mex., University of New Mexico Press, 1940, 2 vols), pp. 213, 218–19; quotation from Judd, p. 34.

27 See Helm (ed.), p. 53.

28 Gossett, pp. 247–8; Bieder, pp. 417–18.

29 Bieder, pp. 417–18; Morgan, *League of the Iroquois*, pp. ix, 33–6, 452; Hays, p. 23; *American Indian Magazine* (quarterly journal of the Society of American Indians) vol. V, no. 2, April–June 1917, pp. 77–8.

30 Borden, p. 94; Priest, *Uncle Sam's Stepchildren*, p. 25.

31 Mardock, *The Reformers and the American Indian*, p. 16; Judd, pp. 53–4; and Nancy Oestreich Lurie, 'Women in early American anthropology' in Helm (ed.) pp. 43–54.

32 *Report of the Twenty-Ninth Annual Lake Mohonk Conference of Friends of the Indian and Other Dependent Peoples, October 18th, 19th and 20th, 1911* (Lake Mohonk Conference, New York, 1911), p. 230; *Proceedings of the Twenty-First Annual Meeting of the Lake Mohonk Conference of Friends of the Indian, 1903* (Lake Mohonk Conference, 1904), pp. 51, 73.

33 Burgess, 'The Lake Mohonk conferences on the Indian', pp. 202–4.

34 Burgess, p. 59, 110; *Proceedings of the Twenty-First Annual Meeting of the Lake Mohonk Conference*, pp. 60, 69, 79–80; Otis, *The Dawes Act*, pp. 38, 66–7, 70, 107; Fritz, 'The Board of Indian Commissioners', in Smith and Kvasnicka (eds), *Indian–White Relations*, pp. 68–9, 70–2; Lurie, 'Women in early American anthropology'; and Alice C. Fletcher, 'Allotment of lands to Indians', *Proceedings of the National Conference of Charities and Correction, 1887* (Boston, Mass., 1887), pp. 172–80.

35 Otis, pp. 37–8.

36 See Moorehead, *An Analysis*, p. 12; Judd, pp. 48–9.

37 *Proceedings of the Twenty-First Annual Meeting of the Lake Mohonk Conference*, p. 73; Haller, pp. viii, 204–10; Borden, p. 94; Gilcreast, 'Richard Henry Pratt', p. 75; Fowler and Fowler, pp. 158–72; Rohner, pp. xxvi–xxvii; Judd, pp. 3–22; and Wallace Stegner, *Beyond the Hundredth Meridian. John Wesley Powell and the Second Opening of the West* (Boston, Mass., Houghton Mifflin, 1954).

38 Schoolcraft, p. 307.

39 Morgan, *League of the Iroquois*, pp. 4, 181; Resek, p. 207.
40 Brinton, *The American Race*, pp. 48–9; J. W. Powell, *Introduction to the Study of Indian Languages*, 2nd edn (Washington DC, Government Printing Office, 1880), pp. 74a, b and c; Thomas and McGee, pp. 417, 420, 429–31; Bieder, pp. 202–3, 215.
41 See Rohner, Introduction; Hays, chs 23, 26; Stocking, chs 7–9, II; Ruth Bunzel's Introduction, pp. 6–10, in Franz Boas, *Anthropology and Modern Life* (New York, Norton, 1962 edn) and ch. II, pp. 50, 55, and ch. IX, especially p. 239.
42 Voget, pp. 335–6; Rohner, p. xxiii.
43 ibid., pp. 336–7; Marden, p. 20.
44 Frank Porter III, 'Anthropologists at work: a case study of the Nanticoke community', *American Indian Quarterly*, vol. 4, February 1978, pp. 1–18, especially p. 7; Marden, p. 20; Gossett, p. 424; Helm (ed.), pp. 196, 200–1; Hazel W. Hertzberg, *The Search for an American Indian Identity. Modern Pan-Indian Movements* (Syracuse, NY, Syracuse University Press, 1971), p. 305; Rohner, p. 301.
45 Hertzberg, pp. 4, 23, 111, 153; Burgess, p. 343; Judd, pp. 50–2.
46 Hertzberg, p. 133; *Quarterly Journal* of the Society of American Indians, vol. I, no. 1, April 1913, pp. 33–5; Vol. I, no. 2, April–June 1913, pp. 138, 173–4; vol. III, no. 2, April-June 1915, p. 127.
47 Hertzberg, pp. 97, 108; *Quarterly Journal*, vol. III, no. 3, July–September 1915, pp. 204–5; editorial in the *American Indian Magazine* (the renamed *Quarterly Journal*), vol. IV, no. 1, January–March 1916, p. 13; and 'A message to Congress', in the *American Indian Magazine*, vol. IV, no. 4, October–December 1916, pp. 282–4.
48 Marden, p. 21.
49 Kvasnicka and Viola (eds), *The Commissioners*, pp. 233, 235, 240, 244.
50 See article by Robin Winks, 'American and European imperialism compared', in Richard H. Miller (ed.), *American Imperialism in 1898. The Quest for National Fulfilment* (New York, Wiley, 1970), pp. 182–3; Mair, pp. 286–7; article by Edward A. Kennard and Gordon MacGregor, 'Applied anthropology in government: United States', in Alfred L. Kroeber (ed.), *Anthropology Today. An Encyclopedic Inventory* (Chicago, University of Chicago Press, 1954 edn), p. 832.
51 See accounts of the work of the Committee of One Hundred in tray 109, BIC files; see also Moorehead, *An Analysis*, pp. 6–7; Marden, pp. 21–3; Philp, *John Collier's Crusade for Indian Reform*, pp. 35, 55: as Philp points out, the Indian Rights Association also opposed the Bursum Bill without admiring Pueblo culture.
52 Chandler, 'Anthropologists and U.S. Indians', pp. 15–18, 31–4, 36, 41–2, 45, 47, 55, 65, 67, 69, 71–2, 76, 79.
53 Study of Redfield, Linton and Herskovits, 1936, quoted in Voget, p. 724; see also Voget, pp. 721–5; B. Malinowski, 'Practical anthropology', *Africa*, vol. II, no. 1, 1929; and B. Malinowski, 'The rationalization of anthropology and administration', *Africa*, vol. III, no. 4, 1931.
54 Voget, p. 724; for the differing British approach, see Mair, pp. 268 ff.
55 See Dr Cole's address, 'The relation of anthropology to Indian and immigrant affairs', 7 March 1930, in BIC Newspaper Clippings.
56 Philp, *John Collier's Crusade for Indian Reform*, pp. 161–2; Marden, p. 23.
57 See paper (24 May 1934) by Allan G. Harper of the American Indian

Defense Association, 'Is the proposed new program, as embodied in the Wheeler-Howard Bill, desirable and feasible?', *op. cit.*, pp. 2, 6.

58 Philp, *John Collier's Crusade for Indian Reform*, pp. 120, 122, 162; Marden, p. 25; William E. Leuchtenburg, *Franklin D. Roosevelt and the New Deal, 1932–1940* (New York, Harper Torchbooks, 1963), pp. 32–3, 63–4; pamphlet of the American Indian Federation, 'To the American citizenship of the United States', in box 1, Office File of Commissioner John Collier.

59 See Collier's 'The unfinished tasks of the Indian Service', p. 6, in Miscellaneous File, Office Files of Assistant Commissioner Provinse; memorandum, 'The greatest unmet practical need in Indian Service', 21 November 1944, by Collier, in box 12, Office File of Commissioner John Collier.

60 Philp, *John Collier's Crusade for Indian Reform*, p. 136; memorandum from H. Scudder MeKeel, 21 April 1936, to Mr Charles Wisdom, Choctaw Agency, Philadelphia, Mississippi, in Subject Files of John Herrick; Alexander Spoehr, 22 August 1939, to Collier, in Seminole File, Office Records of Assistant Commissioner William Zimmerman, Correspondence, box 3; Kennard and MacGregor, p. 833.

61 Letter of Collier to John Evans, General Superintendent, United Pueblos Agency, in Reference File of John Collier.

62 Memorandum to Collier from H. Scudder MeKeel, 21 May 1936, in Office File of Commissioner John Collier, box 16; article by Gertrude Seymour, 13 May 1916, 'Peyote worship – an Indian cult and a powerful drug', pp. 350–1, in tray 119, BIC files; in Office File of Commissioner John Collier, box 12, Peyote 1925–1940 File, Doc. 137817, Statements on Senate Bill 1399, 8 February 1937 by a number of anthropologists, pp. 1, 12–14, 15, 17; and in ibid., Discussion concerning Peyote (Reprinted from Hearings of the Subcommittee of the House Committee on Appropriations Bill for 1936), pp. 689–96, especially p. 691; box 13, letters and memoranda of Collier of 2 January 1942, 16 December 1941, 1 October 1941, 15 January 1941, 6 December 1940; Taylor, *The New Deal and American Indian Tribalism*, p. 47.

63 Clipping from *Rocky Mountain News*, Denver, Colo, 11 November 1930, letter of 10 September 1930 from Dr E. A. Bates to Mrs Joseph Lindon Smith of the General Federation of Women's Clubs, Dublin, New Hampshire, and Address of Charles J. Rhoads, Commissioner of Indian Affairs, Before the Indian Committee of the National Conference of Social Work, in Philadelphia, 19 May 1932, in Office of the Commissioner, Personal and Semi-Official Files; paper by Eliot D. Chapple, Dept of Anthropology, Harvard, on 'Anthropological engineering', pp. 18–19, in Office File of Joseph C. McCaskill, and in ibid., Report of the Committee on Administrative Research of the Society for Applied Anthropology and representatives of the Indian Office, 26 October 1944; details of this meeting are also in box 12 of Office File of Commissioner John Collier. See also Kennard and MacGregor, pp. 833–6.

64 See, in McCaskill File, anthropologists file, including 'Anthropology during the War and after', 10 March 1943, by the Committee on War Service of Anthropologists, Division of Anthropology and Psychology, National Research Council, pp. 5, 7, 9–11, 15; and paper by Eliot D. Chapple, op. cit., pp. 18–19. And see article by Narz R. Haas, 'The application of linguistics to language teaching', in Kroeber (ed.), *Anthropology Today*, pp. 807–18.

65 Memorandum to Collier from H. Scudder MeKeel, Field Representative in charge of Applied Anthropology, 1 December 1937, in Subject Correspon-

dence Files of John Herrick, box 7; Philp, 'John Collier, 1933–45', in Kvasnicka and Viola (eds), *The Commissioners*, p. 276, on the Applied Anthropology Unit's financial difficulties. On the lack of anthropological expertise about the Navajos, see letter by Richard F. Van Valkenburgh, 1945 (?), box 5, Van Valkenburgh Papers, MS 831, Arizona Historical Society Library.

66 Philp, *John Collier's Crusade for Indian Reform*, pp. 206–7.

67 ibid., p. 207.

68 Chandler, ch. 4, especially pp. 81–3, 88, 90–5, 100–1, 103; see letter to Dr Fejos of 21 October 1944 asking for a $6,000 grant for the project from the Viking Fund, in Reference File of John Collier; for more details about the Personality Studies see Personality–Study material in box 12, Office File of Commissioner John Collier; and in ibid., 'Statement made to the Committee on Administrative Research of the Society for Applied Anthropology, October 26, 1944', pp. 1–2, 102897–3; Philp, *John Collier's Crusade for Indian Reform*, p. 208.

69 See paper by Eliot D. Chapple, op. cit., pp. 16–17.

70 Kennard and MacGregor, pp. 837–40; George M. Foster, *Traditional Societies and Technological Change* (New York, Harper & Row, 1973), pp. 256–7.

71 See Chandler, pp. 107–8; Voget, pp. 733–85, especially pp. 745–7, 753–67 and 772–7; Mair, pp. 288–303; and Linton, *Study of Man*, pp. 358 ff.

72 See John J. Bodine, 'Blue Lake: a struggle for Indian rights', *American Indian Law Review*, vol. 1, Winter 1973, pp. 23–32.

73 See, for instance, F. Gearing, R. Netting and L. Peattie (eds), *Documentary History of the Fox Project, 1948–1959. A Program in Action Anthropology* (Chicago, University of Chicago Press, 1960).

74 *Hearings Before the Subcommittee on Indian Affairs of the Committee on Indian Affairs of the Committee on Interior and Insular Affairs, House of Representatives, Ninety-Third Congress, First Session on H.R. 7421* (Washington, DC, US Government Printing Office, 1973), pp. 180–99.

75 Kvasnicka and Viola (eds), p. 312.

76 ibid., pp. 315–20; *Hearings, etc.*, pp. 123 ff.

77 Voget, pp. 777–83; Szasz, *Education and the American Indian*, p. 189; Judd, pp. vii, 34–6.

78 Mario D. Zamora, 'Moral, immoral science. The case for cultural anthropology', *The Indian Historian*, vol. 6, no. 2, Spring 1973, pp. 26–7.

79 See tape 636, pp. 14–17, discussion between Agnes and Brian Ortiz, Bruce Alexander, Irene Silentman and Anna Boyd, University of New Mexico, 22 May 1970, in DD for New Mexico; Szasz, *Education and the American Indian*, p. 227; testimony of Benjamin A. Reifel, Area Director, Aberdeen, 24 July 1956 session, p. 28, in Records of Bureau-Tribal Conference, July 1956, Bureau of Indian Affairs, 68A–2045, no. 369, box 1.

80 Steven Polgar, 'Skills needed in action anthropology: lessons from El Centro de la Causa', *Human Organization*, vol. 33, no. 2, Summer 1974, p. 203.

81 See Helm (ed.), p. 77; Peter Farb, *Man's Rise to Civilization. As Shown by the Indians of North America from Primeval Times to the Coming of the Industrial State* (New York, Dutton, 1968), pp. 243–94; for similar comments by other anthropologists, see Collier article, pp. 339, 347; Harold Driver, *Indians of North America* (Chicago, University of Chicago Press, 1961 and 1969), p. xv; Spencer, Jennings *et al.*, *The Native Americans*; Oswalt, *This*

Land Was Theirs; Roger C. Owen, James F. Deetz and Anthony D. Fisher (eds), *The North American Indians. A Sourcebook* (New York, Macmillan, 1967); and the authors cited by Voget in ch. 19.

82 See Chandler, ch. 5. In the Holt, Rinehart & Winston series, see, for instance, Elizabeth Grobsmith, *Lakota of the Rosebud. A Contemporary Ethnography* (New York, 1981), and Malcolm McFee, *Modern Blackfeet. Montanans on Reservations* (New York, 1972). And see Stephan Thernstrom (ed.), *Harvard Encyclopedia of American Ethnic Groups* (Cambridge, Mass., Harvard University Press, 1981 edn), pp. 58–122.

CHAPTER 8

1 Morgan, *League of the Iroquois,* p. 452.
2 See Mather, *The Life and Death of the Reverend Mr. John Eliot, etc.,* 3rd edn (London, 1694), p. 88; Berkhofer, *Salvation and the Savage,* p. 5; Axtell, *The European and the Indian,* pp. 43–4, 61–2.
3 Lurie, 'Indian cultural adjustment to European civilization', in Smith (ed.), *Seventeenth-Century America,* pp. 37, 39, 43–5, 51, 56–7; Lawrence A. Cremin, *American Education. The Colonial Experience, 1607–1783* (New York, Harper Torchbooks, 1970), p. 158; Axtell, 'The scholastic philosophy', in his *The School upon a Hill,* pp. 245–51.
4 Cremin, *American Education,* pp. 158–63, 194–5, 222–3; Bernard Bailyn, *Education in the Formation of American Society. Needs and Opportunities for Study* (New York, Vintage Books, 1960), pp. 37–8, 69; Norman Earl Tanis, 'Education and John Eliot's Indian utopias, 1645–1675', *History of Education Quarterly,* vol. X, no. 3, Fall 1970, pp. 308–23; Vaughan, *New England Frontier,* pp. 303–7; Wilcomb E. Washburn (ed.), *The Indian and the White Man* (Garden City, Doubleday, 1964), p. 185.
5 Cremin, *American Education,* pp. 328, 341–51, 360; Axtell, 'Dr Wheelock's little red school', in his *The European and the Indian,* pp. 89–109; Margaret Connell Szasz, ' "Poor Richard", meets the Native American: schooling for young Indian women in eighteenth-century Connecticut', *Pacific Historical Review,* vol. XLIX, 1980, pp. 215–35.
6 See *The Society for Propagating the Gospel among the Indians and Others in North America, 1781–1887* (University Press, 1887), p. 19.
7 See Michael B. Katz, *The Irony of Early School Reform. Educational Innovation in Mid-Nineteenth Century Massachusetts* (Cambridge, Mass., Harvard University Press, 1968), Introduction and pt one, especially p. 47; Frederick M. Binder, *The Age of the Common School, 1830–1865* (New York, Wiley, 1974), ch. one; David B. Tyack and Thomas James, 'Education for a republic', *This Constitution: A Bicentennial Chronicle,* Winter 1985, pp. 17–24, esp. p. 17.
8 M. B. Katz, p. 35.
9 See George Catlin, *Letters and Notes on the Manners, Customs and Conditions of the North American Indians, etc.* Vol. I (London, 1841), pp. 8, 10, 210, Vol. II, pp. 244–5; Morgan, *League of the Iroquois,* pp. ix, 4, 35–6, 141–3, 179–81, 446–53; Schoolcraft, *Indian Legends,* pp. xii–xiii, 16–17; McKenney and Hall, *History of the Indian Tribes of North America,* Vol. 1, pp. 4, 64; Vol. 2, p. 200; Vol. 3, pp. 12, 15.
10 See Herman J. Viola's article, 'Thomas L. McKenney, 1824–30', in Kvasnicka and Viola (eds), *The Commissioners* p. 5. The appropriation continued until the repeal of the act in 1873.

11 Tuckerman, *A Discourse, Preached ... November 1, 1821*, pp. 15–16, 23 ff.
12 See Berkhofer, *Salvation and the Savage*, ch. six.
13 See M. B. Katz, pp. 84–5; Berkhofer, *Salvation and the Savage*, p. 18.
14 See Rister, *Baptist Missions Among the American Indians*, p. 67.
15 See, for instance, William T. Hagan, *The Sac and Fox Indians* (Norman, Okla, University of Oklahoma Press, 1958), p. 250.
16 Driver, *Indians of North America*, pp. 361, 379–92.
17 See Cremin, *American Education*, pp. 124–317, 480–91; Driver, pp. 386–9; Binder, *Age of the Common School*, pp. 143–59; Nancy F. Cott, 'Notes towards an interpretation of antebellum childrearing', *The Psychohistory Review*, vol. 6, no. 4, 1978, pp. 4–20.
18 See Berkhofer, *Salvation and the Savage*, ch. two; M. B. Katz, pp. 51–6, 87, 112, 120, 121–3, 125–8, 130–2, 136, 144, 147–8, 153–4, 164, 180, 192, 194–5, 210–11; David Nasaw, *Schooled to Order. A Social History of Public Schooling in the United States* (New York, Oxford University Press, 1979), chs 1–5; Rister, p. 50 and *passim*.
19 On Indian education after removal and up to the Civil War, see Kvasnicka and Viola (eds), pp. 15, 25–6, 30, 43, 50–1, 59, 71, 92; Evelyn C. Adams, *American Indian Education. Government Schools and Economic Progress* (New York, Amo Press, 1971 edn), pp. 34–45; M. T. Bailey, *Reconstruction in Indian Territory*, pp. 15–22; Binder, *Age of the Common School*, pp. 20, 136–8; Hagan, *United States–Comanche Relations*, pp. 14, 18; Edward Everett Dale, *The Indians of the Southwest. A Century of Development under the United States* (Norman, Okla, University of Oklahoma Press, 1971 edn), p. 176; Spicer (ed.), *Perspectives*, p. 354; Danziger, *Indians and Bureaucrats*, Introduction, and pp. 98, 145, 148–9; McReynolds, *The Seminoles*, pp. 131, 281–6; Debo, *Rise and Fall of the Choctaw Republic*, pp. 42–5, 60–3; Debo, *Road to Disappearance*, pp. 33, 65, 84 ff., 87 ff., 92, 94 ff, 97, 99, 110, 116–21, 126, 130–1; Gibson, *The Chickasaws*, pp. 108–14, 136–7, 231–6; Wardell, *A Political History of the Cherokee Nation*, pp. 116–17.
20 Kvasnicka and Viola (eds), p. 92; Debo, *Road to Disappearance*, pp. 146 ff, 155; Gibson, *The Chickasaws*, p. 236, 271; Debo, *Rise and Fall*, pp. 95–7.
21 See William Preston Vaughn, *Schools for All. The Blacks and Public Education in the South, 1865–1877* (Lexington, Ky, University of Kentucky Press, 1974), pp. 22–3, 158–9; and for the later nineteenth century, Jacqueline Fear's excellent study, 'American Indian Education: The Reservation Schools, 1870–1900' (Ph.D. thesis, University of London, 1978).
22 First quotation from W. E. B. DuBois, *The Education of Black People. Ten Critiques, 1906–1960* (ed. Herbert Aptheker; Amherst, Mass., University of Massachusetts Press, 1973), p. 139; Leon F. Litwack, *Been in the Storm So Long. The Aftermath of Slavery* (London, Athlone, 1980), pp. 473–85; Morris, *Reading, 'Riting, and Reconstruction*, pp. ix-xi, 227 and *passim*; David B. Tyack, *The One Best System. A History of American Urban Education* (Cambridge, Mass., Harvard University Press, 1974), pp. 105–6 and *passim*; Nasaw, pp. 68–75, 120, 135, chs 8–9; Horace Mann Bond (source of second quotation), *Negro Education in Alabama. A Study in Cotton and Steel* (New York, Atheneum, 1969 edn), pp. 141–7, 289; Takaki, *Iron Cages*, pt three; (third quotation) Clark Mills, ethnologist of the Smithsonian Institution, to Richard Pratt, 16 December 1878, quoted in Gilcreast, 'Richard Henry Pratt', pp. 22–3; Carleton Mabee, *Black Education in New York State. From Colonial to Modern Times* (Syracuse, NY, Syracuse University Press, 1979), p. 98, ch. 9.

23 See Tucson Indian Industrial Training School, 1888–1953, letter copy
book, Vol. 1, pp. 431, 439, 467; Vol. 2, pp. 33–4, 52, 63–4, 69, 87, 89, 92,
93–6, 108–9, 114, 279–80, 284, 343, 364, 421; Vol. 3, pp. 25, 27, 392, 463,
421–2 (source of quotation about George Enos); and article on the school
in *La Aurora*, vol. IV, no. 8, Albuquerque, N. Mex., 26 March 1903 – all in
MS 809, Arizona Historical Society manuscript collections (hereafter
AHS); report from Superintendent Charles E. Burton to Commissioner of
Indian Affairs, from Moqui Training School, Keam's Canyon, Arizona, 10
July 1903, p. 9, on the good Moqui response to field matrons, in box 6,
Richard F. Van Valkenburgh Papers, 1880–1946, MS 831 in AHS; Tatum,
Our Red Brothers, pp. 81–2, 94–9, 227–30, 234, 237, 240, 243–4, 268, 300–1,
318; Fritz, *The movement for Indian Assimilation*, ch. IV; Adams, *American
Indian Education*, p. 55; Francis Paul Prucha, *The Churches and the Indian
Schools, 1888–1912* (Lincoln, Nebr., University of Nebraska Press, 1979),
pp. 1–9, 41; Ann Douglas, *The Feminization of American Culture* (New York,
Avon Books (Discus), 1977), pp. 86–90, 117–19, 130–1 and *passim*;
Joseph P. Kett, *Rites of Passage. Adolescence in America 1790 to the Present*
(New York, Basic Books, 1977), pp. 114–16; Philip J. Greven, *The Protestant Temperament. Patterns of Child-Rearing. Religious Experience and the Self
in Early America* (New York, New American Library, 1979); Cott, 'Notes
... antebellum childrearing'; D. T. Rodgers, 'Socialising middle-class
children. Institutions, fables and work values in nineteenth-century
America', *Journal of Social History*, vol. 13, no. 3, Spring 1980, pp. 354–64.
24 In 1908 the Supreme Court decided that school contracting using Indian
treaty and trust funds was legal, but it became very uncommon from this
point onwards, and in 1917 Congress forbade the use of US Treasury
funds for sectarian schools. See Burgess, 'The Lake Mohonk conferences
on the Indian', pp. 23–4, 65–7, 78–9, 214–15; Kvasnicka and Viola (eds),
pp. 184, 199, 214, 224–6; see report of Board of Indian Commissioners,
1901, on sectarian schools, in BIC files, tray 122; *A Response to Senator
Pettigrew* (IRA tract no. 40, 1897), p. 2; Prucha, *The Churches and the Indian
Schools*, pp. 204–5 and *passim*; *Shall Public Funds Be Expended For the Support
of Sectarian Indian Schools?* (IRA tract no. 99, 1915), p. 3; *Thirty-Third
Annual Report of the Executive Committee of the Indian Rights Association for
the Year Ending December 15, 1915* (Philadelphia, Pa, 1915), pp. 9–17; and
Report of the same for 1917, pp. 49–50; Gilcreast, ch. VI; Fredric Mitchell
and James W. Skelton, 'The church-state conflict in early Indian education', *History of Education Quarterly*, vol. VI, no. 1, Spring 1966,
pp. 41–51. And on church efforts in education, see Fear, pp. 99 ff.
25 *Annual Meeting and Report of the Women's National Indian Association,
October 27, 1883* (Philadelphia, Pa, 1887), p. 10; *Annual Report of the
Women's National Indian Association, November 17, 1885* (Philadelphia, Pa,
1885), p. 26; *Indians and Other Helpers* (WNIA pamphlet), pp. 6, 8; *First
Annual Report of the Executive Committee of the Indian Rights Association, for
the Year Ending December, 1883* (Philadelphia, Pa, 1884), p. 6; Burgess,
pp. 19, 22, 24, 65–7, and the *Proceedings* of the Conference from 1883; and
*Summary, Work and Recommendations of Board of Indian Commissioners from
Annual Reports, 1869–1915*, pp. 5, 12, 13, 15, 16.
26 Kvasnicka and Viola (eds), pp. 176, 183–4, 189–90. However, in 1889 the
office of superintendent was reduced to an advisory one by an Act of
Congress of 2 March.
27 Kvasnicka and Viola (eds), pp. 196–9; Burgess, pp. 79, 86–7; Kett, p. 142;

Proceedings of the Seventh Annual Meeting of the Lake Mohonk Conference of Friends of the Indian, 1889 (Lake Mohonk Conference, 1889), pp. 16–34; *Proceedings of the Tenth Annual Meeting of the Lake Mohonk Conference of Friends of the Indian, 1892* (Lake Mohonk Conference, 1892), pp. 15–16; Commissioner of Indian Affairs, *Annual Report*, 1889, pp. 93–114; Schmeckebier, *The Office of Indian Affairs*, p. 70; Gilcreast, pp. 285 ff.

28 Kvasnicka and Viola (eds), pp. 231, 233–42; John F. Berens, 'Old campaigners, new realities. Indian policy reform in the Progressive era, 1908–1912', *Mid-America*, January 1977, pp. 51–64.

29 Litwack, *Been in the Storm So Long*, pp. 485–9; Vaughn, *passim*; Fritz, *Assimilation* pp. 114, 116.

30 See F. Leupp, *Notes of a Summer Tour Among Indians of the Southwest* (IRA pamphlet no. 43, Philadelphia, Pa, 1897), pp. 24–6; C. C. Painter, *Extravagance, Waste and Failure of Indian Education* (IRA tract no. 11, 1892), pp. 18–19, 21–2; Herbert Welsh, *How to Bring the Indian to Citizenship, and Citizenship to the Indian* (IRA tract no. 12, 1892), pp. 10–11; Kvasnicka and Viola (eds), pp. 222, 231; Gilcreast, pp. 162–9, 248–9, 364–7; Frederick E. Hoxie, *A Final Promise. The Campaign to Assimilate the Indians, 1880–1920* (Lincoln, Nebr., University of Nebraska Press, 1984), *passim*.

31 Gilcreast, p. 66; Dale, pp. 167, 172–3, 182–3; E. C. Adams, pp. 54–6, 61; Hagan, *United States–Comanche Relations*, pp. 162–4, 195–7, 198; Kvasnicka and Viola (eds), p. 214; letter copy book of Tucson Indian Training School, Vol. 2, pp. 103, 290–1; and Fear, p. 399.

32 Kvasnicka and Viola (eds), p. 225; Stuart, *The Indian Office*, pp. 97, 102, 110 ff.; Prucha, *The Churches and the Indian Schools*, pp. 86–7 and chs 7–9; Hagan, *United States–Comanche Relations*, pp. 199–200.

33 See Otis, *The Dawes Act*, p. 79; complaints about inadequate industrial training and attempts to improve it in letters of 1 August 1891 and 11 November 1891 in folders 1 and 2, Fort Mohave Indian School Collection, MS 267, AHS; Ann M. Keppel, 'The myth of agrarianism in rural educational reform, 1890–1914', *History of Education Quarterly*, vol. II, no. 2, June 1962, pp. 100–12.

34 E. G. Eastman, *Pratt*, pp. 64–6, 69–72; Pratt, *Battlefield and Classroom*, pp. 213–14; Gilcreast, pp. 51–3, 55–6, 60–1, 63, 65–6, 68, 80, 83–6, 91–103, 256–7, 298–9, 325–6; Pratt to Thomas L. Sloan, 21 August 1909, in Carlos Montezuma Papers, 1899–1922, box 1, folder 1, University of Arizona Library; Samuel Chapman Armstrong, *The Indian Question* (Hampton, Va, Normal School Press, 1883).

35 Hertzberg, *The Search for an American Indian Identity*, pp. 18–20, 75, 99; Senator James H. Kyle, 'How shall the Indian be educated?', *North American Review*, vol. CLIX, November 1894, pp. 437–47; Elizabeth Jacoway, *Yankee Missionaries in the South. The Penn School Experiment* (Baton Rouge, La, and London, Louisiana State University Press, 1980), pp. xiv–xv, 253–4, 259, 267; Joe M. Richardson, *A History of Fisk University, 1865–1946* (University, Ala, University of Alabama Press, 1980); Hagan, *United States–Comanche Relations*, pp. 164, 224; Tatum, p. 331; Charles A. Eastman, *From the Deep Woods to Civilization. Chapters in the Autobiography of an Indian* (Lincoln, Nebr., University of Nebraska Press, 1977 edn); Thomas A. Alford, *Civilisation* (Norman, Okla, University of Oklahoma Press, 1936); J. Betzinez, *I Fought with Geronimo* (Harrisburg, Pa, Stackpole, 1959); Moorehead, *The American Indian in the United States, period 1850–1914* (Andover, Mass., Andover Press, 1914), p. 203; letter of

21 April 1891, Vol. 2, p. 472, Tucson Indian Training School, letter copy book; letter of 6 April 1906, Vol. 3, p. 13, ibid.; Robert A. Trennert, Jr, 'From Carlisle to Phoenix. The rise and fall of the outing system, 1878–1930', *Pacific Historical Review*, Vol. LII, 1983, pp. 267–91; Frederick E. Hoxie, 'Redefining Indian education. Thomas J. Morgan's program in disarray', *Arizona and the West*, Vol. XXIV, 1982, pp. 5–18. See also Robert A. Trennert, Jr, 'Educating Indian girls at nonreservation boarding schools, 1878–1920', *Western Historical Quarterly*, vol. 13, July 1982, pp. 271–90.

36 See Gilcreast, p. 365.

37 Dale, pp. 176–7; Hagan, *United States–Comanche Relations*, pp. 133–4, 160–1, 221–3; Spicer (ed.), *Perspectives*, p. 316.

38 See letter of 23 June 1891, folder 1, and letters of 27 December 1892 and 13 April 1893, folder 2, in Fort Mohave Indian School Collection, AHS. See Irving G. Hendrick, 'Federal policy affecting the education of Indians in California, 1849–1934', *History of Education Quarterly*, vol. 16, Summer 1976, pp. 163–85. And on the Santee, see Fear, pp. 222–8.

39 Mitchell and Skelton, p. 47.

40 Morrison, 'Social history of the Choctaw', p. 89; but see also, for the advocacy of practical training schools, message of I. L. Garvin to the Choctaw National Council, summarized in *Indian Journal*, vol. 4, no. 10, 13 November 1879, in Garvin Collection, WHC; and message of Green McCurtain, reported in *Indian Citizen*, vol. 20, no. 7, 29 June 1905, Green McCurtain Collection, box 5, WHC; Debo, *And Still the Waters Run*, pp. 66–8; Spicer (ed.), *Perspectives*, p. 234, 252, 255, 391; Timothy L. Smith, 'Immigrant social aspirations and American education, 1880–1930', *American Quarterly*, vol. XXI, no. 3, Fall 1969, pp. 527–8; Robert G. Sherer, *Subordination or Liberation? The Development and Conflicting Theories of Black Education in Nineteenth-Century Alabama* (University, Ala, University of Alabama Press, 1977), pp. 147–8 and *passim*.

41 Kett, pp. 111, 129–31, 140–3 and ch. 6; Nasaw, pp. 120, 135, and chs 8–9 generally; Keppel, p. 100; Edward H. Clarke, *Sex in Education. Or, a Fair Chance for the Girls* (Boston, Mass., Osgood, 1873).

42 Entry 761, Industries Section, Indian Employment, RG 75, 1914, letters from superintendents of Red Cliff Indian Agency, Wisconsin, and Walker River Agency, Nevada; Schmeckebier, p. 216; Kvasnicka and Viola (eds), pp. 213–14, 217, 224, 231, 235, 248–9; E. C. Adams, pp. 62–5; *Thirtieth Annual Report of the Executive Committee of the Indian Rights Association, 1912* (Philadelphia, Pa, 1912), p. 80; *The Indian Craftsman*, vol. 2, no. 3, pp. 20–2; *The Red Man*, vol. 8, no. 9, May 1916, pp. 310, 312; *Conclusions Arrived at by Indian School Supervisors in Conference at Washington, D.C., 22 June–July 10, 1911*, in BIC files and tray 112; Letter of a Special Committee of Three to the Board, Albany, N.Y., March 10, 1911, p. 6, tray 106, in ibid.; Dale, p. 188; Kett, p. 241; Nasaw, pp. 154–8; *Quarterly Journal* of the Society of American Indians (in future SAI), vol. I, no. 4, October–December 1913, pp. 427–9; vol. II, no. 4, October–December 1914, p. 317; vol. V, no. 1, January–March 1917, p. 100; Debo, *And Still the Waters Run*, pp. 70–4, 276–7; Debo, *Rise and Fall*, pp. 285–6; articles in *Wynnewood New Era*, vol. 6, no. 8, 19 September 1907, in Chickasaw Miscellaneous papers, WHC; in *Muskogee Phoenix*, vol. 7, no. 9, 19 April 1894, in Pleasant Porter Collection, box 1, WHC; in *South McAlister Capital*, vol. 6, no. 10, 26 January 1899, in Green McCurtain Collection, box 2, WHC; *Indian Citizen*,

29 June 1905, in ibid.; Report of the Commissioner to the Five Civilized Tribes to the Secretary of the Interior. For the Fiscal Year Ended June 30, 1910, # 17705, pp. 62, 64, Choctaw Records, OHS; Neighborhood Schools, Choctaw and Chickasaw, Indian Territory, 1901 and 1907, and Day Schools, Cherokee Nation, Indian Territory, 1906–7, entries 736 and 737, in RG 75; also *Third Annual Report of the Supervisor of Indian Education ... 1934*, Office Files of Chief of Education Division, W. Carson Ryan, entry 723, in ibid.; Keppel, pp. 100–1.

43 See, in Office Files of General Superintendent (H. B. Peairs), entry 722, RG 75, Survey of Examination Papers, 1910–11; Assistant Commissioner to Mr Thomas Jackson, Fort Berthold (N. Dak.), Day School no. 2, n.d.; to Superintendent of Haskell Institute, Kan., 24 June 1911; to Superintendent of Tomah Indian School, Wis., 28 June 1911; to Mrs Susan F. Nichols, New York City, 16 June 1911; to Superintendent of Navajo Indian School, Ariz., 1911.

44 Hertzberg, pp. 74, 98–9, 108, 117, 137, 152; *Quarterly Journal* of the SAI, vol. I, no. 1, April 1913, article on Indian Education by Laura Cornelius Kellog (an Oneida), p. 46; vol. I, no. 2, p. 122, comments of Frederick E. Parker (a Seneca) appreciative of Indian schools but on the need to consult the Indians; vol. II, no. 2, April–June 1914, p. 137; vol. III, no. 3, July–September 1915, p. 151–2; vol. IV, no. 3, July–September 1916, pp. 223–4; Fayette A. McKenzie, 'The American Indian of to-day and to-morrow', article of 191 clipped in entry 1395, tray 113, BIC files; article by the Superintendent of Chemawa Indian School, Oregon (O. H. Lipps) in *Chemawa American*, vol. XXXI, no. 24, 26 February 1930, p. 3.

45 See in Carlos Montezuma Papers, box 1, Correspondence, letters by Pratt to Montezuma, 16 September 1909, 27 April 1910, 29 June 1911, folder 1; 11 December 1912, 16 January 1913, 17 July 1913, 20 September 1913, 28 November 1913, and Pratt to F. A. McKenzie, 11 January 1912, folder 2; 24 October 1914, 7 January 1915, folder 3; 2 February 1920, 1 September 1920, Pratt to Gilbert H. Grosvenor, 18 April 1922, folder 4.

46 Trays 107, 120 and 121 on Returned Students, in BIC files; and entry 761, Industries Section, Indian Employment, especially James B. Nash (Digger), Knights Ferry, Stanislaus Co., California, to Dagenett, 13 February 1911; Priscilla La Mote (Monominee), Neopit, Wis., to Dagenett, 8 August 1910; Eva Calhoun, Germantown, Philadelphia, to the Acting Commissioner, 1918 (?); and letters to Dagenett or Commissioner of Indian Affairs on reservation conditions from Truxton Canyon Indian School, 18 February 1914; Shivwits School, Santa Clara, 18 February 1914; Hayward Training School, Wis., 26 February 1914; Fond du Lac School, Minn., 26 February 1914; San Carlos Agency, Ariz., 26 February 1914; Uintah and Ouray Indian Agency, Utah, 20 February 1914; Pueblo Bonito School, N. Mex., 27 February 1914; Lapwai, Idaho, 28 February 1914; Fort Apache Indian School, 3 March 1914; Omaha Agency, Nebraska, 11 March 1914. And see *The Red Man*, vol. 5, no. 5, January 1913, pp. 209–10; *Report of the Twenty-Fourth Annual Lake Mohonk Conference of Friends of the Indian and Other Dependent Peoples ... 1916* (Lake Mohonk Conference, 1916), pp. 138, 140–1; *Wassaja*, vol. 1, no. 3, June 1916, p. 3; vol. 1, no. 5, August 1916, pp. 1–4; letter of Pratt to Montezuma, 15 November 1909, box 1, folder 1, and 20 January 1919, folder 4, box 1, Correspondence, Carlos Montezuma Papers; Christine Bolt, 'Race and the Victorians', in C. C. Eldridge (ed.), *British Imperialism in the Nineteenth Century* (London,

Macmillan, 1984), p. 145; and Christine Bolt, *Victorian Attitudes to Race* (London, Routledge & Kegan Paul, 1971), pp. 190–2 and *passim*.

47 See, in transcripts of the Hualapai Oral History Project, Arizona State Museum Library, interviews at Peach Springs, Hualapai Indian Reservation, with Alma Fielding, 27 June 1968, pp. 18 ff., 33–4, 97; with Tim McGee, Peach Springs, 18 June 1968, pp. 147 ff., 150; with Tim McGee (second interview), Peach Springs, 21 June 1968, pp. 217–18, 220–2, 227; with Frank Beecher, Peach Springs, 19–20 June 1968, pp. 305, 457; with Suwim Fielding, Peach Springs, 25 June 1968, pp. 484–5, 492; with Jane Honga, 11 July 1968, pp. 657 ff.; with Dennis and Rose Butler, Peach Springs, 11 July 1968, pp. 770–1, 773, 781–6; with William Honga, Peach Springs, 12 July 1968, pp. 828 ff.; with Paul Talieje, 26 June 1968, p. 1131; and see, in Havasupai Oral Tradition Project, transcript of interview with Wallen Burro, 24 June 1969, Supai, pp. 12ff.; with Lemuel Paia, 20 June 1969, pp. 325–6. All Arizona State Museum Library oral history records cited are from its Doris Duke Indian Oral History Collection.

48 *Wassaja*, vol. 1, no. 1, April 1916, p. 1; no. 2, May 1916, pp. 2–3; no. 3, June 1916, pp. 3–4; no. 5, August 1916, pp. 1–4; no. 6, September 1916, p. 3; no. 12, March 1917, p. 3.

49 See in Carlos Montezuma Papers, box 1, Correspondence, folder 1, letter to Pratt from Addison E. Johnson, 14 January 1908, and Pratt to Montezuma, 1910; folder 2, Pratt to Montezuma, 11 December 1912, 28 July 1913; folder 3, letters of 24 October 1914 and 7 January 1915; folder 4, Pratt to Thomas L. Sloan, 1 September 1920; folder 7, Montezuma letter of 1894–5 (?) when Agency Physician at the Colville Agency, p. 6; folder 8, letter to Montezuma from Clara Spotted Horse, 22 December 1907, 1 August 1909; folder 10, letters to Montezuma of 8 February 1913 and 19 March 1913 and letter of Montezuma, 10 April 1914; box 2, Correspondence and Manuscripts, folder 3, correspondence of August A. Breuninger with Montezuma; folder 4, correspondence of his cousins with Montezuma.

CHAPTER 9

1 See David K. Cohen, 'Education and race', *History of Education Quarterly*, vol. IX, no. 3, Fall 1969, pp. 284–5; *Fortieth Annual Report of the National Indian Association* (New York, 1919), pp. 34–5; Fritz, *The Movement for Indian Assimilation*, pp. 185–97; and Michael B. Katz, *Class, Bureaucracy and Schools. The Illusion of Change in America* (New York, Praeger, 1975 edn), quotation from p. xviii.

2 See Office of Commissioner, Personal and Semi-Official Files, 1921–32, entry 177, RG 75; Burke/Atwood correspondence, especially Burke to Atwood, 13 September 1922, 4 February 1922, 28 September 1921; and Atwood to Burke, 28 October 1921, 14 April 1921, 25 January 1922, 22 October 1921, 11 April 1922; as well as Atwood, 10 September 1923, to the President of the General Federation.

3 Burke to Atwood, 8 June 1922, and 3 September 1922, op. cit.; and Burke to Oscar H. Lipps, 24 October 1925, in Office Files of General Superintendent (Peairs), entry 722.

4 Kett, *Rites of Passage*, pp. 38–40, 43, 56, 70–1, 74–5, 78, 177, 183, 194, 199–204, 208, 221, 246–54, 258 and *passim*.

5 Burke to Lipps, op. cit.; and in the same collection, *Resolutions* of a

conference held in Spokane, Washington, 2–3 November 1925, p. 3, resolution (3); and *Summary of Conclusions and Recommendations, Adopted by the Conference of District Superintendents of the Indian Field Service, held at Washington, May 3 to 12, 1926*. See letters of Mrs Atwood to Burke, 6 and 23 December 1921, op. cit.; and in BIC files, tray 109, articles of 12 December 1923 in the *Washington Star* and 20 January 1924 in the *New York Times* on the Committee of One Hundred; also, in ibid., *The Native American*, vol. XXIV, no. 2; letter from Malcolm McDowell, 8 January 1924, to members on the subject; and list of members and those attending the committee's meetings. See also *Forty-First Annual Report of the Board of Directors of the Indian Rights Association . . . 1923* (Philadelphia, Pa, 1923), p. 41; Margaret Connell Szasz, *Education and the American Indian. The Road to Self-Determination Since 1928* (Albuquerque, N. Mex., University of New Mexico Press, 1977 edn), pp. 21–2; E. C. Adams, *American Indian Education*, pp. 66–7; Kvasnicka and Viola (eds), *The Commissioners*, pp. 254–6; Schmeckebier, *The Office of Indian Affairs*, p. 216; Lawrence A. Cremin, *The Transformation of the School. Progressivism in American Education, 1876–1957* (New York, Knopf, 1962), pp. 79–80.

6 See Secretary Work's letter, p. 1, tray 109, in BIC files; and article on Burke's 'New general school policy', tray 111, in ibid.

7 See article on Haskell, 1 July 1930, in BIC Newspaper Clippings; Nasaw, p. 163; William E. Leuchtenburg, *The Perils of Prosperity, 1914–32* (Chicago, University of Chicago Press, 1965 edn), p. 202.

8 For Moorehead's comments see in tray 116, in BIC files, his *Analysis of the Problem of Indian Administration*, pp. 1–2, 12; see also *New York Times*, 12/2/28, in BIC Newspaper Clippings.

9 See Kvasnicka and Viola (eds), pp. 258–91; in BIC files, tray 118, on missionary work, letters by H. M. Bowman and H. Fryling, and tray 119, Moral Conditions File; *Indian Truth*, vol. 1, no. 3, February 1924, p. 3; vol. 1, no. 7, August–September 1924, p. 3; vol. 2, no. 2, February 1925, p. 4; vol. 2, no. 4, April 1925, p. 2; Philp, *John Collier's Crusade for Indian Reform*, ch. 3; letter of Montezuma to Richard Pratt, n.d., pp. 6–7, in Carlos Montezuma Papers, University of Arizona Library.

10 Meriam (ed.), *The Problem of Indian Administration*, pp. 9–14, ch. IX.

11 Nasaw, *Schooled to Order*, pp. 102–4; Cremin, *The Transformation of the School*, pp. 201–2 ff, 291–5; Raymond Wolters, *The New Negro on Campus. Black College Rebellions of the 1920s* (Princeton, NJ, Princeton University Press, 1975); Richardson, *A History of Fisk University*, ch. 7; article of 30 January 1929, 'Indian commissioners answer criticisms of Institute of Government Research', in BIC Newspaper Clippings.

12 See, in BIC Newspaper Clippings, articles in *Washington Times*, 18 April 1929; *Saturday Evening Post*, 8 June 1929; *Washington Star*, 11 August 1929; *Christian Science Monitor*, 27 January 1930; *Washington News*, 13 August 1930; *Portland Oregonian*, 28 November 1929. And in Office Files of Chief of Education Division, W. Carson Ryan, entry 723, RG 75, box 1, clippings from the *Spokane Review*, 9/1/1929.

13 See 'Child labor aspects of the Indian question', p. 13, by W. Carson Ryan, in box 1 of Office Files of Chief of Education Division. *American Indian Life*, 8 May 1927, and 16 July 1930, pp. 8–9, in tray 105, BIC files; Wheeler in *Washington Star*, 11 August 1929, in BIC Newspaper Clippings; Szasz, *Education and the American Indian*, pp. 27–8.

14 See Cremin, *The Transformation of the School*, pp. 60 ff, 75, 78, 83–4, 118 and

passim; articles by Ryan in *School Life*, March 1931, 'The new plan for Indian education', and in April 1931, 'From barbarism to civilization in forty-six years', in BIC Newspaper Clippings; article 'New education for Indian adapted to his traditions thought to ease problem', *Christian Science Monitor*, 1 September 1931, in ibid.; 1932 note from Ryan on 'Essential appointments', in box 2, Office Files of Chief of Education Division; in box 6, ibid., note by Ryan on letter of 4 October 1932 to Mr Millington from J. E. Molinray (?); and in box 1, ibid., speech of Lewis Meriam to the Committee on the American Indian of the National Conference of Social Work, Minneapolis, June 1931, p. 10, and 'Cooperation in Indian Education', by W. Carson Ryan, pp. 14, 17–18. See also address by Rhoads to the Indian Committee of the National Conference of Social Workers 1932, p. 4, Office of Commissioner, Personal and Semi-Official Files.

15 See article in *Federal News*, 19 March 1932, in BIC Newspaper Clippings.
16 E. C. Adams, pp. 70–1.
17 See bulletin 380, tray 107, BIC files; and in box 1 in Office Files of Chief of Education Division, memoranda by Thompson, 9/1/31 and 1/7/32; in ibid., 'Cooperation in Indian education', pp. 16–17; in box 6, clip from *The Daily Oklahoman*, 30 April 1931, p. 11, and 1 May 1931; in ibid., note on 'School enrollment in Oklahoma', n.d. but apparently 1932; in ibid., letter from C. L. Crutcher, Day School Representative, Sallisaw, 16 November 1930, to Samuel H. Thompson, Pawnee, Oklahoma; and in ibid., memorandum headed 'Justification' on the need for increased appropriations for public school education – covers 1930–3 period. See also Szasz, *Education and the American Indian*, p. 34; Debo, *And Still the Waters Run*, p. 390.
18 See in Office Files of Chief of Education Division, box 5, article in *Great Falls Tribune*, Montana, 2 March 1930.
19 See in Office Files of Chief of Education Division: box 4, letter from Superintendent Lipps, Sacramento Indian Agency, Calif., 8 December 1931; box 5, article in *Great Falls Tribune*, Montana, 2 March 1930; letter of F. E. Bowers, Supervisor in Secondary Education, State of Nebraska Department of Public Instruction, Lincoln, 19 June 1931; box 7, letter of Peyton Carter, Superintendent of Indian Schools, Madison, Wis., 16 September 1932.
20 See in Office Files of Chief of Education Division: box 1, 'Cooperation in Indian education', pp. 18–19; box 2, George F. Miller's memorandum of 31 March 1932 to Ryan; and box 8, report from the Fort Totten Boarding School; and see Szasz, *Education and the American Indian*, pp. 31–2; E. C. Adams, p. 70; Dale, *The Indians of the Southwest*, pp. 194–5.
21 See in Office Files of Chief of Education Division: box 2, memorandum from Ryan to Mr Armstrong; also box 1, 'Cooperation in Indian education', p. 19; and Debo, *And Still the Waters Run*, p. 392.
22 Kvasnicka and Viola (eds), p. 267.
23 E. C. Adams, pp. 71–3; Cremin, *The Transformation of the School*, pp. 61–2, 124–6; Richardson, ch. 5, especially p. 57; circular letter of 21 May 1931 from Charles J. Rhoads to the Superintendents and All Employees of the Indian Service, tray 118, BIC files; O. H. Lipps in *Chemawa American*, vol. XXXI, no. 24, 26 February 1930, tray 113, BIC files; Dr E. A. Bates reported in *Portland Oregonian*, 17 November 1930, in BIC Newspaper Clippings; and article on 'Tsianina, leader among women of the Indian race', in BIC Newspaper Clippings; see also *The American Indian*, vol. 1, no. 3, December 1926, p. 11; no. 5, February 1927, p. 8; no. 11, August 1927,

p. 4; vol. 3, no. 7, 'Indian schools and education', 1 September 1931, pp. 2, 4, by W. Carson Ryan, in Office File of Commissioner John Collier.

24 See Cremin, *The Transformation of the School*, pp. 250, 261–2, 264, 277, 295–9; and complaints about the state of Indian education in 'Indian primer', by the Committee on Indian Civil Rights of the American Civil Liberties Union, August 1932, p. 7, in Reference File of John Collier, entry 179–80, RG 75.

25 See letter from missionary Mary Crawford to Dr Ward L. Sullivan, 20 October 1933, in Office File of Commissioner John Collier, box 7 (L–M); letter of E. K. Burlew, 14 April 1937, in Office Records of Assistant Commissioner William Zimmerman, Correspondence, box M–P; Beatty's proposed comments (1937) before the Subcommittee of the House Appropriations Committee, pp. 25–8, in box 2, Subject Correspondence Files of John Herrick; in box 7, Office Files of Chief of Education Division, General Statement of Policy Relating to Indian Secondary Schools (1935); E. C. Adams, pp. 80–97; Szasz, *Education and the American Indian*, pp. 61–2, 65–6, 95, and ch. 7.

26 Philp, *John Collier's Crusade for Indian Reform*, p. 129; Szasz, *Education and the American Indian*, p. 42; E. C. Adams, p. 80; 'Highlights of the Roosevelt record in Indian affairs', pp. 1–4, pamphlet of the American Indian Federation, received by the Indian Office, November 1940, in Office File of John Collier, box 6 (H–L).

27 Debo, *And Still the Waters Run*, pp. 391–2.

28 Philp, *John Collier's Crusade for Indian Reform*, pp. 128–9.

29 Report on hostile Navajo opinion in *Washington Post*, 19 June 1937, in Miscellaneous File, box 7 (L–M) in Office File of Commissioner John Collier; and in box 1 (A–B), letter to Collier from J. C. Morgan, a member of the AIF and of the Navajo Tribal Council, 21 January 1933, Office File of Commissioner John Collier.

30 See p. 2 of Statement of John Collier, designed for release on his confirmation as Commissioner, in Reference File of John Collier; 'Is the proposed new program, as embodied in the Wheeler–Howard Bill, desirable and feasible?', pp. 18–21, Harper's paper given to the National Conference of Social Workers in Kansas City, Missouri, 24 May 1934, op. cit.; 'The Indians' attitude toward cooperation', by Mrs Ruth Bronson, pp. 36–8, in box 1, Office Files of Chief of Education Division; Memorandum for the press from John Collier, 6 February 1935, p. 5, replying to American Indian Federation charges, box 6, in ibid.; undated memorandum by Joseph Bruner, president of the AIF, received by the Indian Office, 2 May 1935, in Office File of Commissioner John Collier, box 1 (A–B); 'Highlights of the Roosevelt record in Indian affairs', pp. 1–2, in box 6 (H–L), Office File of Commissioner John Collier; William Collins to Collier, Fort Wingate, New Mexico, 25 May 1933, in box 7 (L–M), Office File of Commissioner John Collier; and talk by Indian informant, 14 October 1970, p. 3, RF. 497, in Arizona State Museum Library, on the negative self-image produced by the Anglo education he received.

31 Note by Collier in his 1944 file, in Reference File of John Collier; Report of the Joint Meeting of the Committee on Administrative Research of the Society for Applied Anthropology and representatives of the Indian Office, 26 October 1944, in Office File of Joseph C. McCaskill; and paper by Eliot D. Chapple, Department of Anthropology at Harvard, on 'Anthropological engineering', pp. 18–19, in Office File of Joseph C.

McCaskill; report of the 1944 meeting in Office File of Commissioner John Collier, box 12 (P), Personality Study File V, and in ibid. Beatty's memo to Collier of 9 November 1944, and *Committee Report on Navajo Education*; Szasz, *Education and the American Indian*, p. 75.

32 See, for instance, letter of John J. McPherson, Red Lake Agency, Minnesota, to Harold Ickes, in box M–P, and memorandum to Collier from Louis Balsam, 3 March 1937 on the failure of formal education among the Florida Seminoles, in box P–W, Office Records of Assistant Commissioner William Zimmerman, correspondence

33 Cremin, *The Transformation of the School*, pp. 258–68.

34 See in Office Files of Chief of Education Division, box 1, letter from Joe Jennings, superintendent of schools, Pine Ridge Agency, S. Dak., 11 April 1934; and in ibid., *Eighty-Seventh Annual Report of the American Missionary Association*, 1933, p. 25; *Composite Annual Administrative and Activity Report. The Board of Home Missions and Church Extension of the Methodist Episcopal Church*, 1934, p. 42; and in Reference File of John Collier, note from Collier to Beatty, 16 October 1944; Philp, *John Collier's Crusade for Indian Reform*, pp. 131–3.

35 See letters of Charles E. Burton to the Indian office, 14 February 1900, 17 March 1900, 10 July 1903, pp. 6–7, 16 March 1905, 20 December 1912, 14 March 1913, and 29 September 1914, from Moqui Training School, Arizona, box 6, Van Valkenburgh Papers.

36 See George F. Miller to W. Carson Ryan, 6 January 1933, Santa Fe School, in box 10, Office Files of Chief of Education Division; William Zimmerman to Adolph Green of Washington, 21 August 1935, box A–M, Office Records of Assistant Commissioner William Zimmerman, correspondence.

37 Collier's memorandum for the press of 6 February 1935, op. cit., p. 5.

38 Interviews with Tim McGee, 18 June 1968, p. 166, with Rupert Parker, 25 June 1968, p. 626 and with Marcus Wellington, 16 July 1968, p. 904, in transcripts of the Hualapai Oral History Project; *Proceedings of the Annual Convention of the National Congress of American Indians*, Oklahoma City, Okla, 22–25 October 1945, pp. 35, 62, 87–8, in section X, OHS; 'A review of Indian education in the state of Oklahoma', *Five Tribes Journal*, vol. 1, no. 4, p. 6, in section X, OHS; letter of S. H. Thompson, Carson City, Nevada, 7 June 1934, in box 5, Office Files of Chief of Education Division; report on Shoshone Agency schools, 24 November 1934, p. 3, in box 7, Office·Files of Chief of Education Division; letter from Samuel H. Thompson to Collier, 11 April 1935, from the Osage Indian Agency, Oklahoma, in box 6, Office Files of Chief of Education Division; Szasz, *Education and the American Indian*, pp. 77–80, ch. 8; E. C. Adams, p. 82; Philp, *John Collier's Crusade for Indian Reform*, p. 134.

39 Paper of Allan C. Harper, op. cit., p. 10; Szasz, *Education and the American Indian*, p. 135.

40 See Gossett, *Race*, pp. 376–7, 425; S. J. MacFadden and J. F. Dashiel, 'Racial differences as measured by the Downey will-temperament individual tests', *Journal of Applied Psychology*, vol. VII, 1922, pp. 30–53; T. R. Garth, *Race Psychology. A Study of Racial Mental Differences* (New York, McGraw-Hill, 1931); O. Klineberg, *Race and Psychology*, UNESCO pamphlet (Paris, UNESCO, 1951); 'Special capacities of American Indians', speech of W. Carson Ryan to the Third International Congress of Eugenics, New York, 23 August 1932, pp. 1–2, 5, in Office of Commissioner, Personal and Semi-Official Files.

41 Letter of E. K. Burlew, op. cit.; 'Address of Dr W. Carson Ryan ... over Station WRC and nation-wide network, Washington, DC, November 14, 1932' in Office of Commissioner, Personal and Semi-Official Files.

42 See article in *The Verstovian* (journal of the Sheldon Jackson school, Alaska), vol. 21, no. 7, April–May 1935, 'Educating the Alaska natives not worthwhile?', in Office Files of Chief of Education Division, box 3; and Annual Report (1933) of New York Agency schools, box 5, Office Files of Chief of Education Division; address to the forum on American Indians of the National Conference of Social Work, Buffalo, NY, 23 June 1939, pp. 5–6, Office File of Joseph C. McCaskill.

43 E. C. Adams, pp. 83–4.

44 See, for instance, letter of Mrs Harvey Wiley, Chairman, Indian Welfare, General Federation of Women's Clubs, 11 October 1940, in Office File of Commissioner John Collier, box 5 (D–H).

45 R. W. Kraushaar, State High School Supervisor, 28 February 1934, on *Second Visit to Some of the Indian Schools of the Rosebud and Pine Ridge Reservations, February 5, 6, 7, 8, 1934*, pp. 4–5, in Office Files of Chief of Education Division, box 7; and memorandum by Lucy Wilcox Adams, Acting Chief, Community Services Branch, 26 February 1941 on 'Adult Education'.

46 See letter to Commissioner William Brophy from Moris Burge, after his first year as superintendent of the (Papago) Sells Agency in Arizona, 27 March 1946, Office Records of Assistant Commissioner William Zimmerman, box D–M; Szasz, *Education and the American Indian*, pp. 107, 110–11.

47 Szasz, *Education and the American Indian*, pp. 73, 75.

48 Radio interview, 22 March 1946, by Mrs J. F. Corletto, Chairman of Indian Welfare for the Sixth District of the Illinois Federation of Women's Clubs, with Randolph McCurtain, pp. 3–5, in Desk Files of Commissioners William A. Brophy and John R. Nichols.

49 First Report on Education to the Navajo Indian Tribe (Department of Interior, Navajo Service, Window Rock, Arizona, 1945), pp. 27–8, and replies of William Brophy to the questions of Hon. Carl Hatch, US Senate, and a number of other politicians, 24 March 1946, in Navajo (Miscellaneous) 1945–8 File of Brophy, in Desk Files of Commissioners Brophy and Nichols.

50 Report to the President on Conditions of the Navajo Indians, pp. 5–6; Comments of the Navajo Tribal Council, 19 March 1948, pp. 3–4, on the Navajo rehabilitation scheme in Navajo Miscellaneous File; and Summary of Navajo Developments, February 1, 1950, in ibid.

51 See note by Beatty, 12 July 1948, in Miscellaneous Activities File in ibid.; Szasz, *Education and the American Indian*, pp. 116–21; Kvasnicka and Viola (eds), pp. 284–6.

52 Statement presented by William Zimmerman, Jr, Acting Commissioner of Indian Affairs before the Senate Committee on Interior and Insular Affairs ... February 3 1949, pp. 5, 8–9, in Desk Files of Commissioners Brophy and Nichols; memorandum from Commissioner Myer to the Secretary of the Interior, 'Information requisition by Mr Charles W. Eliot in letter of November 5, 1951', p. 10, Publicity-Public Relations File in Desk Files of Commissioner Dillon S. Myer; address by Dillon S. Myer, Commissioner of Indian Affairs, at the eighth Annual Convention of the National Congress of American Indians, St Paul, Minnesota, 5 July 1951, pp. 11–12, in Speeches File, Desk Files of Commissioner Myer; and

Superintendents Session 29 January 1958, p. 4, at Tri-Area Resources Conference, op. cit.; and papers of the Tucson Indian Training School, in boxes 10–13, subgroups 9–10, especially article on 'Tucson's Indian training school', p. 34, and 'Products of Tucson Indian School'.

53 Szasz, *Education and the American Indian*, pp. 128, 181–6; Kvasnicka and Viola (eds), pp. 303, 318; and see letter from Elizabeth Roe Cloud, Field Secretary of the NCAI, to Commissioner Myer, 2 November 1951, in Desk Files of Commissioner Myer, Organisation File.

54 Letter of Oscar L. Chapman, Secretary of the Interior, to Hon. J. Hardin Peterson, 25 July 1950, in Miscellaneous File; survey of the work of the Bureau of Indian Affairs, p. 6, Studies and Surveys File; and statement, Indian Bureau Moving to End Federal Supervision, pp. 2–3, Programs, Plans, Policy, etc., File: Desk Files of Commissioner Myer.

55 Report of a Survey of Possibilities of Withdrawal of Federal Supervision and Services in Affairs of the Sac and Fox Indians of Tama, Iowa. Report No. 1, August 1951, pp. 24–5, op. cit.

56 *Hearings Before the Sub-committee on Indian Affairs of the Committee on Interior and Insular Affairs, House of Representatives, Ninety-Third Congress, First Session on H.R. 7421* . . . Serial No. 93–20 (Washington, DC, US Government Printing Office, 1973), pp. 34, 75–8, 99–110; speech by Dr John Nichols at the Conference of Representatives of State Departments of Education and Officials of the Bureau of Indian Affairs, Friday, 17 February 1950, pp. 1–4, Desk Files of Commissioners Brophy and Nichols, Miscellaneous Activities File; Szasz, *Education and the American Indian*, pp. 124, 129, 138–9; Kvasnicka and Viola (eds), pp. 297, 305–6, 318.

57 Memorandum of Commissioner Nichols, 15 August 1949, circular 3704, p. 2, in Desk Files of Commissioners Brophy and Nichols; letter of Elizabeth Roe Cloud, op. cit.

58 See talk by Glenn L. Emmons, Commissioner of Indian Affairs, at a panel discussion held by the Indian Law Committee of the Federal Bar Association, Chicago, Illinois, 1960, op. cit., pp. 3–4, 6–7, File No. 111.

59 See ibid., pp. 3–4; speech, 'The needs of the American Indian', by Myer before the Combined Assemblies of the Division of Christian Life and Work of the National Council of the Churches of Christ, 12 December 1951, pp. 9–10, Speeches File, in Desk Files of Commissioner Myer; Portland Area, Bureau-Tribal Conference, 1956, op. cit., pp. 9–10.

60 Szasz, *Education and the American Indian*, pp. 134–6.

61 Szasz, *Education and the American Indian*, pp. 153–4, 171–80; Tyler, *A History of Indian Policy*, pp. 228–9; and interview with James Hena, former governor of Tesuque Pueblo, 23 February 1970, tape 443, side 1, pp. 9–10, DD for New Mexico.

62 Szasz, *Education and the American Indian*, pp. 145, 150–2, 154–5, 159–61; 'What you should know about N.I.E.A. in 1975', National Indian Education Association pamphlet; interview recorded 25 June 1968, tape 78.57.351, pp. 610–13, in transcripts of the Hualapai Oral History Project, on education in one tribe.

63 Szasz, *Education and the American Indian*, pp. 133, 174–5; Nasaw, pp. 214, 216–17, 222–3 and *passim*; Ravitch, *The Troubled Crusade*; and article on 'Our elders, our children, Indian education for Indians', in *Akwesasne Notes*, vol. 17, no. 3, Summer 1985, pp. 10–11.

64 Szasz, *Education and the American Indian*, pp. 161–3, 165–6; and see interview of 25 June 1968, op. cit., p. 615, Hualapai Oral History Project.

65 See tape of broadcast on Indian education involving Willard Scott, Director of Indian Education (Santa Fe), and Mr Paul Tafoya, Santa Clara Pueblo, tape 499, p. 28, in DD for New Mexico; and in ibid., tape 270, 21 November 1969 (?), side 2, interview with anonymous Navajo women at the University of Arizona. See also talk of Oct. 1970, RF. 497, op. cit., pp. 5–6; and views of Dr Florence Schroeder, University of New Mexico, Dept of Education, 16 March 1970, tape 500, pp. 2, 7–10, 12–13, in DD for New Mexico.

66 See, for instance, interview with Mr Davis, 16 April 1970, tape 626, pp. 1–15, 17–22, in DD for New Mexico.

67 See tape 635, side 2, discussion of Indian students with Commissioner Bruce, May 1970, p. 18, in DD for New Mexico; Szasz, *Education and the American Indian*, pp. 162–4, 166–7; Frank C. Miller, 'Involvement in an urban university', in Jack O. Waddell and O. Michael Watson (eds), *The American Indian in Urban Society* (Boston, Mass., Little, Brown, 1971), pp. 335–9.

68 See Alphonso Pinkney, *Red, Black and Green. Black Nationalism in the United States* (Cambridge, Cambridge University Press, 1976), ch. 9.

69 See, in DD for New Mexico: tape 450, side 2, January 1970, 'The Indian speaks', TV program with Jerry Wilkinson, Sam English, Bill Pensoneau and Seferino Tenorio, speaking about the National Indian Youth Council; tape 596, 21 April 1970, 'The Indian speaks', interview with Sam English and others, pp. 4–6, 8, 11–13, 16; tape 636, 22 May 1970, discussion with Agnes Ortiz (Navajo) and her son Brian, and Bruce Alexander, Creek, University of New Mexico student, pp. 1–2, 15–17, 26, 30; discussion with Commissioner Bruce, op. cit., pp. 3–4, 6–16; tape 497, side 1, March 1970, Kiva Club Members Rap Session Number Two, pp. 19–25; Wilcomb E. Washburn, 'American Indian studies: a status report', *American Quarterly*, vol. XXVII, no. 3, August 1975, pp. 263–74; and Jack Gregory and Bernard Strickland, 'Indian studies must be more than an academic wild West show', in John K. Mahon (ed.), *Indians of the Lower South, Past and Present* (Pensacola, Fla, Gulf Coast History and Humanities Conference, 1975), pp. 42–50.

70 Szasz, *Education and the American Indian*, pp. 199–201.

71 See 'A review of Indian education in the State of Oklahoma', op. cit., pp. 6–7; 'Review of the Johnson O'Malley Program, 1974–75', *Five Tribes Journal*, vol. 1, no. 4, p. 10, section X, OHS; Leonard Bacq and Ofelia Miramontes, 'Bilingual special education teacher training for American Indians', *Journal of American Indian Education*, vol. 24, no. 2, May 1985, pp. 38–47; and Anna Gajar, 'American Indian personal preparation in special education: needs, program components, programs', *Journal of American Indian Education*, vol. 24, no. 2, May 1985, pp. 7–15; Kvasnicka and Viola (eds), pp. 319, 344; Tyler, *A History of Indian Policy*, pp. 230–2; Szasz, *Education and the American Indian*, p. 167; *The Bureau of Indian Affairs Should Do More to Help Educate Indian Students*, United States General Accounting Office, 3 November 1977, HRD–77–155, pp. i–ii; *American Indian Policy Review Commission. Summary, Task Force Reports* (produced by A. T. Anderson, Special Assistant to the Commission, Union Carbide Corporation, 1976), p. 13; 'The American Indian today', *E/SA Forum-31*, July 1977, pp. 30–1; *The Sentinel*, NCAI Bulletin, March 1978, pp. 14–18, 24–6; and Prucha, The Great Father, vol. II, pp. 1142–9.

72 'The American Indian today', op. cit., p. 30; *The Bureau of Indian Affairs*

Should Do More to Help Educate Indian Students, op. cit., ch. 2, pp. 11, 13–15, 17, ch. 5; interviews by Jan Bell with Papago students at the University of Arizona, November 1970–March 1971, 78.57.3 to 7, in Arizona State Museum Library.

73 *Colorado Springs Gazette*, 31 October 1929, in BIC Newspaper Clippings.

CHAPTER 10

1 McKenney and Hall, *History of the Indian Tribes of North America*, vol. 3, p. 43. The reader should consult Beatrice Medicine, 'The role of women in Native American societies. A bibliography', *Indian Historian*, vol. 8, Summer 1975, pp. 50–4. For the argument that white women came to view Indians rather differently from white men, see Glenda Riley, *Women and Indians on the Frontier, 1825–1915* (Albuquerque, N. Mex., University of New Mexico Press, 1984).

2 Vaughan, *The New England Frontier*, pp. 19–20; Vaughan, 'From white man to redskin', p. 927; Axtell, *The European and the Indian*, pp. 55–6, 154.

3 Linda Grant DePauw et al., *Remember the Ladies. Women in America, 1750–1815* (New York, Viking, 1976), p. 19; J. Norman Heard, *White into Red. A Study of the Assimilation of White Persons Captured by Indians* (Metuchen, NJ, 1973), pp. 100–1, on captivity west of the Mississippi; Axtell, *The European and the Indian*, pp. 181–2, 192–5. Francis Parkman, in *The Jesuits in North America*, p. 21, notes the 'remarkable forebearance observed by Eastern and Northern tribes towards female captives', but concludes that this was 'probably the result of a superstition'. See Slotkin, *Regeneration through Violence*, pp. 98, 100–1, on whites' dread of the marriage of white and Indian cultures.

4 Slotkin, pp. 47, 76; also pp. 34–5, 54–5, 59–64, 89, 193–4, 202–3, 442, 490.

5 Ibid., p. 47; and Dunn and Dunn (eds), *The Papers of William Penn*, vol. 2, p. 450.

6 Alice Schlegel, *Male Dominance and Female Autonomy. Domestic Authority in Matrilineal Societies* (New Haven, Conn., HRAF Press, 1972), pp. 88–9, 92.

7 See, for example, Gibson, *The Chickasaws*, p. 20; Debo, *Road to Disappearance*, pp. 16, 22; and Debo, *Rise and Fall of the Choctaw Republic*, p. 18.

8 Karen Ordahl Kupperman, in *Settling with the Indians*, pp. 59–60, maintains that early writers noted polygamy but suggested that it was a status symbol, while later writers minimized 'reports of polygamy' and realized that having 'several wives made up for the high infant mortality rate', besides increasing one's corn supply, which women produced.

9 Nash, *Red, White and Black*, pp. 278–85; Nash 'Red, white and black', in Nash and Weiss (eds), *The Great Fear*, p. 20; Nash, 'The image of the Indian', in Dudley and Novak (eds), *The Wild Man Within*, pp. 76–7, 85; Wilcomb E. Washburn, 'A moral history of Indian–white relations. Needs and opportunities for study', *Ethnohistory*, vol. IV, no. 1, Winter 1957, pp. 50–1; J. H. Johnston, *Race Relations in Virginia and Miscegenation in the South*, pp. 184–5, 269–70; Forbes (ed.), *The Indian in America's Past*, pp. 142–63; Vaughan, 'From white man to redskin', pp. 93–5.

10 Vaughan, 'From white man to redskin', p. 928; Slotkin, p. 65.

11 See Grace Steele Woodward, *Pocahontas* (Norman, Okla, University of Oklahoma Press, 1969).

12 John C. Ewers, 'Mother of the mixed bloods. The marginal woman in the

history of the Upper Missouri', in K. R. Toole, J. A. Carroll, R. M. Utley and A. R. Mortensen (eds), *Probing the American West. Papers from the Santa Fe Conference* (Santa Fe, N. Mex., Museum of New Mexico Press, 1962), pp. 62–3, 65.

13 ibid., p. 68.

14 Debo, *Road to Disappearance*, pp. 38–9; Debo, *Rise and Fall*, pp. 37 ff.; Gibson, *The Chickasaws*, pp. 39, 65–6.

15 Vaughan, 'From white man to redskin', pp. 930–47, 952; Lauber, *Indian Slavery in Colonial Times*, p. 253.

16 Saum, *The Fur Trader and the Indian*, pp. 206–10, 236; J. H. Johnston, *Race Relations in Virginia and Miscegenation in the South*, p. 269; Ewers, pp. 68–9.

17 Harold P. Howard, *Sacajawea* (Norman, Okla, University of Oklahoma Press, 1971), chs 22–4 and *passim*.

18 See Perdue, *Slavery and the Evolution of Cherokee Society*, pp. 9–10.

19 See George Murdock, *Social Structure* (New York, Macmillan, 1949), pp. 184–7; John Fiske, *The Discovery of America. With Some Account of Ancient America and the Spanish Conquest*, Vol. 1 (Boston, Mass., and New York, Houghton Mifflin, 1852, 2 vols), p. 56; see his complaint, pp. 65–8, that husbands were little more than lodgers with their wives.

20 Robin Fox, *Kinship and Marriage* (Harmondsworth, Penguin, 1977 edn), pp. 31–2.

21 See Paula Webster, 'Matriarchy: a vision of power', in Rayna A. Reiter (ed.), *Toward an Anthropology of Women* (New York and London, Monthly Review Press, 1975), pp. 141–56; see also Caroline Fleur-Lobban, 'A Marxist reappraisal of the matriarchate', *Current Anthropology*, vol. 20, 1979, pp. 341–66.

22 See Carol P. MacCormach and Marilyn Strathern, *Nature, Culture and Gender* (Cambridge, Cambridge University Press, 1980); Sherry B. Ortner, 'Is female to male as nature is to culture?', in M. Z. Rosaldo and L. Lamphere (eds), *Woman, Culture and Society* (Stanford, NJ, Stanford University Press, 1974), pp. 67–88; Frances Dahlberg, *Woman the Gatherer* (New Haven, Conn., and London, Yale University Press, 1981); Judith Hoch-Smith and Anita Spring, *Woman in Ritual and Symbolic Roles* (New York and London, Plenum Press, 1978); M. K. Martin and Barbara Voorhies, *Female of the Species* (New York and London, Columbia University Press, 1975); and the various works by Schlegel cited in this chapter, together with Alice Schlegel (ed.), *Sexual Stratification. A Cross-Cultural View* (New York, Columbia University Press, 1979).

23 Webster, p. 144; R. Fox, pp. 88, 93, 95–6.

24 R. Fox, p. 102; Schlegel, *Male Dominance*, p. 80; Martin and Voorhies, pp. 225–7.

25 R. Fox, pp. 111–13; Schlegel, *Male Dominance*, pp. 2–3, 82–4, 98–9, 104; in matrilineal societies, as Schlegel points out, men are the head of descent groups but these are perpetuated by women. Schlegel also notes the existence of matrilocal societies in which women remain under the dominance of men.

26 Eggan, *The American Indian*, pp. 29 (source of quotation), 30, 32, 37, 60–7, 78–85; see also Debo, *Rise and Fall*, p. 77; Wardell, *A Political History of the Cherokee Nation*, p. 7; and Rennard Strickland, *Fire and the Spirits. Cherokee Law from Clan to Court* (Norman, Okla, University of Oklahoma Press, 1975), pp. 3–4, 10, 82, 142–3.

27 Hoch-Smith and Spring, pp. 19–21.

28 See Marilyn Strathern, 'No nature, no culture: the Hagen case', in MacCormach and Strathern, pp. 174–219.
29 Dahlberg, Introduction, pp. 1–27.
30 Physiological obsessions, particularly concerning male attributes, have been noted in Oceanic cultures and seen as being absent from North America by Harriet Whitehead, 'The bow and the burden strap: a new look at institutionalised homosexuality in Native North America', in Sherry B. Ortner and Harriet Whitehead (eds), *Sexual Meanings. The Cultural Construction of Gender and Sexuality* (Cambridge, Cambridge University Press, 1981), pp. 86–7.
31 Ruth M. Underhill, *Red Man's Religion. Beliefs and Practices of the Indians North of Mexico* (Chicago and London, University of Chicago Press, 1974 edn), ch. 6, esp. pp. 49, 51–2.
32 See Axtell, *The European and the Indian*, pp. 56–7; on British and American attitudes, see Elaine and English Showalter, 'Victorian women and menstruation', in M. Vicinus (ed.), *Suffer and be Still. Women in the Victorian Age* (London, Methuen, 1980 edn), pp. 38–44, and John S. Haller and Robin M. Haller, *The Physician and Sexuality in Victorian America* (Urbana, Ill., University of Illinois Press, 1974), ch. II; Carol Smith-Rosenberg, 'Puberty to menopause: the cycle of femininity in nineteenth-century America', in Mary Hartman and Lois W. Banner (eds), *Clio's Consciousness Raised* (New York, Harper & Row, 1974), pp. 28–9, 36.
33 Schlegel, *Male Dominance*, p. 20.
34 William N. Stephens, *The Family in Cross-Cultural Perspective* (New York, Holt, Rinehart & Winston, 1966 edn), pp. 273–8; Elizabeth Fee, 'The sexual politics of Victorian social anthropology', in Hartman and Banner (eds), *Clio's Consciousness Raised*, pp. 86–102; Underhill, pp. 59 ff.; Morgan, *League of the Iroquois*, pp. 322–4; Trenholm, *The Arapahoes, Our People*, pp. 57–8, and Karl N. Llewellyn and E. Adamson Hoebel, *The Cheyenne Way* (Norman, Okla, University of Oklahoma Press, 1967 edn), pp. 190 ff., on arranged marriages in other tribes.
35 Judith K. Brown, 'Iroquois women: an ethnohistoric note', in Reiter (ed.), *Toward an Anthropology of Women;* pp. 241–2; and also Judith K. Brown, 'A note on the division of labor by sex', *American Anthropologist*, vol. 72, 1970, pp. 1073–8; and Judith K. Brown, 'Economic organisation and the position of women among the Iroquois', *Ethnohistory*, vol. 17, 1970, pp. 151–67.
36 See Mary W. Helms, 'Matrilocality, social solidarity, and culture contact: three case histories', *Southwestern Journal of Anthropology*, vol. 27, no. 2, Summer 1970, pp. 198, 203, 205–7.
37 Axtell, *The European and the Indian*, p. 202; Stephens, pp. 342, 364–5, 397–8; Clyde Kluckhohn and Dorothea Leighton, *The Navajo* (Cambridge, Mass., Harvard University Press, 1960), p. 50; Richard Irving Dodge, *The Hunting Grounds of the Great West, etc.* (London, 1877) pp. 307, 314; Gibson, *The Chickasaws*, p. 21; George Bancroft, *History of the United States, from the Discovery of the American Continent*, Vol. III (Boston, Mass., Little, Brown, 1856), pp. 268–9.
38 Axtell, *The European and the Indian*, pp. 100, 160, 281, on the origin of this dislike in the colonial period.
39 Dodge, p. 307; McKenney, *Memoirs, Official and Personal, etc.*, pp. 39, 76–7, 87–92.
40 See Elaine Goodale Eastman, *Sister to the Sioux* (Lincoln, Nebr., University of Nebraska Press, 1978), p. 80, for a view that Sioux women were

'plain-spoken' but 'not offensively so'; for a more conventional view see Mason Wade (ed.), *The Journals of Francis Parkman*, Vol. 2 (London, Eyre & Spottiswoode, 1947), p. 451. And see Parkman, Vol. 3, p. 267, for a condemnation of polygamy.

41 Axtell, *The European and the Indian*, p. 263; Dodge, pp. 301–4, 312–13, for a typically censorious white view of Indian sexual relations; Parkman, in *The Jesuits in North America*, pp. 21–2, though critical of the morals of the Hurons, the Iroquois and the southern tribes, acknowledged that 'chastity in women was recognised as a virtue by many tribes', especially the Algonquins; K. J. Crowe, *Caught . . . Original Peoples of Northern Canada*, pp. 149–50; Priest, *Uncle Sam's Stepchildren*, p. 146; Kluckhohn and Leighton, pp. 54–5; Llewellyn and Hoebel, pp. 181, 187–8, 202 ff., 261–4; Kupperman, p. 59, notes early commentators who stated that there were prostitutes in Indian society, and Parkman, p. 21, makes the same assertion; see also Cotterill, *The Southern Indians*, p. 4, on 'professional prostitution' among the Sioux tribes. And on the smallness of Indian families and the abstemiousness about intercourse of some groups, see Valerie Sherer Mathes, 'A new look at the role of women in Indian society', *American Indian Quarterly*, vol. 2, Summer 1975, pp. 133–4, 138.

42 Kluckhohn and Leighton, p. 47; E. G. Eastman, *Sister to the Sioux*, pp. 35, 49, 59, 100.

43 Axtell, *The European and the Indian*, pp. 48–54; Sheehan, *Savagism and Civility*, p. 94; Dunn and Dunn (eds), Vol. 2, p. 449.

44 Julie A. Matthaei, *An Economic History of Women in America. Women's Work, the Sexual Division of Labour and the Development of Capitalism* (Brighton, Harvester Press, and New York, Schocken Books, 1982), ch. 1; Kupperman, pp. 60–2, stresses early English condemnation of the exploitation of Indian women, while noting 'English writers' ambivalence about the roles of Indian women'; see also R. S. Grumet, 'Sunksquaws, shamans and tradeswomen: Middle Atlantic coastal Algonquin women during the 17th and 18th centuries', in M. Etienne and E. Leacock (eds), *Women and Colonization: Anthropological Perspectives* (New York, Praeger, 1980), pp. 43–62; Lurie, 'Indian colonial adjustments to European civilization', in Smith (ed.), *Seventeenth-Century America*, p. 57; and De Pauw, p. 48.

45 See Mary P. Ryan, 'American society and the cult of domesticity' (PhD thesis, University of California at Santa Barbara, 1971); Barbara Welter, 'The cult of true womanhood, 1820–1860', *American Quarterly*, vol. 18, 1966, pp. 151–74.

46 Manypenny, *Our Indian Wards*, p. xv.

47 See, for instance, Herbert G. Gutman, *The Black Family in Slavery and Freedom, 1750–1925* (Oxford, Blackwell, 1976), pp. 167–8; and Jones, *Labor of Love, Labor of Sorrow*, pp. 58–60.

48 See, for instance, Dodge, p. 297; McKenney and Hall, Vol. 1, p. 22; McKenney, p. 92; Parkman, Vol. III, pp. 270–1.

49 Brinton, *The American Race*, pp. 48–9; E. G. Eastman, *Sister to the Sioux*, p. 104.

50 Dodge, p. 297; Horsman, *Race and Manifest Destiny*, p. 207.

51 Brown, 'Iroquois women'.

52 Eggan, pp. 17–19; Mary E. Young, 'Women, civilization, and the Indian question', in Linda K. Kerber and Jane DeHart Mathews (eds), *Women's America. Refocussing the Past* (New York and Oxford, Oxford University

Press, 1982), p. 151; Gibson, *The Chickasaws*, pp. 2, 6, 7, 28–9; Debo, *Road to Disappearance*, pp. 19–21; Debo, *Rise and Fall*, p. 18.

53   Eggan, pp. 136–7; Alice Schlegel, 'Sexual antagonism among the sexually egalitarian Hopi', *Ethos*, vol. 7, 1979, pp. 124–41; and Alice Schlegel, 'Hopi gender ideology of female superiority', *Quarterly Journal of Ideology*, vol. 8, no. 4, 1984, pp. 3–4.

54   Kluckhohn and Leighton, pp. 55–6; Martin and Voorhies, pp. 99–100.

55   See the traveller Thomas Farnham, quoted in Trenholm, p. 106; and see pp. 66, 126.

56   Eggan, pp. 55, 59–61; Martin and Voorhies, pp. 101, 229 ff.; Llewellyn and Hoebel, p. 78; George Bird Grinnell, *The Cheyenne Indians*, Vol. 1 (New York, Yale University Press, 1923, 2 vols), p. 128.

57   Llewellyn and Hoebel, ch. VIII; Grinnell, p. 212; E. G. Eastman, *Sister to the Sioux*, pp. 111–13.

58   Whitehead, pp. 87–9, 104–5, 107–8, 111; John C. Ewers, 'Deadlier than the male', *American Heritage*, vol. 16, no. 4, June 1965, pp. 10–13; Mathes, pp. 135–6.

59   Underhill, pp. 43, 47–9, 117–18, 207; Hoch-Smith and Spring, Introduction; Morgan, *League of the Iroquois*, p. 161, 165; Kluckhohn and Leighton, pp. 56, 128, 137–8.

60   Slotkin, pp. 45–7; Schlegel, 'Hopi gender ideology', pp. 6–7.

61   Underhill, pp. 177, 277, 215; Alice Schlegel, 'The adolescent socialization of the Hopi girl', *Ethnology*, vol. XII, no. 4, October 1973, p. 452.

62   Brown, 'Iroquois women', p. 241; Underhill, pp. 176–7, 214; Morgan, *League of the Iroquois*, pp. 186, 205; Eggan, pp. 127, 131.

63   Underhill, pp. 83, 91, 94; Mathes, p. 134.

64   Whitehead, p. 105.

65   Trenholm, pp. 80–1.

66   See Karen Sacks, 'Engels revisited: women, the organization of production, and private property', in Reiter (ed.), *Toward an Anthropology of Women*, p. 224.

67   See Schlegel, *Male Dominance*, pp. 9, 24, 80–1.

68   Brown, 'Iroquois women', pp. 238–41, 249–51; O'Donnell, 'Joseph Brant', pp. 22–3, 36, in Edmunds (ed.), *American Indian Leaders*.

69   Schlegel, *Male Dominance*, p. 9; Eggan p. 127; Schlegel, 'Adolescent socialization', p. 452; Schlegel, 'Sexual antagonism', pp. 126–7; Schlegel, 'Hopi gender ideology', p. 5; Peter Mathiessen, *Indian Country* (New York, Viking, 1984), p. 87.

70   Kluckhohn and Leighton, p. 69; see also James F. Downs, *The Navajo* (New York, Holt, Rinehart & Winston, 1972), pp. 22 ff., on the continuing importance of 'the female principle' within the tribe.

71   Gibson, *The Chickasaws*, pp. 28–9; O'Donnell, *Southern Indians in the American Revolution*, p. 11; see also Cotterill, *The Southern Indians*, p. 14.

72   Salisbury, *Manitou and Providence*, pp. 40–1; E. G. Eastman, *Sister to the Sioux*, p. 90; Donald J. Berthrong, *The Southern Cheyennes* (Norman, Okla, University of Oklahoma Press, 1963), pp. 34–6.

73   See McKenney and Hall, p. 102.

74   See Llewellyn and Hoebel, chs IV and V, and *passim*; Trenholm, pp. 77–80.

75   See for a discussion of the correspondence between the autocratic family and autocratic state, Stephens, pp. 326–39.

76　See, for instance, Axtell, *The European and the Indian*, pp. 46–7; Slotkin, pp. 44–5, 200–1, 254.
77　Brinton, *The American Race*, p. 49; Dodge, pp. 390–1; McKenney and Hall, pp. 39–40; Kupperman, p. 61; Mathes, p. 136.
78　Cited in Satz, *American Indian Policy in the Jacksonian Era*, pp. 261–3; and see, on Ward Coachman, *The Indian Journal*, Eufaula, Creek Nation, vol. 2, no. 9, 13 October 1877, Ward Coachman Papers, WHC.
79　See Carlson, *Indians, Bureaucrats and Land*, especially chs 5–6; in order to help women and other groups disadvantaged by the Dawes Act, the equalization of allotments at 80 acres was eventually agreed: see above, Chapter 4, p. 99.
80　See interview with Jane Honga, 11 July 1968, pp. 667–70, 688–90, transcripts of the Hualapai Oral History Project; see also interviews with Alma Fielding, pp. 51–2, and Rose Butler, p. 789, in the same transcripts.
81　Joseph Westermeyer, 'Sex roles and the Indian-majority interface in Minnesota', *International Journal of Psychiatry*, vol. 24, no. 3, Autumn 1978, pp. 189–93.
82　Ibid., pp. 189–90; Stanley Lieberson, *A Piece of the Pie. Blacks and White Immigrants Since 1880* (Berkeley, Calif., University of California Press, 1980), pp. 129, 167; Barbara Miller Solomon, *In the Company of Educated Women. A History of Women and Higher Education in America* (New Haven, Conn., and London, Yale University Press, 1985), ch. Twelve; John A. Price, *Native Studies*, p. 267.
83　See Nancy Butterfield, 'Native American women', *OKC Camp Crier*, Oklahoma City, vol. 3, no. 16, January 1978, pp. 3–4; Westermeyer, p. 193; John A. Price, *Native Studies*, pp. 167, 174, 177.
84　See Downs, *The Navajo*, p. 132.
85　For an introduction to a still raging debate about the black family, the impact upon it of the welfare system and other factors, see Gutman, Afterword; and Charles Murray, *Losing Ground* (New York, Basic Books, 1986 edn).

CHAPTER 11

1　Carlson, *Indians, Bureaucrats and Land*, pp. 155–6.
2　Kvasnicka and Viola (eds), *The Commissioners*, p. 224.
3　See the many letters to Dagenett's office in Industries section, Indian Employment, RG 75; and correspondence in 1917 between Dagenett and Jewell D. Martin, Superintendent of San Xavier Agency, Tucson, Arizona, in ibid.
4　Meriam (ed.), *The Problem of Indian Administration*, ch. 12.
5　See Moorehead, *An Analysis*, p. 19; letters between Mr J. C. H. Reynolds of Spokane, Commissioner Burke and Oscar H. Lipps, Superintendent of Fort Lapwai Agency, 22 and 24 October 1925 and 2 April 1926, and 'Resolutions' of the Spokane Betterment Organisation's first Congress, p. 4, in Office Files of General Superintendent (Peairs), RG 75.
6　Alan L. Sorkin, *The Urban American Indian* (Lexington, Mass., D. C. Heath, 1978), p. 4.
7　See, for instance, Roger Daniels, *Concentration Camps U.S.A. Japanese Americans and World War II* (New York, Holt, Rinehart & Winston, 1971); Dillon S. Myer, *Uprooted Americans* (Tucson, Ariz., University of Arizona

Press, 1974); and 'The needs of the American Indian', Address by Dillon S. Myer, before the Combined Assemblies of the Division of Christian Life and Work of the National Council of the Churches of Christ at Buck Hill Falls, Pennsylvania, on December 12, 1951, pp. 5–8, Speeches File, Desk Files of Commissioner Dillon S. Myer.

8 Walter V. Woehlke to Collier, 26 April 1944, Miscellaneous Correspondence File, in Desk Files of Commissioner John Collier, Bureau of Indian Affairs, Washington DC; and memorandum from C. E. Lamson, Indian Employment, 25 September 1945, to Mr Fickinger, in Office Records of Assistant Commissioner William Zimmerman, Memoranda, 1944–50.

9 Commissioner Myer speaking at Conference of Area Directors, 9 January 1951, p. 5, in Desk Files of Commissioner Myer; Summary of Navajo Development, 1 February 1950, pp. 7–8, in Desk Files of Commissioners William Brophy and John Nichols; and in ibid., statement presented by William Zimmerman, Jr, Acting Commissioner of Indian Affairs before the Senate Committee on Interior and Insular Affairs . . . 3 February 1949, p. 6, and Zimmerman to Sam Akeah of the Navajo Tribal Council, 24 November 1948; Records of Bureau-Tribal Conference, July 1956, meeting with Fort Hall group, pp. 10–11, and with Winnebago, p. 8, 68–2045, no. 369, box 1, Bureau of Indian Affairs, Washington DC.

10 Alan L. Sorkin, *American Indians and Federal Aid* (Washington, DC, the Brookings Institution, 1971), p. 105; memorandum 'Information requested by Mr Charles W. Eliot in letter of November 5 1951', p. 11, in Desk Files of Commissioner Myer. See also Elaine M. Neils, *Reservation to City. Indian Migration and Federal Relocation* (Chicago, Department of Geography, University of Chicago, 1971).

11 Sorkin, *American Indians*, pp. 105–7.

12 Sorkin, *Urban American Indian*, p. 27; Sorkin, *American Indians*, pp. 107–10; Brophy and Aberle (comps), *The Indian. America's Unfinished Business*, pp. 103–4.

13 See Records of Bureau-Tribal Conference, July 1956, op. cit., meeting with Fort Hall group, pp. 10–11, and with Winnebago, p. 8.

14 ibid., meeting with Flandreau group, pp. 2–3; with Fort Hall group, pp. 16–17.

15 Summary of Proceedings, Conference of Area Directors, op. cit., pp. 14–15; Address by Dillon S. Myer, Commissioner of Indian Affairs, at the Eighth Annual Convention of the National Congress of American Indians, St Paul, Minnesota, 25 July 1951, pp. 12–13, in Desk Files of Commissioner Myer.

16 Letter from Hon. Toby Morris, Chairman of Subcommittee on Indian Affairs, to Hon. Frederick J. Lawton, Director, Bureau of the Budget, 19 October 1951, in Desk Files of Commissioner Myer.

17 Statement of Dr John R. Nichols, Commissioner, Bureau of Indian Affairs, Department of the Interior, at the Governor's Conference on Indian Affairs, St Paul, Minnesota, 14 March 1950, p. 6, in Desk Files of Commissioners Brophy and Nichols.

18 Commissioner Emmons in Records of Bureau-Tribal Conference, op. cit., Tribal Council Conference, Second Session, Omaha, Nebraska, pp. 10–11; see also Conference with Lower Brule, pp. 19–20; with Crow Creek, p. 9; with Pine Ridge group, pp. 19–21, 24; with Fort Hall group, p. 25.

19 See comments in ibid., Bob Burnette's group I, pp. 42–3; Cato Valendra's

group, pp. 46–7; Crow Creek group, p. 9; Flandreau group, p. 10; general session, p. 25; records of Conference of Commissioner of Indian Affairs with Oklahoma, Kansas and Mississippi Tribes, 11, 12, 13 December 1956, pp. 38, 40, 43–7; letter to Commissioner Emmons, 14 June 1957, from Jimmie James, Press Agent for the Yakima Indian Nation, Portland, Oregon, and reply by Acting Commissioner Martin P. Mangan, 3 July 1957 file no. 573 1957 (077), Bureau of Indian Affairs, Washington DC; about Indian anxieties over relocation, Conference of Area Directors, 9 January 1951, pp. 2–3, in Desk Files of Commissioner Myer.

20 Talk by Glenn L. Emmons, at a panel discussion held by the Indian Law Committee of the Federal Bar Association, Chicago, Illinois, 1960, op. cit.

21 Sorkin, *Urban American Indian*, pp. 38–42; Sorkin, *American Indians*, pp. 110–19, 120–1, 131, 134–5, 186; Joan Ablon, 'American Indian relocation. Problems of dependency and management in the city', *Phylon*, vol. 26, Winter 1965, pp. 365–6; Lawrence Clinton, Bruce A. Chadwick and Howard M. Bahr, 'Urban relocation reconsidered. Antecedents of employment among Indian males', *Rural Sociology*, vol. 40, no. 2, Summer 1975, pp. 117, 119–22, 129–30; James H. Gundlach, P. Nelson Reid and Alden E. Roberts, 'Migration, labor mobility and relocation assistance. The case of the American Indian', *Social Science Review*, vol. 51, no. 3, September 1977, pp. 466–7, 472; Alan L. Sorkin, 'The economic basis of Indian life', *Annals*, vol. 436, March 1978, pp. 1–7, 12; Bruce A. Chadwick and Lynn C. White, 'Correlates of length of urban residence among the Spokane Indians', *Human Organization*, vol. 32, Spring 1973, pp. 9–16, are unusual in playing down the importance of economic factors in determining Indian migration to and settlement in the city; Sam Stanley and Robert K. Thomas, 'Current demographic and social trends among North American Indians', *Annals*, vol. 436, March 1978, pp. 113, 116–17; and Theodore D. Graves, 'The personal adjustment of Navajo Indian migrants to Denver, Colorado', *American Anthropologist*, vol. 72, February 1970, p. 52.

22 Sorkin, *Urban American Indian*, pp. 21–2.

23 Though some light is thrown on these questions in Theodore D. Graves and Charles A. Lave, 'Determinants of urban migrant Indian wages', *Human Organization*, vol. 31, Spring 1972, pp. 47–61.

24 Clinton, Chadwick and Bahr, pp. 124–5.

25 'Off-reservation Indians', p. 42, in 'The American Indian today', published in *Engage/Social Action*, July 1977, Washington, DC.

26 Sorkin, *Urban American Indian*, p. 40; John W. Olson, 'The urban Indian as viewed by an Indian caseworker', in Waddell and Watson (eds), *The American Indian in Urban Society*, pp. 402–3.

27 Stanley and Thomas, p. 116.

28 Shuichi Nagata, 'The reservation community and the urban community. Hopi Indians of Moenkopi', in Waddell and Watson, (eds), *The American Indian in Urban Society*, pp. 130–6, 144, 148–53; Joann Westerman, 'The Urban Indian', *Current History*, vol. 67, December 1974, pp. 259–61; Roger E. Kelly and John O. Cramer, 'American Indians in small cities', *Rehabilitation Monographs*, no. 1 (Flagstaff, Ariz., Northern Arizona University, 1966); Howard M. Bahr, Bruce A. Chadwick and Joseph Strauss, 'Discrimination against urban Indians in Seattle', *The Indian Historian*, vol. 5, 1972, pp. 5–6; DD for New Mexico, tape 450, side 2; tape 501, pp. 24–5; tape 636, pp. 11–13; tape 497, side 1, pp. 2–8, 10–15; Graves and Lave,

pp. 54, 57–9; Robert S. Weppner, 'Socioeconomic barriers to assimilation of Navajo migrant workers', *Human Organization*, vol. 31, no. 3, Fall 1972, pp. 312–13; Robert S. Weppner, 'Urban economic opportunities. The example of Denver', in Waddell and Watson (eds), *The American Indian in Urban Society*, pp. 261–9; Joan Ablon, 'Relocated Indians in the San Francisco Bay area. Social interaction and Indian identity', *Human Organization*, vol. 23, no. 4, Winter 1964, p. 304; Howard M. Bahr and Bruce A. Chadwick, 'Conservatism, racial intolerance, and attitudes toward racial assimilation among whites and American Indians', *The Journal of Social Psychology*, vol. 94, October 1974, p. 56; J. Milton Yinger and George Eaton Simpson, 'The integration of Americans of Indian descent', *Annals*, vol. 436, March 1978, p. 147; Robert A. Hackenberg and C. Roderick Wilson, 'Reluctant emigrants. The role of migration in Papago Indian adaptation', *Human Organization*, vol. 31, no. 2, Summer 1972, pp. 177, 180.

29 John A. Price, 'The migration and adaptation of American Indians to Los Angeles', *Human Organization*, vol. 27, no. 2, Summer 1968, p. 172; Bruce A. Chadwick and Joseph H. Strauss, 'The assimilation of American Indians into urban society. The Seattle case', *Human Organization*, vol. 34, no. 4, Winter 1975, p. 364.

30 Deward E. Walker, Jr, 'Measures of Nez Percé outbreeding and the analysis of cultural change', *Southwestern Journal of Anthropology*, vol. 23, Summer 1967, pp. 150–2, 155–6; Sorkin, *Urban American Indians*, pp. 73–4, 144; Merwyn S. Garbarino, 'Life in the city. Chicago', in Waddell and Watson (eds), *The American Indian in Urban Society*. p. 175; Ablon, 'Relocated Indians', p. 301; Chadwick and Strauss, p. 364; Gundlach, Reid and Roberts, p. 465.

31 Sol Tax, 'The impact of urbanization on American Indians', *Annals*, vol. 436, March 1978, p. 127; Garbarino, p. 171; Ablon, 'Relocated Indians', pp. 298–303; Sorkin, 'The economic basis', p. 12; Chadwick and Strauss, p. 364; *Red Letter*, Native American Committee, Chicago, August 1975; Joan Dorothy Laxon, 'Aspects of acculturation among American Indians. Emphasis on contemporary pan-Indianism' (PhD thesis, University of California, 1972), pp. 166–7.

32 Laxon, pp. 51–2, 54, 61–4, 71–2, 83, 86, 89, 222; Yinger and Simpson, p. 139.

33 S. Lieberson, *Ethnic Patterns in American Cities* (New York, Free Press of Glencoe, 1963), p. 18.

34 C. Raisch, 'The state of the Indian nation', *Hustler*, January 1978, p. 85; Chadwick and Strauss, p. 362; Peter Z. Snyder, 'The social environment of the urban Indians', in Waddell and Watson (eds), *The American Indian in Urban Society*, p. 218; Sorkin, *Urban American Indians*, p. 72.

35 Snyder, p. 236; Sorkin, *Urban American Indian*, pp. 67 and 144, and ch. 5; and James E. Officer, 'The American Indian and federal policy', in Waddell and Watson (eds), *The American Indian in Urban Society*, p. 62.

36 Theodore D. Graves, 'Drinking and drunkenness among urban Indians', in Waddell and Watson (eds), *The American Indian in Urban Society*, p. 281; Omer Stewart, 'Questions regarding American Indian criminality', *Human Organization*, vol. 23, no. 1, Spring 1964, p. 61; John A. Price, 'An applied analysis of North American Indian drinking patterns', *Human Organization*, vol. 34, no. 1, Spring 1975, pp. 19, 22; Sorkin, *Urban American Indian*, p. 56; Graves and Lave, p. 58; Clinton, Chadwick and Bahr, p. 122; Weppner, 'Urban economic opportunities', p. 264.

37 Patricia D. Mail, 'Hippocrates was a medicine man: the health care of Native Americans in the twentieth century', *Annals*, vol. 436, March 1978, p. 41; J. E. Levy and S. J. Kunitz, *Indian Drinking*, (New York, Wiley, 1974); interview with Rupert Parker, p. 626, in transcripts of the Hualapai Oral History Project; Nancy Oestreich Lurie, 'The world's oldest on-going protest demonstration. North American Indian drinking patterns', *Pacific Historical Review*, vol. 40, 1971, pp. 316, 323 ff.

38 John A. Price, 'An applied analysis', p. 22.

39 John A. Price, 'An applied analysis', pp. 19–20; Graves, 'Drinking and drunkenness', p. 287; Jack O. Waddell, 'For individual power and social credit. The use of alcohol among Tucson Papagos', *Human Organization*, vol. 34, no. 1, Spring 1975, pp. 13–14; Snyder, p. 237; Garbarino, pp. 194–5; Lurie, 'The world's oldest . . . demonstration', p. 315 and *passim*.

40 Graves, 'Drinking and drunkenness', pp. 284, 307; John A. Price, 'An applied analysis', pp. 24–5; Snyder, pp. 233, 235, discovered that among the Navajo he studied in Denver there was a clique which, though least alienated from the city in terms of jobs and attitudes, reported the heaviest drinking; without, however, incurring a high arrest rate. There is no obvious explanation for this finding; see also Snyder, p. 212; Graves, 'Drinking and drunkenness', pp. 290–309; Graves, 'Personal adjustment', pp. 50–1; Garbarino, pp. 187–93; and George Harwood Phillips, 'Indians in Los Angeles, 1781–1875', *Pacific Historical Review*, vol. 49, 1980, pp. 444–7, on Indian drinking and its consequences in a nineteenth-century city, though he also stresses the Indians' contribution to its economy.

41 See interviews with Suwim Fielding, pp. 528 ff., with Dennis and Rose Butler, p. 854, with Marcus Wellington, pp. 870 ff., with Gilbert Butler, pp. 917 ff., 950, with Myrtle Watahomigie, pp. 1001 ff., with Sophie Matapis, p. 1043, and with Laura Majenty, pp. 1096 ff., in transcripts of the Hualapai Oral History Project.

42 Edward P. Dozier, 'Problem drinking among American Indians. The role of sociocultural deprivation', *Quarterly Journal of Studies on Alcohol*, vol. XXVII, 1966, p. 73.

43 Sorkin, *Urban American Indians*, pp. 58–63; Waddell, pp. 14–15; John A. Price, 'An applied analysis', pp. 24–5.

44 Mail, p. 48.

45 Sorkin, *Urban American Indian*, pp. 47–55.

46 ibid., pp. 76–79.

47 ibid., pp. 80–3.

48 See Garbarino, pp. 184–6.

49 See the works by Katz, *Class, Bureaucracy and Schools* and *The Irony of Early School Reform*, and Tyack, *The One Best System*, as well as Colin Greer, *The Great School Legend. A Revisionist Interpretation of American Public Education* (New York, Viking, 1972); Edgar B. Gumbert and Joel H. Spring, *The Superschool and the Superstate, American Education in the Twentieth Century, 1918–1970* (New York, Wiley, 1974); and Henry J. Perkinson, *The Imperfect Panacea* (New York, Wiley, 1968).

50 Garbarino, p. 185.

51 Sorkin, *Urban American Indian*, p. 28.

52 ibid., pp. 87–97; Harry J. Gilman, 'Economic discrimination and unemployment', *American Economic Review*, vol. 55, December 1965, pp. 1077–96; Walter Fogel, 'The effect of low educational attainment on

incomes: a comparative study of selected ethnic groups', *The Journal of Human Resources*, vol. 1, Fall 1966, pp. 22–40; Roy L. Lassiter, 'The association of income and education for males by region, race and age', *Southern Economic Review*, vol. 32, July 1965, pp. 15–22; Steinberg, *The Ethnic Myth*, p. 221; Judith Kleinfeld, 'Positive stereotyping. The cultural relativist in the classroom', *Human Organization*, vol. 34, no. 3, Fall 1975, pp. 269–74; and see above, Chapter 9.

53 Sorkin, *Urban American Indian*, p. 96.
54 See, for instance, *Oklahoma Indian American School Guide* (Southwest Center for Human Relations Studies, University of Oklahoma, 1979); and *The Written and Unspoken Word* (BIA, Indian Education Programs, Andarko, Okla, 1980).
55 Sorkin, *Urban American Indians*, pp. 97–104.
56 Chadwick and Strauss, pp. 365–6.
57 Sorkin, *Urban American Indian*, p. 111.
58 Officer, p. 61; and William H. Hodge, 'Navajo urban migration. An analysis from the perspective of the family', in Waddell and Watson (eds), *The American Indian in Urban Society*, pp. 379–80.
59 See Sorkin, *Urban American Indian*, ch. 9.
60 See Jeanne Guillemin, *Urban Renegades. The Cultural Strategy of American Indians* (New York, Columbia University Press, 1975), on the interrelatedness of the Indians' city and reservation bases.

CHAPTER 12

1 See, for instance, Fiske, *The Discovery of America*, Vol. I, p. 47; Bancroft, *History of the United States*, Vol. III, pp. 274–5, 278, 280; McKenney and Hall, *History of the Indian Tribes*, Vol. 3, pp. 14, 128–9; Morgan, *League of the Iroquois*, p. 4; Edward Channing, *A History of the United States*, Vol. 1 (New York, 1906), pp. 402, 404; Justin Winsor (ed.), *Narrative and Critical History of America*, Vol. 1 (Boston, Mass., Houghton Mifflin, 1889), p. 284; article by Berkhofer, 'Native Americans', in Higham (ed.), *Ethnic Leadership in America*, pp. 121–2.
2 Statement by Calhoun, 5 December 1818, quoted in Prucha (ed.), *Documents of United States Indian Policy*, p. 32.
3 C. A. Eastman, *From the Deep Woods to Civilization*, pp. 164–5; Gilcreast, 'Richard Henry Pratt', pp. 224–5; and see Margot Liberty (ed.), *American Indian Intellectuals* (St Paul, Minn., West Publishing, 1978), which deals with a range of Indian leaders.
4 C. A. Eastman, *From the Deep Woods*, p. 155, chs VIII, X.
5 *Report of the Twenty-Sixth Annual Meeting of the Lake Mohonk Conference of Friends of the Indian and Other Dependent Peoples* (Lake Mohonk Conference, 1908), pp. 47–50, 263, 266; *Report of the Thirty-Third Annual Lake Mohonk Conference on the Indian and Other Dependent Peoples* (Lake Mohonk Conference, 1915), p. 31; *Report of the Thirty-Fourth conference on the Indian and Other Dependent Peoples* (Lake Mohonk Conference, 1916), pp. 54–5. Burgess, 'The Lake Mohonk conferences on the Indian', pp. 91, 97–8, 102–3, 109–10, 121, 123–4, 157, 172, 244, 246, 274, 287–8, 337–8, 343.
6 Burgess, p. 198.
7 See Gilcreast, pp. 177–80.
8 *Report of the Twenty-Ninth Annual Lake Mohonk Conference of Friends of the*

Indian and Other Dependent Peoples (Lake Mohonk Conference, 1911), p. 88; *Report of the Thirty-Second Annual Lake Mohonk Conference of Friends of the Indian and Other Dependent Peoples* (Lake Mohonk Conference, 1914), pp. 105–6.

9 *Thirtieth Annual Report of the Executive Committee of the Indian Rights Association . . . 1912* (Philadelphia, Pa, IRA, 1912), p. 40; also *Report . . . 1911* (Philadelphia, Pa, IRA, 1912), pp. 21–3; *The Present Situation of Indian Affairs* (Philadelphia, Pa, IRA, 1912), p. 2; *Report . . . 1913* (Philadelphia, Pa, IRA, 1913), pp. 46–9; *Report . . . 1915* (Philadelphia, Pa, IRA, 1915), pp. 71–4; *Report . . . 1916* (Philadelphia, Pa, IRA, 1916), pp. 64–6; *Report . . . 1918* (Philadelphia, Pa, IRA, 1918), pp. 66–9; *Quarterly Journal* of the SAI, vol. 1, no. 2, April–June 1913, p. 233; vol. 1, no. 1, April 1913, p. 64; *The Red Man*, vol. 4, no. 1, September 1911, pp. 4–5; vol. 6, no. 3, November 1913, pp. 77–84.

10 Burgess, pp. 299–300, 303; *Quarterly Journal*, vol. 1, no. 4, October–December 1913, p. 338.

11 Charles A. Eastman, *The Indian To-day* (Garden City, NY, Page, 1915), pp. 60–1.

12 *Quarterly Journal*, vol. 1, no. 3, July–September 1913, pp. 270–2; and see Charles Dagenett to F. A. McKenzie, 9 January 1911, box 2, folder 1, Montezuma Papers. I have, in this chapter, drawn and built on my ch. 4 in Barbrook and Bolt, *Power and Protest*.

13 See, for instance, 'Members constituting the Fourth Conference', in *Quarterly Journal*, vol. 2, no. 4, October–December 1914, p. 319.

14 See the fear expressed in a letter of 12 July 1911, box 2, folder 2, Carlos Montezuma Papers, University of Arizona Library, about when 'American whites can be depended upon for contributions to a case in which they do not see themselves leading the procession'.

15 Hertzberg, *The Search for an American Indian Identity*, pp. 57–8, 75, 111; *American Indian Magazine*, vol. 4, no. 3, July–September 1916, p. 213.

16 *Quarterly Journal*, vol. 1, no. 4, October–December 1913, p. 409.

17 Hertzberg, p. 96.

18 *Quarterly Journal*, vol. 1, no. 2, April–June 1913, pp. 141–2; *American Indian Magazine*, vol. IV, no. 3, July–September 1916, pp. 214–15; Hertzberg, p. 133.

19 Hertzberg, p. 111.

20 Ibid., p. 126; *Quarterly Journal*, vol. 2, no. 2, April–June 1914, pp. 159–60.

21 *Quarterly Journal*, vol. 1, no. 2, April–June 1913, pp. 225, 232–3, 238–9; vol. 1, no. 4, October–December 1913, p. 342.

22 *Quarterly Journal*, vol. 2, no. 3, July–September 1914, p. 170.

23 *Quarterly Journal*, vol. 1, no. 1, April 1913, p. 7; vol. 1, no. 2, April–June 1913, p. 224; vol. 1, no. 4, October–December 1913, p. 342; vol. 2, no. 1, January–March 1914, p. 93; *American Indian Magazine*, vol. 4, no. 3, July–September 1916, pp. 227, 230–1; *The Red Man*, vol. 9, no. 3, November 1916, p. 83; Hertzberg, pp. 111–12, 146.

24 *Quarterly Journal*, vol. 2, no. 3, July–September 1914, p. 229.

25 *The Red Man*, vol. 3, no. 7, 1910–11, p. 300; *Quarterly Journal*, vol. 1, no. 1, April 1913, p. 74; vol. 1, no. 2, April–June 1913, p. 101; vol. 2, no. 1, January–March 1914, pp. 27–8.

26 *Quarterly Journal*, vol. 1, no. 1, April 1913, p. 7; vol. 1, no. 2, April–June 1913, pp. 154–5; vol. 1, no. 3, July–September 1913, pp. 275–6.

27 *Quarterly Journal*, vol. 1, no. 1, April 1913, pp. 69, 81; vol. 1, no. 2,

April–June 1913, p. 138; vol. 1, no. 3, July–September 1913, pp. 268, 272–3; vol. 3, no. 3, July–September 1915, pp. 148–9; *American Indian Magazine*, vol. 4, no. 1, January–March 1916, p. 12.

28 *Quarterly Journal*, vol. 1, no. 1, April 1913, p. 46; vol. 4, no. 3, July–September 1916, pp. 223–4; Hertzberg, pp. 98–9, 117, 137, 152.

29 *Quarterly Journal*, vol. 1, no. 2, April–June 1913, p. 106; vol. 2, no. 1, January–March 1914, p. 71; vol. 2, no. 3, July–September 1914, p. 231; vol. 3, no. 4, October–December 1915, p. 252; *American Indian Magazine*, vol. 4, no. 3, July–September 1916, pp. 223–4; vol. 5, no. 4, October–December 1917, pp. 213–15; vol. 7, no. 3, Fall 1919, pp. 127, 140, 151, 153: and see pp. 169–71, for an acknowledgement that the reservations had something to offer the old, poor and ill.

30 *Quarterly Journal*, vol. 1, no. 2, April–June 1913, pp. 233, 238, 261–2; vol. 1, no. 3, July–September 1913, p. 268; vol. 1, no. 4, October–December 1913, pp. 351–2; vol. 2, no. 3, July–September 1914, p. 231; vol. 3, no. 3, July–September 1915, pp. 220–3; *American Indian Magazine*, vol. 4, October–December 1916, pp. 282–4; vol. 5, no. 1, January–March 1917, p. 16.

31 *Quarterly Journal*, vol. 2, no. 3, July–September 1914, pp. 171–2,. 205; vol. 3, no. 3, July–September 1915, p. 177; vol. 3, no. 4, October–December 1915, pp. 286–7; *American Indian Magazine*, vol. 4, no. 3, July–September 1916, pp. 223–4; vol. 4, no. 4, October–December 1916, pp. 311–14; vol. 5, no. 1, January–March 1917, pp. 5–6, 207; vol. 5, no. 2, April–June 1917, p. 69; vol. 5, no. 3, July–September 1917, pp. 137–8, 146–53, 203–4.

32 *Quarterly Journal*, vol. 2, no. 3, July–September 1914, pp. 224–8; *American Indian Magazine*, vol. 4, no. 2, April–June 1916, p. 118.

33 *Quarterly Journal*, vol. 1, no. 1, April 1913, pp. 76–7; vol. 2, no. 2, April–June 1914, article by Professor F. A. McKenzie; vol. 2, no. 3, July–September 1914, pp. 183–4; vol. 2, no. 4, October–December 1914, p. 261; vol. 3, no. 3, June–September 1915, pp. 190–4.

34 Hertzberg, pp. 133, 136, 138–9, 144, 151, 153; *Quarterly Journal*, vol. 1, no. 1, April 1913, pp. 73–4; vol. 1, no. 4, October–December 1913, p. 409; vol. 3, no. 3, July–September 1915, pp. 216–17; vol. 3, no. 4, October–December 1915, p. 287; *American Indian Magazine*, vol. 4, no. 3, July–September 1916, p. 220.

35 See, for instance, Stein, 'The Indian Citizenship Act of 1924', pp. 266 ff.

36 *American Indian Magazine*, vol. 4, no. 2, April–June 1916, p. 118; Hertzberg, pp. 108, 135, 141, 149.

37 *American Indian Magazine*, vol. 4, no. 3, July–September 1916, pp. 230–1.

38 *American Indian Magazine*, vol. IV, no. 2, April–June 1916, p. 113; vol. 7, no. 2, Summer 1919, for an indication of the journal's attempt to attract general interest through less specialist articles; Hertzberg, p. 153; Pratt to Montezuma, 16 December 1921, in box 1, folder 4, Montezuma Papers; *Wassaja*, vol. 1, no. 1, April 1916, p. 3; no. 2, May 1916, pp. 2–4; no. 3, June 1916, p. 3; no. 4, July 1916, pp. 1–4; no. 5, August 1916, pp. 1–4; no. 6, September 1916, p. 3; no. 7, October 1916, p. 3; no. 8, November 1916, pp. 2–3; no. 10, January 1917, pp. 3–4; and Peter Iverson, 'Carlos Montezuma', in Edmunds (ed.), *American Indian Leaders*, pp. 206–20.

39 See F. Svensson, *The Ethnics in American Politics. American Indians* (Minneapolis, Minn., Burgess, 1973), pp. 24–5.

40 Letter of E. B. Merritt, Assistant Indian Commissioner, to the Editor of the *Evening Star*, October 1922, in tray 108, BIC files.
41 See Hertzberg, pp. 71, 98, 118.
42 See Debo, *And Still the Waters Run*, pp. 176, 315, ch. XII, pp. 351–2, 359–60.
43 Article of 1912 on 'The Indian and citizenship' by McKenzie, in tray 108, BIC files.
44 *Indian Truth*, vol. 3, no. 3, March 1926, p. 3; Hertzberg, p. 207; in tray 105, BIC files, *American Indian Life*, bulletin no. 8, May 1927, and no. 16, July 1930, pp. 31–2; Debo, *And Still the Waters Run*, ch. XIII.
45 *The American Indian*, vol. 1, no. 9, June 1927, p. 2; Debo, *And Still the Waters Run*, pp. 331, 337, 344.
46 *The American Indian*, vol. 2, no. 1, October 1927, p. 6; vol. 2, no. 2, November 1927, p. 4; vol. 2, no. 3, December 1927, p. 4; vol. 4, no. 6, March 1930, p. 4; vol. 4, no. 7, April 1930, p. 4.
47 *Indian Truth*, vol. 3, no. 2, December 1926, p. 2; vol. 4, no. 2, February 1927, pp. 3–4; vol. 6, no. 9, October 1929.
48 Quotation from Report of the Sub-Committee on Alaska of the Committee on Objectives, submitted March 15, 1931, Edna R. Voss, Chairman, pp. 12–13, in tray 118, BIC files; Pratt to Hon. Selden Spencer, 29 December 1921, box 1, folder 4, Montezuma Papers.
49 See Philip Drucker, *The Native Brotherhoods* (Washington, DC, Bureau of American Ethnology, Bulletin 168, 1958), pp. 16 ff., 44–59, 131–4, 159–60.
50 Letter of Louis F. Paul, executive committee, Alaska Native Brotherhood, *Portland Oregonian*, 5 May 1931, BIC Newspaper Clippings.
51 Harry B. Hawthorn, Cyril S. Belshaw, S. M. Jamieson *et al.*, *The Indians of British Columbia* (Berkeley and Vancouver, University of British Columbia Press, 1958), pp. 475–6.
52 *The American Indian*, vol. 1, no. 5, February 1927, p. 7; vol. 3, no. 7, April 1929, p. 4.
53 *Indian Truth*, vol. 4, no. 1, January 1927, p. 2.
54 See article, 'Tsianina, leader among women of the Indian race', BIC Newspaper Clippings.
55 See Lawrence M. Hauptman, 'The American Indian Federation and the Indian New Deal. A reinterpretation', *Pacific Historical Review*, vol. 52, 1983, pp. 378–402.
56 Hauptman, pp. 381–4.
57 See articles from the Washington *Star*, in BIC Newspaper Clippings, apparently 21, 22, 23 and 24 April 1933.
58 Jemison in article of 8 August 1935, clipped from the *Washington Times*, box 6, in Office File of Commissioner John Collier.
59 Talk by Jemison, 27 July 1938, p. 2, in Jemison File, box 6, in Office File of Commissioner Collier.
60 'Memorandum for the press', 6 February 1935, op. cit., pp. 4–10; see 'Highlights of the Roosevelt record on Indian affairs', Federation pamphlet, pp. 1–4, received by Indian Office November 1940, in box 6, Office File of Commissioner Collier; 'Indian opinion on the Indian Reorganization Act', pp. 39–40, in ibid.; letter from the Federation, 'To Americans', 23 March 1938, in ibid.; 'Fifth Annual Convention of the American Indian Federation. Resolution no. 2', in box 1, ibid.; clipping from *Southwest Tourist News*, vol. V, no. VII, 12 September 1934, in ibid.; letter from Joseph Bruner to President Roosevelt, 19 June 1936, in ibid.; letter by Bruner 'To the American Citizenship of the United States',

received by Indian Office, 2 May 1935, in ibid.; letter from Secretary of Interior Ickes to Bruner, 16 January 1935, p. 2, in ibid.; in box 6, Office Files of Chief of Education Division. 'Onward to greater things. The American Indian Federation, Sapulpa, Oklahoma, December 21st 1934'.

61 See, for instance, in Office File of Fred Daiker, 1929–43, entry 194, RG 75, American Indian Federation File – notably correspondence about the possibility of taking legal action against the Federation.

62 Letter of Joseph Bruner, 16 October 1936, to Harold L. Ickes, Secretary of the Interior, in box 1 of ibid.; note in ibid. of American Council of Civil Liberties officials Jay B. Nash and Robert Gessner, 31 August 1936, and from M. K. Sniffen, Secretary of the Indian Rights Association to Mrs W. A. Becker, 14 October 1936; 'Memorandum for the press', 6 February 1935, op. cit., pp. 1–3, 10–11, by Collier, in box 6, Office Files of Chief of Education Division; and in box 2, Subject Correspondence Files of John Herrick, Herrick to Richard Rendell, Washington Bureau, *Newsweek*, 7 September 1939; 'Memorandum for the press', 7 September 1939, in ibid.; from Collier to Cato Sells, Fort Worth, Texas, 21 September 1934, in box 1, Office File of Commissioner John Collier; and in box 6, in ibid., letter from Collier to Mrs Mildred W. Leach of Philadelphia; Taylor, *The New Deal and American Indian Tribalism*, p. 107; Hauptman, pp. 398–400; and Kenneth R. Philp, 'The New Deal and Alaskan natives, 1939–1945', *Pacific Historical Review*, vol. 50, 1981, pp. 309–27, especially p. 323.

63 'Memorandum for Secretary Ickes', op. cit.; 'Further Statement Upon Fifth Column Activities in Relation to Indian Legislation', 12 June 1940, box 16, in Office File of Commissioner John Collier; Oliver La Farge to Walter V. Woehlke, Office of Indian Affairs, 9 May 1939, box 6, in ibid.; unheaded note of 14 June 1940, in ibid.; report by F. W. La Rouche on the 1936 Convention of the American Indian Federation, box 1, in ibid.; 'Memorandum for the press', 7 September 1939, op. cit.; account of 'German American Bund Meeting, at San Francisco, May 19, 1939', in Office File of Fred Daiker; Jesse Cornplanter, Basom, New York, to Collier, 12 June 1940, box 6, in Office File of Commissioner John Collier; Hauptman, pp. 396–8.

64 See materials on the group in box 3, in Office File of Commissioner John Collier; and in box 16, in ibid., 6 June 1940, 'Memorandum for Secretary Ickes: re: fifth column activities among Indians. From John Collier, Commissioner of Indian Affairs, through M. W. Strauss.'

65 Hauptman, pp. 400–1.

66 See Jack Nichols, 8 October 1936, to John Collier, box 7, in Office File of Commissioner John Collier.

67 Herrick to Mrs Malvina Thompson, 8 August 1936, box 8, in Subject Correspondence Files of John Herrick; 'To Americans', op. cit., p. 2; 'Highlights of the Roosevelt record in Indian affairs', p. 4; and in box 6, Office File of Commissioner John Collier, note from California Indian Rights Association, Inc., to Michael Harrison of the US Department of Interior, Field Service of CIA, Sacramento, California. And see Kelly, *The Navajo Indians*, pp. 187–9; cases were brought in Arizona and New Mexico in 1947, after which Indians who could show their literacy were allowed to vote.

68 *Proceedings of the First Convention of the National Congress of American Indians, held in Denver, Colorado, 15–18 November 1944*, pp. 2–3, 8, 12, 17, 30–4, 54–9, in OHS, section X; Annual Convention of the National

Congress of American Indians, Bowling, Montana, 22–5 October 1945, pp. 2, 8–9, 21, 36–8, 42, 47, 51, 61, 83–8, OHS, section X; M. L. Wax, *American Indians, Unity and Diversity* (Englewood Cliffs, NJ, Prentice-Hall, 1971), p. 146; Laxon, 'Aspects of Acculturation among American Indians', pp. 168–9, 180; Svensson, pp. 30–1; memorandum to Assistant Commissioner Provinse from Associate Solicitor Cohen, 3 April 1947, 'Policy Statement on Indian Affairs', pp. 1–2 on NCAI, in Office File of Assistant Commissioner Provinse; *The American Indian*, vol. IV, no. 2, 1947, pp. 2, 7–10, 14–18, 28, and NCAI Washington *Bulletin*, vol. 1, no. 4, June–July 1947, pp. 1, 3, 6–7, in Office File of Joseph C. McCaskill.

69 Address by Dillon S. Myer, Commissioner of Indian Affairs, at the Eighth Annual Convention of the National Congress of American Indians, St Paul, Minnesota, 25 July 1951, in Speeches File, Desk Files of Commissioner Dillon S. Myer; appeal for more financial support from the tribes at the twelfth convention of the NCAI reported in *The Christian Century*, 21 September 1955; William H. Kelly, 'The economic basis of Indian life', in George Eaton Simpson and J. Milton Yinger, 'American Indians and American Indian Life', Philadelphia, Pa, *Annals*, Vol. 311, May 1957, pp. 78–9; and in ibid., article by the NCAI's Helen L. Peterson, 'American Indian political participation', pp. 125–6, 123–4. In the Newberry Library, Chicago, microfilm collection: NCAI circular, *To the People Who Have Settled These United States* (no details); Report of the Field Foundation, Inc., National Congress of American Indians Workshop Project, *A New Frontier in American Indian History* (11–23 June 1951, Brigham City, Utah), pp. 1, 4, 9–10, 15–27; *Proposals for Elements to be Included in a 'Point Four Program for American Indians'* (1951 and 1954); *Circular of the Executive Council of the NCAI for Immediate Release, December 14, 1955*, p. 2; *What Indians Want*, article in *The Christian Century*, Spokane, Wash., 21 September 1955; NCAI Thirteenth Annual Convention, 24–28 September 1956, Salt Lake City, Utah; Constitution and By-Laws of NCAI as amended 2 September 1955 and 1 November 1957; NCAI Minutes of the Annual Meeting Executive Council, 1 November 1957, Claremore, Okla, pp. 1–5; *Declaration of Trust Establishing the N.C.A.I. Fund*, 1 November 1957; NCAI Financial Statements, 31 December 1958; *Official American Indian Leaders Wind Up Week-Long Session; Denounce White House Picketing by Unrepresentative Tribe*, 23 March 1959. By 1956 the individual NCAI membership fee was $3, tribal membership, according to the size of the tribe, ranged from $25 plus 5 cents per member to $250 plus half a cent per member; individual associate members were charged $10 and organizations $25. And on the Indian press compare, say, the *Navajo Times TODAY* for 7, 8 and 9 August 1985, even with the long-running Navajo–Hopi dispute an issue again, with *Akwesasne Notes* for Midwinter 1985, vol. 17, no. 1, and for Summer 1985, vol. 17, no. 3.

70 Rachel A. Bonney, 'The role of AIM leaders in Indian nationalism', *American Indian Quarterly*, vol. 3, 1977, pp. 209–24; Vine Deloria, *Behind the Trail of Broken Treaties. An Indian Declaration of Independence* (New York, Delacorte, 1974), *passim*; Prucha, *The Great Father*, Vol. II, pp. 1115 ff.; Robert Burnette and John Koster, *The Road to Wounded Knee* (New York, Bantam, 1974), pp. 196–7, 216, 280–1, and *passim*; NCAI Bulletin, August 1975, pp. 1, 6; *National Indian Youth Council Policy Statement to the American Indian People*, Adopted Annual Meeting, Stewart, Nevada (NIYC Inc., 11 August 1973); Laxon, pp. 170, 178–9, 189; Berkhofer, 'Native Americans',

pp. 134–6; David Murray, *Modern Indians* (BAAS pamphlet 8, 1982), pp. 30–4; Alvin M. Josephy, Jr, *Red Power: The American Indians' Fight for Freedom* (New York, American Heritage Press, 1971), *passim*; Stan Steiner, *The New Indians* (New York, Harper & Row, 1968), *passim*; National Indian Youth Council, Annual Report, 1977; 'Native American Appropriate Technology Action Council', NIYC (n.d. but probably 1978); 'Congressional legislation', NIYC April 1978; Board Report of the NIYC, August 1975; tape 450, side 2, television program, 'The Indian speaks', January 1970, with speakers from the NIYC, in DD for New Mexico.

71 Nancy Lurie in Stuart Levine and Nancy Oestreich Lurie (eds), *The American Indian Today* (Deland, Fla, Everett/Edwards, 1968), pp. 83, 190–3; Laxon, pp. 152–3, 180.

72 Tape 501, February 1970, radio talk involving NIYC staff, pp. 30–1, DD for New Mexico.

73 Burnette and Koster, pp. 174–7, 282, and *passim*; Svensson, pp. 39–45; Laxon, pp. 50–100, 172–4, 184–5, 189, 199 ff.; James Wilson, *The Original Americans: U.S. Indians* (London, Minority Rights Group, report no. 31, 1976), pp. 6–9, 23–4; NTCA membership claim in *NTCA letter, To the President of the United States the Honorable Gerald Ford, the White House*; Raisch, 'The state of the Indian nation', p. 85, on AIM community projects; NCAI pamphlet entitled *The Indians of the United States Seek Together to Attain in their Own Plans and Action the Full Promise of Citizenship* (no details); 'Land at stake: backlash in Congress seen as Indians push claims', *Congressional Quarterly*, 2 December 1978, pp. 3385–8; NCAI *Bulletins*, July 1975, January–February 1977, March 1977, April 1977, March 1978; NIYC Policy Statement, op. cit., p. 3; Mathiessen, *Indian Country*, *passim*, but especially pp. 87 ff. and 321 ff.; Strickland, *The Indians in Oklahoma*, pp. 79–80; *Menominee Restoration Act*, Hearings, etc., op. cit., pp. 36 ff.; Dorothy L. Miller, 'Native American women. Leadership images', *Integrated Education*, vol. 16, January–February 1978, pp. 37–9; and McFee, *Modern Blackfeet*, p. 104. For a statement of the problems of a tribal chairman, see interview (tape 78.57.351) in transcripts of the Hualapai Oral History Project.

74 See Vine Deloria in *Los Angeles Times*, 17 August 1975, part IV, p. 5; Wilson, p. 25; Prucha, *The Great Father*, Vol. II, pp. 1162–70; Anthony D. Brown (intro.), *New Directions in Federal Indian Policy: A Review of the American Indian Policy Review Commission* (Los Angeles, Calif., American Indian Studies Center, UCLA, 1979), *passim*.

75 Tape 450, op. cit., for the NIYC's view of the BIA, and tape 501, op. cit., p. 28; the AIM demand for an independent BIA was one of the demands that came out of the 20-point ultimatum delivered during the 'Trail of Broken Treaties'; and on the federal shift away from direct administration, see George P. Castile, 'Federal Indian policy and the sustained enclave. An anthropological perspective', *Human Organization*, vol. 3, no. 3, Fall 1974, pp. 219–28. See also on attitudes to the BIA, McFee, *Modern Blackfeet*, pp. 125 ff., and Grobsmith, *Lakota of the Rosebud*, pp. 29 ff.

76 NCAI *Bulletin*, July 1975, pp. 17–20; NIYC Policy Statement, op. cit., p. 3.

77 The conflict could be seen particularly clearly at Pine Ridge, during the Wounded Knee troubles.

78 Compare, for example, NCAI Bulletins and Policy Statements with NIYC fliers, Reports and Policy Statement, op. cit., and with *A Program of Action*

for Executive, Legislative, and Judicial Branches of United States Government. Presented by the Board of Directors of National Tribal Chairmen's Association: Wendell Chino, President. March 1975.

79 In 1978, as a result of the Indian Religious Freedom Act, the United States undertook to protect the Indians' right to practise their traditional religions. For a good survey of the problems faced by social movements, see J. Craig Jenkins, *The Politics of Insurgency. The Farm Worker Movement in the 1960s* (New York, Columbia University Press, 1985), chs 1, 8 and 9.

Bibliography

Books, Articles, and Theses

Abbot, Martin, *The Freedmen's Bureau in South Carolina, 1865–1872* (Chapel Hill, NC, University of North Carolina Press, 1967).

Abel, Annie H., 'The history of events resulting in Indian consolidation west of the Mississippi', *American Historical Association, Annual Report for the Year 1906*, vol. 1, 1908.

Abel, Annie H., 'Proposals for an Indian state, 1778–1878', *American Historical Association, Annual Report for the Year 1907*, vol. 1, 1908.

Ablon, Joan, 'Relocated Indians in the San Francisco Bay area. Social interaction and Indian identity', *Human Organization*, vol. 23, no. 4, Winter 1964.

Ablon, Joan, 'American Indian relocation. Problems of dependency and management in the city', *Phylon*, vol. 26, Winter 1965.

Adams, Evelyn C., *American Indian Education. Government Schools and Economic Progress* (New York, Amo Press, 1971 edn).

Adams, Henry, *History of the United States of America during the Administrations of Jefferson and Madison* (abridged and edited by Ernest Samuels; Chicago, University of Chicago Press, 1967, from 1921 edn).

Alderson, Nannie and Smith, Helena Huntington, *A Bride Goes West* (Lincoln, Nebr., University of Nebraska Press, 1975).

Alford, Thomas A., *Civilisation* (Norman, Okla, University of Oklahoma Press, 1936).

Allen, Virginia, 'The white man's road. The physical and psychological impact of relocation on the Southern Plains Indians', *Journal of the History of Medicine*, vol. 30, April 1975.

Allen, Virginia, 'Agency physicians to the Southern Plains Indians, 1868–1900', *Bulletin of the History of Medicine*, vol. 49, Fall 1975.

Altschuler, Glenn, C., *Race, Ethnicity, and Class in American Thought, 1865–1919* (Arlington Heights, Ill., Harlan Davidson, 1982).

Anderson, Gary Clayton, *Kinsmen of Another Kind. Dakota–White Relations in the Upper Mississippi Valley, 1650–1852* (Lincoln, Nebr., University of Nebraska Press, 1984).

Armstrong, Samuel Chapman, *The Indian Question* (Hampton, Va, Normal School Press, 1883).

Axtell, James, 'The scholastic philosophy of the wilderness', in *The School upon a Hill. Education and Society in Colonial New England* (New Haven, Conn, and London, Yale University Press, 1974).

397

Axtell, James, *The European and the Indian. Essays in the Ethnohistory of Colonial North America* (New York, Oxford University Press, 1981).

Bacq, Leonard and Miramontes, Ofelia, 'Bilingual special education teacher training for American Indians', *Journal of American Indian Education*, vol. 24, no. 2, May 1985.

Bahr, Howard M., Chadwick, Bruce A. and Strauss, Joseph, 'Discrimination against urban Indians in Seattle', *The Indian Historian*, vol. 5, 1972.

Bahr, Howard M. and Chadwick, Bruce A., 'Conservatism, racial intolerance, and attitudes toward racial assimilation among whites and American Indians', *The Journal of Social Psychology*, vol. 94, October 1974.

Bailey, L. R., *Indian Slave Trade in the Southwest* (Los Angeles, Calif., Westernlore Press, 1973 edn).

Bailey, M. Thomas, *Reconstruction in Indian Territory. A Story of Avarice, Discrimination and Opportunism* (Port Washington, NY, Kennikat Press, 1972).

Bailyn, Bernard, *Education in the Formation of American Society. Needs and Opportunities for Study* (New York, Vintage Books, 1960).

Baird, W. David, *Peter Pitchlynn. Chief of the Choctaws* (Norman, Okla, University of Oklahoma Press, 1972).

Baird, W. David, 'William A. Jones, 1897–1904', in Kvasnicka and Viola (eds), *The Commissioners of Indian Affairs*.

Bancroft, George, *History of the United States from the Discovery of the American Continent*, Vol. III (Boston, Mass., Little, Brown, 1856).

Bandelier, A. F., *Final Report of Investigations among the Indians of the Southwestern United States, Carried on Mainly in the Years from 1880 to 1885* (Papers of the Archaeological Institute of America, American Series, III, Cambridge, Mass., 1890).

Barbrook, Alec and Bolt, Christine, *Power and Progress in American Life* (Oxford, Martin Robertson, and New York. St. Martin's Press, 1980).

Barclay, W. C., *History of Methodist Missions: Missionary Motivation and Expansion*, Vol. 1 (New York, Board of Missions and Church Extension of the Methodist Church, 1949).

Barsh, Rusel Lawrence and Henderson, James Youngblood, *The Road. Indian Tribes and Political Liberty* (Berkeley, Calif., University of California Press, 1980).

Bastide, Roger, *African Civilizations in the New World* (New York, Harper & Row, 1971).

Beaver, R. Pierce, *Church, State and the American Indians* (St Louis, Mo., Concordia, 1966).

Beloff, Max, *Thomas Jefferson and American Democracy* (Harmondsworth, Penguin, 1972).

Belue, Tessie, 'The black and the red: a result of divide and conquer?', *Wassaja*, vol. 5, no. 8, November–December 1977.

Berens, John F., 'Old campaigners, new realities. Indian policy reform in the Progressive era, 1908–1912', *Mid-America*, January 1977.

Berkhofer, Robert F. Jr, *Salvation and the Savage* (Louisville, Ky, University of Kentucky Press, 1965).

Berkhofer, Robert F. Jr, 'The political context of a new Indian history', *Pacific Historical Review*, vol. 40, August 1971.

Berkhofer, Robert F. Jr, *The White Man's Indian. Images of the American Indian from Columbus to the Present* (New York, Knopf, 1978).

Berkhofer, Robert F. Jr, 'Native Americans', in Higham (ed.), *Ethnic Leadership in America*.

Bery, Brewton, *Almost White* (New York, Macmillan, 1963).

Berthrong, Donald J., *The Southern Cheyennes* (Norman, Okla, University of Oklahoma Press, 1963).

Berthrong, Donald J., *The Cheyenne and Arapaho Ordeal. Reservation and Agency Life in the Indian Territory, 1875–1907* (Norman, Okla, University of Oklahoma Press, 1976).

Betzinez, J., *I Fought with Geronimo* (Harrisburg, Pa, Stackpole, 1959).

Bieder, Robert Eugene, 'The American Indian and the development of anthropological thought: the United States, 1780–1851' (PhD dissertation, University of Minnesota, 1972).

Binder, Fredrick, M., *The Color Problem in Early National America as Viewed by John Adams, Jefferson and Jackson* (The Hague, Moulton, 1968).

Binder, Frederick M., *The Age of the Common School, 1830–1865* (New York, Wiley, 1974).

Bloom, L., 'Role of the Indian in the race relations complex of the South', *Social Forces*, vol. 19, December 1940.

Boas, Franz, *Anthropology and Modern Life* (New York, Norton, 1962 edn).

Bodine, John J., 'Blue Lake: a struggle for Indian rights', *American Indian Law Review*, vol. 1, Winter 1973.

Bolt, Christine, *Victorian Attitudes to Race* (London, Routledge & Kegan Paul, 1971).

Bolt, Christine, 'Red, black and white in nineteenth-century America', in A. C. Hepburn (ed.), *Minorities in History* (London, Edward Arnold, 1978).

Bolt, Christine, 'The anti-slavery origins of concern for the American Indians', in Bolt and Drescher (eds), *Anti-Slavery, Religion and Reform*.

Bolt, Christine, 'Race and the Victorians', in Eldridge (ed.), *British Imperialism in the Nineteenth Century*.

Bolt, Christine and Drescher, Seymour (eds), *Anti-Slavery, Religion and Reform* (Folkestone, Dawson, and Hamden, Conn., Archon, 1980).

Bond, Horace Mann, *Negro Education in Alabama. A Study in Cotton and Steel* (New York, Atheneum, 1969 edn).

Bonney, Rachel A., 'The role of AIM leaders in Indian nationalism', *American Indian Quarterly*, vol. 3, 1977.

Borden, Philip, 'Found cumbering the soil. Manifest destiny and the Indian in the nineteenth century', in Nash and Weiss (eds), *The Great Fear*.

Bowden, Henry Warner, *American Indians and Christian Missions. Studies in Cultural Conflict* (Chicago, University of Chicago Press, 1981).

Bracey, John Jr, Meier, August and Rudwick, Elliott, *Blacks in the Abolitionist Movement* (Belmont, Calif., Wadsworth, 1917).

Brinton, Daniel Garrison, *Races and Peoples. Lectures on the Science of Ethnography* (New York, 1890).

Brinton, Daniel Garrison, *The American Race: A Linguistic Classification and Ethnographic Description of the Native Tribes of North and South America* (New York, 1891).

Brock, William R. (ed.), *The Civil War* (New York, Harper & Row, 1969).

Brock, William R., *Investigation and Responsibility. Public Responsibility in the United States, 1865–1900* (Cambridge, Cambridge University Press, 1984).

Brophy, William A. and Aberle, Sophie D. (compilers), *The Indian, America's Unfinished Business. Report of the Commission on the Rights, Liberties, and Responsibilities of the American Indian* (Norman, Okla, University of Oklahoma Press, 1968 edn).

Brown, Anthony D. (intro.), *New Directions in Federal Indian Policy. A Review of the American Indian Policy Review Commission* (Los Angeles, Calif., American Indian Studies Center, UCLA, 1979).

Brown, Judith, K., 'Economic organisation and the position of women among the Iroquois', *Ethnohistory*, vol. 17, 1970.

Brown, Judith K., 'A note on the division of labor by sex', *American Anthropologist*, vol. 72, 1970.

Brown, Judith K., 'Iroquois women: an ethnohistoric note', in Reiter (ed.), *Toward an Anthropology of Women*.

Burgess, L. E., 'The Lake Mohonk conferences on the Indian, 1883–1916' (PhD dissertation, Claremont Graduate School, 1972).

Burke, Joe, 'The Cherokee cases. A study in law, politics, and morality', *Stanford Law Review*, vol. 21, February 1969.

Burnette, Robert and Koster, John, *The Road to Wounded Knee* (New York, Bantam, 1974).

Burt, Lary W., *Tribalism in Crisis. Federal Indian Policy, 1953–61* (Albuquerque, N. Mex., University of New Mexico Press, 1982).

Butterfield, Nancy, 'Native American Women', *OKC Camp Crier*, vol. 3, no. 16, January 1978.

Cadwalader, Sandra L. and Deloria, Vine Jr (eds), *The Aggressions of Civilization. Federal Indian Policy since the 1880s* (Philadelphia, Pa, Temple University Press, 1984).

Carlson, Leonard A., *Indians, Bureaucrats and Land. The Dawes Act and the Decline of Indian Farming* (Westport, Conn., Greenwood Press, 1981).

Castile, George P., 'Federal Indian policy and the sustained enclave. An anthropological perspective', *Human Organization*, vol. 3, no. 3, Fall 1974.

Catlin, George, *Letters and Notes on the Manners, Customs and Conditions of the North American Indians, etc.*, Vol. I, (London, 1841).

Catterall, Helen T., *Judicial Cases Concerning American Slavery and the Negro*, Vol. I (New York, Negro Universities Press, 1968).

Chadwick, Bruce A. and Strauss, Joseph H., 'The assimilation of American Indians into urban society. The Seattle case', *Human Organization*, vol. 34, no. 4, Winter 1975.

Chadwick, Bruce A. and White, Lynn C., 'Correlates of length of urban residence among the Spokane Indians', *Human Organization*, vol. 32, Spring 1973.

Chambers, Clark, *Seedtime of Reform. American Social Service and Social Action, 1918–1933* (Minneapolis, Minn., University of Minnesota Press, 1963).

Chandler, Joan Mary, 'Anthropologists and U.S. Indians, 1928–1960' (PhD dissertation, University of Texas at Austin, 1972).

Channing, Edward, *A History of the United States*, Vol. 1 (New York, 1906).

Chaput, Donald C., 'Generals, Indian agents, politicians: the Doolittle survey of 1865', *Western Historical Quarterly*, vol. 3, July 1972.

Child, Lydia Maria, *The First Settlers of New-England* (Boston, Mass., Munroe & Francis, 1829).

Child, Lydia Maria, *Letters from New York* (London, 1843).

Child, Lydia Maria, *Letters of Lydia Maria Child* (Boston, Mass., 1883).

Clark, John G. (ed.), *The Frontier Challenge. Responses to the Trans-Mississippi West* (Lawrence, Kans, University of Kansas Press, 1971).

Clark, J. Stanley, 'Ponca publicity', *Mississippi Valley Historical Review*, vol. 29, March 1943.

Clarke, Edward H., *Sex in Education. Or, a Fair Chance for the Girls* (Boston, Mass., Osgood, 1873).

Clinton, Lawrence, Chadwick, Bruce A. and Bahr, Howard M., 'Urban relocation reconsidered. Antecedents of employment among Indian males', *Rural Sociology*, vol. 40, no. 2, Summer 1975.

Cohen, David K., 'Education and Race', *History of Education Quarterly*, vol. IX, no. 3, Fall 1969.

Coleman, Michael C., 'Not race, but grace: Presbyterian missionaries and American Indians, 1837–1893', *Journal of American History*, vol. 67, no. 1, June 1980.

Collier, John, 'Are we making red slaves?', *Survey Graphic*, 1 January 1927.

Collier, John, *From Every Zenith* (Denver, Colo, Sage Books, 1963).

Collier, P., 'The red man's burden', in Frazier (ed.), *The Underside of American History*.

Colson, Elizabeth, *The Makah Indians* (Manchester, Manchester University Press, 1953).

Colton, Calvin (ed.), *The Works of Henry Clay*, Vol. 7 (New York, Putnam, 1904).

Cook, S. F., *The Indian Versus the Spanish Mission*, Vol. III (Berkeley, Calif., University of California Press, 1943).

Cott, Nancy F., 'Notes towards an interpretation of antebellum childrearing', *The Psychohistory Review*, vol. 6, no. 4, 1978.

Cotterill, R. S., 'Federal Indian Management in the South, 1789–1825', *Mississippi Valley Historical Review*, vol. 20, 1933–4.

Cotterill, R. S., *The Southern Indians. The Story of the Civilized Tribes before Removal* (Norman, Okla, University of Oklahoma Press, 1971 edn).

Covington, James W., 'Relations between the eastern Timucuan Indians and the French and Spanish, 1564–1567', in Hudson (ed.), *Four Centuries*.

Craven, Wesley Frank, 'Indian policy in early Virginia', *William and Mary Quarterly*, vol. I, 1944.

Craven, Wesley Frank, *White, Red and Black: The Seventeenth-Century Virginian* (Charlottesville, Va, University Press of Virginia, 1971).

Cremin, Lawrence A., *The Transformation of the School. Progressivism in American Education, 1876–1957* (New York, Knopf, 1962).

Cremin, Lawrence A., *American Education. The Colonial Experience, 1607–1783* (New York, Harper Torchbooks, 1970).

Crockett, Norman L., *The Black Towns* (Lawrence, Kans, Regents Press of Kansas, 1979).

Crosby, Alfred W., 'Virgin soil epidemics as a factor in the Aboriginal depopulation of America', *William and Mary Quarterly*, vol. 33, 1976.

Crowe, C., 'Indians and blacks in white America', in Hudson (ed.), *Four Centuries*.

Crowe, Keith J., *A History of the Original Peoples of Northern Canada* (Montreal and London, Arctic Institute of North America and McGill-Queen's University Press, 1974).

Dahlberg, Frances, *Woman the Gatherer* (New Haven, Conn., and London, Yale University Press, 1981).

Dale, Edward Everett, *The Indian of the Southwest. A Century of Development under the United States* (Norman, Okla, University of Oklahoma Press, 1971 edn).

Daniels, Roger, *Concentration Camps U.S.A. Japanese Americans and World War II* (New York, Holt, Rinehart & Winston, 1971).

Danziger, Edmund Jefferson Jr, *Indians and Bureaucrats. Administering the Reservation Policy during the Civil War* (Urbana, Ill., University of Illinois Press, 1974).

Davis, A. M., 'The employment of Indian auxiliaries in the American War', *English Historical Review*, vol. 2, 1887.

Davis, J. B., 'Slavery in the Cherokee nation', *Chronicles of Oklahoma*, vol. XI, no. 4, December 1931.

De Rosier, Arthur H. Jr, *The Removal of the Choctaw Indians* (Knoxville, Tenn., University of Tennessee Press, 1970).

De Rosier, Arthur H. Jr, 'Myths and realities in Indian westward removal. The Choctaw example', in Hudson (ed.), *Four Centuries*.

Debo, Angie, *And Still the Waters Run* (Princeton, NJ, Princeton University Press, 1970; reprint of 1940 edn).

Debo, Angie, *The Rise and Fall of the Choctaw Republic* (Norman, Okla, University of Oklahoma Press, 1972 edn).

Debo, Angie, *The Road to Disappearance* (Norman, Okla, University of Oklahoma Press, 1979 edn).

Degler, Carl N., 'Slavery and the genesis of American race prejudice', *Comparative Studies in History and Society*, vol. XI, October 1959.

Degler, Carl N., 'Remaking American history', *Journal of American History*, vol. 67, no. 1, June 1980.

Deloria, Vine, *Custer Died for your Sins* (New York, Collier-Macmillan, 1969).

Deloria, Vine, *Behind the Trail of Broken Treaties. An Indian Declaration of Independence* (New York, Delacorte, 1974).

Dennis, Elsie F., 'Indian slavery in the Pacific Northwest', *Oregon Historical Quarterly*, vol. 31, March 1930, June 1930, September 1930.

DePauw, Linda Grant *et al.*, *Remember the Ladies. Women in America, 1750–1815* (New York, Viking, 1976).

Dobyns, Henry F., 'Estimating Aboriginal American population. An appraisal of techniques with a new hemispheric estimate', *Current Anthropology*, vol. 7, October 1966.

Dodge, Richard Irving, *The Hunting Grounds of the Great West, etc* (London, 1877).

Doran, Michael F., 'Population statistics of nineteenth-century Indian territory', *Chronicles of Oklahoma*, vol. 53, Winter 1975–6.

Dorman, James H., 'Ethnicity in contemporary America', *Journal of American Studies*, vol. 15, no. 3, December 1981.

Douglas, Ann, *The Feminization of American Culture* (New York, Avon Books (Discus), 1977).

Downes, Randolph C., 'A crusade for Indian reform, 1922–34', *Mississippi Valley Historical Review*, vol. 32, December 1945.

Downs, James F., *The Navajo* (New York, Holt, Rinehart & Winston, 1972).

Dozier, Edward P., 'Problem drinking among American Indians. The role of sociocultural deprivation', *Quarterly Journal of Studies on Alcohol*, vol. XXVII, 1966.

Drake, Thomas E., 'William Penn's experiment in race relations', *The Pennsylvania Magazine of History and Biography*, vol. LXVIII, no. 4, October 1944.

Drinnon, Richard, *Facing West. The Metaphysics of Indian-Hating and Empire-Building* (Minneapolis, Minn., University of Minnesota Press, 1980).

Driver, Harold, *Indians of North America* (Chicago, University of Chicago Press, 1961 and 1969).

Drucker, Philip, *The Native Brotherhoods* (Washington, DC, Bureau of American Ethnology, Bulletin 168, 1958).

Drucker, Philip, *Cultures of the North Pacific Coast* (San Francisco, Calif., Chandler, 1965).

Drury, Clifford, *Marcus and Narcissa Whitman, and the Opening of Old Oregon* (Glendale, Calif., Arthur H. Clark, 1972).

DuBois, W. E. B., *The Education of Black People. Ten Critiques, 1906–1960* (ed. Herbert Aptheker; Amherst, Mass., University of Massachusetts Press, 1973).

Dudley, Edward and Novak, Maximillian E. (eds.), *The Wild Man Within. An Image in Western Thought from the Renaissance to Romanticism* (Pittsburgh, Pa, University of Pittsburgh Press, 1972).

Dunn, J. P., *Massacres of the Mountains* (London, 1886).

Dunn, Richard S. and Dunn, Mary Maples (eds), *The Papers of William Penn*, Vol. Two, *1680–1684* (Pennsylvania, Pa, University of Pennsylvania Press, 1982).

Eastman, Charles A., *The Indian To-day* (Garden City, NY, Page, 1915).

Eastman, Charles A., *From the Deep Woods to Civilization. Chapters in the Autobiography of an Indian* (Lincoln, Nebr., University of Nebraska Press, 1977 edn).

Eastman, Elaine Goodale, *Pratt. The Red Man's Moses* (Norman, Okla, University of Oklahoma Press, 1935).

Eastman, Elaine Goodale, *Sister to the Sioux* (Lincoln, Nebr., University of Nebraska Press, 1978).

Eccles, W. J., *France in America* (New York, Harper & Row, 1972; 1973 edn).

Edmunds, R. David (ed.), *American Indian Leaders. Studies in Diversity* (Lincoln, Nebr., University of Nebraska Press, 1980).

Edmunds, R. David, 'Old Briton', in Edmunds (ed.), *American Indian Leaders*.

Eggan, F., *The American Indian. Perspectives for the Study of Social Change* (London, Weidenfeld & Nicolson, 1966).

Eldridge, C. C. (ed.), *British Imperialism in the Nineteenth Century* (London, Macmillan, 1984).

Elsbree, Oliver Wendell, *The Rise of the Missionary Spirit in America* (Williamsport, Pa, Williamsport Printing and Binding Company, 1928).

Epstein, Barbara Leslie, *The Politics of Domesticity. Women, Evangelism and Temperance in Nineteenth-Century America* (Middletown, Conn., Wesleyan University Press, 1981).

Essig, James D., *The Bonds of Wickedness. American Evangelicals against Slavery, 1770–1808* (Philadelphia, Pa, Temple University Press, 1982).

Etienne, M. and Leacock, E. (eds), *Women and Colonization. Anthropological Perspectives* (New York, Praeger, 1980).

Evans, W. McKee, *To Die Game: The Story of the Lowry Band, Indian Guerrillas of Reconstruction* (Baton Rouge, La, Louisiana State University Press, 1971).

Ewers, John C., 'Deadlier than the male', *American Heritage*, vol. 16, no. 4, June 1965.

Ewers, John C., 'Mother of the mixed bloods. The marginal woman in the history of the Upper Missouri', in Toole, K. R., Carroll, J. A., Utley, R. M. and Mortensen, A. R. (eds), *Probing the American West. Papers from the Santa Fe Conference* (Santa Fe, N. Mex., Museum of New Mexico Press, 1962).

Fahey, John, *The Flathead Indians* (Norman, Okla, University of Oklahoma Press, 1974).

Fairbanks, Charles Herron, *The Florida Seminole People* (Phoenix, Ariz., Indian Tribal Series, 1973).

Farb, Peter, *Man's Rise to Civilization. As Shown by the Indians of North America from Primeval Times to the Coming of the Industrial State* (New York, Dutton, 1968).

Federal Writers' Project, Slave Narratives (St Clair Shores, Mich., Somerset Publishers, 1976).

Fee, Elizabeth, 'The sexual politics of Victorian social anthropology', in Hartman and Banner (eds), *Clio's Consciousness Raised*.

Fey, Harold E. and McNickle, D'Arcy, *Indians and Other Americans. Two Ways of Life Meet* (New York, Harper & Brothers, 1959).

Filler, Louis, *The Crusade Against Slavery, 1830–1860* (New York, Harper Torchbooks, 1963).

Fischer, Leroy H. (ed.), *The Civil War in Indian Territory* (Los Angeles, Calif., Lorrin L. Morrison, 1974).

Fiske, John, *The Discovery of America. With Some Account of Ancient America and the Spanish Conquest*, Vol. 1 (Boston, Mass., and New York, Houghton Mifflin, 1852, 2 vols).

Fletcher, Alice C., 'Allotment of lands to Indians', *Proceedings of the National Conference of Charities and Correction, 1887* (Boston, Mass., 1887).

Fleur-Lobban, Caroline, 'A Marxist reappraisal of the matriarchate', *Current Anthropology*, vol. 20, 1979.

Flexner, Eleanor, *Century of Struggle. The Woman's Rights Movement in the United States* (Cambridge, Mass., Belknap Press of Harvard University Press, 1973).

Fogel, Walter, 'The effect of low educational attainment on incomes: a comparative study of selected ethnic groups', *The Journal of Human Resources*, vol. 1, Fall 1966.

Foner, Eric, *Tom Paine and Revolutionary America* (London, Oxford University Press, 1976).

Foner, Eric, *Nothing But Freedom. Emancipation and its Legacy* (Baton Rouge, La, and London, Louisiana State University Press, 1983).

Foner, Eric, 'Abolitionism and the labor movement in antebellum America', in Bolt and Drescher (eds), *Anti-Slavery, Religion and Reform*.

Forbes, G., 'The part played by the enslavement of the Indians in the removal of the tribes to Oklahoma', *Chronicles of Oklahoma*, vol. XVI, no. 2, June 1938.

Forbes, Jack D. (ed.), *The Indian in America's Past* (New York, Prentice-Hall, 1964).

Foreman, Carolyn Thomas, *Indians Abroad, 1493–1938* (Norman, Okla, University of Oklahoma Press, 1943).

Foreman, Grant, *The Five Civilized Tribes* (Norman, Okla, University of Oklahoma Press, 1972 edn).

Foster, George M., *Traditional Societies and Technological Change* (New York, Harper & Row, 1973).

Fowler, Don D. and Fowler, Catherine S., 'John Wesley Powell, anthropologist', *Utah Historical Quarterly*, vol. 37, Spring 1969.

Fox, E. L., *The American Colonization Society, 1817–1840* (Baltimore, Md, Johns Hopkins University Press, 1919).

Fox, George, *A Collection of Many Select and Christian Epistles, Letters and Testimonies* (London, 1698).

Fox, George, *Gospel Family-Order, Being a Short Discourse Concerning the Ordering of Families, Both of Whites, Blacks and Indians* (1776, no details).

Fox, Robin, *Kinship and Marriage* (Harmondsworth, Penguin, 1977 edn).

Franklin, W. Neil, 'Pennsylvania–Virginia rivalry for the Indian trade of the Ohio Valley', *Mississippi Valley Historical Review*, vol. 20, March 1934.

Frazier, T. R. (ed.), *The Underside of American History. Other Readings*, Vol. 2 (New York, Harcourt, Brace, Jovanovich, 1971).

Fredrickson, George M., *The Inner Civil War. Northern Intellectuals and the Crisis of the Union* (New York, Harper & Row, 1965).

Fredrickson, George M., *The Black Image in the White Mind. The Debate on Afro-American Character and Destiny, 1817–1914* (New York, Harper & Row, 1971).

Fried, Morton H., *The Notion of Tribe* (Menlo Park, Calif., Cummings, 1975).

Fritz, Henry E., *The Movement for Indian Assimilation, 1860–90* (Philadelphia, Pa, University of Pennsylvania Press, 1963)

Fritz, Henry E., 'The Board of Indian Commissioners and ethnocentric reform, 1878–1893', in Smith and Kvasnicka, *Indian–White Relations*.

Gajar, Anna, 'American Indian personal preparation in special education: needs, program components, programs', *Journal of American Indian Education*, vol. 24, no. 2, May 1985.

Garbarino, Merwyn S., 'Life in the city. Chicago', in Waddell and Watson (eds), *The American Indian in Urban Society*.

Garrison, Wendell Phillips and Francis Jackson, *William Lloyd Garrison, 1805–79*, Vol. 1 (New York, Century, 1885–9).

Garth, T. R., *Race Psychology. A Study of Racial Mental Differences* (New York, McGraw-Hill, 1931).

Gates, Paul W., 'Indian allotments preceding the Dawes Act', in J. G. Clark (ed.), *The Frontier Challenge*.

Gearing, F., Netting, R. and Peattie, L. (eds), *Documentary History of the Fox Project, 1948–1959. A Program in Action Anthropology* (Chicago, University of Chicago Press, 1960).

Genovese, Eugene, *Roll, Jordan, Roll. The World that the Slaves Made* (New York, Pantheon, 1974).

George, Henry, *Progress and Poverty* (London, Kegan, Paul, Trench, 1883).

Gibson, Arrell M., *The Chickasaws* (Norman, Okla, University of Oklahoma Press, 1971).

Gibson, Arrell M., *The American Indian. Prehistory to the Present* (Lexington, Mass., D. C. Heath, 1980).

Gidley, M., *With One Sky Above Us. Life on an Indian Reservation at the Turn of the Century. Photographs by E. H. Latham* (New York, Putnam, and Exeter, Windward/Webb & Bower, 1979).

Gilcreast, Everett Arthur, 'Richard Henry Pratt and American Indian Policy, 1877–1906. A study of the assimilation movement' (PhD dissertation, Yale University, 1967; Ann Arbor, Mich., University Microfilms, 1976).

Gilman, Harry J., 'Economic discrimination and unemployment', *American Economic Review*, vol. 55, December 1965.

Glasrud, Bruce A. and Smith, Alan M. (eds), *Promises to Keep* (Chicago, Rand McNally, 1972).

Godwyn, Morgan, *The Negro's and Indian's Advocate, Suing for the Admission into the Church* (London, 1680).

Goetzmann, William, *Exploration and Empire. The Explorer and the Scientist in the Winning of the American West* (New York, Knopf, 1966).

Gossett, Thomas F., *Race. The History of an Idea in America* (New York, Schocken Books, 1970).

Graham, Otis Jr, *Encore for Reform, the Old Progressives and the New Deal* (New York, Oxford University Press, 1967).

Grant, U. S., *Personal Memoirs of U. S. Grant. In Two Volumes* (London, 1885–6).

Graves, Theodore D., 'The personal adjustment of Navajo Indian migrants to Denver, Colorado', *American Anthropologist*, vol. 72, February 1970.

Graves, Theodore D., 'Drinking and drunkenness among urban Indians', in Waddell and Watson (eds), *The American Indian in Urban Society*.

Graves, Theodore D. and Lave, Charles A., 'Determinants of urban migrant Indian wages', *Human Organization*, vol. 31, Spring 1972.

Graymont, Barbara, *The Iroquois in the American Revolution* (Syracuse, NY, Syracuse University Press, 1972).

Green, Donald E., *The Creek People* (Phoenix, Ariz., Indian Tribal Series, 1973).

Green, Michael D., 'Alexander McGillivray', in Edmunds (ed.), *American Indian Leaders*.

Greene, Lorenzo Johnston, *The Negro in Colonial New England, 1620–1776* (Port Washington, NY, Kennikat Press, 1969).

Greer, Colin, *The Great School Legend. A Revisionist Interpretation of American Public Education* (New York, Viking, 1972).

Gregory, Jack and Strickland, Bernard, 'Indian studies must be more than an academic Wild West show', in Mahon (ed.), *Indians of the Lower South Past and Present*.

Grenfell Price, A., *White Settlers and Native Peoples. An Historical Study of Racial Contacts between English-speaking Whites and Aboriginal Peoples in the United States, Canada, Australia and New Zealand* (Melbourne, Georgian House, and Cambridge, Cambridge University Press, 1950).

Greven, Philip J., *The Protestant Temperament. Patterns of Child-Rearing. Religious Experience of the Self in Early America.* (New York, New American Library, 1979).

Grinnell, George Bird, *The Cheyenne Indians*, Vol. 1 (New York, Yale University Press, 1923, 2 vols).

Grobsmith, Elizabeth, *Lakota of the Rosebud. A Contemporary Ethnography* (New York, Holt, Rinehart & Winston, 1981).

Grumet, R. S., 'Sunksquaws, shamans and tradeswomen: Middle Atlantic coastal Algonquin women during the 17th and 18th centuries', in Etienne and Leacock (eds), *Women and Colonization*.

Guillemin, Jeanne, *Urban Renegades. The Cultural Strategy of American Indians* (New York, Columbia University Press, 1975).

Gumbert, Edgar B. and Spring, Joel H., *The Superschool and the Superstate. American Education in the Twentieth Century, 1918–1970* (New York, Wiley, 1974).

Gundlach, James H., Reid, P. Nelson and Roberts, Alden E., 'Migration, labor mobility and relocation assistance. The case of the American Indian', *Social Science Review*, vol. 51, no. 3, September 1977.

Gutman, Herbert G., *The Black Family in Slavery and Freedom, 1750–1925* (Oxford, Blackwell, 1976).

Haas, Narz R., 'The application of linguistics to language teaching', in Kroeber (ed.), *Anthropology Today*.

Hackenberg, Robert A. and Wilson, C. Roderick, 'Reluctant emigrants. The role of migration in Papago Indian adaptation', *Human Organization*, vol. 31, no. 2, Summer 1972.

Hagan, William T., *The Sac and Fox Indians* (Norman, Okla, University of Oklahoma Press, 1958).

Hagan, William T., *American Indians* (Chicago, University of Chicago Press, 1961).

Hagan, William T., *Indian Police and Judges. Experiments in Acculturation and Controls* (New Haven, Conn., Yale University Press, 1966).

Hagan, William T., 'Kiowas, Comanches, and cattlemen, 1867–1906: a case study of the failure of U.S. reservation policy', *Pacific Historical Review*, vol. 40, August 1971.

Hagan, William T., *United States–Comanche Relations. The Reservation Years* (New Haven, Conn., and London, Yale University Press, 1976).

Hagan, William T., *The Indian Rights Association. The Herbert Welsh Years, 1882–1904* (Tucson, Ariz., University of Arizona Press, 1985).

Hagan, William T., 'The reservation policy: too little and too late', in Smith and Kvasnicka (eds), *Indian–White Relations*.

Hagan, William T., 'Quanah Parker', in Edmunds (ed.), *American Indian Leaders*.

Haller, John S., *Outcasts from Evolution. Scientific Attitudes of Racial Inferiority, 1859–1900* (New York, McGraw-Hill, 1975 edn).

Haller, John S. and Haller, Robin M., *The Physician and Sexuality in Victorian America* (Urbana, Ill., University of Illinois Press, 1974).

Halliburton, R. Jr, *Red over Black. Black Slavery among the Cherokee Indians* (Westport, Conn., Greenwood Press, 1977).

Handlin, Oscar and Handlin, Mary F., 'Origins of the southern labor system', *William and Mary Quarterly*, vol. VII, April 1950.

Handy, Robert T., *A Christian America. Protestant Hopes and Historical Realities* (New York, Oxford University Press, 1971).

Harmon, George Dewey, 'The Indian trust funds, 1797–1865', *Mississippi Valley Historical Review*, vol. 21, 1934–5.

Harmon, George Dewey, *Sixty Years of Indian Affairs: Political, Economic and Diplomatic, 1789–1850* (Chapel Hill, NC, University of North Carolina Press, 1941).

Harris, Marvin, *The Rise of Anthropological Theory. A History of Theories of Culture* (London, Routledge & Kegan Paul, 1968).

Harrison, W. P., *The Gospel among the Slaves. A Short Account of Missionary Operations among the African Slaves of the Southern States* (Nashville, Tenn., Publishing House of the M. E. Church, South, 1893).

Hartman, Mary and Banner, Lois W. (eds), *Clio's Consciousness Raised* (New York, Harper & Row, 1974).

Hatcher, O. E., 'The development of legal controls in racial segregation in the public schools of Oklahoma, 1865–1952' (D.Ed thesis, University of Oklahoma, 1954).

Hauptman, Lawrence M., 'The American Indian Federation and the Indian New Deal. A reinterpretation', *Pacific Historical Review*, vol. 52, 1983.

Hawthorn, Harry B., Belshaw, Cyril S., Jamieson, S. M. *et al.*, *The Indians of British Columbia* (Berkeley and Vancouver, University of British Columbia Press, 1958).

Hays, H. R., *From Ape to Angel. An Informal History of Social Anthropology* (London, Methuen, 1959).

Hayter, Earl W., 'The Ponca removal', *North Dakota Historical Quarterly*, vol. VI, no. 4, July 1932.

Heard, J. Norman, *White into Red. A Study of the Assimilation of White Persons Captured by Indian* (Metuchen, NJ, Scarecrow Press, 1973).

Heizer, Robert and Almquist, Alan F., *The Other Californians* (Berkeley, Calif., University of California Press, 1971).

Helm, June (ed.), *Pioneers of American Anthropology. The Uses of Biography* (Washington, DC, University of Washington Press, 1966).

Helms, Mary W., 'Matrilocality, social solidarity, and culture contact: three case histories', *Southwestern Journal of Anthropology*, vol. 27, no. 2, Summer 1970.

Hendrick, Irving G., 'Federal policy affecting the education of Indians in California, 1849–1934', *History of Education Quarterly*, vol. 16, Summer 1976.

Hertzberg, Hazel W., *The Search for an American Indian Identity. Modern Pan-Indian Movements* (Syracuse, NY, Syracuse University Press, 1971).

Higham, John (ed.), *Ethnic Leadership in America* (Baltimore, Md, Johns Hopkins University Press, 1978).

Hobson, Fred, *Tell About the South. The Southern Rage to Explain* (Baton Rouge, La, Louisiana State University Press, 1983).

Hoch-Smith, Judith and Spring, Anita, *Woman in Ritual and Symbolic Roles* (New York and London, Plenum Press, 1978).

Hodge, F. W. (ed.), *Handbook of American Indians North of Mexico* (New York, Rowman & Littlefield, 2 vols., 1971).

Hodge, William H., 'Navajo urban migration. An analysis from the perspective of the family' in Waddell and Watson (eds), *The American Indian in Urban Society*.

Hodgen, Margaret T., *Early Anthropology in the Sixteenth and Seventeenth Centuries* (Philadelphia, Pa, University of Pennsylvania Press, 1964).

Holmes, Jack D. L., 'Spanish policy toward southern Indians in the 1790s', in Hudson (ed.), *Four Centuries*.

Hood, Susan, 'Termination of the Klamath Tribe in Oregon', *Ethnohistory*, vol. 19, Fall 1972.

Hoopes, Alban W., 'Thomas S. Twiss, Indian agent on the Upper Platte, 1855–61', *Mississippi Valley Historical Review*, vol. 20, 1933–4.

Hoopes, Alban W., *Indian Affairs and their Administration. With Special Reference for the Far West, 1849–1860* (New York, Kraus Reprint Co., 1972).

Hoover, Dwight W., *The Red and the Black* (Chicago, Rand McNally, 1976).

Hoover, Herbert T., 'Sitting Bull', in Edmunds (ed.), *American Indian Leaders*.

Horsman, Reginald, *Expansion and American Indian Policy, 1783–1812* (Lansing, Mich., Michigan State University Press, 1967).

Horsman, Reginald, 'Scientific racism and the American Indian in the mid-nineteenth century', *American Quarterly*, vol. XXVII, no. 2, May 1975.

Horsman, Reginald, *Race and Manifest Destiny. The Origins of American Racial Anglo-Saxonism* (Cambridge, Mass., Harvard University Press, 1981).

Howard, Harold P., *Sacajawea* (Norman, Okla, University of Oklahoma Press, 1971).

Hoxie, Frederick E., 'Redefining Indian education. Thomas J. Morgan's program in disarray', *Arizona and the West*, vol. XXIV, 1982.

Hoxie, Frederick E., *A Final Promise. The Campaign to Assimilate the Indians, 1880–1920* (Lincoln, Nebr., University of Nebraska Press, 1984).

Huddleston, Lee Eldridge, 'Origins of the American Indians. A Study of European Concepts of the Origins of the American Indians, 1492–1729' (PhD dissertation, University of Texas, 1967).

Hudson, Charles M. (ed.), *Four Centuries of Southern Indians* (Athens, Ga, University of Georgia Press, 1975).

Hunt, H. F., 'Slavery among the Indians of Northwest America', *Washington Historical Quarterly*, vol. 9, October 1918.

Hurd, John Codman, *The Law of Freedom and Bondage*, Vol. 1 (New York, Negro Universities Press, 1968 edn).

Ilick, Joseph E., *Colonial Pennsylvania. A History* (New York, Scribner, 1976).

Iverson, Peter, 'Carlos Montezuma', in Edmunds (ed.), *American Indian Leaders*.

Jackson, Helen Hunt, *A Century of Dishonor. The Early Crusade for Indian Reform* (ed. Andrew F. Rolle; New York, Harper Torchbooks, 1965 reprint of 1881 edn).

Jackson, Neeley Belle, 'Political and economic history of the Negro in Indian territory' (MA dissertation, University of Oklahoma, 1960).

Jacobs, Wilbur R., 'The fatal confrontation: early native-white relations on the frontiers of Australia, New Guinea, and America – a comparative study', *Pacific Historical Review*, vol. 40, 1971.

Jacobs, Wilbur R., *Dispossessing the American Indian. Indians and Whites on the Colonial Frontier* (New York, Scribner, 1972).

Jacoway, Elizabeth, *Yankee Missionaries in the South. The Penn School Experiment* (Baton Rouge, La, and London, Louisiana State University Press, 1980).

Jaenen, Cornelius, J., 'Amerindian views of French culture in the seventeenth century', *Canadian Historical Review*, vol. 55, no. 3, September 1974.

Jamieson, S. M. *et al.*, *The Indian of British Columbia* (Berkeley and Vancouver, University of British Columbia Press, 1958).

Jeltz, Wyatt F., 'The relation of the Negroes and Choctaw and Chickasaw Indians, *Journal of Negro History*, vol. 33, January 1948.

Jenkins, J. Craig, *The Politics of Insurgency. The Farm Worker Movement in the 1960s* (New York, Columbia University Press, 1985).

Jenness, Diamond, *The Indians of Canada* (Ottawa National Museum of Canada, Bulletin 65, Anthropological Series no. 15, 1967 edn).

Jennings, Francis, *The Invasion of America. Indians, Colonialism, and the Cant of Conquest* (Chapel Hill, NC, University of North Carolina Press, 1976 edn).

Johannsen, Robert W. (ed.), *The Letters of Stephen A. Douglas* (Urbana, Ill., University of Illinois Press, 1961).

Johnston, Charles M. (ed.), *The Valley of the Six Nations* (Toronto, University of Toronto Press, 1964).

Johnston, James Hugo, *Race Relations in Virginia and Miscegenation in the South, 1776–1860* (Amherst, Mass., University of Massachusetts Press, 1970).

Jones, Jacqueline, *Labor of Love, Labor of Sorrow. Black Women, Work, and the Family from Slavery to the Present* (New York, Basic Books, 1985).

Jones, Maldwyn A., *American Immigration* (Chicago, University of Chicago Press, 1960).

Jordan, Winthrop D., *White over Black. American Attitudes towards the Negro 1550–1812* (Chapel Hill, NC, University of North Carolina Press, 1968).

Jorgenson, Joseph J., *The Sun Dance, Power for the Powerless* (Chicago, University of Chicago Press, 1972).

Josephy, Alvin M. Jr, *The Nez Percé Indians and the Opening of the Northwest* (New Haven, Conn., Yale University Press, 1965).

Josephy, Alvin M. Jr, *The Indian Heritage of America* (Harmondsworth, Penguin, 1968).

Josephy, Alvin M. Jr, *Red Power. The American Indians' Fight for Freedom* (New York, American Heritage Press, 1971).

Judd, Neil M., *The Bureau of American Ethnology. A Partial History* (Norman, Okla, University of Oklahoma Press, 1967).

Kaplan, Sidney, 'The "domestic insurrections" of the Declaration of Independence', *Journal of Negro History*, vol. 61, July 1976.

Katz, Michael B., *The Irony of Early School Reform. Educational innovation in Mid-Nineteenth-Century Massachusetts* (Cambridge, Mass., Harvard University Press, 1968).

Katz, Michael B., *Class, Bureaucracy and Schools. The Illusion of Change in America* (New York, Praeger, 1975 edn).

Katz, William Loren, *The Black West* (New York, Doubleday, 1973).

Keller, Robert H. Jr, 'Christian Indian missions and the American frontier', *American Indian Journal*, vol. 5, April 1979.

Keller, Robert H. Jr, 'Church joins state to civilize Indians, 1776–1869', *American Indian Journal*, vol. 5, July 1979.

Keller, Robert H. Jr, *American Protestantism and United States Indian Policy, 1869–82* (Lincoln, Nebr., University of Nebraska Press, 1983).

Kellogg, Louise Phelps (ed.), *Early Narratives of the Northwest, 1634–1699* (New York, Barnes & Noble, 1959 edn).

Kelly, Lawrence C., *The Navajo Indians and Federal Indian Policy, 1900–1935* (Tucson, Ariz., University of Arizona Press, 1968).

Kelly, Lawrence C., *The Assault on Assimilation. John Collier and the Origins of Indian Policy Reform* (Albuquerque, N. Mex., University of New Mexico Press, 1977).

Kelly, Lawrence, C., 'Cato Sells, 1913–21', in Kvasnicka and Viola (eds), *The Commissioners of Indian Affairs*.

Kelly, Lawrence C., 'Charles Henry Burke, 1921–1929', in Kvasnicka and Viola (eds), *The Commissioners of Indian Affairs*.

Kelly, Lawrence C., 'Charles James Rhoads, 1929–33', in Kvasnicka and Viola (eds), *The Commissioners of Indian Affairs*.

Kelly, Roger E. and Cramer, John O., 'American Indians in small cities', *Rehabilitation Monographs*, no. 1 (Flagstaff, Ariz., Northern Arizona University, 1966).

Kelly, William H., 'The economic basis of Indian life', in George Eaton Simpson and J. Milton Yinger, 'American Indians and American Indian life', Philadelphia, Pa, *Annals of the American Academy of Political and Social Science*, vol. 311, May 1957.

Kelsey, Harry, 'William P. Dole and Mr. Lincoln's Indian Policy', *Journal of the West*, vol. 10, July 1971.

Kelsey, Harry, 'William P. Dole, 1861–65', in Kvasnicka and Viola (eds), *The Commissioners of Indian Affairs*.

Kelsey, Rayner Wickersham, *Friends and the Indians, 1655–1917* (Philadelphia, Pa, Associated Executive Committee of Friends on Indian Affairs, 1917).

Kennard, Edward A. and MacGregor, Gordon, 'Applied anthropology in government: United States', in Kroeber (ed.), *Anthropology Today*.

Kennedy, John Hopkins, *Jesuit and Savage in New France* (New Haven, Conn., Yale University Press, 1950).

Keppel, Ann M., 'The myth of agrarianism in rural educational reform, 1890–1914', *History of Education Quarterly*, vol. II, no. 2, June 1962.

Kerber, Linda K. and Mathews, Jane De Hart (eds), *Women's America. Refocussing the Past* (New York and Oxford, Oxford University Press, 1982).

Kett, Joseph P., *Rites of Passage. Adolescence in America 1790 to the Present* (New York, Basic Books, 1977).

Kinney, Jay P., *A Continent Lost – A Civilization Won. Indian Land Tenure in America* (Baltimore, Md, Johns Hopkins University Press, 1937).

Kiple, Kenneth F. and King, Virginia Himmelsteib, *Another Dimension to the Black Diaspora. Diet, Disease and Racism* (Cambridge, Cambridge University Press, 1981).

Kleinfeld, Judith, 'Positive stereotyping. The cultural relativist in the classroom', *Human Organization*, vol. 34, no. 3, Fall 1975.

Klineberg, O., *Race and Psychology*, UNESCO pamphlet (Paris, UNESCO, 1951).

Kluckhohn, Clyde and Leighton, Dorothea, *The Navajo* (Cambridge, Mass., Harvard University Press, 1960).

Kroeber, Alfred L., *Anthropology* (New York, Harcourt, Brace & World, 1923; 1948 edn).

Kroeber, Alfred L. (ed.), *Anthropology Today. An Encyclopedic Inventory* (Chicago, University of Chicago Press, 1954 edn).

Krupat, Arnold, *For Those Who Came After. A Study of Native American Autobiographies* (Berkeley, Calif., University of California Press, 1985).

Kunitz, Stephen J., 'The social philosophy of John Collier', *Ethnohistory*, vol. 18, Summer 1971.

Kupperman, Karen Ordahl, *Settling with the Indians. The Meeting of English and Indian Cultures in America, 1580–1640* (London, Dent, 1980).

Kvasnicka, Robert M., 'George W. Manypenny, 1853–1857', in Kvasnicka and Viola (eds), *The Commissioners of Indian Affairs*.

Kvasnicka, Robert M. and Viola, Herman J. (eds), *The Commissioners of Indian Affairs, 1824–1977* (Lincoln, Nebr., University of Nebraska Press, 1979).

Kyle, James H., 'How shall the Indian be educated?', *North American Review*, vol. CLIX, November 1894.

Lanctot, Gustave, *Canada and the American Revolution* (Cambridge, Mass., Harvard University Press, 1967).

Lange, Charles H. and Riley, C. L. (eds), *The Southwestern Journals of Adolph F. Bandelier, 1880–1882* (Albuquerque, N. Mex., University of New Mexico Press, 1966).

Lasch, Christopher, *The Culture of Narcissism. American Life in an Age of Diminishing Expectations* (London, Sphere Books, 1982).

Lash, Joseph P., *Eleanor and Franklin* (New York, Norton, 1971).

Lassiter, Roy L., 'The association of income and education for males by region, race and age', *Southern Economic Review*, vol. 32, July 1965.

Lauber, Almon Wheeler, *Indian Slavery in Colonial Times within the Present Limits of the United States* (New York, Columbia University, 1913).

Laxon, Joan Dorothy, 'Aspects of acculturation among American Indians. Emphasis on contemporary pan-Indianism' (PhD thesis, University of California, 1972).

Leckie, William H., *The Buffalo Soldiers. A Narrative of the Negro Cavalry in the West* (Norman, Okla, University of Oklahoma Press, 1967).

411

Lerner, Gerda, *The Grimké Sisters from South Carolina. Pioneers for Women's Rights and Abolition* (New York, Schocken Books, 1973).

Leuchtenburg, William E., *Franklin D. Roosevelt and the New Deal, 1932–1940* (New York, Harper Torchbooks, 1963).

Leuchtenburg, William E., *The Perils of Prosperity, 1914–32* (Chicago, University of Chicago Press, 1965 edn).

Levine, Lawrence W., *Black Culture and Black Consciousness. Afro-American Folk Brought from Slavery to Freedom* (New York, Oxford University Press, 1977).

Levine, Stuart and Lurie, Nancy Oestreich (eds), *The American Indian Today* (Deland, Fla, Everett/Edwards, 1968).

Levitan, Sar A., and Hetrick, Barbara, *Big Brother's Indian Programs – With Reservations* (New York, McGraw-Hill, 1971).

Levy, J. E. and Kunitz, S. J., *Indian Drinking* (New York, Wiley, 1974).

Liberty, Margot (ed), *American Indian Intellectuals* (St Paul, Minn., West Publishing, 1978).

Lieberson, S., *Ethnic Patterns in American Cities* (New York, Free Press of Glencoe, 1963).

Lieberson, Stanley, *A Piece of the Pie. Blacks and White Immigrants Since 1880* (Berkeley, Calif., University of California Press, 1980).

Linton, Ralph (ed.), *Acculturation in Seven American Indian Tribes* (New York, Appleton-Century, 1940).

Linton, Ralph, *The Study of Man. An Introduction* (New York, Appleton-Century-Crofts, 1964 edn).

Littlefield, Daniel C., *Rice and Slaves. Ethnicity and the Slave Trade in Colonial South Carolina* (Baton Rouge, La, and London, Louisiana State University Press, 1981).

Littlefield, Daniel F. Jr, *Africans and Seminoles. From Removal to Emancipation* (Westport, Conn., Greenwood Press, 1977).

Littlefield, Daniel F. Jr, *The Cherokee Freedmen. From Emancipation to American Citizenship* (Westport, Conn., Greenwood Press, 1978).

Littlefield, Daniel F. Jr, *Africans and Creeks. From the Colonial Period to the Civil War* (Westport, Conn., Greenwood Press, 1979).

Littlefield, Daniel F. Jr, *The Chickasaw Freedmen* (Westport, Conn., Greenwood Press, 1980).

Littlefield, Daniel F. Jr, and Littlefield, Mary Ann, 'The Beams family: free blacks in Indian Territory', *Journal of Negro History*, vol. 61, January 1976.

Litwack, Leon F., *North of Slavery. The Negro in the Free States, 1790–1860* (Chicago, University of Chicago Press, 1965).

Litwack, Leon F., *Been in the Storm So Long. The Aftermath of Slavery* (London, Athlone, 1980).

Litwack, Leon F., 'The emancipation of the Negro abolitionist', in Bracey, Meier and Rudwick, *Blacks in the Abolitionist Movement*.

Llewellyn, Karl N. and Hoebel, E. Adamson, *The Cheyenne Way* (Norman, Okla, University of Oklahoma Press, 1967 edn).

Lorimer, D. A., *Colour, Class and the Victorians* (Leicester, Leicester University Press, 1978).

Lurie, Nancy Oestreich, 'The world's oldest on-going protest demonstration. North American Indian drinking patterns', *Pacific Historical Review*, vol. 40, 1971.

Lurie, Nancy Oestreich, 'The Indian Claims Commission', *Annals of the American Academy of Political and Social Science*, vol. 436, March 1978.

Lurie, Nancy Oestreich, 'Indian cultural adjustment to European civilization', in Smith (ed.), *Seventeenth-Century America*.

Lurie, Nancy Oestreich, 'Women in early American anthropology', in Helm (ed.), *Pioneers of American Anthropology*.

Mabee, Carleton, *Black Education in New York State. From Colonial to Modern Times* (Syracuse, NY, Syracuse University Press, 1979).

MacCormach, Carol P. and Strathern, Marilyn, *Nature, Culture and Gender* (Cambridge, Cambridge University Press, 1980).

McCoy, Isaac, *The Annual Register of Indian Affairs within the Indian (or Western) Territory*, Vol. 1 (J. Meeker, Shawanoe Mission, 1835); Vol. 3 (J. G. Pratt, 1837).

McCoy, Isaac, *History of Baptist Indian Missions* (Washington, DC and New York, 1840).

MacFadden, S. J. and Dashiel, J. F., 'Racial differences as measured by the Downey will-temperament individual tests', *Journal of Applied Psychology*, vol. VII, 1922.

McFee, Malcolm, *Modern Blackfeet. Montanans on Reservations* (New York, Holt, Rinehart & Winston, 1972).

McKenney, Thomas L., *Memoirs, Official and Personal* (Lincoln, Nebr., University of Nebraska Press, 1973, reprint of 1846).

McKenney, Thomas L. and Hall, James, *History of the Indian Tribes of North America, etc*, Vol. 3 (Philadelphia, Pa, 1836, 3 vols).

MacLeod, Duncan, *Slavery, Race and the American Revolution* (Cambridge, Cambridge University Press, 1974).

McLoughlin, William G., 'Red Indians, black slavery and white racism: America's slaveholding Indians', *American Quarterly*, vol. XXVI, no. 4, October 1974.

McNickle, D'Arcy, 'Commentary', in Smith and Kvasnicka (eds), *Indian-White Relations*.

McReynolds, Edwin C., *Oklahoma, A History of the Sooner State* (Norman, Okla, University of Oklahoma Press, 1972 edn).

McReynolds, Edwin C., *The Seminoles* (Norman, Okla, University of Oklahoma Press, 1972 edn).

Mahon, John K., 'Anglo-American methods of Indian warfare, 1676–1794', *Mississippi Valley Historical Review*, vol. 45, 1958–9.

Mahon, John K. (ed.), *Indians of the Lower South, Past and Present* (Pensacola, Fla, Gulf Coast History and Humanities Conference, 1975).

Mail, Patricia D., 'Hippocrates was a medicine man: the health care of native Americans in the twentieth century', *Annals of the American Academy of Political and Social Science*, vol. 436, March 1978.

Mair, Lucy, *An Introduction to Social Anthropology*, 2nd edn (Oxford, Clarendon Press, 1975).

Malinowski, B., 'Practical Anthropology', *Africa*, vol. II, no. 1, 1929.

Malinowski, B., 'The rationalization of anthropology and administration', *Africa*, vol. III, no. 4, 1931.

Malone, James H. *The Chickasaw Nation. A Short Sketch of a Noble People* (Louisville, Ky, J. P. Morton, 1922).

Malone, Henry T., *Cherokees of the Old South. A People in Transition* (Athens, Ga, University of Georgia Press, 1956).

Manypenny, George W., *Our Indian Wards* (Cincinnati, Ohio, Robert Clarke, 1980).

Marden, David L., 'Anthropologists and federal Indian policy prior to 1940', *Indian Historian*, vol. 5, Winter 1972.

Mardock, Robert Winston, *The Reformers and the American Indian* (Columbia, Mo., University of Missouri Press, 1971).

Marshall, Lynn L., 'Opposing Democratic and Whig concepts of party organisation', in Pessen (ed.), *New Perspectives*.

Martin, Calvin, *Keepers of the Game. Indian–Animal Relationships and the Fur Trade* (Berkeley, Calif., University of California Press, 1978; 1982 edn).

Martin, M. K. and Voorhies, Barbara, *Female of the Species* (New York and London, Columbia University Press, 1975).

Mather, Cotton, *The Life and Death of the Reverend Mr. John Eliot* (London, 1694 edn).

Mathes, Valerie Sherer, 'A new look at the role of women in Indian society', *American Indian Quarterly*, vol. 2, Summer 1975.

Mathews, Donald G., 'Religion and slavery: the case of the American South', in Bolt and Drescher (eds), *Anti-Slavery, Religion and Reform*.

Mathiessen, Peter, *Indian Country* (New York, Viking, 1984).

Matthaei, Julie A., *An Economic History of Women in America. Women's Work, the Sexual Division of Labour and the Development of Capitalism* (Brighton, Harvester Press, and New York, Schocken Books, 1982).

Maynard, Eileen, 'The growing negative image of the anthropologist among American Indians', *Human Organization*, vol. 33, no. 4, Winter 1974.

Medicine, Beatrice, 'The role of women in native American societies. A bibliography', *Indian Historian*, vol. 8, Summer 1975.

Meier, August and Rudwick, Elliott, 'The role of blacks in the abolitionist movement', in Bracey, Meier and Rudwick, *Blacks in the Abolitionist Movement*.

Meriam, Lewis (ed.), *The Problem of Indian Administration* (Baltimore, Md, Johns Hopkins University Press, 1928).

Metcalf, P. Richard, 'Who should rule at home? Native American politics and Indian–White relations', *Journal of American History*, vol. LXI, no. 3, December 1974.

Meyer, Roy W., 'Ezra A. Hayt, 1877–80', in Kvasnicka and Viola, *The Commissioners of Indian Affairs*.

Meyer, Roy W., *History of the Santee Sioux. United States Indian Policy on Trial* (Lincoln, Nebr., University of Nebraska Press, 1967).

Meyers, Marvin, *The Jacksonian Persuasion. Politics and Belief* (Stanford, NJ, Stanford University Press, 1968 edn).

Miller, Dorothy L., 'Native American women. Leadership images', *Integrated Education*, vol. 16, January–February 1978.

Miller, Frank C., 'Involvement in an urban university', in Waddell and Watson (eds), *The American Indian in Urban Society*.

Miner, H. Craig, *Tribal Sovereignty and Industrial Civilization in Indian Territory, 1865–1907* (Columbia, Mo., University of Missouri Press, 1976).

Mitchell, Fredric and Skelton, James W., 'The church–state conflict in early Indian education', *History of Education Quarterly*, vol. VI, no. 1, Spring 1966.

Montgomery, David, *Beyond Equality. Labor and the Radical Republicans, 1862–1872* (New York, Vintage Books, 1972 edn).

Moorehead, Warren King, *The American Indian in the United States, Period 1850–1914* (Andover, Mass., Andover Press 1914).

Morgan, Lewis Henry, *League of the Iroquois* (New York, Corinth Books, 1962 edn; originally 1851).

Morgan, Lewis Henry, 'The Indian Question', *The Nation*, vol. XXVII, 28 November 1878.

Morris, Robert C., *Reading, 'Riting and Reconstruction. The Education of Freedmen in the South, 1861–1870* (Chicago, University of Chicago Press, 1981).

Morrison, James D., 'Social history of the Choctaw, 1865–1907' (PhD dissertation, University of Oklahoma, 1951).

Moulton, Gary E., *John Ross, Cherokee Chief* (Athens, Ga, University of Georgia Press, 1978).

Murdock, George, *Social Structure* (New York, Macmillan, 1949).

Murray, Charles, *Losing Ground* (New York, Basic Books, 1986 edn).

Murray, David, *Modern Indians* (BAAS pamphlet 8, 1982).

Myer, Dillon S., *Uprooted Americans* (Tucson, Ariz., University of Arizona press, 1974).

Negata, Shuichi, 'The reservation community and the urban community. Hopi Indians of Moenkopi', in Waddell and Watson (eds), *The American Indian in Urban Society*.

Nasaw, David, *Schooled to Order. A Social History of Public Schooling in the United States* (New York, Oxford University Press, 1979).

Nash, Gary B., *Red, White and Black. The Peoples of Early America* (Englewood Cliffs, NJ, Prentice-Hall, 1974).

Nash, Gary B., 'Red, white and black: the origins of racism in colonial America', in Nash and Weiss (eds), *The Great Fear. Race in the Mind of America*.

Nash, Gary B., 'The image of the Indian in the southern colonial mind', in Dudley and Novak (eds), *The Wild Man Within*.

Nash, Gary B. and Weiss, Richard (eds), *The Great Fear. Race in the Mind of America* (New York, Holt, Rinehart & Winston, 1970).

Neil, William M., 'The territorial governor as Indian superintendent in the trans-Mississippi West', *Mississippi Valley Historical Review*, vol. 43, September 1956.

Neils, Elaine M., *Reservation to City. Indian Migration and Federal Relocation* (Chicago, Department of Geography, University of Chicago, 1971).

Nevins, Allan, *The American States during and after the Revolution, 1775–1789* (New York, Augustus M. Kelley, 1969; reprint of 1924 edn).

Nevins, Allan, '1861: a primitive administration' in Brock (ed.), *The Civil War*.

Nevins, Allan, '1863: organization for war', in Brock (ed.), *The Civil War*.

Nicolson, William, 'A tour of Indian agencies in Kansas and the Indian Territory in 1870', *Kansas Historical Quarterly*, vol. 3, 1934.

O'Donnell, James H. III, *Southern Indians in the American Revolution* (Knoxville, Tenn., University of Tennessee Press, 1973.

O'Donnell, James H. III, 'Joseph Brant', in Edmunds (ed.), *American Indian Leaders*.

Officer, James E., 'The American Indian and federal policy', in Waddell and Watson (eds), *The American Indian in Urban Society*.

Olson, James Stuart, *The Ethnic Dimension in American History* (New York, St Martin's, 1979).

Olson, John W., 'The urban Indian as viewed by an Indian caseworker', in Waddell and Watson (eds), *The American Indian in Urban Society*.

O'Neill, William, *Everyone Was Brave. The Rise and Fall of Feminism in America* (Chicago, Quadrangle, 1969).

415

O'Reilly, Kenneth, 'Progressive Era and New Era American Indian policy. The gospel of self-support', *Journal of Historical Studies*, vol. 5, Fall 1981.

Ortner, Sherry B., 'Is female to male as nature is to culture?', in Rosaldo and Lamphere (eds), *Women, Culture and Society*.

Ortner, Sherry B. and Whitehead, Harriet (eds), *Sexual Meanings. The Cultural Construction of Gender and Sexuality* (Cambridge, Cambridge University Press, 1981).

Osthaus, Carl R., *Freedmen, Philanthropy, and Fraud. A History of the Freedman's Savings Bank* (Urbana, Ill., University of Illinois Press, 1976).

Oswalt, Wendall H., *This Land Was Theirs* (New York, Wiley, 1973 edn).

Otis, D. S., *The Dawes Act and the Allotment of Indian Lands* (ed. Francis Paul Prucha; Norman, Okla, University of Oklahoma Press, 1973 edn; originally 1934).

Ourada, Patricia K., 'Glenn L. Emmons, 1953–61', in Kvasnicka and Viola (eds), *The Commissioners of Indian Affairs*.

Ourada, Patricia K., 'Dillon Seymour Myer, 1950–53', in Kvasnicka and Viola (eds), *The Commissioners of Indian Affairs*.

Owen, Roger C., Deetz, James F. and Fisher, Anthony D. (eds), *The North American Indians: A Sourcebook* (New York, Macmillan, 1967).

Parkman, Francis, *The Jesuits in North America in the Seventeenth Century* (Boston, Mass., Little, Brown, 1893).

Parman, Donald J., *The Navajos and the New Deal* (New Haven, Conn., and London, Yale University Press, 1976).

Parman, Donald J., 'Francis Ellington Leupp, 1905–1909', in Kvasnicka and Viola (eds), *The Commissioners of Indian Affairs*.

Partington, F. E., *The Story of Mohonk* (Fulton, NY, Morrill Press, 1911).

Patrick, Rembert Wallace, *Florida Fiasco. Rampant Rebels on the Georgia–Florida Border, 1810–15* (Athens, Ga, University of Georgia Press, 1954).

Patterson, E. Palmer, *The Canadian Indian. A History Since 1500* (Don Mills, Ontario, Collier-MacMillan, 1972).

Pearce, Roy Harvey, ' "The ruines of mankind": The Indian and the Puritan mind', *Journal of the History of Ideas*, vol. XIII, 1952.

Peckham, Howard, *Pontiac and the Indian Uprising* (Princeton, NJ, Princeton University Press, 1947).

'Penn, William' (pseud. Jeremiah Evarts), *Essays on the Present Crisis in the Condition of the American Indian* (Philadelphia, Pa, Thomas Kite, 1830).

Pennanen, Gary, 'Sitting Bull. Indian without a country', *Canadian Historical Review*, vol. LI, no. 2, June 1970.

Perdue, Theda, *Slavery and the Evolution of Cherokee Society, 1540–1866* (Knoxville, Tenn., University of Tennessee Press, 1979).

Perdue, Theda, *Nations Remembered. An Oral History of the Five Civilized Tribes, 1865–1907* (Westport, Conn., Greenwood Press, 1980).

Perkinson, Henry J., *The Imperfect Panacea* (New York, Wiley, 1968).

Peroff, Nicholas C., *Menominee Drums. Tribal Termination and Restoration, 1934–1974* (Norman, Okla, University of Oklahoma Press, 1982).

Pessen, Edward (ed.), *New Perspectives on Jacksonian Parties and Politics* (Boston, Mass., Allyn & Bacon, 1970).

Peterson, John H. Jr, 'Louisiana Choctaw life at the end of the nineteenth century', in Hudson (ed.), *Four Centuries*.

Phillips, George Harwood, 'Indians in Los Angeles, 1781–1875', *Pacific Historical Review*, vol. 49, 1980.

Philp, Kenneth R., *John Collier's Crusade for Indian Reform, 1920–1954* (Tucson, Ariz., University of Arizona Press, 1977).

Philp, Kenneth R., 'John Collier, 1933–45', in Kvasnicka and Viola (eds), *The Commissioners of Indian Affairs*.

Philp, Kenneth R., 'The New Deal and Alaskan natives, 1939–1945', *Pacific Historical Review*, vol. 50, 1981.

Pinkney, Alphonso, *Red, Black and Green. Black Nationalism in the United States* (Cambridge, Cambridge University Press, 1976).

Pole, J. R., *The Pursuit of Equality in American History* (Berkeley, Calif., University of California Press, 1978).

Polenberg, Richard, *One Nation Divisible. Class, Race and Ethnicity in the United States Since 1938* (Harmondsworth, Penguin, 1980).

Polgar, Steven, 'Skills needed in action anthropology: lessons from El Centro de la Causa', *Human Organization*, vol. 33, no. 2, Summer 1974.

Porter, Frank III, 'Anthropologists at work: a case study of the Nanticoke community', *American Indian Quarterly*, vol. 4, February 1978.

Porter, H. C., *The Inconstant Savage. England and the North American Indian, 1500–1660* (London, Duckworth, 1979).

Porter, Kenneth Wiggins, 'The Seminole in Mexico, 1850–61', *Hispanic American Historical Review*, vol. XXXI, February 1951.

Porter, Kenneth Wiggins, 'The Seminole Negro-Indian Scouts, 1870–1881', *Southwestern Historical Quarterly*, vol. 55, January 1952.

Porter, Kenneth Wiggins, 'Negroes and Indians on the Texas frontier, 1831–1876', *Journal of Negro History*, vol. XLI, no. 3, July 1956.

Porter, Kenneth Wiggins, 'Florida slaves and free Negroes in the Seminole War, 1835–1842', in Glasrud and Smith (eds), *Promises to Keep*.

Powell, J. W., *Introduction to the Study of Indian Languages*, 2nd edn (Washington DC, Government Printing Office, 1880).

Pratt, Richard Henry, *Battlefield and Classroom. Four Decades with the American Indian, 1867–1904* (ed. Robert Utley; New Haven, Conn., and London, Yale University Press, 1964).

Price, John A., 'The migration and adaptation of American Indians to Los Angeles', *Human Organization*, vol. 27, no. 2, Summer 1968.

Price, John A., 'An applied analysis of North American Indian drinking patterns', *Human Organization*, vol. 34, no. 1, Spring 1975.

Price, John A., *Native Studies. American and Canadian Indians* (Toronto, McGraw-Hill Ryerson, 1978).

Priest, Loring B., *Uncle Sam's Stepchildren. The Reformation of United States Indian Policy, 1865–1887* (Lincoln, Nebr., University of Nebraska Press, 1975; reprint of 1942 edn).

Prucha, Francis Paul, 'Thomas L. McKenney and the New York Indian Board', *Mississippi Valley Historical Review*, vol. 48, March 1962.

Prucha, Francis Paul, 'Indian removal and the Great American Desert', *Indiana Magazine of History*, vol. 59, December 1963.

Prucha, Francis Paul, 'Andrew Jackson's Indian policy: a reassessment', *Journal of American History*, vol. LVI, December 1969.

Prucha, Francis Paul, *American Indian Policy in the Formative Years* (Lincoln, Nebr., University of Nebraska Press, 1962; 1970 edn).

Prucha, Francis Paul, 'American Indian policy in the 1840s. Visions of reform', in J. G. Clark (eds.), *The Frontier Challenge*.

Prucha, Francis Paul, *Americanizing the American Indians. Writings by Friends of the Indian, 1880–1900* (Cambridge, Mass., Harvard University Press, 1973).

Prucha, Francis Paul *Broadax and Bayonet. The Role of the United States Army in the Development of the Northwest, 1815–1860* (Lincoln, Nebr., University of Nebraska Press, 1973 edn).

Prucha, Francis Paul (ed.), *Documents of United States Indian Policy* (Lincoln, Nebr., University of Nebraska Press, 1975).

Prucha, Francis Paul, *American Indian Policy in Crisis. Christian Reformers and the Indian, 1865–1900* (Norman, Okla, University of Oklahoma Press, 1976).

Prucha, Francis Paul, *The Churches and the Indian Schools, 1888–1912* (Lincoln, Nebr., University of Nebraska Press, 1979).

Prucha, Francis Paul, *The Great Father. The United States Government and the Indians* (Lincoln, Nebr., University of Nebraska Press, 2 vols, 1984).

Putney, Diane T., 'Robert Grosvenor Valentine, 1909–12', in Kvasnicka and Viola (eds), *The Commissioners of Indian Affairs*.

Quarles, Benjamin, *The Negro in the American Revolution* (Chapel Hill, NC, University of North Carolina Press, 1971).

Quinton, A. S., *Indians and Their Helpers* (no details).

Quinton, A. S., *Constitution and By-Laws of the Indian Rights Association* (Philadelphia, Pa, 1883).

Rahill, Peter J., *The Catholic Indian Missions and Grant's Peace Policy, 1870–1884* (Washington, DC, Catholic University Press, 1953).

Raisch, C., 'The state of the Indian nation', *Hustler*, January 1978.

Ravitch, Diane, *The Troubled Crusade. American Education, 1945–1980* (New York, Basic Books, 1983).

Reiter, Rayna A. (ed.), *Toward an Anthropology of Women* (New York and London, Monthly Review Press, 1975).

Resek, Carl, *Lewis Henry Morgan. American Scholar* (Chicago, University of Chicago Press, 1960).

Rich, E. E., *The Fur Trade and the Northwest to 1857* (Toronto, McClelland & Stewart, 1968).

Richardson, Joe M., *A History of Fisk University, 1865–1946* (University, Ala, University of Alabama Press, 1980).

Riley, Glenda, *Women and Indians on the Frontier, 1825–1915* (Albuquerque, N. Mex., University of New Mexico Press, 1984).

Rister, Carl Coke, *Baptist Missions among the American Indians* (Atlanta, Ga, Home Mission Board, Southern Baptist Convention, 1944).

Robe, Stanley L., 'Wild men and Spain's brave new world', in Dudley and Novak (eds), *The Wild Man Within*.

Roberts, Gary L., 'Dennis Nelson Cooley, 1865–66', in Kvasnicka and Viola (eds), *The Commissioners of Indian Affairs*.

Rodgers, D. T., 'Socialising middle-class children. Institutions, fables and work values in nineteenth-century America', *Journal of Social History*, vol. 13, no. 3, Spring 1980.

Rogin, Michael Paul, *Fathers and Children. Andrew Jackson and the Subjugation of the American Indian* (New York, Knopf, 1975).

Rohner, Ronald P. (ed.), *The Ethnography of Franz Boas* (Chicago, University of Chicago Press, 1969).

Roosevelt, Theodore, *The Winning of the West*, Vol. I (New York, Putnam, 1889).

Rosaldo, M. Z. and Lamphere, L. (eds), *Women, Culture and Society* (Stanford, NJ, Stanford University Press, 1974).

Rousseau, Jean-Jacques, *Discourse upon the Origin and Foundation of the Inequality among Mankind* (London, 1761; originally 1755).

Ruchames, Louis (ed.), *The Letters of William Lloyd Garrison*, Vol. IV (Cambridge, Mass., Harvard University Press, 1975).

Russell, John H., *The Free Negro in Virginia* (Baltimore, Md, Johns Hopkins University Press, 1913).

Ryan, Mary P., 'American society and the cult of domesticity' (PhD thesis, University of California at Santa Barbara, 1971).

Sacks, Karen, 'Engels revisited: women, the organization of production, and private property', in Reiter (ed.), *Toward an Anthropology of Women*.

Salisbury, Neal, 'Red Puritans. The "praying Indians" of Massachusetts Bay and John Eliot', *William and Mary Quarterly*, vol. 31, 1974.

Salisbury, Neal, *Manitou and Providence. Indians, Europeans, and the Making of New England, 1500–1643* (New York, Oxford University Press, 1982).

Satz, Ronald N., *American Indian Policy in the Jacksonian Era* (Lincoln, Nebr., University of Nebraska Press, 1975).

Saum, Lewis O., *The Fur Trader and the Indian* (Seattle, Wash., University of Washington Press, 1965).

Savage, W. Sherman, *Blacks in the West* (New York, Greenwood, 1977 edn).

Schlegel, Alice *Male Dominance and Female Autonomy. Domestic Authority in Matrilineal Societies* (New Haven, Conn., HRAF Press, 1972).

Schlegel, Alice, 'The adolescent socialization of the Hopi girl', *Ethnology*, vol. XII, no. 4, October 1973.

Schlegel, Alice, 'Sexual antagonism among the sexually egalitarian Hopi, *Ethos*, vol. 7, 1979.

Schlegel, Alice (ed.), *Sexual Stratification. A Cross-Cultural View* (New York, Columbia University Press, 1979).

Schlegel, Alice, 'Hopi gender ideology of female superiority', *Quarterly Journal of Ideology*, vol. 8, no. 4, 1984.

Schmeckebier, Lawrence F., *The Office of Indian Affairs. Its History, Activities and Organization* (Baltimore, Md, Johns Hopkins University Press, 1927; reprinted New York, AMS Press, 1972).

Schoolcraft, Henry Rowe, *Indian Legends from Algic Researches ... etc* (ed. Mentor L. Williams; Lansing, Mich., Michigan State University Press, 1956).

Schultz, G. A., *An Indian Canaan. Isaac McCoy and the Vision of an Indian State* (Norman, Okla, University of Oklahoma Press, 1972).

Sharp, Wanda Faye, 'The Black Dispatch. A sociological analysis' (MA thesis, University of Oklahoma, 1951).

Sheehan, Bernard W., *Seeds of Extinction. Jeffersonian Philanthropy and the American Indian* (Chapel Hill, NC, University of North Carolina Press, 1973).

Sheehan, Bernard W., *Savagism and Civility. Indians and Englishmen in Colonial Virginia* (Cambridge, Cambridge University Press, 1980).

Sherer, Robert G., *Subordination or Liberation? The Development and Conflicting Theories of Black Education in Nineteenth-Century Alabama* (University, Ala, University of Alabama Press, 1977).

Showalter, Elaine and Showalter, English, 'Victorian women and menstruation', in Vicinus (ed.), *Suffer and Be Still*.

Silver, James W., 'A counter-proposal to the Indian removal policy of Andrew Jackson', *Journal of Mississippi History*, vol. 4, October 1942.

Simon, John Y. (ed.), *The Papers of Ulysses S. Grant*, Vol. 1, *1837–61* (Carbondale, Ill., Southern Illinois University Press, 1967).

Slotkin, Richard, *Regeneration through Violence. The Mythology of the American Frontier* (Middletown, Conn., Wesleyan University Press, 1973).

Smith, James Morton (ed.), *Seventeenth-Century America. Essays in Colonial History* (Chapel Hill, NC, University of North Carolina Press, 1959).

Smith, Jane F. and Kvasnicka, Robert M. (eds), *Indian–White Relations. A Persistent Paradox* (Washington, DC, Howard University Press, 1976).

Smith, Timothy L., 'Immigrant social aspirations and American education, 1880–1930', *American Quarterly*, vol. XXI, no. 3, Fall 1969.

Smith-Rosenberg, Carol, 'Puberty to menopause: the cycle of femininity in nineteenth-century America', in Hartman and Banner (eds), *Clio's Consciousness Raised*.

Snyder, Peter Z., 'The social environment of the urban Indians', in Waddell and Watson (eds), *The American Indian in Urban Society*.

Solomon, Barbara Miller, *In the Company of Educated Women. A History of Women and Higher Education in America* (New Haven, Conn., and London, Yale University Press, 1985).

Sorkin, Alan L., *American Indians and Federal Aid* (Washington, DC, the Brookings Institution, 1971).

Sorkin, Alan L., 'The economic basis of Indian life', *Annals of the American Academy of Political and Social Science*, vol. 436, March 1978.

Sorkin, Alan L., *The Urban American Indian* (Lexington, Mass., D. C. Heath, 1978).

Sowell, Thomas, *Markets and Minorities* (Oxford, Blackwell, 1981).

Sowell, Thomas, *Ethnic America. A History* (New York, Basic Books, 1981).

Spencer, Robert F., Jennings, Jesse D., *et al.*, *The Native Americans. Prehistory and Ethnology of the North American Indians* (New York, Harper & Row, 1965).

Spicer, Edward H., *Cycles of Conquest. The Impact of Spain, Mexico, and the United States on the Indians of the Southwest, 1533–1960* (Tucson, Ariz., University of Arizona Press, 1962).

Spicer, Edward H. (ed.), *Perspectives in American Indian Culture Change* (Chicago, University of Chicago Press, 1966 edn).

Stampp, Kenneth M., *The Peculiar Institution. Negro Slavery in the American South* (London, Eyre & Spottiswoode, 1964).

Stanley, George F. G., *The Birth of Western Canada. A History of the Riel Rebellions* (Toronto, University of Toronto Press, 1963 edn).

Stanley, George F. G., *New France. The Last Phase, 1744–1760* (London, Oxford University Press, and Toronto, McClelland & Stewart, 1968).

Stanley, Sam and Thomas, Roberts K., 'Current demographic and social trends among North American Indians', *Annals of the American Academy of Political and Social Science*, vol. 436, March 1978.

Stanton, W., *The Leopard's Spots. Scientific Attitudes Toward Race in America, 1815–59* (Chicago, University of Chicago Press, 1960).

Starkey, Marion L., *The Cherokee Nation* (New York, Russell & Russell, 1972 edn).

Stegner, Wallace, *Beyond the Hundredth Meridian. John Wesley Powell and the Second Opening of the West* (Boston, Mass., Houghton Mifflin, 1954).

Stein, Gary C., 'The Indian Citizenship Act of 1924', *New Mexico Historical Review*, vol. 47, July 1972.

Steinberg, S., *The Ethnic Myth. Race, Ethnicity and Class in America* (New York, Atheneum, 1981).

Steiner, Stan, *The New Indians* (New York, Harper & Row, 1968).

Steinfels, Peter, *The Neoconservatives. The Men who are Changing America's Politics* (New York, Simon & Schuster, 1980 edn).

Stephens, William N., *The Family in Cross-Cultural Perspective* (New York, Holt, Rinehart & Winston, 1966 edn).

Stewart, Omer, 'Questions regarding American Indian criminality', *Human Organization*, vol. 23, no. 1, Spring 1964.

Stocking, George W., *Race, Culture and Evolution. Essays in the History of Anthropology* (New York, Free Press, 1968).

Strathern, Marilyn, 'No nature, no culture: the Hagen case', in MacCormach and Strathern, *Nature, Culture and Gender*.

Strickland, A. E., 'Toward the Promised Land: the exodus to Kansas and afterward', *Missouri Historical Review*, vol. LXIX, no. 4, July 1975.

Strickland, Rennard, *Fire and the Spirits: Cherokee Law from Clan to Court* (Norman, Okla, University of Oklahoma Press, 1975).

Strickland, Rennard, *The Indians in Oklahoma* (Norman, Okla, University of Oklahoma Press, 1980).

Stuart, Paul, 'United States Indian policy: from the Dawes Act to the American Indian Policy Review Commission', *Social Service Review*, vol. LI, September 1977.

Stuart, Paul, *The Indian Office. Growth and Development of an American Institution* (Ann Arbor, Mich., University Microfilms International, V.M.I. Research Press, 1979).

Svensson, F., *The Ethnics in American Politics, American Indians* (Minneapolis, Minn., Burgess, 1973).

Szasz, Margaret Connell, *Education and the American Indian. The Road to Self-Determination Since 1928* (Albuquerque, N. Mex., University of New Mexico Press, 1977 edn).

Szasz, Margaret Connell, '"Poor Richard" meets the Native American: schooling for young Indian women in eighteenth-century Connecticut', *Pacific Historical Review*, vol. XLIX, 1980.

Takaki, Ronald, *Iron Cages. Race and Culture in 19th-Century America* (London, Athlone, 1980).

Tamarin, Alfred, *We Have Not Vanished. Eastern Indians of the United States* (Chicago, Follett, 1974).

Tanis, Norman Earl, 'Education and John Eliot's Indian utopias, 1645–1675', *History of Education Quarterly*, vol. X, no. 3, Fall 1970.

Tatum, Lawrie, *Our Red Brothers and the Peace Policy of President Ulysses S. Grant* (Lincoln, Nebr., University of Nebraska Press, 1970; originally 1899).

Tax, Sol, 'The impact of urbanization on American Indians', *Annals of the American Academy of Political and Social Science*, vol. 436, March 1978.

Taylor, Graham D., *The New Deal and American Indian Tribalism. The Administration of the Indian Reorganization Act* (Lincoln, Nebr., University of Nebraska Press, 1980).

Teall, Kaye Moulton, *Black History in Oklahoma. A Resource Book* (Oklahoma City, Okla, Oklahoma City Public Schools, 1971).

Thernstrom, Stephan (ed.), *Harvard Encyclopedia of American Ethnic Groups* (Cambridge, Mass., Harvard University Press, 1981 edn).

Thomas, Cyrus and McGee, M. J., *The Indian of North America in Historic Times*, Vol. II of G. C. Lee (ed.), *The History of North America* (Philadelphia, Pa, and London, 1903).

Thrapp, Dan. *The Conquest of Apacheria* (Norman, Okla, University of Oklahoma Press, 1967).

Timmons, David R., 'Elements of prejudice towards Negroes and Indians as found in daily newspapers of Seminole County, Oklahoma, 1950–1959' (MA thesis, University of Oklahoma, 1970).

Tolson, Arthur Lincoln, 'The Negro in Oklahoma Territory 1889–1907; a study in racial discrimination' (PhD dissertation, University of Oklahoma, 1966).

Trelease, Allen W., 'The Iroquois and the western fur trade: a problem in interpretation', *Mississippi Valley Historical Review*, vol. 49, 1962–3.

Trenholm, Virginia Cole, *The Arapahoes, Our People* (Norman, Okla, University of Oklahoma Press, 1970).

Trennert, Robert A. Jr, *Alternative to Extinction. Federal Indian Policy and the Beginnings of the Reservation System, 1846–51* (Philadelphia, Pa, Temple University Press, 1975).

Trennert, Robert A. Jr, 'William Medill 1845–49', in Kvasnicka and Viola (eds), *The Commissioners of Indian Affairs*.

Trennert, Robert A. Jr, 'Educating Indian girls at nonreservation boarding schools, 1878–1920', *Western Historical Quarterly*, vol. 13, July 1982.

Trennert, Robert A. Jr, 'From Carlisle to Phoenix. The rise and fall of the outing system, 1878–1930', *Pacific Historical Review*, vol. LII, 1983.

Trigger, Bruce, 'The French Presence in Huronia: the structure of Franco-Huron relations in the first half of the seventeenth century', *Canadian Historical Review*, vol. XLIX, June 1968.

Trollope, Frances, *Domestic Manners of the Americans*, 5th edn (London, Richard Bentley, 1839).

Tuckerman, Joseph, *A Discourse, Preached Before the Society for Propagating the Gospel among the Indians and Others in North America, November 1, 1821* (Cambridge, Mass., Hilliard & Metcalf, 1821).

Turner, James, 'Understanding the Populists', *Journal of American History*, vol. 67, 1980–1.

Tyack, David B., *The One Best System. A History of American Urban Education* (Cambridge, Mass., Harvard University Press, 1974).

Tyack, David B. and James, Thomas, 'Education for a republic', *This Constitution: A Bicentennial Chronicle*, Winter 1985.

Tyler, S. Lyman, *A History of Indian Policy* (Washington, DC, Dept of the Interior, Bureau of Indian Affairs, 1973).

Tyler, S. Lyman, 'William A. Brophy, 1945–48', in Kvasnicka and Viola (eds), *The Commissioners of Indian Affairs*.

Underhill, Ruth M., *Red Man's Religion. Beliefs and Practices of the Indians North of Mexico* (Chicago and London, University of Chicago Press, 1974 edn).

Unrau, William E., *The Kansa Indians. A History of the Wind People, 1673–1873* (Norman, Okla, University of Oklahoma Press, 1971).

Unrau, William E., 'The civilian as Indian agent: villain or victim?', *Western Historical Quarterly*, vol. 3, no. 4, October 1972.

Utley, Robert M., *Frontiersman in Blue. The United States Army and the Indian 1848–1865* (New York, Macmillan, 1967).

Van Deusen, Glyndon G., *The Jacksonian Era, 1828–1848* (New York, Harper Torchbooks, 1963).

Vaughan, Alden T., *New England Frontier. Puritans and Indians, 1620–1675* (Boston, Mass., Little, Brown, 1965).

Vaughan, Alden T., 'From white man to redskin: changing Anglo-American perceptions of the American Indian', *American Historical Review*, vol. 87, no. 4, October 1982.

Vaughn, William Preston, *Schools For All. The Blacks and Public Education in the South, 1865–1877* (Lexington, Ky, University of Kentucky Press, 1974).

Vicinus, M. (ed.), *Suffer and Be Still. Women in the Victorian Age* (London, Methuen, 1980 edn).

Viola, Herman J., *Thomas L. McKenney. Architect of America's Early Indian Policy, 1816–1830* (Chicago, Swallow, 1974).

Viola, Herman J., 'Thomas L. McKenney, 1824–30', in Kvasnicka and Viola (eds), *The Commissioners of Indian Affairs.*

Voget, Fred W., *A History of Ethnology* (New York, Holt, Rinehart & Winston, 1975).

Vogt, Evon, 'The acculturation of American Indians', *Annals of the American Academy of Political and Social Science*, vol. 311, May 1957.

Waddell, Jack O., 'For individual power and social credit. The use of alcohol among Tucson Papagos', *Human Organization*, vol. 34, no. 1, Spring 1975.

Waddell, Jack O. and Watson, O. Michael (eds), *The American Indian in Urban Society* (Boston, Mass., Little, Brown, 1971).

Wade, Mason (ed.), *The Journals of Francis Parkman*, Vol. 2 (London, Eyre & Spottiswoode, 1947).

Walker, Deward E. Jr, 'Measures of Nez Percé outbreeding and the analysis of cultural change', *Southwestern Journal of Anthropology*, vol. 23, Summer 1967.

Wallace, Anthony F. C., 'New religions among the Delaware Indians, 1600–1900', *Southwestern Journal of Anthropology*, vol. 12, Spring 1956.

Walters, Raymond, *The New Negro on Campus. Black College Rebellions of the 1920s* (Princeton, NJ, Princeton University Press, 1975).

Waltmann, Henry G., 'Ely Samuel Parker, 1869–71', in Kvasnicka and Viola (eds), *The Commissioners of Indian Affairs.*

Walton, Gary M. and Shepherd, James F., *The Economic Rise of Early America* (Cambridge, Cambridge University Press, 1979).

Wanken, Helen M., ' "Woman's sphere" and Indian reform. The Women's National Indian Association, 1879–1901' (PhD dissertation, Marquette University, 1981).

Wardell, Morris L., *A Political History of the Cherokee Nation, 1838–1907* (Norman, Okla, University of Oklahoma Press, 1977 edn).

Washburn, Wilcomb E., 'A moral history of Indian–white relations. Needs and opportunities for study', *Ethnohistory*, vol. IV, no. 1, Winter 1957.

Washburn, Wilcomb E. (ed.), *The Indian and the White Man* (Garden City, NY, Doubleday, 1964).

Washburn, Wilcomb E., 'The moral and legal justifications for dispossessing the Indians' in Smith (ed.), *Seventeenth-Century America.*

Washburn, Wilcomb E., 'American Indian studies: a status report', *American Quarterly*, vol. XXVII, no. 3, August 1975.

Washburn, Wilcomb E. (ed.), *The Assault on Indian Tribalism. The General Allotment Law (Dawes Act) of 1887* (Philadelphia, Pa, Lippincott, 1975).

Wax M. L., *American Indians, Unity and Diversity* (Englewood Cliffs, NJ, Prentice-Hall, 1971).

Way, Royal B., 'The United States factory system for trading with the Indians, 1796–1822', *Mississippi Valley Historical Review*, vol. 6, June 1919–March 1920.

Webster, Paula, 'Matriarchy: a vision of power', in Reiter (ed.), *Toward an Anthropology of Women.*

Weeks, Stephen B., *Southern Quakers and Slavery. A Study in Institutional History* (Baltimore, Md, Johns Hopkins University Press, 1896).

Weiss, Nancy J., *Farewell to the Party of Lincoln. Black Politics in the Age of FDR* (Princeton, NJ, Princeton University Press, 1983).

Welter, Barbara, 'The cult of true womanhood, 1820–1860', *American Quarterly*, vol. 18, 1966.

Weppner, Robert S., 'Socioeconomic barriers to assimilation of Navajo migrant workers', *Human Organization*, vol. 31, no. 3, Fall 1972.

Weppner, Robert S., 'Urban economic opportunities. The example of Denver', in Waddell and Watson (eds), *The American Indian in Urban Society*.

Wesley, John, *Thoughts upon Slavery* (London, 1774).

Westermann, Joann, 'The urban Indian', *Current History*, vol. 67, December 1974.

Westermeyer, Joseph, 'Sex roles and the Indian-majority interface in Minnesota', *International Journal of Psychiatry*, vol. 24, no. 3, Autumn 1978.

Whipple, C. K., *Relation of the American Board of Commissioners for Foreign Missions to Slavery* (Boston, Mass., R. F. Wallcut, 1861).

White, L. A. (ed.), *Pioneers of American Anthropology. The Bandelier–Morgan Letters, 1873–1883*, Vol. 2 (Albuquerque, N. Mex., University of New Mexico Press, 1940, 2 vols).

Whitehead, Harriet, 'The bow and the burden strap: a new look at institutionalised homosexuality in native North America', in Ortner and Whitehead (eds), *Sexual Meanings*.

Wiebe, Robert H., *The Search for Order, 1877–1920* (New York, Hill & Wang, 1968 edn).

Williams, Walter L. (ed.), *Southeastern Indians Since the Removal Era* (Athens, Ga, University of Georgia Press, 1979).

Willis, William S., ' "Divide and rule": red, white and black in the Southeast', *Journal of Negro History*, vol. 48, 1963.

Wilson, James, *The Original Americans: U.S. Indians* (London, Minority Rights Group, Report 31, 1976).

Winks, Robin, 'American and European imperialism compared', in Miller, Richard H. (ed.), *American Imperialism in 1898. The Quest for National Fulfilment* (New York, Wiley, 1970).

Winsor, Justin (ed.), *Narrative and Critical History of America*, Vol. 1 (Boston, Mass., Houghton Mifflin, 1889).

Wolfe, Tom, *Mauve Gloves and Madmen, Clutter and Vine* (Toronto, New York and London, Bantam, 1977).

Wolters, Ronald G., *American Reformers, 1815–1860* (New York, Hill & Wang, 1978).

Woodcock, George, *Peoples of the Coast. The Indians of the Pacific Northwest* (Bloomington, Ind., and London, Indiana University Press, 1977).

Woodward, Grace Steele, *Pocahontas* (Norman, Okla, University of Oklahoma Press, 1969).

Wright, Peter M., 'Washakie', in Edmunds (ed.), *American Indian Leaders*.

Yinger, J. Milton and Simpson, George Eaton, 'The integration of Americans of Indian descent', *Annals of the American Academy of Political and Social Science*, vol. 436, March 1978.

Young, Mary E., 'The Creek frauds. A study of conscience and corruption', *Mississippi Valley Historical Review*, vol. 42, December 1955.

Young, Mary E., *Redskins, Ruffleshirts and Rednecks. Indian Allotments in Alabama and Mississippi, 1830–1860* (Norman, Okla, University of Oklahoma Press, 1961).

Young, Mary E., 'Indian removal and land allotment: the Civilized Tribes and Jacksonian justice', reprinted in Pessen (eds.), *New Perspectives*.
Young, Mary E., 'Women, civilization, and the Indian question', in Kerber and Mathews (eds), *Women's America. Refocussing the Past*.

Zamora, Mario D., 'Moral, immoral science. The case for cultural anthropology', *The Indian Historian*, vol. 6, no. 2, Spring 1973.
Zanger, Martin, 'Red Bird', in Edmunds (ed.), *American Indian Leaders*.

NOTE

Readers interested in Indian education should consult Jacqueline Mary Fear's forthcoming book, *The Little Red Schoolhouse on the Reservation*, which is based on her 1978 University of London Ph.D. thesis, 'American Indian Education: The Reservation Schools, 1870–1900'.

Index

Aberle, S. D. 139
abolitionism 58–9, 94, 95
acculturation
  anthropological studies 201
  black slaves as agents of 7, 162–3, 165
  definition 4
  and Indian education 228–30
  in Canada 89
  through clubs and associations 278–9
  through inter-marriage 254–5
activism see protest movements
Adams, John 44
Adams, J. Q. 55
  favours removal 57
agrarianism
  and confiscation of Indian land 41–2
  and Indian policy 42–3
agriculture
  education programmes 117, 218, 223,
    226
  Indian and white interaction 24
  Indian peoples as peasant
    communities 25–6
  influence of anthropologists 203
  through communal enterprise 118
Alabama
  Indians in 15, 57
Alaska Natives
  Alaska Native Brotherhood 293–4
  post-World War II issues 130–1
alcohol abuse 22
  as an urban problem 280–1
Algonquian tribes confederacy 15
allotment policy 61–2, 79, 97, 104, 114,
    270, 287
  anthropologists, attitude to 197
  Five Tribes post-Civil War 170, 177
  laws revoked 115
  under Dawes Act 99–101
American Anthropological Association
    119, 202, 207
American Association on Indian Affairs
    122
American Board of Commissioners for
    Foreign Missions 51

American Colonization Society 48
American Indian Defence Association
    108
American Indian Federation 121, 184, 295
  achievements 297
  attempts to discredit 297
  criticisms of Indian policy 295–6
American Indian Movement 284, 300
  demonstrations 301
American Indian Policy Review
    Commission 250, 305
anthropology 7, 189–90
  and education 206–7, 241
  development of 198–9
  early 191–8
  influence on Indian policy
    developments 199–201, 202–6
  medical 206
  and politics 207
  terminology definitions 190–1
  theories of Indian origins 191–2
  see also ethnology
Appalachian Mountains
  as settlement boundary 29
Arkansas 49
army 39, 54, 65, 67, 75
  use in Reconstruction 73
  use in reformist policies 80–1
  use in removal 62
  and transfer issue 80
Armstrong, S. C. 224
arts and crafts 242, 262
  Indian Arts and Crafts Board 113, 242
assimilation 3–4, 143
  failures 85, 141, 183, 213–14, 228–30,
    267
  forced 7, 141
  Meriam Report 108–9
  problems 43–4, 50–1
  see also directed change; civilization
    programme
assimilationist campaigns
  Collier seeks to modify 108–10
  through education 218–20
  see also Indian New Deal; 'termination'

Association of American Indian Affairs 132
  opposition to termination 139
Atlantic coastal regions
  Indian population 35
Atwood, S. 232

Baldwin, M. L. 289
Bandelier, A. 194, 198
Banks, D. 301
Baptist General Missionary Convention for Foreign Missions 51
Beatty, W. 206, 239–40
Beeson, J. 71
Bellecourt, C. 301
Bellecourt, V. 301
berdache 263
Black towns *see* settlements
Blacks
  as labour 26
  as slaves 25, 41, 150–1
  colonization proposals 48
  influence of evangelical Christianity 53
  interaction with Indians 5, 7, 155, 278
  post-Revolution collaboration with Indians 38
  see also freedmen; slaves
Bland, T. A. 96, 97
Board of Indian Commissioners 76, 78–9, 108
  abolition 113
  successes 79–80
Boas, F. 198–9, 203
Bodine, J. J. 205–6
Bonnin, G. L. 289, 293
Bonnin, R. T. 293
Brant, J. 36, 40
Brant, M. 266
Brinton, D. 194, 195, 198
Bronson, R. 130, 241
Brookings Institution, Meriam Report 108
Brophy, W. A. 128, 131, 139, 243
Bruner, J. 184, 295
Bureau of (American) Ethnology 195, 197, 206
Bureau of Indian Affairs 3, 55, 73, 110, 305
  administration problems 56, 72, 74, 75
  Applied Anthropology Unit 202
  controls over Indian land 114
  effects of World War II 127–8
  expansion 101–2, 107
  forestry policies 103–4
  in Jacksonian era 55–6
  in New Deal era 119–23, 127
    conflicts with tribal councils 123

Extension Division activities 118–19
  Policy Statement of 1947 132–4
  relations with anthropologists 200
  relocation programme 272–4, 285
  reorganizations 110, 131
  response to Peace Policy 77
  termination programme 134–6
Burke, C. H. 107, 108, 200
  Indian schools programme 232–3
Bursum Bill *see* Pueblo Indians land dispute
Burton, C. 241
Byrd, W. L. 179

Calhoun, J. C. 54–5
California
  reservation policy 68
  termination of federal services 135
Canada
  fur trading 23, 32
  Indian affairs 70, 87, 111
    assimilation programme 136, 140
    effective administration 88–9, 110–11
    effects of World War II 128
    Indian-white relations 89
    problems 88
  Indian population 32
  missionary activities 53–4
captives
  'Indianization' 17
Cass, L. 60
Catawbas 15
Cayugas 15
chapter houses 118
Checote, S. 182
Cherokees 5, 15, 22, 27, 35, 39, 155, 268
  adaptive process 47
  anti-removal lawsuit 61
  black slaves 152, 154, 156
  centralized government 50
  freedmen rights negotiations 173–5
  removal 57
  territory losses 44
Cheschillege, D. 121
Chickahominys 15
Chickasaws 5, 15, 27, 47
  black slaves 151
  freedmen rights negotiations 175–9
  political influence of women 266
  removal 57
Child, L. M. 58
Chippewas 15, 36, 99
Choctaws 5, 15, 27, 33, 35, 47, 50
  black slaves 151
  coercive land losses 46

freedmen rights negotiations 175–9
removal 57
churches
staffing of government peace policy
76–7
inspection system 77–8
citizenship
freedmen rights 171, 174
Indian Citizenship Act 1924 106, 107
Indian rights 82
through allotment policy 99, 100
Civil War
effects on reform efforts 71–2
effects on schools 216
effects on slavery 164–5
Indian participation 6, 36, 39, 40, 71
post-war agreements with Five Tribes
167, 169
post-war reform policies 72–3
Civilization Fund 43, 51, 54
Indian Civilization Act 1819 212
civilization programme 44, 46–8, 64, 65
implementation problems 68
staffing problems 68–9
Clay, H. 48, 58
Cloud, H. R. 288
club movement 294
Coachman, W. 267
Cohen, F. 130
Collier, J. 108, 109–10, 201, 202, 238–9,
271, 295
attempt to discredit AIF 297
Indian New Deal policies 112–17
National Indian Institute director 203
resignation 128
colonial government
relations with Indians 28–9
colonialism
impact on Indian peoples 34–5
see also European settlers; France;
Spain
colonization projects 48
Committee of One Hundred 233
reappraisal of Indian policy 108, 200
community colleges 246–7, 250
Conestogas 15
conflict
Indian versus Indian 21, 22, 71
Indian versus white 18, 37, 67, 72, 80
Connecticut 29
Coolidge, S. 199
cooperative livestock associations 118
cotton trade
in relation to Indian dispossession 57
courts
Court of Indian Affairs proposed 114
Courts of Indian Offences 82, 104

Indian 114, 116
Crawford, T. H. 56, 267
Creeks 5, 15, 27, 35, 40
black slaves 151, 154, 155
civil war 50
freedmen rights negotiations 170–1
land resettlement and allotment 61–2,
171–2
removal 57
-Seminole rift 153–4
cultural values 17, 276
conflicts 20
destructive influence of missionaries
18–19
ethnological studies 192–8
influence of anthropologists 201, 207–8
influence on policy-making 18
pluralism 112, 144, 231, 236, 240, 247,
248–9, 251, 283
recognition of 107

Dagenett, C. E. 228, 288
off-reservation employment projects
270–1
Dawes, H. L. 92, 99
Dawes Commission 172, 178
Dearborn, H. 45
de Buffon, Comte 38
Deer, Ada 304
Delawares 15, 17, 35, 36
Department of the Interior 55
departments of Indian affairs, northern
and southern 28, 39
Depression
effects on education programmes 240
effects on Indian policies 111
'directed change' 7, 82, 165
through political intervention 26
disease
effects on Indian tribes 25
effects of removal 81
on reservations 105–6
Dole, W. P. 72

Eastman, C. 199, 287, 288
Eastman, E. G. 259
economic influences
on reform measures 73
economic problems
as obstacles to Indian policies 40–1
of Indian New Deal 119
on reservations 82–5, 103–4, 129–30
education 8, 45, 114, 246
adult 243, 245–6
bicultural 284
effects of removal policies 214–16
expenditure 80, 136

failures 9
government reform policy
    commitments 220–2
higher 233, 238, 239, 242–3, 246, 250
    problems 251
in Canada 111
innovative developments 247, 250–1
    cultural pluralism 248–9
    local control 248, 250
legislation 247, 249–50
Meriam Report reform proposals 233–5
of freedmen 182
religious origins of 209–14, 220
teacher 240
see also community colleges; schools;
    universities; vocational instruction
Eisenhower, D. 137
Eliot, J. 210
Elk v. Wilkins 82
'emancipation' programme 132
    tribal readiness 133
    see also 'termination'
Emerson, R. W. 58
Emmons, G. 137, 245, 273, 274
employment 270, 274
    off-reservation placement 270–1, 272–3
Eries 15
ethnicity 143–4
ethnocentrism 13
    Indian 19
ethnology
    definition 190
    early studies of Indian peoples 192–4
European settlers
    attitude towards Indians 17
    benefits of trade with Indians 22
    factors influencing population increase
        26
    land acquisition 29
    prejudice against Indians 13–14,
        15
    reliance on Indians 15, 17
Everett, E. 58
expeditions
    information-gathering 47

factionalism 49–50
    on reservations 104
family life
    attempts to alter 10
    see also women
farming
    decline through land loss 100–1
    economic problems 103
    grants 116–17
    irrigation problems 104
    methods, and food production 23–4

New Deal legislation 120–1
federal aid
    during termination programme 136
    for Indian missions and schools 76
federal government
    Articles of Confederation 37
    commitment to Indian schooling 220–1
    Constitution and Indian policies 37–8
    cooperation with anthropologists 197
    Indian policy implementation 39, 140
    Jacksonian policies 55
    withdrawal of tribal supervision 132–5
feminism 10, 90, 125, 256
Fitzgerald, J. J. 92
Five Civilized Tribes 5, 6, 99
    adoption of black slavery 151–3
        relations with slaves 155, 161–2,
            165
        slave codes 158–9
    land losses and destructive white
        economic interests 84–5
    post-Civil War treaties government
        agreements 167, 169
    removal
        and education endeavours 215
        and slave labour 156–8
    white inter-marriage advantages 254
    see also Cherokees; Chickasaws;
        Choctaws; Creeks; Seminoles
Fletcher, A. 196–7
Florida 37, 49
    early Spanish mission activities 31
    termination of federal services 135
food production 23–4
forestry policy 103–4
Fox Indians 15
    termination opposition 138
France
    charter of the company of New France
        34
    early exploration and exploitation 32–3
    missionary activities 33–4
freedmen 166–7, 179–80
    education 182
    land resettlement and allotment 170,
        172, 175
    rights negotiations 169–70, 170–1,
        173–5, 175–9
Freedman's Savings Bank 75
Freedmen's Bureau 73–4, 217, 228
Frelinghuysen, T. 58
fur trade
    Indian and white trading 21, 22–3, 32

Gallatin, A. 195, 198
Garrison, W. L. 58
Gates, M. E. 92

General Federation of Women's Clubs 117, 132, 232
Georgia
 Cherokee anti-removal lawsuit 61
 cotton trade and removal policies 57
 independent relations with Indians 37, 57
 Indians 15
Ghost Dance movement 84
government *see* colonial government; federal government; state government
government trading houses 43, 54
Grand Council of Fire of American Indians 294
Grant, U. S. 75
 Peace Policy 75–81
Grayson, E. B. 169
Grimké sisters 58

Hall, J. 48, 195
Harris, C. A. 56
Harris, LaDonna 304
Harrison, B. 222
Hayes, R. B. 77
Herring, E. 56
Hewitt, J. N. B. 199
home economics
 4-H club programme 117–18
 vocational instruction 117, 218, 236, 240
Hoover, E. 109
housing
 in urban areas 279
Houston, S. 58
Hrdlicka, A. 203
Hudson River Valley Indians 15
Hulputta Micco 179
Hunt, J. 194
Hurons 21

Ickes, H. 130
Illinois 49
Illinois confederacy 15, 21, 27
Indian centres 268–9
Indian Claims Commission 130–1, 205, 299
Indian country 59, 63, 64, 66, 142, 168
 post-Civil War racial social interaction 180–1
Indian Department 43–4
Indian Health Service 282, 299
 alcohol abuse treatment projects 281
Indian New Deal 112, 117–18, 126–7
 administrative problems 119–20
 agencies and organizations 113

anthropological analyses 204
 communal enterprises 118
 criticisms of 119–20, 122, 125, 295
 economic policies 119
 education policies 239
 farming legislation 120–1
 Navajo rejections 120–2
 see also Indian Reorganization Act 1934
Indian peoples
 basic culture areas 14–15, 16
 characteristics 17, 141, 276
 citizenship rights 82
 current population figures 32
 definition 115–16
 debate about origins 191–2
 early population figures 32
 ethnological studies 192–8
 hostility towards missionaries 52
 interaction with blacks 5, 7, 38, 167–83, 184–8, 278
 interaction with whites 19–20, 21–3
 nomadic 15
 response to World War II 128
 tribal readiness for emancipation 133
 see also individual tribes
Indian policy *see* Bureau of Indian Affairs; Indian New Deal; Meriam Report; policy implementation; policy-making; removal policies; 'termination'
Indian Reorganization Act 1934 114, 115–16, 202, 239
 criticisms of 115, 125
 grants 116–17
 Indian response and approval 116
 Navajo rejection 120–2
Indian Rights Association 90, 91–2, 125, 199, 287, 288
 opposition to termination 139
Indian studies 248–9
Indian Territory 6, 7, 79, 81, 84, 85, 90, 97, 156ff., 166ff., 215
Indiana 49
intermarriage 5, 10, 185, 254, 277
 and acculturation 255
 in Canada 89, 254
Iroquois confederacy 15, 27, 35, 36
 conflict with the fur trade 21
 trade with white settlers 21
 women
  high status and economic role 261
  political influence 265–6
  religious influence 264–5

Jackson, A. 55
 removal policy 59–60
Jackson, H. H. 86–7

Japanese-American evacuees 127–8, 272
Jefferson, T. 38, 42
  assimilation policies 45–6
  removal policies 47–8
  and slavery 44
Jemison, A. L. 295
Johnson, C. 179
Johnson, W. 266
Johnson-O'Malley Act
  federal-state cooperation for health,
    education and welfare 114
Jones, W. 92

Kendall, A. 55
Kickapoos 15
Kennedy Task Force on Indian Affairs
  206
Kennedy, R.
  SubCommittee on Indian Education
    247
Klamaths
  termination 137, 138, 139, 140
Knox, H. 39
Kroeber, A. L. 203

La Flesche, F. 199, 288
Lake Mohonk Conference of Friends of
  the Indian 90, 92–3, 196, 288
land
  as Indian trading commodity 23
  confiscation 41
  in political dealings 27, 29, 39, 40, 41
  loss through allotment 60–1, 99–100
  loss through coercion 46, 49
  needs 119, 132
  soil conservation policies 118, 121
  treaties 36, 43
land rights
  Alaska Natives dispute 130–1
  protective legislation 107
  Pueblo Lands dispute 107, 200, 231
  threats to 106
  see also Indian Claims Commission
Lansa, M. 266
Latimer, J. 295
Le Farge, O. 122, 200
leadership 27
  office of head chief 27–8
  power struggles 26
  voluntary local Indian leaders 118
legislation
  citizenship 106
  education 247, 249–50, 273
  Navajo-Hopi Long Range
    Rehabilitation Act 129
  oil leasing 107
  removal 59–60

reorganization under the
  Wheeler-Howard Act 114–16
severalty 97–101
slave codes 158–60
to regulate trade and commerce 43
Leupp, F. E. 91, 92, 222, 270
Lincoln, A. 47, 72
Linnaeus, C. 38
Logan, J. 18
Louisiana Purchase 46, 47
Lovejoy, E. P. 58
Lurie, N. 206

McCoy, I. 51, 60
McCurtain, G. 177
McCurtain, R. 243
McGee, W. J. 194, 198
McGillivray, A. 40, 50
McKenney, T. L. 48, 54, 55, 60–1, 212
Mankiller, W. 268
Manypenny, G. 86–7
Martinez, M. 262
Maryland 29
Massachusets 15
  impact of smallpox epidemic 25
Massachusetts 29
Mattaponis 15
Means, R. 301
medical services 105–6, 136
  in Canada 111
  private clinics 282
  urban 281–2
Medill, W. 56, 65
Mekeel, H. S. 203
Menominees 15
  effects of termination 140
  restoration to federal control 140
  termination opposition 137, 138, 139,
    206
Meriam Report on Indian policy 108–9,
  200, 271
  proposals on educational reform 233,
    234–5
Miamis 15, 17
  Chief 'Old Briton' and trading
    strategies 21
Michigan 49
Miles, J. 77
military alliances 21
  and political alliances 27
  French-Indian 32
missionaries 51–2, 68–9
  during Reconstruction 74
  friction with Indian service personnel
    31, 74, 238, 241
  Protestant-Catholic tensions 54
  relations with black slaves 153

missionary activities 3, 211
  achievements 54
  attempted influence on Indian culture
    19
  during removal 214–15
  early French activities 33–4
  early Spanish activities 31
  in Canada 53, 111
  in first half of nineteenth century 51
  on reservations 104–5, 181
Mississippi
  Indians 15
  Indian removal west of the Mississippi
    57
Missouri 49
Mitchell, G. 301
Mitchell, J. 38
Mohawks 15, 40
Mohegans 15
Monroe, J. 48
  favours removal 57
Montezuma, C. 229–30, 288, 292
Moorehead, W. K. 233
Morgan, J. C. 121
Morgan, L. H. 192, 193, 195, 196, 198
Morgan, T. J. 92, 221
Morton, S. 193, 195
Mott, J. 58
Mott, L. 58
Myer, D. S. 128, 134, 135
  War Relocation programme 272

Nanticokes 15, 35
Narragansets 15, 19
Nash, P. 206
National Advisory Council on Indian
    Education 249
National Association for the
    Advancement of Colored People
    289
National Congress of American Indians
    132, 244, 289, 303, 304–5
  effectiveness 299–300
  objectives 298–9
  opposition to termination 139
National Council of American Indians
    293
National Council on Indian Opportunity
    247
National Federation of Women's Clubs
    294
National Indian Defense Association 96,
    97
National Indian Education Advisory
    Commission 247
National Indian Education Association
    247

National Indian Institute 203
  research studies 204
National Indian Youth Council 300,
    301–2
National Society of Indian Women 294
National Tribal Chairmen's Association
    303
Native American Church *see* religion
Navajo Indian Rights Association 121
Navajos
  day schools resistance 225, 240
  Navajo Community College 246–7, 250
  post-war reservation crisis 129–30
  rejection of Indian New Deal 120–2
  social organization 262
  Special Education Program 244
  women 259, 266
    female deities 264
New England
  effects of epidemics 25
  effects of fur trading 23
  European 'captives' 17
  Indians 15
New England Company 53
New Mexico
  reservation policy 68
New York 49
  independent relations with Indians 37
  Indian Society for the Propagation of
    Indian Welfare 293
  termination of federal services 135
Niantics 15
Nichols, J. R. 128
North Carolina 29
  Indians 15
Nott, J. 193, 195
Nottaways 15

Occom, S.
  fund-raising tour 211
Office of Economic Opportunity
  education funding 246
Office of Indian Education 249
Officer, J. E. 206
Ohio 49
oil
  Indian Oil Leasing Act 1927 107
  on reservations 106
Oklahoma Territory 6, 183
  Oklahoma Society of Indians 293
  Tushkahoma League 293
Oneidas 15, 40
Onondagas 15
Oregon
  reservation policy 68
Oskison, J. 288
Ottawas 15, 36

Painter, C. C. 91
Pamlicos 15
Pamunkeys 15
Pancoast, H. S. 91
Parker, A. C. 199–200, 288, 298
Parker, E. S. 75–6, 79, 192
Payne, J. H. 58
Peace Policy 75–81, 218
Peltquestangue, E. M. de 289
Penn, J. 18
Penn, W. 17, 18
Pennacooks 15
Pennsylvania 17, 29
    independent dealings with Indians 37
Penobscots 15
Pequots 15
    leadership struggles 26
    white attack on 18
Peters, S. 105
peyote cult 123–5
Pocahontas 254
police
    Indian 287
    Indian tribesmen 82
policy implementation 39–40
    and radical agrarianism 41–3
    problems 40–1, 136–7
    progress 110
policy-making 69
    BIA Policy Statement 1947 132–4
    colonial 28–9
    current 140
    in education 247
    influence of early anthropological
        studies 194–5
    influence of Wheeler-Howard Act 127
    post-colonial 35
    post-Civil War 36–7, 65
    post World War I 108
    role of anthropologists 7–8, 199–201,
        202–8
political systems
    early Indian access to 287–8
    factionalism 22, 26, 27
    Indian-European relations 26–8
    Indian representation 292–3
    women in 265–7
Poncas
    removal sufferings and compensation
        case 86, 232
Populism 94, 101
Porter, P. 6
Potawatomis 15
poverty
    among urban Indian populations 41,
        275
Powell, J. W. 193, 196, 197, 198

power
    in Indian communities 28
    of women 257
Powhatan confederacy 15, 27
Pratt, R. H. 197, 222, 224, 228, 229, 288,
        292
prejudice
    against blacks 38, 182–3
    against Indians 13–14, 15, 19, 38, 43,
        44, 57, 70
    between Indians and Blacks 187–8
    in employment 271
    in schools 237
Preston-Engle Report 108, 110
Progressive Education 114, 234, 235–6,
        238, 239, 240, 241
Progressive reform and reformers 94, 95,
        102, 107, 109, 200, 222, 288, 292
property
    concept of, and Indian policy 41, 42
    see also land rights
protection measures
    in Indian policy 43, 65
protest movements 11–12, 285, 306
    demonstrations 301
    early 287–8
    external relations 305–6
    local associations 293
    political influence 292–3
    youth 301–2
    see also American Indian Federation;
        National Congress of American
        Indians; Society of American Indians
public expenditure
    cuts effects on Indian New Deal 119
    on education 239, 240, 245, 246
    on Indian affairs 39, 43, 46, 115
    on land 117
Pueblo Indian lands dispute 106–7, 200,
        231–2
Puritans
    attitude to human sexuality 253
    educational endeavours 210
    see also European settlers
Pushmataha 50

Quakers 51
    as Indian Commissioners 109
    attitude towards Indians 17–18
Quinton, A. S. 90

race relations 5–6, 38
    tripartite systems 184–8
racism
    versus ethnocentrism 13–14
ranching 104
    livestock purchases 117

Reconstruction treaties 167–79
reform
'coercive' 4
impact of Civil War 71–2
twentieth century 103–11
see also Peace Policy
reform movements 43, 44, 46, 51, 65,
86–7, 90–6, 101, 102, 107–9, 132,
211–12, 217–18, 221–2
achievements 96–7
difficulties 68–9, 73
see also abolitionism, protest
movements, Populism, Progressive
education, Progressive reform and
reformers
religion 17, 19, 45
charter of the Company of New France
34
in abolition and reform movements 95
in anthropological enquiry 193
Indian 53, 84, 123
of slaves 161
see also missionary societies; peyote
cult
relocation programme 11, 59, 270, 272–4
failures of 275
forced removal 62–4
of Japanese-Americans 128, 272
problems 64–5
return rates 274, 276–7
see also urbanization
removal policies 47–8, 58, 81
effects on education 214–16
effects on slave labour 156–8
Ponca Indian sufferings 86
Removal Act 1830 59–60
voluntary 57
see also abolitionism; relocation
programme
reservations 29, 67–8
adjustment problems 83–4
administration 108
and tribal disruption 81
anthropological studies 202–3
cooperative livestock associations 118
effects of relocation programme 274
failures of 85, 270
farming efforts 83
government 104
government jurisdiction over 82
lack of welfare services 132
law enforcement disputes 134
oil exploration 106
survey of conditions 108

Reynolds, G. A. 169
Rhoads, C. 109, 112, 235

Rhode Island
Indians and white settlers 19
rights
activism 303
citizenship 82, 171, 174
Colonial defence of Indians 18
problems in Canada 111
under Indian Reorganization Act
115–16
see also land rights
Rolfe, J. 254
Romans, B. 38
Roosevelt, E. 126
Roosevelt, F. D. 112, 126
Ryan, W. C. 234, 235, 239

Sacajawea 255
Sanborn, J. B. 170
Sauk 15, 49–50
termination opposition 138
Scattergood, J. 109, 112, 235
Schoolcraft, H. R. 56, 192, 196, 198
schools 9–10, 209, 212–13, 231
Catholic 220
community day school problems
225–6, 240–1, 243–4, 248
effects of Civil War 216
failures 214, 228–30, 241
freedmen's aid society 217
in assimilation activities 217–18
Indian 214, 222, 232, 233, 238, 242
all-Indian school boards 248
boarding schools 223–5, 234, 235–6
loss of 227, 283
resistance to 222–3
missionary 215, 216, 218–20, 241
public school policies 226–7, 232–3,
235–7, 239, 242, 244–5
urban problems 283
segregation strategies 185
for menstruating women 257–8
in schools 237
self-determination 140
in education 246, 249–51
see also protest movements
self-government 6, 114
see also tribal councils
Sells, C. 200
Seminoles 5
black slaves 151, 154, 157–8
-Creek rift 153–4
freedmen rights agreement 169–70
removal 57
Senate Committee on Indian Affairs
survey of reservation conditions
108
Senecas 15, 40

settlements
  all-black 180
severalty legislation 97–101 (*and see*
  allotment)
sexual mores 15, 253–5, 259
Shawnees 15, 17, 36, 49
Sherman, J. 92
Sioux
  allotment policy 99
  attempt to settle on Canada 87–8
  Ghost Dance movement 84
Sitting Bull 84, 87–8
Skinner, A. B. 199
slavery
  anti-slavery in Indian Territory 163–4
  attempts at ending 43
  black African 25, 41, 150–1
  Creek-Seminole rift 153–4
  early 18, 30, 149–50, 151
  impact of Civil War 164–5
  Quaker involvement 18
  similarities between Indian and
    Southern white 160–1
slaves
  as agents of acculturation 162–3,
    165
  as intermediaries between Indians and
    whites 153
  codes 158–60
  in the removal process 156–8
  lifestyles 154
  prices 161
  revolts 38, 159, 164–5
smallpox epidemics 25
Smiley, A. K. 92
Smith, S. S. 195
social development
  between black, white and Indian
    communities 180–1
social problems
  as effects of 'termination' 140
  attempts to alleviate 120
  conservative approaches toward 144
  see also alcohol abuse
social services 282–3
Society for Applied Anthropology 204
Society for the Propagation of the Gospel
  in Foreign Parts 53, 210
Society for the Propagation of the Gospel
  in New England 210
Society of American Indians 199, 227,
  287, 288–90
  aims 290–1
  education proposals 228
  internal disputes 292
  problems 291–2
Society of Friends 76, 77

sodalities
  instructional learning groups 213
South America
  early Spanish exploration 30
  Indian population 32
South Carolina 29
  independent relations with Indians 37
  Indians 15
Spain
  early exploration and exploitation
    30–1
  missionary activities 31
Speck, F. G. 199
Spinden, H. 200
Squier, E. 195
Stanton, E. 72
state government
  and administration of Indian affairs
    108, 114, 135
status
  and band membership in Canada
    89–90
  and colonists' view of Indians
    14
  and segregation strategies 185
  of mixed-blood blacks 186
Strong, W. D. 202

Taliaferro, L. 56
Tatum, L. 77
Tecumseh 49–50
Tennessee
  independent Indian relations 57
'termination'
  anthropological criticisms of 206
  BIA programme 134–6
  educational consequences of 245–6
  effects of 136–7, 138, 140
  legislation 137
  problems 138, 139–40
territories
  Appalachian Mountain boundary 29
  see also reservations, Indian Territory
Thomas, C. 194, 198
Thompson, H. 244
Thompson, N. 172
trade 5
  and inter-marriage 254
  between Indians and white settlers
    20–1, 22, 32
  conflicts 21–2
  legislation 43
  see also fur trade
treaties 36, 39, 43
  American land acquisition 49, 59–60,
    68
  tribal authority constraints 7

tribal councils 134, 266–7
  conflicts 123
  Navajo 129, 130
  powers 115, 127
  relocation procedures 274
tribal economy 7
tribal organization 116, 129, 267
  anthropological studies 202
  sodalities 213
  see also tribal councils
tribal sovereignty
  and white land purchases 40
tribute relationship 27
Trollope, F. 58–9
Trudell, J. 301
Truman, H. S. 129–30
Tuscaroras 15, 17

unemployment rates 275
United Foreign Mission Society 51
United States Indian Commission 71
United States v. Kagama 82
Universal Peace Society 71
universities 247–8
  Indian studies courses 248–9
uprisings
  Virginia 18
urbanization 11, 273, 274–5
  adjustment to 176–8, 285–6
  and alcohol abuse 280–1
  and housing patterns 279

Valentine, R. 200
Virginia 29
  Algonquian tribes confederacy
    15
  impact of smallpox epidemic 25
  native decline 35
  native uprising 18
vocational instruction 238, 239,
  246
  Adult Vocational Training Programme
    273
  in agriculture 117, 218, 223, 226
  in home economics 117, 218, 236,
    240
  Navajo Special Education Program
    244
  Tucson Indian Training School 244
  Vocational Education Act 250

Wampanoags 15
wampum 20
War Department
  coordination of Indian matters
    54–5

Washington
  reservation policy 68
Washington, G.
  civilization programme 44
weapons
  firearms 21, 22
Webster, D. 58
Welsh, H. 91
Welsh, W. 75, 91
Wheeler-Howard Act *see* Indian
  Reorganization Act
Wheelock, E. 211
Whipple, H. B. 71, 75
Whites
  attitude towards black and Indian
    interaction 5
  cultural influences 6
  destructiveness 20
  economic interests in reservations 84
  in Indian protest organizations 289
  'Indianized' 19
  post-Revolution prejudice towards
    non-whites 38
  pressures to end Indian independence
    182–3
  use of black slaves 160–1
  views of Indian assertiveness 187–8
  see also European settlers
Whittesley, E. 92
Wilber, Silvia 304
Wilbur, R. L. 109, 235
Williams, R. 19
Winnebagos 15
Wisconsin 49
women 10–11, 252
  activism 304
  child-rearing practices 258–9, 282
  clubs 294
  conservatism and white reform
    programme 105
  emancipation through education 8,
    267, 268
  marriage and inter-marriage 253–5,
    259
  matriliny 255–7, 261–2, 268–9
  menstrual power 257
  political influence and power
    265–8
  religious powers 264–5
  segregation 257–8
  special societies 265
  widowhood 263
  within division of labour strategies
    260–1, 262
Women's National Indian Association
  90–1
Work, H. 108

World War I
  impact of 9
  Indian participants 106
World War II
  effects on education 9, 243
  effects on Indian policies 127–8

  Indian participation 128
Wyandots 36

youth clubs 117, 202

Zimmerman, W. 132